Freque

p. 285, 12a ortant words

p. 291, 12d Action con… through verbs rather than nouns

p. 292, 12e Active voice usually preferred

p. 301, 13c Clarity through free subordination

p. 390,

p. 397, and coordinating

p. 399, 19b Avoidance of run-on senten

p. 411, 20c Subject-verb agreement

p. 428, 20o No comma between subject and verb

p. 433, 21c Avoidance of dangling modifier

p. 445, 21l Comma on both sides of an interrupting element

p. 447, 21m Restrictive versus nonrestrictive element

p. 476, 23i Pronoun antecedent included

p. 477, 23j No competition for role of antecedent

p. 533, 28b No fragment following a semicolon

The Random House Handbook

The Random House Handbook

SIXTH EDITION

Frederick Crews
University of California, Berkeley

McGraw-Hill, Inc.
New York St. Louis San Francisco Auckland Bogotá
Caracas Lisbon London Madrid Mexico Milan
Montreal New Delhi Paris San Juan
Singapore Sydney Tokyo Toronto

This book was developed by STEVEN PENSINGER, Inc.

THE RANDOM HOUSE HANDBOOK

Permissions acknowledgments appear on pages 735–736, and on this page by reference.

2 3 4 5 6 7 8 9 0 FGR FGR 9 0 9 8 7 6 5 4 3 2

ISBN 0-07-013636-X

This book was set in Times Roman by Monotype Composition Company.
The editors were Steve Pensinger and James R. Belser;
the production supervisor was Kathryn Porzio.
The cover was designed by Armen Kojoyian.
Arcata Graphics/Fairfield was printer and binder.

Library of Congress Cataloging-in-Publication Data

Crews, Frederick C.
Random House handbook / Frederick Crews.—6th ed.
p. cm.
Includes index.
ISBN 0-07-013636-X
1. English language—Rhetoric. 2. English language—Grammar—1950- I. Title.
PE1408.C715 1992 91-31851
808′.042—dc20

About the Author

FREDERICK CREWS, Professor of English at the University of California, Berkeley, received the Ph.D. from Princeton University. In his career he has attained many honors, including a Guggenheim Fellowship, appointment as a Fulbright Lecturer in Italy, an essay award from the National Council on the Arts and Humanities, election to membership in the American Academy of Arts and Sciences, and, from his own university, recognition as a Distinguished Teacher and as Faculty Research Lecturer. His writings include the widely used *Borzoi Handbook for Writers* (with Sandra Schor) as well as highly regarded books on Henry James, E. M. Forster, and Nathaniel Hawthorne, the best-selling satire *The Pooh Perplex,* and two volumes of his own essays entitled *Out of My System* and *Skeptical Engagements*. Professor Crews has published numerous articles in *Partisan Review, The New York Review of Books, Commentary, Tri-Quarterly, The American Scholar,* and other important journals. He has twice been Chair of Freshman Composition in the English Department at Berkeley.

FOR BETTY
again and always

Contents

Preface

Since its original publication in 1974, *The Random House Handbook* has continually evolved toward greater clarity, ease of use, and responsiveness to the concerns of composition instructors and students. Like previous revisions, the sixth edition attempts to retain the *Handbook*'s distinctive outlook and tone, including its sometimes whimsical sample sentences. Once again, however, I have made some fundamental changes as well as many smaller ones. Instructors who know the fifth edition will want to be alert to the following developments among others:

1. Much of the represented student writing is new, including a fresh research essay, a new example of "One Essay from Start to Finish," and a complete essay illustrating the assessment of a published text.
2. The number of exercises in the Usage section has been considerably increased, with more emphasis on the student writer's own original sentences as opposed to right/wrong choices.
3. A new Chapter 3, "Planning an Essay," conveniently combines advice on developing a topic and thesis with advice on organization.
4. Material on the presenting of evidence, formerly scattered through three chapters, has been consolidated in a new Chapter 4, "Supporting a Thesis."
5. Chapter 5, now called "Collaborating and Revising," devotes a good deal of emphasis to peer editing, including a Peer Editing Worksheet that instructors can adapt to their own assignments.
6. The segment of chapters on "The Research Essay" has been moved forward to occupy Part III (Chapters 6, 7, and 8), so that it can naturally follow the advice on "Composing Whole Essays."
7. Chapter 6, "Finding and Mastering Sources," now places more emphasis on on-line catalogs and CD databases, provid-

ing fuller information about the latter than any handbook to date.

8. Chapter 7, "Documenting Sources," now keeps the MLA and APA citation styles separate instead of juxtaposing them. (Since only one style will be used in a given paper, close comparisons are not helpful.)
9. With separate chapters on paragraph unity and continuity (9), paragraph development (10), and opening and closing paragraphs (11), instructors can now more easily choose what to emphasize.
10. Similarly, the old chapter on "Sentences" has become Chapters 12, 13, and 14, on "Writing Distinct Sentences," "Subordination," and "Sentence Emphasis and Variety."
11. Again, the old chapter on "Words" is now Chapters 15, 16, and 17: "Appropriate Language," "Efficient Language," and "Figurative Language."
12. Chapter 15 now includes a new point, "Master idioms," showing which prepositions go with certain common phrases. Students for whom English is a second language should find this advice helpful.
13. I have included a whole chapter (19) on "Joining Independent Clauses," thus enabling the key usage problems of sentence fragments and run-on sentences to be highlighted and treated more extensively in chapters of their own (18 and 19, respectively).
14. Chapter 23 has been considerably expanded to cover pronoun agreement as well as pronoun reference.
15. Fifteen separate, and potentially cumbersome, comma rules in the fifth edition are now consolidated and graphically illustrated in three convenient boxes (27a–c).
16. Chapter 38 now shows how to prepare not only business letters but also cover sheets for facsimile transmissions.
17. A new Part XI, "Tools," includes a chapter entitled "Writing with a Word Processor."
18. Throughout the book I have simplified alphanumeric head-

ings to replace difficult grammatical concepts with concrete, readily grasped examples.

19. Highlighted passages in examples are now shown by unmistakable boldface type.

20. Finally, the index, which now devotes separate lines to subtopics, is much easier to consult than before.

These and other changes have brought *The Random House Handbook* closer in content and format to the second edition of *The Borzoi Handbook for Writers,* which the late Sandra Schor and I published in 1989. But whereas *Borzoi* is intended chiefly as a reference tool, this present book gives special attention to rhetorical strategies for the college writer. It is also distinguished by a greater number of examples (including some droll ones) and by the inclusion of exercises.

Since this text can be ordered shrink-wrapped with Michael Hennessy's superb *Random House Practice Book,* instructors who want to go beyond the exercises in the *Handbook* can do so without causing their students much additional cost or any inconvenience. I have prepared a new *Instructor's Manual* explaining alternative ways to use the book and providing answers to the exercises.

There are other supplements as well: the *Random House On-Line Handbook* (IBM Version), *The Random House Diagnostic Tests,* and an *Answer Key for the Random House Practice Books.*

I remain sincerely grateful to everyone who has been mentioned in previous acknowledgments. Space permits me to single out only those generous people who have enriched this edition in distinctive and indispensable ways: James R. Belser, Gladys M. Craig, Alice Jaggard, Judith C. Kohl, Steve Pensinger, Sandra Schor, Jo-Ann M. Sipple, and Anita Wagner.

Frederick Crews

The Random House Handbook

Introduction

Looking ahead

If you are like most students entering a composition course, you arrive with a mixture of hope and worry. The hope is that the course will help you to put your thoughts into written words with greater precision and effect. The worry is that nothing of the sort will happen and that you will have to go through a painful, humiliating ordeal. Essays, you know, will be required of you on short notice. Will you be able to write them at all? Looking ahead, perhaps you experience a feeling that assails every writer from time to time—the suspicion that words may fail you. (And if words fail you, the instructor may fail you, too.)

It may seem odd at first that putting your thoughts into words should be so challenging. Since childhood, after all, you have been speaking intelligible English. When you talk about things that matter to you, the right words often come to your lips without forethought. Again, in writing letters to friends you scribble away with confidence that you will be understood. But in writing essays you find yourself at a disadvantage. You know that your prose is expected to carry your reader along with a developing idea, but you don't have a clear notion of who that reader is. Instead of exchanging views with someone who can see your face, interpret your gestures, and tell you when a certain point needs explanation or support, you have to assume a nonexistent relationship and keep on writing. It is almost like composing love letters "to whom it may concern" and mailing them off to "Occupant" or "Boxholder."

Faced with this real but manageable challenge, some students make matters worse by conceiving of "good writing" as a brass ring to be seized or, more probably, missed on their first and only try. Condemning themselves in advance as people who lack a writer's mysterious gifts, they imagine that their function in the months ahead will be merely to produce errors of expression so that their instructor can continue to believe that the language is going downhill. For them, the game is over before its rules have been explained.

To stave off such defeatism you need only realize that effective prose is not like a brass ring at all; it is more like the destination of a journey, approachable by steps that anyone can follow. People who turn out dazzling work without blotting a line are so rarely found that you can put them out of your mind. Everyone who writes for a living knows what you too should remember: by and large, *writing is rewriting*. Even the most accomplished authors start with drafts that would be woefully inadequate except *as* drafts—that is, as means of getting going in an exploratory process that will usually include a good many setbacks and shifts of direction. To feel dissatisfied with a sample of your prose, then, is not a sign of anything about your talent. The "good writer" is the one who can turn such dissatisfaction to a positive end by pressing ahead with the labor of revision, knowing that niceties of style will come more easily once an adequate structure of ideas has been developed.

Thus it is also a mistake to think of yourself as either having or not having "something to say," as if your head were a package that could be opened and inspected for inclusion of the necessary contents. We do not *have* things to say; we acquire them in the process of working on definite problems that catch our attention. If you grasp that crucial fact, you can stop worrying about writing in general and prepare yourself for writing *within a context*—that is, inside a situation that calls for certain ways of treating a typical range of questions.

Everything you encounter in a college course provides elements of context, helping to make your writing projects less like all-or-nothing tests of your inventiveness and more like exercises in the use of tested procedures. Before long, in any course that calls for written work, you will have picked up important clues about characteristic subject matter and issues, conventions of form and tone, and means of gathering and presenting evidence. And as you do so, you will find yourself not only writing but also thinking somewhat like a historian, an economist, or whatever. That practice in operating within the idiom, or accepted code, of various disciplines is a good part of what a successful college experience is about.

In a composition course, most of your contextual clues will be gleaned not from readings or lectures but from your instructor's way of explaining assignments, discussing common problems, and commenting on your submitted work. It is essential, therefore, that you get over any lingering image of the composition teacher as a mere fussbudget, hungry to pounce on comma faults and dangling modifiers. If you arrive with that stereotype in mind, you may start out by writing papers that are technically careful but windy and devoid of feeling. In other words, you may think that the game is to be won through negative means, by producing the lowest possible number of mistakes. You should realize instead that your instructor's standards, like your own when you pick up a magazine, are chiefly positive. It is perfectly true that English teachers prefer correctly formed sentences to faulty ones; so do you. But you also expect an article to engage you in a lively and well-conceived topic, to support a consistent central idea, and to convey information clearly and efficiently, without needless pomp. Your instructor will hope for nothing less—and nothing fancier—from your own essays.

Nevertheless, like many another freshman student, you may feel ill at ease addressing this still unknown and potentially troublesome person. Very well: don't even try. You can get the desired results if, while you compose, you think of your classmates, not the instructor, as your audience. This is not to say that you should write in dormitory slang. The point is that if you think of trying to convince people of your own age and background, you will get a reliable sense of what needs proving, what can be taken for granted, and what tone to adopt. If the student sitting next to you would probably choke on some contrived generalization, leave it out. If you suspect that the class as a whole would say "Make that clearer" or "Get to the point," do so. Your instructor will be delighted by any paper that would impress most of your classmates.

Writing to achieve different effects

Many college-bound students have been taught to aim at a prissy, rule-conscious, rigidly formal notion of "good English." The outcome is prose that sounds as if it were meant to pass a parade inspection rather than to win a reader's sympathy or agreement. In college and beyond you will find that no single formula can suit the variety of writing contexts you will meet. The rules you may have memorized in high school—*avoid the passive voice*, *never use* I *and* me, *do not begin a sentence with a conjunction or end it with a preposition*—must now be reconsidered in the light of shifting audiences and purposes.

You will always want to adjust your **rhetoric** to the specific audience and purpose you have in mind. That advice may leave you uneasy if you think of rhetoric in its casual meaning of insincere, windy language, as in *Oh, that's just a lot of rhetoric*. But in its primary meaning rhetoric is simply *the strategic placement of ideas and choice of language*—the means of making an intended effect on a reader or listener. Rhetoric need never call for deceptive prose; it calls, rather, for making a strong case by satisfying your audience's legitimate expectations.

Confronting the essay

By the end of your composition course you will almost certainly be better able to write papers for any other course, regardless of its subject matter. But your composition instructor will not be assigning such "disciplinary" papers. You will be asked instead to create *essays* conveying a characteristic blend of opinion and evidence, of intimacy and objectivity.

An **essay** can be defined as a *fairly brief piece of nonfiction that tries to make a point in an interesting way*:

1. *It is fairly brief.* Some classic essays occupy only a few paragraphs, but essays generally fall between three and twenty typed pages. Under that minimum, the development of thought that typifies an essay would be difficult to manage. Above that maximum, people might be tempted to read the essay in installments, like a book. A good essay makes an unbroken experience.

2. *It is nonfiction.* Essayists try to tell the truth; if they describe a scene or tell a story, we presume that the details have not been made up for effect.

3. *It tries to make a point . . .* An essay characteristically tells or explains something, or expresses an attitude toward something, or supports or criticizes something—an opinion, a person, an institution, a movement. A poem or a novel may also do these things, but it does them incidentally. An essay is directly *about* something called its **topic**, and its usual aim is to win sympathy or agreement to the point or **thesis** it is maintaining.

4. *. . . in an interesting way.* When you write an answer to a question on an exam, you do not pause to wonder if the reader actually *wants* to pursue your answer to the end; you know you will succeed if you concisely and coherently satisfy the terms of the question. But a full-fledged essay tends to be read in another way. Its reader could agree with every sentence and still be displeased. What that reader wants is not just true statements, but a feeling that those statements support an idea worth bothering about.

As an essayist, then, you should aim to harmonize reason and rhetoric, trying to be at once lively, fair, and convincing. You must

tell the truth →	but first make people interested in hearing it;
write with conviction →	but consider whether the ideas will stand up under criticism;
supply evidence →	but not become a bore about it;
be purposeful →	but not follow such a predictable pattern that the reader's attention slackens.

But why, you may ask, should you have to write essays at all? No doubt they provide good training for students who want to become professional essayists, but what about future nurses or computer programmers or social workers? I think there are four reasons for the persistence of the essay in freshman English:

1. In a population of freshmen who have varying career plans (including, in some cases, no plan at all), it is impossible to have all students write the kinds of specialized papers or reports they will be producing in their majors.

2. Writing that draws chiefly on opinion and personal experience can spare you the inconvenience of having to do outside reading for every writing assignment.
3. All college writing tasks place a premium on certain common points that are highlighted by the essay: coherence, clarity, persuasive order of presentation, and correctness of usage, punctuation, and other conventions.
4. More generally, practice in supporting opinions is also practice in forming them—in thinking clearly, weighing objections, and preferring solid evidence to prejudice.

Still, there is that anxiety triggered by the blank page or blank screen. How can you master it? Beyond reminding you that such a feeling is normal, this book proposes a two-step remedy. First, we begin with specific writing tasks that will sharpen the skills you need in creating whole essays; you can develop a knack for essay prose in a piecemeal fashion. And second, when you do arrive at the total work of composing, we will break that process into manageable parts, showing how you can get started purposefully and, in the drafting stage, exit from an occasional blind alley. Nothing can spare a writer from meeting obstacles; but with your instructor's participation and your own effort, the advice and exercises that follow ought to convince you that strong, consecutive, even graceful prose lies within your reach.

I

EXPLORING PROSE STRATEGIES

EXPLORING PROSE STRATEGIES

This section covers the most common techniques that skillful writers use to gain a reader's involvement, trust, and agreement. Whole essays always combine such strategies, typically setting a descriptive scene, comparing one thing to another, showing how a narrated incident lends support to an opinion, conceding one objection to that opinion but then refuting another. If you get to feel comfortable with a full array of strategies, you will be able to make shrewd and varied choices at the appropriate time.

Prose strategies fall into two natural categories according to their relation to physical experience. The "immediate" strategies, ***description*** *and* ***narration****, are alike in that they appeal directly to the senses, calling scenes or episodes to the reader's mind. Chapter 1 covers principles for imparting an air of reality and drama to the objects and events you will want your reader to picture. Chapter 2, by contrast, introduces two strategies that belong together because they appeal primarily to the reader's understanding and judgment:* ***analysis*** *and* ***argument****. To analyze is not to present the physical actuality of an experience but to explain something so that the reader will appreciate its function, its importance, or its relation to something else. And to argue is to justify a position on an issue so that the reader will come to share that position instead of a rival one.*

None of these aims is inherently superior to the others. We begin with description and narration not because there is anything rudimentary about them, but because they require a sharpness of language that can serve to keep your prose lively even when you are dealing with abstract and complex issues.

1

Strategies of Description and Narration

DESCRIPTION

1a Aim for vividness in describing.

When you write a passage of **description**, you want to *make vivid* a place, an object, an animal, a character, or a group. That is, instead of trying simply to convey facts about the thing described, you want to give your readers a direct impression of it, as if they were standing in its presence. Your task is one of translation: you are looking for words to capture the way your senses have registered the thing, so that a reader will have a comparable experience.

Early in a composition course you may be asked to write a descriptive sketch of one provocatively simple thing, such as a pencil or an apple. If so, your first move should be to open your senses to its physical characteristics. As soon as you do, you will be surprised by the object's endless particularity: the lopsidedness of the apple, its creases and scars and speckles, the fuzziness of

descr
1a

its stem, and so forth. And you will begin to appreciate the real lesson your instructor has in mind: the value of language that conveys vividness by being both concrete and specific.

Concrete versus Abstract Language

A **concrete** word or phrase denotes an actual, observable thing or quality such as *skin* or *crunchy*. Words of the opposite sort, like *nutrition* or *impossible assignment*, are called **abstract**; they address the mind without calling the senses into play. To familiarize yourself with this distinction, study p. 000, 16a. You will see that concrete (also called *sensuous*) terms are essential to most description because they are the only ones that can bring the perceived thing to life in your reader's imagination.

Specific versus General Language

Among the possible concrete terms you might use, the relatively *specific* ones will call up sharper images than the relatively *general* ones. Specific language gets down to particulars: not *red* but *greenish-red*, not *too soft* but *dented by my thumbprint*. Note, incidentally, that although we can distinguish clearly between concrete and abstract language by the test of "appeal to the senses," a word is specific only by contrast with a more general one. Thus, *hound* is specific by contrast with *dog* but general by contrast with *bloodhound*.

Note how the writer of the following paragraph uses specific terms—*deteriorating shingles*, *tarpaper*, *peeling clapboard*, and so on—to make her description come alive:

> It was an unattractive low-rent building in the Winter Hill section of Somerville. A strange exterior of deteriorating shingles, tarpaper, peeling clapboard, and weathered plywood gave the house a haunted look. When my young daughter and I moved in, the outer doors were never locked and the back hall was filled with old chairs and underbrush. In our apartment the ceilings were peeling, wallpaper buckled off the walls, and a mouse lived behind the stove. There were code violations too numerous to count. But light streamed in through the windows. It warmed the rooms, created brilliant patterns on the floor, made our houseplants thrive. When the sun was out it was easy to understand why this had once been the most beautiful house in the neighborhood.[1]

Creating a Picture

Detail alone, however, does not make for vividness, as you can tell from these opening sentences of a book about baseball:

> It weighs just over five ounces and measures between 2.86 and 2.94 inches in diameter. It is made of a composition-cork nucleus encased in two thin layers of rubber, one black and one red, surrounded by 121 yards of tightly wrapped blue-gray wool yarn, 45 yards of white wool yarn, 53 more yards of blue-gray wool yarn, 150 yards of fine cotton yarn, a coat of rubber cement, and a cowhide (formerly horsehide) exterior, which is held together with 216 slightly raised red cotton stitches.[2]

Here we have an abundance of concreteness and specificity. The baseball is not just *made of different materials inside* but *made of a composition-cork nucleus encased in two thin layers of rubber . . .* ; it is not merely *stitched* but *held together with 216 slightly raised red cotton stitches*; etc. Yet the effect created is not descriptive but remote. Why?

The answer is that the writer has made no effort as yet to *show* us the baseball. Rather, he is analyzing its components in the spirit of a statistical review. Note, for example, how little appeal to our senses is made by the difference between 2.86 and 2.94 inches or by the idea of 150 yards of wound yarn or of 216 stitches. Even though the stitches are on the surface of the ball, we could never see more than a fraction of them at a time. The implied point of view, then, is not that of someone who is looking at a baseball, but of someone who knows the manufacturer's secrets.

This writer, who knows how to be as vivid as anyone, is here deliberately adopting a dry analytic stance, holding in check his enthusiasm for baseballs and baseball so that we will be struck by the release of that enthusiasm a few sentences later:

> Pick it up and it instantly suggests its purpose; it is meant to be thrown a considerable distance—thrown hard and with precision. Its feel and heft are the beginning of the sport's critical dimensions; if it were a fraction of an inch larger or smaller, a few centigrams heavier or lighter, the game of baseball would be utterly different. Hold a baseball in your hand. As it happens, this one is not brand-new. Here, just to one side of the curved surgical welt of stitches, there is a pale-green grass smudge, darkening on one edge almost to black—the mark of an old

descr
1a

> infield play, a tough grounder now lost in memory. Feel the ball, turn it over in your hand; hold it across the seam or the other way, with the seam just to the side of your middle finger. Speculation stirs. You want to get outdoors and throw this spare and sensual object to somebody or, at the very least, watch somebody else throw it. The game has begun.[3]

Once again we find highly concrete and specific diction: *just to one side of the curved surgical welt of stitches, there is a pale-green grass smudge, darkening on one edge almost to black. . . .* But now the definite language presents something we can take in, moment by moment, with our senses; the writer *is* being vivid. Even though quite a bit of his language is abstract (*purpose, precision, the sport's critical dimensions, memory, speculation,* etc.), our attention is occupied not by analytic findings but by the ball itself as we would see and feel it.

The key to vividness, then, lies less in a certain range of language than in a certain relationship with one's reader. The idea is to invite the reader into the scene and make it believable as immediate experience.

One way to stimulate vivid description is to pretend that you have no prior idea about the nature and function of the object in view. Thus a student writer begins a descriptive essay in this way:

> The object stands as high as one's knee, a foot and a half wide, a cylinder of deep gray metal. It is topped by a somewhat transparent plastic dome, of a dark tint, which looks uniformly dirty, as though it had been left in a smoky room for a few months. The object may look at first like a wastecan. On further inspection it might be mistaken for a bomb.
>
> On the side of the cylinder, at ankle height, white squares of plastic as big as one's palm bulge from a strip of blue metal in a row around the entire girth. There are eight of them, protruding half an inch and spaced two inches apart, as if they were somehow protecting the cylinder. Choosing one, I kick it. It springs back, a sort of huge button. But the object itself remains still.

As the essay continues beyond this point, we gradually infer that the object is a robot. By delaying that identification, the writer has usefully obliged himself to rely on precise details and points of comparison to better-known things.

EXERCISES

1. Write a descriptive paragraph about an object you can see as you sit at your desk. Begin the paragraph with a sentence supplying an idea to cover the details that follow.

2. Choose any convenient outdoor location, and go there as early in the morning as you can manage, taking notes on what you observe. Return to the same spot at night and repeat the process. Then write and submit two descriptive paragraphs corresponding to the two scenes. Try to make your reader feel how daylight and darkness (or artificial light) change the way objects are perceived.

3. Like the writer of the "robot" passage above, choose an object that your reader will not immediately recognize. Take two or three paragraphs to describe it, as if you yourself were trying to identify it by noting its features and relating them to more familiar things.

1b Establish a descriptive point of view.

The term **point of view** can have two meanings, both of which are relevant to effective description within an essay. First, a point of view is literally a place of observation, a stationary or moving vantage from which the reader is invited to look. Instead of presenting a scene as if it stood apart from any perceiver, you can heighten involvement by setting up such a vantage. Note, for instance, how Joan Didion enlists her reader to be the driver of a car—a role that is deeply appropriate to a tour of southern Californian subdivisions:

> Imagine Banyan Street first, because Banyan is where it happened. The way to Banyan is to drive west from San Bernardino out Foothill Boulevard, Route 66: past the Santa Fe switching yards, the Forty Winks Motel. Past the motel that is nineteen stucco tepees: "SLEEP IN A WIGWAM—GET MORE FOR YOUR WAMPUM." Past Fontana Drag City and the Fontana Church of the Nazarene and the Pit Stop A Go-Go; past Kaiser Steel, through Cucamonga, out to the Kapu Kai Restaurant-Bar and Coffee Shop, at the corner of Route 66 and Carnelian Avenue. Up Carnelian Avenue from the Kapu Kai, which means "Forbidden Seas," the subdivision flags whip in the harsh wind. "HALF-ACRE RANCHES! SNACK BARS! TRAVERTINE ENTRIES! $95 DOWN." It is the trail of an intention gone haywire, the flotsam of the

descr
1b

> new California. But after a while the signs thin out on Carnelian Avenue, and the houses are no longer the bright pastels of the Springtime Home owners but the faded bungalows of the people who grow a few grapes and keep a few chickens out here, and then the hill gets steeper and the road climbs and even the bungalows are rare, and here—desolate, roughly surfaced, lined with eucalyptus and lemon groves—is Banyan Street.[4]

Similarly, these sentences by Mark Twain invite you not just to contemplate a sunset but to scan the Mississippi River and its banks as if you, too, were a cub pilot on the bridge of a steamboat:

> Now when I had mastered the language of this water, and had come to know every trifling feature that bordered the great river as familiarly as I knew the letters of the alphabet, I had made a valuable acquisition. But I had lost something, too. I had lost something which could never be restored to me while I lived. All the grace, the beauty, the poetry, had gone out of the majestic river! I still kept in mind a certain wonderful sunset which I witnessed when steamboating was new to me. A broad expanse of the river was turned to blood; in the middle distance the red hue brightened into gold, through which a solitary log came floating, black and conspicuous; in one place a long, slanting mark lay sparkling upon the water; in another the surface was broken by boiling, tumbling rings, that were as many-tinted as an opal; where the ruddy flush was faintest, was a smooth spot that was covered with graceful circles and radiating lines, ever so delicately traced; the shore on our left was densely wooded and the somber shadow that fell from this forest was broken in one place by a long, ruffled trail that shone like silver; and high above the forest wall a clean-stemmed dead tree waved a single leafy bough that glowed like a flame in the unobstructed splendor that was flowing from the sun. There were graceful curves, reflected images, woody heights, soft distances, and over the whole scene, far and near, the dissolving lights drifted steadily, enriching it every passing moment with new marvels of coloring.[5]

The other meaning of *point of view* is an attitude or mental perspective, a way of "seeing things" more judgmentally. To be psychologically compelling, your essayistic descriptions should reflect a consistent point of view in this sense. Sometimes you can state your judgment directly, in Didion's manner: *It is the trail of an intention gone haywire, the flotsam of the new California.* Or, like Mark Twain, you can let the overtones of your language do the work of creating an attitude. The vagueness and abstractness of Twain's final sentence, for example, are deliberate; they convey a rapt inattentiveness to those particulars that the river pilot must learn to read not as a sublime whole but as specific perils to navigation.

Again, consider how another writer, N. Scott Momaday, establishes a strong point of view in both meanings of the term:

> A single knoll rises out of the plain in Oklahoma, north and west of the Wichita Range. For my people, the Kiowas, it is an old landmark, and they gave it the name Rainy Mountain. The hardest weather in the world is there. Winter brings blizzards, hot tornadic winds arise in the spring, and in summer the prairie is an anvil's edge. The grass turns brittle and brown, and **it cracks beneath your feet**. There are green belts along the rivers and creeks, linear groves of hickory and pecan, willow and witch hazel. **At a distance in July or August the steaming foliage seems almost to writhe in fire**. Great green and yellow grasshoppers are everywhere in the tall grass, popping up like corn **to sting the flesh**, and tortoises crawl about on the red earth, going nowhere in the plenty of time. **Loneliness is an aspect of the land**. All things in the plain are isolate; **there is no confusion of objects in the eye,** but one **hill** or one **tree** or one **man. To look upon that landscape in the early morning, with the sun at your back, is to lose the sense of proportion. Your imagination comes to life, and this, you think, is where Creation was begun.**[6]

Everything we have changed to boldface here enlists the reader's participation in a mood, beginning with a sense of physical hardship and ending with awe at a landscape that frustrates every wish for comfort, moderate weather, gentle scenery, sociability, and human scale. The writer's point of view has become our own.

EXERCISES

4. Choose an activity with which you are very familiar, and write a paragraph describing it in a way that gives your reader a sense of being present as the activity is performed. You can make the reader either a performer or an observer.

5. Think of a place you are fond of; it could be as small as your bedroom or as large as your home town. Write two descriptive paragraphs about that place. In the first one, try simply to "give the facts" in a neutral, precise way, without any special emphasis. Then convey the same

information in a vivid, engaging paragraph in which your point of view (attitude) is strongly apparent. Try to convey your point of view through descriptive commentary rather than through direct statements of opinion.

6. Choose any scene and think how it would look from the vantage of a certain moving vehicle (a truck, a plane, a boat, etc.). Making your reader into a passenger, write and submit a paragraph or two registering the reader's experience of that passing scene. Remember that you can make use of any sense impressions, not just visual ones.

7. In *Life on the Mississippi*, Mark Twain's romantic description of the river (p. 14) is followed by a hard-boiled paragraph which reviews the same scene with the mentality of an experienced river pilot: *that slanting mark on the water refers to a bluff reef which is going to kill somebody's steamboat one of these nights*, etc. Think of a scene that would look very different from two points of view—a hermit's, say, and a weekend backpacker's. (Choose a different contrast from that one.) Submit two paragraphs describing the scene from those two psychological outlooks. Remember that your two observers are actively making judgments, not just taking in the scenery.

1c Describe through a revealing action.

When the thing to be described is a person or animal, you should try to include a characteristic action—either a revealing incident or a habit. Note, for example, how a student writer characterizes her stepfather by telling a little story which puts his best-remembered quirk into a form that the reader, too, will be likely to remember:

> Poor Harvey meant well by all of us, but the truth is that we made him uncomfortable—especially as we grew into gangly adolescence and began changing shapes and voices. Youthful bosoms and peach-fuzz mustaches across the dinner table were too much for his suspicious, uptight nature to bear. He could hardly criticize us for getting older, but he *could* take his nervousness out on Blacky the dog, who was forever scratching wherever he pleased in a carefree, immodest way, as dogs will do even while grace is being said at Thanksgiving. Harvey would sit at the head of the table, not knowing how to control the squirming and giggling teenagers he had acquired as relatives, but then he would spot Blacky off in the corner scratching away most indecently, and he couldn't contain himself. "Blacky, Blacky!" he would yell, "*Stop it! Stop that right now!*" Blacky would stop scratching for just a

moment—long enough to stare back at Harvey as you would too if a lunatic were trying to interrupt your normal life for no reason—but when he started up again, he had a large and appreciative audience.

You can also describe by putting together a series of characteristic actions. In the following passage, the writer makes us feel a once-prosperous woman's homelessness by giving us glimpses of her daily routine:

Don't worry about Joanna—she'll be warm tonight. She'll park in her old neighborhood, on a street with no security patrol and tall hedges in front of the houses, so no one will notice her car.

She'll open the window a crack, lock the doors, curl up in warm clothes beneath blankets. Tomorrow she'll do the Beverly Center. Or maybe Westside Pavilion. She'll wash her hair and underwear in Nordstrom's ladies' room, dry them under the hand blower, apply makeup from testers at the cosmetic counter downstairs.

She'll nibble her way through Vons, her cart piled with items useless to a woman with no home in which to use them. While pretending to shop she'll munch roast beef, potato logs, and salad from the deli counter—then abandon the cart before she checks out with only two apples, which is all she can afford.

You won't know her if you see her. She looks and acts the well-heeled woman. She knows the Westside ropes. It's where she can survive—someone the census never counts, the regulars never notice. Not even her children, now in college, know she has no home. She will get back on her feet by herself, she says—or die in the attempt.[7]

EXERCISE

8. Write a descriptive paragraph or two about someone you know well, using an act of characteristic behavior to show your reader what impression that person usually makes on others. Before submitting your paragraph, revise it to make it as lively as possible, short of silliness.

1d Describe through figurative language.

Figurative, or *metaphorical*, language is a means of making something imaginatively striking by presenting it in terms of something that is very different in kind but appropriate in at least one limited respect. In essay prose, an effective description may well contain

descr
1d

some sharply figurative language. Consider examples in passages already studied:

> It is . . . the flotsam of the new California (Didion).
>
> A broad expanse of the river was turned to blood (Twain).
>
> the surface was broken by boiling, tumbling rings, that were as many-tinted as an opal (Twain).
>
> a single leafy bough that glowed like a flame (Twain).
>
> in summer the prairie is an anvil's edge (Momaday).
>
> the steaming foliage seems almost to writhe in fire (Momaday).

As readers, we instinctively ignore the literal absurdity of such statements and take them in the intended spirit. River water, we know, is not blood, but we ourselves have probably seen a river turn blood-red at sunset, and so the implied comparison brings the scene to life. That is what is remarkable about strong figurative language: by taking us momentarily away from the literal scene, it makes our participation in that scene more intense.

To see how figurative language can enliven a description, note the emphasized expressions in this passage:

> The road to Msinga begins in white South Africa and runs for hours through neat and orderly white farm land, not so different in appearance from parts of central California. Some ten miles beyond the last white town, you cross the border between the First and Third Worlds, between white South Africa and black kwaZulu. The border isn't marked; there is no need. You know you are coming into a different country, a different world. The white centerline vanishes, and the road itself starts **rearing and plunging, like a turbulent river rushing towards a waterfall.** The very mood of the landscape changes. And then you round a bend, and the tar falls away beneath the wheels, and you're looking down into Africa, into a vast, sweltering valley strewn with broken hills, mud huts, and tin-roofed shanties. From the rim of the escarpment, **it looks as though some mad god has taken a knife to the landscape, slashing ravines and erosion gullies into its red flesh and torturing its floor into rugged hills.** This is Msinga, a magisterial district in the self-governing homeland of kwaZulu, the place of Zulus.[8]

The notion of radically contrasting black and white "worlds" is dramatized here by the highlighted elements, which suggest more than they explicitly say. Where the road starts *rearing and plunging* like a horse and seemingly drawing the driver toward a *waterfall*, we know that danger and violence are imminent. And how "self-governing" can kwaZulu really be, if a *mad god* (apartheid?) appears to be *slashing* and *torturing* its landscape? This introductory paragraph braces us for serious trouble ahead.

Similarly, another writer combines precise literal details with figurative effects in order to rivet our attention on the object described—in this case, a performer who dives from a forty-foot ladder into a play pool of twelve-inch-deep water:

> LaMothe dives, however—doesn't jump—into water that scarcely reaches his calves as he stands up, his hands in a Hallelujah gesture. His sailor hat never leaves his head, his back stays dry unless the wash wets him, and yet so bizarre is the sight of a person emerging from water so shallow that one's eye sees him standing there as if with his drawers fallen around his feet. As he plummets, his form is as ugly and poignant as the flop of a frog—nothing less ungainly would enable him to survive—and, watching, one feels witness to something more interesting than a stunt—a leap for life into a fire net, perhaps.[9]

This writer combines sharply rendered particulars with a continual appeal to our imagination. First LaMothe is said to assume *a Hallelujah gesture*, as if he were in a revival meeting. Then we see him *as if with his drawers fallen around his feet*; nothing of the sort has actually occurred. Then LaMothe's fall is likened to *the flop of a frog*, and finally we regard the whole jump as if it were *a leap for life into a fire net*. The writer has gained effect not just from close observation, but also from freely relating what he perceives to other forms of experience.

For a fuller discussion of figurative language, see Chapter 17.

EXERCISES

9. Photocopy and submit any passage (for example, one taken from the assigned readings in this course) that describes by means of effective figurative language. Underline the relevant parts and submit a brief discussion of the effects achieved. Be specific in treating the author's particular choice of image in each instance.

10. Resubmit any passage you have written for a previous exercise in this chapter. Along with it, submit a second version in which you have tried to appeal to your reader's imagination through figurative language. Underline the sentences that aim at that effect.

1e Sharpen a description through contrast.

As the "South Africa" passage (p. 18) illustrates, one way you can make a description more pointed is to set the scene against a very different one. Note, for instance, how one writer makes us feel the devastation of strip mining in the Great Plains:

> Like other arid but inhabited parts of the world, the plains sometimes hold pieces of the past intact and out of time, so that a romantic or curious person can walk into an abandoned house and get a whiff of June 1933, or can look at a sagebrush ridge and imagine dinosaurs wading through a marsh. In the presence of strip-mined land, these humble flights fall to the ground. Scrambled into the waste heaps, the dinosaur vertebrae drift in chaos with the sandstone metate, the .45-70 rifle cartridge, the Styrofoam cup. It is impossible to imagine a Cheyenne war party coming out of the canyon, because the canyon is gone.[10]

EXERCISE

11. Submit a paragraph or two of description in which you guide your reader's feelings by sharply contrasting the described object with a very different one. If you prefer, you can base your contrast on the same object in a different state—a lake during calm and stormy weather, say, or a sick dog versus a healthy and frisky one.

1f Try different ways of ordering a description.

Note these principles for arranging the elements of a description:

1. If you give the observer a means of locomotion, as in Joan Didion's drive to Banyan Street (pp. 13–14), arrange the details in their "trip sequence."

2. If you are describing a landscape or an object, ask yourself what is most impressive about it, and try to save that feature for last. If it is a small detail, begin with larger ones; if it lies in the foreground, begin in the distance; and so on.
3. Similarly, if one fact about a described person stands out as more imposing than the others, look for a way of leading up to it.
4. If you are recounting a characteristic action, follow that action to its climax or conclusion. If it is a single incident, give it an introductory context so that your reader will understand why it is typical (Harvey's yelling at the dog, pp. 16–17). Alternatively, you can plunge your reader into the incident and then supply the context, as in a baited opener (p. 269, 11c).
5. If you want to convey a certain mood or idea, look for an order that will gradually develop and intensify the desired response (the mysterious effect of Rainy Mountain, p. 15).

EXERCISE

12. Choose any two of the five listed principles for ordering a description, and submit two descriptive passages, each following one of those principles. Indicate which principle you are illustrating in each instance. If you wish, you may use some of the same descriptive material in both passages.

NARRATION

Much that bears saying about description in essay prose applies equally to **narration**, or storytelling, for both modes aim at reproducing experience. Indeed, we have already seen that the recounting of characteristic actions is a common means of describing. Since all the virtues of a good description apply to narration as well, begin your mastery of narrative strategies by reviewing points 1a–f above.

1g Choose an appropriate tense for your narration.

Your choice of either the customary narrative past tense (*went*, *did*) or the less usual present tense (*goes*, *does*) should rest on

narr
1g

whether or not you are after a special effect. Since narrated actions are always "over," the past tense is generally appropriate and expected. (To see how such a past-tense framework governs the use of related tenses, look at p. 506, 25b.)

For past actions that were typical or recurrent, employ the **auxiliaries** *would* and *could*: *I would cry every Saturday night*, etc. The following student paragraph shows the auxiliaries in typical use:

> When I was a child I could always tell what the next day's weather would be. If, for example, rain was on the way, I would know it many hours in advance, without having to listen to weather forecasts. Sometimes I would notice a small change in the sky, such as the arrival of the first wisps of cirrus clouds that come before a front. Or again, I would realize that the flies around our apartment were acting sluggish in a way that usually spelled rain to me. Most often, though, I would simply feel "rainy inside," as I called it; the drop in barometric pressure would take down my mood and my energy level before there were any visible signs of a storm.

Choosing the present tense, by contrast, creates a more immediate effect, giving readers a sense of participating directly in the scene. Here, for example, someone who had idolized Bruce Lee in childhood tells of visiting the actor's grave:

> The hunger is eased this gray morning in Seattle. After asking directions from a policeman—Japanese—I easily locate Bruce's grave. The headstone is red granite with a small picture etched into it. The picture is very Hollywood—Bruce wears dark glasses—and I think the calligraphy looks a bit sloppy. Two tourists stop but leave quickly after glancing at me.
>
> I realize I am crying. Bruce's grave seems very small in comparison to his place in my boyhood. So small in comparison to my need for heroes. Seeing his grave, I understand how large the hole in my life has been, and how desperately I'd sought to fill it.[11]

Sometimes, too, a narrator will choose the present tense to suggest that the events being told are still fresh in memory and that they are accompanied by strong feelings. Thus a student writes:

> I turn on the public television station, expecting to hear a thoughtful program on Africa scheduled for this hour. But tonight there is a fund-

raising "special" instead. I am annoyed, but I try to be understanding; after all, the station needs extra contributions to survive. But before long I am completely fed up with the whole undertaking. It seems that the station manager has asked every unemployable comedian and punk band in town to put in an appearance. They are "special," yes—in just the way that marked-down loaves of yesterday's bread are "special" in the supermarket.

Notice how the writer's impatience is made more convincing by his telling the story as if it were occurring as he writes.

EXERCISES

13. Think of a significant incident in your life and narrate it in one or two paragraphs, using a straightforward time sequence and the past tense.

14. Choose a person to write about—either someone you know or someone in public life—and write a narrative paragraph that (a) shows the person in action, and (b) uses the present tense.

1h Choose between direct and indirect discourse.

One frequently used feature of narration is the reporting of speech or thought. When the language is quoted, the result is **direct discourse**. Direct discourse involving two or more people constitutes **dialogue**:

> "Mayday! Mayday! We're going down!" Those were the captain's last recorded words.
>
> "Try to make it to the runway," pleaded the flight controller. "We've got the fire trucks on line for you." But there was no reply; the plane had already begun its fatal plunge.

The obvious advantage of such quotation is that you give your reader the impression of being right on the scene.

Note that a paragraph of dialogue can be as brief as one speaker's remark. You should begin a new paragraph with every change of speaker.

If your purpose is merely to convey *what* was said, without reproducing speech patterns and tone, you can use **indirect discourse** instead of dialogue:

> In his last recorded words the captain declared that the plane was going down. There was no reply to the flight controller's plea that he try to reach the runway; the plane had already begun its fatal plunge.

Compared with the dialogue version, this is colorless. But no writer needs to be colorful at every moment—and no reader could stand it. In many situations you will find that indirect discourse suits your purpose well. You may also want to keep relatively incidental remarks in indirect discourse, shifting into dialogue when you feel that the speaker's exact words are dramatic or important.

Since a person's unspoken thoughts are less precise than statements, it is generally best to render them without quotation marks. Note, however, that you can do so in direct discourse:

> I can't keep up this pretense much longer, thought Kate. In another week or so, anyone will be able to read my face like a billboard.

Alternatively, you can put a character's thoughts into the past tense and thus render them indirectly:

> Friedland felt a wave of sadness, a sense of loss made sharper by the fact that he had been away; he could have contributed *something*, he thought, if he had stayed. But you couldn't be on call 24 hours a day, 365 days a year, and death, he mused, has never waited on the convenience of doctors. He found some comfort in having arranged the end of Maria's life as she had wanted it and having prepared her family adequately—or, anyway, extensively—for it. He felt that there was—he chose the word carefully—an *appropriate* time to die, and that that time had come for Maria. It ran cross grain with his training and his heart to say so; it was like asking a soldier on a battlefield to lay down his arms and admit defeat, even when it made no sense to fight on. He knew what had lain ahead for Maria and her family had she lingered. The spectacle of her death, he thought, would have distorted her in memory for her survivors. She would have become, in her deepening dementia, a nonperson. She would have ceased being Maria.[12]

For the problem of mixing direct and indirect discourse within a single sentence, see p. 511, 25d. For punctuation rules governing the presentation of dialogue, see pp. 550–52, 30d–30e.

EXERCISES

15. Write three paragraphs of narration in which two speakers are represented. Make use of both direct and indirect discourse, saving the former for utterances that deserve to be highlighted.

16. Write a paragraph in which you represent someone's thoughts and feelings about any subject. Put some of those reflections into direct discourse and others into indirect discourse, as in the "Friedland" paragraph above (*The spectacle of her death, he thought, would have distorted her in memory for her survivors*).

1i Experiment with the order of events.

Because every story occurs in a time sequence, the most natural order of telling is a chronological (straightforward) one, from the first incident to the last. That order, which characterizes all the examples of narration we have thus far reviewed, is the easiest one to master.

Once you feel at home with straightforward narrating, you can experiment with an order that requires more planning but also offers greater possibilities for inspiring your reader's curiosity. Instead of starting at the earliest moment, choose a more dramatic scene and reveal just enough about it to provoke interest. After that act of anticipation, you can skip back to the earliest relevant moment, filling in the circumstances that led to the climactic dramatic scene, and then carry the story through to its end.

Here, for instance, are the opening paragraphs of an essay about a brilliant scientist who developed sophisticated artillery and secretly sold it to Iraq:

> On a quiet evening this March, in the leafy Brussels suburb of Uccle, Gerald Bull walked down the hallway leading to his apartment and pulled out the key to his door. It was the last thing he ever did. Behind him, hidden in the shadows, an assassin stepped forward and fired two 7.65-millimeter rounds at point-blank range into the back of his skull.
>
> The killing bore all the hallmarks of a professional job. No one heard the silenced shots or the sound of the body slumping to the floor. No one saw the gunman. The $20,000 in cash Bull was carrying remained untouched.

narr 1i

> Gerald Vincent Bull, the world's greatest artillery expert, did not die alone. As the 62-year-old scientist fell to the floor, his lifetime obsession died with him: the dream of building a Supergun, a huge howitzer able to blast satellites into space or launch artillery shells thousands of miles into enemy territory.[13]

Note how the initial recounting of Gerald Bull's murder arouses curiosity and sets the stage for a story of high-stakes international intrigue.

Even within the scope of a single paragraph, you can double back in time with good effect. In the following case, the writer whimsically "explains the need for" the first *Dick Tracy* comic strip by referring to an event of the previous day:

> The original Dick Tracy, compounded of a few right angles and a pun, made his first appearance in the color cartoon section of the *Detroit Mirror* on October 4, 1931. He was presented as a detective attached to the police force of a city like Chicago, which was then enduring the Depression, the last years of Prohibition, and the prime of Al Capone. Only the day before, on October 3, Big Al himself had gone to a football game in suburban Evanston, Illinois, attended by eight overdressed bodyguards, chief among whom was a Sicilian called Machine Gun Jack McGurn. Witnesses recall a cheering throng and the gangster's slack smile and the courtly wave of his stubby-fingered hand as he acknowledged the multitude. Most sobering to responsible observers was the conduct of the Boy Scouts at the game, who reportedly ran around Capone shouting, "Yea-a-a, Al!" Obviously, in the autumn of 1931, with much of the police force in Al's pocket and the Boy Scouts plainly wavering, the time had come for extraordinary measures.[14]

EXERCISE

17. Look through some newspapers and magazines for a story that tells the outcome of previous events. (For example, a murder trial obviously follows a murder; the banning of a dangerous drug follows the harm it has been causing; the resumption of fishing in a once-polluted lake follows a crackdown on polluters.) Photocopy and hand in the story. Using your own words, write and submit several paragraphs of narration in which you begin by anticipating the most recent development in that story and then fill in relevant events from the more distant past. Feel free to invent details if necessary.

1j Use a story to make a point.

Essayists rarely tell stories without having in mind a general reflection or lesson that the story illustrates. Sometimes the point is actually learned by a figure within the narrative, as in this account of a foreigner's efforts to accustom himself to the ugly sprawl of Tokyo:

> Disappointed by the dismal panorama of the city as a whole, Boon began to suspect that he might be looking at it in the wrong way, judging it by standards that did not apply. And he recalled an incident that he had experienced about a week after his arrival.
>
> He had seen an old lady kneeling by the side of the road, cleaning out the gutter in front of her house. As he passed by, he noticed to his astonishment that she carried out this task with a pair of chopsticks. Most Japanese would themselves have regarded this use of chopsticks as eccentric, but the scrupulous attention to detail which it demonstrated would probably have gone without comment. On Boon it left a lasting impression. Discarding those large-scale expectations which the city failed to live up to, he set about exploring Tokyo with the old lady's chopsticks. He ignored the general and searched for the particular, in time discovering that for the loss of a spectacular urban panorama he was richly compensated by an inexhaustible fund of detail. It was a city made interesting solely by its people, customs, and the terrific vitality of its street life.[15]

Alternatively, you can draw the lesson yourself, as in the following lighthearted account of Sunday morning waffles prepared by the writer's father:

> After a while we would be summoned to the breakfast room where we would confront, not the geometrically perfect waffle of the Aunt Jemimah ads, but a great junk pile of a waffle that to a child of the forties looked like a target of the London Blitz. No one complained. Instead, we proceeded to salvage the rubble by adding gobs of syrup poured from log cabin-shaped tins. The waffles looked terrible but tasted fine. I learned from this to confront the waffle at hand and not worry much about Aunt Jemimah. This principle has guided my life.[16]

EXERCISE

18. Submit a paragraph or two in which you tell a story and include its point, either spelling out that point yourself or including it in the thoughts or words of a character.

1k Allow a story to imply its point.

If all narratives were accompanied by "morals," the balance between pleasure and instruction would be tipped too far to the grim side. In most cases it is better to leave your point *implicit*, or lurking within the story without ever being openly stated. The trick is to allow the very manner of your telling to convey what you leave unsaid.

Look, for instance, at this opening paragraph of an essay:

> A muskrat, also called musquash, or technically, *Ondatra zibethica zibethica* Linn. 1766—the creature didn't give a hoot about nomenclature—fell into our swimming pool, which was empty except for a puddle of winter water. It huddled in a corner, wild frightened eyes, golden brown fur, hairless muddied tail. Before I could find instruments suitable for catching and removing muskrats, a passing neighbor (unfamiliar with rodents per se, or even with rodents living in Czechoslovakia since 1905), deciding he'd come across a giant rat as bloodthirsty as a tiger and as full of infections as a plague hospital, ran home, got his shotgun, and fired at the muskrat until all that was left was a shapeless soggy ball of fur with webbed hind feet and bared teeth. There was blood all over the sides and bottom of the pool, all over the ball of fur, and the puddle of water was a little red sea. The hunting episode was over, and I was left to cope with the consequences. Humankind can generally be divided into hunters and people who cope with consequences.[17]

Without directly condemning his neighbor, this writer distances himself from the rodent-hating mentality. He does so not only in his icy final sentence but also at the outset in his droll show of respect for muskrats as fellow creatures.

For a more extended example of an implied narrative point, consider the following complete essay by a freshman student:

> "You should fix everyone's coffee or tea. You know, add the sugar, etc., and pour it. If the meat is hard to handle, you should cut it for the patient," instructed my predecessor. "After you've passed out the trays, you feed Irene and Molly."
>
> "That's Granny Post in there. She's 106. Even though she's not particularly senile, she's lost her teeth and must be fed with a giant eyedropper." I discovered just how clear Granny Post's mind was when I tried to feed her. The dear old lady wasn't hungry and spat it back at me.
>
> After that first day at the convalescent hospital, I was on my own.

Irene was eager to please and partially fed herself, but I dreaded feeding Molly. She was blind and pitifully thin. "I'm sick. I'm sick," she'd cry. "Don't make me eat any more. Please, I'm sick."

"But Molly, you've got to eat so you can get well. Come on, one more bite. Here, hold my hand. It's not so bad." And I'd coax one more bite down her before gathering the sixty trays onto their racks and wheeling them back to the safety of the kitchen. The rest of the evening I cleaned the coffee pot, set up the breakfast trays, scoured sinks, and mopped the floors. I didn't mind sitting on the floor scrubbing at the oven or making the juices and sandwiches for the evening nourishment. It was when I confronted the elderly people on the other side of that kitchen door that I became nervous and awkward.

In a few weeks I mastered the hospital routine, the names of most of the patients, and their idiosyncrasies.

Opposite the kitchen was what was fondly called "the ward." Dora, a small, white-haired woman who was continually nearly slipping out of the bottom of the wheelchair to which she was tied, was the ringleader of this group. She cussed up a storm at anyone who came near her and perpetually monotoned, "What can I do? Tell me, what can I do?" May accompanied her with "Put me to bed. I want to go to bed." One evening as I entered with dinner, the woman across from Dora was gaily slinging her waste matter about the room, especially at anyone who threatened to come near her. A nurse and some aides calmed her down.

As far as the two sisters in room twelve were concerned, they were traveling on a huge ocean liner. When I brought their trays, they always asked, "How long till we get to port?" or "I'm sorry. We can't eat today because we're seasick."

John mumbled perpetually about the batty ladies in the TV room. He liked his smokes and his sports magazine.

Mr. Harrison fed a stray cat that stayed outside his sliding-glass door. He loved his cat and I gave him leftovers to feed it. One day a car rushed down the hill and struck his cat. Mr. Harrison told me his cat ran away, but it would come back as always. He stood at his door watching for it.

There were two Ethels. Dora advanced to feeding herself so I began feeding Ethel Irene. Ethel Irene was small, roly-poly, and had gray-black hair cut short like a little boy's. She liked to joke and use large words. Sometimes when she grasped for a word, it just wouldn't come and great big tears would form in her eyes. She liked sunshiny days and the sound of birds singing. She liked me to sing to her, too. Always clamped tightly in her hand was the buzzer to call the nurse. It was Ethel Irene's lifeline. Occasionally it fell out of her hand and she became so frantic she couldn't speak, only pointing and crying.

I tried to regard the other Ethel as just one of the many patients to whom I delivered food. When I brought dinner, I fixed Ethel's tea,

narr
1k

cut her meat, and tucked in her napkin. Then I'd clearly shout, "Enjoy your dinner." But instead of letting me leave, she'd pull me down to her and in a low, halting voice struggle out, "I like you. Can I kiss you?"

It became increasingly difficult to leave Ethel. She'd refuse to release my arm, purposely eat slowly so I was forced to return just to retrieve her tray, and cry when I succeeded in making my exit. To avoid upsetting her, I began sneaking into the room to take her tray or sending someone else. If she realized the deception, she'd let out an anguished cry and begin sobbing. I couldn't bear to pass Ethel's room and see her arms reaching out for me.

Many of the patients were lonely like Ethel and starved for attention. Some were on welfare and had few or no relatives. Most were just forgotten.

Ethel's son visited one day. Roaring drunk, he first tried to get fresh with me and then stomped into the kitchen demanding food.

Molly had visitors once, too. When I reached work and dropped by to see Molly, two or three of her relatives were standing about her. Molly was breathing laboriously, her nose and mouth were attached to an oxygen tank. She was dying now. The relatives left shortly. Molly's bed was empty when I returned the next day.

I worked in the convalescent hospital only sixteen hours a week for eight months. The old people remained there twenty-four hours a day for months or years, depending on how "lucky" they were. They were fed, diapered at night, and sponge-bathed in the morning. But what they needed most . . .

The age is gone when three generations occupy the same house. Young people want a life of their own.

My parents are nearly fifty now.

This essay has some minor flaws, but they are outweighed by its compassion and control. The memorable description of Ethel Irene with her *lifeline* buzzer and the understated recounting of Molly's death seem like reality itself. And the apparent disorganization covers a subtle and effective movement engaging the reader in the writer's own ordeal of first learning her chores, then coping with the patients' oddities, then facing the ultimate fact of death, and finally turning her thoughts to her own parents, who *are nearly fifty now* and may someday be like Molly and Mr. Harrison. Will she look after them in their senility? The abrupt ending leaves us troubled, not only by grotesque and tender images from the convalescent hospital, but also by conflicting feelings toward parents who deserve our care but who threaten to invade *a life of* [our] *own*.

EXERCISES

19. From your assigned readings or any other source, photocopy a passage that strikes you as effectively conveying a stated or implied point. Submit the passage along with a paragraph of your own analyzing how the writer has achieved that effect. Be specific about the writer's choice of language.

20. Think of a real or imaginary story that would lead to some perception or generalization. Put that point into a sentence at the top of a page. Then skip some lines and write the story in several paragraphs (or more, if you use dialogue) so that the story implies your point without completely stating it.

NOTES

[1] Beverly Belfer, "Stealing the Light," *Boston Review* Dec. 1987: 3.

[2] Roger Angell, *Five Seasons: A Baseball Companion* (New York: Simon, 1977) 11.

[3] Angell 12.

[4] Joan Didion, *Slouching Towards Bethlehem* (1968; New York: Washington Square, 1981) 20–21.

[5] Mark Twain, *Life on the Mississippi* (1883; New York: Signet, 1961) 67–68.

[6] N. Scott Momaday, *The Way to Rainy Mountain* (Albuquerque: New Mexico UP, 1969) 5.

[7] Bettijane Levine, "Living in the Shadows," *Los Angeles Times* 2 Dec. 1990: E1.

[8] Rian Malan, *My Traitor's Heart: A South African Exile Returns to Face His Country, His Tribe, and His Conscience* (New York: Atlantic Monthly, 1990) 283.

[9] Edward Hoagland, *Red Wolves and Black Bears* (New York: Random, 1972) 19–20.

[10] Ian Frazier, *Great Plains* (New York: Farrar, 1989) 90.

[11] Shanlon Wu, "In Search of Bruce Lee's Grave," *New York Times Magazine* 5 Apr. 1990: 20.

[12] Peter Goldman and Lucille Beachy, "One Against the Plague," *Newsweek* 21 July 1986: 50.

[13] Kevin Toolis, "The Man behind Iraq's Supergun," *New York Times Magazine* 26 Aug. 1990: 46.

[14] Robert Stone, "Sunday Mornings with Fly Face," *Times Literary Supplement* [London] 13–19 July 1990: 752.

[15] John David Morley, *Pictures from the Water Trade: Adventures of a Wanderer in Japan* (Boston: Atlantic Monthly, 1985) 65–66.

[16] Art Peterson, "Me and Barbara Stanwyk," unpublished essay, n.d.

[17] Miroslav Holub, "Shedding Life," trans. Dana Hábová and Patricia Debney, *Science* 86 (1986): 51–52.

2

Strategies of Analysis and Argument

Narrowly construed, **analysis** is a means of explanation whereby something is separated into its parts. But in common use, the word covers a number of ways to grapple with a problem. When one instructor asks you to "analyze the effects of the *Challenger* explosion on the American space program," while another wants an "analysis of the differences between problems of school discipline in 1992 and those in 1952," and still another says, "analyze the last scene of *Macbeth*," you can gather that *analysis* has become a roomy term. Here we will take it to include every customary means of explanation.

Argument, or the use of persuasive reasoning to convince others that a certain position on an issue is justified, has traditionally been recognized as an essay mode in its own right. And with good reason: since argument always involves opposing someone else's position, an argumentative essayist must be unusually alert to objections. Actually, though, all the merits of a sound argument can be found in many analytic essays as well. And conversely, every strategy of analysis is serviceable in argumentation.

Rather than insist on fine distinctions before we have arrived at the full essay, then, we can think of analysis and argument together here. As opposed to the *physical immediacy* of description and narration (Chapter 1), analysis and argument make up the strategies of *mental operation*—those designed to show that the writer's understanding of a given problem is a reasonable one.

2a Clarify the meaning of a key term or concept.

Many student writers recall having been told that they should always define their terms at the outset of an analysis or argument. The result, usually, is the hapless "dictionary definition opener" (p. 275, 11g)—a stiff exercise in belaboring the obvious, leaving an impression that the writer is casting about for something, anything, to say. You should define only those terms that are both crucial to your point and seriously in need of clarification. And you should do so in a vivid, helpful way, avoiding the tone that says in effect, "We interrupt this graceful essay to bring you the following bulletin from *Webster's Unabridged*."

Definition becomes a truly serviceable tool when it brings to light a misunderstanding that the writer wishes to correct. Suppose, for example, you find yourself arguing against the idea, upheld by some social scientists, that intelligence is unevenly distributed across ethnic groups. The very first question you should ask yourself is what those social scientists mean by *intelligence*. In all likelihood, they mean simply a capacity to achieve high scores on standardized IQ tests, which in turn are based on a concept of intelligence as an indivisible, quantifiable thing. But that concept happens to be outmoded; most authorities now hold that intelligence is made up of many capacities falling within broad groupings—linguistic, logical-mathematical, musical, bodily-kinesthetic, spatial, interpersonal, and intrapersonal.[1] Though there are other weighty points that you can make against IQ tests as measures of intelligence, you can give your essay a strong beginning by redefining the key term to reflect the current state of understanding.

Here is a carefully thought-out example of this strategy, deployed by a writer who wants to challenge the popular belief in extrasensory perception:

> ESP, "extrasensory perception," has become the most widely known term from the general field of psychical phenomena. Of all the borderline effects, ESP comes closest to scientific respectability by being perceived as similar to the paradigms of normal science. However, confusion exists because ESP has two quite different meanings. One school of thought believes that information may be transmitted from one individual or object to another individual or object by means of physical signals that we have not as yet discovered. These carriers may be electromagnetic waves in some little-studied spectral range, or gravity waves, or some other type of ill-characterized energy transmission. Such a postulate has the virtue of being within the framework of contemporary physics. Other advocates of ESP believe that transmission involves methods that are totally outside the range of measurement of physical devices and are not energy dependent in the thermodynamic sense.
>
> The first concept of ESP does not fit the ordinary meaning of the words, for if a physical signal is sent from a source with a sending device to an individual with a receiver, there is nothing extrasensory about the process. It is de facto sensory; we have only failed so far to locate and characterize the sense organ. Such phenomena may be very interesting, but nothing revolutionary is being explored that is likely to change our philosophical concepts or science. . . .
>
> The second type of ESP, or true extra sensory perception, is an entirely different kind of idea. If it is proved to exist, it will seriously alter our ideas about physics and biology. This kind of ESP would, as we will show, violate the Second Law of thermodynamics and force a basic reformulation of most of science.[2]

These paragraphs shrewdly use definition as an argumentative wedge. If proponents of ESP believe in transmission through physical signals, the writer says, then they are not talking about ESP at all. And if they don't, they are defying much of what is known about physics.

Defining by Example

Often the best way to define a tricky term is to use a concrete example, as in this preliminary attempt to fix the meaning of "complexity":

> So, what is a complex thing? How should we recognize it? In what sense is it true to say that a watch or an airliner or an earwig or a person is complex, but the moon is simple? The first point that might occur to

us, as a necessary attribute of a complex thing, is that it has a heterogeneous structure. A pink milk pudding or blancmange is simple in the sense that, if we slice it in two, the two portions will have the same internal constitution: a blancmange is homogeneous. A car is heterogeneous: unlike a blancmange, almost any portion of the car is different from other portions. Two times half a car does not make a car. This will often amount to saying that a complex object, as opposed to a simple one, has many parts, these parts being of more than one kind.[3]

EXERCISES

1. Ask yourself which, if any, of the following activities ought to be regarded as *sports:* hiking, chess, bowling, bodybuilding. Then write a paragraph or two in which you resolve that issue by carefully defining what you mean by the term *sports*. (Must a sport be physical, competitive, etc.?)

2. Choose a term, such as *freedom* or *democracy* or *patriotism*, that you find to be interpreted *positively but very differently* by different individuals or groups. (For example, leaders of nations with entirely opposed political systems regard those nations as *democracies*.) Using your dictionary, your memory, and any other handy sources, gather as many different senses of your chosen term as you can. Then submit several paragraphs in which you define the term as *you* think it should be construed, showing why you prefer that definition to other possibilities.

2b Divide an object or idea into its parts.

In **division** the work of analysis consists of spelling out the parts or stages that make up some whole. Since the parts of one thing will always differ in some way from those of anything else, division can be close in function to definition; naming all the parts is a means of grasping what is unique about the object or idea. Thus the writer who specified all the ingredients of a baseball (p. 17) was using division to indicate what the ball *must* contain to be properly considered a baseball and not, for example, a softball.

Especially when used near the beginning of an essay, division can perform the simple but useful function of indicating the scope of a subject:

> The predators—insects that kill and consume other insects—are of many kinds. Some are quick and with the speed of swallows snatch their prey from the air. Others plod methodically along a stem, plucking off and devouring sedentary insects like the aphids. The yellowjackets

capture soft-bodied insects and feed the juices to their young. Mud-dauber wasps build columned nests of mud under the eaves of houses and stock them with insects on which their young will feed. The horse-guard wasp hovers above herds of grazing cattle, destroying the bloodsucking flies that torment them. The loudly buzzing syrphid fly, often mistaken for a bee, lays its eggs on leaves of aphid-infested plants; the hatching larvae then consume immense numbers of aphids. Ladybugs or lady beetles are among the most effective destroyers of aphids, scale insects, and other plant-eating insects. Literally hundreds of aphids are consumed by a single ladybug to stoke the little fires of energy which she requires to produce even a single batch of eggs.[4]

Observe how the writer has first defined predator insects and then divided them into various kinds. Yet instead of making a dry, listlike effect, she has sustained interest by descriptively capturing each species' most typical action. More important, she has demonstrated her wide knowledge and laid a foundation for her main point, disclosed in a later paragraph: that indiscriminate spraying of pesticides kills a great many insects that would otherwise help to control agricultural pests.

By dividing a subject into its parts, you can also bring order out of apparent confusion. Look, for example, at how a student writer leads into a discussion of buying a ten-speed bicycle:

> What should you look for when shopping for a ten-speed bike? It is easy to get confused by glossy advertisements saying that you can't do without the latest molybdenum frame and cantilever brakes. But you can bring some sense into the matter if you keep in mind that all ten-speed bikes are designed primarily either for *touring* or for *racing*. Which activity do you prefer? The answer will tell you whether to go for a stiff frame or a more comfortable one; whether you want tight steering or a capacity for no-hands cruising on the highway; whether you should be more interested in quickness of shifting or in having a low enough bottom gear for hauling luggage up a mountain road.

Here the act of division—separating all ten-speed bikes into touring and racing cycles—leads to a series of further distinctions, each of which can be developed in a subsequent paragraph.

EXERCISES

3. Submit several paragraphs in which you divide college or high school teachers into a number of main types. (If you want to be humorous, go

ahead.) Try to include at least one characteristic action to illustrate each of your types.

4. Take a public problem or issue, such as air pollution or gene transplants or the arms race, and break that problem or issue into what you consider to be its component parts—namely, the narrower issues that go to make it up. (If the issue were abortion, for example, the subissues might be the rights of the unborn, how to determine when human life begins, parents' right to control family size, religious prohibitions, health risks to mothers, and the effects of making abortion legal or illegal. But now that this example has been supplied, you should choose a different issue.) Underline the items on your list that strike you as deserving the most concern, and then write the introductory paragraph to an essay about the issue, emphasizing the important subissues. Hand in your underlined list along with the paragraph.

2c Illustrate a point with details.

The heart of analysis and argument consists of making general points and backing them up with examples and/or reasons (2d below). As the writer of the following paragraph understood, readers expect a broad assertion to be fleshed out with specific instances:

> Dictators tend to like movies. Benito Mussolini ordered the construction, in 1938, of Cinecittá, the most monumental film studios in Europe. Stalin, according to his daughter's biography, presided over the outfitting of a magnificent private projection room in his Kremlin apartments; the rise and fall of Soviet filmmakers depended on his tastes and his moods. Juan Perón and Mao Zedong shared the fascination, to the extent that each married an actress of the silver screen. Francisco Franco was not known for his literary achievement, apart from his speeches, but he seems to have had the fantasy of being a writer for the movies; in 1940, under the pseudonym Jaime de Andrade, he wrote a film script entitled, significantly, *Race*. It was filmed on a huge budget in the first days after the victory of the "glorious national movement," and it opened with great pomp, as the model for an epic Spanish cinema. The Maximum Leader of the Cuban revolution does not escape the rule. Having created, in 1979, the International Film Festival of Havana (it drew many people to the Cuban capital this past December), he inaugurated a film school, too.[5]

A humorous or whimsical thesis stands in just as much need of illustration as a serious one:

> "I eat bread sparingly," writes Tom Osler. "In the summer, I consume large quantities of fruit juices. . . . I do not use salt at the table or at the stove. I do not use sugar, because it seems to make my skin break out in acne." In an article titled "Running Through Pregnancy" in *Runner's World*, we learn that runners "have little trouble with irregularity. Some even experience a frequency increase in bowel movements." In the pages of the same magazine Joe Henderson reports that he thinks of a running high "as the way we're supposed to feel when not constipated." If one did not know what was being talked about—running—one might feel like an eavesdropper listening in on conversations in a nursing home for the elderly.[6]

EXERCISES

5. Scan the readings for this or any other course until you find an analysis that uses substantial illustration of a point. (If your example comes from outside this course, submit a photocopy of it.) Hand in a paragraph of your own in which you state the writer's point and back it up with several of the illustrative examples cited. Be careful to use your own language.

6. Think of some general statement you would feel comfortable justifying (e.g., *Students on this campus are more interested in parties than in books*), and jot down as many illustrative instances as you can think of. Then write and submit a paragraph in which you set forth and illustrate your idea.

2d Support a point with reasons.

Analysis and argument often require you to supply not only instances of your point (2c) but also reasons why it ought to be believed. After an opening assertion, for example, the following paragraph is devoted entirely to showing the plausibility of that assertion.

> Not only is putting the most difficult skill in the game, it's by far the most important. If par for a course is 72 strokes, 36 of those strokes are allotted for putts. Thus a round is evenly divided between putting

and all the other skills combined that are needed to move a ball from tee to green. Further, from the standpoint of scoring, sinking a putt is always worth more than hitting a perfect drive or lofting a lovely iron. Every time you sink a putt you save a stroke; for all the brilliance of a drive or an approach, what you earn is a leg up on your next shot, which won't necessarily be worth a thing on the scorecard. Another way of saying this is that putting is important because it comes last. "You can recover from a bad shot," notes Chi Chi Rodriguez, the former P.G.A. player who dominated the senior tour last year. "But you can't recover from a bad putt."[7]

For a fuller discussion of reasoning and its functions, see Chapter 4.

EXERCISE

7. Think of a non-obvious assertion that you would like your reader to believe, and submit a paragraph making that assertion and backing it up with reasons.

2e Establish causes and effects.

Most writing about cause and effect proceeds from known effects—that is, from facts such as a burst dam or an economic recession or a change in climate—to supposed causes, which are usually multiple. The following student paragraph shows a common pattern of beginning with the effect, disposing of relatively minor causal factors, and then treating the factors that seem weightiest:

the effect to be explained In recent decades the reported death rate from cancer has been rising dramatically. How alarmed should we be by this **cause #1** statistical change? One cause of the mounting curve is probably the simple fact that we are more conscious of cancer now than we used to be, and less ashamed to mention **cause #2** the feared disease. Another cause may be the fact that more and more people are dying in hospitals and undergoing autopsies: in earlier times the comparable deaths at home from cancer might have been attributed to "old age." But factors like these take us only so far. Eventually we have to admit that cancer has been gaining on us in an absolute sense. If so, the real causes must be environmental: the

the more serious causes: #3, #4, #5

> continued increase in smoking, the use of dangerous pesticides and food additives, and increased pollution from automobiles and industry. Some of those sources must be more responsible than others, but until we know more than we do, we had better give urgent attention to all of them.

After this strong introduction, which showed a proper caution about making one-to-one connections between causes and effects, the writer devoted the rest of her essay to the three causes she had identified as most significant.

Again, note how another writer begins with a condition—the scarcity, in Southern California cities, of cafés in which neighbors can linger and converse—and goes on to propose the sources of that condition:

> There are simple economic explanations why cafés of community don't exist in Southern California urban centers. Rent is dear and coffee cheap; the turnover would be too slow to make a profit. Lingering also doesn't fit the image of a city on the move, especially if the clientele arrives in unmatched pants and jackets.
>
> Yet economic explanations are not the dominant reasons. Lack of common grounds—communities of interest—are the larger trouble. Angelenos or Orange County residents are either too new or too unsettled to develop the sense of shared geography that holds on in places like Riverside or Barstow.[8]

Correlation

Much treatment of causes and effects wisely steers away from flat assertions that *x* is *the* cause of *y*. Instead, the writer significantly associates, or *correlates*, *x* with *y*, leaving open the possibility that factors *a*, *b*, and *c* may also have played a part in bringing about *y*.

Consider the following student passage, which correlates a popular dance style with various characteristics of the 1970s:

> The clearest example of all is provided by disco dancing, which became a national craze in 1978. In several respects disco was the perfect expression of the decade that produced it. For one thing, the seventies combined a rediscovery of "roots" with an easing of the racial tensions that were so explosive in the sixties. Black and Latin in its origins, disco remained somewhat ethnic in flavor, yet it was accepted by the whole society. Second, disco was a high-technology form; its amplified

sounds and its dazzling lights suggested the network of electronics that many people had come to regard as their real environment. Third, disco expressed "the me decade" both in its demand for physical fitness and in its emphasis on display. And finally, disco was more disciplined than the do-your-own-thing dances of the sixties. Disco swept the country at a time when nearly everyone who had once joined "the counterculture" was ready to give the sense of order a second chance.

Observe that in this passage, cause-and-effect reasoning merely *associates* a complex of factors with a certain result. The writer wisely refrains from risking everything on only one of four possible sources of the 1970s' disco craze—the emphases on race, technology, self, and discipline.

EXERCISES

8. Think about something you have done that now strikes you as wrong; it can be either a specific act or the adoption of a habit or prejudice. What were the probable causes, or determining factors, leading to your act or habit? Submit a paragraph in which you proceed from *what* you did to *why* you think you did it.

9. To explore relations between intended causes and effects, find an advertisement that implies a strong but farfetched connection between an advertised product and an appealing image, personality, or style of living. Submit the advertisement or a photocopy of it along with two or three paragraphs analyzing what you take to be the intended effect of the ad. (Of course, the ultimate intended effect is that people buy the product. You should concentrate on the immediate intended effect—for example, to link the product with a certain pleasurable feeling.)

10. Find a news story about an event that probably had at least three separate causes, and submit two or three paragraphs summarizing the event and explaining what you take to have been its main causes.

2f Developing comparisons and contrasts.

In a sense, we could say that all thinking comes down to comparing (matching things that are alike) and contrasting (pointing out differences). We cannot have an idea about anything without setting that object of thought beside similar things and then asking ourselves how it differs from them. Not surprisingly, then, **comparison** and **contrast** can be found at all levels of writing, from the structure of sentences and paragraphs through the central purpose of an essay or book.

One tidy way of handling a contrast is to devote one paragraph to item *x* and a second paragraph to the contrasting item *y*, as in this passage:

> Formerly the movies sold a vision of utopia, allowing—indeed, exploiting—the impulse to escape into another place: a balmy land of plenty, where the people would be kind (and, in most movies, all the same). This vision often made the movies memorable. In 1939, for instance, the best big productions ended, albeit naively or dishonestly, with their gazes outward, looking past the whole dispiriting mechanism of production toward that place "across the border" where Dallas and the Ringo Kid are headed, or toward that paradise beyond the snows where Heathcliff will love Cathy for all time, or toward Jefferson Smith's rejuvenated nation, or toward that new Union wherein Rhett and Scarlett will now go their separate ways, or toward that homey farm where Dorothy will now find her "heart's desire."
>
> Today's movies offer no utopia, because, they say, everything you'd ever want is here on sale. The movies make this pitch first by concentrating on, and glamorizing, the closed sites of shopping and consumption: nice restaurants and luminous department stores, and the clean and roomy cell wherein the star keeps his or her posters, sweaters, jackets, copper pots, appliances. And the movie makes the pitch by packaging *itself* as a commodity. Like any smoke or Coke or fast-food burger, it is an item whose appeal fails to outlast the moment that it takes to suck it in.[9]

So, too, you can devote a whole paragraph to resemblances, as a student writer does in this richly detailed comparison between two characters in Shakespeare's *Hamlet:*

> We need only abstract Laertes' five brief appearances in order to see that he and Hamlet are meant to be taken as parallel figures. In Act I, scene 2, Laertes asks the King for permission to return to France; in the same scene we learn that Hamlet has asked the King for permission to return to Wittenburg. In Laertes' second appearance he reproaches his sister for her receptivity to Hamlet; Hamlet later gives a comparable lecture to Gertrude. Hamlet's loss of a father through murder is mirrored by Laertes' loss of Polonius to Hamlet's own sword, and in Act IV, scene 1, Laertes reappears with the Hamlet-like idea of killing his father's murderer. Again, Laertes' cries of grief at Ophelia's funeral are

an/ arg 2f

> travestied by Hamlet, who leaps after him into the grave. And in Laertes' fifth appearance, in Act V, he and Hamlet square off for a duel of offended sons—and the result of the scene is that both of them die and both are avenged. Laertes, we might say, scarcely exists apart from Hamlet. Superficially, at least, they harbor the same desires and grievances, love the same woman, behave alike, and are drawn into a single fate at the end.

Having established these strong parallels, the writer went on to show how the reckless passion of Laertes stands out against Hamlet's doubts and hesitations.

Alternatively, you can combine resemblances and differences within a single paragraph, as this student writer does:

resemblances

> The authors of our Bill of Rights and of the *Communist Manifesto* shared an idea that previous forms of government had protected injustice and inequality. Both were determined to write a charter for a new kind of society in which ordinary people would be free from tyranny.

differences

> The two documents, however, are absolutely opposed in their conceptions of human liberty. The Bill of Rights seeks to limit the powers of government by specifying the rights of individuals, whereas Marx's *Manifesto* seeks—chiefly by denying the rights of inheritance and private property—to protect the masses from powerful individuals. We will see that this difference of philosophy runs straight through the two documents, making one of them, the *Manifesto*, a list of what *must* be done and the other, the Bill of Rights, a list of what *must not* be done to interfere with the will of citizens.

The pivotal word *however* doesn't simply divide this writer's paragraph in two; it correctly predicts that in her essay the differences between the *Communist Manifesto* and the Bill of Rights will outweigh the characteristics they share. Readers intuitively know that the second of two elements will always be the more emphatic one.

The following paragraph, finally, makes particularly strong use of this principle:

> To get a sense of the scale of what happened at Hanford, consider this: The most serious release of radioactivity from a nuclear complex in the western world was thought to have occurred in 1957 at England's plutonium production plant at Windscale. There, 20,000 curies of iodine-

131 escaped into the atmosphere as a result of a fire in the reactor. British authorities, suspecting that cows grazing on contaminated forage might pass the hot iodine on in their milk, impounded all fresh milk within a 200-mile radius—a prudent step given that dairy products turn out to be the main way that humans pick up radioactive iodine. The 1979 Three Mile Island accident in Pennsylvania vented 15 to 24 curies of iodine-131 from the reactor containment building; pregnant women and pre-school children were evacuated. But at Hanford, more than *half a million* curies went up the plutonium separation plants' stacks in the decade following start-up in 1944. With not a word of warning or the slightest effort to protect local food sources.[10]

For a complete essay of comparison and contrast, see page 111.

EXERCISES

11. Looking through magazines and newspapers, find two editorials or columns expressing opinions about the same public issue. Submit copies along with two or three paragraphs of your own in which you compare and contrast the two pieces, emphasizing the points of opinion or style or tone that you find most significant.

12. Write two paragraphs about two movies that seem to you alike in certain ways and different in others. Use your two paragraphs to establish the most important resemblances and differences. You can deal with themes, leading characters, techniques, or effects.

13. Think of two individuals or groups that are often considered to be extremely different (e.g., two famous public figures, men and women, babies and old people, Texans and New Yorkers). Jot down all the ways in which you could show that the seeming opposites are really alike. Then submit a paragraph in which, beginning with the obvious points of difference, you emphasize the little-noted similarities.

2g Cover the steps of a process.

Sometimes the stages to be covered in an analysis are actions or steps which, performed correctly and in a certain fixed order, make up a routine for accomplishing some end. The strategy of laying out such steps is called **process analysis**.

A process analysis can serve its purpose only if all of the

essential steps appear in their necessary order. If, for instance, you were teaching your reader how to drive a stick-shift car, you might decide that the essential parts of the process are (1) familiarizing oneself with ignition, clutch, brake pedal, accelerator, and emergency brake; (2) starting and stopping; (3) steering while remaining within one gear; (4) shifting gears; (5) making turns; and (6) backing up. If item 1 appeared farther down the list, or if item 4 were missing, or if a triviality like *reading the odometer* were thrown in, the analysis would be flawed.

Process analyses occur frequently in technical writing—for example, in reports of experimental procedures or in operating instructions for new equipment. When essayists use the same strategy, they usually have some further idea in mind. Thus one writer analyzes a motorcycle mechanic's diagnostic steps, not in order to teach motorcycle repair, but to show that the mechanic uses exactly the same principles of reasoning as a scientist:

> Skill at this point consists of using experiments that test only the hypothesis in question, nothing less, nothing more. If the horn honks, and the mechanic concludes that the whole electrical system is working, he is in deep trouble. He has reached an illogical conclusion. The honking horn only tells him that the battery and horn are working. To design an experiment properly he has to think very rigidly in terms of what directly causes what. This you know from the hierarchy. The horn doesn't make the cycle go. Neither does the battery, except in a very indirect way. The point at which the electrical system *directly* causes the engine to fire is at the spark plugs, and if you don't test here, at the output of the electrical system, you will never really know whether the failure is electrical or not.
>
> To test properly the mechanic removes the plug and lays it against the engine so that the base around the plug is electrically grounded, kicks the starter lever and watches the spark-plug gap for a blue spark. If there isn't any he can conclude one of two things: (a) there is an electrical failure or (b) his experiment is sloppy. If he is experienced he will try it a few more times, checking connections, trying every way he can think of to get that plug to fire. Then, if he can't get it to fire, he finally concludes that *a* is correct, there's an electrical failure, and the experiment is over. He has proved that his hypothesis is correct.[11]

What distinguishes such a paragraph from sheer narrative is its reference, not to something that happened once, but to a procedure that must be followed every time a certain problem arises.

Sometimes, however, you can include elements of process analysis within prose that *is* primarily narrative, saying in effect, "This is how I used to do x." Notice, for example, how one writer zeroes in on a process while recalling his boyhood days as a yo-yo champion:

> The greatest pleasure in yo-yoing was an abstract pleasure—watching the dramatization of simple physical laws, and realizing they would never fail if a trick was done correctly. The geometric purity of it! The string wasn't just a string, it was a tool in the enactment of theorems. It was a line, an idea. And the top was an entirely different sort of idea, a gyroscope, capable of storing energy and of interacting with the line. I remember the first time I did a particularly lovely trick, one in which the sleeping yo-yo is swung from right to left while the string is interrupted by an extended index finger. Momentum carries the yo-yo in a circular path around the finger, but instead of completing the arc the yo-yo falls on the taut string between the performer's hands, where it continues to spin in an upright position. My pleasure at that moment was as much from the beauty of the experiment as from pride. Snapping apart my hands, I sent the yo-yo into the air above my head, bouncing it off nothing, back into my palm.[12]

EXERCISES

14. Think of some result that is usually arrived at by stages (e.g., developing a conscience, losing one's innocence, understanding computers, becoming an alcoholic). Write a paragraph of process analysis in which you set forth those stages in their usual order.

15. Think of some process that you have mastered or are trying to master (e.g., juggling, cooking an omelet, writing computer programs), and jot down the stages of that process—either the stages of learning it, or, if you prefer, the stages of executing it. Then write a paragraph or two in which you analyze the process by describing those stages as accurately as possible.

16. Think of a general point that could be supported by one of the analyses you wrote for Exercises 14 and 15 (e.g., *There are no shortcuts to learning how to program computers* or *Anyone can become a juggler, but only by mastering the relevant skills in their necessary order*). Submit a paragraph in which you make that point, including as much process analysis as you find necessary for illustration.

---

an/
arg
2h

2h Develop an analogy.

When you use an **analogy**, you are asking your reader to apply principles from one situation to another one that needs to be explained or reinterpreted. An analogy is much like an extended figure of speech (p. 376, 17c), and it may in fact employ one of those figures of speech. In analogizing, though, you don't merely liken one thing to something quite different; you extract a rule from *x* and carry it over to *y*. Thus analogizing is truly a form of reasoning—though not one that can substitute for the presentation of real evidence.

Consider, for example, this brief passage:

> A *New York Times* editorial describes methadone as a drug that "blocks the craving for heroin." You might as well say that a Coke blocks the craving for a Pepsi.[13]

The writer takes situation *x*, the relation between Coke and Pepsi, and applies it to situation *y*, the relation between methadone and heroin. In doing so, he vividly conveys his sense that methadone is chemically akin to heroin, no less addictive, and therefore ill-advised as a therapy. Of course, the analogy doesn't prove the writer's case; it only dramatizes it in a way that the reader can readily grasp. (Knowing this, the writer went on to include other forms of support for his stand.)

You can use an analogy not only to argue but also to make an explanation clearer. Here, for example, a writer who wants to explain a disastrous conjunction of weather fronts uses the more readily apprehended image of an automobile crashing into a wall:

> The real problem with forecasting the generation of a storm such as this is gauging its severity. It is not like following a fully developed storm for several days as it moves across the ocean, watching it weaken or strengthen with some sort of regularity. It is more like watching a car about to crash into a brick wall; you know there is going to be a crash, there is an 80 percent chance the gas tank will explode, but you don't know how much gas is in the tank! Just as with the car, the measure of a storm's severity is gauged by its ingredients; the existence of a front (the brick wall), the amount of cold air coming down behind the front (speed of the car), and the degree of circulation in the upper air approaching the front (amount of gas in the tank).[14]

Note how carefully this writer has developed the elements of his analogy, drawing out its lesson without pursuing it to the point of tedium or pedantry.

EXERCISES

17. Examine and, in a paragraph or two, evaluate the use of analogy in the following paragraph by a writer who wants the oil industry to be subject to fewer regulations:

> To return to our analogous world of the entertainment industry, we may ask why it is fair that someone earn a fortune because he is born with flexible hips and durable vocal cords. To my knowledge, most people do not chastise entertainers for making a fortune rocking in the jailhouse in blue suede shoes. We accept that market outcome and fuss very little about its equity. Why is it that we place emphasis on political justice in petroleum but not in amusement? When we have answered that question, if we can, and when we have decided to allow petroleum companies and consumers the same rights we grant rock musicians and their audiences, I strongly suspect we will find the public better served.[15]

18. Think of an activity, hobby, sport, or business that you might want to explain to someone who knew nothing about it. Jot down as many analogies as you can think of, and write a paragraph in which you use the most promising-looking of those analogies to make the topic clear to an outsider.

NOTES

[1] These are the categories preferred by a leading expert on intelligence, Howard Gardner. For discussion, see Marie Winn, "New Views of Human Intelligence," *Good Health* [supplement to *New York Times Magazine*] 29 Apr. 1990: 16+.

[2] Harold Morowitz, "ESP and dQ over T," *BASIS* Apr 1990: 2.

[3] Richard Dawkins, *The Blind Watchmaker* (New York: Norton, 1986) 6.

[4] Rachel Carson, *Silent Spring* (Boston: Houghton, 1962) 249–50.

[5] Nestor Almendros, "Lights, Camera, Communism," *New Republic* 29 Feb. 1988: 28.

[6] Joseph Epstein, *Familiar Territory: Observations on American Life* (New York: Oxford UP, 1979) 159–60.

an/
arg
2h

[7] Peter de Jonge, "When the Putting Goes Bad," *New York Times Magazine* 13 Mar. 1988: 32.

[8] David Glidden, "Café California: A Lack of Common Ground," *Los Angeles Times* 10 Dec. 1989: M4.

[9] Mark Crispin Miller, "Hollywood: The Ad," *Atlantic* Apr. 1990: 68.

[10] William Boly, "Downwind," *In Health* July–Aug. 1990: 63.

[11] Robert M. Pirsig, *Zen and the Art of Motorcycle Maintenance: An Inquiry into Values* (New York: Morrow, 1974) 110.

[12] Frank Conroy, *Stop-time* (New York: Viking, 1967) 114–15.

[13] Stephen J. Gould, "Taxonomy as Politics," *Dissent* Winter 1990: 74.

[14] Rob Mairs, "How the Storm Developed," *Yachting* Nov. 1979: 120.

[15] Edward J. Mitchell, "Oil, Films, and Folklore," *Chevron World* Fall 1978: 25.

II

COMPOSING WHOLE ESSAYS

COMPOSING WHOLE ESSAYS

Having surveyed the main paragraph-by-paragraph strategies that essayists employ to generate the four modes of nonfiction prose, we turn now to the conceiving, drafting, and revising of full essays. In college writing, such essays are rarely descriptive or narrative in purpose. Though we have already seen (Chapter 1) that description and narration can be put to excellent use in any kind of writing, the dominant college strategies are ***analysis*** *and* ***argument*** *(Chapter 2). Accordingly, we will focus on them here.*

In analysis and argument the ***thesis****, or central point, is of paramount importance. We will highlight the process of searching for a thesis and organizing an essay around it (Chapter 3), of supporting it with reasoning and evidence (Chapter 4), and of revising to make sure that it has the best chance of being persuasive (Chapter 5). Nonetheless, these chapters are not meant to dictate just how you must proceed in composing. Think of them rather as putting into an ideal order the problems that good writers typically solve, whether through sudden intuition or laborious reworking.*

3

Planning an Essay

3a Recognize the differences between a subject area, a topic, and a thesis.

The key to writing a successful college essay is a strong and clear *thesis*—that is, a central idea to which everything else in your essay will contribute. You cannot get by with only a *topic* or, worse, a *subject area*.

Subject Area

A **subject area** is a large category within which you hope to find your actual topic—the specific question you will address. Thus, if you are asked to "recount a personal experience" or "discuss open admission to college" or "write an essay about *Catch-22*," you have been given not topics but subject areas: a personal experience, open admission to college, *Catch-22*.

Topic

The **topic** of an essay is the particular, focused issue or phenomenon being addressed. Thus, within the subject area "open admission to college," some workable topics might be:

The effect of open admission on "high potential" students

My debt to the policy of open admission

Why did open admission become popular in the late 1960s?

The success (or failure) of open admission

Is open admission a means to social equality?

Notice that these topics take up considerably more words than "open admission to college." Potential "topics" that are expressed in few words may be subject areas in disguise.

Thesis

Your **thesis** is the one ruling idea you are going to propose *about* your topic. Thus a thesis is never material to be investigated. It is always an *assertion*—an idea you will support in the body of your essay. And because it always makes a claim, a thesis lends itself to expression in one clear sentence.

Here is a chart that illustrates the contrast between a subject area, a topic, and a thesis. Notice that two possible theses are given for each topic.

SUBJECT AREA	TOPIC	THESIS
Open admission to college	The success of open admission	1. The success of open admission in my large urban college can be measured by the effectiveness of our basic instruction in reading and writing. 2. Unconventional students admitted under a policy of open admission have had a positive influence on the education of traditional students.
A personal experience	My night in jail	1. After my night in jail I will have more respect for prisoners' rights. 2. My night in jail helped to make me a safer driver.

SUBJECT AREA	TOPIC	THESIS
Agricultural production	The effect of mechanization on farm employment	1. The typical farm employee has changed from a migrant laborer to a sophisticated regular with the skills to operate large machines. 2. Many migrant farm laborers have become the unskilled unemployables of the cities.
Civil liberties	Phone tapping as an issue of civil liberties	1. When government officials place innocent citizens under observation and routinely tap one another's phones, everyone's civil liberties are threatened. 2. Despite its infringement of civil liberties, phone tapping is the most effective device the government has for procuring evidence in criminal cases.

EXERCISE

1. Each of the following is either a *subject area*, a *topic*, or a *thesis:*

   A. Mass urban transportation.
   B. The space shuttle should not be used primarily for military research.
   C. Protection of rape victims from harmful publicity.
   D. Network news programs.
   E. The return of the convertible car.

Submit a whole sheet of paper that you have first marked as follows, leaving ample space between the horizontal lines:

Subject Area	Topic	Thesis
A.		
B.		

Subject Area	Topic	Thesis
C.		
D.		
E.		

topic 3b

For each letter matching the items listed, (a) put a check in the appropriate column, and (b) fill in examples for the two remaining columns. Thus, if you think that item A is a topic, check the "Topic" column and add a related subject area and thesis.

3b Recognize the flexibility of the composing process.

Many students believe that good writing is a matter of sheer inspiration or luck; they furrow their brows and hope that a light bulb will flash over their heads. When it does not, they lose heart. But experienced writers know that good ideas, instead of dropping (or not dropping) from the sky, must be generated by activities that place one thought into relation with another. And one of those activities is writing itself. In the labor of writing you will be forced to zero in on connections, comparisons, contrasts, illustrations, contradictions, and objections, any of which may point you toward a central idea or alter the one you began with.

Thus the finding of that idea, or *thesis*, is not a fixed early stage of the composing process, but a concern that is urgent at first and will probably become urgent again when you run into trouble or realize that a better idea has come into view. The sooner you arrive at a thesis—by any means, including random writing—the better; but your choice will be continually tested until you are ready to type up the final copy of your essay. At any moment you may find yourself having to take more notes, to argue against a point you favored in an early draft, or to throw away whole pages that have been made irrelevant by your improved thesis. Do not imagine that such annoyances set you apart from other writers; they put you in the company of the masters.

So, too, the other "stages of composing" normally leak into one another. Although you cannot complete your organizing, for example, until you have arrived at a thesis, unexpected problems of organization may point the way to a better thesis. Even a simplified diagram of your options at such a moment would look complex:

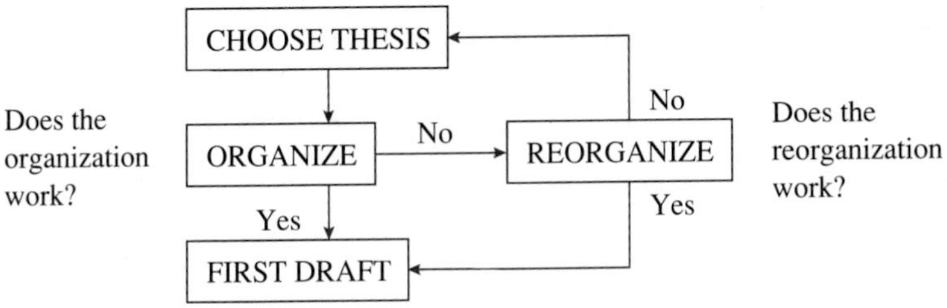

And even the revising of paragraphs for internal unity may prompt a more fundamental change of direction. Writing is almost never a linear process; it typically doubles back on one phase because a later one has opened new perspectives.

Thus, though we will discuss composing as a logical sequence of steps, its actual order in any one instance defies summary. At nearly every point you are free either to move ahead or to reconsider a previous decision. A reasonably ample flow chart for composing, then, would look like this:

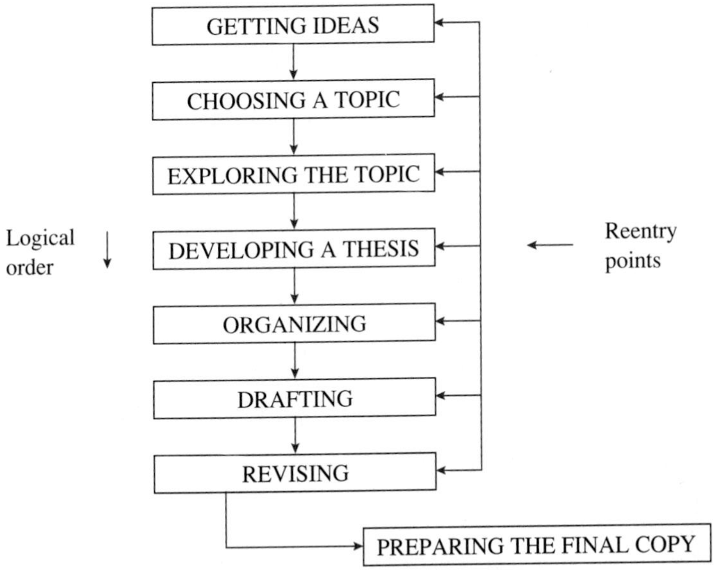

The lesson here is that, wherever your composing hits a snag, it is normal and useful to double back. Such rethinking is nothing to be alarmed about; it is the usual means by which weak ideas and structures give way to stronger ones.

TOPIC

3c Narrow your subject area.

Once you recognize that you have been given a subject area rather than a topic, you can work toward possible topics by dividing and subdividing the subject area. That maneuver will not in itself present you with a topic. *Chicago*, for instance, is narrower than *Illinois*, and *Lakeshore Drive* is narrower still, but all three lack a suitable focus; they remain subject areas because no question has yet been asked about them. Yet the process of breaking a large subject area into several smaller ones may bring such questions into mind.

If all you have to go on is the vast subject area *Education*, for example, you can start by noting as many *categories* of education as you can. It may help to think of the categories as sets of opposites:

Education:

private/public

religious/secular

vocational/academic

lower/higher

Which of these categories do you feel most comfortable with? Write it down and run through the categorizing operation again:

Higher education:

undergraduate/graduate

science/humanities/engineering

privately supported/state-supported/federally supported

Now study each item in your second list and ask what *issues or questions* it raises in your mind. One of them should prove to be an acceptable topic. Thus, if you are looking at *federally supported higher education*, you might ask these questions:

1. How much influence does the government exercise on admission policies?
2. Do professors in a federally supported institution enjoy greater academic freedom than those in a privately supported institution?
3. Has the program of federal loans to students been cut back too far?
4. To what extent can the government insist that men's and women's athletic programs be equally funded?
5. What is the effect of tying federal aid to student responsibilities, such as registering for the draft?

EXERCISE

2. Take any subject area other than "education" and subdivide it twice, in the manner of the example above. In your second list, check the item that looks most promising to you, and add three questions about it, each of which might prove to be a good topic. Submit this page of work.

3d Use notes to develop your thoughts.

You should take notes throughout the composing process, raising previously unforeseen questions, commenting on earlier notes, jotting down changes of plan, and reminding yourself of the next two or three points you ought to cover. Even if you are working from an outline (p. 85, 3q) your notes can overrule any segment of it.

When your essay is supposed to deal with an assigned text, your note taking should begin during your reading of the text. Do you own the book? If so, mark it up. Underline passages that look significant and write comments and questions in the margins. Wherever one part of the text helps you to understand another part, make a marginal cross-reference such as "see p. 134." And as soon as you have finished reading or, preferably, rereading, get your miscellaneous impressions onto paper so that you can begin dealing with *them* instead of with the whole text. Of course you will need to keep returning to the text, but now you can do so with specific, pointed questions in mind.

Some writers use uniform-sized index cards for all their notes, restricting themselves to one idea per card, but you may prefer full pages of scratch paper. In either case, you can use your notes to quote passages from your reading, record or summarize facts, make comparisons, launch a trial thesis as it occurs to you, express doubts or warnings, or comment on your comments, developing a dialogue of pros and cons.

3e Get ideas from your experience.

Instructors sometimes assign essays of a certain structural type (for example, comparison and contrast) without specifying a subject area or a topic. When you find yourself thus free to choose a topic, think at once about your own interests and areas of special knowledge—activities, skills, attitudes, problems, and unique or typical experiences. The reason is simple: what doesn't interest you is not likely to engage a reader, whereas it is easy to be convincing when you can draw on firsthand information.

Reviewing Course Work and Recent Reading

One source of interest may be your course work in composition or any other discipline. Have you come across a significant problem in the assigned reading? If you have been taking notes during class, do the notes contain questions or observations that could lead to a thesis? Wherever you have recorded doubts or strong agreement or connections with ideas of your own, you may have in hand the beginnings of an essay.

So, too, you can search for topics in the books and magazines that happen to be within easy reach. The goal, of course, is not to copy someone else's words or ideas (see p. 000, 7a), but to find an issue that meets up with experience or knowledge or an opinion of your own.

Keeping a Journal

Your search for ideas will be easier if you keep a *journal*. Unlike a diary, which has no restriction of focus, a journal is a daily record of your experience and thoughts within a certain area. A typical journal, for example, might trace your progress in understanding musical theory or mastering computer skills. Alternatively, it could store your reflections about life in general, your plans and ambitions, your ideas for short stories you hope to write, and so forth. You may even be asked to keep a journal about your efforts and problems in this very course. Whatever material it deals with, a journal can point you toward a topic by reminding you of already developed interests and opinions.

EXERCISES

3. Take some notes reflecting on any recent experience of yours that you think you could make interesting to readers. Submit the notes along with a paragraph developing one idea you have selected from those notes.

4. Writing once a day for a week, keep a journal of your thoughts about any one subject that interests you—a world crisis, for example, or your own work habits, or the problems you face as a student writer. Submit your entries along with a paragraph or two about the experience of journal keeping. Did you find that one day's entry responded to the previous one? Did your ideas become more definite as you went along? Did the existence of the journal affect the rest of your life in any way? Have you found the possible makings of an essay?

5. Using either cards or pages, take notes on anything you find significant in a piece of writing assigned by your instructor. Submit your notes along with a paragraph that develops one idea you have selected from those notes.

3f Try freewriting or brainstorming.

If you have ever told yourself or others, "I don't know what I want to say until I've written it out," consider yourself normal. Writing is a primary way of arriving at ideas, and teachers have increasingly been recognizing that fact. By forcing yourself to hook up nouns and verbs, subjects and predicates, you can draw forth insights that you didn't know you possessed.

You can even begin writing before having any idea of what your topic will be. When you feel stymied, assign yourself a ten- or fifteen-minute stint of **freewriting**. The trick is to put pen to paper at "Go" and to keep writing until "Stop" without pausing between your sentences or fragments of sentences. If you get stuck, just repeat a key word in the last sentence you have written and build a further statement around it. And even if one freewriting session appears to take you nowhere, a second one, started a few minutes later, may pick up on thoughts that were not quite ready for expression in a first effort.

Here, for example, are two passages of freewriting that a student produced in quick succession:

FIRST FREEWRITING:

Well, what do I have to say? Not much it appears! Sitting here "free" writing, so they tell me. How free is freewriting on demand, with the stopwatch ticking? Freedom in general—it always confuses me. I never know whether it's supposed to be freedom to go out and do something you'd like to, or freedom to keep somebody else from doing something mean to you. Anyway, would sure like to be free from freewriting! What is so sacred about exactly ten minutes worth of this stuff? How about nine or eleven? Stuck for ideas—ugh! Well, just keep pushing this pencil until time's up. . . .

SECOND FREEWRITING:

OK, maybe something here after all. Idea of freedom. *Total* freedom is empty, unattractive, boring—we always have something in mind to be free *for*—i.e. something that won't leave us so free any more. E.g., religious freedom usually means spending that freedom on some belief and/or practice—some "service." Or does it? What about unbelievers? I guess they have a right to a freedom that stays negative: no, thanks. . . . But historically, the fighters for freedom have always been people with strong beliefs of their own. Luther, Jefferson, Lincoln, King . . . Maybe an essay here? "Freedom For or Freedom From"?

Although neither of these passages has the grammatical completeness and the logical continuity of finished essay prose, and although the writer is clearly uncomfortable with an imposed task, his struggle to keep writing finally yields a likely-looking idea.

With a Word Processor: To keep yourself from pausing to edit, turn down the brightness control knob for your monitor. Turn it back up again when the time has expired. You may also want to use your computer's alarm function as a stopwatch.

Whereas freewriting teases forth ideas by means of our urge to link one sentence with the previous one, **brainstorming** works by the opposite principle, discontinuity. To brainstorm is to toss out suggestions without regard for their connections with one another. Since no development is called for, nothing stands in the way of your leaping from one notion to a completely unrelated one.

You can brainstorm by yourself, listing random words and phrases as they occur to you, scribbling across a notepad, or talking into a tape recorder. Or you can work in a group, either among friends or in the classroom, where the "notepad" is a shared chalkboard. In discussion or reflection, certain ideas will begin to look more fruitful than others—and you are on your way toward a topic.

When brainstorming works, it sometimes evolves naturally into freewriting as one hastily mentioned idea starts to look more interesting than the others:

> Freedom / freedom fighters / free-for-alls / freed slaves / "free gifts" / I.e., come-ons for renting (or buying) a car, going to grand opening, etc. What's really free—nothing! Who pays? The customers, of course; extra costs added back into prices. Notice that "free gifts" come only when the customers aren't buying. . . .

By this point the writer already has a clear topic in view: the hidden costs and motives behind "free" merchandise.

EXERCISE

6. Write freely for ten minutes without planning or pausing. After a brief rest, read what you have written and then write for ten more minutes, this time taking off from any promising-looking idea in the first passage. Submit both passages along with a carefully revised paragraph that turns the second passage into typical essay prose, with consecutive development of a central idea.

3g Test your trial topic.

Once you are sure you have arrived at a topic rather than a subject area, you may feel so relieved that you yearn to start the actual writing of your essay. But that would be a mistake. In the first place, your writing will quickly bog down if you still lack a thesis—a main point that answers the question implied or stated in your topic. And second, how do you know that the first topic to come to mind is the best one for your purpose? Your **trial topic** should stay on probation until you are sure it can pass six tests:

1. Is this trial topic narrow enough?
2. Is it likely to sustain my interest?
3. Is it appropriate to my intended audience?
4. Can it lead to a reasonable thesis?
5. Does it involve enough complexity—enough "parts"—for development at essay length?
6. Do I have enough supporting material to work with?

If, without further thought, you can answer all of these questions positively, consider yourself lucky. More probably, you will need to explore your trial topic by one or more of the following means.

Focused Freewriting or Brainstorming

If freewriting and brainstorming can lead to preliminary ideas for an essay, they can also help you to explore a trial topic. The same rules apply (see pp. 61–63). The only difference is that now you begin with a definite focus and try to keep it—developing, not miscellaneous thoughts about anything, but specific features of the trial topic. As before, the idea is to set aside worries about correctness of organization and expression and to see what happens.

Asking Reporters' Questions

Another simple yet surprisingly helpful way to expand your view of the trial topic is to run through the standard list of questions reporters are supposed to answer in covering a story: *who? what?*

when? where? how? why? Unlike a reporter, of course, you are not trying to make sense of a single event, yet the procedure can work because it keeps returning you to the same material from fresh perspectives.

Suppose your trial topic were the merits of a proposed law that encouraged recycling of glass by requiring a five-cent returnable deposit on all bottles. Asking the six standard reporters' questions, you might come up with answers like these:

Who? The elected official of your community or state.

What? Pass a law requiring a five-cent deposit on every returnable bottle.

When? At the next session of the city council or legislature; law to take effect at start of next calendar year.

Where? Only within the boundaries of this community or state.

How? Fix penalties for noncompliance by sellers of bottles, give the law wide publicity, warn first offenders, then begin applying penalties.

Why? Reduce waste and pollution; raise public consciousness about conservation; cut prices through use of recycled glass.

Any of these brief notes could carry you beyond your first thoughts and lead to an adequately focused thesis. For example, will a five-cent deposit be large enough to ensure returns? Will there be special problems associated with putting the law into effect so soon? If the law applies only within a small geographic area, will consumers take their business elsewhere? Are the penalties for noncompliance too strict? Not strict enough?

Applying Analytic Strategies

Whether or not you intend to write a whole essay of analysis, you can explore your trial topic by considering it in the light of some classic analytic strategies (Chapter 2), which can hardly fail to stimulate new trains of thought.

Definition: How does a law differ from a regulation? A misdemeanor from a felony? What kinds of containers would be included or excluded?

Division: What are the separate provisions of the bill? What types of stores would be affected?

Illustration: Which communities and states have already established deposit laws? What reports of success or failure are available? Do we have case histories of bottling companies and grocery chains that have accommodated themselves to the law, of individuals who were prosecuted, of others who have made a subsistence living by collecting other people's empty bottles for refund?

Cause and effect: What events and trends have made passage of the law likely or unlikely? What differences in consumers' behavior would the law bring about? Would littering be significantly curtailed? In the long run, would prices of bottled products go up or down?

Comparison and contrast: In what ways does this law resemble others that have been enacted elsewhere? How does it differ from them? Are the conditions (commercial, political, environmental) in this community or state like those elsewhere, or must special factors be taken into account? Do young and older people hold different views of the law?

Process analysis: How will violations of the law come to public notice, arrive at a prosecutor's desk, and be subsequently handled? Does the law allow unknowing violations to be treated differently from outright defiance? If so, at what point would such a difference be recognized? And what flow of payments and reimbursements is expected between the consumer, the grocer, and the distributor?

EXERCISES

7. Return to Exercise 2, p. 59, and choose one of your "subdivisions" as a trial topic. Submit a paragraph of focused freewriting about that idea.

8. Take another of your subdivisions from Exercise 2 and apply the six reporters' questions to it. Submit this page of work.

9. Choosing any of your subdivisions from Exercise 2, submit a page of notes in which you apply any *three* analytic strategies (definition, division, etc.) to that trial topic, posing questions like those supplied above for the bottle bill.

THESIS

3h Write out a one-sentence trial thesis.

When you have arrived at a **trial thesis**, or preliminary idea for an essay, put it into one clear sentence that you can then consider from several angles. That sentence may or may not eventually find its way into the body of your essay. Its function for now is to let you make sure that you have *one* central idea—not zero, not two—and that it looks sufficiently challenging and defensible. To these ends it is important that you keep to the one-statement limitation. Though your trial thesis can contain several considerations, one point should control all the others.

Typical trial theses for an essay about instituting a bottle law (p. 65) might be these:

ANALYTIC TRIAL THESES:

Increased fear that the environment is becoming polluted and that raw materials are growing scarce has provided broad-based support for laws requiring deposits on returnable bottles.

The passage or failure of bottle-deposit legislation in any given state or community can be directly correlated with the proportion of voters under age thirty.

ARGUMENTATIVE TRIAL THESES:

The minor inconvenience of paying a deposit and having to return empty bottles to a store is far outweighed by the benefits that all citizens would receive from a well-drafted law requiring the deposits.

A deposit law would not only hurt small business people by adding to their expenses and reducing their sales but also result in more, not less, pollution because of the increased trucking it would require.

None of these four examples is good or bad in itself; everything would depend on whether the writer had appropriate material on hand to make a convincing case. But all four trial theses meet the requirement of presenting just one main idea.

EXERCISE

10. Return to Exercise 9 on page 66. Using the work you did there, submit three trial theses, each making a single statement. Add a paragraph explaining why one of those trial theses looks more promising to you than the others.

3i Give your thesis definite content.

To secure your reader's interest, you must propose an idea that will require support and illustration to be made convincing. Avoid the unassertive **weaseling thesis**, which expresses nothing more than a desire to stay out of trouble.

DON'T:

x A deposit law is very controversial.

x Although some people approve of a deposit law, others do not.

Compare these vacant assertions with the "deposit law" theses above, which do take the necessary degree of risk.

EXERCISE

11. Invent and submit two examples of a weaseling thesis, and briefly explain what is wrong with each. Then submit two revised, improved theses.

3j Limit the scope of your thesis.

A thesis that quickly proves unworkable may suffer from too broad a scope. Remember that you have only a short essay in which to develop your idea successfully. Instead of discarding a thesis that seems to lead nowhere, try recasting it in narrower terms, replacing vague, general concepts with more definite ones.

TOPIC	THESIS TOO BROAD	THESIS IMPROVED
The popularity of garage sales	Garage sales reflect the times we live in.	Garage sales circulate goods during periods of high inflation and high unemployment. ["The times" are carefully defined.]
A "Star Wars" missile defense system	We need to invest in a "Star Wars" missile defense system.	Although extremely costly, a "Star Wars" missile defense system may be our only safeguard against nuclear war. [Considerations of cost and safeguarding our future are both expressed in the thesis.]
Late marriages and the changing American family	Late marriages are creating a different kind of American family life.	Because marriage is often postponed to accommodate careers, Americans are creating a new kind of family in which parents are old enough to be their children's grandparents. [Reason for late marriage and a detailed explanation of "different" belong in the thesis.]

Faulty Generalization

When you write out a trial thesis, examine it for telltale danger words like *all, none, no, any, always, never, only*, and *everyone*. Such all-inclusive terms usually signal the presence of **faulty generalization**, the illegitimate extension of *some* instances to cover *all* instances of something. Suppose, for example, you want to argue that *There is no reason to delay immediate adoption of a national health insurance program*. Ask yourself: no reason at all? Will I be anticipating *all* possible reasons in my essay? Perhaps I can avoid unnecessary trouble by making my thesis more modest: *Adoption of a national health insurance program would answer needs urgently felt by the poor, minorities, and the chronically ill.*

You should be especially wary of faulty generalization if you find that you have written a thesis that covers centuries of history or makes sweeping judgments of right and wrong.

DON'T:

x The decay of our culture has been accelerating every year.

x The West is guided by Christian morals.

x The purpose of evolution is to create a higher form of human being.

Encyclopedias of support could not establish the plausibility of such theses. Consider: (1) What universally recognized indicators of *cultural decay* do we have, and how could anyone show that cultural decay has been *accelerating every year*? (2) Can something as vague and various as *the West* be said to be *guided* by certain *morals*? How will the writer explain away all the brutalities of the past twenty centuries? (3) How has the writer been able to discover a purpose hidden from all professional students of evolution?

Avoiding *Post hoc* Explanation

Bear in mind that two events or conditions can be associated in time without being related as cause and effect. Perhaps this seems obvious, but most of us become superstitious when partisan feelings or pet beliefs are involved. Democrats claim that Republican administrations "cause" economic recessions; Republicans call their rival "the war party" because most wars have erupted when Democrats were in power; and some people support their beliefs by arguing that their dreams were fulfilled or that a certain result followed their witnessing an unusual phenomenon: "I saw a black cat and then lost control of the car"; "I landed my job after I saw a rainbow." This fallacy goes by its Latin name, ***post hoc, ergo propter hoc***: "after this, therefore because of it." It was most memorably exemplified by the Canadian humorist Stephen Leacock: "When I state that my lectures were followed almost immediately by the union of South Africa, the banana riots in Trinidad, and the Turco-Italian war, I think the reader can form some opinion of their importance."

POST HOC THESIS:

x Aspirin cures colds, as can be seen from the fact that a cold will disappear just a few days after you begin taking regular doses of aspirin.

REVISED THESIS:

• Though aspirin relieves some cold symptoms, the idea that any currently available medicine "cures" a cold is not supported by evidence.

EXERCISES

12. Invent and submit three deliberately defective trial theses that suffer from faulty generalization, including at least one example of overgeneralizing from personal experience. For each defective statement, add a brief explanation of its weakness. Then supply three versions that remedy the problem.

13. Submit three defective trial theses that illustrate *post hoc* explanation, and briefly explain what is wrong with each. Add three versions that remedy the problem.

3k State your thesis fairly.

Just as there is little point in choosing a thesis with which no one could disagree (3i), so it is vital to avoid artificially shielding a *controversial* thesis by trying to shut off the very possibility of disagreement. The best posture to assume is one of inviting fair-minded attention to everything that can be said on both sides of the issue. If, instead, you resort to special pleading or dirty tricks, you are signaling to an astute reader that you lack confidence in the merits of your case.

Begging the Question: Reasoning in Circles

Technically speaking, to beg the question is to arrive at a conclusion that is essentially the same as a premise used to support it. More informally, you are begging the question, or indulging in *circular reasoning*, whenever you state a point in such "loaded" terms that your language itself prejudges the issue.

thesis
3k

DON'T:

x A. It is inadvisable to let hardened criminals out of prison prematurely so that they can renew their war on society.

x B. Society has no right to lock up the victims of poverty and inequality for indefinite periods, brutalizing them in the name of "rehabilitation."

Writers A and B are addressing the same issue, but each of them has settled it in advance. The word *prematurely* already contains the idea that many convicts are released too soon, and other terms—*hardened criminals, renew their war*—reinforce the point. For writer B there is no such thing as a criminal in the first place. Prisoners have already been defined as *victims,* and imprisonment is equated with *brutalizing*. Similarly, the quotation marks around *rehabilitation* dismiss the possibility that a criminal might be taught to reform. The trouble here is that both writers A and B, in their eagerness to sweep away objections, are portraying themselves as close-minded. No one will want to read an essay whose very thesis forbids all disagreement.

Of course your thesis should convey an attitude, but it should do so in fair language.

DO:

• A. The policy of releasing prisoners on probation has not justified the social risks it involves.

• B. If the goal of prisons is to rehabilitate, the prison system must be considered on balance to be a failure.

Note that these two versions are just as hard-hitting as the ones they replace; the difference is that their language does not beg the question.

Either-Or Reasoning: Believe It or Else

Make sure your thesis does not pull the alarmist trick of **either-or reasoning**—that is, pretending that the only alternative is something awful. Thus a writer favoring legal abortion might claim, x *We must legalize abortion or the world will become disastrously overpopulated*, and a writer on the opposite side might reply, x *We must prevent legal abortion or the family will cease to exist*. Both writers would be delivering an ultimatum. *Which do you choose, overpopulation or legal abortion? What will it be, legal abortion or the survival of the family?* The choice is supposed to be automatic. All a reader must do, however, to escape the bind is to think of one other possibility. Is there no means to control population except through abortion? Might legal abortion have some lesser consequence than the destruction of family life? Your wisest course would be to admit that people favoring an opposite stand from yours have good reasons for their view—reasons that you do not find decisive. If the issue *were* one of total right versus total wrong, you would probably be wasting your time writing about it.

EXERCISES

14. Invent and submit three defective trial theses that beg the question, and briefly explain what is wrong with each. Add three versions that remedy the problem.

15. Invent and submit three defective trial theses that illustrate either-or reasoning, and briefly explain what is wrong with each. Add three versions that remedy the problem.

3l Try developing your trial thesis into a full thesis statement.

Let us suppose that your thesis is no longer on trial: it has passed the tests of definiteness and reasonable scope, and you are ready to go with it. At this point you would do well to take an extra step that may look unnecessary at first. Cast your thesis into a **full thesis statement**—a sentence that not only names your main point but also includes its most important parts, supplies reasons why that point deserves to be believed, and/or meets objections to it. This statement will probably be long and cumbersome. Never mind: it will not appear anywhere in the body of your essay. It is simply a private guide which will help you (a) be completely sure that you are in control of your material and (b) choose a sound organization for your essay's parts (p. 83, 3p).

Sometimes your unexpanded thesis will possess the complexity that can carry you into the work of organizing. We have already met one such thesis/thesis statement: *A deposit law would not only hurt small business people by adding to their expenses and reducing their sales but also result in more, not less, pollution because of the increased trucking it would require*. Here we see three crucial factors begging to be made structurally prominent: added expense, reduced sales, increased pollution. The writer is ready to decide on an effective order for these main supporting points.

thesis
3l

More often than not, though, a thesis will be too simple in form to serve as a thesis statement. The remedy is to spell out some of the large considerations that made you adopt the thesis in the first place. You can add *main details, reasons,* and/or *objections,* all of which will become prominent units of your organization.

Including Main Details

Suppose your tested and approved thesis is a sentence as plain as this: *Chinese farming methods differ strikingly from American ones*. Fine—but are you sure you know exactly which differences you will be emphasizing in your essay? Now is the time to clear up any lingering doubt by working those differences into a full thesis statement.

Since you will eventually have to choose an order of presentation for your main details, why not decide right now, as you are drawing up your thesis statement? The final position is generally the most emphatic one, whether the unit be a sentence, a paragraph, or a whole essay. Think, then, about the relative importance of your points and arrange them accordingly within your thesis statement:

DO:

- Chinese farming differs strikingly from American farming in its greater concern for using all available space, its handling of crop rotation, its higher proportion of natural to manufactured fertilizers, and, above all, its emphasis on mass labor as opposed to advanced machinery.

Here you already have a complete blueprint for a brief essay, which you could begin writing without delay.

Supplying Reasons

In some theses the main statement does not !end itself to the kind of expansion we have just considered. Yet you can always find more "parts" for your essay—and thus for your full thesis statement—by listing the reasons why you think the thesis deserves to be believed. Suppose, for example, you intend to maintain that *The first year of college often proves to be a depressing one*. That is a fair beginning, but it tells you only that *x proves to be y*. How is a whole paper going to result from such a simple declaration? Ask yourself, then, why or in what ways you find that year typically depressing.

If you tell why in one or more *because* clauses, your thesis statement becomes an organizational blueprint:

- The first year of college often proves to be a depressing one, because many students have moved away from their parents' homes for the first time, because it is painful to be separated from established friends, and because homework and grading are usually more demanding than they were in high school.

Now you have laid out the nature of your analysis: you are reasoning from an effect (depression) to its causes, which you will discuss one by one in your essay.

Mentioning Objections

If your thesis is controversial—and all argumentative theses and many analytic theses are—you should expect to deal with at least one major objection to it. Typically, you will want to handle that point either through **refutation** or through **concession**—that is, either by showing that the objection is wrong or by granting its truth while showing that it does not overrule your thesis (p. 107, 4i).

If the objection will be discussed in your essay, it should also appear in your full thesis statement. Include that objection in an *although* clause:

- Although some students find their freshman year exciting and rewarding, many others find it depressing, because they have moved away. . . .

Again, suppose you intend to maintain that the government should not insist on equal expenditures for men's and women's athletic programs in college. You know that to be convincing you will have to blunt the force of at least one strong point on the opposing side. Get that point into your full thesis statement, add your positive reasons, and you are ready to go:

- Although men and women in college should certainly have equal opportunities to participate in sports, the government should not insist on equal expenditures for men's and women's athletic programs, because in colleges where a football program exists it requires disproportionately high expenditures, and because such a program can produce income to support the entire spectrum of men's and women's athletics.

A mouthful! But, again, a thesis statement is only a road map, not an excerpt from your essay. You need not try to make it concise. It will succeed in its purpose if it allows you to move confidently to the next phase of planning.

EXERCISES

16. In the left column of a sheet of paper, write out any three of the revised trial theses you prepared for Exercises 11-15. In the right column, write three corresponding *full thesis statements* possessing enough complexity to serve as organizational guides for the writing of brief essays.

17. Submit a full thesis statement whose main details, like those in the expanded "Chinese farming" statement on page 74, give the statement an adequate degree of complexity.

18. Jot down an analytic trial thesis that, like *The first year of college often proves to be a depressing one,* lacks the complexity of a full thesis statement. Then expand that core thesis by surrounding it with an *although* clause and one or more *because* clauses. Hand in your complete thesis statement.

VOICE AND STANCE

3m Choose between a personal and an impersonal voice.

Voice refers to the "self" projected by a given piece of writing. The relevant question to ask is not "What am I really like?" but "What is the nature of this occasion?" For certain occasions you will want to maintain a formal, impersonal air, while for others you will want readers to feel much closer to you as an individual.

Consider the following deliberately impersonal paragraph:

IMPERSONAL VOICE:

Much of the long-term and continuing controversy over subliminal perception (see Dixon, 1971, 1981; Holender, 1986, for extensive reviews) has centered on definitional issues concerning how conscious perceptual experience is best defined and measured. Given that stimulation of the sense organs typically leads to subjective phenomenal experiences that can be described in some detail, the problem has been to find a behavioral measure that accurately reflects the presence or absence of phenomenal experience. Unfortunately, there is no general agreement as to the most appropriate measure, and depending on the measure selected, it is possible to obtain evidence under laboratory conditions that either supports the existence of subliminal perception or indicates that subliminal perception is a very improbable phenomenon.[1]

aud
3m

The writer of this passage wants to show a serious, well-informed audience that he has looked at the problem of subliminal perception from all sides and is reluctant to draw hasty conclusions about it. He does not refer to his own experiences or feelings. The absence of intimacy here is a deliberate stylistic effect; the **impersonal voice** suits the writer's task of "allowing the facts to speak for themselves."

The following student paragraph illustrates an opposite effect.

PERSONAL VOICE:

Eating the catered meals they serve on airplanes is always a memorable experience. In the first place, you have to admit it is exciting to open that little carton of salad oil and find a stream of Thousand Islands dressing rocketing onto your blouse. Then, too, where else would you be able to dig into a *perfectly* rectangular chicken? And let's not forget the soggy, lukewarm mushrooms which are accused by the menu of having "smothered" the geometrical bird. They look and taste exactly like the ear jacks that are forever falling off your rented headset. Come to think of it, what *do* they do with those jacks when the flight is over?

This writer, using a **personal voice**, everywhere implies that she is drawing on her private experience, and she insists on an involved response by addressing her reader as an individual: *you have to* *admit; your blouse; where else would you be able; your rented headset.* Since the "facts" in this passage are not facts at all but witty exaggerations of widely shared inconveniences, the writer wants us to gather that she is saying at least as much about her own wry, mildly cynical attitude toward life as she is about airline food.

By choosing an appropriate voice, you also help to establish the **tone**, or quality of feeling, of your essay, paper, or report. An impersonal voice necessarily carries a dry, factual tone, but a personal voice can be intense, respectful, supportive, fanciful, mocking, worldly, or authoritative, depending on your purpose. Compare the wry tone of the "airline food" passage, for example, with that of the following lines by Martin Luther King, Jr., addressing a "letter" to eight Alabama clergymen who had urged him to proceed cautiously in seeking racial justice. Both voices are personal, but King's tone is noble and angry:

> We know through painful experience that freedom is never voluntarily given by the oppressor; it must be demanded by the oppressed. Frankly, I have yet to engage in a direct-action campaign that was "well timed" in the view of those who have not suffered unduly from the disease of segregation. For years now I have heard the word "Wait!" It rings in the ear of every Negro with piercing familiarity. This "Wait" has almost always meant "Never." We must come to see, with one of our distinguished jurists, that "justice too long delayed is justice denied."[2]

Here is the rhetoric of a writer who knows that he cannot bank on much agreement from his immediate readers; after all, they had just written *him* a highly critical letter. Instead of swallowing his feelings, King defiantly stands on his own authority: *I have yet to engage in a direct-action campaign that was "well timed"* and *For years now I have heard the word "Wait!"* He and other black activists *know through painful experience* what the eight timid clergymen will never know about how freedom is won.

Choice of Governing Pronoun

Notice that the **governing pronoun** you choose for your essay helps to establish a consistent voice. If you call yourself *I*, you are guaranteeing at least a degree of personal emphasis. Even greater intimacy is implied if, like the "airline food" writer, you presume to call your reader *you*. That pronoun can quickly wear out its welcome, however; a reader resents being told exactly what to think and feel. If, like King, you occasionally shift from the personal *I* to the community *we*, you can imply a sense of shared values between yourself and all fair-minded readers. And if you want a strictly formal, impersonal effect, you should refer to yourself rarely, if at all—and then only as a member of the indefinite "editorial" *we*, as in *We shall see below. . . .*

EXERCISE

19. Using any handy source—for example, a science textbook—locate some facts or ideas that might bear on a controversial topic (creation, evolution, energy development, environmental protection, abortion, foreign aid, etc.). Submit two connected paragraphs dealing with some of that material. In the first, make use of an *impersonal voice*. In the second, continue to develop a position, now using a *personal* voice to indicate your involvement or conviction. Use a change in governing pronoun to help convey the shift in voice.

3n Generally prefer a forthright stance.

Most essays and nearly all college papers, like the prose of this present book, are meant to be taken "straight." Readers sense that the writer is taking a **forthright stance**—a straightforward, trustworthy rhetorical posture. Thus they assume that the writer is being sincere in making assertions and in endorsing certain attitudes while disapproving of others.

The following paragraph from a freshman essay shows the usual features of the forthright stance:

> When this University switched from quarters to semesters, my first reaction was dismay over my shortened summer. The last spring quarter ended in mid-June; the first fall semester began in August. Was this what the new order would be like—a general speed-up? It took me a while to realize that my lost vacation was not a permanent feature of the semester system but a one-time inconvenience. Now that I have survived nearly two whole semesters, I am ready to admit that there is much to be said for the changed calendar. As for vacations, those five weeks of freedom around Christmas have turned my vanished summer into a trivial, faded memory.

Note how this writer, using readily understandable language and maintaining an earnest manner, carefully lays out the reasons why she had first one reaction and then another to the semester system. She gives us no cause to doubt any of her statements.

aud
3o

EXERCISE

20. Submit any paragraph of your own prose that uses a forthright stance. You may write a new paragraph or make use of previous work. (Note, however, that you may be asked to modify this same paragraph in Exercise 21, page 83; plan accordingly.)

3o Note the special effect of an ironic stance.

Once in a while, instead of taking the usual forthright stance (3n), a writer may strike an *ironic stance*, saying one thing in such a way as to express a different or even opposite meaning. **Irony** is delicious when it works and disastrous when it does not. Before practicing it, you should understand what kinds of opportunities and difficulties it typically presents.

Irony can be either subtle or broad and either local or sustained. Local and subtle irony, lasting only for a sentence or two and scarcely striking the reader's attention, can enter into any essay possessing a personal voice (3m). Take, for example, the sentence *Recovery from an all-out nuclear attack would not be quite the routine project that some officials want us to believe*. The irony here, barely noticeable at first, is concentrated on the word *quite*. Taken at face value, the sentence claims that recovery from an all-out nuclear attack would be *almost* routine. But of course the writer means just the reverse—that there would be nothing routine about it. The word *quite* serves two ironic functions, twitting the business-as-usual mentality of the bureaucrats and hinting, through *understatement*, at the unspeakable horror of an actual nuclear attack. After such a sentence, the writer would want to shift to a straightforward stance and paint the gruesome details.

Broad irony, in contrast to the subtle kind, is deliberately outrageous in turning the world upside down to make fun of some disapproved policy or position. We can hardly escape the ironic point, for example, when an opponent of the "Star Wars" program writes:

To do this we will need a vast array of radars, infrared sensors, and technologies that do not exist. All of this will be controlled by large computers, like the ones used by the telephone company to generate wrong numbers.[3]

Irony can also be gradually increased in obviousness or intensity. You can begin on a subtle note and build to a broadly ironic punch line, as this passage does:

A world economic conference can always point up the rational way to do things. Is Japan overloaded with dollars? Let the Japanese lend the dollars to the Third World, which needs propping up so it can buy things again. Let Japan spend more money on roads and housing. Let the German economy expand a bit more. Let the sloppy, undisciplined Americans finally curb their spending, and let them save up so they can stop borrowing so much from the rest of the world; really, they are like teenagers with a new credit card. And by the way, let them also learn to be more productive, improve their level of education—maybe they should start to work on Saturdays like the Japanese. Now, what's for lunch, and when is the next conference?[4]

Only at the very end of this paragraph are we completely sure that the writer's real, ironically conveyed point is not the "rationality" of international economic conferences but their futility—all talk and no results.

In a whole essay of broad irony, the idea is to pretend to take seriously a ridiculous extension of some dubious policy or position and to run through its consequences with seeming enthusiasm. Thus, in the most famous example of broad irony, Jonathan Swift's "A Modest Proposal" suggested that the Irish children who were being starved by English absentee landlords could be profitably butchered and sold as meat for their persecutors' tables. Swift was not of course putting forward any such plan; he was ironically exposing the landlords' inhumanity.

For a modern sample of broad and sustained irony, consider the following passage by a writer who has recently dined at an elegant, trend-conscious country restaurant:

Comes the menu. It's time to idly, in the manner of certain doges, select from the bounty of the earth some particularly fragrant and ornamental nutrition bundle. Here's one entry: "Heart Healthy Swordfish."

Let's see, that would be swordfish prepared in such a way that it contains no substances detrimental to the smooth workings of your

> circulatory system. That would be swordfish without cloying animal fats, cholesterol-laden gobs of yellowish gunk that enter your arteries and move directly to the entrance to a ventricle, where they coalesce into an implacable substance the size of a grapefruit that stops all flow entirely, leading to spasms and fibrillation and unconsciousness and final death on the quaint hardwood floors of the main dining room, your head just inches from the rich purplish surface of the antique breakfront.
>
> Is that right?
>
> Does every meal really have to begin with a discussion of methods of forestalling mortality? If so, why stop at the menu? Why not have a strolling doctor, sort of like a sommelier, dressed in a lab coat with a stethoscope stuffed into one pocket, to advise the diners on the possible consequences of their choice of entree?
>
> Patrons would, of course, routinely carry photocopied summaries of their family histories and current medical status to allow the doctor to personalize his recommendations. Sure, a brisk discussion of colon cancer might leach the antic joy out of the early part of the evening, but isn't it worth it in the long run?
>
> And think of the joy you'll feel when the doctor says, "You know, Janet, the theory that sugar somehow triggers the onset of Bell's palsy has not been scientifically proven, so go ahead and have that berry tart with my blessings."[5]

The first paragraph of this passage tips off the writer's ironic stance through its wild shifting in levels of diction (pp. 351–53, 15h), from the slangy *Comes the menu* to the pompous, gas-filled *select from the bounty of the earth some particularly fragrant and ornamental nutrition bundle*. The writer then follows the classic strategy of "A Modest Proposal," pushing the satirized idea to absurd limits in order to expose and mock the error he finds in it.

If you have a fruitful premise to work with—one like "Let's pretend that Irish children can be sold as table meat" or "Let's pretend that restaurant going ought to be a grim medical experience"—you can build a whole essay upon broad irony, working out the various implications of the absurd situation you have created. But if you are just poking fun at others or yourself, you would do well to keep your irony relatively low-keyed. A whole essay taking the stance of the "airplane food" passage (p. 77), for example, would become tiresome.

If you plan to submit an essay of broad irony, check with your instructor first. Many writing assignments have important purposes that cannot be met once you have adopted the broad-ironical stance.

Beware of reaching for irony simply because you would rather not fulfill the terms of the assignment.

For a further discussion of ironic language, see page 352, 15h.

EXERCISE

21. Submit a new version of the paragraph you wrote for Exercise 20, now making use of an ironic stance. If you decide to try local ironic touches rather than broad irony throughout, indicate with marginal checks which sentences you expect your reader to take ironically.

ORGANIZING

3p Find the most effective organization for your ideas.

The key to arriving at a sound essay structure is to put yourself in your reader's place. Beginning in ignorance, your reader wants to know certain things that fall into a natural order:

1. what is being discussed;
2. what the writer's point is;
3. why objections, if any, to that point are not decisive;
4. on what positive grounds the point should be believed.

As a diagram, then, the most reliable essay structure would look like this:

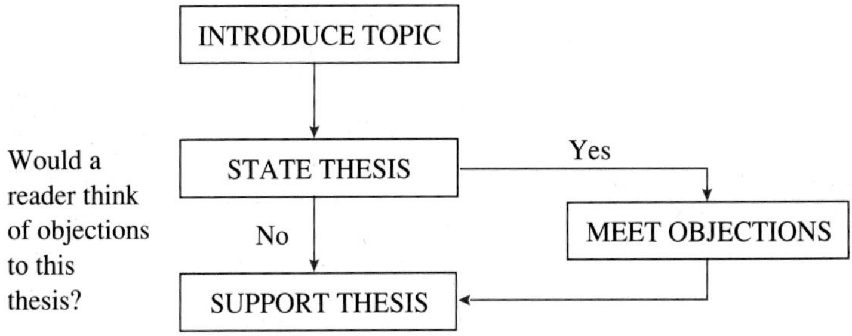

If you try to rearrange this common order, you will find it difficult. How, for example, could a reader want to know the writer's thesis before knowing the issue at stake? Why ask for supporting evidence before knowing what it is evidence *for*? Even the optional part of the sequence, the handling of objections, falls into a logical place. When (as in any argument) it does become important to address objections, the handiest place to do so is right after the thesis has been revealed—for that is where the objections are most likely to occur to the reader and hence to threaten the writer's credibility.

Using the Full Thesis Statement as a Guide

By following the simplified model just discussed, you can derive the structure of a brief essay directly from your full thesis statement.

1. The *topic*, the first element of the model, is known from the thesis statement because it is the question answered by the thesis.
2. The *thesis* is directly named in the thesis statement.
3. If the thesis contains an *although* clause, at least one important *objection* has been isolated.
4. *Because* clauses in the thesis statement specify the final element of structure, the main points of support for the thesis.

Moving beyond a Fixed Pattern

The principles of organization mentioned above will serve you best if you take them as a starting point rather than as an inflexible guide. There are things the model cannot do—choices you must settle either through a detailed outline (3q) or through problem solving as you struggle with your draft. Specifically, the model

—does not tell you how to catch a reader's interest;

—does not say how many objections, if any, you should deal with, or whether they should be met by concession or by refutation (p. 105, 4h);

—does not indicate which analytic strategies you should rely on (Chapter 2);

—does not say how much space you should devote to any single point; and

—does not indicate whether you will need a formal concluding paragraph.

Thus your developing sense of problems, opportunities, and paragraph-by-paragraph tactics should be your final guide.

Suppose, for instance, you notice that the best positive evidence for your thesis consists of points that also answer main objections. In that case it would be wasteful to treat objections and supporting evidence separately. Or, again, the decision to include or skip a summary paragraph at the end is a matter of weighing available alternatives. If your essay is long and complex, a conclusion is probably called for. But if you have saved a decisive point of evidence, a revealing incident, or a striking sentence, you may be well advised to end dramatically with that clincher and omit a concluding paragraph.

EXERCISE

22. Suppose you wanted to write essays based on the following five theses. In which instances would you include a discussion of *objections* to the thesis? Briefly justify each of your answers.

    A. Recurrent images of rottenness and disease help to convey Shakespeare's thematic emphasis in *Hamlet*.
    B. In the interest of public safety, Congress should pass a law requiring the installation of restraining air bags in all new automobiles.
    C. Although soccer has grown enormously in popularity, it is still largely boycotted by the major television networks.
    D. The decline of the Roman Empire, so often attributed to loose living and military errors, was in reality caused chiefly by lead poisoning from toxic earthenware.
    E. Airlines should not be held financially liable for problems of hearing loss experienced by people who live close to major airports.

3q Suit an outline to your purpose.

An outline can be an important aid to your composing, but to make good use of it you must first appreciate what it *cannot* do. Briefly, it cannot replace a sound thesis.

Some writers, equating an outline with "good organization," are tempted to go directly from a subject area or topic (p. 53, 3a) to an outline:

DON'T:

x Topic: Commercial Airlines

I. Relation to Military
II. The Jet Age
III. Fare Wars in the 1990s
IV. Future of the Industry

An analytic or argumentative essay, you recall, must pursue a point from beginning to end. In contrast, the outline above merely identifies assorted subtopics that the writer hopes to cover. It is actually doing the writer a disservice by giving a false appearance of order and purpose. Be sure, then, that any outline of your own is preceded by and derived from a thesis statement. Even if some parts of your outline look like subtopics, you will know that they represent necessary steps in the case you will be making for your thesis.

Competent writers differ greatly in their fondness for an outline. If, like some of them, you find that you simply cannot work from an outline in writing your first draft, you should nevertheless make an outline of that draft when you have finished it. There is no better way of spotting redundancies and inconsistencies that need fixing.

Scratch Outline

If your essay is going to be brief and you simply need to decide on an order for several paragraphs, you will be adequately served by a **scratch outline**—that is, one showing no subordination of some points to others.

Suppose, for instance, you had hit upon the following thesis statement for an analytic 600-word essay: *Although television and radio both cover news developments and sports events, their styles are necessarily different, TV leaning toward "editorial" and radio toward "reportorial" coverage.* A serviceable scratch outline of your paragraphs might look like this:

1. TV and radio cover many of the same happenings, e.g., news developments and sports events.
2. Thesis: But the two styles differ. Because TV can show what radio has to describe, TV has more air time to comment on events.
3. News developments (film clips of speeches, interviews, battles, election returns, etc.): only on TV are the events partly allowed to speak for themselves, with occasional or follow-up commentary by news analysts.
4. Sports events: TV, relatively free from reporting what is happening, includes more commentary than radio does.
5. In summary: TV coverage doesn't abolish the spoken word, but because we can *see*, the balance tips toward "editorial" as opposed to radio's "reportorial" coverage.

Subordinated Outline

For longer and more complex essays you may want to use a **subordinated outline**—one that shows, through indention and more than one set of numbers, that some points are more important than others.

Suppose, for instance, you had decided to write a thousand-word argument opposing rent control of off-campus housing, and you were satisfied with the following thesis statement: *Although off-campus rent control is aimed at securing reasonable rents for students, it would actually produce four undesirable effects: establishment of an expensive, permanent rent-control bureaucracy; landlord neglect of rental property; a shortage of available units; and a freezing of currently excessive rents.* Knowing that your argument would be fairly complex, you might want to draw up a full outline:

I. The Problem Is That Students Now Face Hardships in Securing Adequate Housing.
   A. Students are currently subject to rent gouging.
   B. High rents force many students to live far from campus.

II. The Promise Is That Rent Control Will Guarantee Reasonable Rents near Campus.

III. The Reality Is That the Actual Effects of Rent Control Would Be Undesirable.
   A. An expensive, permanent rent-control bureaucracy would be established.
   B. Landlords would neglect rent-controlled property.
   C. The shortage of units would *worsen*, because:
      1. Owners would have no incentive to increase the number of rental units.
      2. Competition for rent-frozen units would be more intense.
   D. Currently excessive rents would be frozen, thus ruling out any possible reduction.

Notice that this outline establishes three degrees of importance among your ideas. The Roman numerals running down the left margin point to the underlying structure of the essay, a movement from problem to promise to reality. These main categories come straight from the thesis statement. The *problem* is the topic itself; the *promise* is the "although" consideration, which is taken care of early; and the *reality*, the thesis itself, consists of the "four undesirable effects" of off-campus rent control.

At the next level of subordination, the indented capital letters introduce ideas that contribute to these larger units. The problem, says Part I of the outline, has two aspects: rent gouging and the forcing of students to seek lower rents far from campus. By listing those aspects as *A* and *B*, you assign them parallel or roughly equivalent status in your argument.

Points A through D in Part III are also parallel, but one of them, C, is supported in turn by two narrower points. By assigning those two points Arabic numerals and by a further indention from the left margin, you indicate to yourself that these considerations go to prove the larger idea just above them. Thus the three sets of numbering/lettering and the three degrees of indention display the whole logic of your essay.

Sentence versus Topic Outline

The example just given is a *sentence outline*, using complete sentences to state every planned idea. A sentence outline is the safest kind, because its complete statements ensure that you will be making assertions, not just touching on subjects, in every part of your essay.

But if you are confident of keeping your full points in mind, you can use the simpler *topic outline*, replacing sentences with concise phrases:

I. The Problem
  A. Rent Gouging
  B. Students Forced to Live Far from Campus (etc.)

The form you choose for an outline is hardly an earthshaking matter; just be sure the outline gives you enough direction, and do not waste time making it more intricate and hairsplitting than your essay itself will be.

Keeping Outline Categories in Logical Relation

If you do use subordination in an outline, observe that each heading or subheading should have at least one mate—no *I* without *II*, no *A* without *B*. The reason is that headings and subheadings represent divisions of a larger unit, either a more general point or the thesis of the whole essay. It is of course impossible to divide something into just one part. If you have a lonesome *A* in a draft outline, work it into the larger category:

ILLOGICAL:
x I. Problems
  A. Excessive Noise
II. Cost Factors
  A. Overruns

BETTER:
• I. Problems of Excessive Noise
II. Cost Overruns

In addition, you should always check a draft outline to make sure that all the subheadings under a given heading logically contribute to it. Do not try to tuck in irrelevant items just because you find no other place for them; that would defeat the whole purpose of outlining, which is to keep your essay coherent and logical in moving from one idea to the next.

With a Word Processor: If your word-processing program allows you to place "windows" on the screen beside your developing draft, fill one window with your outline. Consult the outline as you proceed from paragraph to paragraph. When you see that your essay must deviate from the outline (3r), stop to revise the entire rest of the outline, double-checking it for coherence.

EXERCISES

23. For any of the theses appearing in Exercise 22 (p. 85), submit a full thesis statement (p. 73, 3l) and a scratch outline for an essay.

24. Submit a subordinated sentence outline and a subordinated topic outline that would constitute two fuller alternatives to the scratch outline you prepared for Exercise 23.

25. Suppose you have been taking notes for an essay defending the private automobile against those who regard it as a social menace. Your notes include the following miscellaneous statements:

    We could find new fuels and impose limits on horsepower.

    Cars waste precious energy.

    We don't have to make all-or-nothing choices between private cars and mass transit.

    Congestion and smog are real problems.

    Cars give people initiative and individualism.

    Thousands of people are killed every year in traffic accidents.

    Without cars, no one could live outside major population centers.

    The government can require stricter safety standards.

    Abolish the dangers and inconveniences, not the cars themselves.

    Using some or all of these statements—and a few more, if you like—write a full thesis statement for your essay, and submit that thesis statement along with a subordinated outline of the type (sentence or topic) preferred by your instructor.

3r Mix improvising with planning in writing your first draft.

Even after much preparation, you may feel some resistance to committing your first draft to paper. If the opening paragraph looms as an especially big obstacle, try skipping it and starting with a later one. If you seem to be losing momentum in the middle of a sentence, shift into a private shorthand that will keep you from worrying about the fine points of expression; you can return to them later. And instead of writing, you may find it easier to talk into a tape recorder and then transcribe the better parts. Whether you write or dictate, do not be afraid to include too much, to leave blank spaces, or to commit errors of usage and punctuation. What matters is that you move ahead, understanding that you will have a substantial job of revision to do (Chapter 5).

Do not be alarmed if you find new possibilities coming into view as you finish one sentence and struggle to begin the next one. Some of your best ideas—perhaps even a radically improved thesis—can be generated by that friction between the written sentence and the not-yet-written one. So long as you anticipate the need to reconsider and reorganize after your first draft is complete, the tug of war between plans and inspirations should result in a subtler, more engaging paper than you originally expected to submit.

NOTES

[1] Philip M. Merikle, "Subliminal Auditory Messages: An Evaluation," *Psychology and Marketing* 5 (1988): 357–58.

[2] Martin Luther King, Jr., *Why We Can't Wait* (New York: Harper, 1964) 82–83.

[3] Fred Reed, "The Star Wars Swindle: Hawking Nuclear Snake Oil," *Harper's* May 1986: 39.

[4] Adam Smith, "Is the Dollar Doomed?" *Esquire* Jan. 1987: 52.

[5] Jon Carroll, "The Picture of Good Health," *San Francisco Chronicle* 9 Nov. 1990: E18.

4

Supporting a Thesis

Whenever you write an analysis or argument (p. 33), the heart of your essay will be the support you provide for your thesis. The more controversial that thesis is, the greater your need to back it with **evidence**—reasons, facts, and authoritative testimony. In addition, you can strengthen your essay by carefully controlling its tone. If you not only present solid evidence but also give a general impression of thoughtfulness and trustworthiness, your reader will be inclined to give you the benefit of the doubt on any points of remaining controversy.

MAKING A POSITIVE CASE

4a Use reasoning to reach well-founded conclusions.

In a sense, all the advice in this chapter has to do with offering reasons why the thesis of your essay deserves to be believed. By **reasoning**, however, we mean something narrower: the drawing of a conclusion from accepted facts that lead logically to that conclusion. You have already seen that this procedure is a classic tool of analysis and argument (p. 39, 2d). Here we will look more closely at the logical relation between a writer's offered reasons, or *premises*, and the *conclusions* that follow from them.

Study the following student paragraph, written before Congress repealed the 55-miles-per-hour speed limit:

> Most people believe that the lower speed limit has saved many thousands of lives—but can we be sure? Highway fatalities certainly dropped after the 55-mph limit was imposed in 1974. Yet they have continued to drop in subsequent years, as drivers' speeds have been creeping steadily *upward* toward the old 65-mph norm. This can only mean that other factors—safer cars and roads, less reckless driving habits, mandatory seat belt laws, harsher penalties for drunken driving—have been influencing the statistics. Thus, strictly speaking, we have no way of knowing how much the lower speed limit has actually contributed to safety.

We could restate this writer's reasoning more formally using **syllogisms**, or chains of deduction from premises to conclusions:

Opponents believe:

Premise: If highway deaths decline, the lower speed limit deserves the credit.
Premise: Highway deaths have declined.
Conclusion: Therefore the lower speed limit deserves the credit.

But: The lower speed limit has been gradually disregarded by drivers, while deaths have continued to decline. So:

Premise: If actual speeds have been increasing while deaths have been declining, we cannot say for sure that the lower speed limit is responsible for the savings in lives.
Premise: Speeds *have* increased, and deaths *have* declined.
Conclusion: We cannot say for sure that the lower speed limit is responsible for the savings in lives.

Needless to say, the "speed limit" paragraph itself is more appealing than these x-rays of its logic. As a writer, you rarely if ever need to spell out both of the premises that lead to a given conclusion. You need only credit your reader with the same commonsense grasp of reasoning that you yourself possess. In practice, then, reasoning within an essay boils down to the presentation of facts or considerations that *would* enter into a full, formal proof if you were to supply the missing, but implicitly understood, premise. Just be sure that the reasons you cite are widely known to be true and that they do, indeed, speak directly to your thesis.

Principles of sound reasoning are violated by **fallacies**, or illegitimate ways of reaching a favored conclusion. See the discussions of **faulty generalization** (p. 69, 3j), ***post hoc* explanation** (p. 70, 3j), **begging the question** (p. 71, 3k), **either-or reasoning** (p. 72, 3k), **straw man reasoning** (p. 100, 4f), and ***ad hominem* reasoning** (p. 101, 4f).

EXERCISE

1. Find an article or chapter that supplies at least three instances of reasoning to support a claim. Submit a concise analysis of the author's reasoning. Do you find that reasoning satisfactory? If not, why not? Make sure that you yourself employ sound reasoning instead of merely asserting your agreement or disagreement with the author's opinions. Accompany your analysis with a photocopy of the relevant page or pages.

4b Cite available facts and figures.

When most people think of evidence, they call to mind "facts and figures"—statements and numerical data that are regarded as well established. Though useful evidence goes well beyond such items, they can have a compelling effect on a reader. Suppose, for example, you were intuitively convinced that life has recently become more dangerous for young people in American cities. Personal testimony could be dramatic, but it wouldn't settle the point. But suppose you knew, from well-authenticated sources, that twice as many minors were murdered in 1988 as in 1965, when there were more than 6.5 million *more* Americans under the age of 18, and that homicide is now the number one cause of childhood death in many inner cities?[1] Armed with those facts, you could make your case with confidence.

Note the authoritative effect produced by the following introductory paragraph, written by a woman who believes that medical research has shown favoritism toward males:

> Heart disease kills women and men in almost equal numbers: it has no gender bias. Medical researchers have. In clinical trials for any number

> of health problems, including heart disease, they usually employ only male subjects—whether humans or rodents. In 1988, research on 22,071 male doctors revealed that aspirin reduces the risk of heart attacks. The benefit for women? Who knows? A study published this fall indicated that heavy coffee intake did not increase the incidence of heart attacks or strokes. The 45,589 subjects, aged 40 to 75, were men.[2]

Picture the effect of this writer's accusation without the supporting data, and you will see how facts and figures can make a crucial difference in gaining your reader's confidence.

EXERCISE

2. Browse through available newspapers and magazines until you find an authoritative-looking array of facts and/or figures. Make a photocopy of the relevant page or pages, and submit it with a paragraph of your own in which, using your own language, you support a point with some of the data you have found.

4c Cite authorities who share your position.

In theory, the least impressive evidence ought to be the citing of authority; after all, authorities are often proved to have been wrong. In practice, however, we all wisely respect the judgment of people who are better placed than we are for understanding a given issue or technical field. Thus, if a committee of distinguished scientists declares that a proposed weapons system lies beyond the reach of existing technology, we have to be impressed—even if we may harbor some doubts about their unstated political motives. Again, an opponent of placing warning labels on alcoholic beverages could score a telling point by mentioning that the prestigious American Council on Alcoholism *disapproves* of such labeling. Such citation of authority does not by itself win an argument, but it can leave your reader favorably disposed toward your more substantial evidence.

The more subjective and controversial your claim, the more important it is to cite some respected figure who agrees with you. Thus the writer of the following lines, knowing that she has a world-famous scientist on her side, feels that she can draw up a sweeping indictment of American schools:

> It's not as if the schools were failing to *create* budding scientists. No one could fault them for that. The scandal is much worse. Educators take children who demand "Why?" and "How?", who poke and drop and squeeze like the most exuberant experimenters—and turn them off to science completely and irreversibly. As Nobel Prize-winning physicist Leon Lederman of the University of Chicago puts it, schools take "naturally curious, natural scientists and manage to beat that curiosity right out of them."[3]

Even when your case is plausible enough on its merits, you can still strengthen it by concisely citing an informed opinion. For instance:

> The marginalization of sub-Saharan Africa in the 1980s has been relentless. Its share of world trade is half what it was thirty years ago. Private investment is virtually nonexistent. Aid money from the United States is dropping, and total global aid to Africa has stagnated. With the Cold War winding down, superpower competition in sub-Saharan Africa is on the wane—a welcome development in certain ways, no doubt, but one guaranteed to make Africa seem all the more irrelevant. General Olusegon Obasanjo, a former President of Nigeria and a highly respected voice in African affairs, said in a speech last year that "Africa has become peripheral to the rest of the world on global issues. Everywhere in Africa the evidence is of dereliction and decay, and we are rapidly becoming the Third World's Third World.[4]

Observe how the writer allows the authoritative quotation to come last, after we have had a chance to review more tangible evidence of the *marginalization of sub-Saharan Africa*.

EXERCISE

3. Reread the material you reviewed for Exercise 2. Find a statement, written (not quoted) by the author of one piece, that strikes you as especially convincing and important. Then submit a paragraph of your own in which you provide evidence for a claim, including among that evidence a citation of the author's authoritative statement. (If the previously used sources look unsuitable, find a different one and submit a photocopy of the relevant page.)

4d Use quotations sparingly and pointedly.

Quotation can serve not only to invoke authority (4c) but also to provide material for your own analytic reasoning. Observe, for example, how a skeptical observer of "New Age consciousness" handles a key statement and two revealing phrases used by New Age enthusiasts:

> The bedrock of New Age thought now is the fulfillment of individual potential, with the implicit consequence of bringing the New Age closer. How fulfillment is achieved—whether through meditation, pop psychology, physical fitness, est, whatever—and what form it takes (money, power, sex) doesn't matter. What counts is the awareness that one has such potential and can exploit it. Thus *Pathways*, a New Age newspaper in Washington, D.C., defines itself with this credo: "The world public has become disenchanted with both the political and financial leadership. . . . All the individuals of humanity are looking for the answers to what the little individual can do that can't be done by great nations and great enterprises." *Pathways* then encourages the "'little individual' to join together in the dynamic process of personal and sociological transformation."
>
> If all of this makes New Age sound like a religion, that's because for many adherents it is. Like most religions, it attempts to address believers' spiritual concerns with the promise of an afterlife (or rather, another life). And it demands that its believers have faith in things that cannot be scientifically proven—channeling, for instance. But there is no God in the New Age church. Rather, god is within everyone, a universal characteristic New Agers sometimes refer to as "god-force" or "pure-consciousness." Reaching the god-force within you is easy if you know how to do it, like knowing the combination to a bank vault. And if you don't know how to do it, there are plenty of New Age teachers to show you how—for a price.[5]

In his first paragraph this writer, concerned to expose the New Age movement as pseudoreligious, quotes language that conveys religious overtones, and in his second paragraph he dwells on that connection, adding the corroborative terms *god-force* and *pure-consciousness*. The quotations make his reasoning more believable.

Note, however, how the writer has kept that reasoning in the foreground, quoting only enough language to allow him to make his point. Some student writers, in contrast, look to quotation as a readily available form of stuffing that can allow them to meet a minimum word limit. They typically begin a paragraph with an introductory sentence and complete it with a long indented passage that they leave unanalyzed. And then they do the same thing again, rapidly accumulating precious words—but not ideas. An instructor need only glance through such a paper in order to see that the truly important language, the writer's own consecutive discourse, is a bare, inadequate skeleton.

sup 4e

When you are telling a story, quoted dialogue is almost always effective. But especially in analytic and argumentative writing, you should ask what a proposed quotation will be doing *for your reader*. Does the quoted language convey something that wouldn't be apparent in a summary or paraphrase (p. 176, 6f)? Quote only where that language makes a difference.

One place where it always makes a difference is in literary analysis. When you make a claim about the language of a text—a claim, for instance, that Hemingway's sentences are more complex than most people suppose, or that Robert Frost's nature imagery often carries sinister undertones—you ought to quote representative samples of that language. If the quotations alone do not make your point, follow them with passages of analysis. For examples, see the essay of literary interpretation beginning on page 111 below.

For proper acknowledgment of sources, see Chapter 7. For advice about punctuating a quotation, see Chapter 30.

EXERCISE

4. Using new material or the same material you drew upon for Exercises 1 and 2, photocopy and submit a passage of analytic or argumentative prose that you consider worthy of attention. With that passage, submit a paragraph or two of analytic comment in which you succinctly quote parts of the passage in order to make your own points about it. Do not worry about proper citation form; just be sure that you are efficiently using the quoted material instead of merely allowing it to fill up space.

4e Draw on personal experience where you can.

We have said that personal experience can be an important source of ideas for a college essay (p. 60, 3e). In theory, of course, one person's testimony carries no more evidential weight than another's.

Yet all of us are inclined to lend extra credence to a writer's assurance that she herself has witnessed or undergone examples of the phenomenon she describes—outbursts of anger among frazzled motorists, courage among the homeless, delays in "911" response, the effects of racial discrimination, or whatever.

Consider the following passage from an editorial letter protesting the Environmental Protection Agency's declaration that Love Canal, New York—once evacuated because of extreme toxic contamination—is once again safe for habitation:

sup 4e

> In late November 1980, five other scientists and I were conducting field investigations on behalf of the Environmental Protection Agency . . . when we stopped to visit Love Canal. . . . As we made our way by foot between 95th and 96th Streets just north of Colvin Boulevard, which your map describes as an "area declared habitable," a team member shrieked. The object of the shriek was two blooming weeping willows. We ran to our vehicles, got masks, shovels, a volatile organic gas sniffer and a temperature probe. After conducting a preliminary safety analysis, we began to dig at the base of the trees. We had not got more than a foot and a half below the surface when we felt the soil beginning to heat up.
>
> After digging a little further, we stopped and inserted the temperature probe into the ground. It read 120 degrees Fahrenheit. We quickly concluded that the chemical reactions between the numerous constituents dumped into Love Canal were generating substantial heat that caused the roots of these trees to "believe" that it was time for them to regenerate themselves. However, at the surface the temperatures were so cold that the tree's biological system would naturally lead it to conclude it was time for winter hibernation.
>
> I convey this story because I believe it important that people like . . . , who "thinks it's all a lot of hooey," know what disinterested parties at Love Canal in 1980 saw. I believe the area should not be inhabited now or in the future.[6]

By themselves, this writer's ten-year-old recollections cannot settle the question of whether Love Canal has now become habitable. Even so, they would make any reader think twice about accepting assurances that all danger has passed.

But you should also recognize the risks of putting too much weight on personal testimony. If the question, for instance, is whether the human species has an innate aggressive instinct, you may feel inclined to look in your heart and say either yes or no. To do this, however, would be to rely on guesswork and an inadequate sample of just one case. The same lapse occurs when a foreign-born writer asserts, *The idea that immigrants want to become "Americanized" is contradicted by all experience*, meaning *I, for one, do not want to be "Americanized."* Someone else writes, *Professors actually enjoy making students suffer*, meaning *I had an ugly experience in History 10*. Personal experience can usefully illustrate a thesis, but the thesis itself should rest on more public grounds.

fair 4f

EXERCISE

5. Think of an experience—something you have witnessed or undergone—that bears on a question of general interest. (Example: Hospitalized, you were given an incorrect dosage of a prescribed medicine by an intern who had been awake for two days; you regard this mistake as evidence against the policy of deliberately depriving interns of sleep.) Submit two paragraphs in which you take a position and support it. In the first paragraph, give "public" reasons for your stand. In the second, use your personal story as further evidence.

ALLOWING FOR DISAGREEMENT

4f Be fair to an opposing position.

Misstating the Opposing Case: The Straw Man

When struggling to provide adequate support for a stand, you may find yourself tempted to distort the position contrary to your own. Such distortion creates a so-called **straw man**—that is, an imaginary opponent that can be all too easily knocked over. Thus, if the question is whether students should be allowed to serve on faculty committees, a writer would be creating a straw man with this thesis:

x Faculty efforts to keep the student body in a state of perpetual childhood must be resisted.

Here the specific issue—the pros and cons of student participation—

has conveniently disappeared behind the straw man of wicked faculty intentions. A fairer statement would be:

- If faculty members really want to make informed judgments about conditions on campus, they ought to welcome student voices on their committees.

fair
4f

Attacking Personalities: *Ad Hominem* Reasoning

Still another fallacious shortcut is to attack the people who favor a certain position rather than the position itself. This is known as ***ad hominem*** (Latin, "to the man") reasoning. Sometimes such an argument tells us real or invented things about somebody's character or behavior. The implication is that if we disapprove of certain people, we had better reject the idea that has become linked with them. More often the writer simply mentions that a despised faction such as "Communism" or "big business" supports the other side.

DON'T:

x By now we should all recognize the dangers of national health insurance, a scheme for which subversives have long been agitating.

x The benefits of home videotaping are obvious to everyone except the money-crazed Hollywood moguls who stand to lose by it.

DO:

- To judge from the British example, national health insurance might impose an intolerable burden on our economy.
- Although movie executives are understandably worried about competition from home videotaping, they would do better to adapt to the new technology instead of trying to have it banned.

As politicians realize, *ad hominem* attacks do often have their desired effect. Because none of us has time to think through the pros and cons of every public issue, we sometimes rely on surface clues; if certain "bad guys" are revealed to be on one side, we automatically favor the other. As citizens, though, we ought to recognize that the *ad hominem* appeal is a form of bullying. And as writers, we ought to get along without the cheap advantage it affords. If you *can* win an argument on its merits, do so; if you cannot, you should change your position or even your whole topic.

EXERCISE

6. Invent and submit four unfair statements, two creating a straw man and two indulging in *ad hominem* reasoning. Briefly explain what is wrong with each statement, and add four satisfactory versions.

4g Control your tone.

The **tone**, or quality of feeling, conveyed by an essay can be somber or playful, formal or informal, earnest or droll, excited or deliberate, angry or appreciative. But whatever tone you are aiming for, you must check your draft to see that you have sustained it throughout.

Avoiding Emotionalism

Strong emotions have their place in essay rhetoric. Sometimes, for example, righteous sarcasm works better than a studiously neutral weighing of pros and cons—provided the writer can count on the reader's sympathy. Hence the abrupt and cutting tone in much commentary found in magazines whose audience consists of a single political faction. But in college writing there is rarely a good reason for sounding as if you couldn't possibly be wrong.

The chief threat to an adequately controlled tone comes not from strong emotions but from **emotionalism**, the condition of someone who is too upset to think clearly. Compare, for instance, the following passages:

A. The slaughter of whales is butchery pure and simple! Can you imagine anything more grotesque than the hideous, tortured death of a whale, shot with a grenade-tipped harpoon that *explodes* deep inside its body? *And for what?* Why the sadistic murder? Because certain profiteers want to turn the gentlest creature on this planet into *crayons, lipstick, shoe polish, fertilizer, margarine*, and *pet food*, for God's sake! If this doesn't make you sick—well, all I can say is that you must be ripping off some of those obscene profits yourself.

The second passage shows at least as much conviction—probably more—but the emotionalism of passage A is nowhere to be seen:

• B. The killing of a whale at sea isn't pleasant to witness or even to contemplate. Hunted down through sonar and other highly specialized equipment, the whale has no more chance of escape than a steer in a slaughterhouse. The manner of his death, however, is very different. A grenade-tipped harpoon explodes deep within his body, often causing prolonged suffering before the gentle giant, whose intelligence may be second only to our own, is reduced to a carcass ready for processing into crayons, lipstick, shoe polish, fertilizer, margarine, and pet food.

The inhumane manner of death, however, is the least part of the scandal known as the whaling industry. Much more important is the fact that the killing is quite unnecessary. Adequate substitutes exist for every single use to which whale carcasses are currently put, and although some 32,000 whales are killed every year, the sum of commodities they provide is insignificant in the world's economy. Indeed, two already wealthy nations, Russia and Japan, account for eighty percent of all the whales "harvested" annually. Though the Japanese claim that whale meat is a vital source of protein for them, less than one percent of the Japanese protein diet actually comes from that source. Yet the slaughter goes on unchecked. The alarming truth is that one of the noblest species on earth is being pressed toward extinction for no justifiable reason.

If you already agree with the author of passage A, you may find yourself aroused by his overemphatic prose. In that case nothing has been gained or lost. If you disagree, you find yourself insulted as a profiteer. And if you are neutral, wondering which side possesses the strongest argument, you may notice how little relevant information is being offered. Should whaling be stopped because of the mere fact that whales are slaughtered and turned into commodities? So are many other animals. In his outrage the writer has neglected to supply a reasoned analysis that would keep him from being regarded as a sentimentalist.

The measured language of passage B is much more effective than the exclamations and italics of passage A. Take the description of a whale's death: we see, not the writer emoting over the fact, but the fact itself, which becomes more impressive without the signs of agitation. Similarly, by not calling special attention to the list of commodities from *crayons* through *pet food*, passage B achieves a powerful quality of **understatement**, whereby the mere reality appears more expressive than any editorializing about it would be. And above all, note that writer B provides detailed evidence for the belief that whale slaughter, whether or not it revolts us, is economically unnecessary. In reading passage A, our only options are to share or reject a fit of temper. But even if we lean at first toward a pro-whaling stance, we find it hard to dismiss writer B's objectively reported facts. Here and elsewhere, reasons prove to be not just fairer but also more persuasive than fits of sentiment.

For more advice on controlling your tone through revision, see page 126, 5d.

EXERCISES

7. Here are three passages illustrating very different tones:

   A. Yes, you CAN stop drinking! I tell you it's really possible! The fact that you're reading these words means that you have the MOTIVATION, the WILL POWER, to make the change now—*today!*—and to STAY ON THE WAGON FOREVER!! Think and believe, *I am just as good as everybody else! I don't NEED that bottle!* It's really true. You have more potential than the HYDROGEN BOMB! Just take yourself in hand *today*, and by tomorrow you'll start feeling like a NEW PERSON—the person that you really are inside!

   B. While it has seemed probable that addiction to alcohol is at least in part due to the development of physiological tolerance to the drug, there have been to date no clear demonstrations that alterations in the blood level of alcohol alone (without concomitant experiential factors of taste and ingestion) were sufficient to produce a lasting enhancement of alcohol preference subsequent to treatment. Here we report a method capable of producing a lasting enhancement of alcohol preference without concomitant oral stimulation. . . .

      This enhancement of preference has been achieved by prolonged passive infusion of alcohol into the stomach of rats. After recovery from surgical preparation, the rats were placed in a Bowman restrainer cage to adapt for 24 hours. After this initial period each rat was connected to a pump. . . .[7]

   C. A man who once developed printed circuits for computers begs on street corners for enough coins to buy another bottle of cheap port.

A woman whose husband walked out when she couldn't stop drinking at home sits stupefied on a park bench, nodding senselessly at passers-by. An anxious teenager raids her parents' liquor closet at every opportunity. These people, though they have never met, suffer from the same misfortune. If they were placed together in a room, each of them might recognize the others as alcoholics. Yet what they have most in common is their inability to see *themselves* as alcoholics—and this is the very worst symptom of their disease. For until the alcoholic's self-deception can be broken down, not even the most drastic cure has a chance of success.

Study passages A, B, and C, and then submit an essay in which you discuss their differences of tone, pointing to specific uses of language in each case. Include an assessment of each writer's probable audience and purpose.

8. The following passage may serve as an extreme example of emotionalism in prose:

> Supermarket prices are a damn ripoff! The middlemen and store managers take us customers for a bunch of suckers! Hamburger "extended" with soybeans but labeled as pure meat costs more than steak did a few years ago! Hey, man, don't try to tell me it's just inflation! The filthy con artists shake you down for all you're worth! "Specials" in bins turn out to cost more per item than the cans on the shelves, for God's sake! I've *had* it with those dudes! Have you seen the way they put candy right by the checkout counter, where your kid will grab it and throw a tantrum if you don't buy it?

Write a paragraph of your own in which you express some or all of this writer's grievances, but in a tone suitable for a typical college essay.

4h Handle objections through concession and refutation.

If you think of likely objections to your central claim, you should pause over them attentively. A writer who simply ignores an opposing reason is gambling that it won't occur to the reader. But the gamble is risky. A wiser course would be to grant, or make a **concession** of, minor points that count against your case and to disprove, or make a **refutation** of, points that lack merit. The more persuasive-looking and damaging the objection, the more care you should devote to it.

When you do decide to concede an objection, you must go on

to restore your own positive point of view. Observe the two essential steps in this passage advocating population control:

> He who says "The earth can support still more people" is always right; for, until we reach absolute rock bottom, we can always lower the standard of living another notch and support a larger population. The question is, which do we want: the maximum number of people at the minimum standard of living—or a smaller number at a comfortable, or even gracious, standard of living?[8]

fair
4h

Always take care to state objections fairly instead of sneering at them. Leave your reader with the impression that you are compelled by fairmindedness, not by prejudice, to adhere to the judgment you have chosen. Notice, for example, how a student writer calmly summarizes the case against her view and then addresses it with an effective refutation:

objections are summarized . . .

> Opponents of antismoking laws greet such proposals with several answers, some of which look very impressive at first glance. The new laws would be unenforceable, they say; smoking is an irrational addiction, and millions of smokers would simply defy the law. The government, we are told, should direct its efforts not to hiring Smoke Police but to developing harmless cigarettes. Furthermore, we are reminded that regulation of smoking would cause economic hardship for tobacco growers, advertisers, and people connected with bars and arenas—places where smoking is so customary that a ban on smoking would affect patronage. Above all, the defenders of smoking point out that no studies have yet demonstrated a connection between lung cancer and *accidentally* inhaled smoke. Perhaps, then, we who favor new laws have failed to distinguish between a mere annoyance and a health hazard.

. . . and then refuted

> Let us review these arguments in turn. Is it obvious, first of all, that antismoking laws couldn't be enforced? People said the same thing about "pooper scooper" ordinances directed at dog owners, but those ordinances are actually working in New York City and elsewhere. It is not a question of hiring more police, but of using the law to raise consciousness, make violators feel criticized, and bring about voluntary compliance. To say that the government should try to develop safe cigarettes is true but beside the point; we must decide what to do *until* such cigarettes are on the market.

Again, the "hardship" argument has some merit but is not decisive. If smoking did decrease, farmers could be compensated and aided in switching crops; advertisers would surely continue to get cigarette accounts; and bars and arenas could be exempted from the law on the grounds that most of their patrons *voluntarily* expose themselves to smoke. As for the lack of proven connection between second-hand smoke and lung cancer, we should remember that lung cancer is by no means the only disease associated with cigarette smoke. It *has* been proven that people who suffer from heart and respiratory diseases can be seriously affected by a smoke-filled environment. It is these people—not the rest of us who just find smoking distasteful—whose rights are at issue.

EXERCISES

9. Choose a topic of controversy about which you feel strongly. In one sentence, write down your position on that issue. Then list below it as many objections as you can, and place check marks beside the points that you would feel obliged to raise if you were defending your position in an essay. Submit this page of work, and be prepared to explain why you checked certain points instead of others.

10. Write and submit a paragraph or two in which you deal with one of the checked objections (Exercise 9) by means of *concession*. Show your reader that this negative point, though true enough, is less important than another, positive, consideration.

11. Take any of the checked objections (Exercise 9) and submit a paragraph or two in which you *refute* that objection.

DEALING WITH A TEXT

4i Assess the merits of a presented case.

Often, a college writing assignment will ask you to read someone else's analysis or argument and make a response to it—not a gut reaction of approval or disapproval but a careful consideration of stronger and weaker points. To meet this challenge, you must go through several steps:

1. Read and reread the work to be quite sure you "have it right."
2. Take notes, using separate cards or pages for positive and negative features as you perceive them. Use page references to remind yourself where the key passages are found.
3. Decide whether you are going to put primary emphasis on the "pros" or the "cons," and organize your essay accordingly. (See pp. 83–89, 3p and 3q.)
4. Make your case, being sure to summarize the writer's position fairly before beginning to assess it. Quote from the text wherever the writer's language is important to your point.

The advice we gave in the previous section, "Allowing for Disagreement," might lead you to think that you should go out of your way to include both positive and negative considerations. But a *text*, as opposed to an *issue of general controversy*, won't always give you an opening for such evenhandedness. You needn't pull your punches; just set forth the merits and/or defects exactly as you find them.

The complete student essay below, for example, has scarcely a kind word to say about the British scientist Richard Dawkins's proposal, in his book *The Selfish Gene*, that we can usefully think of human culture as being transmitted by gene-like "memes."[9] The writer feels no obligation to toss in compliments where she doesn't find them justified. She does, however, try to be consistently fair, steering clear of both **straw man** and ***ad hominem*** **reasoning** (pp. 100–102, 4f) and maintaining a rational tone.

This essay was written for a class in which *The Selfish Gene* had been assigned. If you haven't read that book yourself, you will find the essay hard to follow. Don't worry about the details; just note the businesslike way in which the writer accomplishes her task.

DREAMS OF SELFISH MEMES

In his book *The Selfish Gene*, Richard Dawkins says that while the genetic makeup of plants and animals dictates their behavior to a great degree, human behavior is additionally influenced by an evolving social culture. More controversially, he asserts that "cultural transmission is analogous to genetic transmission" (189). Thus he coins the term "meme," a name for "a unit of cultural transmission, or a unit of *imitation*" (192). "Tunes, ideas, catch-phrases, [and] clothes-fashions" (192) are examples of memes. Dawkins maintains that these units, just like genes, exist as self-copying entities, or replicators; that an analogue of natural selection is seen in the different success rates of meme transmission; and that the competitive nature, or selfishness, of memes deters new memes from entering the meme pool.

Dawkins finds it convenient to think of memes, like genes, as "active agents, working purposefully for their own survival" (196). But when his anthropomorphic (humanizing) language is translated into realistic language, we see that meme theory ignores the possibility of *human* intervention in shaping human culture. In conferring the powers of will and action on memes, Dawkins avoids consideration of the human power struggle as a leading factor in cultural evolution.

Dawkins says that "all life evolves by the differential survival of replicating entities" (192), and he extends this argument to culture. "Memes propagate themselves in the meme pool by leaping from brain to brain via a process which . . . can be called imitation," and when "the idea catches on, it can be said to propagate itself" (192). Furthermore, just as genes are changed by mutation, "memes are being passed on to you in altered form" (195), since they are subject to interpretation by the brains in which they replicate themselves.

The spread of these units of imitation—of cultural transmission—is suspiciously identical to the spread of all units of information. But while memes are supposed to spread themselves, most of us understand that information is spread by *people*. When anthropomorphism is removed from the phrase "memes propagate themselves," we shouldn't be too surprised to find that "memes are propagated." Because cultural information is not self-replicating, Dawkins's analogy between memes and genes lacks explanatory force.

In Dawkins's view of physical evolution, nature favors the survival of aggressive, selfish genes. Altruistic, unselfish genes cannot compete with selfish genes; they eventually become extinct. Memes, in order to have a function analogous to that of genes, must also be competitive and selfish. As Dawkins puts it, "selection favours memes which exploit their cultural environment to their own advantage" (199). When we subtract the humanizing language, however, we find a trivial and circular meaning: some ideas are more popular than others because they are more culturally useful.

But Dawkins carries his gene analogy further. He suggests that memes link themselves, forming groups when it is mutually advantageous. Meme complexes thus supposedly "have the attributes of an evolutionarily stable set, which new memes find it [sic] hard to invade" (199). As history shows, however, when one group of people is able to force its culture on another, the memes being spread need not be any "stronger" than the memes that are destroyed. Bad ideas can drive out good ones if they have a superior army championing their cause.

The theory of selfish memes is a thought-provoking analogy between biological and cultural evolution. Unfortunately, however, that is all it is. Richard Dawkins's attempt to explain why certain ideas and traditions survive lacks solid data and is filled with unjustifiable assumptions. Selfish memes belong in daydreams, not in serious science.

EXERCISE

12. Choose a piece of analytic or argumentative writing to assess; if it falls outside the assigned reading for your composition course, submit a photocopy of it. Write a brief essay in which you clearly summarize the writer's case and provide a critique of it, setting forth whatever strengths and weaknesses you perceive. Refer to specific passages from the text, and make sure that you provide objective grounds for your judgments.

4j Reveal a pattern in a literary work.

What should you do when asked to "analyze" a poem, a short story, a scene from a play, or a passage from a novel? First, you should realize what kind of task is involved: **interpretation**. Interpretation is the making of judgments about the meaning or coherence of a piece of writing, a work of art, or an event or a movement. By its nature, interpretation can never be definitive. Thus, though you will be looking for a way in which the work "hangs together," you must understand that different observers will see other patterns that may be as legitimate as yours. And second, precisely because interpretation is so open-ended, you should gather every clue as to what kind of interpretive analysis is expected. Find out whether you are to concentrate on meaning (thematic emphasis) alone or on formal qualities (features of expression such as poetic meter or significant images) as well. Be sure you know whether your instructor wants you to treat the text by itself or to relate it to other texts you have been reading lately.

All good literary interpretations do have one important thing in common: they get down to specifics about the author's language. A work of verbal art is not a direct message—even when it is phrased like one—but a structure of words which arouses a certain range of thoughts and feelings through its manner of expression. The most fundamental advice about interpretation, therefore, is this: *stay close to the text* instead of skipping quickly to your own ideas. If a poem, for example, deals with the sorrow of parting, don't use up space telling about your own sorrows; show your reader how this particular artistic structure makes (or fails to make) its intended effect.

In looking for meaning, read and reread the text in search of its underlying idea. If a certain theme catches your notice, check to see whether it recurs. When you find a deliberate insistence, go over the text again in the light of your half-formed interpretation, taking notes on further details that fit the pattern—or that conspicuously don't. (As one example of the kind of evidence you may come across, look again at the "Laertes" paragraph on page 43.)

Another hint: always discuss formal features *in relation to meaning*, not for their own sake. Your reader will have little interest, for example, in a mechanical run-through of a poem's stanza length, rhyme scheme, and meter, yet any one of those qualities could be usefully brought into a wider interpretation. Keep in mind that you are trying to show what is unique, not what is commonplace, about the text.

To get a more concrete idea of how interpreters work, study the following complete student essay comparing and contrasting two poems written in different eras.

DEATH, WITH AND WITHOUT THE TRIMMINGS

In juxtaposing Tennyson's "Crossing the Bar" and Stevens's "The Death of a Soldier," we get some sense of the chasm separating the late-Victorian era from modern times. The common subject matter—dying and its aftermath, if any—only sharpens the contrast. Tennyson, writing in 1889, makes of death something downright attractive, a peaceful and passive transition to eternal reward. Stevens, writing in the ominous year 1918, has said goodbye to all that. Death, for his soldier, is just itself, the Big Stop that will be followed by nonexistence.

We are told in history courses that World War I struck a heavy blow against Christian faith. These two poems could provide some indirect evidence for that thesis. In 1889 Tennyson can still "hope," at least, that his "Pilot" will welcome him into heaven. But when Stevens says that the soldier "does not become a three-days personage" (is not resurrected like Christ), he is ironically understating the case. An anonymous victim of the so-called Great War will presumably not be in line for any kind of salvation, much less for being made divine. Stevens's indifferent clouds pass, significantly, "over the heavens."

Tennyson's poem has proved far more popular than Stevens's, but sometimes mass appeal can be a sign that a poet has made things too easy for himself. Considered in the light of "The Death of a Soldier," "Crossing the Bar" strikes me as rather sentimental and self-indulgent. The poet says, in effect, *Hold back your tears, everybody; my passing will be nothing more painful or final than floating out through the harbor on an ebb tide*. It sounds humble at first, but on rereading, it comes to seem quite self-centered: "And one clear call for me!" A century's-worth of lulled readers have gladly entertained the daydream that they, too, may be granted such a tasteful exit from this world.

"Lulled" does appear to be the appropriate word. "Crossing the Bar" begins like an incantation, with two strong beats introducing a free-standing phrase that puts us into a dim half-light, and then the incantation is renewed in the exact middle of the poem:

> Súnsét an̆d évenin̆g stár.
>
> . . . .
>
> T́wilíght an̆d évenin̆g béll. . .

Meanwhile, the very tide "seems asleep," and all the usual agony of real dying is smothered under a drowsy ease, pleasantly "full" and "boundless." This atmosphere really is enchanting—so much so that we aren't bothered by the absurdity of the old poet's asking a sand bar to kindly refrain from "moaning" on his behalf, or by the apparent confusion of his floating out to sea and *then* perhaps coming across the ship's pilot. "Crossing the Bar" is a great emotional success, though of a kind that a conscientious modern poet wouldn't dare to strive for.

"The Death of a Soldier" illustrates the modern reticence and tough-mindedness to an exceptional degree. Victorian self-dramatization is ruled out from the start by Stevens's choice of the third person instead of the first; the poet's own eventual death isn't even remotely contemplated. Until the closing lines, the poem remains pointedly abstract and cold: "Life contracts and death is expected"; "Death is absolute and without memorial." Instead of Tennyson's full boundlessness, we get the barest of reports ("The soldier falls") followed by negation: "He does not become. . . ." All is prosaic here, in contrast to Tennyson's delicately hushed language, predictable rhymes, and mostly regular meter, flowing like the benevolent tide. And though both poets finish every stanza with a very short line, the effects achieved are opposite. Tennyson's stanzas end succinctly because, with the comfort of salvation in view, little more need be said. In "The Death of a Soldier," each stanza seems to "run out of poetry" in the presence of a final nothingness.

But this is not to say that "The Death of a Soldier" lacks artfulness. On the contrary, the poem hinges on a brilliant surprise. The simile "As in a season of autumn" sets up a trite anticipation: the soldier falls, we assume, as do autumn leaves. In the third stanza, with the strange repetition of line 2, we begin to see that something more unusual is brewing: death is somehow like the stopping of autumn *wind*. Only in the final stanza do we grasp why. What matters about death, for Stevens, is not that a life ceases but that everything else proceeds as before: "The clouds go, nevertheless, / In their direction." Thus even the absoluteness of death is, we might say, nothing to write home about.

Why does Stevens repeat the clause "When the wind stops"? I think he is playing a subtle game with us. At the end of stanza 3 we still suppose that everything ends with the hapless soldier's death. Dying, then, is like the sudden stopping of a breeze. But by immediately repeating "When the wind stops" and then *continuing*, the poem catches its breath, as it were, passing right by the soldier's meaningless corpse. Thus "The Death of a Soldier" mirrors its own message by keeping going, nevertheless, in its direction.

Although "The Death of a Soldier" suits my taste better than "Crossing the Bar," it would be unfair to say that Stevens has written the better poem. Each work is well suited to the spirit of its age, and even today many readers must find Tennyson's outlook on death to be not only more reassuring but also more plausible than Stevens's. Each poet offers us a curiously complete experience. Instead of choosing between them, we might do better to grant both poets their initial assumptions—and let the poetry do its expert work on our feelings.

This is a very sophisticated essay, but it follows principles that can be applied to any literary analysis. Note, for example, that although the writer clearly prefers one poem (Stevens's) to the other, he allows for differences of taste. Instead of dwelling on his likes and dislikes, he gives his major emphasis to examining the language of the two works. Note, too, that the writer avoids merely listing traits such as the presence or absence of rhyme and the short closing lines in each poem's stanzas. With both poems, he is concerned to show how specific features of expression yield precise—or, in Tennyson's case, vague—emotional effects. It is this use of detail in the service of carefully developed ideas that chiefly distinguishes the essay from a routine performance.

EXERCISE

text 4j

13. Choose a concise literary text—a poem, short story, or one-act play—and submit a brief essay analyzing some of its key features. If the work falls outside your assigned reading for this course, include a photocopy of it.

NOTES

[1] See Karl Zinsmeister, "Growing Up Scared," *Atlantic* June 1990: 51.

[2] Katrine Ames, "Our Bodies, Their Selves," *Newsweek* 17 Dec. 1990: 60.

[3] Sharon Begley, "Rx for Learning," *Newsweek* 9 Apr. 1990: 55.

[4] David Ewing Duncan, "The Long Good-bye," *Atlantic* July 1990: 20.

[5] Richard Blow, "Moronic Convergence," *New Republic* 25 Jan. 1988: 26.

[6] Itzchak E. Kornfeld, Letter, *New York Times* 15 Aug. 1990, national ed.: A18.

[7] J. A. Deutsch and H. S. Koopmans, "Preference Enhancement for Alcohol by Passive Exposure," *Science* 179 (1973): 1242.

[8] Garrett Hardin, *The Limits of Altruism: An Ecologist's View of Survival* (Bloomington: Indiana UP, 1977) 58–59.

[9] See Richard Dawkins, *The Selfish Gene*, 2nd ed. (Oxford: Oxford UP, 1989).

5

Collaborating and Revising

Many students are willing enough to revise their work but are held back by two misconceptions. First, they suppose that revision begins only when an essay is nearly ready to be turned in; and second, they think that revision involves only a tidying up of word choice, spelling, punctuation, and usage. But experienced writers revise their prose even while they are first producing it—adding, deleting, replacing, and rearranging material at every opportunity (p. 56, 3b). They never assume that any given draft will be the last one. And they stand ready to make conceptual and organizational changes as well as editorial ones.

5a Learn to give constructive advice as a peer editor.

Increasingly, composition instructors have been enlisting their students as **peer editors** of one another's work. Either in pairs or in small groups, students are asked to take turns examining drafts and making appropriate suggestions for revision. Although such exchanges have only recently become standard procedure in the college classroom, conscientious writers—student and nonstudent alike—have always known how important it is to solicit outside opinions about their work. Precisely because they stand outside your thoughts and feelings, your classmates may be able to spot both major and minor problems in short order.

If you take your duties as a peer editor seriously, you will find yourself becoming a keener critic of your own work. Though it will always be harder to apply objective standards to your prose than to someone else's, peer editing will make you more consistently aware of what those standards are. To some extent, you can learn to anticipate your editor's point of view while making changes in your first draft.

There is just one key difference between the ways in which you should treat your own writing and that of a fellow student. It has to do with tact. Since you probably think too well of your freshly written draft, you should try to be as hard on it as possible. But with classmates, you want to offer encouragement and support as well as criticism. The human ego is fragile; if you simply mock or condemn a fellow student's efforts, you will cause only bitterness, not improvement.

Try, then, to find something praiseworthy in your classmate's draft, and mention that feature before offering any criticisms. For example: *You have a promising topic here* or *Your strong feelings about animal rights keep this essay lively throughout*. When you do criticize, put your stress on possibilities for further development or clarification. Don't, for example, write *This is a mess!* Try something like *Doesn't this paragraph contradict paragraph 3?* or *Your argument seems to get lost somewhere around here. Provide some signposts?* Questions can be especially helpful because they sound polite and unthreatening and because they pass the initiative for revision back to the writer.

As a peer editor, you want to emphasize large issues such as the believability of the writer's thesis, the adequacy of presented evidence, and the suitability and consistency of the essay's tone. Don't shrink from pointing out errors of usage, punctuation, and spelling, but make sure you don't leave the impression that you were simply waiting to pounce on mistakes.

A Peer Editing Worksheet

To make sure you cover major categories and maintain a sense of proportion, copy the following items onto both sides of a sheet of paper, leaving more space between them than you see below. (For convenience, you may want to make enough photocopies of this two-sided worksheet to see you through all the peer editing tasks that lie ahead.) After reading the draft essay at least twice, fill out the answers. When you return the writer's draft, attach the completed worksheet to it.

coll/
rev
5a

Peer Editing Worksheet

Writer's name: ______________________________

Title of paper: ______________________________

Peer editor: ______________________________

1. What is the main impression this draft makes? What appear to be its strongest and weakest features?

2. Is the thesis clearly and prominently stated?

3. Is the thesis in its present form worth defending, or does it seem too obvious or too implausible? Explain.

4. Is the tone consistently appropriate to the writer's purpose? If not, explain.

5. Is the thesis adequately supported? What points, if any, need further evidence?

6. Do the writer's points appear in the most effective order? If not, explain.

7. Does the draft essay repeat or contradict itself? If so, explain here, or mark the relevant passages.

8. Are all the paragraphs fully developed and well organized? If not, explain.

9. Are the opening and closing paragraphs effective in arousing curiosity and giving a sense of completion? If not, how could they be improved?

10. Are a significant number of expressions erroneous in meaning, tone, spelling, or correctness of usage? Mark examples on the draft.

11. Does the draft have an appropriate title? If not, explain.

12. Do you have any concluding thoughts?

To see how this worksheet can help a writer to revise effectively, study pages 139–49 below, showing a typical progress from first thoughts to a final draft. The completed worksheet for that essay can be found on pages 145–46. Another completed worksheet appears on pages 122–23.

For a fuller Checklist for Revision, meant for application to your own drafts, see the inside front cover.

EXERCISE

1. Find a completed essay of your own, written for this or any other course. If none is available, borrow an essay from a classmate. Using a copy of the Peer Editing Worksheet, draw up a critique of the essay as if you were helping the writer with a draft. Submit the completed worksheet along with a copy of the paper.

5b Welcome suggestions for improvement of your draft.

Professional writers know that the difference between effective and dreary prose is often made not by sheer talent but by the writer's willingness to seek and accept criticism. To be sure, you can't count on a peer editor to give you the crucial guidance you need; you will have to weigh your classmate's perceptions against your own and decide which suggestions have hit the mark. But if your peer editor lets you down, you should keep showing your draft to others until you get an objective judgment.

Insofar as possible, stay in personal contact with your peer editor and make it known that you want no punches pulled. Without reassurance on that point, some peer editors—especially if they happen to be your friends—will waffle, hoping to avoid an embarrassing confrontation. If your peer editor is not equipped with a Peer Editing Worksheet (p. 117), supply one yourself, adding any questions you yourself have about the adequacy of your draft. You may find some of your peer editor's observations painful, but if they lead to revisions that clarify your thesis and trim the fat from your rhetoric, you will end by being grateful.

EXERCISE

2. Show one of your drafts to a classmate, friend, or roommate. Include a Peer Editing Worksheet (p. 117), and ask for a critique of the draft. If you find the critique helpful in important ways, submit original and revised versions of two or three paragraphs that were shown to be among the weakest. Otherwise, submit an analysis of your peer editor's work, showing how that effort fell short of what you needed. What kind of critical attention do you think your writing typically calls for?

5c Be open to conceptual and organizational revision.

Because sentence-by-sentence composing often leads to new ideas (p. 91, 3r), you must read through your completed draft to be sure it makes a consistent impression. Do not hesitate to alter your thesis or even reverse it if you become more swayed by objections than by supporting points. Such a shift can be painful and time-consuming, but in the long run it will spare you many hours of trying to show interest in ideas that you now consider fatally weak.

You should be prepared to make less sweeping conceptual changes as well. Have you exaggerated your claims? Are your explanations clear? Do you need to supply more evidence? Give your conceptual revisions top priority; there is no reason to tinker with phraseology if the whole direction of your essay has to be changed.

coll/rev 5c

After you have made necessary changes in your ideas, check your draft to see whether your points appear in a logical and persuasive order. Have you placed your thesis prominently? Have you waited to unveil it until you have attracted the reader's interest and clearly identified the topic? Have you avoided digressions, or passages that stray from the issue at hand? Have you avoided redundancy, or needless repetition of assertions? Are all of your quotations succinct and necessary? And have you included all necessary information—for example, the setting for your discussion of an event, the rules of a little-known game, or the plot of an unassigned novel? Here as elsewhere the key to successful revision is to "play reader" and probe for sources of puzzlement or dissatisfaction.

To see how a student, making use of peer criticism, can arrive at fundamental changes of idea and organization, consider the following draft essay and its sequel:

Opposites Attract

If given a choice of location in which to travel, I would like to visit the USSR. Many myths surround my impressions of the Soviet Union, impressions that are certain to be false. The false images are mostly due to obvious considerations of geographical location. I envision the USSR as cold, scarce, and populated with people who seem inhuman. Out of this curiosity, I would like to travel and see for myself that the country and the people are very similar to the typical American life. The influence of the news media, radio, and television are to blame for my current feeling.

In the state of world affairs, issues and politics

between the U.S. and the Soviets dominate the stage. As a result of the inner competition between the two powers of the world, many of the aspects and beauties of the Soviet Union are never spotlighted. I have seen film and pictures of the people and the climate which resemble places in the United States.

Geographically, I would be inclined to think that the landscape and climate is comparable to Canada and the United States. The Soviet Union is located approximately the same distance above the equator as North America, meaning that there is a diversity in scenery ranging from extremely cold to desert heat. This is an obvious observation, but to the American people an observation which is given little thought. The American people are too often cluttered with implications made by the media and as a result develop impressions on limited evidence.

Another misconception is the people. Since the media only concerns itself with the political powers of the USSR, the politicians are the only people we have to associate with our image of the country. On the contrary, I get a different idea whenever I see an interview with someone who has defected or emigrated. I find the Soviets are very similar to the typical American, which leads me to believe that Soviet society is really very much like our own.

My curiosity is shared by many of my fellow students. With the positions that the U.S. and the Soviets hold, we are interested in just where the average Soviet stands in relation to ourselves. Also, the evidence of knowing what the country looks like in different areas would help in the overall feelings I have for the Soviet Union.

A classmate gave this student the following advice on a Peer Editing Worksheet:

1. What is the main impression this draft makes? What appear to be its strongest and weakest features?

   Bill—this is a good start toward a strong essay. Right now, though, I think you're struggling a bit. Although it's a great idea to want to go to the USSR and find out for yourself what things are like, you seem bogged down here in your quarrel with the American media. On the one hand, you accuse them of withholding the truth from you; on the other hand, your contrary ideas about the USSR come mostly from those same media—e.g., interviews with defectors. Also, I wonder how accurate your criticisms are; they seem to apply more to the Cold War period than to now. All in all, the "media" aspect of this draft seems like it's holding you back from the more interesting stuff about the Soviets.

2. Is the thesis clearly and prominently stated?

   Well . . . yes, if the thesis is that you want to go to Russia! See below.

3. Is the thesis in its present form worth defending, or does it seem too obvious or too implausible? Explain.

   "I want to visit the USSR" seems more like a personal remark—like "I like skateboarding"—than a thesis I can agree or disagree with. But you have the makings of a better thesis here—something along the lines of new opportunities to take a fresh view of the Soviets, now that the Cold War's over?

4. Is the tone consistently appropriate to the writer's purpose? If not, explain.

   The tone will be fine, I think, once you let up a bit on the media bashing.

5. Is the thesis adequately supported? What points, if any, need further evidence?

   See above. With a meatier thesis, you'll have to face this question again.

6. Do the writer's points appear in the most effective order? If not, explain.

   If it's geography first, people second, then yes, that looks like the right order. But actually, I have a problem with the geography stuff. You're treating latitude as if it were the only thing determining scenery and climate; I don't think that's right. And it seems like you're saying, "I want to go there to find out what I'm already sure is true—that the USSR is just like America and Canada."

7. Does the draft essay repeat or contradict itself? If so, explain here, or mark the relevant passages.

   I just mentioned one contradiction above, and there's another one under point 1—about the media. You do repeat yourself somewhat, too; I'll mark examples.

8. Are all the paragraphs fully developed and well organized? If not, explain.

   Here and there you seem to be spinning your gears, but I don't think it's because you have trouble with ¶ structure in itself. If you take my hint and shift your thesis, ¶ development will probably take care of itself.

9. Are the opening and closing paragraphs effective in arousing curiosity and giving a sense of completion? If not, how could they be improved?

   Again, a new thesis will make for a new beginning and end. In this draft, the last ¶ in particular seems to run out of gas.

10. Are a significant number of expressions erroneous in meaning, tone, spelling, or correctness of usage? Mark examples on the draft.

    You do run into some problems with parallelism and predication (the people are similar to the life; pictures of the people . . . resemble places; Another misconception is the people) and with subject-verb agreement (the influence . . . are; the landscape and climate is . . .). But there's no point in fixing these passages until you see whether they make it into your next draft!

11. Does the draft have an appropriate title? If not, explain.

    Your title is clever, but you may need a new one if you change emphasis.

12. Do you have any concluding thoughts?

    Yes. . . . In writing this, I've come to feel more strongly that there's something funny about the curiosity you keep mentioning. As I said under #6, you want to learn what the Soviets are like, but somehow you already know that they're just like us—both the people and the landscape. If so, how interesting, really, is that? And is this really curiosity on your part—or are you making up your mind in advance? Maybe you should project a more open attitude toward the traits that you don't know about yet.

The writer was disagreeably surprised to get this response, but after sitting down and rereading his draft, he saw that the criticisms were justified. Before revising, he took note of everything he heard and saw about the Soviet Union in newspapers and magazines and on television. Eventually, he was able to produce a better-informed and more concrete essay that completely reversed his early assumptions about the underlying sameness of Soviets and Americans:

After the Evil Empire

The news from the Soviet Union, according to what I see and read these days, has notably changed its character. It wasn't very long ago that the Evil Empire, as one recent American president called it, came across in the media as awesomely powerful, ruthless, and bent on destroying our socioeconomic way of life in general and our nation in particular. Every image of "the Russians"--usually rugged Cosmonauts, drab-looking Party bosses, and fat generals weighted down with medals--was darkened in our minds by the shadow of the Bomb. Today, however, the collapse of the Red Menace has allowed the media to give us at least a little insight into ordinary Soviet people.

But there is a catch. On closer inspection, the new coverage of the USSR seems to be a lot like what we saw in the bad old days. What remains the same is the American media's habit of showing everything and everyone foreign not as they are but only as they have a bearing on America's self-interest. Back then, every "Russian" was someone who might want to reduce us to radioactive dust. Now, the one big question is: "How far have the Soviets gotten toward totally accepting the American way of life?" Thus, even while millions of people throughout the USSR face near-famine conditions and a drastic shortage of winter heating oil, we are bombarded with images of Moscow citizens eating Big Macs, drinking Pepsi, and crowding around visiting American economists and plant managers to learn how capitalism works.

For me, the number one question is different: "Are those people really like us?" In one sense, obviously, they are. The United States consists mostly of immigrants and their descendants; the Soviets we see on TV are typical of the discontented people from the USSR and many other countries who flee to the West, continuing to make American society the most diverse on earth. And when we hear what those Soviet citizens are worried about--jobs and housing, health care and nutrition, crime and corruption--we can easily imagine that their lives are a lot like ours.

I have come to understand, though, that traditions are at least as important as present-day needs in shaping the way people think and act. Whatever we may once have thought from watching spy movies and the evening news, "the Russians" are not one people but many. They speak many languages; they follow several major religions, from Russian Orthodox Christianity to Islam to Judaism; they live in regions ranging from Arctic frost to scorching desert heat; and they belong to rival ethnic groups that never wanted to be drawn into a "Union" in the first place. If we study Russian history, furthermore, with its traditions of feudalism and absolute rule, we may be able to understand why the people closest to the heart of Soviet power are still slow to accept democratic forms of government and the work ethic.

Back in 1989, the Iron Curtain separating eastern and western Europe fell apart in a matter of weeks. Before it did, Americans had the luxury of thinking about "the Soviet bloc" as if it were one thing--a vast system of oppression radiating out from Moscow. Today, there is no excuse for not learning about the many groups that kept their identity and their beliefs throughout the period when they were forced to be satellites of the USSR. And now we realize--or ought to realize--that the USSR itself is a coalition in the act of dissolving into its constituent parts. The old saying "Know your enemy" is certainly good advice; but when your enemy ceases to pose a threat, you understand for the first time how little you have really known about him.

For another example of conceptual and organizational revision, see pages 139–49 below.

EXERCISE

3. Reread the original and revised versions of the essay above, and submit a brief analysis showing how the writer has reconceived his topic and thesis. In what ways has he reversed the emphasis of his draft? Is it "insincere" of him to have done so, or do you consider such changes a normal part of the revision process? If you have found yourself making similar adjustments to your own drafts, cite a relevant example.

5d Revise for appropriateness and consistency of tone.

We have already seen (p. 102, 4g) that college writing generally calls for a reasonable, measured tone—one that inspires confidence in your cool judgment. But tone is not something to fuss over in the early stages of writing an essay. It is more important to work out your ideas and decide how you are going to support them than to worry about whether you are creating exactly the right kind of impression with your language.

Once you have finished a draft, however, try to reread it as if you didn't know the writer, and ask yourself, "What is this person's mood?" Frequent underlining, dashes, and exclamation points, for example, are signs of excitement. Is that the effect you want to create in the final version? In revising, you may decide you would rather show composure and control. On the other hand, if your draft sounds like the work of a bored and listless writer, you can look for ways of showing more engagement.

Here is a typical instance of revision for tone. The student's draft began as follows:

```
So you're having trouble deciding what major to pursue?  Why
not consider Business Administration?  If you have not even
bothered to inform yourself about it, you are making the
biggest mistake of your life.  This major is not only
academically challenging and diverse, it is also practical
and economically rewarding.  Business Administration is the
answer to all the problems facing today's student.
```

On her Peer Editing Worksheet, a classmate commented:

> 4. Is the tone consistently appropriate to the writer's purpose? If not, explain.
>
> *Your opening paragraph sounds kind of aggressive/defensive. And how do you know what's right for all students? Consider more of a live-and-let-live approach?*

After reflecting on this criticism, the student modified his tone:

```
So you're having trouble deciding what major to pursue?  Join
the crowd!  For some of us, though, this decision isn't
really agonizing.  In Business Administration we are finding
just what we need: academic challenge, diversity, and a good
prospect of economic reward in the long run.  Though
Business Administration isn't for everyone, quite a few
```

bewildered freshmen could do themselves a favor by checking it out.

Again, here is a draft paragraph and a peer comment on its tone:

Everyone in college could use a hobby or sport to take some of the academic pressure off. In my case, the sport of choice is hang gliding. It isn't as dangerous as most people seem to think, but it certainly takes your mind off studying.

4. Is the tone consistently appropriate to the writer's purpose? If not, explain.

   The rest of your paper is full of intriguing details about hang gliding, but the opening paragraph seems flat. How about moving some of the lively material up front?

The student revised accordingly:

Have you ever felt like a "launch potato"? Do you quail at the thought of "turn and burn"? Members of the UC Hang Gliding Club have a chance to consider such obscure notions in their weekly pursuit of the stuff dreams are made of. Every Saturday, before the sun has burned off the dew, twenty people from Berkeley are checking parachutes, adjusting straps, pulling on extra socks. If the weather and the equipment cooperate, a magical transformation occurs. Chemical engineers, political scientists, and French majors leave their earthbound identities behind and fly.

EXERCISE

4. Looking through previously written work, find a paragraph of your own that seems "off" in tone. Submit a brief explanation of the problem and a revised paragraph whose tone seems more appropriate and effective.

5e Attend to editorial revision.

Though editorial revision—improvement of wording and conventions—is rarely the most important kind, it does cover the greatest number of problems. In every case, effective editorial revision means putting the reader's convenience ahead of your own.

FEATURE	REVISE FOR	HELPS READER TO
paragraphs	unity, continuity, development	see relations between major and minor points
sentences	distinctness, subordination, emphasis, variety	follow ideas, avoid tedium
words	appropriateness, liveliness	get clear information, avoid jarring effects
usage, punctuation, spelling, other conventions	conformity with standard written practice	concentrate on substance of essay
citation form	fullness, exactness, consistency	have access to secondary information

For an idea of how instructors and peer editors typically draw attention to editorial problems and how students then revise, consider the following made-up paragraph and the symbols for comment and revision (see the inside back cover) that have been added to it:

> Once people [have gone to the trouble of acquiring the capacity to treat everyone as equals,] they can work with others for the common good. A great example is how the Los Angeles area handled it's pollution problem. Everyone was aware of the stifling smog. But the majority of these people were willing only to complain. One group of

(Margin annotations: wdy; exag; pred; sp; chop; ref; ¶ un)

coll/ rev 5e

```
p     citizens, however^ came up with a creative plan
      for carpooling. Providing an incentive, one lane        dm
      of freeway was set aside for cars carrying three
      or more people. [But after a short period of
sp    time,] the committment was abandoned. [Because of       wdy
collog the godawful traffic jams in the other lanes.]        frag   ¶un
ref   It was a promising idea, but most people are made      pass
comp  [less upset by smog so that] they actually prefer
      it to traffic jams in freeway lanes.                    red
```

The most important of these markings is ¶*un*, since it calls for a substantial rewriting that would automatically eliminate some of the smaller problems. But if the student were to address those problems as they stand, the diagnoses and the most likely remedies would be these.

SYMBOL	PROBLEM AND SOLUTION	UNREVISED VERSION	REVISION
wdy	the expression is wordy; make it more concise	Once people have gone to the trouble of acquiring the capacity to treat everyone as equals	Once people can recognize others as equals
		after a short period of time	soon
exag	the expression is overstated; tone it down	A great example	One example
pred	faulty predication; do away with the mismatch between subject and predicate	A great example is how . . .	One example is the handling . . . ; *or* Consider, for example, how Los Angeles handled . . .

SYMBOL	PROBLEM AND SOLUTION	UNREVISED VERSION	REVISION
sp	spelling error; look the word up and spell it correctly	it's committment	its commitment
chop	choppy sentences; several plain, brief sentences in a row; introduce variety of structure	A great example is how Los Angeles . . . willing only to complain.	Consider, for example, how Los Angeles handled its pollution problem. Even though everyone was aware of the stifling smog, few people were willing at first to do anything more than complain.
ref	pronouns or demonstratives lack clear, explicitly stated antecedents; make the reference clear	these people It was a promising idea	residents The carpooling plan was a promising idea
p	punctuation error; correct it	One group of citizens, however came up with	One group of citizens, however, came up with
dm	dangling modifier; supply an agent to perform the action	Providing an incentive, one lane of freeway was set aside	Providing an incentive, county officials set aside
colloq	the expression falls beneath the level of diction appropriate to this paper; find a middle-level substitute	godawful	serious

SYMBOL	PROBLEM AND SOLUTION	UNREVISED VERSION	REVISION
frag	sentence fragment; rewrite or combine to form a grammatically complete sentence	Because of the godawful traffic jams in the other lanes.	But because of serious traffic jams in the other lanes, the commitment was soon abandoned.
pass	unnecessary use of passive voice; shift to active voice	most people are made less upset	most people would rather
comp	faulty comparison; match the compared terms or completely recast the expression	most people are made less upset by smog so that	most people prefer smog to traffic jams; *or* most people find smog less offensive than traffic jams
red	this expression repeats an earlier one; rephrase it	traffic jams in the other lanes . . . traffic jams in freeway lanes	. . . can't take lung congestion any more seriously than they do traffic congestion

As for ¶un, notice that the writer began by asserting that *people can work for the common good* but then went on to illustrate a nearly opposite point, that *most people cannot put the public interest before their immediate convenience*. Until that contradiction is resolved, no amount of tinkering can make the paragraph effective.

To weigh the writer's options, ask yourself which idea shows more regard for real experience, the initial one or the one that surfaced in the drafting process. It is really no contest. *Working with others for the common good* is a limp "motherhood" concept, wishful and bland. The conflict between selfish private habits and the common good is a more balanced, less simplistic notion—one that indicates an ability to face facts. Thus the writer would do well to skip the moralizing and rethink the whole thesis. An eventual, radically improved version of the paragraph might look like this:

> When selfish private habits and the common good come into conflict, the outcome is likely to be all too predictable. Take a recent example from Los Angeles, where everyone's health would be safeguarded by a significant reduction in automobile exhausts. Acting on the suggestion of a citizens' group, county officials tried to promote carpooling by setting aside one lane of each freeway for cars carrying three or more people. If it had worked, this plan would have enabled everyone to breathe more easily. The plan had to be dropped, however, when so few people cooperated that motorists refusing to share rides were hopelessly clogging the remaining lanes. Los Angelenos, it seems, can't take lung congestion any more seriously than they do traffic congestion.

EXERCISE

5. Using your instructor's and/or peer editors' comments on previously submitted work, decide *which three* kinds of editorial problems you have least under control. List them and then, in two columns, provide several of the marked examples of each weakness, with improved versions in the right column. Submit this work.

5f Check your quotations and citations.

To avoid unintentional **plagiarism** (p. 181, 7a) and to be sure you are fairly representing your sources, you will need to check your draft against the original passages you are using. If you are summarizing a passage, see the discussion of summary on page 176, 6f. For the form of quotations, see Chapter 30.

If you are taking notes on library materials that you may not have on hand by the time you draft your essay, it is important to check your quotations and summaries on the spot, before letting those documents out of your possession. But if you can keep them, always compare your draft to those documents, not to your notes. Take care to reproduce everything in a quotation exactly as you find it in the published source.

With a Word Processor: A chief source of error in quoting is the recopying of passages from one draft to another. But if you can take notes on your word processor and check for accuracy at that point, the risk of error will greatly decrease. Save the quoted passage or passages as a document, and simply lift the quotation into your draft when you need it. If you copied it correctly the first time, it will stay accurate through any number of subsequent drafts.

5g Make your title definite.

Do not bother thinking of a title until you have finished at least one draft, and be ready to change titles as your later drafts change emphasis. If you begin with a title, it will probably indicate little more than the subject matter treated in your essay. Replace it later with a title expressing your *view of* that subject matter, or at least posing the question answered by your thesis. Thus, asked to write about revision, do not remain satisfied with "Revision" or "Revising College Essays"; such toneless titles suggest that you have no thesis at all. Instead, try something like "The Agony of Revision," "Revision as Discovery," or "Is an Essay Ever Really Finished?" Each of those versions tells the reader that you have found something definite to say.

That impression will be especially strong if you can make your title surprising and vivid. Look for a striking figure of speech (p. 368, 17a) that could suggest your thesis with pointed wit. One common device is to combine such a phrase with a more straightforwardly informative subtitle:

- Downhill All the Way: My Melting Career as a Ski Racer

- Going High for the Rebound: Drugs as a Menace to Athletes' Careers

If your essay contains especially significant phrases (original or quoted), see whether any of them could be borrowed for your title. One freshman student, for example, began a prizewinning essay about *Hamlet* with the following paragraph:

> While showing Guildenstern how to play the recorder, Hamlet remarks that it is "as easy as lying" (III.ii.343). In a sense, much of the play's meaning is expressed in this line. Almost every character in Hamlet is to some extent living a lie: hiding thoughts, playing a role, trying to deceive another character. Claudius conceals his crime; Hamlet feigns madness; private schemes prevail. In the end, Hamlet may even be deceiving himself, forcing himself into a role of avenger when he may not actually fit.

For a title, the writer chose "As Easy as Lying"—a phrase that stirred curiosity and gave promise of a well-considered, original thesis.

EXERCISES

6. Look through available magazines and newspapers for titles of articles that are both definite and inviting. Submit three such titles along with brief analyses of why they work.

7. Look through your own previously submitted papers for this or any other course until you find a title that could be significantly improved. Submit a brief discussion of the problem and include one or more new titles that now seem more satisfactory.

5h Test your draft against a Checklist for Revision.

Since you cannot always count on having a friendly critic available, and since even a peer editor will see only a preliminary version of your essay, you yourself will need to test your drafts against commonly held standards. A Peer Editing Worksheet (p. 117, 5a) can help you to begin seeing how those standards apply to an early draft, but eventually you will want more thorough guidance. For this purpose, consult the Checklist for Revision found on the inside front cover of this book. Running through its twenty-one questions, you should be able to pinpoint remaining problems and locate the relevant discussions of them elsewhere in this book.

EXERCISE

8. In preparing an assigned essay, pause after completing a draft and run through the Checklist for Revision, using the page references to look up any unclear points. Evaluate and revise your draft accordingly, keeping notes on the changes you are making at this stage. Then submit a paragraph or two explaining what weak features of your draft became apparent to you in light of the checklist.

5i Follow standard typescript form in your final copy.

No matter how many changes you make between drafts, the essay you eventually submit should look unscarred, or nearly so. It should also meet certain technical requirements of form. The following advice reflects general practice and should be followed whenever your instructor does not specify something different.

1. Type your essay if possible, using standard-sized (8½″ × 11″) unlined white paper of ordinary weight, not onionskin. If you must write longhand, choose paper with widely spaced lines or write on every other line. Type with an unfaded black ribbon or write in dark ink. Use only one side of the paper.

2. If you are submitting a title page, arrange it like the model on page 217, and repeat *the title only* on your first page of text, as on page 219.

3. If you are not submitting a title page, treat your first page like the model on page 147.

4. If you are asked to supply a thesis statement and/or an outline, put them on a separate page, as on page 218.

5. Allow at least one-inch margins on all four sides of each page of your main text. Your right margins need not be even. In a handwritten essay, be sure to leave as much space as in a typewritten one.

6. Unless you have a separate title page, leave the first page of text unnumbered, but put your last name and unpunctuated Arabic numerals (2, 3, 4) in the upper right corners of subsequent pages, including your endnotes (p. 207, 7e) and reference list (p. 188, 7c), if any.

7. Double-space your whole essay, including any reference list, endnotes, or bibliography (p. 213, 7e). Single-space any footnotes. Follow your instructor's specifications for the spacing of indented quotations (p. 554, 30h).

8. Indent the first line of each paragraph by five type-spaces; that is, press the space bar five times and then begin typing. In a handwritten essay, indent by about an inch. Do not skip extra lines between paragraphs. When a quoted passage is long enough to require indention (see p. 554, 30h), generally indent it by ten spaces—fewer if a quoted poem uses very long lines.

9. Retype any pages on which you had to make more than a few last-minute changes. Otherwise, type those changes or write them clearly in ink, using the following conventions:

   a. Remove unwanted letters with a diagonal slash:

      `indigestio`~~n~~`n`

   b. Remove unwanted words by running a line through them:

      ~~nasty~~ `slur`

c. Replace a letter by putting the new letter above your slash:

```
     s
compo/ition
```

d. Replace words by putting the new word above your canceled one:

```
             writer
please every ~~reader~~
```

e. Add words or letters by putting a caret (∧) at the point of insertion and placing the extra words or letters above it:

```
          notable
Another ∧ feature of this device
```

f. Separate words or letters by placing a vertical line between them:

```
steel and|iron
```

g. Close up separated letters with a curved line connecting them from above:

```
hic cup
```

h. Transpose (reverse) letters or words with a curved enclosing line:

```
Aldie; Carroll Lewis
```

i. Indicate a paragraph break by inserting the paragraph symbol before the first word of the new paragraph:

```
depends on development. ¶ Transitions, too, have a
certain importance.
```

j. Run two paragraphs together by connecting them with an arrow and writing *no ¶* in the margin:

```
    She has found a way of turning "nothing" time into
    pleasure or learning.
no ¶
    Isn't that better than having some trivial chitchat
    on the sidewalk?
```

10. Carefully proofread your final copy, looking especially for typing errors. Check all quotations against your notes or, better, against the printed passages.

11. Make sure you have assembled your pages in order. Fasten them with a paper clip or, second best, with a staple.

12. Make a photocopy of your essay, and retain the copy until you get the original back. Keep the graded original at least until the course is over. These steps will protect you if your instructor should mislay an essay or misrecord a grade.

For citation form, see Chapter 7. For the forming and spacing of punctuation marks, see Chapter 31.

5j Observe the composition of one essay from start to finish.

A freshman student, Becky Alexander, found that her next writing assignment was a 500-word essay about "a topic of current controversy." Scanning magazines in her campus bookstore, she came up with several preliminary ideas, and later sorted out her thoughts about them in a note:

"Educational" TV, but with commercials, in the grade-school classroom. ("Channel One.") Not a bad topic—but what do I really know about it? Would have to speculate about effects on kids. . . . No relevant experience.

"Does the Mac Make You Stupid?" (Macworld article.) Good possibilities: writing with a "friendly" computer may not be good for students' prose. But again—how can I tell? And the article already lays out both sides pretty fully.

Home schooling—big new movement. Sounds great for parents who already have the time, $, and education to substitute for a whole school. But that's the problem!—not relevant to the mass of kids who aren't getting an education either at school or at home.

Lotteries, pro and con. Should states be running a gambling ring? Maybe so, if taxpayers won't pay enough. . . . Good arguments on both sides. Explore? . . .

To follow up her first thoughts about state lotteries, Becky tried a session of freewriting (p. 61, 3f):

Lotteries produce "tax money" without actually taxing anybody—sounds fine, esp. if Congress and state legislatures lack guts to raise taxes. But revenue doesn't amount to much. Meanwhile, state becomes a hustler—pretty seamy! Trick the poor and minorities into betting their *grocery $—yuck! Still, some lotteries seem OK: army draft, sports drafts, etc. . . . But big difference: those don't promote a dangerous habit. You could say, though, that the govt permits alcohol and gets tax $ from it; same sort of deal. Wait, though—the govt doesn't beg you to drink, does it? But why be so uptight, Becky? Lotteries entertain—distract people from their misery. They choose to bet. If they're going to bet anyway, let's put the profit to good use.*

Becky could see that she was going to have plenty to say on both sides of the lottery question. She wasn't sure, though, which position she would finally favor. To advance her thinking, she drew a line down the center of a page and listed pros and cons on either side:

PROS	*CONS*
People will gamble anyway—why not get revenue from legal activity?	*Got to be a better way to balance state budget.*
Congress can't face unpopular taxes, but $ is needed.	*Revenue produced is trivial, esp. compared to negative effects.*
Voluntary "taxation" for entertainment is fair.	*Burden falls on poor, minorities—greater proportion of their budget is gambled.*
Poor, minorities get many of the services funded by lotteries.	*Don't want to promote compulsive gambling.*
NBA draft, army draft, etc.—legitimate lotteries.	*Get-rich-quick message—just what people don't need.*
Why get upset by people's dreams of wealth? It's their choice.	*The chances against winning are so great that it's a hoax.*
Some people actually will get rich and be relieved of a tough situation.	*State advertising budget—up to 3/4!—squandered on enticing people to bet. Cf. AIDS, smoking, etc.*
Over 28 states already have lotteries. Where are the bad effects? Everybody seems reasonably happy about fun & revenue.	*The state itself becomes a "compulsive gambler."*
	Deceptive pitch—no mention of odds, taxes, risks of betting too much.

Examining these columns, Becky felt that although she herself wasn't favorably inclined toward the idea of state lotteries, the arguments for and against them seemed about equally weighty. For a trial thesis statement (p. 73, 3l), then, she came up with the following:

TRIAL THESIS STATEMENT:

> Since there appear to be excellent considerations on both sides of the lottery question, it might be best in the short run neither to cancel existing state lotteries nor to rush into creating new ones, but to collect more evidence about their social effects.

To make use of peer criticism in the composing process, Becky's instructor asked all students to bring their trial thesis statements and their notes to class and to discuss them in small groups. Becky's group was not enthusiastic about her first try at a governing idea for the essay. Some comments:

> "This looks kind of wishy-washy to me. On the one hand, on the other hand . . . it's just not very committed to anything."
>
> "Lotteries have been around for a long time. What are we going to learn from the wait-and-see approach?"
>
> "This statement seems to overlook the fact that individual states make the choice as to whether they'll have a lottery or not. Who is it who's supposed to decide on 'more' or 'fewer' lotteries? You're just not talking about the real world here."
>
> "In your notes, you show strong feelings about state governments indulging in deceptive advertising. Maybe you should concentrate on that. It would help you get off dead center."

These criticisms found an echo in Becky's own misgivings about the current state of her project. But the last comment gave her a ray of hope: if she shifted her topic toward deceptive enticements to gamble, she could "get off dead center" and develop a real commitment to her thesis. Hence her second try at a thesis statement:

REVISED THESIS STATEMENT:

> Although state lotteries produce some benefits, both in entertainment and in revenue, that offset at least some of their disadvantages, there is no excuse for advertising the lotteries in a way that disguises the odds against winning, overstates the take-home jackpots, and encourages people to become compulsive gamblers.

This version struck Becky and her classmates alike as showing both the decisiveness and the complexity that could lead to an engaging yet carefully reasoned essay. For a title to accompany it, she chose the hard-hitting phrase "Turning Citizens into Suckers."

Since her essay was to be fairly short, Becky decided to try a simple scratch outline (p. 86, 3q):

1. What's bad enough: TV displays deceptive ads for lotteries, encouraging people to gamble against nearly impossible odds.
2. What's worse: This is your state government, spending most of its advertising budget on the merchandising of a possibly destructive fantasy.
3. To be sure, much can be said in favor of having the lotteries themselves.
4. If lotteries are here to stay, however, the governments sponsoring them should inform citizens, not deceive them, about the odds against winning, the actual size of after-tax jackpots, and the dangers of compulsive gambling.

In her discussion group, one student suggested that this outline might be too sketchy; point 3 looked more like a vague promise than a real guide to arguments favoring lotteries. Becky, however, knew from her sheet of pros and cons (p. 140) that she had those arguments at her fingertips. She was ready to begin writing her first draft.

Here is the draft that Becky submitted to a peer editor, Reina César, and received back with Reina's notes and comments:

Turning Citizens into Suckers

A person who watches a lot of television will certainly see a lot of commercials, and you soon get used to the idea that people are always trying to sell you something you don't need. However, you may never get entirely used to the idea that your own state government is trying to trick you. What I have in mind here is advertisements for lotteries, in the states (like mine) that have them. [I am sure you have seen these ads.] They make fun of people who don't gamble on the lottery--even though the odds against winning are literally astronomical. And they don't tell you how much (perhaps half) of your jackpot, if you do win, will be kept for taxes. They also don't tell you that the rest will be doled out to you in installments while the state--not you!--earns interest on the unpaid balance. And perhaps worst of all, they try to extract money from poor and uneducated people, who may need that money for groceries, doctor bills, etc. They actually help to create a certain number of compulsive gamblers!

rep — pr shift — rep — ¶? — no-see RHH, p. 697 — p. — inappropr. for main text

Up to three-quarters of a typical state budget, if that state has a lottery, goes into advertising the lottery. So, instead of spending money warning people about AIDS, drunken driving, etc., the state is putting its emphasis on selling dreams of something-for-nothing.

¶ dev

Of course, there are things to say on the

coll/ rev 5j

see RHH p. 685

other side, at least as far as having the lotteries in the first place. You aren't going to stop Americans from gambling; they bet over $1 billion on football alone! Some people say that lotteries actually reduce the incidents of illegal gambling, and this is good because the public gets its hands on the money that illegal gamblers would just keep for themselves. It's a good idea to take that money and spend it on transportation, education, care for the elderly, etc. Though it is too bad that most Americans resist being openly taxed for all the social services they demand. Still, if that's the way it's going to be, the lottery is a pretty painless way of making up the difference. Even so, a government shouldn't be in the business of deceiving its citizens.

sp

frag

too many "pivots"

Although we probably have to accustom ourselves to having lotteries whether we like them or not, I think the state should always be in the position of serving and protecting us, not trying to corrupt us. It shouldn't be trying to trick people in taking food out of their children's mouths to put into the lottery. I think there should be a law to make sure that lottery ads be truthful, with full disclosure of the odds against winning, the taxes and installments involved, and with warnings (like the Surgeon General's warnings against smoking) about the dangers of compulsive gambling.

into?

fig—the food goes into the lottery

//

Essay just stops here. Wrap it up?

And here is the completed Peer Editing Worksheet that Becky got back from Reina:

Peer Editing Worksheet

Writer's name: *Becky Alexander*

Title of paper: *"Turning Citizens into Suckers"*

Peer editor: *Reina César*

1. What is the main impression this draft makes? What appear to be its strongest and weakest features?

   Becky—This is a really strong and balanced argument. The fact that you grant some usefulness to lotteries makes your attack on the false advertising more believable. I think some of the prose can be tightened up, though.

2. Is the thesis clearly and prominently stated?

   Yes, although it's unusual to save your main point for the last paragraph. I guess it works in a four-paragraph paper.

3. Is the thesis in its present form worth defending, or does it seem too obvious or too implausible? Explain.

   Seems fine to me.

4. Is the tone consistently appropriate to the writer's purpose? If not, explain.

   No problem!

5. Is the thesis adequately supported? What points, if any, need further evidence?

   Support is OK as you have it, though paragraph 2 looks a bit lame.

6. Do the writer's points appear in the most effective order? If not, explain.

   No problem.

7. Does the draft essay repeat or contradict itself? If so, explain here, or mark the relevant passages.

   No, but some of your language is repetitive. See my comments.

8. Are all the paragraphs fully developed and well organized? If not, explain.

   Paragraph 2 looks badly undeveloped to me. And paragraph 3 ends with material that probably belongs in #4.

9. Are the opening and closing paragraphs effective in arousing curiosity and giving a sense of completion? If not, how could they be improved?

   First paragraph is OK but seems rather wordy. Last paragraph ends suddenly with the statement of your thesis. Too abrupt, I think.

10. Are a significant number of expressions erroneous in meaning, tone, spelling, or correctness of usage? Mark examples on the draft.

    I've marked everything I could find, but in addition, you should try to phrase things more economically and vividly.

11. Does the draft have an appropriate title? If not, explain.

    Nice title!

12. Do you have any concluding thoughts?

    You're close to a first-rate paper here, Becky. Go for it!

With the help of this criticism and the Checklist for Revision (inside front cover), Becky finally submitted the following version:

Becky Alexander
English 1A, section 7
Mr. Marks
3 December 1991

Turning Citizens into Suckers

Since our state is among the majority that now run an official lottery to supplement tax revenue, your television screen is probably as saturated with lottery come-ons as it is with ads for toothpaste, beer, and deodorant. The lottery commercials, you may have noticed, dangle incredibly huge sums before your eyes and leave the impression that the only real fools are the people who won't try their luck at becoming richer than kings. No mention is made of the odds against winning. There is no way to tell that if (by a near miracle) you do choose all the right numbers, about half of your prize will be kept for taxes and that the rest will be doled out over many years, while the state continues to earn interest on the unpaid balance. And the ads never refer to the problem of compulsive gambling--an addiction that ranks just behind substance abuse as a social problem. On the contrary, the state seems determined to _create_ a certain number of compulsive gamblers from among its poorest and least educated citizens.

coll/ rev 5j

2

A stranger from a non-lottery state, turning on a motel TV and seeing those upbeat commercials, might wonder at first why the government was allowing them to be shown. Only gradually would it dawn on her that the state itself is "the house," enticing and fleecing its own people. Even then, she might not realize that up to three-fourths of the state's advertising budget is spent on promoting the lottery. Very little is left over, therefore, to warn citizens about the risks of AIDS, drunken driving, smoking, and pollution. The state focuses nearly all its publicity effort on merchandising a get-rich-quick fantasy--one that will come true for only a handful of people while encouraging millions of others to think of success as a product of luck, not honest work.

I admit, however, that I have been presenting only one side of a complex issue. There are, after all, perfectly sound arguments for allowing state lotteries to continue and spread. Americans are going to gamble anyway; for example, they now bet more than $1 billion yearly on football alone. Lotteries may actually reduce the incidence of illegal gambling, and they certainly do produce extra funds for transportation, education, care of the elderly, and so forth. Though it is too bad that Americans resist being openly taxed to cover all the social services

3

they demand, the lottery is a relatively painless and even entertaining way of making up the deficit.

Even so, there is a fundamental difference between merely supervising a game and actively manipulating and deceiving the public. I think we should insist that tax dollars not be spent on the recruiting of players who will put lottery tickets ahead of groceries and shelter for their families. I recommend, therefore, that a law be passed requiring truth in lottery advertising--by which I mean full disclosure of the odds against winning, an explanation of the taxes and installment payouts that apply to the prizes, and warnings against compulsive gambling. If these reforms cause fewer dollars to flow into the state treasury, they should also help to keep some marginally solvent families self-sufficient--and thus off the welfare rolls. The point of state government, after all, is not to get and spend as much money as possible but to improve the quality of life. Refraining from turning citizens into suckers would be one small but welcome step toward that goal.

III

THE RESEARCH ESSAY

THE RESEARCH ESSAY

When assigned a research essay, some students feel they must set aside everything they have learned about writing essays and concentrate instead on showing how much library reading they can do. The result may be a paper crammed with references but lacking a clear point or concern for the reader's patience. A research essay is above all an essay—one that happens to be based in part on library materials (Chapter 6), duly documented (Chapter 7). The advice that follows should be regarded not as a self-sufficient unit but as a supplement to Chapters 1–5. If you are undertaking a research essay and have not gone through those chapters, it would be good to do so now.

6

Finding and Mastering Sources

A college library is in essence an information retrieval system. As with a computer, the knack of using it successfully consists in knowing the right questions to present it with. Searching through the stacks without any questions at all would be as senseless as trying to browse in the computer's memory bank; you have to be looking for something from the outset. And the more specific your question, the more shortcuts you can take. Experienced researchers do not run through all the ways of seeking information described in this chapter. Rather, they find a few key works as early as possible and then allow those works—especially those containing a **bibliography**, or list of further books and articles on the topic—to suggest how to proceed.

6a Get acquainted with the parts of your library.

Perhaps your college library strikes you as mysterious or even vaguely threatening. If so, bear in mind that you do not have to understand the whole system—just some procedures for retrieving the books and articles you need. Watch for free library tours and information packets, and do not hesitate to ask a *reference librarian* for help in getting an efficient start on your project.

No two libraries are quite alike, and your own may be much simpler than the model we summarize here. Even so, you will find the same functions met within a more consolidated floor plan. Here, then, are the key rooms and services found in an ample college library:

1. *Stacks*. These are shelves on which most books and bound periodicals are stored. In the "open stack" system, all users can enter the stacks, find materials, and take them to a check-out desk. If your library has "closed stacks," access to the stacks is limited by status; see the next item.

libr
6a

2. *Circulation desk*. You can check out a book or bound periodical by submitting a *call slip*—a card identifying what you need—to the *circulation desk*, to which a clerk will return either with the book or with an explanation that it is on reserve (see item 5), out to another borrower, or missing. If it is out to another borrower, you can "put a hold" on it—that is, indicate that you want to be notified as soon as the book has been returned. Since you may have to wait as long as two weeks for some items, it is important to begin your research early.

3. *Catalog*. Near the circulation desk you will find cabinets full of alphabetically filed cards, listing all the library's printed holdings (books, periodicals, pamphlets, and items on microfilm, but no manuscripts, records, or tapes). This is the *card catalog*. Its listings are by author, title, and subject. In some libraries the card catalog has been supplemented or replaced by a *microfiche catalog*, consisting of miniaturized photographic entries on plastic cards that can be read when placed in a microfiche reader, available nearby. Your library may also have an *on-line catalog*—that is, a continually updated computer file. If so, you will see computer terminals, accompanied by appropriate instructions, near the circulation desk. Whatever its form, the catalog is your master key to the stacks, for it gives you call numbers enabling you or a clerk to locate the books you need.

4. *Reference room*. In the *reference room* (or behind the reference desk) are stored sets of encyclopedias, indexes, dictionaries, bibliographies, and similar multipurpose research tools. You cannot check out reference volumes, but you can consult them long enough to get the names of promising-looking books and articles that you *will*

be able to get from the main collection. The reference room usually doubles as a *reading room*, enabling you to do much of your reading near other sources of information.

5. *Reserve desk*. Behind the *reserve desk* (or in the reserve book room) are kept multiple copies of books that are essential to current courses. The distinctive feature of reserved books is that they must be returned quickly, usually within either an hour or a day or a week. When you learn that a book is "on reserve," even for a course other than your own, you can be reasonably sure of finding an available copy.

6. *Periodical room*. In the *periodical room* you can find magazines and journals too recent to have been bound as books. Thus, if you do research on a topic of current interest, you are certain to find yourself applying to the periodical room for up-to-date articles.

7. *Newspaper room*. Take your call slips to this room to get a look at newspaper articles and editorials. Most newspapers are stored on *microfilm*, which can be read only with a microfilm reader. Ask a clerk to show you how the machine works.

Thus your research is likely to take you back and forth between various sites:

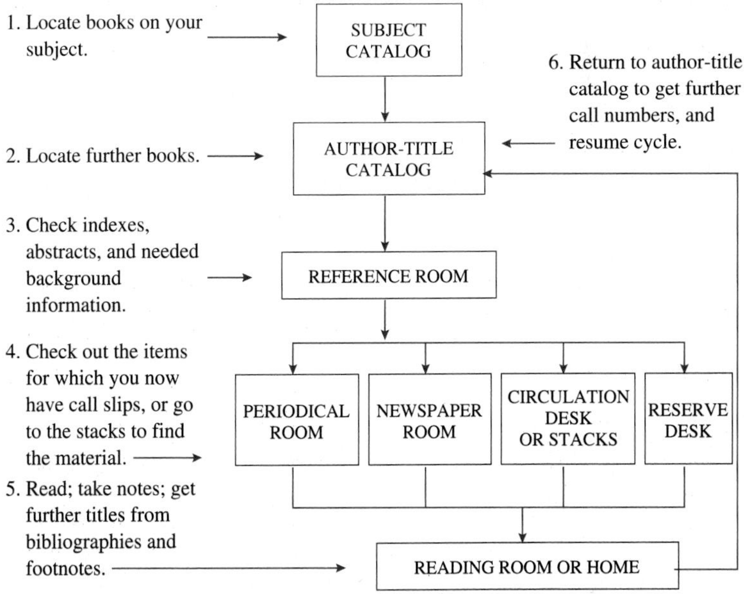
1. Locate books on your subject.
SUBJECT CATALOG
6. Return to author-title catalog to get further call numbers, and resume cycle.
2. Locate further books.
AUTHOR-TITLE CATALOG
3. Check indexes, abstracts, and needed background information.
REFERENCE ROOM
4. Check out the items for which you now have call slips, or go to the stacks to find the material.
PERIODICAL ROOM
NEWSPAPER ROOM
CIRCULATION DESK OR STACKS
RESERVE DESK
5. Read; take notes; get further titles from bibliographies and footnotes.
READING ROOM OR HOME

At some point, obviously, this cycle has to be interrupted; the first draft beckons. But even as you write successive drafts, you may find yourself dipping back into library sources to check new leads and follow up ideas that now look more fruitful than they did at first.

EXERCISES

1. Find out—if necessary by asking a reference librarian—what catalogs your main campus library has, where they are located, and whether they are equally up-to-date. Submit a paragraph that supplies these pieces of information.

2. If your library offers guided tours, take one. If not, check the various rooms and functions on your own. (Never mind about branch libraries or special collections; look for the rooms discussed above.) Submit a brief report of what you have learned, including any questions that remain unresolved for you.

6b Learn the most efficient ways to search for books.

Subject Catalog

If you are searching for a topic within a general subject area, the first thing you want to do is check your library's holdings within that area. You can do so by consulting the *subject catalog*, which is arranged not by authors and titles of books but by fields of knowledge, problems, movements, schools of thought, and so forth. Once you locate an array of relevant titles, you should fill out call slips for the most recent appropriate-looking works. If you get hold of just one recent book that has a **bibliography**—a list of consulted works—in the back, you may discover that you already have the names of all the further books and articles you will need.

Guide to Subject Headings

But how do you know which headings your subject catalog uses to classify the entries you will want to review? You can try your luck, sampling a number of alternative phrases, or you can take a more systematic and reliable approach. Your subject catalog follows the headings adopted by the Library of Congress in Washington, D.C. Ask your reference librarian where a book called *Library of Congress Subject Headings* is to be found. That book is heavily *cross-indexed*; in other words, if you look up a plausible-sounding phrase, you will not only learn whether it constitutes a Library of Congress subject heading, you will also be directed to other phrases that do serve as headings.

Thus the student who wanted to investigate animal intelligence for his research paper (pp. 217–29) began by going to the *Library of Congress Subject Headings*, where he found these headings and symbols:

Animal intelligence
1—— [QL785]
2——UF Intellect of animals
Intelligence of animals
3——RT Animal psychology
Instinct
Psychology, Comparative
4——SA *subdivision* Psychology *under individual animals and groups of animals, e.g.* Cattle—Psychology
5——NT Animal behavior
Cognition in animals
Learning, Psychology of
Learning in animals
Tool use in animals

Observe that:

1. The entry provides the Library of Congress call number of a key work on the subject. Armed with this number, the reader can consult the Library's *shelf list*—a catalog arranged in order of call numbers—and be sure of finding relevant material near card QL785.

2. The symbol *UF* ("used for") alerts the reader to topic headings that will not be used elsewhere in the reference work. Thus there would be no point in searching for further information under "Intellect of animals."

3. The symbol *RT* ("related topics") sends the reader to other headings that may prove useful.

4. The symbol *SA* ("see also") gives further advice about finding relevant information from other entries.

5. The symbol *NT* ("narrower topics") gives more specific headings that can be consulted. If a subentry had been marked with *BT* ("broader topics"), the reader would be sent to topics that would put the subject matter in a wider perspective.

Author-Title Catalog

When you conduct a subject search using Library of Congress headings (above), you won't necessarily be consulting a separate subject catalog (p. 156 above). In many libraries, subject entries are interfiled within the *author-title catalog*.

If you know that your paper will deal with a certain author or public figure, you can bypass a subject search and go directly to the author-title catalog, which lists works alphabetically by both author and title. The last entries in your author's listing, after his or her own works, may be useful books of biography, criticism, and commentary. Thus the author-title catalog is itself a kind of subject catalog, with the treated figures as subjects.

The most important piece of information in any catalog entry is the *call number* in the upper left corner; it tells exactly where the book or bound journal is shelved. But you can also get several other kinds of information from a card, as did a student who was doing research for a paper on computer crime. The cards she consulted are shown on the opposite page. In addition to some coded information chiefly of interest to librarians, the author card contains six potentially useful kinds of knowledge:

1. The author's name.

2. The call number, enabling someone to apply for the book at the circulation desk or to locate it in the stacks.

3. The title of the book, the author's name as it appears on the title page, the fact that this is a first edition, the place of publication, the publisher, and the date of copyright. A researcher would want to get all this information (except "1st ed.") recorded on a bibliography card (p. 173, 6e).

4. Physical features of the book. It contains 164 pages, is illustrated, and is 21 centimeters in height. The key point here

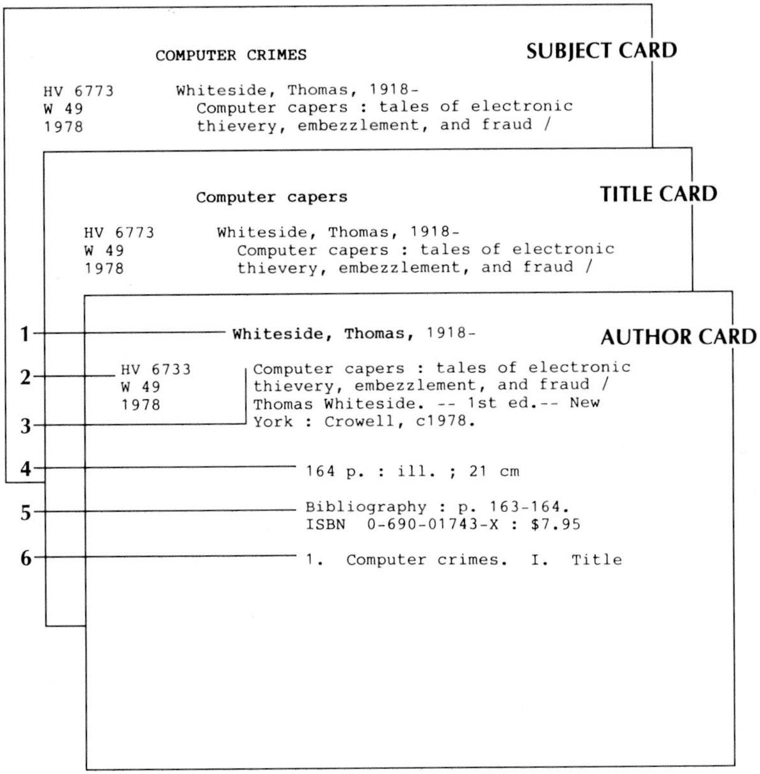

is the length; this book will be more worth looking into than, say, a forty-page pamphlet would be.

5. Notes on the contents of the book. In this case we are promised a bibliography—that is, a list of other related materials—which could prove extremely helpful for a research paper.

6. A list of all the headings under which this book is filed in the library's catalogs. By going to "Computer crimes" in the subject catalog, a researcher might find several items of related interest.

Once in a while you may come across a reference to an apparently indispensable book that is unlisted in your library's catalog. Since there are some sixty thousand new volumes published each year in English alone, no library but the Library of Congress itself could acquire more than a minority of them. You can get essential information about the book's author, title, publisher, and date of publication from the *National Union Catalog*, which reproduces the Library of Congress Catalog and includes titles from other libraries as well. If you cannot visit a library that has the book, you can probably borrow it through *interlibrary loan*. The same holds for journals. By consulting the *Union List of Serials in Libraries of the United States and Canada*, you can discover which libraries own sets of hard-to-find journals.

libr 6b

On-Line Catalog

Most card catalogs are now being supplemented or replaced by *on-line* (computer) *catalogs* that serve the same function, but with greater efficiency for both catalogers and users. A writer of a research paper on Chinese-American business relations, for example, guided by the *Library of Congress Subject Headings* (p. 157 above), used a library terminal to run a subject search on "China—Economic conditions—1976– ." This is what came up on the screen:

Your search for the Subject: CHINA ECONOMIC CONDITIONS 1976– retrieved multiple records.

Title List
1. China trade: a guide to doing business with the People's Re
2. China's economy in global perspective/A. Doak Barnett
3. China takes off: technology transfer and modernization/E.E.
4. The second economy of rural China/Anita Chan and Jonathan
5. China's allocation of authority and responsibility in ener
6. China's economic development: growth and structural change/
7. Mainland China: why still backward?/by Cheng Chu-Yuan
8. China among the nations of the Pacific/edited by Harrison
9. China and Southeast Asia: contemporary politics and economi
10. China, economic structure in international perspective.
11. China in transition: papers/Kenneth Lieberthal . . . [et al.

By requesting further information about item 3, the student was shown the equivalent of a catalog card for a book that eventually proved useful to him:

Call #:	HC430.T4.B381 1986 Chinese Stdy, Main Stack, Business/SS
Author:	Bauer, E. E.
Title:	China takes off : technology transfer and modernization / E.E. Bauer ; introduction by Michel Oksenberg. Seattle : University of Washington Press, © 1986. xvi, 227 p. : ill. ; 25 cm.
Notes:	Includes bibliographical references.
Subjects:	Technology transfer-China. China-Economic conditions-1976–

For more information about on-line searching, see pages 165–68.

EXERCISES

3. Choose a sample research project—preferably one that you hope to carry out in the weeks ahead. Go to the *Library of Congress Subject Headings* and find what appears to be the main heading for your topic. Copy out a passage beginning from that heading (as on page 157) and submit it along with an explanation of the symbols accompanying the entries.

4. The passage you have copied for Exercise 3, like the example on page 157, contains further headings that may be relevant to your topic. Using one or more of those categories, consult your library's subject catalog, its author-title catalog, and its shelf list (if any), looking for key books on your subject. Submit a paragraph or two explaining the steps of your search and the relative usefulness of the catalogs you examined.

5. List what you take to be the three most important books to consult for the sample research project you undertook for Exercise 3. For each book, explain which information on the entry card (or in the microfiche or on-line entry) made you eager to see that book.

6. Check out the three books you discussed in Exercise 5. When you have been able to scan two of those books, submit a paragraph about each of them, explaining how acquaintance with that book could influence the direction of your sample research project. Are you closer than before to having a precisely focused topic? What sources would you want to investigate next?

6c Learn how to find recent articles and reviews.

If you have chosen a topic of current interest—the spread and control of a new disease, say, or the changing American family structure—you will want to review the latest available information. You cannot find it in even the most recently published books, which will necessarily be a year or two behind the times. Newspaper articles will be best for following events as they occur. Magazine articles, such as those in *Harper's* or *The Atlantic*, will give you a general perspective that may be just right for the audience and level you have in mind. And in professional journals—specialized scholarly periodicals such as the *New England Journal of Medicine* or the *Bulletin of the Atomic Scientists*—you will get access to detailed knowledge and theory that may not yet have appeared in hard cover. You may also want to check expert reviews of books you hope to use. Digests of reviews (p. 164) can show you how much trust you should place in a given book.

Indexes and Abstracts

Obviously, you would be wasting your time poring over the handiest newspapers, magazines, and journals in the hope of finding relevant items. The efficient thing is to consult indexes and abstracts, which you will find shelved (or on compact discs; see page 166) in your library's reference room. *Indexes* are books, usually with a new volume each year, containing alphabetically ordered references to articles on given subjects. And *abstracts* are summaries of articles, allowing you to tell whether or not a certain article is important enough to your project to be worth tracking down. It is the reference room, then—not the newspaper room or the periodical room—that holds the key to your search for pertinent articles and reviews.

1. *To newspapers*. The only newspaper index you may ever need to consult is the *New York Times Index* (1913–), which covers a vast array of news and commentary having national or international importance. Since it is issued every two weeks before being bound into annual volumes, you can be sure of staying current with developments in your subject. For coverage of newspapers in Chicago, Los Angeles, New Orleans, and Washington, D.C., try the *Newspa-*

per Index (1972–). And for international and especially British coverage, consult the *Index to the* [London] *Times* (1906–).

2. *To magazines.* If you want to find an article in a general-interest magazine, go to the *Reader's Guide to Periodical Literature* (1900–), which covers about 160 magazines on a twice-monthly basis. Indeed, the *Reader's Guide* is so useful for the typical research essay that many students begin their investigation there, saving the subject catalog until they have seen whether their topic has engaged the public lately. Browsing through the headings in the *Reader's Guide* may help you focus your topic better. If you draw a blank from the *Reader's Guide*, ask yourself whether your topic is too broad, too narrow, too specialized, or too outdated to merit pursuing.

A typical segment of a column in the *Reader's Guide* looks like this:

a — **Heme**
Long-range electron transfer in heme proteins. S. L. Mayo and others. bibl f il *Science* 233:948-52 Ag 29 '86

b — **Hemingson, Peter**
The composter's Cuisinart. il *Mother Earth News* 101:52-3 S/O '86

c — **Hemingway, Ernest, 1899–1961**
about
For whom the bell tolled. J. Hart. *Commentary* 82:59-62 D '86
Hemingway, Mary, 1908–1986
about
UNCF to receive gift from Hemingway will. *Jet* 71:60 D 29 '86-Ja 5 '87

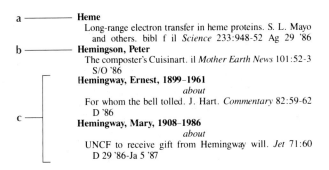

a. *An entry listed by subject.* The article about heme proteins appeared in the journal *Science*, volume 233, August 29, 1986, on pages 948 through 952, and it contained a bibliography, footnotes, and illustrations.

b. *An entry listed by the author's name.*

c. *Two entries listed by the individuals who are discussed.*

3. *To journals.* While the *Reader's Guide* gives you good access to such popular magazines as *Time* and *Business Week*, it does not cover journals such as *Science* and *Modern Language Quarterly*. Journals are issued less often than magazines and are far more

technical in nature. Although you probably want to keep a general-interest focus in your paper, an important piece of information may be accessible to you only in a journal. The key indexes for access to journal articles in a variety of fields are the *Humanities Index* (1974–) and the *Social Sciences Index* (1974–). The *Humanities Index* should be your first choice for post-1973 articles in archaeology, area studies, classics, folklore, history, language and literature, literary criticism, performing arts, philosophy, religion, and theology. Use the *Social Sciences Index* for post-1973 articles in anthropology, economics, environmental science, geography, law and criminology, medicine, political science, psychology, public administration, and sociology. For years before 1973, consult the *International Index* (1907–1965) and the *Social Sciences and Humanities Index* (1965–1974); the latter was the parent of the now separate *Humanities Index* and *Social Sciences Index*.

libr
6c

4. *To Book Reviews*. If you want to know how reliable a certain book is, you can quickly learn what some of the book's original reviewers had to say by consulting *Book Review Digest* (1905–). For other guides to book reviews, consult *Book Review Index* (1965–), *Current Book Review Citations* (1976–), and *The New York Times Book Review Index* (1896–1970).

Here is a list of useful indexes and abstracts:

Abstracts in Anthropology (1970–)
Abstracts of Health Care Management Studies (1978–)
Accountant's Index (1944–)
America: History and Life: A Guide to Periodical Literature (1964–)
American Statistics Index (1973–)
Applied Science and Technology Index (1913–)
Art Index (1947–)
Arts and Humanities Citation Index (1978–)
Astronomy and Astrophysics Abstracts (1969–)
Bibliographic Index (1933–)
Biography Index (1947–)
Biological Abstracts (1926–)
Biological and Agricultural Index (1964–)
Bioresearch Index (1967–)
British Humanities Index (1962–)
Business Periodicals Index (1958–)
Chemical Abstracts (1907–)
Child Development Abstracts and Bibliography (1927–)

Computer and Control Abstracts (1967–)
Congressional Digest (1921–)
Current Index to Journals in Education (1969–)
Dissertation Abstracts International (1938–)
Education Abstracts (1936–)
Education Index (1929–)
Engineering Index (1920–)
Environment Abstracts (1971–)
Essay and General Literature Index (1934–)
Film Literature Index (1973–)
General Science Index (1978–)
Geo Abstracts (1972–)
Historical Abstracts (1955–)
Index Medicus (1961–)
Index to Legal Periodicals (1908–)
MLA Abstracts of Articles in Scholarly Journals (1971–)
MLA International Bibliography (1921–)
Monthly Catalog of United States Government Publications (1895–)
Music Index (1949–)
Philosopher's Index (1967–)
Physics Abstracts (1895–)
Psychological Abstracts (1927–)
Public Affairs Information Service Bulletin (1915–)
Religious and Theological Abstracts (1958–)
RILA Abstracts (International Repertory of Art Literature) (1975–)
RILM Abstracts (International Repertory of Music Literature) (1967–)
Science Abstracts (1898–)
Science Citation Index (1961–)
Social Sciences Citation Index (1973–)
Sociological Abstracts (1977–)
Urban Affairs Abstracts (1971–)
Women's Studies Abstracts (1972–)

Electronic Databases

In increasing numbers, printed indexes, abstracts, reports, conference proceedings, and government documents are being gathered in the alternative form of *databases*—that is, computer files that can be instantly scanned. If your library has an on-line catalog (p. 160), then that catalog is itself a database. But that is just the beginning. If your library subscribes to such databases as, say,

Pharmaceutical News Index, Population Bibliography, and *Pollution Abstracts*, you can instruct the computer to retrieve every relevant article from one or more of those sources.

Such *on-line searching* can save time, unearth very recent references, and ferret out specific topics that do not constitute subject headings in the index itself. Suppose, for example, you are interested in the connection between child abuse and alcoholism. Instead of asking for all items within each of those large subjects, you can tell the computer to display only those items whose titles refer to *both* problems. The outcome will be a relatively short but highly efficient list, fairly free of "dumb mistakes" on the computer's part.

To gain access to some electronic databases—for example, RLIN, the powerful Research Libraries Information Network—you will need to pay a fee and ask a trained technician to connect you to a national computer network. Increasingly, however, libraries have been purchasing specialized, frequently updated *CD-ROM* (compact disk—read only memory) databases that you can consult gratis at a library workstation. With very little practice, you can learn to make thorough, efficient, and up-to-date searches of CD-ROM sources for articles, dissertations, statistics, and films and videotapes, eliminating the tedium of hunting through multiple printed volumes. Note, however, that in many instances the CD-ROM coverage begins in a later year than in the printed version.

To find out which CD-ROM databases your library possesses, ask a reference librarian. Some of the most useful sources that might be available are the following.

GENERAL DATABASES

A-V Online. Annually updated directory of over 200,000 media items, including films, videotapes, audio cassettes, and slides. 1986– .

Academic Index. Bibliographic references to 390 scholarly and general-interest periodicals in the humanities, social sciences, and general sciences. Covers journals for latest three to four years; *New York Times* for latest six months.

CIS Statistical Masterfile. Combines three printed indexes:

American Statistics Index, Statistical Reference Index, and *Index to International Statistics*. Covers early 1970s through 1989.

Dissertation Abstracts. Cites over 900,000 U.S. and foreign doctoral dissertations and masters' theses. 1861– .

National Newspaper Index. Covers *New York Times, Wall Street Journal, Christian Science Monitor, Washington Post,* and *Los Angeles Times*. Covers latest four years.

HUMANITIES AND SOCIAL SCIENCES

ABI/Inform. Indexes 850 business and economics journals, with abstracts. Covers latest five years.

Art Index. Indexes over 200 periodicals, yearbooks, and museum publications in art, art history, architecture, graphic art, design, photography, etc. 1984– .

ERIC. Cites published and unpublished articles in education and related topics. 1980– .

MLA International Bibliography. Indexes articles in literature, language, and folklore published in all modern languages in over 3000 journals. 1981– .

PAIS. Public Affairs Information Service. Citations and abstracts of articles, books, and reports in public policy, economics, and government, in several languages. 1972– .

PsycLIT. The CD-ROM version of *Psychological Abstracts*. Gives citations and abstracts for articles in psychology and related fields. 1974– .

Social Sciences Index. Indexes articles from over 353 journals in area studies, political science, geography, sociology, psychology, etc. 1983– .

Sociofile. The CD-ROM version of *Sociological Abstracts*. For journals, 1974– . For dissertations, 1986– .

GOVERNMENT AND LAW

Census Data. Statistical data from the U.S. Bureau of the Census.

CIS Congressional Masterfile. Indexes almost 400,000 congressional hearings, reports, etc. 1789– .

LegalTrac. Indexes over 800 legal journals and newspapers. 1980– .

SCIENCE AND TECHNOLOGY

Agricola. Indexes citations from over 5000 international journals, reports, etc., dealing with agriculture. 1970– .

Applied Science and Technology Index. Indexes 335 journals in chemistry, engineering, computer science, physics, etc. 1983– .

Life Sciences Collection. Citations and abstracts from over 5000 journals, books, and conference reports on animal behavior, biochemistry, biotechnology, microbiology, toxicology, and other life sciences. 1982– .

Science Citation Index. Covers over 3300 worldwide science and technical journals. 1986– .

EXERCISES

7. Resume the sample research project you began for Exercise 3, or begin a new one. Using the *New York Times Index*, locate two relevant articles or editorials in the *Times*. Find those items (probably on microfilm) in your library's newspaper room, and take notes on their content. Submit a paragraph or two in which you give precise references to those items, and summarize what you learned from them.

8. Repeat Exercise 7, this time using magazine articles traced through the *Reader's Guide*. One of your two articles should be so recent that it can be found in an unbound copy of a magazine; the other should be at least two years old.

9. Repeat Exercise 7, this time using journal articles traced through one or more of the indexes or abstracts listed above. If your library possesses a relevant CD-ROM database, make use of it for this task. As in Exercise 8, retrieve one of your two items from an unbound issue of a journal.

10. Use *Book Review Digest* to find summaries of the reviews of any one book that looks promising for your sample research project. Submit a paragraph or two referring specifically to some of the reviews and explaining how they have affected your assessment of the book.

6d Consult background sources as necessary.

The steps we have already covered should be enough to give you all the information you need for a typical research essay. Sometimes, however, you may want an out-of-the-way bit of knowledge or a broad introduction to the field you are going to treat. Where should you turn? Most of the works mentioned below can be found in the reference room.

If you know an author's name but not the title of the book, if you have the title but not the author, or if you want to know when a certain book appeared, try consulting *Books in Print* (1948–), *Cumulative Book Index* (1898–), *Paperbound Books in Print* (1955–), or *Subject Guide to Books in Print* (1957–). The last of these volumes can give you a quick idea of what you could hope to find under a given subject heading of your card catalog. If you see an essential item in the *Subject Guide* that is missing from your catalog, you may be able to send for it through interlibrary loan.

Reference works—books that survey a field and tell you how to find materials within that field—are now so numerous that you may need to consult an even more general book that lists reference works and explains their scope. Try especially Eugene P. Sheehy, *Guide to Reference Books* (1976, with later supplements), which can lead you to the most appropriate bibliographies and indexes to articles.

For a college research paper, however, you will probably need at the most one survey of your field and one guide to sources. Here is a representative sample of titles to consult:

ART

Encyclopedia of World Art (1959–83)

BUSINESS AND ECONOMICS

Dictionary of Economics and Business, ed. Erwin E. Nemmers (1978)

DRAMA

McGraw-Hill Encyclopedia of World Drama (1984)

How to Locate Reviews of Plays and Films, by Gordon Samples (1976)

EDUCATION

A Dictionary of Education, by Derek Rowntree (1982)

FILM

The World Encyclopedia of the Film (1972)

FOLKLORE AND MYTHOLOGY

Funk & Wagnalls Standard Dictionary of Folklore, Mythology, and Legend (1972)

Motif-Index of Folk-Literature, by Stith Thompson (1955–58)

HISTORY

An Encyclopedia of World History, ed. William L. Langer (1972)

LITERATURE

A Handbook to Literature, by C. Hugh Holman (1986)

Literary Research Guide, by James L. Harner (1989)

MUSIC

The New Oxford Companion to Music (1983)

PHILOSOPHY

The Encyclopedia of Philosophy, ed. Paul Edwards (1972)

PSYCHOLOGY

Encyclopedia of Psychology, ed. Raymond J. Corsini (1984)

RELIGION

A Reader's Guide to the Great Religions, ed. Charles J. Adams (1977)

SCIENCE AND TECHNOLOGY

McGraw-Hill Encyclopedia of Science and Technology (1987)

SOCIAL AND POLITICAL SCIENCE

International Encyclopedia of the Social Sciences, ed. David L. Sills (1977–79)

WOMEN'S STUDIES

Handbook of International Data on Women (1976)

When you need to draw on a particular fact—the population of a country, an event in someone's life, the origin of an important term, the source of a quotation—you can go to one of the following sources:

GENERAL ENCYCLOPEDIAS

Encyclopaedia Britannica (1986)

Encyclopedia Americana (revised annually)

COMPILATIONS OF FACTS

The World Almanac and Book of Facts (1868–)

ATLASES

National Geographic Atlas of the World (1990)

The Times Atlas of the World (1985)

DICTIONARIES (See p. 333 for college dictionaries.)

A Comprehensive Etymological Dictionary of the English Language, by Ernest Klein (1979)

The Oxford English Dictionary (1989)

BIOGRAPHY

Who's Who in the World (1976–)

The McGraw-Hill Encyclopedia of World Biography (1973)

QUOTATIONS

Familiar Quotations, by John Bartlett and E. M. Beck (1980)

The Oxford Dictionary of Quotations (1980)

EXERCISES

11. For each of the following proposed topics, list two or three sources (a dictionary, the subject catalog, etc.) that you would *begin* by consulting:

    A. The reception of Don DeLillo's 1991 novel *Mao II.*
    B. Should abortions be automatically granted on demand?
    C. Pickett's Charge.
    D. The wave of terrorism in France in 1986.
    E. Recent advances in semiconductor memory systems for computers.
    F. The development of logical positivism as a philosophical school.
    G. Beethoven's reputation today.
    H. Beethoven's childhood.
    I. The origin and evolving meaning of the word *wit* in English.
    J. Who wrote the line "The proper study of mankind is man"?

12. Which of the following books are still in print? Which ones are available in paperbound editions? (See p. 169.)

    A. Milan Kundera, *The Book of Laughter and Forgetting*
    B. Oliver Perry Medsger, *Edible Wild Plants*
    C. James Herndon, *Sorrowless Times: A Narrative*
    D. Maria Lemnis and Henryk Vitry, *Old Polish Traditions in the Kitchen and at the Table*
    E. Flannery O'Connor, *The Habit of Being*

13. Read one article in a general encyclopedia (p. 171) encompassing the problem treated in your sample research project (Exercise 3 and/or Exercise 7), and look up the same problem in any two of the reference sources listed on pages 169–71. Submit two or three paragraphs identifying the three sources you used and indicating what you have learned from them.

14. Check two biographical sources (p. 171) for information about any one prominent figure in the field of knowledge that includes your sample research project. Submit a paragraph or two identifying the sources you checked and comparing their usefulness in this one instance.

6e Take full and careful notes from your reading.

A typical library book or journal will be available to you for a few hours or days or weeks, depending on its importance to other borrowers. When you try to get it again, you may find that it is on loan to someone else, or has been sent to the bindery or even misplaced or stolen. Thus you have to be sure to get everything you need from the work on your first try.

One means of doing so is to photocopy important pages, either in the library or at a copy center. If you use this method, make sure you have gathered all the bibliographical information you will need. You can write that information on your first photocopied sheet or make copies of title and copyright pages to accompany the text.

When you do take notes, those notes must be clear and full enough to be your direct source when you write. Although it is always a good idea to keep the work before you and recheck it for accurate quotation and fair summary, you should assume that this will not be possible. You should make sure your notes are error-free before you let the book or article out of your hands.

Bibliography Cards and Content Cards

The notes you take from your reading will serve two distinct purposes: to keep an accurate list of the works you have consulted and to record key information you have found in them. Sooner or later most researchers understand that these purposes demand different kinds of notecards. To compile a *bibliography* or list of works consulted, one card per entry is ideal; but *content* (or informational) notes may run through many cards. To avoid confusion use 3″ × 5″ bibliography cards to identify the works you have consulted, and larger (usually 4″ × 6″) content cards for quotations, summaries, and miscellaneous comments. Or, if you prefer, use cards of different colors.

You may choose to jot down ideas on sheets of paper rather than on cards. For quoting and summarizing published statements, however, cards are easier to keep track of and to rearrange as the organization of your essay takes shape.

Observe the sample cards on page 174. (Note that once a separate bibliography card has been prepared, the researcher can give the briefest of references on a content card: *Mountjoy*, p. 27.)

Form of Notecards

The more systematic you are about note taking, the less likely you will be to misquote, summarize unfairly, or supply inaccurate references. Here are some tips about form:

1. Use cards of one uniform size or color for all bibliography notes, and cards or sheets of another uniform size or color for all your content notes. This will make for easy filing and reshuffling.

BIBLIOGRAPHY CARD

Ed/P
BF 1
P. 68

Mountjoy, Paul T., and Alan G. Lewandowski
"The Dancing Horse, a Learned Pig, and Muscle Twitches."
Psychological Record 34 (1984): 25–38

(Relates Clever Hans effect to two documents—17th & 19th c's—describing the training of animals to mimic human intelligence)

CONTENT CARD

Mountjoy, p. 27 Forerunners of Clever Hans
"Marocco [horse in Elizabethan England] purportedly could count money, single out of an audience any person named by [his trainer], count the number of spots exposed by the roll of a pair of dice, ..."
(Note that this was show business; cf. Hans, who fooled his trainer!)

2. Write in ink. Penciled notes smudge when pressed against other notes.
3. Never put entries from different sources on one card or page, and never write on the reverse side. Otherwise, you will probably lose track of some of your work.
4. Include the call number of any book or magazine you have found in the library. You never know when you may want to retrieve it for another look.
5. Quote exactly, including the punctuation marks in the original, and check each quotation as soon as you have copied it.
6. Use quotation marks only when you are actually quoting verbatim, and check to see that the marks begin and end exactly where they should. Use the dots known as ellipses (p. 560, 30o) to indicate where you have skipped some material within a quotation. If you have inserted any of your own words into the quoted passage, enclose them in brackets, as in the content card on page 174.
7. Be attentive to oddities of spelling and punctuation in quoted material. If, for instance, the original text omits a comma that you would have included, you can place a bracketed [*sic*], meaning *this is the way I found it*, at the questionable point in your notes; this will remind you not to improve the quotation illegitimately when reproducing it in your essay. But do not retain the *[sic]* in your paper unless it refers to an obvious blunder.
8. Supply page references not only for all quotations but for paraphrases and summaries as well.
9. Do not allow any ambiguities in your system of abbreviations. If two of your symbols mean the same thing, change one of them.
10. Distinguish between your own comments and those of the text you are summarizing. Use slashes, brackets, or your initials to show that the following remarks are yours, not those of the author.
11. When copying a passage that runs from one page to another, mark on your notecard where the first page ends: "*One other*

point might be noted, in view of the White / House concern over the military implications of lasers." If you finally quote only a portion of the excerpt in your paper, you will want to know where it ended in the original.

12. Use a portion of the card or page to evaluate the material and to remind yourself of possibilities for further study. You might say, for example, *This looks useless—but reconsider chapter 13 if discussing astrology.*

13. Leave some space in the margin or at the top for an indexing symbol, so that you can easily keep related items together.

EXERCISE

15. Using any books or articles you have handy, submit two sample bibliography cards and two content notes. One of your notes should quote a passage; the other should summarize that same passage. Be sure your two bibliography cards give full and exact citations.

6f Summarize or paraphrase relevant passages that you do not intend to quote.

The most accurate way of noting what you have read is to quote it exactly (Chapter 30) or to photocopy it. But in your notes you can only quote a fraction of the important material you have seen, and once you have photocopied many pages, you still face the task of drawing from them what is essential to your own purpose. Here is where *summary*, or brief restatement, and *paraphrase*, or more ample restatement, can come to your aid. Remember that summary and paraphrase require the same accurate documentation that quotation does. You must cite the source of someone else's ideas, even when you express those ideas in your own words (see p. 180, 7a).

A **summary** of a text concisely presents the author's key ideas, omitting examples and descriptive detail. Insofar as possible you should use your own language, though some repetition of the author's terms may be inevitable. The knack of efficient summary is to strip away everything but the essential content.

ORIGINAL TEXT:

The modern world began on 29 May 1919 when photographs of a solar eclipse, taken on the island of Principe off West Africa and at Sobral in Brazil, confirmed the truth of a new theory of the universe. It had been apparent for half a century that the Newtonian cosmology, based upon the straight lines of Euclidean geometry and Galileo's notions of absolute time, was in need of serious modifications. It had stood for more than two hundred years. It was the framework within which the European Enlightenment, the Industrial Revolution, and the vast expansion of human knowledge, freedom and prosperity which characterized the nineteenth century, had taken place. But increasingly powerful telescopes were revealing anomalies. In particular, the motions of the planet Mercury deviated by forty-three seconds of arc a century from its predictable behaviour under Newtonian laws of physics. Why?

libr 6f

In 1905, a twenty-six-year-old German Jew, Albert Einstein, then working in the Swiss patent office in Berne, had published a paper, "On the electrodynamics of moving bodies," which became known as the Special Theory of Relativity. Einstein's observations on the way in which, in certain circumstances, lengths appeared to contract and clocks to slow down, are analogous to the effects of perspective in painting. In fact the discovery that space and time are relative rather than absolute is comparable, in its effect on our perception of the world, to the first use of perspective in art, which occurred in Greece in the two decades c. 500–480 B.C.

The originality of Einstein, amounting to a form of genius, and the curious elegance of his lines of argument, which colleagues compared to a kind of art, aroused growing, world-wide interest. In 1907 he published a demonstration that all mass has energy, encapsulated in the equation $E = mc^2$, which a later age saw as the starting point in the race for the A-bomb. Not even the onset of the European war prevented scientists from following his quest for an all-embracing General Theory of Relativity which would cover gravitational fields and provide a comprehensive revision of Newtonian physics. In 1915 news reached London that he had done it. The following spring, as the British were preparing their vast and catastrophic offensive on the Somme, the key paper was smuggled through the Netherlands and reached Cambridge, where it was received by Arthur Eddington, Professor of Astronomy and Secretary of the Royal Astronomical Society.[1]

SUMMARY:

Johnson dates "the modern world" from the solar eclipse observations of 29 May 1919, confirming Albert Einstein's General Theory of Relativity. The world had already shown great interest in Einstein after his 1905 publication of the Special Theory of Relativity, indicating that space and time are relative categories, and his 1907 demonstration that mass possesses energy ($E=mc^2$). The General Theory, embracing gravitational fields, completed the overthrow of Newtonian physics, based in its turn on Euclid's geometry and Galileo's absolute time. The Einsteinian revolution affected our perception of the world as radically as the ancient Greek discovery of perspective in art.

libr
6f

A **paraphrase** is a running restatement of the original passage in your own words. You should follow the order of the text and include important detail. Since a paraphrase is closer to the original than a summary, you must be careful not to repeat the author's wording without quotation marks; that practice could lead you into accidental **plagiarism** (p. 181, 7a), or the presentation of someone else's words (or ideas) as your own.

PARAPHRASE:

Johnson dates "the modern world" from the 29 May 1919 observations of a solar eclipse, taken in Africa and Brazil, confirming Einsteinian cosmology. For fifty years the existing Newtonian conception, based on Euclid's geometry and Galileo's absolute time, had been in trouble. It had been the set of assumptions behind the Enlightenment, the Industrial Revolution, and nineteenth-century progress in learning, democracy, and wealth, but it had been placed in doubt by unaccountable telescopic data such as the deviated motion of Mercury.

The new universe began to take shape with Albert Einstein's 1905 paper, "On the electrodynamics of moving bodies" (the Special Theory of Relativity), showing how in some conditions time and space are variable. This discovery affected our way of seeing the world as profoundly as did the Greeks' use of artistic perpsective in the fifth century B.C.

In 1907 Einstein proposed that all mass has energy ($E=mc^2$), an idea later seen as having begun the race to develop the atomic bomb. Not even the outbreak of World War I could stop scientists from participating in his search for a General Theory of Relativity that would include gravitational fields. Word of Einstein's having completed that theory arrived in London in 1915, and in 1916, at the height of the awful war, the key paper reached Arthur Eddington, Secretary of the Royal Astronomical Society, in Cambridge.

EXERCISE

16. Photocopy and submit a paragraph from a book or article that you expect to be using in your research project. (If you have not yet settled on a project, choose any handy source.) Also submit (a) a summary, and (b) a paraphrase, of that same paragraph.

NOTE

[1] Paul Johnson, *Modern Times: The World from the Twenties to the Eighties* (New York: Harper, 1983) 1–2.

7

Documenting Sources

DOCUMENT A SOURCE IF . . .
you quote the passage verbatim
you paraphrase the passage
you summarize the passage
you include information not generally known
you borrow someone else's opinion

7a Learn where documentation is called for.

If you have done research for a paper, there are several reasons why you should cite your sources, using a standard form of documentation. You want credit for your efforts, and your documentation will help to show a reader that your ideas are consistent with facts and expert judgments that have already appeared in print. In some cases you may even want to pose a challenge to received views, showing that you know what those views are and where they can be found. And documentation is also a courtesy to your readers, who ought to be able to check your sources either to see whether you have used them responsibly or to pursue an interest in your topic.

Avoiding Plagiarism

A further reason for providing documentation is to avoid **plagiarism**—the serious ethical violation of presenting other people's words or ideas as your own. Plagiarism does tempt some student writers who feel too rushed or insecure to arrive at their own conclusions. Yet systematic dishonesty is only part of the problem. For every student who buys a term paper or copies a whole article without acknowledgment, there are dozens who indulge in "little" ethical lapses through thoughtlessness, haste, or a momentary sense of opportunity. Though nearly all of their work is original, they too are plagiarists—just as someone who robs a bank of $2.39 is a bank robber.

Unlike the robber, however, some plagiarists fail to realize what they have done wrong. Students who once copied encyclopedia articles to satisfy school assignments may never have learned the necessity of using quotation marks and citing sources. Others may think that by *paraphrasing* a quotation or *summarizing* an idea (p. 176, 6f)—that is, by putting it into their own words—they have turned it into public property. Others acknowledge the source of their idea but fail to indicate that they have borrowed words as well as thoughts. And others plagiarize through sloppy note taking (p. 172, 6e). Since their notes do not distinguish adequately between personal observations and the content of a consulted book or article, their papers repeat the oversight. And finally, some students blunder into plagiarism by failing to recognize the difference between fact and opinion. They may think, for example, that a famous critic's opinion about a piece of literature is so authoritative that it belongs to the realm of common facts—and so they paraphrase it without acknowledgment. All these errors are understandable, but none of them constitutes a good excuse for plagiarism.

What to Acknowledge

Consider the following source and three ways that a student might be tempted to make use of it.

SOURCE:

The joker in the European pack was Italy. For a time hopes were entertained of her as a force against Germany, but these disappeared under Mussolini. In 1935 Italy made a belated attempt to participate in the scramble for Africa by invading Ethiopia. It was clearly a breach of the covenant of the League of Nations for one of its members to attack another. France and Great Britain, as great powers, Mediterranean powers, and African colonial powers, were bound to take the lead against Italy at the league. But they did so feebly and half-heartedly because they did not want to alienate a possible ally against Germany. The result was the worst possible: the league failed to check aggression, Ethiopia lost her independence, and Italy was alienated after all.[1]

doc 7a

VERSION A:

Italy, one might say, was the joker in the European deck. When she invaded Ethiopia, it was clearly a breach of the covenant of the League of Nations; yet the efforts of England and France to take the lead against her were feeble and halfhearted. It appears that those great powers had no wish to alienate a possible ally against Hitler's rearmed Germany.

Comment: Clearly plagiarism. Although the facts cited are public knowledge, the stolen phrases are not. Note that the writer's interweaving of his own words with the source does *not* make him innocent of plagiarism.

VERSION B:

Italy was the joker in the European deck. Under Mussolini in 1935, she made a belated attempt to participate in the scramble for Africa by invading Ethiopia. As J. M. Roberts points out, this violated the covenant of the League of Nations (Roberts 845). But France and Britain, not wanting to alienate a possible ally against Germany, put up only feeble and halfhearted opposition to the Ethiopian adventure. The outcome, as Roberts observes, was "the worst possible: the league failed to check aggression, Ethiopia lost her independence, and Italy was alienated after all" (Roberts 845).

Comment: Still plagiarism. The two correct citations of Roberts serve as a kind of alibi for the appropriating of other, unacknowledged, phrases.

VERSION C:

```
Much has been written about German rearmament and militarism
in the period 1933–1939.  But Germany's dominance in Europe
was by no means a foregone conclusion.  The fact is that the
balance of power might have been tipped against Hitler if one
or two things had turned out differently.  Take Italy's
gravitation toward an alliance with Germany, for example.
That alliance seemed so very far from inevitable that Britain
and France actually muted their criticism of the Ethiopian
invasion in the hope of remaining friends with Italy.  They
opposed the Italians in the League of Nations, as J. M.
Roberts observes, "feebly and half-heartedly because they did
not want to alienate a possible ally against Germany"
(Roberts 845).  Suppose Italy, France, and Britain had
retained a certain common interest.  Would Hitler have been
able to get away with his remarkable bluffing and bullying in
the later thirties?
```


Comment: No plagiarism. The writer has been influenced by the public facts mentioned by Roberts, but he has not tried to pass off Roberts's conclusions as his own. The one clear borrowing is properly acknowledged.

There *is* room for disagreement about what to acknowledge; but precisely because this is so, you ought to make your documentation relatively ample. Provide citations for all direct quotations and paraphrases, borrowed ideas, and facts that do not belong to general knowledge.

Ask yourself, in doubtful cases, whether the point you are borrowing is an opinion or a fact. Opinions are by definition ideas that are not yet taken for granted; document them. As for facts, do not bother to document those that could be found in any commonly used source—for example, the fact that World War II ended in 1945. But give references for less accessible facts, such as the numbers of operational submarines that Nazi Germany still possessed at the end of the war. The harder it would be for readers to come across your fact through their own efforts, the more surely you need to document it.

If you are quoting, paraphrasing, or making an **allusion** to statements or literary passages that are not generally familiar, cite the source. A phrase from Lincoln's Gettysburg Address could get by without a citation, but a remark made in a presidential news conference could not.

DO NOT DOCUMENT	DOCUMENT
the population of China	the Chinese balance of payments in 1987
the existence of a disease syndrome called AIDS	a possible connection between AIDS and the virus that carries cat leukemia
the fact that Dickens visited America	the supposed effect of Dickens's American visit on his subsequently written novels
the fact that huge sums are wagered illegally on professional football games	an alleged "fix" of a certain football game
a line from a nursery rhyme	a line from a poem by Yeats

EXERCISE

1. If you intended to make the following statements in college papers, which ones would require documentation? What kind of documentation, if any, would be appropriate in each case? Briefly explain each of your decisions.
   A. The "black hole" hypothesis, once generally dismissed, has been steadily gaining favor among astronomers in recent years.
   B. To be or not to be: that is indeed the central question for anyone who experiences suicidal feelings.
   C. There can be no denying the fact that industrialization and lung disease are inseparable twins; where you find the first, you are bound to find his grim brother.
   D. The oppressed people of the world must often feel like those who cried out, "How long, O Lord, holy and true, dost thou not judge and avenge our blood . . . ?"
   E. The first direct act of atomic warfare occurred at Hiroshima in August 1945.

7b Observe the differences between parenthetic citation form and footnote/endnote form.

In your reading you will encounter many documentation styles, but every version will belong to one of two general schemes. In *parenthetic citation form*, citations within parentheses in the main text are keyed to a list of "Works Cited" or "References" appearing at the end of the paper, article, chapter, or book. In *footnote/endnote form*, raised numbers in the main text—usually at the ends of sentences—are keyed to notes appearing either at the foot of the page (**footnotes**) or at the end of the whole text (**endnotes**). Both forms allow for **substantive** or **bibliographic notes** (p. 213, 7f) that make comments or mention further references.

PARENTHETIC CITATION FORM	FOOTNOTE/ENDNOTE FORM
No note numbers are used (except for supplementary notes.)	Raised numbers appear in text.
No notes are used to cite works.	Notes appearing at foot of page or at end of text give citations corresponding to note numbers in text.
All references are made through parenthetic citations within text.	Parenthetic citations within text are used only for "subsequent references" to frequently cited works.
Substantive and bibliographic notes, if any, appear after main text but before reference list.	Substantive and bibliographic notes, if any, are integrated into footnotes or endnotes.
A reference list, identifying only works cited or consulted, appears at the end. The listed works match the parenthetic citations in the text.	A bibliography, idenifying both works cited and works consulted, may appear after all the notes.

Until recently, parenthetic citation form has generally prevailed in the physical and social sciences and footnote/endnote form in the humanities. Today, however, parenthetic citation form is gaining ground in the humanities as well; it is recommended, for example, by the Modern Language Association. But if your instructor prefers footnote/endnote form, you should know how it works; see page 207, 7e.

In some disciplines—for example, mathematics, chemistry,

physics, biology, and engineering—the textual citations are Arabic numerals that correspond to numbered items in the **reference list**. A numbered item may mention any number of works.

SENTENCE IN TEXT:

It appears that female choice is frequently involved in the evolution of the conspicuous acoustic signals that precede mating (2, 3).

ITEMS IN REFERENCE LIST:

2. L. Fairchild, *Science 212*, 950 (1981); R. D. Howard, *Evolution 32*, 850 (1978); M. J. Ryan, *Science 209*, 523 (1980).

3. R. D. Alexander, in *Insects, Science, and Society*, D. Pimentel, Ed. (Academic Press, New York, 1975), p. 35; P. D. Bell, *Can. J. Zool. 58*, 1861 (1980); W. Cade, *Science 190*, 1312 (1975); in *Sexual Selection and Reproductive Competition in Insects*, M. S. Blum and N. A. Blum, Eds. (Academic Press, New York, 1979); A. V. Popov and V. F. Shuvalov, *J. Comp. Physiol. 119*, 111 (1977); S. M. Ulagaraj and T. J. Walker, *Science 182*, 1278 (1973).[2]

In other disciplines—for example, botany, geology, zoology, economics, psychology, and sociology—the parenthetic citations include the author(s) and date of publication *(Comstock & Fisher, 1975)*, and the reference list is ordered alphabetically.

If you are writing for publication in any field, look at a relevant journal and adopt its conventions. You can also consult one of the following style manuals if it corresponds to your subject matter.

BIOLOGY:

CBE Style Manual: A Guide for Authors, Editors, and Publishers in the Biological Sciences (1983)

BUSINESS:

Report Writing for Business, by Raymond V. Lesikar (1986)

CHEMISTRY:

Handbook for Authors of Papers in American Chemical Society Publications (1978)

EDUCATION:

NEA Style Manual for Writers and Editors (1974)

GEOLOGY:

Guide to Authors: A Guide for the Preparation of Geological Maps and Reports, by Robert G. Blackadar et al. (1980)

HISTORY:

Historical Journals: A Handbook for Writers and Reviewers, by Dale R. Steiner (1981)

JOURNALISM:

The UPI Stylebook: A Handbook for Writers and Editors, by Bobby Ray Miller (1977)

LAW:

A Uniform System of Citation, ed. Harvard Law Review Association (1986)

LIBRARY SCIENCE:

A Style Manual for Citing Microform and Nonprint Media, by Eugene B. Fleisher (1978)

LINGUISTICS:

LSA Bulletin, Dec. issue, annually

MATHEMATICS:

A Manual for Authors of Mathematical Papers, ed. American Mathematical Society (1984)

MEDICINE:

American Medical Association Manual of Style, by Cheryl Iverson et al. (1989)

PHYSICS:

Style Manual for Guidance in the Preparation of Papers for Journals, ed. Publication Board, American Institute of Physics (1978)

7c Learn how to present a reference list and parenthetic citations according to MLA style.

doc 7c

Most research papers for composition courses are now written in parenthetic citation form, following the style of either the Modern Language Association (**MLA style**) or the American Psychological Association (**APA style**). You will find the essential features of MLA style described below; for APA style, see page 198, 7d. For an extended example of MLA style, see the sample research paper on pages 217–29. And if you need to explore MLA style in further detail, see Joseph Gibaldi and Walter S. Achtert, *MLA Handbook for Writers of Research Papers* (3rd ed., 1988).

Place your MLA-style "Works Cited" list after your main text and any substantive or bibliographic notes (p. 213, 7f). Start on a new page, consecutively numbered with the foregoing ones. Space your list like the sample on page 228.

Order of Entries

Order your MLA reference list alphabetically by authors' last names or, when no author appears, by the first significant word of the title (omitting *A*, *An*, and *The*). If the author is an institution—for example, SRI International—list it by the first letter in the corporate name's first significant word (in this case *S*).

If you are citing more than one work by a given author, observe the following MLA rules:

1. Follow the alphabetical order of that author's titles.
2. If a cited author is also the coauthor of another cited work, put the single-author work first.
3. If a cited author has different coauthors for two cited works, place the works according to the alphabetical order of the coauthors' last names.

Order within Entries

In MLA style, present information (where relevant) within each entry in the following order:

BOOKS	ARTICLES
1. Author's name	1. Author's name
2. Title of part of book	2. Title of article
3. Title of book	3. Name of periodical
4. Name of editor, translator, or compiler	4. Series number or name
5. Edition used	5. Volume number
6. Number of volumes	6. Date of publication
7. Name of series	7. Page numbers
8. Place of publication, shortened name of publisher, date of publication	
9. Page numbers	

Here are sample entries covering typical kinds of works that might appear in your reference list.

Books

A BOOK BY A SINGLE AUTHOR:

Kendall, Elizabeth. The Runaway Bride: Hollywood Romantic Comedy of the 1930s. New York: Knopf, 1990.

TWO OR MORE BOOKS BY THE SAME AUTHOR:

Michaels, Leonard. I Would Have Saved Them If I Could. New York: Farrar, 1975.

---. The Men's Club. New York: Farrar, 1981.

A BOOK BY TWO AUTHORS:

Liehm, Mira, and Antonin J. Liehm. The Most Important Art: Soviet and Eastern European Film after 1945. Berkeley: U of California P, 1977.

A BOOK BY THREE AUTHORS:

Burns, James MacGregor, J. W. Peltason, and Thomas E. Cronin. Government by the People. 12th ed. Englewood Cliffs: Prentice, 1984.

A BOOK BY MORE THAN THREE AUTHORS:

Lauer, Janice, M., et al. Four Worlds of Writing. 2nd ed. New York: Harper, 1985.

A BOOK BY A CORPORATE AUTHOR:

American Society of Hospital Pharmacists. Consumer Drug Digest. New York: Facts on File, 1982.

AN ANONYMOUS BOOK:

Chicago Manual of Style. 13th ed. Chicago: U of Chicago P, 1982.

A WORK IN AN ANTHOLOGY:

Herbert, George. "The Pulley." The Bedford Introduction to Literature. Ed. Michael Meyer. New York: St. Martin's, 1987: 790–91.

THE ANTHOLOGY ITSELF:

Meyer, Michael, ed. The Bedford Introduction to Literature. New York: St. Martin's, 1987.

A WORK FROM A COLLECTION BY ONE AUTHOR:

Mill, John Stuart. On Liberty. Three Essays: On Liberty, Representative Government, The Subjection of Women. New York: Oxford UP, 1975. 1–141.

THE EDITED WORK OF AN AUTHOR:

Plato. The Collected Dialogues of Plato: Including the Letters. Ed. Edith Hamilton and Huntington Cairns. Princeton: Princeton UP, 1961.

A BOOK EDITED BY TWO OR THREE PEOPLE:

White, George Abbott, and Charles Newman, eds. Literature in Revolution. New York: Holt, 1972.

A BOOK EDITED BY MORE THAN THREE PEOPLE:

Kermode, Frank, et al., eds. The Oxford Anthology of English Literature. 2 vols. New York: Oxford UP, 1973.

A TRANSLATION:

Soseki, Natsume. The Miner. Trans. Jay Rubin. Stanford: Stanford UP, 1988.

A REPUBLISHED BOOK:

Conroy, Frank. Stop-time. 1967. New York: Penguin, 1977.

Articles in Journals, Magazines, and Newspapers

AN ARTICLE IN A JOURNAL WITH CONTINUOUS PAGINATION:

Cooper, Arnold M. "Psychoanalysis at One Hundred: Beginnings of Maturity." Journal of the American Psychoanalytic Association 32 (1984): 245–67.

AN ARTICLE IN A JOURNAL THAT DOES NOT IDENTIFY THE EXACT DATE OF EACH ISSUE:

Langford, Larry L. "How Many Children Had Molly Bloom? Sons and Lovers in Ulysses." Literature and Psychology 34.2 (1988): 27–40.

AN ARTICLE IN A MAGAZINE WITH SEPARATE PAGINATION FOR EACH ISSUE:

Havel, Václav. "The New Year in Prague." New York Review of Books 7 Mar. 1991: 19–20.

A REVIEW:

Singer, Brett. "Husbands at Bay." Rev. of Only Children, by Rafael Yglesias. New York Times Book Review 17 July 1988: 19.

AN UNSIGNED MAGAZINE ARTICLE:

"On a Clear Day You Can See. . . ." Newsweek 25 Feb. 1991: 54–55.

A SIGNED NEWSPAPER ARTICLE:

Nevius, C. W. "When Choices Were Simpler." San Francisco Chronicle 20 Feb. 1991, five-star ed.: D1.

AN UNSIGNED NEWSPAPER ARTICLE OR EDITORIAL:

"For Lasting Peace: Tougher Terms." New York Times 20 Feb. 1991, national ed.: A14.

Other Written Works

AN ENCYCLOPEDIA ENTRY:

L[ustig], L[awrence] K. "Alluvial Fans." Encyclopaedia Britannica: Macropaedia. 1985.

The author's initials appear at the end of the entry; they are identified elsewhere. Note that volume and page numbers are unnecessary when items appear in alphabetical order. But since the *Britannica* from 1974 onward has three sets of contents, the note should indicate which one is intended—in this case the "Macropaedia."

A PAMPHLET OR MANUAL:

Wiggins, Robert R., and Steve Brecher, with William P. Steinberg. Suitcase User's Guide. Sunnyvale: Software Supply, 1987.

A DISSERTATION:

Boudin, Henry Morton. "The Ripple Effect in Classroom Management." Diss. U of Michigan, 1970.

A PUBLIC DOCUMENT:

United States Dept. of Agriculture. "Shipments and Unloads of Certain Fruits and Vegetables, 1918–1923." Statistical Bulletin 7 (Apr. 1925).

A PUBLISHED LETTER:

McFann, Winfried S. Letter. Popular Photography Aug. 1988: 8.

AN UNPUBLISHED LETTER:

Graff, Gerald. Letter to the author. 18 Jan. 1989.

Nonwritten Works

A THEATRICAL PERFORMANCE:

Six Degrees of Separation. By John Guare. Dir. Jerry Zaks. With Stockard Channing, Courtney B. Vance, and John Cunningham. Vivian Beaumont Theatre, New York. 20 Feb. 1991.

A FILM:

The Hard Way. Dir. John Badham. With Michael J. Fox and James Woods. Universal, 1991.

A RADIO OR TELEVISION PROGRAM:

Knocking on Armageddon's Door. Prod. and dir. Torv Carlsen and John R. Magnus. PBS. 19 July 1988.

A RECORDING:

Beethoven, Ludwig van. Symphony no. 8 in F, op. 93. Cond. Pierre Monteux. Vienna Philharmonic Orch. Decca, STS 15238, 1964.

MLA requires that names of musical works be underlined except when (as here) the work is identified by its form, number, and key rather than by a title.

A LECTURE:

Hirsch, E. D., Jr. "Frontiers of Critical Theory." Wyoming Conference on Freshman and Sophomore English, U of Wyoming. Laramie, 9 July 1979.

AN INTERVIEW:

Collier, Peter, and David Horowitz. Personal interview. 5 Jan. 1991.

COMPUTER SOFTWARE:

Word. Release 4.0. Computer software. Microsoft, 1988. Macintosh.

MLA Parenthetic Citations

The idea behind all parenthetic citations is to give the minimum of information that will send a reader to the correct item in the reference list and, where applicable, to the cited portion of the work. As you might expect, MLA citations rely on authors' *names* and, if necessary for clarity, the *titles* of their works.

If you are referring to a whole work and if the author's name appears in your sentence, MLA style does not require you to supply any further information:

```
Cooper's presidential address struck a gloomy note.
```


But the same sentence would require a parenthetic page reference—without repeating the author's name—if you had in mind only part of the item:

```
Cooper's presidential address struck a gloomy note (249-52).
```

Where the author's name does not appear in your sentence, supply it in the citation:

```
One prominent authority has expressed serious doubt about the
current health of the profession (Cooper 249-52).
```

For an indented quotation (p. 554, 30h), place your end punctuation before rather than after the parenthesis.

The following sample MLA citations cover a variety of features in the cited works:

A MULTIVOLUME WORK:

```
In "An Apology for Poetry," Sidney shows a healthy distrust
of what he calls "that honey-flowing matron Eloquence"
(Abrams et al. 1:503).
```

A WORK LISTED BY TITLE:

The word "Saint" is disregarded in the alphabetizing of saints' names (Chicago Manual 18.103).

Note the shortened title; compare page 190 above. No edition number is needed, since the reference list contains only one entry under this name. Note, too, the citing of a section, rather than a page, of a reference work thus ordered.

A WORK BY A CORPORATE AUTHOR:

The American Society of Hospital Pharmacists considers methicillin "particularly useful" in treating hospital-acquired infections (89).

"Corporate" names are usually too long to be inserted into a parenthetic citation without distracting the reader. Make an effort to get the name into the main part of your sentence. Here the remark about methicillin is attributed to page 89 of the book in the reference list named under *American Society of Hospital Pharmacists*.

TWO OR MORE WORKS BY THE SAME AUTHOR:

"I feel you're feeling anger," says Kramer after his wife has clobbered him with an iron pot (Michaels, Men's Club 172).

The title of the work is included in the citation when two or more works by the same author appear in the reference list (p. 189).

AN INDIRECT SOURCE:

Writing in Temps Modernes in 1957, Woroszylski expressed surprise at "how much political nonsense we allowed ourselves to be talked into" (qtd. in Liehm and Liehm 116).

If you have no access to the original text, use *qtd. in* to show that your source for the quotation is another work.

A CLASSIC VERSE PLAY OR POEM:

"I prithee, daughter," begs Lear, "do not make me mad" (II.iv.212).

Cite acts, scenes, and lines instead of pages. The capital and lowercase Roman numerals here help to distinguish the act and scene from the line number; however, *2.4.212* would also be acceptable.

MORE THAN ONE WORK IN A CITATION:

The standard view of "scientific method" has come under concentrated attack in recent years (Kuhn; Lakatos; Laudan).

But if your parenthetic citation becomes too cumbersome, consider replacing it with a bibliographic note (p. 213, 7f).

EXERCISES

2. Submit a sample MLA-style list of "Works Cited" containing five items, preferably from your actual research project. Choose a different kind of source (edited book, translation, journal article, etc.) for each entry.

3. Using MLA style, submit five sentences containing references to the works you used in Exercise 2. Make each citation illustrate a different kind of circumstance (single author, two authors, two works by the same author, etc.)

7d Learn how to present a reference list and parenthetic citations according to APA style.

The sample citations below follow specifications found in *Publication Manual of the American Psychological Association* (3rd ed., 1983). To see how a typical APA reference list looks, study the sample "References" on pages 230–31 below.

Place your "References" after your main text and any substantive or bibliographic notes (p. 213, 7f). Start on a new page, consecutively numbered with the foregoing ones.

Order of Entries

Order your APA reference list alphabetically by authors' last names or, when no author appears, by the first significant word of the title (omitting *A*, *An*, and *The*). If the author is an institution—for example, SRI International—list it by the first letter in the corporate name's first significant word (in this case *S*).

If you see that you will be citing more than one work by a given author:

1. Follow the order of that author's dates of publication.
2. If a cited author is also the coauthor of another cited work, put the single-author work first.
3. If a cited author has different coauthors for two cited works, place the works according to the alphabetical order of the coauthors' last names.
4. If you are citing two works showing the same author(s) and date, follow the alphabetical order of the titles and add lowercase letters to the dates:

   Mauldin, C., & Valle, R. (1988a). Apple-Growing . . .
   Mauldin, C., & Valle, R. (1988b). Bee-Keeping . . .

Order within Entries

In APA style, present information (where relevant) within each entry in the following order:

BOOKS	ARTICLES
1. Author's name	1. Author's name
2. Date of publication	2. Date of publication
3. Title of part of book	3. Title of article
4. Title of Book	4. Name of periodical
5. Name of editor, translator, or compiler	5. Series number or name
6. Edition used	6. Volume number
7. Number of volumes	7. Page numbers
8. Name of series	
9. Place of publication, shortened name of publisher	
10. Page numbers	

Here are sample entries covering typical kinds of works that might appear in your APA reference list.

Books

A BOOK BY A SINGLE AUTHOR:

Kendall, E. (1990). The runaway bride: Hollywood romantic comedy of the 1930s. New York: Knopf.

TWO OR MORE BOOKS BY THE SAME AUTHOR:

Michaels, L. (1975). I would have saved them if I could. New York: Farrar, Straus & Giroux.

Michaels, L. (1981). The men's club. New York: Farrar, Straus & Giroux.

A BOOK BY TWO AUTHORS:

Liehm, M., & Liehm, A. J. (1977). The most important art: Soviet and eastern European film after 1945. Berkeley: University of California Press.

A BOOK BY THREE AUTHORS:

Burns, J. M., Peltason, J. W., & Cronin, T. E. (1984). Government by the people. (12th ed.). Englewood Cliffs, NJ: Prentice-Hall.

A BOOK BY MORE THAN THREE AUTHORS:

Lauer, J. M., Montague, G., Lunsford, A., & Emig, J. (1985). Four worlds of writing. (2nd ed.). New York: Harper & Row.

A BOOK BY A CORPORATE AUTHOR:

American Society of Hospital Pharmacists. (1982). Consumer drug digest. New York: Facts on File.

AN ANONYMOUS BOOK:

Chicago manual of style. (1982). (13th ed.). Chicago: University of Chicago Press.

A WORK IN AN ANTHOLOGY:

Herbert, G. (1987). The pulley. In M. Meyer (Ed.), The Bedford introduction to literature (pp. 790–791). New York: St. Martin's.

If you are citing more than one work from an anthology, provide an entry for the anthology itself, and cite it along with the references to the separate works, as follows. Note that APA uses no quotation marks around the titles of items within an anthology.

THE ANTHOLOGY ITSELF:

Meyer, M. (Ed.). (1987). The Bedford introduction to literature. New York: St. Martin's.

A WORK FROM A COLLECTION BY ONE AUTHOR:

Mill, J. S. (1975). On liberty. In Three essays: On liberty, Representative government, The subjection of women (pp. 1–141). New York: Oxford University Press. (Original work published 1859).

THE EDITED WORK OF AN AUTHOR:

Plato. (1961). The collected dialogues of Plato: Including the letters. (E. Hamilton & H. Cairns, Eds.). Princeton: Princeton University Press.

A BOOK EDITED BY TWO OR THREE PEOPLE:

White, G. A., & Newman, C. (Eds.). (1972). Literature in revolution. New York: Holt.

A BOOK EDITED BY MORE THAN THREE PEOPLE:

Kermode, F., Hollander, J., Bloom, H., Price, M., Trapp, J. B., & Trilling, L. (Eds.). 1973. The Oxford anthology of English literature. (Vols. 1–2). New York: Oxford University Press.

A TRANSLATION:

Soseki, N. (1988). The miner. (J. Rubin, Trans.). Stanford: Stanford University Press.

A REPUBLISHED BOOK:

Conroy, F. (1977). Stop-time. New York: Penguin. (Original work published 1967).

Articles in Journals, Magazines, and Newspapers

AN ARTICLE IN A JOURNAL WITH CONTINUOUS PAGINATION:

Cooper, A. M. (1984). Psychoanalysis at one hundred: Beginnings of maturity. Journal of the American Psychoanalytic Association, 32, 245–267.

AN ARTICLE IN A JOURNAL THAT DOES NOT IDENTIFY THE EXACT DATE OF EACH ISSUE:

Langford, L. L. (1988). How many children had Molly Bloom? Sons and lovers in Ulysses. Literature and Psychology, 34(2), 27–40.

AN ARTICLE IN A MAGAZINE WITH SEPARATE PAGINATION FOR EACH ISSUE:

Havel, V. (1991, March 7). The new year in Prague. New York Review of Books, pp. 19–20.

A REVIEW:

Singer, B. (1988, July 17). Husbands at bay. [Review of Only children, by R. Yglesias]. New York Times Book Review, p. 19.

AN UNSIGNED MAGAZINE ARTICLE:

On a Clear Day You Can See. . . . (1991, February 25). Newsweek, pp. 54–55.

A SIGNED NEWSPAPER ARTICLE:

Nevius, C. W. (1991, February 20). When choices were simpler. San Francisco Chronicle, sec. D, p. 1.

AN UNSIGNED NEWSPAPER ARTICLE OR EDITORIAL:

For lasting peace: Tougher terms. (1991, February 20). New York Times, sec. A, p. 14.

Other Written Works

AN ENCYCLOPEDIA ENTRY

L[ustig], L. K. (1985). Alluvial fans. Encyclopaedia Britannica: Macropaedia.

Note that volume and page numbers are unnecessary when items appear in alphabetical order. But since the *Britannica* from 1974 onward has three sets of contents, the note should indicate which one is intended—in this case the "Macropaedia."

doc 7d

A PAMPHLET OR MANUAL:

Wiggins, R. R., & Brecher, S., with Steinberg, W. P. (1987). Suitcase User's Guide. Sunnyvale, CA: Software Supply.

A DISSERTATION:

Boudin, H. M. (1970). The ripple effect in classroom management. Unpublished doctoral dissertation, University of Michigan, Ann Arbor.

A PUBLIC DOCUMENT:

United States Dept. of Agriculture. (1925, April). Shipments and unloads of certain fruits and vegetables, 1918–1923. Statistical Bulletin, 7.

A PUBLISHED LETTER:

McFann, W. (1988, August). [Letter to the editor]. Popular Photography, p. 8.

AN UNPUBLISHED LETTER:

Graff, G. (1989, January 18). [Letter to the author].

Nonwritten Works

A THEATRICAL PERFORMANCE:

Zaks, J. (Director). (1991, February 20). Six degrees of separation. Vivian Beaumont Theatre, New York City.

A FILM:

Badham, J. (Director). (1991). The Hard Way. Universal.

A RADIO OR TELEVISION PROGRAM:

Carlsen, T., & Magnus, J. R. (Producer & Director). (1988, July 19). Knocking on Armageddon's door. PBS.

A LECTURE:

Hirsch, E. D., Jr. (1979, July). Frontiers of critical theory. Paper presented at the Wyoming Conference on Freshman and Sophomore English, University of Wyoming, Laramie.

AN INTERVIEW:

Collier, P., & Horowitz, D. (1991, January 5). [Interview with the author.]

COMPUTER SOFTWARE:

Word. (1988). [Computer program]. Microsoft, Macintosh, Version 4.0.

APA Parenthetic Citations

In a first APA citation, include the date of publication:

> Cooper (1984) struck a gloomy note in his address.

Observe that in APA style the parenthetic date comes immediately after the author's name. In this example the whole work is being cited. If, on the other hand, you wanted to cite a specific passage, you would put the page numbers into a separate, later, parenthesis:

> Bercovitch (1986) mentions a growing sense among critics that race, class, and gender are essential categories of textual analysis (p. viii).

The following examples show further APA rules in action:

> "I feel you're feeling anger," says Kramer after his wife has clobbered him with an iron pot (Michaels, 1981, p. 172).

Even though the reference list may contain more than one work by Michaels, the date alone suffices to show which one is meant.

> Karsh (1987b) has proposed a rival explanation.

The date-plus-letter shows which work is meant among two or more by the same author in the same year.

> Preston and Martini (1988) examined the backgrounds of 234 schizophrenic patients.

If there are two authors, always mention both.

> A study of 234 patients produced no support for the idea that schizophrenia is caused by unusual family tensions (Preston & Martini, 1967).

Note the use of the ampersand ("&") within the parenthetic citation but not in the main sentence (previous example).

```
Lauer, Montague, Lunsford, and Emig (1985) emphasize that
writers must make their evaluative standards known to their
readers (p. 200).
```

```
Writers must make their evaluative standards known to their
readers (Lauer, Montague, Lunsford, & Emig, 1985, p. 200).
```

In a first citation, APA requires that all coauthors, unless there are six or more, be mentioned.

doc 7d

```
Lauer et al. (1985) acknowledge their debt to Kinneavy (1971)
for key rhetorical terms.
```

```
The authors acknowledge their debt to Kinneavy (1971) for key
rhetorical terms (Lauer et al., 1985, p. 21).
```

Both of these sentences illustrate a "subsequent citation"; that is, the four coauthors have already been named. Consequently, the *et al.* ("and others") formula can now be used to save space. Note also how each of these sentences efficiently cites *two* items from the writer's reference list.

```
According to Nietzsche, Greek tragedy arose "out of the
spirit of music" (cited in Merquior, p. 83).
```

This sentence shows how to cite a quotation from an indirect source.

EXERCISES

4. Submit a sample APA-style list of "References" containing five items, preferably from your actual research project. Choose a different kind of source (edited book, translation, journal article, etc.) for each entry.

5. Using APA style, submit five sentences containing references to the works you used in Exercise 4. Make each citation illustrate a different kind of circumstance (single author, two authors, two works by the same author, etc.)

7e Observe the features of "alternative MLA" footnote/endnote style.

If your instructor prefers the "alternative MLA" style of citation, you will use either **footnotes** or **endnotes** instead of parenthetic citations and a reference list. A footnote appears at the bottom of the page on which its corresponding number appears within the text; see page 221 for a sample of text and notes together. Endnotes, by contrast, appear in sequence at the end of the paper, article, chapter, or book.

Wherever you decide to put your notes, you should follow these rules for handling the note numbers within your text:

doc 7e

1. Number all the notes consecutively (1, 2, 3, . . .).
2. Elevate the note numbers slightly, as here.[8]
3. Place the numbers after, not before, the quotations or other information being cited: not X `As Rosenhan says,`[11] `"the evidence is simply not compelling,"` but ● `As Rosenhan says, "the evidence is simply not compelling."`[11]
4. Place the numbers after all punctuation except a dash; even parentheses, colons, and semicolons should precede note numbers.

Endnotes versus Footnotes

Type endnotes on a new page after your main text, but before a bibliography if you are supplying one. Here is the standard form for endnotes.

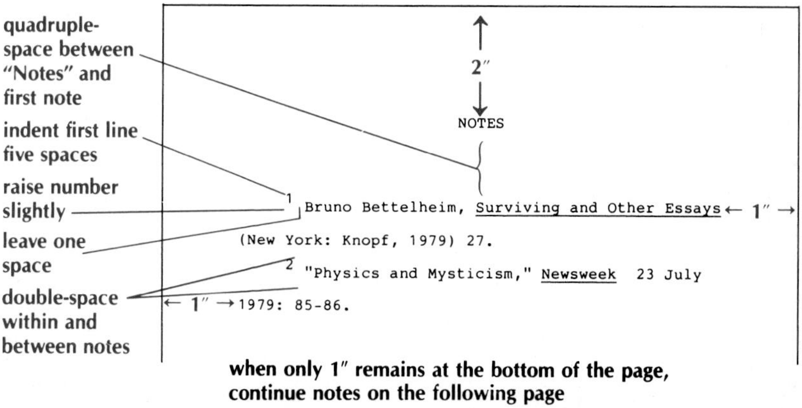

Handle footnotes just like endnotes except for these differences:

1. On each page where you will have notes, stop your main text high enough to leave room for the notes.
2. Quadruple-space between the end of the text and the first note on a page.
3. Single-space within the notes, but double-space between them.
4. If you have to carry a note over to the next page, type a solid line a full line below the last line of text on that new page, quadruple-space, and continue the note. Then add any new notes.

Thus, footnotes at the bottom of a page look like this.

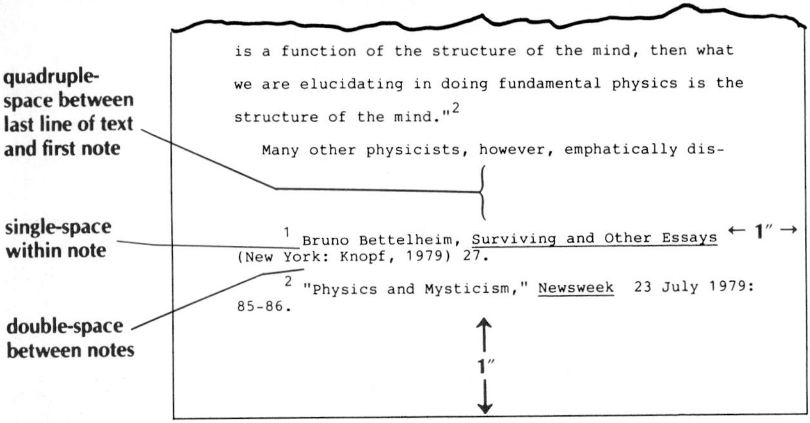

And here is a footnote carried over from a preceding page.

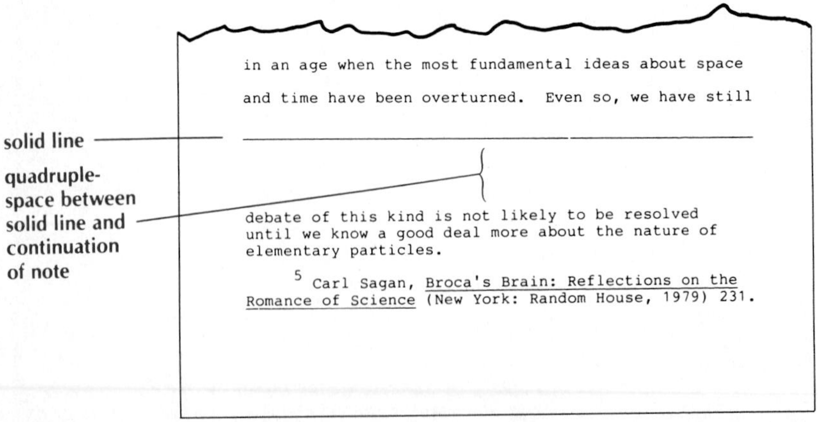

First Notes

To see how notes differ from reference list entries, compare the following sample notes with the corresponding entries on pages 189–94.

[1] Elizabeth Kendall, The Runaway Bride: Hollywood Romantic Comedy of the 1930s (New York: Knopf, 1990) 107.

[2] Mira Liehm and Antonin J. Liehm, The Most Important Art: Soviet and Eastern European Film after 1945 (Berkeley: U of California P, 1977) 234–45.

[3] American Society of Hospital Pharmacists, Consumer Drug Digest (New York: Facts on File, 1982) 107.

[4] Chicago Manual of Style, 13th ed. (Chicago: U of Chicago P, 1982) 18.103.

[5] George Herbert, "The Pulley," The Bedford Introduction to Literature, ed. Michael Meyer (New York: St. Martin's, 1987) 790–91.

[6] Plato, The Collected Dialogues of Plato: Including the Letters, ed. Edith Hamilton and Huntington Cairns (Princeton: Princeton UP, 1961) 327.

[7] Frank Kermode et al., eds., The Oxford Anthology of English Literature, 2 vols. (New York: Oxford UP, 1973) 1:209–11.

[8] Natsume Soseki, The Miner, trans. Jay Rubin (Stanford: Stanford UP, 1988) 99–103.

[9] Frank Conroy, Stop-time (1967; New York: Penguin, 1977) 8.

[10] Arnold M. Cooper, "Psychoanalysis at One Hundred: Beginnings of Maturity," Journal of the American Psychoanalytic Association 32 (1984): 250.

[11] Larry L. Langford, "How Many Children Had Molly Bloom?

Sons and Lovers in Ulysses," Literature and Psychology 34.2 (1988): 27–28.

[12] Václav Havel, "The New Year in Prague," New York Review of Books 7 Mar. 1991: 20.

[13] Brett Singer, "Husbands at Bay," rev. of Only Children, by Rafael Yglesias, New York Times Book Review 17 July 1988: 19.

[14] "On a Clear Day You Can See . . . ," Newsweek 25 Feb. 1991: 54.

[15] C. W. Nevius, "When Choices Were Simpler," San Francisco Chronicle 20 Feb. 1991, five-star ed.: D1.

[16] "For Lasting Peace: Tougher Terms," New York Times 20 Feb. 1991, national ed.: A14.

[17] L[awrence] K. L[ustig], "Alluvial Fans," Encyclopaedia Britannica, 1985, Macropaedia.

[18] Robert R. Wiggins and Steve Brecher, with William P. Steinberg, Suitcase User's Guide (Sunnyvale, Software Supply, 1987).

[19] Henry Morton Boudin, "The Ripple Effect in Classroom Management," diss., U of Michigan, 1970, 78–93.

[20] United States. Dept. of Agriculture, "Shipments and Unloads of Certain Fruits and Vegetables, 1918–1923," Statistical Bulletin 7 (Apr. 1925): 208.

[21] Winfried S. McFann, letter, Popular Photography Aug. 1978: 8.

[22] Gerald Graff, letter to the author, 18 Jan. 1989.

[23] John Guare, Six Degrees of Separation, dir. Jerry Zaks, with Stockard Channing, Courtney B. Vance, and John Cunningham, Vivian Beaumont Theatre, New York, 20 Feb. 1991.

[24] The Hard Way, dir. John Badham, Universal, 1991.

[25] Knocking on Armageddon's Door, prod. and dir. Torv Carlsen and John R. Magnus, PBS, 19 July 1988.

[26] Ludwig van Beethoven, Symphony no. 8 in F, op. 93, cond. Pierre Monteux, Vienna Philharmonic Orch., Decca, STS 15238, 1964.

[27] E. D. Hirsch, Jr., "Frontiers of Critical Theory," Wyoming Conference on Freshman and Sophomore English, 9 July 1979.

[28] Peter Collier and David Horowitz, personal interview, 5 Jan. 1991.

[29] Word, release 4.0, computer software, Microsoft, 1988, Macintosh.

Subsequent References

After you have provided one full endnote or footnote, you can be brief in citing the same work again:

[24] Kendall 197.

If you refer to more than one work by the same author, add a shortened title:

[25] Michaels, Men's Club 45.

[26] Michaels, I Would Have Saved Them 89–91.

If you cite the same work a third time, do not use the obsolete abbreviations *ibid.* or *op cit.;* repeat the identifying information given in your first shortened reference. If the title of the whole work is cumbersome, abbreviate it.

FIRST NOTE:

[27] The McGraw-Hill Encyclopedia of World Biography. 12 vols. (New York: McGraw-Hill, 1973) 6: 563; hereafter cited as MEWB.

SUBSEQUENT NOTE:

[28] MEWB 8: 354.

If the same work comes up repeatedly in your notes, provide one full reference and then shift to parenthetic citations.

FIRST NOTE:

[29] William Shakespeare, The Merchant of Venice, ed. Louis B. Wright and Virginia LaMar (New York: Washington Square, 1957) II.iii.43.

SUBSEQUENT PARENTHETIC REFERENCE:

Portia tells Nerissa that she will do anything "ere I will be married to a sponge" (I.ii.90–91).

Bibliography

A **bibliography** is a list of works that you have consulted or that you recommend to your readers for further reference. Research papers, dissertations, and scholarly books that do not follow a parenthetic citation style of documentation (7b–d) typically contain bibliographies at the end. If you are supplying endnotes or footnotes, you can decide whether or not to include a bibliography by asking whether your notes have given a sufficient idea of your sources.

For bibliographical form, follow the conventions specified for an MLA reference list of "Works Cited" (p. 188). In practice, the only differences between a bibliography and a reference list are that (a) parenthetic citations are not keyed directly to a bibliography, and (b) a bibliography may include some works that were consulted but are not actually cited in the text.

EXERCISES

6. Write sample first endnotes (double-spaced) giving the usual amount of information about the following sources:

   A. A quotation from page 228 of this present book.
   B. A book by Herman Ermolaev called *Soviet Literary Theories 1917–1934: The Genesis of Socialist Realism.* The book was published in 1963 by the University of California Press, whose offices are in Berkeley and Los Angeles, California.
   C. A 1940 pamphlet issued by the United States Department of the Interior, Bureau of Indian Affairs, called *Navajo Native Dyes: Their Preparation and Use*. The pamphlet was published by the U.S. Government Printing Office in Washington, D.C.
   D. A story by Philip Roth called "On the Air," published in Number 10 of *New American Review*, on pages 7 through 49. This magazine did not carry dates, and its pagination began anew with each issue.
   E. A two-volume book called *American Literary Masters*, edited by Charles R. Anderson and seven other people. The work was published in 1965 by Holt, Rinehart and Winston, whose places of publication are listed on the back of the title page as New York, Chicago, San Francisco, and Toronto.

7. If you are now working on a research project, supply first endnotes (double-spaced) to five items you have examined, including at least one article in a magazine or newspaper. In addition, supply a subsequent note or parenthetic citation for each item, using the MLA style shown above.

7f Learn the uses of substantive and bibliographic notes.

If you are using parenthetic citations (pp. 184–206, 7b–d), you will not be routinely supplying footnotes or endnotes. But you may nevertheless want to include some notes—usually endnotes, placed between the final paragraph of your main text and the beginning of your reference list—to make substantive comments (**substantive notes**) or to supply more references than you could gracefully fit into one set of parentheses (**bibliographic notes**). Although APA generally discourages use of such supplementary notes, MLA does not.

SUBSTANTIVE NOTE:

[1] According to Jalby, the peasants of Languedoc dressed lightly on the whole, but on feastdays, regardless of the heat, they wore their best winter clothes over their best summer ones to demonstrate their sense of luxury (194).

BIBLIOGRAPHIC NOTE:

doc 7f

[2] See also E. R. Dodds, The Greeks and the Irrational (Berkeley: U of California P, 1951) 145–62; Richard Stillwell, "The Siting of Classical Greek Temples," Journal of the Society of Architectural Historians 13 (1954): 5; and Robert Scranton, "Group Design in Greek Architecture," Art Bulletin 31 (1949): 251.

If the works cited in this note appeared in the reference list, the note could be briefer:

[2] See also Dodds 145–62; Stillwell 5; Scranton 251.

If you have been following a footnote/endnote form, your substantive and bibliographic notes should be integrated with the others. But whichever form you use, beware of demoting important points from your main text to your notes. Remember that readers would be annoyed by having to lurch back and forth between text and notes in order to follow your reasoning.

EXERCISE

8. Using either MLA or APA style, submit a bibliographic note that mentions all five of the items you included in Exercise 7 (p. 213).

NOTES

[1] J. M. Roberts, *History of the World* (New York: Knopf, 1976) 845.

[2] The example is taken from Christine R. B. Boake and Robert R. Capranica, "Aggressive Signal in 'Courtship' Chirps of a Gregarious Cricket," *Science* 218 (1982): 580–82.

8

A Sample Research Essay

8a Note the features of a research essay following MLA parenthetic citation style.

To illustrate the fruits of library research, here is an analytic student paper about the origin and importance of a key principle in experimental psychology.

"Clever Hans and His Effect: Horse Sense about Communicating with Animals"

Mode	Analysis
Title page	Page 217
Thesis statement and outline	Page 218
Documentation style	MLA parenthetic citation
List of sources	"Works Cited" reference list (pp. 228–229)
Sample reference list in APA style	Pages 230–231
Sample page in "alternative MLA" footnote style	Page 232

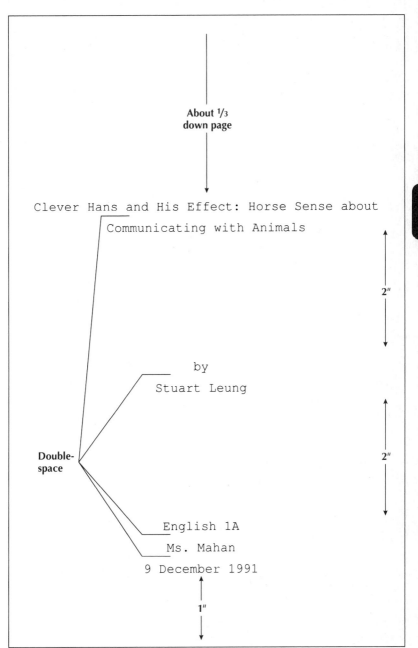

About 1/3 down page

Clever Hans and His Effect: Horse Sense about

Communicating with Animals

2″

by

Stuart Leung

Double-space

2″

English 1A

Ms. Mahan

9 December 1991

1″

Thesis: From Oskar Pfungst's debunking of the "counting horse" Clever Hans, experimental psychology took an enduringly important, but still frequently violated, principle of caution against inadvertent cueing of subjects.

The writer uses a topic outline (p. 89).

res essay 8a

Outline

I. Clever Hans and His "Powers"
   A. Initial Disbelief in the Claims of Hans's Trainer
   B. Acceptance of Hans's Alleged Powers
      1. Mathematical
      2. Linguistic and musical
   C. Hans's Uniqueness: No Conscious Deception by the Trainer
II. The Explanation
   A. Occult versus Naturalistic Possibilities
   B. A Champion of Rational Standards: Oskar Pfungst
   C. Pfungst's Demonstration of Hans's Incapacities
   D. The Solution: Unconscious Cueing by Hans's Interrogator
   E. The Clever Hans Effect Defined
III. Applying the Clever Hans Effect Today: Primate Language Studies
   A. Insufficient Precautions against the Effect
   B. A Classic Instance: Koko, the "Talking Gorilla"
   C. Increasing Doubts about Imparting Human Language to Captive Animals
   D. The Importance of the Clever Hans Effect to Any Future Experimental Studies

Leung 1

For a sample first page when a title page is not supplied, see page 147.

Clever Hans and His Effect: Horse Sense about Communicating with Animals

4 spaces

At first the drama featured just two characters--a man and a horse--and its only spectators were jeering neighbors surrounding a courtyard in central Berlin. There each day the man, a retired schoolteacher named Wilhelm von Osten, would attempt to teach his Russian stallion Hans how to think and calculate like a human being. In his long white coat and floppy broad-brimmed hat, worn in every kind of weather, and with his teacher's slate and chalk at hand, urging Hans to tap out answers to math problems with a raised hoof, von Osten seemed ridiculous to his neighbors (Fernald 7). Surely, they told each other, he had to be crazy to waste his time for months and finally years attempting to break through barriers established by nature itself.

The writer begins with an engaging and centrally important story.

Parenthetic citations are keyed to the "Works Cited" on page 10.

Everything changed, however, in 1904, when word spread rapidly in Berlin, and then through all Europe and across the Atlantic, that Hans was not just another long-suffering pet with a crackpot master. He was Clever Hans, the equine genius. The visitors who now packed von Osten's courtyard, without ever being charged for the privilege, verified for themselves that the horse could manage virtually any problem in arithmetic. As one observer recalled,

res essay 8a

Ellipsis indicates material omitted from quotation.

Block quotation (more than 4 typed lines) indented 10 spaces

> The four fundamental processes were entirely familiar to him. Common fractions he changed to decimals, and vice versa. . . . The following problems are illustrations of the kind he solved. "How much is 2/5 plus 1/2?" Answer: 9/10. . . . "What are the factors of 28?" -- Thereupon Hans tapped consecutively 2, 4, 7, 14, 28. "In the number 365287179 I place a decimal point after the 8. How many are there now in the hundreds place?"--5. "How many in the ten thousandths place?"--9. (Pfungst 20-21)

But that wasn't all. Hans, it turned out, could read and spell German words; he appeared to have memorized the calendar, so that he could supply the date of any mentioned day; he could be told a German sentence and, twenty-four hours later, correctly tap out the code for its fifty-eight letters; and, still using taps for letters, he could perform astounding feats of musical analysis and judgment (Pfungst 21-23). Moreover, an investigative committee headed by

Carl Stumpf, the distinguished director of Berlin's Psychological Institute, disproved any deceptive intent on the part of the trainer von Osten, whose passionate faith in Hans's intelligence prompted him to cooperate fully with the committee's tests for fraud.

res essay 8a

It was this apparent scientific validation that set Clever Hans apart from any number of other performing animals dating back to the sixteenth century (Mountjoy and Lewandowski 27), including "composing and chess-playing dogs, calculating cats, [and] a learned pig . . . " (Hövelmann 203) among many others.[1] The ruling out of deception, however,

Citation of a work by two authors

[1] Even Hans's fame was outshone, a decade later, by the alleged feats of an airedale terrier named Rolf, who was thought to have written letters to people and fellow dogs. What is certain is that some of the people wrote back to him. As one historian recounts, "Imagine . . . a distinguished German university professor who, with full Teutonic earnestness, writes respectful letters to a dog inquiring about the dog's views on the political implications of the first World War (which Rolf dutifully explains to him by return mail), and asking the dog to convey his greetings to his wife and children!" (Hövelmann 203). Regrettably, Rolf caught

Substantive footnotes can be combined with reference list documentation.

only made Hans's powers more mysterious. Had he truly, thanks to von Osten's extraordinary diligence and patience, broken through to a human plane of understanding? Or, as Sigmund Freud among others suspected (Fernald 213), was he receiving messages through mental telepathy or some other occult mechanism?

The central issue is posed.

res essay 8a

The writer prepares us for a solution.

The bewildered Professor Stumpf, for one, felt that the explanation must lie within the range of commonly known phenomena, and so he directed one of his graduate students, Oskar Pfungst, to seek for such an answer (Fernald 47). The choice was inspired. Pfungst, not Hans or von Osten or Stumpf, was destined to become the real hero of the drama--the debunker of Hans's alleged gifts and the setter of enduring standards for rigor in the conduct of experimental psychology.

As he later recounted in his classic study Clever Hans, Pfungst began by putting Hans to a sterner test than any devised by Stumpf's committee. To determine

---

pneumonia and had to be put to sleep before his announced autobiography could be completed (Hövelmann 203-4).

whether the horse was actually capable of independent thought, he offered Hans problems whose answers were unknown to the questioner (Pfungst 32). The results were unequivocally negative: "Hans can neither read, count nor make calculations. He knows nothing of coins or cards, calendars or clocks, nor can he respond, by tapping or otherwise, to a number spoken to him but a moment before. Finally, he has not a trace of musical ability" (Pfungst 40).

The mystery is explained.

Instead, Pfungst reasoned, Hans must have acquired an exceptional responsiveness to unconscious cueing by those questioners who did know what answers to expect. By carefully watching von Osten and others in the act of interrogation, he discovered that "as soon as the questioner gave the problem he bent forward--be it ever so slightly--in order to observe the horse's foot the more closely, for the hoof was the horse's organ of speech" (Pfungst 57). And when Pfungst himself succeeded, simply by inclining his torso, in making Hans start "counting" in the absence of any question, the whole mystery evaporated. Hans's talent was not for mathematics or music but for "pantomime" (Pfungst 141), or a mimicry of human bowing in the hope of earning sugar cubes.

Thesis: the Clever Hans effect and its importance

Yet along with Hans's demotion from a wizard to a well-trained horse came the birth of a fundamentally important concept. This was to become known as the "Clever Hans effect"--the inadvertent communication from an experimenter to an experimental subject through what Pfungst called "the tension of expectation" (Pfungst 147). After Pfungst, no experiment dealing with animal or human intelligence could be considered trustworthy unless it showed strict precautions against the Clever Hans effect.

res essay 8a

Applying the Clever Hans effect to recent research

This is not to say, however, that later scientists have always kept the Clever Hans effect in mind. In the 1970s, several celebrated researchers in what Thomas A. Sebeok has named "zoosemiotics" (Sebeok, "Semiotics," 200), or animal communication, based far-reaching conclusions about primate language acquisition on studies that failed to match Pfungst's rigor in 1904. One such researcher, Herbert A. Terrace, eventually came to see that "the teacher's coaxing and cueing have played much greater roles in so-called 'conversations' with chimpanzees than was previously recognized" (Terrace 196). And according to Gerd H. Hövelmann in 1989, "not a single ape language study" has as yet taken sufficient precautions against cueing (Hövelmann 207).

Citing one of several works by the same author

Leung 7

One need only read Pfungst's Clever Hans of 1911 to see why, for example, no faith should be invested in Francine Patterson's "talking gorilla" Koko, sponsored and publicized in the seventies by the National Geographic Society. Koko, Patterson tells us, is not just "the focus of [her] career" but also her "dear friend" (Patterson 438); in other words, the experimenter has a strong emotional investment in her subject's success at learning American Sign Language. Predictably, both photographs (Patterson 442–43) and film clips (Terrace 196) of Koko's "speech" show Patterson unmistakably cueing the gorilla's signs. And if Patterson had taken Clever Hans to heart, she might have thought twice about interpreting even Koko's mistakes as proving a knack for "lies," "brattiness," and "jokes" (Patterson 440, 449, 462).[2]

An extended example

Significantly, an increasing number of researchers now challenge the whole strategy of

Larger issue raised by the Clever Hans effect

[2] Compare Pfungst 145–46. For discussion of Koko's "jokes," see Sebeok, "Clever Hans," 108.

removing animals from their habitats and turning them into human "artifacts" (Hediger 5). "In neither the natural nor domesticated state," as one expert on the body language of horses has remarked, "has [a horse] any occasion to push buttons or turn labyrinthine corners in quest of a snack" (Ainslie and Ledbetter 27). What one species can learn from being forced to use another's language may, after all, be of relatively minor scientific interest (Walther 371). The future of studies in animal intelligence probably lies in the wild, where communication systems reflect not the impoverished stimulus-response model of the laboratory but "social organization involving many speakers and many listeners of different age-sex classes" (Todt et al. v; see also Bright 233).

To be sure, efforts to impart human language to animals continue in the 1990s. Some of them, it is thought, may actually have demonstrated a limited capacity of imprisoned dolphins, seals, and apes to handle symbolic concepts (Crowley 54). Yet Oskar Pfungst would have wanted to remind us of the gulf separating the performing of conditioned stunts and the active use of words to express ideas. As the parlor magician James Randi has said, scientists who think they cannot be deceived by apparent human language on the part of captive animals "should listen more carefully. From a distance of many decades comes a sound that they should heed; it is the sound of that ubiquitous horse, and he is laughing" (Randi 296).

A striking quotation reinforces the thesis and makes for a lively ending.

A reference list according to MLA style

Leung 10

Works Cited

Title centered

Ainslie, Tom, and Bonnie Ledbetter. The Body Language of Horses. New York: Morrow, 1980.

Bright, Michael. Animal Language. Ithaca: Cornell UP, 1984.

Crowley, Geoffrey. "The Wisdom of Animals." Newsweek 23 May 1988: 52–59.

Fernald, Dodge. The Hans Legacy: A Story of Science. Hillsdale, N.J.: Erlbaum, 1983.

Hediger, Heini K. P. "The Clever Hans Phenomenon from an Animal Psychologist's Point of View." In Sebeok and Rosenthal 1–17.

Hövelmann, Gerd H. "Animal 'Language' Research: The Perpetuation of Some Old Mistakes." Semiotica 73 (1989): 199–217.

Mountjoy, Paul T., and Alan G. Lewandowski. "The Dancing Horse, A Learned Pig, and Muscle Twitches." Psychological Record 34 (1984): 25–38.

Patterson, Francine. "Conversations with a Gorilla." National Geographic 154 (1978): 438–65.

Pfungst, Oskar. Clever Hans (The Horse of Mr. von Osten): A Contribution to Experimental Animal and Human Psychology. New York: Holt, 1911.

Entry begins at left margin.

Subsequent lines indented 5 spaces

Titles listed alphabetically by authors' last names

res essay 8a

Leung 11

Randi, James. "Semiotics: A View from behind the Foot Lights." In Sebeok and Rosenthal 291–98.

Sebeok, Thomas A. "Clever Hans and Smart Simians." Anthropos 76 (1981): 89–165.

---. "Semiotics and Ethology." In Sebeok and Ramsay 200–31.

---, and Alexandra Ramsay, eds. Approaches to Animal Communication. The Hague: Mouton, 1969.

---, and Robert Rosenthal, eds. The Clever Hans Phenomenon: Communication with Horses, Whales, Apes, and People. Annals of the New York Academy of Sciences 364 (1981).

Terrace, H. S. "'Language' in Apes." In Rom Harré and Vernon Reynolds, eds. The Meaning of Primate Signals. Ed. Rom Harré and Vernon Reynolds. London: Cambridge UP, 1984. Pp. 179–203.

Todt, D., P. Goedeking, and D. Symmes, eds. Primate Vocal Communication. Berlin: Springer-Verlag, 1988.

Walther, Fritz R. Communication and Expression in Hoofed Mammals. Bloomington: Indiana UP, 1984.

Multiple works by one author or editor

8b Note how the reference list would look in APA style.

res essay 8b

Leung 10

References

Ainslie, T., & Ledbetter, B. (1980). The body language of horses. New York: Morrow.

Bright, M. (1984). Animal language. Ithaca: Cornell University Press.

Crowley, G. (1988, May 23). The wisdom of animals. Newsweek, pp. 52–59.

Fernald, D. (1983). The Hans legacy: A story of science. Hillsdale, NJ: Erlbaum.

Hediger, H. K. P. (1981). The clever Hans phenomenon from an animal psychologist's point of view. In Sebeok & Rosenthal, pp. 1–17.

Hövelmann, G. H. (1989). 'Animal language' research: The perpetuation of some old mistakes. Semiotica, 73, 199–217.

Mountjoy, P. T., & Lewandowski, A. G. (1984). The dancing horse, a learned pig, and muscle twitches. Psychological Record, 34, 25–38.

Patterson, F. (1978). Conversations with a gorilla. National Geographic, 154, 438–465.

Pfungst, O. (1911). Clever Hans (the horse of Mr. von Osten): A contribution to experimental animal and human psychology. New York: Holt.

Leung 11

Randi, J. (1981). Semiotics: A view from behind the foot lights. In Sebeok & Rosenthal, pp. 291–298.

Sebeok, T. A. (1981). Clever Hans and smart simians. _Anthropos_, _76_, 89–165.

Sebeok, T. A. (1969). Semiotics and ethology. In Sebeok & Ramsay, pp. 200–231.

Sebeok, T. A., & Ramsay, A. (Eds.). (1969). _Approaches to animal communication_. The Hague: Mouton.

Sebeok, T. A., & Rosenthal, R. (Eds.). (1981). _The clever Hans phenomenon: Communication with horses, whales, apes, and people_. _Annals of the New York Academy of Sciences_, _364_.

Terrace, H. S. (1984). 'Language' in apes. In Harré, R., & Reynolds, V. (Eds.) _The meaning of primate signals_ (pp. 179–203). London: Cambridge University Press.

Todt, D., Goedeking, P., & Symmes, D. (Eds.). (1988). _Primate vocal communication_. Berlin: Springer-Verlag.

Walther, F. R. (1984). _Communication and expression in hoofed mammals_. Bloomington: Indiana University Press.

res essay 8b

8c Note how the sample paper would look in "alternative MLA" footnote style.

Leung 6

This is not to say, however, that later scientists have always kept the Clever Hans effect in mind. In the 1970s, several celebrated researchers in what Thomas A. Sebeok has named "zoosemiotics," or animal communication, based far-reaching conclusions about primate language acquisition on studies that failed to match Pfungst's rigor in 1904.[6] One such researcher, Herbert A. Terrace, eventually came to see that "the teacher's coaxing and cueing have played much greater roles in so-called 'conversations' with chimpanzees than was previously recognized."[7] And according to Gerd H. Hövelmann in 1989, "not a single ape language study" has as yet taken sufficient precautions against cueing.[8]

[6] Thomas A. Sebeok, "Semiotics and Ethology," in Approaches to Animal Communication, ed. Sebeok and Alexandra Ramsay (The Hague: Mouton, 1969) 200.

[7] H. S. Terrace, " 'Language' in Apes," in The Meaning of Primate Signals, ed. Rom Harré and Vernon Reynolds (London: Cambridge UP, 1984) 196.

[8] Gerd H. Hövelmann, "Animal 'Language' Research: The Perpetuation of Some Old Mistakes," Semiotica 73 (1989): 199–217.

IV

PARAGRAPHS

PARAGRAPHS

Once you have mastered paragraph form, you have an invaluable means of keeping your reader's interest and approval. Although each sentence conveys meaning, an essay or paper or report is not a sequence of sentences but a development of one leading point through certain steps of presentation. Those steps are, or ought to be, paragraphs.

The sentences within an effective paragraph support and extend one another in the service of a single unfolding idea, just as the paragraphs themselves work together to make the thesis persuasive. In key respects, then, you can think of the paragraph as a mini-essay. Like the full essay, a typical paragraph

1. *presents one main idea;*
2. *conveys thoughts that are connected both by logical association and by word signals;*
3. *often reveals its main idea in a prominent statement, usually but not always toward the start;*
4. *usually supports or illustrates that idea;*
5. *may also deal with objections or limitations to that idea, but without allowing the objections to assume greater importance than the idea itself; and*
6. *may begin or end more generally, taking an expanded view of the addressed topic.*

In one sense, nothing could be easier than to form paragraphs; you simply indent the first word of a sentence by five spaces. But those indentions must match real divisions in your developing thought if you are to keep your reader's respectful attention. All readers sense that a new paragraph signals a shift: a new subject, a new idea, a change in emphasis, a new speaker, a different time or place, or a change in the level of generality. By observing such natural breaks and by signaling in one paragraph how it logically follows from the preceding one, you can turn the paragraph into a powerful means of communication.

9

Paragraph Unity and Continuity

PARAGRAPH UNITY

9a Highlight your leading idea.

As a rule, every effective paragraph has a **leading idea** to which all other ideas in the paragraph are logically related. A reader of your essays or papers should be able to tell, in any paragraph, which is the **main sentence** (often called *topic sentence*)—the sentence containing that one central point to be supported or otherwise developed in the rest of the paragraph.

It is true that in some prose—for example, descriptions, narratives, and the parts of a report that present data or run through the steps of an experimental procedure—many paragraphs contain no single sentence that stands out as the main, controlling one. Such a paragraph can be said to have an implied main sentence: "This is the way it was," or "These are the procedures that were followed." But in college essays and term papers that call for analysis and argument (Chapter 2), you should try to see that each paragraph contains not only a leading idea but an easily identified main sentence as well.

We will see (Chapter 10) that a main sentence can occur anywhere in a paragraph if the other sentences are properly subordinate to it. More often than not, however, a main sentence comes at or near the beginning, as in this student example:

> Walt Whitman's "A Noiseless Patient Spider" is built on a comparison of the poet's soul to a spider. Both of them, he says, stand isolated, sending something from inside themselves into the surrounding empty space; in their obviously different ways they are both reaching for *connection*. Whitman does not say what the spiritual connection may be, except that his soul hopes to find "the spheres to connect" the "measureless oceans of space" out there. He is vague—but so is the unknown realm toward which he yearns.

¶ un
9a

The heart of this paragraph is its opening sentence, which reveals the leading idea: Whitman's poem is built on a comparison of the poet's soul to a spider. Reread the other three sentences and you will see that each of them contributes to that leading idea, remaining within its organizing control.

EXERCISES

1. Write out a main sentence for a paragraph on any topic. (That is, state a leading idea.) Follow it with three sentences that develop, explain, or illustrate your leading idea. Number all four sentences and, beneath your paragraph, briefly explain each sentence's function. (E.g., "Sentence 4 gives an example of the idea proposed in sentence 3.")

2. Since a paragraph can be regarded as a mini-essay (p. 234), you ought to be able to boil down an essay to paragraph size. Try that experiment with an essay you have already read for this course. Your paragraph should have as its main sentence a statement of the essay's thesis, and your other sentences should cover the author's most important supporting points.

3. Suppose you have been writing an essay about the difficulties people face when they try to write essays. You have just ended a paragraph with this sentence: *Writing provides rich confirmation of Murphy's Law: "If anything can go wrong, it will."* Your next paragraph will supply an example from your own experience as a student writer. Submit that paragraph, including

(a) a main sentence stating what your experience taught you, and (b) several supporting sentences describing that experience. (If you have no relevant story to tell, make one up.)

9b Keep to your point.

A paragraph can include negative as well as positive considerations, but it should never "change its mind," canceling one point with a flatly contrary one.

DO:

- A. The seepage of dioxin into a community's water supply always terrifies everyone once it has been discovered. Citizens naturally expect the Environmental Protection Agency and the guilty industry to remove the source of risk as soon as possible. Unfortunately, however, this chemical is so incredibly toxic in small doses that decades may pass before the threat to public health is truly over.

¶ un
9b

DON'T:

x B. The seepage of dioxin into a community's water supply always terrifies everyone once it has been discovered. Citizens naturally expect the Environmental Protection Agency and the guilty industry to remove the source of risk as soon as possible. Yet many people react to the crisis quite calmly, refusing to worry about cancer, birth defects, and other proven results of contact with dioxin.

Each of these paragraphs ends with a sentence that "goes against" the preceding two sentences. In paragraph A, however, there is no contradiction; the writer simply turns from one aspect of the dioxin problem (citizens' demand for a speedy solution) to a more serious aspect (long-term toxicity). But in paragraph B the writer says two *incompatible* things: that everyone is alarmed and that some people are not alarmed. The writer of paragraph B could eliminate the contradiction by rewriting the opening sentence:

- The seepage of dioxin into a community's water supply provokes mixed reactions once it has been discovered. Citizens naturally expect the Environmental Protection Agency and the guilty industry to remove the source of risk as soon as possible. Yet many people react to the crisis quite calmly, refusing to worry about cancer, birth defects, and other proven results of contact with dioxin.

A paragraph that shows strong internal continuity, hooking each new sentence into the one before it, can cover a good deal of ground without appearing disunified. Every sentence, however, should bear some relation to the leading idea—either introducing it, stating it, elaborating it, asking a question about it, supporting it, raising a doubt about it, or otherwise reflecting on it. A sentence that does none of those things is a **digression**—a deviation. Just one digression within a submitted paragraph may be enough to sabotage its effectiveness.

Suppose, for example, paragraph A on dioxin contained this sentence: *The Environmental Protection Agency, like the Federal Communications Commission, is an independent body.* Even though that statement deals with the EPA, which does figure in the paragraph, it has no bearing on the paragraph's leading idea: that dioxin can remain hazardous for decades. Thus the statement amounts to a digression. Unless the writer decided to shift to a different leading idea, the digression would have to be eliminated in a later draft.

EXERCISES

4. Find the digressive sentence that has been inserted into the following paragraph. Submit an explanation of why that sentence interferes with paragraph unity.

   In 1886 Grinnell suggested in the pages of *Forest and Stream* that concerned men and women create an organization for the protection of wild birds and their eggs, its administration to be undertaken by the magazine's staff. Grinnell did not have to grope to name this organization. He had grown up near the home that the great bird painter, John James Audubon, had left to his wife and children at his death. As a boy Grinnell had played in an old loft cluttered with stacks of the red muslin-bound copies of the *Ornithological Biography* and boxes of bird skins brought back by Audubon from his expeditions. He had attended a school for small boys conducted by Lucy Audubon nearby. All his life he would remain an avid reader. Grinnell quite naturally called the new organization the Audubon Society.[1]

5. Choosing any topic not already used in Exercise 1 (p. 236), write two paragraphs that suffer, respectively, from self-contradiction and digression.

Label and submit the faulty paragraphs along with a third, adequately unified, paragraph on the same topic.

9c Give your leading idea the last word.

Although it is sometimes useful to include statements that limit the scope of a paragraph's leading idea or that raise objections to it (p. 255, 10b), you should try never to *end* a paragraph with such a statement. Final positions are naturally emphatic. If your last sentence takes away from the main idea, you will sound indecisive or uncomfortable, and the paragraph will lack emphasis.

INDECISIVE:

x A. One reason for the recent popularity of Hollywood autobiographies must surely be the decline of serious fiction about important, glamorous people. We know that readers crave intimacy with the great, and we also know that modern novelists have ignored that craving. What people no longer get from fiction, they now seek in true confessions from Tinseltown. Of course, other factors must be at work as well; literary fads are never produced by single causes.

¶ un
9c

FIRM:

• B. One reason for the recent popularity of Hollywood autobiographies must surely be the decline of serious fiction about important, glamorous people. Of course, other factors must be at work as well; literary fads are never produced by single causes. But we do know that readers crave intimacy with the great, and we also know that modern novelists have ignored that craving. What people no longer get from fiction, they now seek in true confessions from Tinseltown.

Notice that these paragraphs say the same thing but leave the reader with different impressions. Paragraph A trails off, as if the writer were having second thoughts about the leading idea. Paragraph B gets its "negative" sentence about *other factors* into a safely unemphatic position and then ends strongly, reinforcing the idea that was stated in the opening sentence. The confident treatment of an objection makes the paragraph supple rather than self-defeating.

EXERCISE

6. Write and submit a paragraph that fails to give its leading idea the last word, and accompany it with a revised version that fixes the problem.

PARAGRAPH CONTINUITY

9d Use one sentence to respond to the previous one.

¶ con 9d

To maintain **continuity**, or linkage between sentences or whole paragraphs, you need to write each new sentence with the previous one in mind. You want your reader to feel that one statement has grown naturally out of its predecessor—an effect that comes from picking up some element in that earlier sentence and taking it further.

If, for example, the most recent sentence in your draft reads *The economic heart of America has been shifting toward the Sunbelt*, you could maintain continuity in any of the following ways, depending on the point you wish to make:

- The economic heart of America has been shifting toward the Sunbelt. But how much longer will this trend continue? [Ask a question.]
- The economic heart of America has been shifting toward the Sunbelt. The recent history of Buffalo, New York, is a case in point. [Illustrate your point.]
- The economic heart of America has been shifting toward the Sunbelt. It may be, however, that the country also has a quite different kind of heart—one that is not so easily moved. [Limit your point.]
- The economic heart of America has been shifting toward the Sunbelt. Without forgetting that trend, let us turn now to less obvious but possibly more important developments. [Provide a transition to the next idea.]
- The economic heart of America has been shifting toward the Sunbelt. If so, it can only be a matter of time before the moral

or spiritual heart of the country is similarly displaced. [Reflect on your point; speculate.]

In short, reread the sentence you have just written and ask yourself, "All right, what follows from this?" What follows may be

1. a question (or further question);
2. an answer (if the sentence above is a question);
3. support or illustration of the point just made;
4. a limitation or objection to the point just made;
5. further support or illustration of an earlier point, or further limitation or objection to an earlier point;
6. a transition; or
7. a conclusion or reflection appropriate either to the sentence above or to the whole idea of the paragraph.

EXERCISE

7. Write out a sentence stating an idea about any topic. Then, on separate lines, write five numbered sentences, *each* of which could be the next sentence following that one in a paragraph. (Your numbered sentences are not meant to form a sequence; they are five alternative ways of maintaining continuity with the first sentence.) Give your five numbered sentences the form of (1) a question, (2) a supporting point or illustration, (3) a limitation or objection, (4) a transition, and (5) a conclusion or reflection.

9e Include signal words and phrases.

Though you may sometimes want to delay stating your paragraph's leading idea (pp. 255–59, 10b–c), you should never put your reader to the trouble of puzzling out hidden connections. By using unmistakable **signals of relation** from sentence to sentence, you can let the reader see at a glance that a certain train of thought is being started, developed, challenged, or completed.

Those signals are chiefly words or phrases indicating exactly how a statement in one sentence relates to the statement it follows. The possible types of relation, along with examples of each type, are these:

CONSEQUENCE:

- therefore, then, thus, hence, accordingly, as a result

LIKENESS:

- likewise, similarly

CONTRAST:

- but, however, nevertheless, on the contrary, on the other hand, yet

AMPLIFICATION:

- and, again, in addition, further, furthermore, moreover, also, too

EXAMPLE:

- for instance, for example

CONCESSION:

- to be sure, granted, of course, it is true

INSISTENCE:

- indeed, in fact, yes, no

SEQUENCE:

- first, second, finally

RESTATEMENT:

- that is, in other words, in simpler terms, to put it differently

RECAPITULATION:

- in conclusion, all in all, to summarize, altogether

TIME OR PLACE:

- afterward, later, earlier, formerly, elsewhere, here, there, hitherto, subsequently, at the same time, simultaneously, above, below, farther on, this time, so far, until now

In addition to signal words that show logical connections, you can gain continuity through words indicating that something already treated is still under discussion. Such signal words make sense only in relation to the sentence before.

PRONOUNS:

- Ordinary people know little about the causes of inflation. What **they** do know is that **they** must earn more every year to buy the same goods and services.

DEMONSTRATIVE ADJECTIVES:

- Mark Twain died in 1910. Since **that** date American literature has never been so dominated by one writer's voice.

REPEATED WORDS AND PHRASES:

- We should conserve fossil fuels on behalf of our descendants as well as ourselves. Those **descendants** will curse us if we leave them without abundant sources of light and heat.

IMPLIED REPETITIONS:

- Some fifty Americans were trapped in the embassy when the revolution broke out. **Six more** managed to scramble onto the last helicopter that was permitted to land on the roof.

Notice how a careful use of relational signals (boldfaced) brings out the logical connectedness of sentences in the following paragraph:

> What was most distinctive about late-60s popular music, **though**, was not that some of its performers used drugs, or that some of its songs were about drugs. **It** was that late-60s rock was music designed for people to listen to while they were *on* drugs. **The music** was a prepackaged sensory stimulant. **This** was a new development. Jazz

musicians might sometimes be junkies, **but** jazz was not music played for junkies. A lot of late-60s rock music, **though**, plainly advertised itself as a kind of complementary good for recreational drugs. **This** explains many things about the character of popular music in **the period—particularly** the unusual length of the songs. There is really only one excuse for buying a record with a twelve-minute drum solo.[2]

One key word, repeated several times, can do much to knit a paragraph together. Thus in the following paragraph the name *Ottawa* (boldfaced here for emphasis) is artfully plucked out from other names:

¶ con 9e

Perhaps a visitor cannot truly understand the country until he has traveled from the genteel poverty of the Atlantic coast with its picturesque fishing villages and stiff towns through the Frenchness of sophisticated Quebec cities and rural landscapes, past the vigorous bustling Ontario municipalities and industrial vistas, over mile after mile of wheat fields between prairie settlements into the lush and spacious beauty of British Columbia; but he must also visit **Ottawa** and the House of Commons. **Ottawa** the stuffy, with its dull-looking houses, its blistering summer heat, its gray rainy afternoons; **Ottawa** the beautiful, on a snowy day when the government buildings stand tall and protective, warmly solid above the white landscape; on a sunny spring afternoon with the cool river winding below, and people moving easily through the clean streets, purposeful but not pushed. Even during the morning and evening traffic rushes, **Ottawa** seems to remain sane.[3]

In the first sentence *Ottawa* belatedly emerges as the key name among several; it gains importance by being weighted singly against all the "travelogue" references before the semicolon. In the second sentence (or intentional sentence fragment) the name is used insistently and fondly. And the author exploits this effect in her final sentence, using the name yet again to reinforce her idea that Ottawa stands apart from the rest of Canada.

EXERCISES

8. Take (or write) a paragraph of your own on any topic and revise it until you are satisfied that it shows adequate continuity from sentence to sentence. Number the sentences. Submit your paragraph along with a sentence-by-sentence explanation of its elements of continuity. (E.g., "Sentence 3: *furthermore* shows that another supporting statement will be added to the one in sentence 2.")

9. Revise the following paragraph for continuity, adding signal words to show relations between sentences:

   Most people hesitate to enter photo contests because they are sure that professionals will take all the prizes. Professional photographers are barred from most photo contests. When professional photographers are permitted to enter photo contests, they hardly ever win the top prizes. There is no reason for a competent amateur photographer to feel handicapped in competing against professionals.

10. Choosing any topic, submit a paragraph which, like the "Ottawa" paragraph, gains continuity from the repetition of a key word or phrase.

9f Keep related sentences together.

You can serve continuity by keeping together sentences that all bear the same relation to the paragraph's leading idea. To simplify, let us reduce all such relations to *support* and *limitation* (qualification). Sentences that support the leading idea by restating it, illustrating it, offering evidence for its truth, or expanding upon it belong in an uninterrupted sequence. So do all sentences that limit the leading idea by showing what it does *not* cover or by casting doubt on it.

Continuity is especially threatened when a paragraph contains two isolated sets of limiting sentences. To see why, examine the following draft paragraph:

limitation	x Not many people would want to endure the lonely hours, the aches and pains, and the probable injuries awaiting anyone who trains seriously for a marathon.
main sentence	The pride, however, that comes from finishing one's first marathon makes all the struggle seem worthwhile.
limitation	But is it really worthwhile? What does running twenty-six miles in glorified underwear have to do with real life?
support	But for veteran marathoners, long-distance racing *is* real life, while all other claims on their time are distractions or nuisances.

Here the direction established by the main sentence is pro-marathon. But that direction is opposed twice in the course of the paragraph; the main sentence is hemmed in by qualifications, and the reader is bounced back and forth between "pro" and "con" points. Compare:

limitation	• Not many people would want to endure the lonely hours, the aches and pains, and the probable injuries awaiting anyone who trains seriously for a marathon. Is all the effort worthwhile? More than once, no doubt, exhausted beginners must ask themselves what running twenty-six miles in glorified underwear has to do with real life. Yet
main sentence	the pride that comes from finishing one's first marathon makes all the struggle seem worthwhile. And for veteran
support	marathoners, long-distance running *is* real life, while all other claims on their time are distractions or nuisances.

Now the paragraph's shuffling between pros and cons has been replaced by *one* definitive pivot on the signal word *Yet*. One such turn per paragraph is the maximum you should allow yourself. To observe that principle, make sure that your limiting and supporting sentences remain within their own portion of the paragraph—with the limiting sentences first to keep them from "having the last word."

For further discussion of the kind of paragraph that pivots to its leading idea, see p. 255, 10b.

EXERCISE

11. Write a brief analysis of the effectiveness or ineffectiveness of the order of sentences in the following paragraph. If you believe the order could be made more effective, rewrite the paragraph, keeping nearly all the same language but changing words as needed to bring out relations between supporting and limiting remarks.

> 1. Some of the most haunting music of our century was composed by the eccentric Parisian Erik Satie. 2. Once you have acquired a taste for his fanciful and melancholy works, you will find it hard to keep them out of your head. 3. But not everyone can take Satie seriously; his modesty makes him appear trivial compared, say, to the bold and colorful Stravinsky.

9g Create linkage through varied and repeated sentence structure.

A further means of making the sentences of a paragraph flow together is to give them some variety of structure. In particular, avoid an unbroken string of choppy sentences, each consisting of one statement unmarked by pauses (see p. 318, 14f).

Within certain limits, however, you can show continuity by *repeating* a sentence pattern. Those limits are that (a) only parts of paragraphs, not whole paragraphs, lend themselves comfortably to such effects, and (b) the sentences so linked must be parallel in meaning. When you want to make their association emphatic, you can give them the same form.

The following paragraph relates American history textbooks to a transformed society. Notice how the writer makes use of identical structures (here boldfaced) in two of her sentences to call attention to the changes in America that have made history books less predictable than they used to be:

> But now the texts have changed, and with them the country that American children are growing up into. **The society that was once uniform is now** a patchwork of rich and poor, old and young, men and women, blacks, whites, Hispanics, and Indians. **The system that ran so smoothly** by means of the Constitution under the guidance of benevolent conductor Presidents **is now** a rattletrap affair. The past is no highway to the present; it is a collection of issues and events that do not fit together and that lead in no single direction.[4]

¶ con
9g

And observe how a critic of urban planning gains emphatic continuity through two sets of identical structures:

> But look what we have built with the first several billions: Low-income projects that become worse centers of delinquency, vandalism and general social hopelessness than the slums they were supposed to replace. Middle-income housing projects which are truly marvels of dullness and regimentation, sealed against any buoyancy or vitality of city life. Luxury housing projects that mitigate their inanity, or try to, with a vapid vulgarity. Cultural centers that are unable to support a good bookstore. Civic centers that are avoided by everyone but bums, who have fewer choices of loitering place than others. Commercial centers that are lackluster imitations of standardized suburban chain-store shopping. Promenades that go from no place to nowhere and have no promenaders. Expressways that eviscerate great cities. This is not the rebuilding of cities. This is the sacking of cities.[5]

The body of this paragraph consists of intentional sentence fragments (p. 394, 18e), each of which takes its sense from the writer's opening words: *But look what we have built. . . .* An entirely different parallelism of structure brings the paragraph to its emphatic end: *This is not the rebuilding of cities. This is the sacking of cities.* The writer has risked annoying us with relentless hammer blows, but her shifting to a second variety of patterning prevents monotony.

EXERCISES

12. Choosing any topic, submit a paragraph which, like the "urban renewal" paragraph above, gains continuity from reuse of the same structure in sentences or intentional sentence fragments.

13. Beginning with the writer's handling of sentence structure, submit a discussion of the way she has given continuity to the following paragraph:

> We like to think that we are finely evolved creatures, in suit-and-tie or pantyhose-and-chemise, who live many millennia and mental detours away from the cave, but that's not something our bodies are convinced of. We may have the luxury of being at the top of the food chain, but our adrenaline still rushes when we encounter real or imaginary predators. We even restage that primal fright by going to monster movies. We still stake out or mark out our territories, though sometimes now it is with the sound of radios. We still jockey for position and power. We still create works of art to enhance our senses and add even more sensations to the brimming world, so that we can utterly luxuriate in the spectacles of life. We still ache fiercely with love, lust, loyalty, and passion. And we still perceive the world, in all its gushing beauty and terror, right on our pulses. There is no other way. To begin to understand the gorgeous fever that is consciousness, we must try to understand the senses—how they evolved, how they can be extended, what their limits are, to which ones we have attached taboos, and what they can teach us about the ravishing world we have the privilege to inhabit.[6]

¶ con
9h

9h Link one paragraph to the previous one.

Just as linked sentences help to establish the internal continuity of a paragraph, so linked paragraphs help to establish the continuity of a whole essay or paper. Of course your paragraphs must actually *be* logically connected, not just appear so. But once again you can bring out the connections through conjunctions like *but* or *yet* and through sentence adverbs and transitional phrases like *thus*, *however*, *in fact*, and *on the contrary*. And the linkage is surest of all in a paragraph whose first sentence refers directly to a point made in the previous sentence: *These problems, however, . . . ; Nevertheless, that argument can be answered;* and so forth.

Note, for instance, how, in the sample essay about lotteries on pages 147–49, each paragraph "answers" the one before it:

> A stranger from a non-lottery state, turning on a motel TV and seeing **those** upbeat commercials, . . .
>
> I admit, **however**, that **I have been presenting** only one side of a complex issue.
>
> **Even so**, there is a fundamental difference. . . .

Enumeration

One rather formal but occasionally helpful way of linking paragraphs is to enumerate points that have been forecast at the end of the earlier paragraph. If you assert, for example, that there are three reasons for favoring a certain proposal or four factors that must be borne in mind, you can begin the paragraphs that follow with *First, . . . , Second, . . . ,* and so on.

Conciseness in Making Transitions

Try not to devote a substantial paragraph to explaining how much of your outline has been covered so far:

> DON'T:
>
> x We have now seen that the question of human rights posed at the beginning of this essay cannot be easily answered, and that, specifically, two serious considerations stand in our way. The first of those considerations has now been dealt with, though not perhaps as fully as some readers might prefer. It is time now to go on to the second point, after which we can return to our original question with a better sense of our true options.

Such a paragraph merely tells your reader that you are having trouble making things fit together smoothly.

From time to time, however, you may want to devote a *brief* paragraph to announcing a major shift of direction. Do so with a minimum of distraction from the sequence of ideas.

DO:

- But how can such violations of human rights be swept under the rug? Unfortunately, as we will see, the method is simple and practically foolproof.

With a Word Processor: If you have an editing program that can highlight the first and last sentences of every paragraph, make use of it. (If you don't, you can still "select" those sentences and make a document out of them.) Check to see that the connections between last and next (paragraph-opening) sentences are clear, and revise if necessary to make effective use of these naturally strong positions.

EXERCISE

14. Look through a completed essay, either for your present course or for another, and check the relation between the last sentence of each paragraph and the first sentence of the next one. Did you always make that relation apparent with your language? Revise where necessary. When you are satisfied that all your sets of last-and-first sentences make for easy and logical transitions, copy those sentences, numbering each set of two, and hand them in.

9i Link several related paragraphs in a block.

A relatively long essay typically develops in groups of paragraphs that address major points. Within each of these **paragraph blocks**, one paragraph will usually state the dominant idea and the others will develop it. A writer working, for example, from the "rent control" outline on pages 87–88 might decide to introduce Part III, the heart of the argument, with a "thesis" paragraph marking a major shift in emphasis:

> Such is the promise that advocates of rent control offer to students who are weary of expensive housing and long trips to campus. If the promise could be even partially realized, it might be worth giving rent control another try. Unfortunately, there is no reason to think that another experiment would work better than all previous ones. However bad the present housing crisis is, you can be sure that rent control would make it worse.

Then four paragraphs, covering points A through D in the outline, would follow, making a single paragraph block about the disappointing results of rent control.

EXERCISE

15. Think of a point you would like to make about any topic. Write out that point in one sentence, and then ask yourself how you could best support it. Write at least two sentences that would help establish your main idea. You need not submit any of these sentences. Using them as a starting point, however, do submit a three-paragraph block in which the first paragraph *states* your idea and the other two *support* it.

NOTES

[1] Adapted from Carl W. Buchheister and Frank Graham, Jr., "From the Swamps and Back: A Concise and Candid History of the Audubon Movement," *Audubon* Jan. 1973: 7.

[2] Louis Menand, "Life in the Stone Age," *New Republic* 7 & 14 Jan. 1990: 41.

[3] Edith Iglauer, "The Strangers Next Door," *Atlantic* July 1973: 90.

[4] Frances Fitzgerald, *America Revised: History Schoolbooks in the Twentieth Century* (Boston: Little, 1979) 10–11.

[5] Jane Jacobs, *The Death and Life of Great American Cities* (New York: Vintage, 1961) 4.

[6] Diane Ackerman, *A Natural History of the Senses* (New York: Random, 1990) xviii–xix.

10

Paragraph Development

Most of the advice you may have seen about constructing paragraphs deals with just one kind of development, which we will call *direct* (10a). Direct paragraphs are indeed the most common type. Capable writers, however, also feel at home with other ways of putting a paragraph together. For simplicity's sake we will recognize three patterns—the *direct*, the *pivoting*, and the *suspended* paragraph. They illustrate classic ways of combining the types of sentences most frequently found in paragraphs:

1. a **main sentence**, which carries the paragraph's leading idea;
2. a **limiting sentence**, which "goes against" the leading idea by raising a negative consideration either before or after that idea has been stated; and
3. a **supporting sentence**, which backs or illustrates the leading idea.

10a Master the direct pattern.

In a **direct paragraph**, the most usual pattern, you place the main sentence at or near the beginning, before you have mentioned any limiting (negative or qualifying) considerations. The second "Hollywood" paragraph (p. 239), the "Ottawa" paragraph (p. 244), the "urban planning" paragraph (p. 247), and this present paragraph all exhibit the direct pattern.

The following example is typical:

> **There is a paradox about the South Seas that every visitor immediately discovers.** Tropical shores symbolize man's harmony with a kind and bountiful nature. Natives escape the common vexations of modern life by simply relaxing. They reach into palms for coconuts, into the sea for fish, and into calabashes for poi. But when the tranquilized tourist reaches Hawaii, the paradise of the Pacific, he finds the most expensive resort in the world and a tourist industry that will relieve him of his traveler's checks with a speed and ease that would bring a smile to the lips of King Kamehameha.[1]

Here the main sentence (boldfaced) announces a *paradox*—that is, a seeming contradiction—and the rest of the paragraph consists of supporting or explanatory sentences that develop the two halves of that paradox, harmonious nature and commercial exploitation. The result is extreme clarity: the structure of the paragraph fulfills the promise given in the main sentence, and the reader feels guided by that structure at each moment.

Again, look at the way the opening sentences of the following two paragraphs control everything that follows:

> **Custer's life demonstrates the power of a person having fun.** Why, for example, were his superiors never able to restrain him successfully, or to keep this repeat offender away from important command? Maybe because they secretly looked up to him; maybe because a career of cavalry charges and danger and glory was something they had dreamed about as boys; maybe because he more closely resembled the soldier they had dreamed of being than they now did. Or maybe they simply loved him—Custer was good at being loved. The congressman who appointed him to West Point remembered him as "beautiful as Absalom with his yellow curls." Several now-forgotten Army officers did a better job fighting Indians on the plains, but Custer's fame is the victory of fun and myth over complicated history. Pursuing his boy's dream of a life on the Great Plains, a land which was itself a dream in many people's minds, Custer finally ran into the largest off-reservation gathering of Indians ever in one place on the continent, and gave them what was possibly the last really good time they ever had.[2]

There is a window on our disorder in the movie *Wall Street*. It comes in a scene in which Charlie Sheen, the poor boy who made good as the protegé of Michael Douglas, and Daryl Hannah, the woman who is determined never to be a loser, engage in an orgy of acquisition to decorate his newly purchased Manhattan apartment. They fill it with extravagantly expensive modern art, furnishings, and the most up-to-date culinary gadgets. The only thing they lack is the time to enjoy the things they've worked so hard to acquire. They have a life-style but no life.[3]

Note that a direct paragraph, just like an essay whose thesis is stated near the outset, can comfortably include *limiting* considerations—those that "go against" the leading idea. In the following student paragraph, for example, the writer can afford to offer a "con" remark, which is placed strategically between the main sentence and two final sentences of support for that statement:

main sentence	The "greenhouse effect," whereby the temperature of the atmosphere rises with the increased burning of hydrocarbons, may have devastating consequences for our planet within one or two decades.
limiting sentence	Similar scares, it is true, have come and gone without leaving any lasting mark.
supporting sentences	Yet there is an important difference this time. We know a good deal more about the greenhouse effect and its likely results than we knew, say, about invasions from outer space or mutations from atomic bomb tests. The greenhouse effect is already under way, and there are very slender grounds for thinking it will be reversed or even slowed without a more sudden cataclysm such as all-out nuclear war.

Direct paragraphs, then, can follow two models, one including and one omitting limiting sentences:

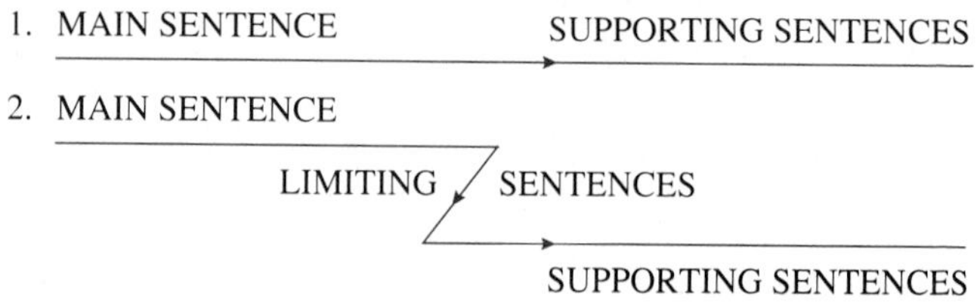

Main Sentence Delayed

The main sentence in a direct paragraph need not be the first one; it must simply precede any limiting sentences. Note, for example, how the following student paragraph puts the main sentence second, after an introductory sentence that prepares for a shift of emphasis:

introductory sentence	But the statistics do not tell the whole story.
main sentence	If we set aside the government reports and take the trouble to interview farm workers one by one, we find an astounding degree of confidence in the future.
supporting sentences	The workers are already thinking a generation ahead. Even if they have little expectation of improving their own lives, most of them are convinced that their children will begin to participate meaningfully in the American dream.

EXERCISE

1. Submit a direct paragraph on any topic. Your paragraph should consist of an opening main sentence followed by two or three sentences of support. Below it, provide a version of the same paragraph that includes (a) an introductory sentence preceding the main sentence, and (b) one or two limiting sentences. You need not make changes in the other sentences, but do make sure that your new version is still a direct paragraph and that it "gives its leading idea the last word" (p. 239, 9c).

¶ dev
10b

10b Master the pivoting pattern.

A **pivoting paragraph** not only delays the main sentence but begins by "going against it" with one or more limiting sentences. Characteristically, the pivoting paragraph then turns sharply ("pivots") toward the main sentence, usually announcing that shift of emphasis with a conspicuous signal word such as *but*, *yet*, or *however*. The leading idea, once announced, then dominates the rest of the paragraph. The opening paragraph of this chapter (p. 252) typifies the pattern. Its third sentence, containing the pivoting word *however*, reverses the paragraph's direction while stating the leading idea, which is then illustrated in the remaining sentences.

Notice how the following student paragraph pivots neatly on the word *But* and then develops its leading idea:

limiting sentence When we think of Gandhi fasting, plastering mud poultices on his belly, and testing his vow of continence by sharing a bed with his grand-niece, we can easily regard him as a **pivot to the main sentence** fanatic who happened to be politically lucky. **But** the links between his private fads and his political methods turn out to be quite logical. **supporting sentences** Gandhi's pursuit of personal rigors helped him to achieve a rare degree of discipline, and that discipline allowed him to approach political crises with extraordinary courage. The example of his self-control, furthermore, was contagious; it is doubtful that a more worldly man could have led millions of his countrymen to adopt the tactic of nonviolent resistance.

Similarly, the classic pivoting signal *however* shows us that the third sentence of this next paragraph is making a reversal of emphasis:

¶ dev 10b

> Health experts always seem to be telling Americans what *not* to eat. Cholesterol, salt and sugar are but a few of the dietary no-no's that threaten to make dinnertime about as pleasurable as an hour of push-ups. In a report last week on the role of nutrition in cancer, **however**, a blue-ribbon committee of the National Academy of Sciences offered a carrot—as well as oranges, tomatoes and cantaloupes—along with the usual admonitory stick. While some foods appear to promote cancer and should be avoided, said the panel, other comestibles may actually help ward off the disease.[4]

The further you venture from the direct pattern, the more important it is to guide your reader with signal words such as *but* or *however*. You can also make your pivot, if you prefer, by means of a whole sentence such as *That is no longer the case*. You can even make your pivot in the very last sentence, as this writer does to give her opening paragraph a powerful sense of irony and drama:

> The Shining Path threw a square dance any mother could love. The hall was freshly painted, decorated with balloons filled with confetti and colored-paper snowflakes. As Javier and I walked in, young people were eating plates of chicken and rice or square dancing in Andean folk style as men in ponchos played guitars and flutes. We had picked our

way through the rubble in the unlit streets outside, filled with broken glass and fermenting garbage; few places are as menacing as a Lima barrio at night. But inside was all light and laughter, good clean fun—**except that the band's lyrics were a hymn to the People's War, and among the young dancers were people who attached bombs to dogs and slit policemen's throats.**[5]

A scheme of the pivoting paragraph would look like this:

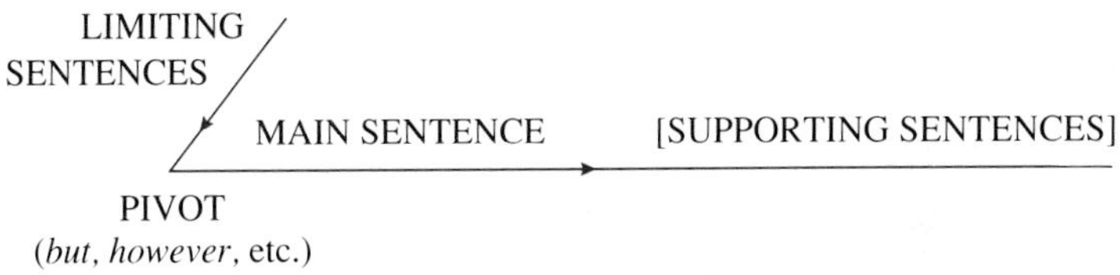

The brackets around "Supporting Sentences" indicate that a pivoting paragraph can end with its main sentence. More commonly, though, the main sentence is supported by one or more following sentences. In pivoting paragraphs already used as sample passages, for instance, the main sentence of the first "dioxin" paragraph (p. 237) comes at the end, whereas the main sentence of the second "marathon training" paragraph (p. 246) is followed by support. So are the main sentences of the "Gandhi" and "nutrition" paragraphs just examined.

For an extension of the pivoting principle to whole paragraphs that oppose the emphasis of the paragraph before, see page 272, 11e.

EXERCISES

2. Reusing as many sentences as you please from Exercise 1 (p. 255), submit a pivoting paragraph that proposes the same leading idea. Use a pivoting word or phrase to indicate where your paragraph is turning toward the leading idea, and underline the expression.

3. Think of resemblances and differences between two of your recent teachers. Then write a pivoting paragraph of about six sentences comparing and contrasting those teachers.

10c Master the suspended pattern.

Once you have a feeling for the direct and pivoting patterns, you can turn to the more taxing **suspended paragraph**—that is, a paragraph building to a climax or conclusion by some means other than a sharp reversal of direction. In a suspended paragraph the main sentence always comes at or near the end. Instead of taking a sharp turn, like the pivoting paragraph, it moves from discussion or exemplification to leading idea, maintaining the reader's sentence-by-sentence interest until it arrives at a statement that brings things together at last:

DISCUSSION → MAIN SENTENCE

Here are two examples:

discussion / main sentence

On the morning of August 7, 1987, a battery of emergency X-rays was run in the diagnostic unit of Executive Health Examiners in Manhattan. Five men nervously waited outside the twenty-first-floor radiology room while technicians inside went through their paces. When the film was processed, the pictures were snapped onto a light box for study. The X-rays were negative. Everyone breathed a collective sigh of relief. **New York Mets third baseman Howard Johnson's bat was indeed a solid piece of wood.**[6]

discussion / main sentence

Shortly after dawn, at the Saint-Antoine produce market in the ancient French city of Lyons, a white pickup truck screeches around a corner, double-parks impatiently and disgorges a rugged man wearing a rumpled windbreaker. As if by prearranged signal, prize raspberries, dewy spinach and pristine baby carrots suddenly emerge from hiding places below the trestle tables where they've been saved for inspection by this very special customer. "*Viens ici, Paul,*" shouts a fruit vendor. "I've got some melons you won't believe." Slicing a sample in half, the man in the windbreaker rejects the melons and some string beans as well ("too fat"). But thirty-five minutes later, he has sniffed, nibbled, pinched, prodded, and fondled his way through the choicest fruits and vegetables, loaded fifteen crates of produce into his van and hummed off toward his next quarry: plump chickens from Bresse, Charolais beef and fresh red mullet. **Paul Bocuse, the most visible, the most influential—and possibly the best—chef in the world, has begun another working day.**[7]

Looking back on the "discussion" sentences in these paragraphs, we could regard them as providing support for the leading idea. But we cannot perceive a sentence as "supporting" if we have not yet been told what it supports. By withholding that information until the end, the suspended paragraph establishes itself as the most dramatic pattern as well as the hardest to manage.

Once you feel at ease with the suspended paragraph, you will find it especially useful as a means of introducing or concluding an essay (Chapter 11). An opening paragraph that ends with its main sentence—a sentence revealing either your topic or your thesis—can gradually awaken the reader's interest and eagerness to move ahead. And a suspended final paragraph allows you to finish your essay with a "punch line"—an excellent tactic if you have saved a strong point for the end.

EXERCISES

4. Write a two- or three-paragraph analysis of the following paragraph, showing what effects the writer has gained from use of a suspended pattern:

> Knowing that it is possible to see too much, most doormen in New York have developed an extraordinary sense of selective vision: they know what to see and what to ignore, when to be curious and when to be indolent; they are most often standing indoors, unaware, when there are accidents or arguments in front of their buildings; and they are usually in the street seeking taxicabs when burglars are escaping through the lobby. Although a doorman may disapprove of bribery and adultery, his back is invariably turned when the superintendent is handing money to the fire inspector or when a tenant whose wife is away escorts a young woman into the elevator—which is not to accuse the doorman of hypocrisy or cowardice but merely to suggest that his instinct for uninvolvement is very strong, and to speculate that doormen have perhaps learned through experience that nothing is to be gained by serving as a material witness to life's unseemly sights or to the madness of the city. This being so, it was not surprising that on the night when the Mafia chief, Joseph Bonanno, was grabbed by two gunmen in front of a luxury apartment house on Park Avenue near Thirty-sixth Street, shortly after midnight on a rainy Tuesday in October, the doorman was standing in the lobby talking to the elevator man and saw nothing.[8]

5. Think of someone you know or would like to know. Then write a suspended paragraph which, like the "Paul Bocuse" example on page 258, reveals that person's identity at the end. In the preceding sentences, take your reader through an action or sequence of actions that is

characteristic of that person. Make your account as vivid as you can (p. 9, 1a).

10d Keep to a manageable paragraph length.

There is no single "right" size for all paragraphs. In newspaper reporting, where the purpose is to communicate information with a minimum of analysis, paragraphs consist of one, two, or three sentences at the most. Paragraphs of dialogue also tend to be short; most writers indent for every change of speaker. So, too, scientific and technical journals favor relatively brief paragraphs that present facts and figures with little rhetorical development. And essayists vary considerably among themselves, both in their preference for short or long typical paragraphs and in the paragraph sizes they use within a given essay.

Even so, it is possible to tell at a glance whether your essay paragraphs fall within an acceptable range. If you hardly ever write paragraphs of more than three brief sentences, you are erring on the side of choppiness. Readers will suspect that you have no great interest in exploring your ideas. And if your typical paragraph occupies nearly all of a typewritten, double-spaced page, you are being long-winded, making your reader work too hard to retain the connection between one leading idea and the next. The goal is to show careful sentence-by-sentence thought within a paragraph without allowing the main idea to lose its prominence.

Avoiding the Choppy Paragraph

If you have a tendency to write brief, stark paragraphs in which the main sentence is accompanied by just one or two other short sentences, reread one of your main sentences and ask yourself what else a reader might want to know about its implications. Do any of its terms need explaining? Where does it lead? What questions or objections does it call to mind? The new statements thus generated can become supporting or limiting sentences (p. 245) that will flesh out the skeleton of your draft paragraph.

Suppose, for example, your draft paragraph looks like this.

CHOPPY DRAFT PARAGRAPH:

x Acid rain has been destroying the forests of Canada. Although it blows northward from the United States, no one is sure that American factories are the only guilty ones. The damage is extensive, and it may take a court case to find out who is liable.

To gather material for a more developed paragraph, ask yourself what else your reader might profit from knowing:

—What questions might be asked about acid rain? What is it? Is the damage irreversible? Can it be prevented?

—What objections might be raised to the charge that American factories are responsible for destroying the forests of Canada? Are there other causes? Are American factory emissions mixed with those from Canada itself?

—Where does the issue of acid rain lead? For example, to questions of legal liability for "pollution at a distance."

Your revised, adequately developed paragraph might look like this:

ADEQUATELY DEVELOPED PARAGRAPH:

• American factories, we are told, have been discharging atmospheric wastes that drift northward and fall on Canada as acid rain, destroying valuable forests. We cannot yet tell for certain how extensive the damage is, whether it is irreversible, and whether the pollution could be effectively stopped at its source. Indeed, we cannot be sure that American factories are the only guilty ones. Yet there is little reason to doubt that those factories are the primary source of acid rain and that the damage being caused is very considerable. If so, a landmark case of liability for "pollution at a distance" would seem to be in the offing.

Exception: The Emphatic Brief Paragraph

If you establish a norm of paragraphs containing three or more sentences, you can make a powerful rhetorical effect through a rare paragraph consisting of only one sentence or even an intentional sentence fragment. In an essay about his alcoholic father, for example, one writer charged such a paragraph with emotional implication:

> Three years ago, my recovering alcoholic father called me into my mother's kitchen to apologize for all the pain he inflicted on me for so many years. "One of the things I've learned through Alcoholics Anonymous is that you have to admit that you've hurt people and have to let them know how sorry you are," he explained to me. "Son, I'm sorry for anything I may have done to harm you." He then shook my hand.
>
> **"*May* have done" was the part I liked.**[9]

Here a choked sarcasm, confined to just eight bitter words, conveys the writer's feeling that old wounds cannot be healed with a mere apology and handshake. The one-sentence paragraph is rendered even more effective by being sandwiched between more ample and reasoned paragraphs.

Avoiding the Bloated Paragraph

¶ dev
10d

If you see that your draft essay or paper contains a bloated paragraph—one that goes on and on without a strong sense of purpose—seek out its main sentence. If you cannot find it, decide what you want your leading idea to be. As soon as you are sure you have a leading idea, check to see that every sentence has some bearing on it. In some cases your long paragraph will split neatly into two new ones, but you should never indent for a fresh paragraph without verifying that both units are internally complete.

Many draft paragraphs begin purposefully but bloat as the writer gets absorbed in details.

BLOATED DRAFT PARAGRAPH:

limiting sentence	x 1. If a person feels guilty about something, the obvious thing to do is to get that guilt out in the open.
main sentence	2. But many people take a different approach, one that only makes matters worse: they try to stifle their bad feelings by means of depressants or stimulants such as alcohol, methedrine, or marijuana.
supporting sentences	3. A friend of mine felt guilty about getting low grades. 4. Her solution was to stay high nearly all the time. 5. But of course that made her get even lower grades and it thus redoubled her guilt, so she had even more bad feelings to hide in smoke. 6. I tried to talk to her about her problems, but she was already too depressed to allow

supporting sentences: anyone to get through to her. 7. Finally, she left school. 8. I lost touch with her, and I never did learn whether she straightened herself out. 9. I think that people like her deserve a lot of pity, because if she hadn't been so sensitive in the first place, she wouldn't have had the guilt feelings that sent her into a tailspin. 10. People who just don't care are sometimes better off.

This begins as a competent pivoting paragraph (p. 255, 10b) contrasting two approaches to the problem of handling guilty feelings and providing an example of the second, self-defeating, approach. The momentum, however, begins to drag as the writer shifts attention to herself in sentence 6, and the paragraph falls apart completely at sentence 9, which escapes the control of the main sentence, number 2. Revising for economy and relevance, the writer decided to do without the sentences about herself and her compassionate attitude.

ADEQUATELY FOCUSED PARAGRAPH:

limiting sentence: • If a person feels guilty about something, the obvious thing to do is to get that guilt out in the open.

main sentence: But many people take a different approach—one that only makes matters worse.

supporting sentences: They try to stifle their bad feelings with stimulants or depressants such as alcohol, methedrine, or marijuana. A friend of mine, for example, feeling guilty about her low grades, tried to stay high nearly all the time. The result was that she got even worse grades, felt guiltier still, smoked even more dope, and eventually dropped out of school. Her supposed remedy had become a major part of her problem.

EXERCISES

6. Write out a main sentence for a paragraph on any topic you have not treated in a previous exercise. Beneath that sentence, write out answers to the three questions that can usually lead to a remedy for choppy paragraph structure: (a) Where does the main sentence lead? (b) What questions might be asked about the terms it contains? (c) What objections might be raised? Then, using some of the material you have developed, write an adequately full paragraph about your leading idea, using either a direct, a pivoting, or a suspended pattern.

7. Look through the readings assigned for this course, or any other prose you may have handy, until you find a paragraph that, in your opinion, goes on too long to be readily grasped by a reader. Rewrite the paragraph to make it more compact and comprehensible, and submit your version with the original—or with a page reference if you found the original in an assigned text. Be sure that the material you omit is not essential support for the main sentence.

NOTES

[1] Timothy E. Head, *Going Native in Hawaii: A Poor Man's Guide to Paradise* (Rutland, Vt.: Tuttle, 1965) 7.

[2] Ian Frazier, *Great Plains* (New York: Farrar, 1989) 179–80.

[3] Suzanne Gordon, "A National Care Agenda," *Atlantic* Jan. 1991: 65.

[4] Matt Clark and Mary Hager, "A Green Pepper a Day," *Newsweek* 28 June 1982: 83.

[5] Tina Rosenberg, "Guerrilla Tourism," *New Republic* 18 June 1990: 23.

[6] Dan Gutman, "The Physics of Foul Play," *Discover* Apr. 1988: 71.

[7] "Food: The New Wave," *Newsweek* 11 Aug. 1975: 50.

[8] Gay Talese, *Honor Thy Father* (1971; Greenwich, Ct.: Fawcett, 1972) 16.

[9] Joseph M. Queenan, "Too Late to Say, 'I'm Sorry,' " *Newsweek* 31 Aug. 1987: 7.

11

Opening and Closing Paragraphs

OPENING PARAGRAPHS

A good introductory paragraph customarily accomplishes three things. It catches your reader's interest; it establishes the voice and stance of your essay or paper (pp. 76–83, 3m–o); and—usually but not always—it reveals the one central matter you are going to address. Only rarely does a shrewd writer begin by blurting out the thesis and immediately defending it. The standard function of an introduction is to *move toward* disclosure of the thesis in a way that makes your reader want to come along. We begin with possible strategies for achieving that effect.

But if your mind goes blank when you try to write the opening paragraph, delay the opener until you have drafted subsequent paragraphs. Some writers routinely compose in that order, and nearly all writers return to adjust and polish their opening to suit the rest of the essay.

11a Establish a context for your topic or thesis.

Perhaps the most usual function of an opening paragraph is to put the topic or thesis into a setting of some kind. Typically, the writer begins by sketching that context and then introduces the topic or thesis as an instance of the wider principle or subject area. In a brief essay, you will want to accomplish all this work within the first paragraph, as in the following example:

> Remember when Europe was just Europe? When it meant a trans-Atlantic crossing, a weekend in London to see the changing of the guard and the Harrods food halls, then to Paris for the clothes and the perfumes, Vienna for the opera and the Sacher torte, Rome for the Pope, and then back with a load of booty and a vague feeling of having seen the land of your (or probably someone else's) ancestors? Simple days, long gone. If you want to know Europe—*really* know Europe—it's not so easy anymore. Now it's no longer just a holiday destination. Europe is a *community*.[1]

In an ampler essay, you can consider devoting the entire first paragraph to establishing a context. In this passage, the topic is revealed only at the outset of the second paragraph:

> There are a few rare and troubled souls in this world who find ordinary living nearly impossible. They keep bumping into the edges of life, they keep barking their shins on obstacles that others do not even notice, they give the appearance of struggling through water when the rest of us are striding through the air. They are anguished by what the rest of us accept as the facts of life, and unreconciled to cruelties that the rest of us have shrugged off as the normal lot of the world. Most of us take social life as the only existence there can be, but these souls pine for something better. Our attitude toward such people is always a mixture of admiration for their insight, pity for their suffering, and (it must be admitted) some contempt for the mess they usually make of their lives.
>
> **Simone Weil was one of these rare people.** In her lifetime, she evoked all of these emotions. . . .[2]

Or again:

> At different times in our history, different cities have been the focal point of a radiating American spirit. In the late eighteenth century, for example, Boston was the center of a political radicalism that ignited a shot heard round the world—a shot that could not have been fired any other place but the suburbs of Boston. At its report, all Americans, including Virginians, became Bostonians at heart. In the mid-nineteenth century, New York became the symbol of the idea of a melting-pot America—or at least a non-English one—as the wretched refuse from all over the world disembarked at Ellis Island and spread over the land their strange languages and even stranger ways. In the early twentieth

century, Chicago, the city of big shoulders and heavy winds, came to symbolize the industrial energy and dynamism of America. If there is a statue of a hog butcher somewhere in Chicago, then it stands as a reminder of the time when America was railroads, cattle, steel mills, and entrepreneurial adventures. If there is no such statue, there ought to be, just as there is a statue of a Minute Man to recall the Age of Boston, as the Statue of Liberty recalls the Age of New York.

Today, we must look to the city of Las Vegas, Nevada, as a metaphor of our national character and aspiration, its symbol a thirty-foot-high cardboard picture of a slot machine and a chorus girl. . . .[3]

The Funnel Opener

One way of establishing a context is to begin on a general level and then narrow your focus to the topic. The middle passage on page 266 illustrates such a **funnel opener**; we are asked to contemplate a type of person and then introduced to an example of that type, Simone Weil. For another instance of this strategy, turn back to page 38, 2c, and study the paragraph about movies and dictators; the topic of the writer's essay, Fidel Castro, appears only at the end.

More rarely, the opening paragraph or paragraphs will take us through more than one stage of progressive narrowing:

> Only a few politicians have taken a craftsman's pride in self-expression, and fewer still—Caesar, Lord Clarendon, Winston Churchill, De Gaulle—have been equally successful in politics and authorship. Of these, Churchill may be the most interesting, for he was not only among the most voluminous of writers, but also commented freely on the art of writing. He was, in fact, a writer before becoming a politician.[4]

By the end of this paragraph we know that the topic will be Churchill's writing, but we arrive at that knowledge by sliding down the funnel:

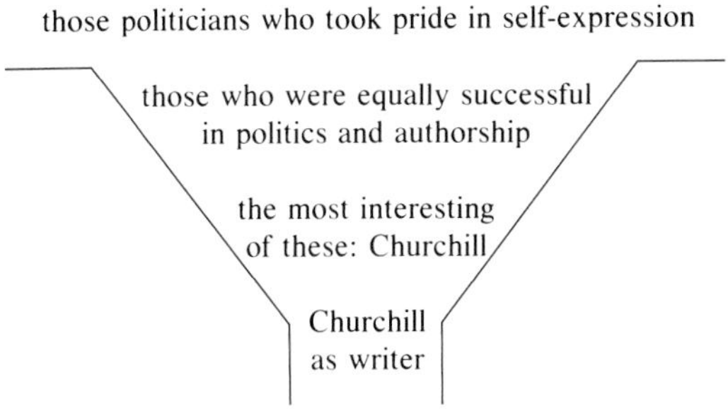

EXERCISES

1. Choose someone you know personally or through the media, and write an opening to an essay about that person, using the same technique of generalizing that you see in the passage introducing Simone Weil (p. 266). In other words, characterize the person's *type* and then present the person him- or herself. You can accomplish this within one paragraph or, as in the Weil example, complete the task at the start of a second paragraph.

2. Suppose you have been asked to write an essay about any topic of your choice. Pick a topic that you know quite well, and take notes on the way that topic relates to larger ones. (For example, if the topic is a meltdown of a nuclear reactor, think of such an event as one particular kind of disaster among all the possible other ones.) Using your sense of these broader relations, write and submit a funnel opener for your essay, beginning on the broadest level and narrowing to your actual topic. Give your reader a sense of what is special and important about your topic.

11b Pose a question and address it.

If you find that your draft opener sounds vague, windy, and spiritless, try revising to begin with a blunt question—not any question, but one that leads directly or indirectly to your thesis. Jolted to attention, your reader will realize at once that you have been thinking analytically about the topic and have something definite to say:

> **How can good science be distinguished from bad?** Philosophers of science call this the "demarcation problem." Like most problems about distinguishing parts of spectra, sharp definitions are impossible, but from hazy borders it doesn't follow that distinctions between extremes are useless. Twilight doesn't invalidate the contrast between day and night. The fact that top scientists disagree about many things doesn't mean that terms like pseudoscience, crank, and charlatan have no place in the history of science.[5]

It is not necessary, of course, to pose your question in the very first sentence. In the following paragraph, the writer *ends* with three questions that set up the subsequent discussion:

> As German reunification proceeds on its apparently inevitable course, and Chancellor Kohl scrambles with almost indecent haste to write his name into the history books as the second Bismarck, images spring to mind of that previous unification, over a century and a quarter ago, and the consequences it brought to Europe and the world in the following decades. **After Charlemagne's First Reich, Bismarck's Second, and Hitler's Third, are we now in for a Fourth Reich of equally imposing dimensions and equally uncertain duration? Does the new and seemingly unstoppable drive to reunify Germany in our own day mark the resumption of a submerged but ultimately ineradicable tradition of German national feeling and identity? Or does it merely register a stampede by the East Germans, their consumerist appetites whetted by years of watching West German television advertisements?**[6]

EXERCISE

3. Think of a topic that needs explaining or an issue on which you can take a position. Using one or more paragraphs, write an introduction to an essay that uses a question (or more than one question) to pose the problem. You can pose the question first, as in the "good science" paragraph, or lead up to it, as in the "German reunification" paragraph.

11c Try a baited opener.

A **baited opener** is an introductory passage of one or more paragraphs that not only saves its main idea for last (p. 258, 10c) but also teases the reader by withholding a clear sense of the essay's topic. We are drawn ahead in the hope of getting our bearings:

> At the funeral, the priest read from Ecclesiastes: "One generation cometh and another passeth away, but the land abideth forever." He stopped short of the words, "The sun also rises." Three men sat in the front pew, listening. Each had come into this old Idaho valley on a light plane, fixing on his own mortality. Afterward these three sons, who now had children of their own, received the news that their father had disinherited them.
>
> The stone the family picked was flat to the ground and wide, as if to accommodate the special bulk beneath it. You can see this stone, between two thirty-foot-high pines, in the town cemetery just north of Ketchum, and there is also a rough-made white wooden cross at the

> head of its smooth gray marble. There is only the name, "Ernest Miller Hemingway," and his dates, 1899–1961, cut carefully in.
>
> Fathers and sons. It is a conflict that haunts literature—but life far more. And what is it like when your father is a kind of totem for the twentieth century, an icon for maleness and grace under pressure, when he owns a terrifying unconscious and, not least, is gnawed on as you grow up, secretly and not so secretly, in ever larger bites, by fame and his own demons, until that Sunday morning in July when he blows away his entire cranial vault with a double-barreled twelve-gauge Boss shotgun he had once shot pigeons with?[7]

Readers who know their Hemingway can already guess whose funeral is being described in the first of these paragraphs. Only in the third paragraph, however, does the writer remove all doubt as to his topic: not Hemingway but his surviving, troubled sons.

Again, notice how firmly "hooked" we are by the following two-paragraph opening of a brief essay:

> Natasha Crowe, a close acquaintance of mine, recently received an unsolicited invitation from Joanne Black, senior vice president of the American Express Co.'s Card Division. "Quite frankly," the letter began, "the American Express Card is not for everyone. And not everyone who applies for Card membership is approved." Tasha (as she is affectionately called) ignored the letter. A few weeks later she received a follow-up offer from a different vice president, Scott P. Marks Jr. "Quite frankly," Mr. Marks reminded her, "not everyone is invited to apply for the American Express Card. And rarer still are those who receive a personal invitation the second time."
>
> Despite the honor, Tasha has continued to disregard this and similar invitations she has lately been receiving. For one thing, she has no job. Her savings are minimal. Her credit history is essentially a vacuum and therefore her credit rating, I'd imagine, is lousy. She doesn't even speak English. She's my cat, and I love her.[8]

For further examples of the baited opener, see pages 273–74, 11f.

EXERCISE

4. Choosing any topic, think of an unusual and surprising way of introducing it, and submit a baited opener of one or more paragraphs. If you go beyond a single paragraph, you can stop, with an ellipsis mark (. . .), as soon as you have revealed the topic.

11d Try speaking directly to your reader.

Perhaps the hardest thing about composing an opening paragraph is the sense that you do not really know your reader. One simple, effective remedy is to pretend that the reader is standing right before you, awaiting your instruction to think of a scene or issue. In effect, you *command* your reader to share your responses—as, for example, in this beginning to an essay about motorcycle touring:

> The road glides beneath you. The sky flows over you. The wind rushes past, bringing new sounds and smells. Uninsulated, you touch the world as you press through it unencumbered by a cage. Beneath you, the machine hums and throbs, almost alive. It blends with you, telling you of the road surface and responding to your every movement.[9]

Again, study this opening to an essay about dinosaurs who, it has been found, were able to survive winters near the North and South Poles. Since the very existence of dinosaur fossils in those localities is just now coming to light, the writer begins by demanding that we get over a misconception:

> Picture a dinosaur in your mind. Then take a look at the surrounding landscape. What do you see?
>
> The images that come to mind are probably reminiscent of horror movies with either "lagoon" or "swamp" in the title. Clouds of fog blanket the still surface of some tropical waterway. Overhead, some mushy growth, the consistency of cooked spinach, hangs off lush, drooping leaves.
>
> Snow just doesn't seem to fit into the picture.[10]

Observe that one or two very brief, pointed paragraphs, like the first and third ones here, can sometimes make for an energetic beginning.

EXERCISE

5. Choosing any topic, submit one or more paragraphs that address the reader directly as a way of introducing that topic.

11e Begin on an opposite tack.

The "dinosaur" example on page 271 illustrates a very common and useful way of getting started. Think about how your thesis significantly *differs from* some pattern, and begin with that pattern. Thus you are approaching your point by isolating its boundaries, showing its uniqueness:

> Back in the 1970s I thought I could make my 14-month-old baby safe from drowning: I signed him up for swimming instruction. Virginia Hunt Newman's book *Teaching an Infant to Swim* had appeared not long before, and infant "waterproofing" programs were springing up at YMCAs and aquatic organizations everywhere. It was all the rage, with photos in national magazines of tiny "waterbabies" bubbling and bobbing in backyard pools. I was swept along in the movement: we were saving the nation's toddlers from the perils in their own backyards.
>
> During that time, however, the statistics on childhood drowning accidents didn't decline; they went up. And now most swimming experts admit that this buoyant national experiment failed: swimming lessons in infancy do not make for waterproof toddlers. In fact, the popular waterproofing programs may actually have led to even more tragedies by giving youngsters and their parents a false sense of security.[11]

op ¶ 11e

This writer could have begun by declaring flatly that "waterproofing" doesn't work. Instead, she devotes her opening paragraph to the contrary possibility and then turns toward her thesis in the second paragraph. Her "opposite tack" opener provides historical background and a sense of dramatic reversal and control. Note that such a two-paragraph introduction serves the same purpose as a single **pivoting paragraph** (p. 255, 10b).

The same principle is illustrated by this introduction to an essay about an amazing tribe in New Guinea:

> The Gebusi, a society of around 450 persons living in a New Guinea rain forest, are a strikingly gentle lot. They revel in *kog-wa-yay*, roughly translated as "good company." Togetherness, casual talk, and exuberant humor are daily staples. There is no central political structure and no jockeying for power among the stronger men; matters of concern to Gebusi, who live in communal "longhouse" settlements, are decided by consensus. Food, including bananas grown in small gardens and the occasionally hunted wild pig, is routinely shared among all the residents of a settlement. Anger, violence, and warfare are frowned upon.
>
> **But behind this aura of serenity and conviviality lurks a brutal**

paradox: The Gebusi murder one another at a rate among the highest ever reported, about forty times greater than the 1980 homicide rate in the United States. . . .[12]

EXERCISE

6. Choosing any topic, submit one or more paragraphs that introduce that topic by beginning on an opposite tack.

11f Begin with a story.

op ¶ 11f

Look back to the "Hemingway" passage on pages 269–70. Would you find it possible to stop reading the writer's essay after those three paragraphs? Everyone loves a story, and one of the best ways to introduce an essay—even if your main purpose is not a narrative one—is to recount an intriguing incident. Here, for example, is the first paragraph of an essay-review about a seemingly undramatic topic, dictionaries and other books about language:

> In 1897 James Murray, the first editor of *The Oxford English Dictionary*, paid a courtesy visit to one of the most prolific of his "voluntary readers"—the army of retired curates, amateur philologists, widows, and other people with time on their hands who supplied the dictionary with the hundreds of thousands of quotations needed to illustrate the history of words. The reader was a Dr. W. C. Minor, who gave his address as Crowthorne in Berkshire. When Murray arrived, he was driven from the station to an imposing brick building that seemed too large to be a house. In fact, he discovered, it was not a house; it was the Broadmoor Criminal Lunatic Asylum. Dr. Minor was an inmate.[13]

The reader, needless to say, will eagerly plunge ahead to learn more. But like all thoughtful storytellers, this writer is not simply "baiting" us; he has a larger point to make. As he says in his next sentence, "The story has piquancy not only because it suggests the ad hoc conditions in which the world's most famous dictionary was produced, but because the enterprise itself had something of a lunatic quality."

Again:

> The steam from four outdoor lobster pots rose toward the blue sky and danced like happy ghosts in a balsam-scented breeze over Mount Desert

Island, Maine. It was a perfect Maine day. A lobster kind of day. And a line of station wagons and campers, sports cars and Jeeps, pulled into the Bar Harbor Snack Bar.

The crunch of gravel under tires, the distant surf, the lip-smacking clamor of lunch orders was punctuated by the splash of live lobsters being tossed into the vats of boiling sea water and by the thumping staccato of the lobsters flailing inside the pots.

"This is starting to gross me out," murmured Larraine Brown, a forty-year-old radio producer at WERU in nearby Blue Hill who had stopped by for lunch.

She might as well have screamed "Jaws!" The crowd of vacationers did double takes. The splash-thump swelled like a dirge. "I'm sorry," Ms. Brown said to the fourteen people around the pots. She had ordered a two-pounder, but the sound of her lunch cooking changed her appetite.

She is not alone.

The wellspring of humane sentiment tapped by recent anti-fur campaigns is trickling toward America's dinner tables. In grocery stores and restaurants and in national advertising campaigns, animal rights advocates—some concerned with the quality of animal life, others defending the sanctity of animal life—are confronting consumers.[14]

The last of these six paragraphs, stating the writer's topic in general terms, could have made an acceptable introduction by itself. By preceding it with a vivid story, however, the writer has involved her readers and made them begin thinking, uncomfortably, about their own feelings toward the boiling of live creatures.

EXERCISE

7. Choosing any topic, submit one or more paragraphs that introduce that topic by telling a story.

11g Avoid the deadly opener.

An experienced reader can usually tell after two or three sentences whether the writer commands the topic and will be able to make it engaging. Never reach for one of the following classic sleeping pills:

1. *The solemn platitude:*

    x Conservation is a very important topic now that everyone is so interested in ecology.

Ask yourself whether *you* would continue reading an essay that began with such a colorless sentence.

2. *The unneeded dictionary definition:*

x The poem I have been asked to analyze is about lying. What is lying? According to *Webster's Eighth New Collegiate Dictionary*, to lie is "1: to make an untrue statement with intent to deceive; 2: to create a false or misleading impression."

Ask yourself whether your reader is actually in the dark about the meaning of the word you are tempted to define. *Lie* obviously fails that test.

3. *Restatement of the assignment, usually with an unenthusiastic declaration of enthusiasm:*

x It is interesting to study editorials in order to see whether they contain "loaded" language.

If you are actually interested, you would do well to *show* interest by beginning with a thoughtful observation.

4. *The bald statement of the thesis:*

x In this essay I will prove that fast-food restaurants are taking the pleasure out of eating.

But you are also taking the pleasure out of reading. You want to *approach* your thesis, not to drop it on the reader's foot like a bowling ball that has slipped out of your grasp.

5. *The "little me" apology:*

x After just eighteen years on this earth, I doubt that I have acquired enough experience to say very much about the purpose of a college education.

Is this going to whet your reader's appetite for the points that follow?

EXERCISE

8. Look through the essays you have already written for this or any other course, and find a first paragraph that you would now regard as a "deadly opener." If you cannot find one, choose the weakest opening paragraph you have handy. Copy and submit it along with a revised version that leads engagingly toward your thesis. Briefly explain what was wrong with the first version and why the second is better.

11h Sharpen your opening sentence.

op ¶ 11h

If your first paragraph is the most important one, its first sentence is your most important sentence as well. When that sentence betrays boredom or confusion, you reduce your chances of gaining the reader's sympathy. If your first sentence is crisp and tight and energetic, its momentum can carry you through the next few sentences at least. This is why some people take pains to make that first sentence *epigrammatic*—pointed and memorable. Thus one writer begins a review of a book about Jewish immigrants by declaring:

> The first generation tries to retain as much as possible, the second to forget, the third to remember.[15]

Another wittily begins an essay on divorce:

> There was a time when a woman customarily had a baby after one year of marriage; now she has a book after one year of divorce.[16]

And a student writer advocating gun control begins:

> Thousands of people in this country could make an overwhelming case for the banning of handguns, except for one inconvenient fact: they aren't so much *in* the country as *under* it, abruptly sent to their graves with no chance to protest or dissuade. Arguing with a gun nut may be futile, but have you ever tried arguing with a gun?

EXERCISES

9. Looking through any handy materials—magazines, anthologies, newspapers, or essays by you or someone else—find an opening paragraph that

begins with a particularly effective sentence. Copy or photocopy the paragraph and submit it, along with a brief explanation of why you think the opener makes a strong impression.

10. Submit an introductory paragraph of your own that begins with a concisely worded sentence that is calculated to arouse interest. You can write on a new topic or adapt any paragraph you have used for other exercises.

CLOSING PARAGRAPHS

11i Save a clinching statement for your closing paragraph.

Remember that the final position within any structure—sentence, paragraph, or whole essay—is naturally emphatic. To take advantage of that fact, delay writing your conclusion until you have found material that bears reemphasizing or expanding. Look especially for a striking quotation or story that might drive your point home. Thus, for example, an essay about the revival of interest in roller coasters ends with this paragraph:

> For the legion of admirers who queue up to ride, however, getting terrified is what coasters are all about. "It's the ultimate daring adventure that pushes the edge of our own bravery," explains Randy Geisler, president of the American Coaster Enthusiasts, which has tripled its membership to 3,200 in five years. That sentiment was echoed by Greg Blum, 15, of Dallas as he bounded off the Texas Giant recently. **"That was almost too much to stomach," he cried. "Let me on again."**[17]

A striking image, whether figurative (p. 368, 17a) or drawn directly from observation, can also be an effective closer. Here, for instance, is how one writer ends an essay on the bustling entrepreneurial colony of Hong Kong, which is already experiencing the disintegrating effects of its scheduled incorporation into China:

> As I prepare my own departure, I often think of an image that captures the melancholy of this slowly breaking city. **It is a scene I saw on the television news, almost surreal in its violent intensity, the scene of a great**

bulldozer crushing a mountain of fake gold watches, all made in Hong Kong, until there was nothing left but dust.[18]

And even if you aren't introducing a new image or story, you should try—as this writer does in concluding an essay about the practicality of cattle worship in India—to end with an emphatic and memorable sentence:

> The higher standard of living enjoyed by the industrial nations is not the result of greater productive efficiency, but of an enormously expanded increase in the amount of energy available per person. In 1970 the United States used up the energy equivalent of twelve tons of coal per inhabitant, while the corresponding figure for India was one-fifth ton per inhabitant. The way this energy was expended involved far more energy being wasted per person in the United States than in India. Automobiles and airplanes are faster than oxcarts, but they do not use energy more efficiently. In fact, more calories go up in useless heat and smoke during a single day of traffic jams in the United States than is wasted by all the cows of India during an entire year. The comparison is even less favorable when we consider the fact that the stalled vehicles are burning up irreplaceable reserves of petroleum that it took the earth tens of millions of years to accumulate. **If you want to see a real sacred cow, go out and look at the family car.**[19]

EXERCISE

11. Among your own essays or, if necessary, someone else's, find a concluding paragraph that now strikes you as ending in a relatively flat, unemphatic way. Submit the paragraph along with a rewritten version that ends with a more striking, conclusive sentence.

11j Try recalling your opening paragraph in your closing one.

Look for ways of making your concluding paragraph show some evident, preferably dramatic, relation to your introductory one. If you already have a sound first paragraph and are groping for a last one, reread that opener and see whether it contains some hint that you can now develop more amply. Here, for instance, is the concluding paragraph of the essay (quoted on p. 256) that began by asking whether Mahatma Gandhi was nothing more than a fanatic:

> Gandhi's arguments reveal an underlying shrewdness. Far from betraying the dogmas of a fanatic, they are at once moral and cunningly practical. His genius, it seems, consisted in an unparalleled knack for doing right—and, what isn't quite the same, for doing the right thing. It is hard to come up with another figure in history who so brilliantly combined an instinct for politics with the marks of what we call, for lack of a better name, holiness.

Note how the writer has put his opening question into storage until it can be answered decisively, with a pleasing finality, in his closing lines.

EXERCISE

12. Photocopy and submit the first and last paragraphs of an essay that does *not* recall its opening paragraph in its closing one. (The essay can be your own or anyone else's.) Add an alternative final paragraph that does develop a hint or recall an image from that opening one.

11k Try looking beyond your thesis in a closing paragraph.

Just as you can lead to your thesis by beginning on a more general plane (pp. 265, 11a), so you can end by looking beyond that thesis, which has now been firmly established. Thus, in a paper defending the thesis that unilateral disarmament is a dangerous and unwise policy, a student writer concluded as follows:

> There is no reason to expect, then, that the world would be safer if we laid down our arms. On the contrary, we could do nothing more foolhardy. **We must look to other means of ensuring our security and that of the nations we have agreed to protect.**

The sentence we have emphasized "escapes" the thesis, posing a relevant goal for future investigation. But note that it does so without embarking on a new topic; it provokes thought by looking further in the direction already taken.

11l Avoid the deadly conclusion.

Readers want to feel, at the end of a piece of writing, that it has truly finished and not just stopped like some toy soldier that needs rewinding. Further, they like to anticipate the end through a revealing change in tone or intensity or generality of reference. If you end by sounding bored or distracted or untrustworthy or even hesitant, you are encouraging your reader to discount everything you have worked so hard to establish.

Though you may not always come up with a punchy conclusion, you can avoid certain lame devices that would threaten your good relations with your reader. Check your draft endings against the following cautions:

1. Do not merely repeat your thesis.
2. Though you can look beyond your thesis (11k), do not embark on a completely new topic.
3. Do not pretend to have proven more than you have.
4. Do not apologize or bring your thesis into doubt. If you find anything that requires an apology, fix it!

11m If your essay is brief, feel free to omit a formal conclusion.

A short essay may make its point thoroughly within five hundred words; your readers will be insulted or bored by a heavy-handed reminder of the points they have just finished reading. Sometimes a brief concluding paragraph—consisting of no more than one or two sentences—can effectively end a short essay. But you can also save one of your strong supporting points for the last paragraph, counting on an emphatic final sentence to give a feeling of completion.

EXERCISES

13. Photocopy and submit *any two* effective conclusions to articles or chapters that you can find in any source. For each conclusion, supply a

paragraph of analysis explaining why the conclusion succeeds as rhetoric. In each case, be specific about the writer's language and the relation between the conclusion and the rest of the piece.

14. Repeat the procedure of Exercise 8 (p. 276), this time using a *concluding* paragraph that strikes you as relatively ineffective. Use your revised paragraph to *expand upon*—not to repeat—the thesis of your essay, and try to make your language vivid and pointed.

NOTES

[1] Malcolm Bradbury, "All Aboard for the New Europe," *New York Times Magazine* 3 Feb. 1991: 22.

[2] Michael Ignatieff, "The Limits of Sainthood," *New Republic* 18 June 1990: 40.

[3] Neil Postman, *Amusing Ourselves to Death: Public Discourse in the Age of Show Business* (New York: Penguin, 1985) 3.

[4] Manfred Weidhorn, "Blood, Toil, Tears, and 8,000,000 Words: Churchill Writing," *Columbia Forum* Spring 1975: 19.

[5] Martin Gardner, "Bumps on the Head," *New York Review of Books* 17 March 1988: 8.

[6] Richard J. Evans, "Towards Unification," [London] *Times Literary Supplement* 4–10 May 1990: 463.

[7] Paul Hendrickson, "Papa's Boys," *Washington Post* 29 July 1987: D1.

[8] Steven J. Marcus, "How to Court a Cat," *Newsweek* 22 Mar. 1982: 13.

[9] Art Friedman, "Uninsulated, Unencumbered," *Forbes* 21 Mar. 1988: 178.

[10] Richard Monastersky, "Dinosaurs in the Dark," *Science News* 133 (1988): 184.

[11] Diane Divoky, "Waterproofing Your Baby: Too Good to Be True," *Hippocrates* May/June 1988: 28.

[12] Bruce Bower, "Murder in Good Company," *Science News* 133 (1988): 90.

[13] Louis Menand, "Talk Talk," *New Republic* 16 Feb. 1987: 28.

[14] Molly O'Neill, "Will Too Many Sentiments Spoil the Cook?" *New York Times* 8 Aug. 1990, national ed.: B1.

[15] Theodore Solotaroff, rev. of *World of Our Fathers*, by Irving Howe, *New York Times Book Review* 1 Feb. 1976: 1.

[16] Sonya O'Sullivan, "Single Life in a Double Bed," *Harper's* Nov. 1975: 45.

[17] Richard Woodbury, "Eeeeeyyooowiiii!!!!" *Time* 6 Aug. 1990: 62.

[18] Ian Buruma, "The Last Days of Hong Kong," *New York Review of Books* 12 April 1990: 46.

[19] Marvin Harris, *Cows, Pigs, Wars, and Witches: The Riddles of Culture* (New York: Vintage, 1974) 26–27.

V

SENTENCES

SENTENCES

Strong sentences have much in common with strong paragraphs and whole essays, including a clear idea, emphatic placement of that idea, and subordination of other elements. You can think of the fully developed sentence as a skeletal paragraph containing major and minor components that ought to be easy for a reader to spot:

	ESSAY		PARAGRAPH		SENTENCE
MAJOR	Thesis	=	Main Sentence	=	Independent Clause
MINOR	Supporting Paragraphs		Supporting Sentences		Free Elements

On each level—essay, paragraph, sentence—your chief purpose in redrafting should be to highlight the major element and to see that it is adequately backed by minor elements that are clearly subordinate to it.

The chapters in Part V assume that you can already recognize the parts of sentences—subjects and verbs, for example, or independent and subordinate clauses—and put together grammatically coherent statements of your own. If you feel uncertain about fundamentals of usage, you may want to begin by reviewing several chapters in Part VII. But since you have already succeeded in getting countless sentences onto paper, we start our discussion not with the blank page but with draft sentences that a student writer might want to improve. Our keynote will be revising to make your meaning easier to grasp and your sentences more fluent and varied.

12

Writing Distinct Sentences

12a Put your meaning into grammatically important words.

Writing proceeds not word by word but sentence by sentence—an obvious point, but one with crucial implications for your relation to your reader. That reader wants above all to grasp the point of each sentence, to take in your idea without difficulty. Even if the idea is a clear one, you must be sure to make it **distinct**—that is, readily comprehended on a first reading. While such a task sounds easy enough, in practice most draft sentences, even those written by very accomplished writers, are to some extent indistinct. Left unrevised, they would put their reader to extra trouble, thus sapping precious energy and attention.

When you think of revising a draft sentence, start by looking for its main idea—the point that *ought* to be conveyed by a clear, concise **independent clause** (p. 387, 18c). If, instead, you see that the point goes on and on or is trapped in a subordinate part of the sentence, you are ready to make your most essential improvement. Move your idea into an independent clause, making sure that the grammatically strongest parts of that clause convey important information.

The strongest parts of a clause are generally a *subject* and a *verb*, possibly linked to either a *direct object* or a *complement* (pp. 384–85, 18a):

- S V
The **committee exists.**
- S V
The **committee meets** on Tuesdays.
- S V D OBJ
The **committee is drafting** a **report.**
- S V COMPL
The **committee is** an official **body.**
- S V COMPL
The **committee seems prepared.**

Consider the "correct" but unimpressive sentence that follows:

S V
x The **departure** of the fleet **is thought** to be necessarily conditional on the weather.

Here the essential grammatical elements are a subject and verb, *The departure . . . is thought*. This is scanty information; we must root around elsewhere in the sentence to learn what is being said *about* the departure. The idea is that bad weather—here tucked into a prepositional phrase, *on the weather*—may delay the fleet's departure. Once we recognize that point, we can get *weather* into the subject position and replace the wishy-washy construction *is thought to be conditional on* with a verb that transmits action to an object.

DO:

- S V D OBJ
Bad weather may keep the **fleet** at anchor.

Notice that we now have three grammatically strong elements—a subject, a verb, and a direct object—that do carry significant meaning.

DON'T:

S V
x The **thing** the novelist seems to say **is** that the human race is lacking what is needed to keep from being deceived.

Notice how little information is conveyed by this subject and verb: *The thing is*. To find the writer's meaning, we must disentangle various embedded infinitives, subordinate clauses, and a prepositional phrase, each of which adds a little more strain to our memory.

DO:

S V
- **Human beings**, the novelist seems to say, necessarily **deceive**
D OBJ
themselves.

Now the subject and verb do convey information. The key grammatical elements, subject-verb-direct object, bear the chief burden of meaning: *Human beings deceive themselves*. And as a result of this realignment, the sentence core now takes up just a few words instead of twenty-two. Notice, too, how the commas make it easy for a reader to tell where the central statement is being interrupted.

Avoiding Clusters of Prepositional Phrases

clear sent 12a

Prepositions—*to, with, toward*, and so forth—are essential function words that combine with nouns and pronouns to form prepositional phrases such as *to the contrary, with gusto*, and *toward nightfall*. Though they are rarely emphatic, isolated prepositional phrases constitute no threat to efficient sentence structure. Closely bunched, however, they sometimes make for an annoyingly clogged, stop-and-start effect:

x A lot **of journalists of different points of view** were there.

x They learned a lesson **from her conclusions from the incident.**

Compare:

- Many journalists holding different points of view were there.
- Her conclusions from the incident taught them a lesson.

Consider, too, the following unrevised student sentences:

> When health science was **in its stages of development before the modern age**, the publicity received **in the press by this branch of science** was negligible. Accordingly, the public was unaware **of the significance of balanced nutrition for the maintenance of good health.**

These sentences contain no errors, but their clusters of (boldfaced) prepositional phrases try the reader's patience. Compare the student's revision:

> Many years ago, when health science was still largely undeveloped, the public heard little about this branch of science. Accordingly, the connection between balanced nutrition and good health remained generally unknown.

The improvement here is subtle, but if you learn to spot your own clusters of prepositional phrases and revise wherever they sound awkward, you will automatically be curing several of the other faults covered in this chapter.

EXERCISES

1. Type out (double-spaced) the following student paragraph, and submit it with letters above its grammatically essential elements to mark every subject (S), verb (V), direct object (DO), and complement (C):

    > Our society has always prided itself on having an impersonal, unemotional system of justice. Supposedly, we imprison criminals not to take revenge on them but to "rehabilitate" them under safe conditions. Prisons, however, do not rehabilitate; if anything, they are training schools for further crime. If, knowing this, we leave people in prisons anyway, we evidently do care about revenge. Perhaps the state as a collective body has no vengeful feelings, but its individual members demand punishment, not rehabilitation.

2. The passage used in Exercise 1 shows a good alignment of meaning and grammatically strong elements. To get a better feeling for the difference between distinct and indistinct expression, rewrite that passage to make it *less* distinct. Submit your deliberately weakened paragraph.

3. Go over your own papers or drafts written for this or any other course, looking for insufficiently distinct expressions that show a weak alignment of grammar and meaning. Revise five sentences to make them more distinct, and submit both the original sentences and the revisions.

12b Avoid an overstuffed sentence.

Check your drafts for formless sentences that do not distinguish primary from subordinate elements.

DON'T:

x It is what she recalled from childhood about the begonia gardens that were cultivated in Capitola that drew her to return to that part of the coastline one summer after another.

Since such a sentence demands that all of its elements be kept in mind until the point eventually becomes clear, the sentence often will require two readings. The solution, as we will see more fully below (13a–d), lies in shortening the core of the sentence and setting the minor elements apart.

DO:

- Summer after summer, drawn by her childhood recollections of the Capitola begonia gardens, she returned to that portion of the coastline.

> Note how, through the separating out of a key assertion, the sentence becomes more dramatic and easier to grasp. Its key element, instead of being thirty-one words jostling together in a mass, is a readily understood eight-word statement: *she returned to that portion of the coastline*.

Again:

DON'T:

x To think that an answer that would be satisfactory had taken so long to arrive was something that put him into a state of deep resentment.

DO:

- He deeply resented the long wait for a satisfactory answer.

Note that every overstuffed statement will also show a misalignment of meaning and grammatically strong sentence elements (p. 285, 12a).

EXERCISE

4. Look through any handy sources, including your own writing, until you have located five overstuffed statements. Watch especially for long strings of words with little or no punctuation, especially if they contain *what* or *that* clauses. (If your search fails, make up new overstuffed statements.) Submit the five examples along with adequately revised versions.

12c Be sparing with the verb *to be*.

You can make your prose more expressive by cutting down on the colorless, actionless verb *to be* (*is, are, were, had been*, etc.) and substituting action verbs.

"CORRECT" BUT ACTIONLESS:

x It **was** clear that the soprano **was** no longer in control of the high notes that **had been** a source of worry to her for years.

STRONGER:

• Clearly, the soprano **had lost** control of the high notes that **had been worrying** her for years.

clear sent 12c

The action-bearing verbs in the revised version trim away needless words—notably the plodding prepositional phrases *in control, of worry*, and *to her*—and convey the key activities of losing and worrying.

"CORRECT" BUT ACTIONLESS:

x One source of tension in Dickinson's poetry **is** the fact that her shyness **is** in conflict with a tendency **to be** stagey.

STRONGER:

• In Dickinson's poetry, tension **arises** when shyness **conflicts** with staginess.

You need not worry about eliminating every last instance of *to be*; that would be pointless and impossible. Forms of *to be* are often justified, as in this very sentence and the previous one. But you can combat weakness and woodenness in your drafts by circling each use of that verb and seeing where you could replace it with a more vivid expression.

With a Word Processor: Instruct your word processor to highlight every example of *to be* in your draft: *am, is, have been, would be,* and so forth. If you cover all forms in all tenses, you can be sure that you won't miss any relevant instances.

EXERCISE

5. Find or invent five sentences that would show more distinct expression if they avoided forms of *to be*. Submit those sentences along with adequately revised versions.

12d Convey action through a verb, not a noun.

As the examples in 12a–c show, a sentence with an indistinct main idea typically uses nouns instead of verbs to express action. That in itself is no crime, but you can do your prose a favor by habitually moving the action into verbs: Not *was no longer in control* but *had lost control*; not *is a source of worry to her* but *worries her*. You gain a little energy with each such shift. Notice the relative vitality of the "stronger" examples below:

"CORRECT" BUT COLORLESS:

x Some young single people are in a financial arrangement that enables them to have joint ownership of a house.

STRONGER:

• Some young single people have been pooling their resources and buying houses together.

"CORRECT" BUT COLORLESS:

x A single parent stands in need of occasional relief from the endless responsibilities of workplace and household.

STRONGER:
- Sometimes a single parent must get away from the endless responsibilities of workplace and household.

EXERCISE

6. Find or invent five sentences which would show more distinct expression if their action were conveyed through verbs rather than nouns. Submit those sentences along with adequately revised versions.

12e In most contexts, prefer the active voice.

In addition to choosing verbs that show action (12d), you can make your sentences more distinct by generally putting your verbs into the active rather than the passive voice: not *was done* but *did*, not *is carried* but *carries*. (For further illustration of the active and passive voices, see p. 574, 32b, and p. 580, 32d.)

Passive verbs typically saddle you with three problems. First, they make the sentence a little longer, risking an effect of wordiness. Second, since they can never take direct objects, their energy isn't conveyed to another element in the sentence. And third, they oblige the performer of the deed to go unnamed or to be named only in a postponed and grammatically minor element. All three features go to make up a wan and evasive effect.

DON'T:

x **It is believed** by the candidate that a ceiling **must be placed** on the budget by Congress.

DO:
- The candidate **believes** that Congress **must place** a ceiling on the budget.

DON'T:

x Their motives **were applauded** by us, but their wisdom **was doubted.**

DO:
- We **applauded** their motives but **doubted** their wisdom.

In scientific writing, which often stresses impersonal, repeatable procedures rather than the individuals who carried them out, passive verbs are common. You can also use them in essay prose whenever you want your emphasis to remain on the person or thing acted upon. Suppose, for example, you are narrating the aftermath of an accident. Both of the following sentences would be correct, but you might have good reason to prefer the second, passive one:

ACTIVE VERB:
- Then three hospital attendants and the ambulance driver **rushed** Leonard into the operating room.

PASSIVE VERB:
- Then Leonard **was rushed** into the operating room.

Although the second sentence is less vivid, it keeps the focus where you may want it to be, on the injured man.

Passive verbs, then, are not automatically "wrong." As you revise your prose, look at each passive form and ask yourself whether you have a good justification for keeping it.

EXERCISE

7. Study the passive verbs in each of the following sentences. Indicate with an "OK" which sentences use the passive voice justifiably, and rewrite the others to cast the verbs in the active voice.

   A. The defendant was brought to trial after a delay of eleven months.
   B. The ball was kicked out of bounds by Biff on his own four yard line.
   C. Novosibirsk has been called the most important city in Siberia.
   D. Pollution of lakes and rivers is deeply resented by the typical Minnesotan.
   E. The Declaration of Independence was called by Thomas Jefferson "the holy bond of our union."

12f Use formulas like *it is* and *there are* only for special emphasis.

If one of your sentences begins with a subject-deferring expression such as *it is* or *there were*, take a close look at the subject (it is the *weather*; there was a *princess*). That "announced" word stands out emphatically in its unusual position. If you have a special reason for highlighting it, your delaying formula may be justified:

- It is the weather that causes her arthritis to act up.
- There was a princess whose hair reached the ground.

In the first of these sentences, *weather* is isolated as the cause of the arthritis acting up; in the second, the writer succeeds in getting an intended "fairy tale" effect.

More often than not, however, delaying formulas show up in first-draft prose simply because the writer is postponing commitment to a clearly stated assertion. The price of delay is that, without any gain in emphasis, the writer is pushing essential information further back into subordinate parts of the sentence (p. 285, 12a). Frequently the result is an awkward and indistinct statement.

DON'T:

x **There is** no reason to suspect that **there is** much difference between what she wrote in her last years and what she felt when **it was** not so easy for her to be candid in her thirties.

DO:

- Her statements in her last years probably express ideas she already held, but was censoring, in her thirties.

Note how much more easily you can take in the revised sentence; you do not have to hold your breath until you can discover what the statement is about. The complete grammatical subject, *Her statements in her last years*, immediately gives us our bearings.

EXERCISE

8. Indicate which of the following sentences use delaying formulas to good effect, and be prepared to explain what has been gained in each case. Revise the other sentences to achieve more direct expression.

   A. It was exactly at two A.M. that the killer would always strike.
   B. In 1985, there was just 4.6 percent of Americans' after-tax income that they put into savings.

C. There can be little doubt that immigration has been enormously beneficial to our economy.
D. There is something that helps to make the literature of the South distinctive, and that is the attempt to represent the exact cadence of local speech.
E. It was the hard truth, not some syrupy evasion, that she now required of her ashen-faced doctor.

12g Avoid an unnecessary *that* or *what* clause.

Look at the DON'T example on page 294 *(There is no reason to suspect that . . .)*. Part of the indistinctness of that sentence comes from its *that* and *what* clauses, which further tax the reader's patience. Such clauses can, it is true, serve a good purpose—for example, arousing a curiosity that can then be emphatically answered:

- **What he needed** above all, after eight hours of steady questioning, was simply a chance to close his eyes.

In much first-draft prose, however, *that* and *what* clauses serve only to nudge the intended statement along in little jerks.

DON'T:

x At the present time, the realities of nuclear terror are such **that** countries **that** possess equal power find, when they oppose each other, **that** the weapons **that** carry the most force are precisely the weapons **that** they cannot use.

DO:

- In this age of nuclear terror, equal adversaries are equally powerless to use their strongest weapons.

Here thirty-nine words have been compressed into sixteen, and a slack, cud-chewing sentence has become tight and balanced (*equal adversaries are equally powerless*). And notice how the grammatical core of the sentence (p. 285, 12a) has been given something definite to convey: not *realities are such* but *adversaries are powerless*. Strong, message-bearing elements of thought have been moved into the positions where they normally belong.

EXERCISES (12a–12g)

9. The following paragraph, adapted from an excellent student essay, has been doctored to *prevent* an effective alignment of subjects, verbs, and direct objects with performers of action, actions, and receivers of action, respectively. (See 12a.) Submit a revised version in which you correct that problem wherever it occurs.

   It is within the graveyard that Hamlet's final revelations about mortality are made. The function of the graveyard setting is operative in several ways. First, Hamlet's continuing confrontation with death receives highly dramatic emphasis here. Second, the digging up of buried motives, which has been a concern of Hamlet's from the beginning, is related to the literal digging of a grave. The buried skulls which are unearthed by the gravedigger are like the secrets toward which Hamlet's investigative efforts have been directed. Finally, Hamlet's realization of his earthly limits is appropriate to a setting in which an abundance of anonymous bones is evident.

10. Here is a draft paragraph containing ideas that could be made more distinct. Submit a revised version, numbering your sentences to correspond to those below. Do not hesitate to break long sentences into shorter ones if you find it necessary, but if so, avoid falling into choppiness (see p. 318, 14f).

    1. It has been said by some people in recent years that the problem of low-frequency magnetic emissions from personal computers is a serious one. 2. Whether or not this problem is one that ought to be of grave concern is dependent on a larger question: do electromagnetic fields in certain frequencies have an effect on what happens within the human immune system? 3. That this larger issue is not yet within the range of quick resolution may be suggested by the fact that there have recently been editorials in major newspapers in which opposing positions have been maintained. 4. The experience of better-established health hazards such as asbestosis and black lung disease is such as to imply that nothing is likely to be done until large numbers of people who are suffering ill effects from electromagnetic computer emissions are banded together into an effective political force which is like a trade union. 5. It is an unfortunate aspect of such controversies as the one under consideration here that adequate resources for the conduct of necessary research into the alleged ill effects are largely under the control of the very industries that are being accused of dangerous practices, instead of being available to the threatened consumers who may not even know about one another's complaints.

13

Subordination

The first thing to do with any draft sentence—even an adequate-looking one—is to see whether you can make its idea more distinct (Chapter 12). In doing so, you will often find yourself using **subordination**—that is, giving secondary grammatical emphasis to certain parts of the sentence. As a rule, the act of subordinating brings out the primary importance of the elements that remain unsubordinated. We will see some interesting exceptions, however; on occasion a subordinated element, shrewdly placed, can pack a curious wallop (pp. 306–7).

Our discussion emphasizes the usefulness of *free subordination* (13c–d), which typically gets set off by commas. Once you can manage free subordination effectively, you have in hand one of the most fruitful of all revision strategies.

13a Subordinate to highlight the key idea of your sentence.

When one of your thoughts in a sentence is less important than another, you should put it into a subordinate structure. Thus, if your draft sentence says *The government collects billions of dollars in taxes, and it must meet many obligations*, you should recognize that by using *and* you have given equal weight to two independent remarks. Are they of equal importance in your own mind? If you decided that you really meant to stress the collecting of money, you would want to turn the statement about meeting obligations into a subordinate element:

SUBORD EL

- **Because it has many obligations to meet,** the government collects billions of dollars in taxes.

But if you wanted to stress the meeting of obligations, you would subordinate the remark about collecting money:

SUBORD EL

- **By collecting billions of dollars in taxes,** the government is able to meet its obligations.

When you make an element subordinate, it will usually fit into one of the following (left-column) categories. Note how subordinating words like *because, where*, and *although* (p. 387, 18c) not only spare us the trouble of locating the main idea but specify the relation between that idea and the subordinate element.

	WITHOUT SUBORDINATION	WITH SUBORDINATION
Time	The earthquake struck, and then everyone panicked.	Everyone panicked **when** the earthquake struck.
Place	William Penn founded a city of brotherly love. He chose the juncture of the Delaware and Schuylkill rivers.	**Where** the Schuylkill River joins the Delaware, William Penn founded a city of brotherly love.
Cause	She was terrified of large groups, and debating was not for her.	**Because** she was terrified of large groups, she decided against being a debater.
Concession	He claimed to despise Vermont. He went there every summer.	**Although** he claimed to despise Vermont, he went there every summer.
Condition	She probably won't be able to afford a waterbed. The marked retail prices are just too high.	**Unless** she can get a discount, she probably won't be able to afford a waterbed.

	WITHOUT SUBORDINATION	WITH SUBORDINATION
Exception	The grass is dangerously dry this year. Of course I am not referring to watered lawns.	**Except for** watered lawns, the grass is dangerously dry this year.
Purpose	The Raiders stayed in Los Angeles. Their deal to return to Oakland fell through.	**Since** their deal to return to Oakland fell through, the Raiders stayed in Los Angeles.
Description	The late Edward Steichen showed his reverence for life in arranging the famous exhibit "The Family of Man," and he was a pioneer photographer himself.	The late Edward Steichen, **himself a pioneer photographer**, showed his reverence for life in arranging the famous exhibit "The Family of Man."

sub 13a

EXERCISE

1. Combine each pair of sentences below to form two new sentences using subordination. First subordinate element 1 to element 2 and then vice versa. Be prepared to explain the difference in emphasis between your sentences in each new pair.

   A. 1. Unemployment is beginning to look like a permanent problem in America.
      2. Every student wants assurance that a job will be waiting after graduation.

   B. 1. Postage rates are discouragingly high.
      2. There are few real alternatives to using the mails.

   C. 1. Hang gliding is growing in popularity.
      2. It will never catch on in Kansas.

   D. 1. I am an avid sports fan.
      2. I do not intend to watch next Sunday's underwater tug of war between the Miami Dolphins and a team of alligators.

   E. 1. The alligators will do all they can to win the prize.
      2. It is hard to imagine what the alligators would do with $500,000.

13b Avoid such vague subordinators as *in terms of* and *being as*.

Sometimes you can make a sentence more distinct not by adding subordination but by sharpening a vague subordinate element or eliminating it altogether. In rereading your drafts, watch especially for formulas like *in terms of, with regard to*, and *being as*. Such expressions are inherently woolly; they fail to specify exactly *how* the subordinated element relates to the primary one.

DON'T:
x **In terms of swimming,** she was unbeatable.

Here a rather pompous subordinate element hints at a cloudy connection between swimming and being unbeatable. The connection can be stated more straightforwardly.

DO:
• **As a swimmer** she was unbeatable.

or

• She was an unbeatable swimmer.

DON'T:
x He felt sympathetic **with regard to their position.**

DO:
• He sympathized with their position.

DON'T:
x **Being as it was noon,** everyone took a lunch break.

DO:
• Everyone took a lunch break at noon.

Other potentially vague subordinators include *with, as, as to, in the area of, in connection with, in the framework of, along the lines of, pertaining to*, and *as far as*.

DON'T:

x **With all that he says about the English,** I believe he has misrepresented them.

DO:

• I believe he has altogether misrepresented the English.

DON'T:

x **As far as finals,** I hope to take all of them in the first two days of exam week.

To be correct in usage the writer would have to say *As far as finals are concerned,* . . . But unless there is some special reason for singling out *finals*, a more concise statement would be preferable.

DO:

• I hope to take all of my finals in the first two days of exam week.

EXERCISE

2. Each of the following sentences shows vague subordination. Submit revised versions that eliminate the problem.

   A. In the framework of chocolate consumption, the British probably take first place.
   B. Regarding the weather, it has been unusually mild in recent weeks.
   C. She left nothing to be desired in terms of her eagerness to learn.
   D. As far as ethics, that is a subject of very little interest to them.
   E. With reference to the obligations facing him this semester, volunteer work would seem to be out of the question.

13c Gain clarity through free subordination.

Note, in the right-hand column of the chart on pages 298–99, that all but one of the italicized elements are set apart from the main statements by commas. They are **free elements** in the sense of standing alone. By contrast, the sentence *Everyone panicked when the earthquake struck* contains a **bound element**; that is, the subordinate clause *when the earthquake struck* is "bound together" with the main statement. Here are some further contrasts:

BOUND	FREE
The Germany that he remembered with horror had greatly changed.	Germany, **which he remembered with horror**, had greatly changed.
Germany was now inclined toward neutralism **instead of being fiercely militaristic**.	**Instead of being fiercely militaristic**, Germany was now inclined toward neutralism.
Hitler had vanished from the scene **along with everything he stood for**.	**Along with everything he stood for**, Hitler had vanished from the scene.

In general, bound elements are **restrictive**, or defining, and thus they should not be set off by commas (see p. 447, 21m). Free elements, being **nonrestrictive**, or nondefining, should be set apart. But since any phrase or subordinate clause at the beginning of a sentence can be followed by a comma (p. 443, 21i–j), a restrictive element that comes first can be free—that is, followed by a comma:

RESTR AND FREE

• **In September or October**, heating bills begin to rise.

sub 13c

The distinction between free and bound elements is a valuable one for mastering an efficient style. When one of your draft sentences is clumsily phrased, you can often attack the problem by looking for bound elements and then setting them free.

WITH BOUND SUBORDINATION:

x The censorship **that is not directly exercised by a sponsor when a program is being produced** may be exercised in many instances by the producers themselves.

WITH FREE SUBORDINATION:

• **Even when a sponsor does not directly censor a program**, the producers often censor it themselves.

Note the importance of the comma after *program*, leaving the reader in no doubt about where the shortened main statement begins. Observe, too, that the revised sentence shifts from passive to active verbs (p. 292, 12e). Use of the passive voice almost always results in the addition of bound prepositional phrases (*by a sponsor, by the producers*).

EXERCISES

3. Each of the following sentences uses the coordinating conjunction *and* inappropriately, allowing a subordinate meaning to be lost. Rewrite the sentences, using a free element that stands clearly apart from the single main statement in each case.

   A. He is going to apply for the job, and he doesn't have a chance.
   B. She hopes to quit work early today, and she wants to get to the mountains ahead of the weekend traffic.
   C. Farmers want the price of corn to rise this year, and otherwise many of them will be driven out of business.
   D. There has been very little snow this year, and most of the ski resorts are closed.
   E. Most species of American animals have recently been declining in population, and the sea otter is one exception to the rule.

4. Each of the following sentences is clogged with bound subordinate elements that make the statement indistinct. Without trying to cover every last bit of information in the original sentences, submit revised versions using free subordination to convey each assertion more distinctly. For example:

ORIGINAL:

× Any time that an accident that involves a spill of toxic substances occurs is a time that could reasonably cause alarm to everyone who lives in the area that surrounds the scene where the accident occurred.

REVISION:

● Whenever a spill of toxic substances occurs, everyone in the surrounding area has cause for alarm.

   A. It is an interesting fact that in America the statistics show that for every adult member of the population there is approximately one automobile.
   B. The use of these 130 million vehicles results every day in the consumption of 5.5 million barrels of gasoline coming partly from domestic sources while the rest is made up from foreign ones.

sub
13c

C. Standards for the fuel economy of new cars that the government put into effect for domestic auto makers beginning in 1978 brought about a steady rise in the number of miles per gallon of new cars in each year until the return of the "muscle car" in the mid-eighties.
D. The total consumption of oil in the United States is now less by 3.5 million barrels of oil a day than it was at the time that the new fuel economy standards were passed.
E. Yet it is unfortunately true that the advantage in terms of reduction of dependence on foreign sources of oil has been largely offset by the fact that the domestic production of oil has been declining at about the same rate as the decline in the demand for gasoline.

5. The following passage lacks adequate subordination. Rewrite it, combining sentences and making ample use of free elements.

> Hippocrates used garlic as a pharmaceutical. He used it to treat different diseases, and so did other early doctors. They believed that a plant or herb had a very penetrating odor so it must have a lot of therapeutic value. Tuberculosis and leprosy are not at all alike but garlic was used to treat both of them. There was a Roman naturalist named Pliny. He listed sixty-one diseases; garlic was supposed to cure them all. And he added the information that garlic has very powerful properties and you can tell this because serpents and scorpions are driven away by the very smell of it.[1]

13d Follow sentence logic in placing a subordinate element.

One important feature of free subordinate elements is that they can be moved without a radical loss of meaning. How can you tell where a free element would be most effective? If you do not trust your ear, you can apply one of the following three principles:

1. *Explain or place conditions on an assertion*. If your free element explains your main statement or puts a condition on it, you should consider placing the free element *first*. In that position it will allow your reader to follow your logic from the start:

- **Unless scientists come up with a better explanation,** we will have to lend our belief to this one.
- **Although he finished the test in time,** he missed many of the answers.

- **Because he becomes nervous whenever he isn't listening to music,** he wears earphones while he works.

In first-draft prose, main statements tend to come first, with limiting or explanatory elements dragging behind. Get those elements into early positions; they will show that you have the entire logic of the sentence under control. And since last positions tend to be naturally emphatic, you can generally make a stronger effect by putting your main statement after your free subordinate element.

2. *Add to an assertion.* If your free element, instead of explaining the main statement or placing a condition on it, merely adds a further thought about it, you should place that free element *after* the main statement:

- Her smile disguised her fierce competitiveness, **a trait revealed to very few of her early teammates.**
- His life revolved around his older brother, **who never ceased making unreasonable demands.**

3. *Modify one part of an assertion.* If your free element modifies a particular word or phrase, consider placing it *right after* that element:

sub 13d

- Cézanne's colors, **earthy as his native Provence,** are not adequately conveyed by reproductions.
- They gave me, **a complete newcomer**, more attention than I deserved.

A less usual but sometimes effective position is *right before* the modified element:

- **Earthy as his native Provence**, Cézanne's colors are not adequately conveyed by reproductions.

Placing Sentence Adverbs and Transitional Phrases

A **sentence adverb** (p. 403, 19c) such as *however, nevertheless*, or *furthermore* constitutes a movable subordinate element in its own right. The placement of a sentence adverb is highly flexible, but different positions suggest different emphases. In general, a sentence adverb puts stress on the word that precedes it:

- I, **however,** refuse to comply. [I contrast myself with others.]
- I refuse, **however,** to comply. [My refusal is absolute.]

In the first and last positions of a sentence, where a sentence adverb cannot be set off on both sides by commas, it makes a less pointed effect:

- **However**, I refuse to comply.
- I refuse to comply, **however**.

} No single element within the main statement is highlighted.

The final position is the weakest—the one that gets least stress from the logical force of the sentence adverb. In some sentences, however, this may be just the effect you are seeking.

The same principles of emphatic placement apply to **transitional phrases** like *in fact, on the contrary*, and *as a result*, which are really multiword sentence adverbs. Note how meaning as well as emphasis can sometimes be affected by different placement of the same transitional phrase:

sub 13d

- **In fact,** Marie was overjoyed. [Marie was not unhappy. No, indeed. . . .]
- Marie, **in fact,** was overjoyed. [Others were happy, but one person—singled out here—was more so.]

For fuller lists of sentence adverbs and transitional phrases, see page 403, 19c.

Emphatic Subordination

Once you are sure of your control over subordination, you can occasionally surprise your reader by saving a "bombshell" for a late, subordinate element:

> There was nothing unusual in the visit **except that Thoreau fell utterly in love with her as soon as she arrived.**[2]

In one sense, this statement means what it starts out to say; nothing outwardly noteworthy happened during Ellen Sewell's visit to Concord, Massachusetts, in July 1839. But something privately momentous did happen: Henry Thoreau fell in love. The writer gains an effect of **irony** (p. 80, 3o), or incongruity between what is said and meant, by tucking that important news into an "afterthought" subordinate clause.

Free subordinate elements, "casually" appended to straightforward-looking sentences, are especially suited to ironic effects:

> Perhaps the Las Vegas wedding industry achieved its peak operational efficiency between 9:00 P.M. and midnight of August 26, 1965, **an otherwise unremarkable Thursday which happened to be, by Presidential order, the last day on which anyone could improve his draft status merely by getting married.**[3]

This writer mocks the "peak operational efficiency" of the Las Vegas wedding industry by explaining it away in an "unremarkable" sequence of subordinate clauses and phrases. Her sentence is an exploding cigar, with the explosion timed to occur when we could least expect it.

We have previously advised you to "subordinate to highlight the key idea of your sentence" (p. 297, 13a). Here you see, however, that the rule can be twisted for purposes of irony or humor; you can put your key idea into the subordinate structure if you know exactly why you are doing so.

EXERCISES

6. Submit three original sentences illustrating, in turn, the three numbered principles explained on pages 304–5.

7. In earlier papers or in a draft that you have been preparing, find three sentences that now strike you as lacking adequate subordination or as using subordination awkwardly. Submit those sentences along with three revised versions that clear up the problem. Be prepared to justify your placement of subordinate elements in one part of each sentence instead of another.

NOTES

[1] Adapted from Michael Field, *All Manner of Food* (New York: Knopf, 1970) 4–5.

[2] Robert D. Richardson, Jr., *Henry Thoreau: A Life of the Mind* (Berkeley: U of California P, 1986) 57.

[3] Joan Didion, *Slouching Towards Bethlehem* (New York: Farrar, 1968) 79–80.

14

Sentence Emphasis and Variety

SENTENCE EMPHASIS

14a Use parallelism to show that elements belong together.

You can write more effective sentences by making your statements more distinct (Chapter 12) and by highlighting their key elements through subordination (Chapter 13). In addition, you can revise to give the same grammatical structure to elements that are closely related in meaning. Such a use of **parallelism** (Chapter 24) is emphatic because it makes logical relations immediately apparent to your reader. The idea is to have your grammar reinforce your meaning, not only through the choice of a main subject and verb but also through the aligning of key words, phrases, and clauses.

To appreciate the advantage that parallelism brings, compare two passages that convey the same information:

A. Animals think *of* things. They also think *at* things. Men think primarily *about* things. Words are symbols that may be combined in a thousand ways. They can also be varied in the same number of ways. This can be said of pictures as well. The same holds true for memory images.

B. Animals think, but they think *of* and *at* things; men think primarily *about* things. Words, pictures, and memory images are symbols that may be combined and varied in a thousand ways.[1]

Passage A, a classically choppy paragraph, takes seven sentences and fifty-one words to say what passage B says in two sentences and thirty-one words. In passage B, seven statements are condensed to four, with a corresponding gain in understanding. And the key to this concentration is parallelism—of paired clauses (*Animals think, but they think. . .*), of conspicuously equal halves of a sentence marked by a semicolon, of nouns in a series (*Words, pictures, and memory images*), and of verb forms (*combined and varied*). Passage B inspires confidence in the writer's control; we feel that she could not have packed her sentences with so much parallel structure if she had not known exactly what she wanted to say.

Most instances of parallelism involve two items that are manifestly equivalent in emphasis. The following table shows how such items can be made parallel, with or without conjunctions (joining words such as *and* and *or*).

PATTERN	EXAMPLE
x and *y*	She was tired of [*x*] **waiting** and [*y*] **worrying**.
x or *y*	If he had continued that life, he would have faced death [*x*] **in the electric chair** or [*y*] **at the hands of the mob**.
x, *y*	He strode away, [*x*] **the money in his hand**, [*y*] **a grin on his face.**
x: *y*	He had [*x*] **what he wanted**: [*y*] **enough cash to buy a new life**.
x; *y*	[*x*] **He wanted security**; [*y*] **she wanted good times.**

As you can see from these examples, parallelism can involve units as small as single words (*waiting* and *worrying*) or as large as whole statements (*he wanted security* and *she wanted good times*).

For problems of usage and punctuation arising with parallelism, see pages 484–503, Chapter 24.

EXERCISE

1. Looking through earlier papers or a draft that you have been working on, find a paragraph of your own prose that now strikes you as lacking in the conciseness that parallel structures can provide. Type out or photocopy that paragraph, and submit it along with a revised version that is concise and rich in parallelism. In the revised version, underline the words that constitute the matched items.

14b Use anticipatory patterns.

In the boxed sentences on page 310, each *y* element comes as a mild surprise; we discover that a matching structure is in process only when we reach the second item. But other matching formulas, known as **anticipatory patterns**, announce the pairing of items by beginning with a "tip-off" word.

PATTERN	EXAMPLE
both *x* and *y*	**Both** guerrillas (*x*) **and** loyalists (*y*) pose a threat to the safety of reporters covering foreign revolutions.
either *x* or *y*	**Either** reporters should be recognized as neutrals (*x*) **or** they should not be sent into combat zones (*y*).
neither *x* nor *y*	**Neither** the competition of networks (*x*) **nor** the ambition of reporters (*y*) justifies this recklessness.
whether *x* or *y*	Reporters must wonder, when they wake up each

PATTERN	EXAMPLE
	morning in a foreign city, **whether** they will be gunned down by the loyalists **or** kidnapped by the guerrillas.
more (less) *x* than *y*	It is **more** important, after all, to spare the lives of journalists **than** to get one more interview with the typical freedom fighter.
not *x* but *y*	It is **not** the greed of the networks, however, **but** the changed nature of warfare that most endangers the lives of reporters.
not only *x* but also *y*	Now reporters covering a guerrilla war find it hard **not only** to distinguish "friendly" from "unfriendly" elements **but also** to convince each side that they are not working for the other one.
so *x* that *y*	Such reporting has become **so** risky **that** few knowledgeable journalists volunteer to undertake it.

emph 14b

Note how the first word of the anticipatory formula prepares us for the rest. As soon as we read *both* or *either* or *so*, we know what kind of logical pattern has begun; we are ready to grasp complex paired elements without losing our way. Anticipatory matching always means improved readability—provided, of course, that the grammar and punctuation of your sentence make the intended structure clear.

To see how anticipatory patterns can aid a reader, compare an imagined first-draft passage with the actual finished version:

A. He swore a lot. He would swear at absolutely anybody. For him it was just the natural thing to do. The people who worked for him probably thought he was angry at them all the time, but it wasn't necessarily true. A man like that could have been just making conversation without being angry at all, for all they knew.

B. He swore so often and so indiscriminately that his employees were sometimes not sure whether he was angry at them or merely making conversation.[2]

Passage A uses more words to make more assertions, yet it never lets us see where it is headed. Nora Ephron's more economical passage B uses two anticipatory structures—*so x and so y that z* and *whether he was x or y*—to pull elements of thought into alignment without squandering whole sentences on them.

EXERCISE

2. Using any paper or draft, find three of your own sentences that you can make more readable through the use of anticipatory patterns. Submit the original sentences along with the improved versions.

14c Make your series consistent and climactic.

One indispensable form of parallelism (14a) is the **series** of coordinated items, three or more elements in grammatically aligned sequence. A series tells your reader that the items it contains each bear the same logical relation to some other part of the sentence.

• $\overbrace{\textbf{Declining enrollments}}^{x}$, $\overbrace{\textbf{obsolete audio equipment}}^{y}$, and $\overbrace{\textbf{hostility from the administration}}^{z}$ have hurt the language departments.

This says that *x*, *y*, and *z* are comparable factors, each making its contribution to the effect named. Such a condensed, immediately clear statement could replace as many as three rambling sentences in a draft paragraph.

Although the parts of a series must be alike in form, they may have different degrees of importance or impact. Since the final position is by far the most emphatic one, that is where the climactic item should go:

- He was prepared to risk everything—**his comfort, his livelihood, even his life.**

  If you try to put *his life* into either of the other positions in the series, you will see how vital a climactic order is.

Again:

- For a week and a half, it has been so hot across the South that (w) **chickens in their sheds,** (x) **fish in their ponds,** (y) **ancient oaks in their woods,** and (z) **people in their homes** have died of the heat.[3]

  The writer would have looked monstrously insensitive if he had placed the *z* element, *people in their homes*, any earlier.

emph 14c

As you can see from the first of these two examples above, you do not always have to put *and* or *or* before the last member of a series. Omitting the conjunction can give the series an air of urgency or condensed thought:

- A moment's **distraction, hesitation, impatience** can spell doom for an aerialist.
- The last words, the blessings of the young, the washing of the body, the coins on the eyelids, the deathbed confession, the deathbed reconciliation, and the deathbed farewell have been succeeded or crowded by **the IV, the respirator, the feeding tubes in the nostrils, the living will, the hospital roommate, the nurses.**[4]

EXERCISES

3. For each item A through E, compose a sentence that places the three terms in a series. Be sure to choose the most emphatic, climactic order of arrangement for those terms:

A. courage   cheerfulness   patience
B. the neighborhood   the county   the city
C. grade school   college   high school
D. terrors   worries   fears
E. an inconvenience   an outrage   a disturbance

4. Submit three sentences containing series. In the first, omit a conjunction before the final item in the series. In the second, join all items in the series with conjunctions, not commas. And in the third, include two series, using *both* of the devices practiced in the first two sentences. Beneath each of your three sentences, briefly explain why the optional form or forms you are illustrating suit the idea or mood of this particular statement.

14d Use balance for special emphasis.

emph
14d

When a sentence uses emphatic repetition to achieve parallelism (p. 309, 14a), it shows **balance.** A balanced sentence usually does two things: (1) it repeats a grammatical pattern, and (2) it repeats certain words so as to highlight key differences. Thus the two halves of *He wanted security; she wanted good times* use the same subject-verb-object pattern and the same verb, *wanted*, in order to contrast *he* with *she* and *security* with *good times*.

You can see the ingredients of balance in the following **aphorisms,** or memorable sentences expressing very general assertions:

- What is **written without effort** is in general **read without pleasure.** (Samuel Johnson)
- We must indeed **all hang together**, or, most assuredly, we will **all hang separately.** (Benjamin Franklin)
- Democracy substitutes **election by the incompetent many** for **appointment by the corrupt few.** (George Bernard Shaw)

Notice in each instance how the writer has used identical sentence functions to make us confront essential differences: *written/read, effort/pleasure, together/separately, election/appointment, incompetent/corrupt, many/few.*

The art of creating balance consists in noticing elements of sameness and contrast in a draft sentence and then rearranging your grammar so that those elements play identical grammatical roles.

DRAFT SENTENCE:

- Love of country is a virtue, but I think that it is more important today to love the human species as a whole.

BALANCED VERSION:

- Love of country is a virtue, but love of the human species is a necessity.

  The first sentence is adequately formed, but it still reads like an idea-in-the-making, the transcript of a thought process. The second, radically concise, sentence uses balance to convey authority and finality.

Again:

DRAFT SENTENCE:

- One aspect of Garrison Keillor's prose is that it is wry and slightly crackpot, which allows it to rely more on humor.

This sentence, with its weak main verb *is* (p. 290, 12c), its classically vague pronoun *which* (p. 479, 23k), its muddled cause-and-effect relations (being crackpot allows Keillor's prose to rely on humor?), and its incomplete comparison (more than what?), typifies the problems of first-draft sentence construction. All of those defects vanish in the more concise and emphatic balanced version:

BALANCED VERSION:

- Wry and slighly crackpot, Garrison Keillor's prose relies more on humor that pleases than on argumentation that persuades.

EXERCISES

5. Submit a paragraph analyzing all the elements of balance in the following sentence about a proposed "missile shield" program. What general effect does the writer achieve?

Star Wars will roll ever on, opposed by liberals who don't know why they oppose it, supported by conservatives who don't know why they support it, spending money we can't afford to do what can't be done.[5]

6. Using any paper or draft, find three of your own sentences that you can revise to achieve the effect of balance. Submit both the original and the revised versions.

14e Take advantage of the emphatic final position in a sentence.

If you want to make an expression dramatic and memorable, try putting it at the end of its sentence. With a proper buildup, the final position is naturally punchy. Notice, for example, how every sentence in the following paragraph about "snap books"—that is, books by "name" authors who write about countries they have scarcely visited—saves its most biting expressions (boldfaced here) for the end:

> What really distinguishes snap books from other genres is not so much their length as **their self-consciousness.** They are the creation of individuals who, thrust into a wrenching world of death squads and land mines, **profess to know terror through having been forced to eat dinner in the dark.** In snap books, war and revolution serve primarily as backdrops **against which star writers can shine.**[6]

emph 14e

The same effect is even more apparent in the following passage, with its one-word punch line:

> No wonder the TV industry is finally wooing black audiences. They've come to embody its favorite color, which is, of course, **green.**[7]

Wherever, in your own drafts, you find a sentence that seems to trail off weakly, reread it to see whether its most important element is hidden away somewhere in the middle. Consider this student example and its revision:

UNREVISED SENTENCE:

- Tom Wolfe establishes a stamp of authority as a writer who can describe "the right stuff" because of his use of a technical vocabulary that a pilot would know.

Notice, here, how two "bound" subordinate clauses (p. 302, 13c) at the end—*because of his use of a technical vocabulary* and *that a pilot would know*—reduce the energy and pointedness of the writer's sentence. In the revision, the key idea comes last, after a "free" subordinate clause (p. 301) that leaves us ready for an emphatic statement:

REVISED SENTENCE:

- Because he has mastered the technical vocabulary of aviation, Tom Wolfe convinces us that he is in possession of "the right stuff."

EXERCISE

7. Using any paper or draft, find three of your own sentences that you can make more emphatic by moving a naturally strong element to the end. Submit the three sentences with appropriate revisions.

SENTENCE VARIETY

var
14f

14f Combine choppy sentences to set off related elements.

Bear in mind that your prose will be read not in isolated sentences but in whole paragraphs. You, too, should read your drafts that way, checking to see that the sentences within each paragraph sound comfortable in one another's company. If they seem abrupt and awkward, the problem may be a discontinuity of thought. Yet your sentences can be related in thought and still feel unrelated because they are too alike in structure. Watch especially for **choppy sentences**—a monotonous string of brief, plain statements containing few if any internal pauses. What you want instead is movement between relatively plain sentences and sentences that do contain pauses.

You can break up monotony just by adding one punctuated modifier—a *however* or a *furthermore*—to a sentence in a choppy sequence: *The storm, however, was not expected to end the drought.*

But you can also look for ways to combine two or more choppy sentences into one. Ask yourself what the logical relation between those sentences is, and then turn one statement into a punctuated modifier of the other.

CHOPPY:

x The president serves a four-year term. He must seek reelection when it is over.

COMBINED:

• After serving a four-year term, the president must seek reelection.

The first sentence in the choppy sequence has been turned into a **free element** (p. 301, 13c), duly set off by punctuation.

CHOPPY:

x Some experts favor a six-year term of office. They say that reelection causes too many pressures. Long-term problems get neglected. These problems are both domestic and foreign.

COMBINED:

• Some experts, maintaining that both domestic and foreign problems get neglected in the rush for reelection, favor a six-year term of office.

Here four abrupt, disjointed sentences, each as unemphatic as the next, have been transformed into one sentence that sorts out major and minor elements and gets its key point into the emphatic final position (see 14e).

CHOPPY:

x Some knowledgeable observers do think that the present arrangement is superior. One of them is the noted historian Arthur Schlesinger, Jr. He argues that a president must be accountable to the people. It is the core of our democracy. Schlesinger says that a four-year term answers this need.

COMBINED:

• Some knowledgeable observers, among them the noted historian Arthur Schlesinger, Jr., believe that the present arrangement is superior. In Schlesinger's opinion, a four-year term answers our fundamental democratic need to keep the president accountable to the people.

To appreciate the gain in stylistic control that comes with eliminating choppiness, look first at the following, extremely monotonous, passage:

x The high snow in the Wasatch Mountains is light and dry. You can't make a snowball out of it. This is Utah powder. It makes for some of the West's greatest skiing. The numerous slopes are regularly groomed. The snow crunches under your skis. It forgives your rusty technique. It gives gently under your fall. There is deep, new powder in the back bowls. You float up and over the ground. Plumes of white mist curl around your waist like smoke.

Here every sentence consists entirely of a brief independent clause. The passage goes almost nowhere in little jerks, like a stalled snowmobile being nudged by its starter motor. Now compare the actual published text:

- The snow that falls high in the Wasatch Mountains is so light and dry that you can't make a snowball out of it. This is Utah powder, and it makes for some of the West's greatest skiing. On the numerous slopes that are regularly groomed, the snow crunches under your skis, forgiving if your technique is rusty, giving gently if you fall. On the deep new powder of the back bowls, you float up and over the ground, plumes of white mist curling around your waist like smoke.[8]

These four sentences contain more words than the eleven above—their average length is twenty-two words, not seven—yet their message is more comprehensible, and certainly more pleasant to take in, than exactly the same message delivered in Dick-and-Jane sentences. Why? Since the words used are almost identical, the difference in effect must be entirely due to sentence variety. Three features are especially noteworthy:

1. The second passage requires us to deal with only five independent clauses, not eleven.
2. The second passage, therefore, spares us the bothersome work of deciding which among the eleven assertions are the important ones.

3. Because the five independent clauses are not bunched together, we enjoy some "breathing space" between emphatic statements and a sense of increasing freedom as we progress.

EXERCISE

8. Here are several choppy sentences in a row. Using much of the same language but adding and subtracting where necessary, write a revised version that eliminates the problem of choppiness. You need not keep the same number of sentences.

   Atari was the pioneer in video games. The company ran into serious problems in the early 1980s. The trouble was that the real profits lay in software. Atari had invented the hardware. Any rival company could market programs that could run on Atari's console. Activision, Imagic, and Mattel's Intellivision quickly exploited that advantage. This happened as soon as they realized the opportunity before them. Atari's managers were so used to leading the field that they failed to realize they were being overtaken.

14g Try an occasional interruption.

var 14g

To lend a conversational yet subtly controlled air to your prose, you can occasionally insert a surprise element into your sentence, interrupting the normal linkage of subject, verb, and direct object:

- The street Jerry lived on—**it was more like an alley than a street**—was so neighborly that he scarcely ever felt alone.
- The hot, moist summer air of Florida—**people call it an instant steambath**—makes an air conditioner a necessity in every home and office.
- A woman of strong opinions—**her last movie grossed $50 million, and she calls it a turkey**—she is not exactly a press agent's dream come true.

As you can gather, dashes are the normal means of punctuating an interruption.

The "False Start"

In a variation on the interruptive pattern, you can begin your sentence with a lengthy element—for example, a series (p. 313,

14c)—and follow it with a dash announcing that the grammatical core of the sentence is about to begin:

- **Going to hairdresser school, marrying the steady boyfriend, having the baby, getting the divorce**—everything in her life seemed to follow some dreary script.

Such a sentence takes the reader off guard by making a "**false start.**" We assume at first that the opening element will be the grammatical subject, but we readjust our focus when we see that the true subject will come after the dash. (The first element is actually in apposition to the subject; see page 451, 21n.)

EXERCISE

9. Submit five original sentences in which you interrupt your own sequence of grammatical elements to insert a new element.

14h Practice the cumulative sentence.

var
14h

A **cumulative sentence** is one whose main statement is followed by one or more free subordinate elements (p. 301, 13c). It is called *cumulative* because it "accumulates," or collects, modifying words, phrases, or clauses at the end. The following sentences, encountered earlier, are typical:

- Her smile disguised her fierce competitiveness, **a trait revealed to very few of her early teammates.**
- He was prepared to risk everything—**his comfort, his livelihood, even his life.**

The beauty of the cumulative pattern is that it offers refinement without much risk of confusing the reader. Since the basic structure of the sentence is complete before the end-modifiers (boldfaced above) begin, your reader has a secure grasp of your idea, which you can then elaborate, illustrate, explain, or reflect on. And since much of our speech follows the cumulative model of statement-plus-adjustment, a cumulative sentence on the page can make a pleasantly conversational effect, as if one afterthought had brought the next one to mind.

To see just how ambitious a cumulative sentence can be without losing its way, consider the following example from a book about the Great Plains:

> If you ask the flight attendant about those green and brown rectangles, chances are he or she will not say that in the spring of 1885 a wheat farmer on the Canadian plains named Angus Mackay was unable to plant a field which had already been plowed when his hands left to suppress a rebellion of frontiersmen of French and Indian ancestry against the Dominion of Canada, and so he left the field fallow, cultivating it occasionally to kill the weeds; that when he planted it the following year, it weathered a drought to produce thirty-five bushels of wheat per acre, thirty-three bushels more than continuously cropped land; that the practice he had initiated, called summer fallow, was an effective way to conserve moisture in the soil in a semi-arid climate, and many other farmers adopted it; that the one problem with summer fallow was the tendency of fields with no crop cover sometimes to dry up and blow away; that in 1918 two other Canadian farmers, Leonard and Arie Koole, experimented successfully with crops planted in narrow sections at right angles to the prevailing winds, to protect sections of fallow ground in between; and that this refinement, called strip farming, turned out to be the best way to raise wheat on the northern plains.[9]

Here is a sentence of 215 words, yet it unfolds in readily grasped units, connected by six parallel *that*'s. Although such a sentence is far longer than normal, it makes a pleasant break from convention while demonstrating a high degree of writerly control.

EXERCISES

10. Find five relatively plain sentences in your own writing, and submit them along with five expanded versions that have been made cumulative.

11. Study the "Great Plains" passage above, and, choosing any topic, submit an original sentence of comparable length and complexity. You can use that sentence's structural devices or try another means of making everything hang together.

14i Try an occasional question or exclamation.

Usually a paragraph develops as a succession of statements, or **declarative sentences.** But to show strong feeling, to pinpoint an issue, to challenge your reader, or simply to enliven a string of sentences, you can make use of a strategically placed question or exclamation:

- **What are we to make of such turmoil over the narrow, arid Gaza Strip?** A full answer would take us back to the era of the Roman emperors.
- And this is all the information released so far. **Does anyone doubt that the Congressman has something to hide?**
- **A million tons of TNT!** The power of this bomb was beyond anyone's imagination.
- Once the grizzlies were deprived of garbage, their population declined steeply. **So much for the "back to nature" school of bear management!**

var 14i

Note, in the second of these examples, that the writer asks the question without expecting an answer, for the question "answers itself." Such a **rhetorical question** can work well for you in driving home an emphatic point. Since rhetorical questions have a coercive air, however, you should use them sparingly. The same holds true for exclamations; see page 523, 26j.

Here are two further examples of questions that add liveliness to the paragraphs in which they occur:

> **What do dandelions and certain species of fish have in common?** There's not a male among them—yet they do very well, thank you. As one of several procreation options available in nature, all-female species are intriguing. **But can this extreme form of asexual independence teach us anything about the evolution of sexual behavior in higher animals, including *homo sapiens*?** Maybe, maybe not, say scientists who study lizards lacking the true male touch.[10]

> In the 1980s more paper wealth was generated in New York than in any other city at any other time in human history. Greenmail, junk bonds, leverage, and the precarious liquidity of an overgeared credit economy transformed the art world into the Art Industry, turnover immense,

regulations none. **What was a picture worth?** One bid below what someone would pay for it. **And what would that person pay for it?** Basically what he or she could borrow. **And how much art could dance for how long on that particular pinhead?** Nobody had the slightest idea. What is certain is that nobody foresaw the hyperinflation of the market; and that when the bubble bursts, or softly deflates, as bubbles do, nobody will have foreseen that either.[11]

EXERCISE

12. Submit five numbered sets of two sentences each. In each pair, include one question or exclamation that is closely related to the point of the other sentence.

14j Try reversing normal word order.

Readers normally expect subjects to come before verbs, but for that very reason you can gain emphasis by occasionally reversing that order. The subject becomes more prominent as a result of such **inverted syntax:**

var
14j

- In the beginning was the **Word.**
- Most important of all, for the would-be tourist, is a **passport** that has not expired.

Similarly, any sentence element that has been wrenched out of its normal position and placed first gets extra attention:

- **Not until then** had he understood how miserable he was.
- **Never again** will she overlook the threat of an avalanche.

Again:

- **About such a glaring scandal** nothing need be said.

  The subject and verb, *nothing* and *need*, are in the usual sequence, but the writer begins with a prepositional phrase that would normally come last.

EXERCISE

13. Submit five sentences illustrating the principle of inverted syntax. In each case underline the word or words that you have made more emphatic by means of the inverted structure.

14k Use delaying tactics to build toward a climax.

If you substantially delay completing your main statement, forcing your reader to wait for the other shoe to drop, you have written a **suspended sentence** (often called a *periodic sentence*). Through its use of delaying elements (boldfaced in the following examples), a suspended sentence can be an effective means of leading to a climax:

- It appears that their success was due more to the influence of their father, **so dominant in the worlds of business and politics that every door would open at his bidding,** than to any merits of their own.
- The states argued that they had indeed complied, **if compliance can mean making a good-faith effort and collecting all the required data,** with the federal guidelines.
- If you are still unused to the idea of gasohol, you will certainly not be ready to hear that some diesel engines will soon be running on **that most humble and ordinary of products, taken for granted by homemakers and never noticed by auto buffs,** vegetable oil.

Suspended sentences are especially appropriate when you have a reason for wanting to build tension, as this writer does:

> As I sat reading Derickson's chapter describing how miners died of black lung, how car painters died of fumes from some of the first autospraying machines, how felt-hat makers went slowly mad, how radium dial painters became palsied, I came to realize that we are, just as our grandparents before us, in the midst of the latest technological/industrial maelstrom, facing a new set of health-related issues little understood by our peers.[12]

Finally, as a remarkable student passage demonstrates, suspended sentences can work to keep readers engrossed in the unfolding details of a narrative—in this case a humorous one:

> Crouching behind a fortress made from pillows and both mattresses of the bunk bed, feverishly gathering rubber bands—the big, thick, red ones which are tight when pulled yet don't fly far; the rare blue and green ones found and pocketed on the walk home from school; and the skinny brown ones, which are the best because they whirr and zing, stinging the skin and leaving puffy, reddish marks (these brown ones are also easiest to find, wrapped twice around the morning newspaper—unless it's raining, then the paper arrives dry in a plastic bag without a rubber band—or scattered in a jackpot on the corner of Longest Avenue and Willow in Louisville, Kentucky, where the paperboy assembles his papers at 4 A.M.)—and loading his black plastic Slammer 36, a rubber-band gun, with sixteen rubber bands—six is considered the safe maximum—my father, age fifteen, waits to ambush his younger brother Guy in their ongoing rubber-band war.
>
> Meanwhile, in the bathroom on the second floor, a bathroom that links my dad's old bedroom with the guest room, also known as the green room because of the lime-green walls and matching shag rug, the squeaking of the cold-water faucet, the closing of the medicine cabinet, and the turning of the brass doorknob warn my father of Guy's imminent entrance through the bathroom door into the soon-to-be shambles. Guy unknowingly opens the door, and my dad opens fire. Instead of shooting sixteen rubber bands in rapid succession, as he intended, the entire notched wheel—this wheel, where the rubber bands hook, resembles the hammer of a real gun—under the pressure of ten overloaded rubber bands, breaks off, hitting my uncle on the bridge of his nose, breaking his glasses and blackening both eyes. This incident happened years ago; my dad, however, still holds the memory, my uncle the scar.[13]

var 14k

EXERCISES (14f–14k)

14. Starting from any five sentences, perhaps including some already used in recent exercises, add the subordinate elements necessary to create five suspended sentences. Submit only the revised versions.

15. Study the use of sentence variety in the following paragraph, and then submit a three-sentence paragraph of your own, on any topic, making use of the same patterns you perceive here:

> Men wear their belts low here, there being so many outstanding bellies, some big enough to have names of their own and be formally introduced. Those

men don't suck them in or hide them in loose shirts; they let them hang free, they pat them, they stroke them as they stand around and talk. How could a man be so vain as to ignore this old friend who's been with him at the great moments of his life?[14]

16. Taking the numbered sentences one by one, analyze all the elements of sentence variety that you find in the following paragraph:

> 1. In desperate fantasy one thinks, at times, of escaping. 2. From childhood there remains a faint memory, nearly lost, of a stream in a Northern forest; a stone dam, a trickling sluice, a hut of some sort where the dam-keeper lives. 3. The loon cries over a lake, the pines stretch endlessly, black against the sky. 4. And then one thinks of *The New York Times* on Sunday, five pounds of newsprint, a million-and-a-half copies a week. 5. How many miles of forest, birds flung from their nests, the work of honey bees wasted, does our Sunday paper, thrown aside between breakfast and lunch, consume?[15]

17. Study the structure of the following sentence, and, choosing any topic you find congenial, submit an original sentence that imitates that structure fairly closely:

> The reason that Madonna does not possess much intrinsic sexual appeal, in spite of having raided the symbolic vanity cases of every icon from Harlow to Dietrich to Hayworth to Monroe (and throwing in Elvis for good measure), is that she lacks any trace of vulnerability, a quality that, it should be noted, is essential to the charms of both sexes.[16]

NOTES

[1] Susanne K. Langer, "The Lord of Creation," *Fortune* Jan. 1944: 140.

[2] Nora Ephron, "Seagrams with Moxie," *New York Times Book Review* 11 Mar. 1979: 13.

[3] Dudley Clendinen, "Even the Fish Die in Streams As the Dust-Dry South Bakes," *New York Times* 17 July 1986, national ed.: 1.

[4] Robert Pinsky, "Letting Go," *New York Times Book Review* 6 Jan. 1991: 30.

[5] Fred Reed, "The Star Wars Swindle: Hawking Nuclear Snake Oil," *Harper's* May 1986: 48.

[6] Michael Massing, "Snap Books," *New Republic* 4 May 1987: 25.

[7] Harry F. Waters, "TV's New Racial Hue," *Newsweek* 25 Jan. 1988: 52.

[8] "Skiing Utah Powder," *Sunset* Jan. 1976: 39.

[9] Ian Frazier, *Great Plains* (New York: Farrar, 1989) 5.

[10] Diane D. Edwards, "Leaping Lizards and Male Impersonators: Are There Hidden Messages?" *Science News* 131 (1987): 348.

[11] Robert Hughes, "The Decline of the City of Mahagonny," *New Republic* 25 June 1990: 35.

[12] Jerry Borrell, "Is Your Computer Killing You?" *Macworld* July 1990: 24.

[13] Meg Furnish, "Another '59," unpublished essay.

[14] Garrison Keillor, *Lake Wobegon Days* (New York: Penguin, 1986) 5.

[15] Jason Epstein, "Living in New York," *New York Review of Books* 6 Jan. 1966: 15.

[16] Luc Sante, "Unlike a Virgin," *New Republic* 20 & 26 Aug. 1990: 27.

VI

WORDS

WORDS

To convey your ideas successfully, you need to know words well and to respect their often subtle differences from one another. Specifically, when revising your drafts you should make sure that your words

1. *mean what you think they mean;*
2. *are appropriate to the occasion;*
3. *are concise;*
4. *are neither stale, roundabout, nor needlessly abstract; and*
5. *show control over figurative, or nonliteral, implications.*

Chapters 15–17 discuss these requirements of ***diction,*** *or word choice. For an alphabetically arranged treatment of problem expressions, see the Index of Usage beginning on page 682.*

15

Appropriate Language

15a Know how to use your college dictionary.

To make progress in your control of **denotation**, or the dictionary meaning of words, it is essential that you own a college dictionary such as *The Random House College Dictionary, Funk and Wagnalls Standard College Dictionary, Webster's New World Dictionary of the American Language, Webster's New Collegiate Dictionary*, or *The American Heritage Dictionary of the English Language*. These volumes are large enough to meet your daily needs without being too cumbersome to carry around. Once you learn from the prefatory guide to your dictionary how to interpret its abbreviations, symbols, and order of placing entries, you can find in it most—perhaps all—of the following kinds of information:

spelling	capitalization	biographical and given names
parts of speech	derivations	places and population figures
definitions	usage levels	weights and measures
synonyms	syllable division	names and locations of colleges
antonyms	principles of usage	
alternate forms	abbreviations	
pronunciation	symbols	

To see what a college dictionary can and cannot do, look at *Random House*'s entry under *fabulous:*

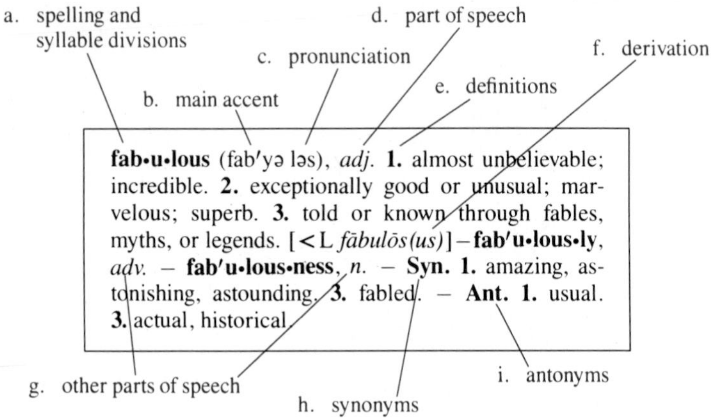
a. spelling and syllable divisions
d. part of speech
c. pronunciation
f. derivation
e. definitions
b. main accent
fab•u•lous (fab′yə ləs), *adj.* **1.** almost unbelievable; incredible. **2.** exceptionally good or unusual; marvelous; superb. **3.** told or known through fables, myths, or legends. [< L *fābulōs(us)*] – **fab′u•lous•ly**, *adv.* – **fab′u•lous•ness**, *n.* – **Syn. 1.** amazing, astonishing, astounding. **3.** fabled. – **Ant. 1.** usual. **3.** actual, historical.
g. other parts of speech
i. antonyms
h. synonyms

The entry shows, in the following order:

a. how the word is spelled and the points where syllable divisions occur *(fab•u•lous);*

Comment: The lowercase *f* shows that *fabulous* is not normally capitalized.

If this word could be spelled correctly in different ways, the less common form would appear in a separate entry with a cross-reference to the more common form; thus the entry for *reenforce* merely sends you to *reinforce*. In your writing, use the spelling under which a full definition has been given.

app lang 15a

Syllable division is not completely uniform from one dictionary to another, but you cannot go wrong by following your dictionary's practice in every case. (You can also spare yourself trouble by not breaking up words at all; a little unevenness in right-hand margins is normal.)

b. where the main accent falls *(fab′);*

Comment: If the word had another strongly stressed syllable, like *hand* in *beforehand*, you would find it marked with a secondary accent: *bi•for′ hand′*.

c. how the word is pronounced;

Comment: The pronunciation key at the bottom of every pair of pages reveals, among other things, that ə = *a* as in *alone*. (One dictionary's key will differ from another's.) College dictionaries make no attempt to capture regional or nonstandard pronunciations, like x *nōō'kul ər* for *nōō'klē ər (nuclear)*.

d. the **part of speech** *(adj.* for *adjective);*

Comment: Some words, like *can* and *wait*, occupy more than one part of speech, depending on the context. Definitions are grouped according to those parts of speech. Transitive verbs (those that take an object—p. 383, 18a) are usually listed separately from intransitive verbs (those that take no object). Thus *Random House* gives all the intransitive senses of *wait (v.i.)*, as in *Wait for me*, before the transitive senses *(v.t.)*, as in *Wait your turn!*

e. three definitions of *fabulous;*

Comment: No dictionary lists definitions in the order of their acceptability. The dictionary illustrated here begins with the most common part of speech occupied by a given word and, within each part of speech, offers the most frequently encountered meaning first. Some other dictionaries begin with the earliest meaning and proceed toward the present. The system used in your dictionary is clearly set forth in the prefatory material, which you should read through at least once.

f. the word's derivation from the first three syllables of the Latin word *fabulosus;*

app lang 15a

Comment: The derivation, or *etymology*, of a word is given only if its component parts are not obviously familiar—as they are, for example, in *freeze-dry* and *nearsighted*. Many symbols are used in stating etymologies; look for their explanation in the prefatory material of your dictionary.

g. an adverb and a noun stemming from the main word;

Comment: Fabulously and *fabulousness* are "run-on entries," words formed by adding a suffix (p. 731, 34e) to the main entry.

h. synonyms of definitions 1 and 3;

Comment: In most dictionaries a word with many apparent synonyms—words having the same or nearly the same meaning—is accompanied by a "synonym study" explaining fine differences. Thus, this dictionary's entry for *strength* concludes:

> **–Syn. 4.** STRENGTH, POWER, FORCE, MIGHT suggest capacity to do something. STRENGTH is inherent capacity to manifest energy, to endure, and to resist. POWER is capacity to do work and to act. FORCE is the exercise of power: *One has the power to do something. He exerts force when he does it. He has sufficient strength to complete it.* MIGHT is power or strength in a great degree: *the might of an army.*

This would be useful information if you were wondering which of the four similar words to use in a sentence. If you looked up *power, force*, or *might*, you would find a cross-reference to the synonym study under *strength*.

i. antonyms (words with the opposite meaning) of definitions 1 and 3.

Comment: If you are searching for a word to convey the opposite of a certain term, check its listed antonyms. But if you still are not satisfied, look up the entries for the most promising antonyms and check their synonyms. This will greatly expand your range of choice.

So much for *fabulous*. But other sample entries would reveal still further kinds of information:

1. *inflected forms*. Some entries show unusual inflected forms—that is, changes in spelling expressing different syntactic functions. You will find unusual plurals *(louse, lice);* unusual principal parts of verbs (*run, ran, run*—see p. 576, 32b); pronoun forms (*I, my, mine*, etc.); comparative and superlative degrees of adjectives (*good, better, best*—see p. 431, 21a).

2. *restrictive labels*. The entry will show how a word's use may be limited to a region *(Southern U.S., Austral., Chiefly Brit.);*

to an earlier time or a kind of occasion *(Archaic, Obs., Poetic);* to a subject *(Bot., Anat., Law);* and, most important for the writer, to a level of usage for words not clearly within standard American English *(Nonstandard, Informal, Slang).*

3. *usage study.* Beyond its usage levels, your dictionary may offer especially valuable discussions of usage problems surrounding certain controversial words or meanings, such as *ain't, different from/than*, or *hardly* with negative forms:

> —**Usage.** HARDLY, BARELY, and SCARCELY all have a negative connotation, and the use of any of them with a supplementary negative is considered nonstandard, as in *I can't hardly wait* for *I can hardly wait.*

EXERCISES

1. After consulting your dictionary, use your own words to write brief definitions of both terms in each of the following pairs:

   A. accent, accentuate *(verbs)*
   B. accused, suspected *(adjectives)*
   C. adverse, averse
   D. barbaric, barbarous
   E. childish, childlike
   F. elemental, elementary
   G. exhausting, exhaustive
   H. healthful, healthy
   I. infect, infest
   J. possible, feasible

2. Using your dictionary as necessary, explain the chief differences of denotation, or dictionary meaning, between the following paired words:

   A. ample, excessive
   B. avenue, road
   C. cunning, politic
   D. overhear, spy
   E. ecstatic, happy
   F. bold, brash
   G. erotic, lustful
   H. impartial, indifferent
   I. stimulate, fake
   J. opponent, enemy

15b Keep a vocabulary list.

The only way to be certain that you have broadened your written vocabulary is to try out new words in your papers, risking an occasional inaccuracy while gradually building your store of useful words. But how are you to acquire those words in the first place?

Many student writers rely on a *thesaurus*, or dictionary of synonyms and antonyms, to learn new words and to jog their memory of words already known. A thesaurus can be especially handy if it is included in the word processing program you happen to be using with a computer. You should realize, however, that the synonyms found in a thesaurus are only approximate. To use the thesaurus shrewdly in composing a given sentence, you must already be familiar with the term you select.

The best way to build vocabulary, with or without a thesaurus, is to notice how words are being used by published authors and to keep a record of your growing knowledge. Specifically:

1. Keep a section of your notebook for listing and defining words that you didn't previously know, words whose meanings you misunderstood, and words you understand and admire but haven't yet had occasion to use in your writing.
2. Begin your list by going over the Index of Usage on pages 682–705, making an entry for each expression whose indicated meaning is new to you. Note especially those terms that get easily confused (*affect* versus *effect, imply* versus *infer*, etc.).
3. Add to your notebook continually as you keep reading and receiving comments on your written work.
4. Every time you make an entry, quickly scan the previous entries to see whether you have mastered them yet. Cross out or asterisk terms that you now consider to be part of your normal working vocabulary.

EXERCISE

3. Once your vocabulary list has begun to grow, copy and submit any five entries, including a definition for each word.

15c Master idioms.

An **idiom** is a fixed expression whose meaning cannot be deduced from its elements—for example, *put up with*, as in *She put up with his complaining*. For foreign students of English (or any other language), idioms are a continual source of worry. No amount of grammar study or knowledge of the separate meanings of *put, up*, and *with* will yield the right meaning; the idiom, like all others, must simply be learned as a unit. It is not just foreigners, however, who stumble over idioms in their writing. Every composition teacher is familiar with essays by native speakers who write *I was bored of being sick* or *in regards to traffic* (it should be *bored by* or *bored with* and *in regard to* or *with regard to*).

As these examples suggest, most of the mischief caused by idioms centers on prepositions—words like *down, up, in, out, by, of*, and *with*. What can you do to make sure you are choosing the right preposition to go with a given expression? The answer is threefold:

1. Consult your dictionary; in many cases you will find the idiom covered there.
2. Study the list of common idioms below.
3. Beginning with unfamiliar items in that list and adding problem expressions that turn up in your edited drafts and submitted papers, insert idioms into your ongoing vocabulary list (15b).

Prepositions in Idioms

abide *by* a promise
abide *in* a place

acquiesce *in* a wish or request

adapt *from* a model
adapt *to* new conditions

affinity *with* a person

afraid *of* someone or something

agree *on* a strategy
agree *to* a proposal
agree *with* an opinion

analogy *with* something comparable
analogous *to* something comparable

angry *at* a situation
angry *with* a person

annoyed *with* or *by* a persistent bother or person

apropos *of* a topic

aptitude *for* a skill

at peace *with* oneself

in behalf of someone's interest
on behalf of someone absent

capacity *to* do something
capacity *of* that thing

charge *for* a purchase
charge *with* an offense

compare x *to* y [they are alike]
compare x *with* y [make the act of comparison]

concur *in* a judgment
concur *with* someone who has made a judgment

conform *to* a rule
in conformity *with* a rule

contend *for* a prize
contend *with* an obstacle or adversary

cooperate *with* authority

correspond *to* something equivalent
correspond *with* a letter writer

depart *from* tradition
depart *for* a destination

dependent *on* favors or persons

differ *about* or *over* an issue
differ *from* something different
differ *with* someone holding a contrary opinion

equal *to* something
equally *with* something

equivalent *to* a like case

fired *from* a job
fired *with* enthusiasm

free *from* interference or bondage
free *of* charge

frightened *by* something or someone

identical *to* or *with* something that is the same

impatient *at* a delay
impatient *for* a desired outcome
impatient *with* a person

independent *from* another country's rule
independent *of* support or supporting persons

inferior *to* something else

infer *from* a source

meet *with* an obstacle

oblivious *of* something forgotten
oblivious *to* an ignored circumstance

occupied *by* a tenant
occupied *in* deep thought
occupied (or preoccupied) *with* a concern

part *from* a friend
part *with* a possession

partake *of* a feast

participate *in* an activity

prior *to* something later

prohibit x *from* doing y

a report *of* an event
a report *on* a topic

rewarded *by* an outcome or person
rewarded *for* a good deed
rewarded *with* a prize

superior *to* something lesser

sympathy *for* the oppressed
sympathy *with* someone with like feelings

tired *of* an annoyance

wait *at* a bus stop
wait *for* a result
wait *on* a customer

EXERCISE

4. Consulting the list above and your dictionary as necessary, fill in the missing prepositions in the following sentences:

   A. Tired _______ waiting for a raise, she marched into the boss's office and announced that she was fed up _______ the delay.
   B. The appellate judge, after conferring _______ the attorneys from both sides, announced that he concurred _______ the original verdict.
   C. After contending _______ a typhoon and a broken rudder, the captain was gratified _______ the sight of land; and later he was rewarded _______ a commendation from the admiral.
   D. The couple differed _______ every political question, but they differed _______ their neighbors in never arguing in public.
   E. Although he was getting increasingly bored _______ television, he was reluctant to part _______ his set.

15d Use words in established senses.

English is probably the fastest-changing of all languages, and yesterday's error often becomes today's standard usage. As a writer, however, you should be concerned not with anticipating shifts in taste but with communicating your ideas effectively. Many readers are upset by diction that is being used in some capricious or momentarily popular way. By being conservative in your choice of words, you can avoid arousing automatically negative responses to the content of your work.

Many fad words have a common feature: they usually belong to one part of speech but are being used as another. Sometimes a suffix (p. 731, 34e) such as *-wise* or *-type* has been added to turn a noun into an adjective or adverb.

DON'T:
x **Gaswise**, the car is economical.

DO:
• The car gets good mileage.

DON'T:
x **Preferencewise,** she is looking for a **commuter-type** car.

DO:
• She wants a car suitable for commuting.

More often, one part of speech simply takes over another.

DON'T:
x It was a **fun** party.

x She **authored** the book in 1989.

x We **gifted** the newlyweds with a toaster.

x Mark is a **together** person.

x I would give anything for an **invite** to the party.

DO:
• The party was **fun.**

• She **wrote** the book in 1989.

• We **gave** the newlyweds a toaster.

• Mark is a **confident, competent** person.

• I would give anything for an **invitation** to the party.

The use of nouns as adjectives deserves special mention in an age of spreading bureaucracy. Standard English allows many such **attributive nouns,** as they are called, as in *mountain time, night vision, cheese omelet*, and *recreation director*. But officials have a way of jamming them together in a confusing heap. A frugal governor, for example, once proposed what he called a *community work experience program demonstration project*. This row of nouns was meant to describe, or perhaps to conceal, a policy of getting welfare mothers to pick up highway litter without receiving any wages. As a student writer, you would be wise to avoid changing the customary part of speech of a word or piling up attributive nouns.

EXERCISE

5. Study the following entries in the Index of Usage (pp. 682–705): *enormity, enthuse, fortuitous, fulsome, hopefully, imply/infer, literally, mad, militate/mitigate, otherwise, part/portion, phenomena, plus, possible, rebut/refute, reticent,* and *usage*. Choose the five expressions that you yourself tend to use most often in the criticized ways. If you have to stop before five items, fill out the quota with those expressions that you think are most commonly misused by other writers. For each of the five terms, submit a pair of original sentences, first showing a typical misuse and then a correct one.

15e Control connotations.

The prime requirement for controlling meaning is to know the *denotations*, or dictionary definitions, of the words you are using. (See 15a–d.) But words also have important **connotations**—further suggestions or associations derived from the contexts in which the words have been habitually used. By and large, you will not find connotations in your dictionary; you have to pick them up from meeting the same words repeatedly in reading and conversation. Of course you cannot expect to learn all the overtones of every English word. But as a writer you can ask yourself whether the words you have allowed into your first drafts are appropriate to the occasion. When you are unsure, think of related words until you find one that conveys the right associations.

Take, for example, the words *store, shop*, and *boutique*. Because of the contexts in which the words most often appear, they *connote* different things. When we think of a *store*, we picture an establishment where merchandise is sold. A *shop* suggests a smaller establishment selling a specific type of goods, or a department in a larger store, such as the *card shop* at Field's. A *boutique* is a small shop that specializes in fashionable items, often clothing or accessories for women. If you were writing about the corner grocery that keeps your neighborhood in bread, milk, and other staples seven days a week, you would want to call it a *store*. To call it a *shop* or a *boutique* would undercut your purpose in pointing out the establishment's diverse and ordinary stock.

Consider two further examples, *complex* versus *complicated* and *workers* versus *employees*. Although the members of each pair are close in denotation, their connotations differ. Suppose you wanted to characterize an overelaborate instruction manual. Would you call it *complex* or *complicated*? We hope you would choose *complicated*, which can imply not just intricacy but more intricacy than is called for. And if you were criticizing harsh factory conditions, you would want to write about mistreated *workers*, not mistreated *employees*. These words denote the same people, yet *employees* characterizes them from a corporate point of view, whereas *workers* calls to mind laborers whose interests and loyalties may be quite different from those of the company.

Note that there is such a thing as getting connotations too lopsidedly in favor of your own position on an issue. Suppose, for example, you were writing an essay about discourtesy among adolescents. If you chose the term *young thugs* to characterize teenagers, you would certainly be making your feelings clear, but you would also be *begging the question* (p. 71, 3k), forcing your reader to respond emotionally with you or against you. In revising your essays, tone down any inflammatory language that seems to convey ready-made conclusions.

EXERCISES

6. Explain whatever differences of connotation you find between the following paired words:

   A. stout, fat
   B. express, communicate
   C. hasten, scurry
   D. talented, gifted
   E. investigate, inquire

7. Submit a paragraph of your own prose written for this or any other course. Circle three words whose connotations strike you as appropriate to your precise intention. Then, beneath the paragraph, briefly discuss the connotations of all three words, contrasting them with the connotations of three other words that would have proved less appropriate. (Your rival choices should be "near misses," not wildly implausible terms.)

15f Avoid racist and sexist language.

Since you are writing to convince, not to insult, nothing can be gained from using offensive terms. Racial slurs like *nigger, honky*, and *wop*, demeaning stereotypes like *pushy Jew* and *dumb Swede*, and sexually biased phrases such as *lady driver, female logic*, and *typical male brutality* make any fair-minded reader turn against the writer.

The problem of sexism in language deserves special discussion because it goes beyond any conscious wish to show prejudice. In recent decades people have been increasingly realizing that long-accepted conventions of word choice imply that women are inferior or are destined for restricted roles. To keep sexist language out of your prose, then, it is not enough to avoid grossly insulting terms; you must be watchful for subtler signs of condescension as well.

If, for example, you call William Shakespeare *Shakespeare*, why should you call Emily Dickinson *Miss Dickinson* or, worse, *Emily*? Such names imply that a woman who writes poems is not really a poet but a "poetess," a "lady poet," or even a "spinster poet." Write about *Dickinson's poetry*, thus giving it the same standing you would the work of any other author. Similarly, use *sculptor* and *lawyer* for both sexes, avoiding such designations as *sculptress* and *lady lawyer*. And do without *coed*, which suggests that the higher education of women is an afterthought to the real (male) thing. Make your language reflect the fact that, in North America at any rate, men and women are now considered equally eligible for nearly every role.

Tact is necessary, however, in deciding how far to go in changing traditional expressions. The ideal is to avoid sexism without sacrificing clarity and ease of expression. If you wrote *actor* for *actress* and *waiter* for *waitress*, for example, your readers would be confused; rightly or wrongly, common usage still recognizes separate terms for male and female performers of those functions. But when in doubt, choose a sex-neutral term: not *mankind* but *humanity*, not *man-made* but *artificial*.

-Person

Try to find nonsexist alternatives to awkward *-person* suffixes, which sound ugly to many readers of both sexes.

SEXIST	NONSEXIST BUT AWKWARD	PREFERABLE
chairman	chairperson	chair, head
Congressman	Congressperson	Representative
mailman	mailperson	letter carrier
policeman	policeperson	police officer
weatherman	weatherperson	meteorologist

The Pronoun Dilemma

Perhaps the sorest of all issues in contemporary usage is that of the so-called **common gender**. Which pronouns should you use when discussing an indefinite person, a "one"? Traditionally, that indefinite person has been "male": *he, his, him*, as in *A taxpayer must check his return carefully*. For the centuries in which this practice went unchallenged, the masculine pronouns in such sentences were understood to designate not actual men but people of either sex. Today, however, many readers find these words an offensive reminder of second-class citizenship for women. Remedies that have been proposed include using the phrase *he or she* (or *she or he*) for the common gender, treating singular common words as plural (*A taxpayer must check their return*), combining masculine and feminine pronouns in forms like *s/he*, and using *she* in one sentence and *he* in the next.

Unfortunately, all of these solutions carry serious drawbacks. Continual repetition of *he or she* is cumbersome and monotonous; many readers would regard *A taxpayer must check their return* as a blunder, not a blow for liberation; pronunciation of *s/he* is uncertain; and the use of *she* and *he* in close alternation, though increasingly common, risks confusing the reader by implying that two indefinite persons, a female and a male, are involved.

To avoid such awkwardness, follow these seven guidelines:

1. Use *she* whenever you are sure the indefinite person would be female (a student in a women's college, for example):

   • Someone who enters a nunnery must sacrifice everything from **her** former life.

2. Do not use *she* for roles that have been "traditionally female" but are actually mixed: secretary, school teacher, laundry worker, and so forth. Female pronouns in such contexts imply an offensive prejudgment about "women's place." Use plural forms to show a sex-neutral attitude.

   DON'T:
   x A kindergarten teacher has **her** hands full every day.

   DO:
   • Kindergarten teachers have **their** hands full every day.

3. Use an occasional *he or she* or *she or he* to indicate an indefinite person:

   • When a driver is stopped for a traffic violation, **he or she** would do well to remain polite.

   But be sparing with this formula; it can become annoying.

4. Try, throughout an essay, using *she* consistently as the "common gender" pronoun. Your reader will become quickly adjusted to the change, especially if you yourself are female.
5. If your uses of the common gender are few and widely spaced, try alternating the masculine and feminine forms.
6. Avoid the singular whenever your meaning is not affected.

   DON'T:
   x A taxpayer must check **his** return.

   DO:
   • Taxpayers must check **their** returns.

7. Omit the pronoun altogether whenever you can do so without awkwardness.

ACCEPTABLE:
- Everyone needs **his or her** vacation.

BETTER:
- Everyone needs **a** vacation.

EXERCISE

8. Rewrite each of the following sentences, removing sexist implications without creating an awkward effect:

   A. A nurse's heavy responsibilities can eventually cause her to experience what is known as "nurse's burnout."
   B. You had better take those soiled sheets to the nearest laundress.
   C. Someone who drives too slowly on the freeway is a menace to his fellow drivers.
   D. A policeman in that neighborhood had better be prepared to defend himself against muggers.
   E. All mankind is eager for peace.

15g Avoid jargon.

Jargon is specialized language that appears in a nonspecialized context, thus giving a technical flavor to statements that would be better expressed in everyday words. When you are writing a paper in, say, economics, anthropology, or psychology, you can and should use terms that are meaningful within the field: *liquidity*, *kinship structure*, *paranoid*, and so forth. But those same terms become jargon when used out of context.

DON'T:
x My liquidity profile has been weak lately.

DO:
- I have been short of cash lately.

DON'T:
x Her kinship structure extends from coast to coast.

DO:
• Her family is scattered from coast to coast.

DON'T:
x Roland was really paranoid about the boss's intentions.

DO:
• Roland was suspicious of the boss's intentions.

Most jargon today comes from popular academic disciplines such as sociology and psychology, from government bureaucracy, and from the world of computers. Here is some of the more commonly seen jargon, accompanied by everyday equivalents that would usually be preferable.

JARGON	**ORDINARY TERM**
access (v.)	enter, make use of
behaviors	acts, deeds, conduct
correlation	resemblance, association
cost-effective	economical
counterproductive	harmful, obstructive
dialogue (v.)	talk, converse
ego	vanity, pride
facilitate	help, make possible
feedback	response
finalize	complete
input	response, contribution
interface (v.)	meet, share information with
maximize	make the most of
obsession	strong interest
parameters	borders
prioritize	prefer, rank
reinforcement schedule	inducements
sociological	social
syndrome	pattern
trauma	shock
user-friendly	uncomplicated

You can put jargon to good comic or ironic use, but when you find it appearing uninvited in your drafts, revise.

EXERCISE

9. Here is a fictitious letter making fun of a certain "official" style. Pick out several examples of jargon and submit comments on the way they convey or disguise meaning:

Dear Miss Dodds:

Thank you for your letter deploring the 14,000 fish deaths apparently related to thermal outflow into Long Island Sound from our nuclear power facility at Squaw Point. While the blame for this regrettable incident might most properly be ascribed to the fish, which swam closer to the Connecticut shore than is their normal habit, we believe that the ultimate solution must be found in terms of "the human element." Specifically, it is a task of public education in this era when customer demand for power markedly exceeds the deliverability capability of the electrical segment of the energy usage industry.

Do you ever stop to think, Miss Dodds, where the power comes from when you flick on your air-conditioner, your hair dryer, your cake mixer, your vacuum cleaner, and the myriad other appliances that enable you to live in "the lap of luxury" vs. the meager subsistence standard enjoyed by most of the peoples of the world? Until the American housewife is willing to go back to the egg beater and the broom, the utilities industry cannot be made the scapegoat for occasional episodes of ecological incompatibility.

Many consumers today advocate "zero growth" and a turning back of the clock to a simpler agrarian past. Quite frankly, if the rural American of 1900 had been as counter-oriented to the ongoing thrust of technology as certain romantic elements are in 1973, the outhouse would never have been supplanted by the flush toilet.

Very truly yours,

NORMAN R. HOWELL
Vice President for Consumer Relations
AFFILIATED UTILITIES COMPANY[1]

15h Aim for middle diction in most contexts.

SLANG	MIDDLE DICTION	FORMAL DICTION
mug	face	visage
kicks	pleasure	gratification
threads	clothes	attire
specs	glasses	spectacles
rip off	steal	expropriate
big-mouthed	talkative	voluble

Different situations call for different levels of diction (word choice), from the slang that may be appropriate in a letter to a friend, to the formal language expected in a legal document, to the technical terms demanded by a scientific report. But whenever you are writing outside such special contexts, you should aim for *middle diction*—language that is neither too casual to convey serious concern nor too stiff to express feeling.

The best way to recognize levels of diction is to be an observant reader of different kinds of prose and a close listener to conversations. But if you have studied Latin or a "Latinate" modern language such as Spanish, French, or Italian, you have a head start toward spotting formal English diction. All the words in the right column on page 351 are both formal and Latinate.

Deliberately Extreme or Mixed Diction

If you have a firm sense of diction levels and want to create an effect of **irony** (p. 80, 3o), you can do so by playing with fancy language or with slang. Look back, for example, at the long passage about "heart healthy swordfish" that begins on page 81. Except for a few offhand expressions like *let's see* and *sure*, both the sentence structure and the diction of that passage are deliberately "high": *It's time to idly, in the manner of certain doges, select from the bounty of the earth some particularly fragrant and ornamental nutrition bundle*. Such a style establishes a comic distance between the writer and his subject; he is winking at us and saying, "Is this stuff pretentious, or what?"

Similarly, you can achieve irony by nudging your reader with a combination of high and low language, as this writer does in mocking government officials who announce that they are "taking the blame" for mistakes and misdeeds:

> Except, of course, that the executive officeholder or other **bigwig** who has employed this language usually hasn't taken the blame at all. This is the second key feature of the **gambit** and its particular **beauty**. For the leader to refuse all further discussion of who did what, as they usually do, insistently meeting every request for elaboration instead with the **ostentatiously** clipped and wooden **reiteration** ("I have already said that I accept the responsibility. I am just not going to get into that") is to powerfully suggest that in fact *somebody* else did it. **Our hero** now looks even better; he is seen to be **stoically taking heat** for his subordinates—**what a guy!** This suggestion will likely be reinforced

> **pretty** quickly by **a sudden spring shower** of unattributed **inside-dope** stories saying which subordinate's **foul-up** it really was.[2]

The contrast between sixty-four-dollar words like *reiteration* and slangy ones like *inside-dope* helps the writer to show that, in her view, nothing said in Washington should be taken at face value.

EXERCISES

10. Use your dictionary, if necessary, to help you decide which level of diction (formal, middle, or informal) is illustrated by each of the following words. Whenever you label a word as formal or informal, provide a middle-level equivalent:

    A. irritate
    B. hyperbole
    C. birdbrain
    D. zonked
    E. fluoridate
    F. refractory (*adjective*)
    G. indemnify
    H. gal
    I. oafish
    J. resist

11. For each of the following middle-level words, give one formal and one informal equivalent:

    A. friend
    B. understand
    C. smell (*noun*)
    D. clothes
    E. rob
    F. see
    G. idea
    H. change (*verb*)
    I. leave (*verb*)
    J. good

12. Return to the "airline food" passage on page 77 and examine its language. Submit a paragraph or two explaining how the writer has achieved her effect in part by controlling levels of diction. Be specific in citing her words.

NOTES

[1] William Zinsser, "Frankly, Miss Dodds," *Atlantic* Apr. 1973: 94.

[2] Meg Greenfield, "The No-Fault Confession," *Newsweek* 15 June 1987: 80.

16

Efficient Language

16a Be concrete.

Concrete words name observable things or properties like *classroom* and *smoky*; **abstract** words convey ideas like *education* and *pollution*—nonphysical things that we can grasp only with our minds, not with our senses. Of course there are gradations between the extremes: a *university* is more concrete than *education* but less so than a *classroom*, a distinct physical place. The more concrete the term, the more vivid it will be to a reader.

Whenever you are describing something or telling a story, you can hardly go wrong by making your successive drafts more concrete. Suppose you are trying to characterize your new typewriter, which you have praised in your first draft as *extremely modern*. That is an abstract judgment that could mean anything to anyone. What precisely is modern about the machine? In revising, think about *the daisy wheel printing unit, the automatic return, the automatic correction, the sixteen-character memory, the programmable margin settings*, and so forth. Get the concrete details into your essay, convincing your reader that your general statements rest on observations.

Even in papers of analysis and argument, where the thesis is necessarily an abstract idea, concrete language will help you provide supporting details and retain your reader's interest. Here, for example, are two versions of a student paragraph. In drafting the first, the writer was evidently thinking of himself as a social science major. When asked to revise for an essay audience, he looked for ways of turning abstract statements into concrete ones:

A. Lasting trauma from early stress is probably causally related to two factors: heritability of susceptibility and the age at which the stress occurs. In infant rhesus monkeys, certain members of the experimental population prove more susceptible to permanent disturbance than others; heritability is thus an indicated factor. Furthermore, the entire population yields a finding of greater vulnerability when administration of stress occurs between the precise ages of two and seven months. Such a finding suggests that among humans, too, a period of maximum vulnerability may obtain.

B. A recent study of rhesus monkeys may offer us some clues to the way people react—and sometimes don't react—to early stress. Baby monkeys who have been put into solitary cages tend to become feisty and to stay that way. We might have expected as much. But some monkeys, oddly, act normal again almost as soon as they have rejoined their fellows; it seems that they have inherited a resistance to trauma. Furthermore, the most aggressive monkeys turn out to be those who were isolated within a precise period, between the ages of two and seven months. If these findings carry over to humans, we can see why it is risky to generalize about the effects of *all* early stress. What matters may not be whether you suffered in infancy, but who your parents were and exactly when your ordeal occurred.

effic lang 16a

Neither of these paragraphs abounds in concrete language, but the relative concreteness of passage B helps to explain why it is easier to grasp and more pleasurable to read. Note that weighty, awkward abstractions like *heritability of susceptibility* have disappeared and that we now see *Baby monkeys . . . in solitary cages*, not a *population* that has undergone *administration of stress*.

EXERCISES

1. Make the following sentences more vivid by substituting concrete language where it is appropriate:

    A. She attended scheduled sessions at the institution of higher learning with unfailing regularity.

B. Daytime serial dramatic programs had his undivided concentration.
C. The small rodents are of lasting interest to cats, who would never willingly forgo an opportunity for the pursuit and seizure of same.
D. In northern regions, conspicuous display of emotions on the part of members of the populace is rather the exception than the rule.
E. Loss of control of one's sense of reality has come to be recognized by courts of law as a factor tending to favor the acquittal of a defendant who was afflicted in that manner.

2. Professor X describes himself as follows in a classified advertisement:

> Sophisticated, debonair college prof., 35, recently divorced, with liberal values and classical tastes, seeks broadminded female companion for travel and cultural pursuits. Knowledge of vintage wines and modern verse desirable. Send photo. Box 307, NYR.

What do you think Professor X is really like? Write a paragraph describing him vividly, and then underline all the concrete diction you have used.

16b Be concise.

Your reader's attention will depend in large part on the ratio between information and language in your prose. Wordiness, or the use of more words than are necessary to convey a point, is one of the most common and easily corrected flaws of style. The fewer words you can use without harm to your meaning, the better.

WORDY	CONCISE
among all the problems that exist today	among all current problems
an investment in the form of stocks and bonds	an investment in stocks and bonds
at the present time	now
due to the fact that	because
during the course of	during
for the purpose of getting rich	to get rich
for the simple reason that	because
in a very real sense	truly
in spite of the fact that	although
in the not too distant future	soon
in view of the fact that	since

WORDY	CONCISE
it serves no particular purpose	it serves no purpose
majoring in the field of astronomy	majoring in astronomy
my personal preference	my preference
on the part of	by
owing to the fact that	because
proceeded to walk	walked
rarely ever	rarely
seldom ever	seldom
the present incumbent	the incumbent
to the effect that	that

Avoiding Redundancy

A **redundancy** is an expression that conveys the same meaning more than once—for example, *circle around*, which says "go around around." The difference between writing *She circled the globe* and X *She circled around the globe* is that in the second version the word *around* delivers no new information and thus strains the reader's patience.

Examine your drafts to see whether they contain redundancies, and be uncompromising in pruning them. The following examples are typical:

REDUNDANT	CONCISE
adequate enough	adequate
advance planning	planning
both together	both
but yet	but
contributing factor	factor
deliberate lie	lie
equally as far	as far
exact same	same
few in number	few
final outcome	outcome
free gift	gift
join together	join
large in size	large

REDUNDANT	CONCISE
past experience	experience
past history	history
refer back	refer
set of twins	twins
share in common	share
shuttle back and forth	shuttle
two different	two

Redundancy also occurs when you unnecessarily repeat an expression that may not be redundant in itself. Every writer has favorite words that tend to get overused in the course of an essay. Reread your drafts to ferret out such terms, and consult your dictionary or thesaurus if necessary to explore alternative ways of conveying the same meaning.

With a word processor: When you suspect that you have been using a certain expression too often in a draft essay, run a "Find All" search for that term, and revise accordingly.

Avoiding Circumlocution

All redundancies fall into the broader category of **circumlocutions**—that is, roundabout forms of expression. But some circumlocutions, instead of saying the same thing twice, take several words to say almost nothing. Formulas like *in a manner of speaking* or *to make a long story short*, for example, are simply ways of making a short story long. Watch especially for cumbersome verb phrases like *give rise to, make contact with*, and *render inoperative;* prefer *arouse, meet, destroy*. And if you mean *because*, do not reach for *due to the fact that*. When five words do the work of one, all five are anemic.

CIRCUMLOCUTION	CONCISE EXPRESSION
He was of a kindly nature.	He was kind.
It was of an unusual character.	It was unusual.

CIRCUMLOCUTION	CONCISE EXPRESSION
My father and I have differences about dating.	My father and I differ about dating.
I finally made contact with my supervisor.	I finally met my supervisor.
The copy that is pink in color is for yourself.	Keep the pink copy.
She suspected she would be in an unemployment-type kind of situation when the overflow of customers due to the Christmas shopping circumstances was no longer in effect.	She suspected she would be laid off after the Christmas rush.

EXERCISES

3. Look through your own prose—earlier exercises, papers, or drafts—until you have found five sentences that seem deficient in conciseness. Submit the five sentences along with five adequately concise revisions.

4. Write a paragraph in which you deliberately use wordy expressions, redundancies, and circumlocutions. Underline the offending expressions, and submit the paragraph along with a revised version that is adequately concise.

16c Prune intensifiers.

In conversation most of us use **intensifiers**—"fortifying" words like *absolutely, basically, certainly, definitely, incredibly, intensely, just, of course, perfectly, positively, quite, really, simply, so, too,* and *very*—without pausing to worry about their meaning. And in telling stories or expressing opinions, we veer toward the extremes of *fantastic, terrific, sensational, fabulous*, and *awful, horrible, terrible, dreadful*. Our listeners know how to allow for such exaggeration. Most written prose, however, aims at a more measured tone. Look through your drafts for intensifiers, and see how many of them you can eliminate without subtracting from your meaning. Your revised work will not only be more concise and therefore less taxing to read, it will also sound more assured. Readers sense that intensifiers are morale-building words meaning *maybe* or *I hope;* doing without such terms is a sign of your confidence that you are making a sound case for your ideas.

WITH INTENSIFIERS:

x It was another **very** routine start to a two-week vacation. I **definitely** had no fixed plans other than **simply** flying to Denver. I knew Colorado was a **fantastic** state, and **basically** that is all I thought about as I settled into my assigned seat. As the aircraft door was about to be closed, a man walked in and occupied the vacant seat next to me. He mumbled something to me in an **absolutely** foreign accent. The departure was **very** uneventful. All we **really** did was try to kill time, but the book he was reading **just** attracted my interest: *Cave Exploring in the USA*. I was **so** curious and asked him if cave exploring interested him. That was when he explained—**incredibly**—that in France he was a professional cave explorer. After the dinner service ended, we talked, and his stories of days underground were **too** fascinating. Finally, he invited me to join him, and I **quite** happily accepted.

WITHOUT INTENSIFIERS:

- It was another routine start to a two-week vacation. I had no fixed plans other than flying to Denver. I knew Colorado was an exceptional state, and that is all I thought about as I settled into my assigned seat. As the aircraft door was about to be closed, a man walked in and occupied the vacant seat next to me. He mumbled something in a foreign accent. The departure was uneventful. All we did was try to kill time, but the book he was reading attracted my interest: *Cave Exploring in the USA*. I was curious and asked him if cave exploring interested him. That was when he explained that in France he was a professional cave explorer. After the dinner service ended, we talked; his stories of days underground were fascinating. Finally, he invited me to join him, and I happily accepted.

EXERCISE

5. Submit an original paragraph in which you use, and underline, unnecessary intensifiers. You need not include a revised version.

16d Put your statements in positive form.

Negative ideas are just as legitimate as positive ones; you may have to point out that something did not happen or that an argument leaves you unconvinced. But the negative modifiers *no* and *not* sometimes make for wordiness and a slight loss of readability. If you write *We are not in agreement*, you are asking your reader to go through two steps, first to conceive of agreement and then to negate it. But if you simply write *We disagree*, you have saved three words and simplified the mental operation. The gain is small, but good writing results from a sum of small gains.

Of course you need not develop a phobia against every use of *no* or *not*. Observe, however, that negatively worded sentences tend to be slightly less emphatic than positive ones. Compare:

NEGATIVE	POSITIVE
She did not do well on the test.	She did poorly on the test.
He was not convicted.	He was acquitted.
They have no respect for rationing.	They despise rationing.
It was not an insignificant amount.	It was a significant amount.

EXERCISE

effic lang 16d

6. Submit an original paragraph in which you use, and underline, unnecessary negative forms. Below the paragraph, supply a list of positively worded alternatives to those expressions.

16e Avoid euphemisms.

A **euphemism** is a squeamishly "nice" expression standing in the place of a more direct one. Some words that began as euphemisms, such as *senior citizen* and *funeral director*, have passed into common usage, but you should try to avoid terms that still sound like ways of covering up a meaning instead of conveying it. Euphemisms often conceal a devious political or commercial motive. If you want to be regarded as candid and trustworthy, do not write *discomfort* for *pain*, *memory garden* for *cemetery*, *pass away* for *die*, *relocation center* for *concentration camp*, *revenue enhancement* for *tax raise*, *adult* for *pornographic*, *deployment of forces* for *invasion*, and so forth.

DON'T:

x The governor is extremely concerned about **human resources development.**

DO:

• The governor is extremely concerned about **unemployment.**

DON'T:

x The candidate issued a press release declaring that her earlier remarks about her opponent were now to be considered **inoperative.**

DO:

• The candidate issued a press release admitting that her earlier remarks about her opponent were **untrue.**

DON'T:

x We are recalling all late models because the bearings **at variance with production code specifications** may **adversely affect vehicle control.**

DO:

• We are recalling all late models because the **defective** bearings may cause drivers to **lose control of the steering**.

EXERCISES

7. Submit revised versions of the following sentences, substituting direct language for any euphemisms that you find:

   A. The departed one is now receiving visitors in the adjacent slumber chamber, prior to journeying to his final resting place in the memory garden.
   B. Repair of defective underground wastewater conveyance devices constituted her mode of employment.

C. The chairman of the board declared that certain facilities, along with their attendant personnel, would be granted an indefinite furlough from utilization in view of demand slackness throughout the consumer sector.
D. The Raiders have been known to get physical near the end of a hopelessly disadvantageous contest, provoking incidents of a questionably sportsmanlike nature.
E. In the absence of an affirmative sign of compliance with our repeated solicitations for appropriate reimbursement, we have no alternative to the regrettable option of terminating the dispensation of utilities to your residential fixtures.

8. The following classic paragraph by George Orwell deals with euphemism in political language. Write a paragraph of your own about this passage, showing how it embodies or exemplifies its author's belief in the need for vivid diction.

> In our time, political speech and writing are largely the defence of the indefensible. Things like the continuance of British rule in India, the Russian purges and deportations, the dropping of the atom bomb on Japan can indeed be defended, but only by arguments which are too brutal for most people to face, and which do not square with the professed aims of political parties. Thus political language has to consist largely of euphemism, question-begging, and sheer cloudy vagueness. Defenceless villages are bombarded from the air, the inhabitants driven out into the countryside, the cattle machine-gunned, the huts set on fire with incendiary bullets: this is called *pacification*. Millions of peasants are robbed of their farms and sent trudging along the roads with no more than they can carry: this is called *transfer of population* or *rectification of frontiers*. People are imprisoned for years without trial, or shot in the back of the neck or sent to die of scurvy in Arctic lumber camps: this is called *elimination of unreliable elements*. Such phraseology is needed if one wants to name things without calling up mental pictures of them.[1]

16f Avoid clichés.

A **cliché** is a trite, stereotyped, overused expression such as *throw money around* or *bring the house down*. Clichés are **dead metaphors**—that is, they are figures of speech that no longer sound figurative. When someone writes *off the wall* or *the bottom line*, no reader sees a wall or a line. On the other hand, a writer could blunder into causing people to see real bricks by saying *On the first* *day that June worked in the construction crew, Steve fell for her like a ton of bricks.* (For such accidentally revived clichés, see page 375, 17b.) But the usual effect of clichés is not unintended comedy but simple boredom. The reader feels that the writer is settling for prepackaged language instead of finding the exact words to convey a particular thought. And matters are not improved by the apologetic addition of *so to speak* or *as the saying goes*. When you need to apologize for any expression, change it.

The worst thing about cliché-ridden prose is its predictability. As soon as we register one element of the cliché, the rest of it leaps to mind like an advertising jingle:

pleasingly . . . plump

lines of . . . communication

the foreseeable . . . future

the pieces . . . of the puzzle . . . fall into place

The resultant prose—*to be brutally frank*—is a *far cry* from being a *sure winner* in the *hearts and minds* of readers *from every walk of life*.

Three lists of clichés follow. List A includes examples of gross clichés, which you can spot fairly easily and eradicate as you revise. List B includes less obvious clichés, pairs of seemingly inseparable adjectives and nouns, clusters that choke out your originality as a writer. List C consists of pat expressions that say too little in a wordy and predictable manner.

LIST A: GROSS CLICHÉS	
a needle in a haystack	one in a million
blind as a bat	quiet as a mouse
carve a niche for oneself	rule with an iron fist
drive one to distraction	sly as a fox
happy as a lark	smart as a whip
live like a king	sow one's wild oats
make a beeline for	the top of the heap
old as the hills	tough as nails

LIST B: "INSEPARABLE" PAIRS	
bounce back	supreme moment
flawless complexion	tempestuous affair
grave danger	tender mercies
high spirits	unforeseen obstacles
integral part	vicious circle
nuclear holocaust	vital role

LIST C: PAT EXPRESSIONS	
after all is said and done	in this day and age
at this point in time	it goes without saying
far be it from me	it stands to reason
in a very real sense	once and for all
in the final [last] analysis	when push comes to shove

EXERCISES

9. With classmates or friends, draw up a list of clichés supplementing those mentioned above. Then submit five sentences in which you call attention to the clichés by treating them literally.

   Examples:

   - She will **string him along** until he agrees to **tie the knot.**
   - Never trust ventriloquists; they **talk out of both sides of their mouth.**

effic lang 16g

10. Look through your own prose—earlier exercises, papers, or drafts—until you have found five clichés. Copy and submit the sentences in which they occur, adding revised versions in each case. If your own prose doesn't yield five instances, make up the quota from any published source.

16g Watch for distracting sound patterns.

Knowing that repeated sounds draw attention, you can sometimes use them deliberately, as Mark Twain did in referring to

- the **calm confidence** of a **Christian** with four aces, or as Thomas Paine did in writing

- These are the **times** that **try** men's souls.

In these examples the "poetic" quality goes along with the effort to make a concisely emphatic statement.

Unless you are after some such effect, however, beware of making your reader conscious of rhymes (*the side of the hide*) or alliteration (*pursuing particular purposes*) or repeated syllables (*apart from the apartment*). These snatches of "poetry" usually result from an unconscious attraction that words already chosen exert on subsequent choices. Having written *the degradation*, you write *of the nation* because the *-ation* sound is in your head. You may have to read your first draft aloud, attending to its sound and not its sense, in order to find where you have lapsed into jingling.

Abstract Latinate words—the ones that usually end in *-al, -ity, -ation*, or *-otion*—are especially apt to make a repetitive sound pattern. It is worth the pains to rewrite, for example, if you find bunched words like *functional, essential, occupational*, and *institutional* or *equality, opportunity, parity*, and *mobility*.

EXERCISE

11. Submit five sentences in which patterns of repeated sound cause an unwelcome distraction. Be original in your choice of words. Circle the words that cause the problem of bothersome "poetry." Then add five revised sentences that eliminate the problem.

NOTE

[1] George Orwell, "Politics and the English Language," *A Collection of Essays* (Garden City, N.Y.: Anchor, 1954) 172–73.

17

Figurative Language

17a Become alert to figures of speech and their uses.

Consider the following two sentences:

LITERAL:

- I ate until I wasn't hungry any longer.

FIGURATIVE:

- I ate until I was as stuffed as a taxidermist's owl.

The first statement is **literal** because it makes its point without requiring us to call up any picture, or **image,** of something other than the matter at hand. The second statement is **figurative** (also called *metaphorical*); it asks for an effort of imagination on our part. The writer wants us to see the point in different terms—specifically, to compare a person to a stuffed owl. The comparison is appropriate because, though exaggerated, it is relevant to the intended effect: a person's full stomach is likened to the mounted owl's entire body, as if the person's insides consisted altogether of packing. Whenever your language makes such a nonliteral appeal, you are using what is known as a *figure of speech*.

The more closely we examine common terms, the more figurative they come to appear. Take, for example, a phrase used in the previous paragraph: *the matter at hand.* In that expression, both *matter* and *at hand* could be called metaphorical, since the sentence that contained them wasn't literally about either matter (physical material) or anybody's actual hand. But you almost certainly didn't notice this figurative quality at the time. Practically speaking, then, *the matter at hand* doesn't call on our imagination; it is not experienced as figurative language. In this chapter, we will call an expression figurative or metaphorical only if it makes its reader conscious of a departure from the literal plane.

Why should you bother incorporating figures of speech into your prose? The answer is that such language, when thoughtfully managed, achieves an impressive effect of vividness, condensation, and wit. Note the striking differences of appeal between the following literal and figurative passages.

LITERAL:

The primary Whitman, psychologically speaking, is the Whitman who, at some point in his thirties, made a new connection between two kinds of energy, that of his sensuality and that of language. Thenceforth, his identity was defined by his ability to reconcile those opposite forces.

FIGURATIVE:

The primary Whitman, psychologically speaking, is the Whitman who, at some point in his thirties, opened a new circuit between the energies of sensuality and the energies of language, making them the electric poles of his identity.[1]

LITERAL:

Chicago used to have a great vitality in its downtown area, but by now the city has deteriorated. Much of its life has been transferred to the suburbs, occupying a larger area but lacking that optimism and concentration for which the original Chicago was known.

FIGURATIVE:

Chicago's rising star is now a worn-out supernova, which has exploded all over suburbia.[2]

LITERAL:

In New England in autumn, the leaves on the trees are dying. Another common feature of that season is that the Red Sox have typically failed to fulfill people's expectation that they would win their league championship.

FIGURATIVE:

Dying leaves and dead Red Sox—that's the New England autumn.[3]

In each figurative expression above, we feel ourselves to be as far from the groping of first-draft prose as we can get. The writer has reduced a complex thought not only to relatively few words but also to a mental picture that lingers in our minds, giving pleasure and information at the same time.

Again, note how the boldfaced figurative expressions in the following passages bring our imagination into play:

> Seeing Tina Turner onstage is **like watching a demented child who stamps her feet, twirls in circles, and bops around bow-legged as though she's wearing a diaper.**[4]

> One of the world's favorite views of Orson Welles in later life . . . shows him inside a limousine, sucking imperiously on **a torpedo-sized cigar.** The venomous intentness of his profile is explained by what we can see in the background: a giggling, gawping multitude pressing against the side windows of the vehicle. Being inside it with Welles, we can participate a little in his visible scorn. . . . **It is like sharing an aquarium with a very large ocean-going predator of uncertain appetite.**[5]

> This generation thinks—and this is its thought of thoughts—that nothing faithful, vulnerable, fragile can be durable or have any true power. **Death waits for these things as a cement floor waits for a dropping light bulb. The brittle shell of glass loses its tiny vacuum with a burst, and that is that.**[6]

EXERCISES

1. Look through available printed materials until you have found three figures of speech that strike you as effective vehicles of the writer's meaning. Copy or photocopy the relevant sentences, and submit them along with a brief analysis of each figure's appropriateness.

2. Submit a paragraph or two analyzing the use of figurative language in the following passage. In addition to pointing out where the writer is being figurative, assess the aptness of her figures of speech to her meaning.

   > Our skin is a kind of space suit in which we maneuver through an atmosphere of harsh gases, cosmic rays, radiation from the sun, and obstacles of all sorts. Years ago, I read about a boy who had to live in a bubble (designed by NASA) because of the weakness of his immune system and his susceptibility to disease. We are all that boy. The bubble is our skin. But the skin is also alive, breathing and excreting, shielding us from harmful rays and microbial attack, metabolizing vitamin D, insulating us from heat and cold, repairing itself when necessary, regulating blood flow, acting as a frame for our sense of touch, aiding us in sexual attraction, defining our individuality, holding all the thick red jams and jellies inside us where they belong.[7]

17b Aim for unstrained similes and metaphors.

Two closely related figures of speech allow you to draw imaginative likenesses. A **simile**, by including the word *like* or *as*, explicitly acknowledges that a comparison is being made.

SIMILE:

- **Like** a patio rotisserie, George's mind always keeps turning at the same slow rate, no matter what is impaled on it.

  George's mind is explicitly compared to a rotisserie.

fig lang 17b

A **metaphor** omits *like* or *as*.

METAPHOR:

- George's hedgeclipper mind gives a suburban sameness to everything it touches.

  George's mind is compared to hedgeclippers, but without either of the explicit terms of comparison, *like* or *as*.

In theory a metaphor is a more radical figure of speech than a simile, for it asserts an identity, not just a likeness, between two things (George's mind "is" a gardening tool). But in practice one kind of figure can be as striking as the other. What counts is not the choice between simile and metaphor but the suitability of the image to your intended meaning. The two images about George, for example, call to mind not only his conformism but also his specifically suburban background (the carefully tended hedge, the patio rotisserie).

Simile and metaphor predominate among the figures of speech you have already studied in this chapter:

SIMILE	METAPHOR
• I ate until I was **as** stuffed **as** a taxidermist's owl. • Seeing Tina Turner onstage is **like** watching a demented child who stamps her feet, twirls in circles, and bops around bow-legged **as though** she's wearing a diaper. • It is **like** sharing an aquarium with a very large ocean-going predator of uncertain appetite.	• The primary Whitman . . . opened a new circuit between the energies of sensuality and the energies of language, making them the electric poles of his identity. • Chicago's rising star is now a worn-out supernova, which has exploded all over suburbia. • Dying leaves and dead Red Sox—that's the New England autumn.

fig lang 17b

When a simile or metaphor succeeds, it usually bears a stamp of naturalness and transparency; the reader can immediately see through the chosen figure to the intended resemblance. Consider, for instance, the image (boldfaced) that concludes this paragraph:

> The ideals of the revolutions in Poland, Hungary, Czechoslovakia, and even Bulgaria owe much to the American model, with its combination of political freedom and an economic system that seems to guarantee an ever-rising standard of living. It is important to recognize that it is a version of American political democracy, and not Japanese discipline or German efficiency, that the new leaders of these countries say they are striving for. Whether and how they will succeed is impossible to predict; their struggle will be long and may not always be peaceful. It is worth examining, however, whether the American system is all that they think it is, or whether **they are seeing the light of a distant star which, some time ago, may have ceased to shine so brightly.**[8]

This writer, believing that the American socioeconomic system has entered a hard period and knowing that eastern Europeans have little accurate knowledge of our present condition, wonders whether their ideas about us aren't obsolete. If so, the metaphor says, perhaps what the Poles, Czechs, and others see in the American way is comparable to what all people see in a star—a light given off long ago, before the star itself began to fade. The image appears precisely and effortlessly suited to the thought behind it.

Occasionally, however, instead of looking uncontrived, a successful figure of speech will startle us with its boldness. Only after a double take do we realize that the image is not just fresh but also apt. Consider this passage, written by a literary journalist who knew that he had only weeks to live and who longed for good conversation with his taciturn doctor:

> Whether he wants to be or not, the doctor is a storyteller, and he can turn our lives into good or bad stories, regardless of the diagnosis. If my doctor would allow me, I would be glad to help him here, to take him on as *my* patient. Perhaps later, when he is older, he'll have learned how to converse. Astute as he is, he doesn't yet understand that all cures are partly "talking cures." **Every patient needs mouth-to-mouth resuscitation, for talk is the kiss of life.**[9]

Here two metaphors are daringly combined. The first one startles us by seeming to be bizarrely literal; *what do you mean*, we want to protest, *"every patient needs mouth-to-mouth resuscitation"?* Only when we have digested the second, plainly figurative, image of talk as the kiss of life do we realize that the other image is figurative as well: the mouth-to-mouth resuscitation being evoked is simply talk itself. Yet with this delayed insight the imaginative brilliance of the whole sentence becomes apparent. What eloquence, and from the deathbed at that!

This example shows that careful writers can defy the English teacher's maxim that figures of speech should keep their distance from one another. For further evidence, look at this dizzying but tightly controlled sequence of images:

> When you write, you lay out a line of words. The line of words is a miner's pick, a woodcarver's gouge, a surgeon's probe. You wield it, and it digs a path you follow. Soon you find yourself deep in new territory. Is it a dead end, or have you located the real subject? You will know tomorrow, or this time next year.[10]

fig lang 17b

In this passage one metaphor, the *line of words*, is subdivided into three others, the *pick*, the *gouge*, and the *probe*. And still the writer isn't through; her verbal tool *digs a path* leading to *new territory* that may or may not prove a *dead end*. The passage flirts with absurdity but survives, barely, by virtue of its cunning. All of those images work together to represent the point being made—that writing is a risk-taking enterprise that can lead anywhere, or in some cases nowhere.

The danger of **mixed metaphor** is not that images will rub shoulders but that they will take a pratfall together. And it arises not when writers deftly reconcile two or more figures but precisely when they fail to do so, allowing one image's implications to clash disastrously with the other's. Consider:

MIXED METAPHOR:

x A tiger in the jungle of politics, he was a cream puff around the house.

> The reader's mind strains unsuccessfully to grasp how a *tiger* is meaningfully related to a *cream puff*—that is, how a wild animal can be changed into a dessert.

EFFECTIVE METAPHOR:

● A tiger in the jungle of politics, he was a pussycat around the house.[11]

> The images of *tiger* and *pussycat* are closely related, and the writer (characterizing his father-in-law, Harry Truman) fully controls the different implications of the two terms.

fig lang 17b

Again, note how the following paragraph jumbles several figures of speech.

MIXED METAPHOR:

x Although some analysts feel that the presidential primary system is the wrong game plan for choosing the best nominee, they forget that primaries are an important mirror and proving ground of our democracy. To be sure, candidates can get burned out on the hustings. But by diving into the very heart of state and county politics, the survivors of this pressure cooker can acquire a hands-on feeling for the people they hope to govern.

This passage begins with a sports metaphor, *game plan*, but before the first sentence is over we have been taken through two more incompatible images, a *mirror* and a *proving ground*. The next sentence tells us that candidates can get *burned out on the hustings* (literally, speaking platforms)—a mixed metaphor that unintentionally suggests a public execution. And finally, those candidates who survive the *pressure cooker* are said to be *diving into a heart* where they can get a *hands-on feeling*. Emergency surgery in the kitchen? Clearly, this writer likes to reach for the handiest figurative language without taking responsibility for its implications.

Perhaps you feel that you can avoid mixed metaphors by shunning figurative language altogether. But insofar as you do, your prose will be flat and colorless. Besides, it is not really possible to be completely unfigurative. Many ordinary terms and nearly all clichés (p. 364, 16f) are **dead metaphors**—that is, they contain the faint implication of an image which we are not supposed to notice as such (the *leg* of a table, a *blade* of grass). When clichés are used in close succession, they mischievously come back to life as mixed metaphors:

x **Climbing to the heights** of oratory, the candidate **tackled** the issue.

x Either we **get a handle** on these problems or we are all **going down the drain.**

x You can't **sit on your hands** if a recession is developing, because **you don't know where the bottom is.**

Figurative language, then, can be tricky. When you intend an abstract meaning, you have to make sure that your dead metaphors stay good and dead. But when you do wish to be figurative, see whether your image is vivid, fresh, and consistent. Literal statement may be safe, but a striking figure carried through consistently can unify and intensify your sentences.

EXERCISES

3. List all the figures of speech you find in the following passage, and briefly discuss the relation of each image to the one preceding it. Do you find any problems of mixed metaphor? If so, explain.

> Academics, it has been said before, are very much like people who drive their cars by looking through their rear-view mirrors. Looking backward does offer certain satisfactions and provides splendid intellectual vistas, but it hardly brings into focus the best view of the road ahead. Academics may seem to bemoan the fact that the federals now hold the cards, and that they must do their bidding, however reluctantly. But the facts would appear to be otherwise: it is the federals who are at least trying to game-plan an extremely delicate future, while most academics remain on the sidelines, seized by fits of moral indignation about the felt deprivation of their intellectual autonomy. It would rarely occur to them that the federal planners would like nothing better than a showing of academia's own imaginative initiatives and social vision, if only they would gird themselves for that sort of resolve.[12]

4. Look through your own prose—earlier papers or drafts—until you find five examples of figurative language. Copy the complete sentence in each instance, and submit it with a brief comment on the appropriateness or inappropriateness of the image you chose. If you now think a different image would have served better, present and justify that image. If your own writing doesn't yield five examples, make up the difference from any published source.

17c Practice the extended figure of speech.

If you have hit upon a suitable image to convey your meaning, you can sometimes add a sentence or two, or even a whole paragraph, that will draw further implications from it. Such an **extended figure of speech** is very much like an **analogy** (p. 48, 2h). The difference is that whereas an analogy typically compares two literal objects or situations by extracting a rule from one and applying it to the other, an extended figure elaborates a metaphorical comparison.

fig lang 17c

One such extended figure of speech is the "light bulb" passage on page 370. Here, from a student writer, is another:

> For me, the idea of going on for an advanced degree is like that of rowing across the ocean. Perhaps I could do it and perhaps I couldn't. But what, I wonder, is waiting for me on the other side, and isn't there some faster and safer way of getting there? Until I know the answers to these questions, I intend to keep my feet planted on familiar soil.

This writer begins with a simile (*the idea of going on for an advanced degree is <u>like</u> that of rowing across the ocean*) and then extends it through three more sentences, making sure that the rest of her language remains compatible with that initial image.

Again, note how a reviewer wittily employs an extended figure to convey her displeasure with a self-important book of essays:

> . . . I would say these essays are like a false pregnancy. In a typical first trimester the author explains how she came to write the essay: what the weather was like and where she had lunch and what the furniture mover had to say about it all. In the second she forecasts what she is about to say on the next page but intimates that it might not, after all, be more than a sketch—it is a work in progress and you must please see the next book, and also the earlier ones. The third consists of a long review of the first two. By now everything has got very big and fat, but there is no actual baby.[13]

To be effective, an extended figure must above all be apt. That is, the chosen image ought to convey natural-looking resemblances to the situation it is meant to express, so that the writer can draw out those resemblances without seeming to labor over them:

EFFECTIVE:

> I am a kind of human snail, locked in and condemned by my own nature. The ancients believed that the moist track left by the snail as it crept was the snail's own essence, depleting its body little by little; the farther the snail toiled, the smaller it became, until it finally rubbed itself out. That is how perfectionists are. Say to us Excellence, and we will show you how we use up our substance and wear ourselves away, while making scarcely any progress at all. The fact that I am an exacting perfectionist in a narrow strait only, and nowhere else, is hardly to the point, since nothing matters to me so much as a comely and muscular sentence. It is my narrow strait, this snail's road: the track of the sentence I am writing now; and when I have eked out the wet substance, ink or blood, that is its mark, I will begin the next sentence.[14]

The key question about an extended figure of speech, beyond its aptness, is when to abandon it. As soon as your reader becomes conscious of the pains you are taking to keep the image self-consistent, the extended figure starts to become a liability. Consider the following passage, which stretches a rather unpromising image through a fully developed paragraph:

OVEREXTENDED:

> The ivory tower, as college students—and psychiatrists—across the country will testify, is not nearly so pleasant an abode as it appears

> from the outside. It shelters its inhabitants from some of life's pedestrian difficulties, but at the same time creates new traumas and problems, which take on, in such closed quarters, an importance of which the real world cannot conceive. The legendary tower of learning is not a stable structure: it is buffeted by the high winds of exam periods, by the gales of preprofessional competition; it shakes with the constant underground rumblings of adolescent crises. What shall I be? What shall I do? Will I succeed? At times it sways so forebodingly that the unfortunate standing on top sees his future in a heap of broken bones and ivory rubble.[15]

This is accomplished prose, but the writer's *ivory tower*, unlike Cynthia Ozick's *snail*, threatens at every moment to revert to its original status as a cliché. By the final sentence we may feel that the writer has become a prisoner of her own image. Wisely, she drops the ivory tower figure altogether in the next paragraph of her essay.

EXERCISE

5. Look through available materials until you have found three figures of speech other than the ones you used in Exercise 4. Submit copies of them along with extended versions in which you flesh out the implications of each image.

---

fig lang 17d

17d Experiment with understatement and hyperbole.

Language that conspicuously minimizes an extreme state of affairs can also be regarded as figurative, even if it doesn't draw a comparison. Thus imaginative effects are at work in the following examples of **understatement:**

- You get **a little sweaty** out there fighting a forest fire.
- To be born with a cocaine addiction is **not necessarily the most advantageous way to enter the world.**
- She worked at the office from nine until five, endured a second rush-hour traffic jam, cooked the dinner, and rushed off to the

emergency room with her suddenly feverish child—**just a routine day in the life of a single mother.**

Similarly, you can get a figurative effect through **hyperbole**, or overstatement:

- . . . sucking imperiously on **a torpedo-sized cigar.**
  (See the "Orson Welles" passage, p. 370.)
- They won't do a thing about smokestack pollution **until the view from their penthouses is a solid wall of soot.**
- The moths on the Puerto Vallarta coast **were as big as B-52s, and the cockroaches looked like Winnebagos.**
- " 'Mind if I smoke?' might once have been a rather routine query. **Today it's about the same as Iraq asking, 'Mind if I drop in?' "**[16]

As you can see, understatement and hyperbole produce an effect of **irony** (p. 80, 3o), or the conveying of something quite different from what one's words seem to say. Like other successfully handled figures of speech, these devices tell the reader that the writer has been confident enough to play with language while still maintaining rhetorical control. The effect would be ruined, of course, if it were carried through an entire serious essay.

EXERCISE

fig lang 17d

6. Submit three original sentences containing understatement and three containing hyperbole.

NOTES

[1] Helen Vendler, "Body Language: *Leaves of Grass* and the Articulation of Sexual Awareness," *Harper's* Oct. 1986: 64.

[2] Thomas Geoghegan, "Chicago, Pride of the Rustbelt," *New Republic* 25 Mar. 1985: 23.

[3] Russell Baker, "New England Gray," *New York Times Magazine* 1 Dec. 1985: 24.

[4] Mick LaSalle, "She's Her Own Best Imitator," *San Francisco Chronicle* 14 Dec. 1987: F1.

[5] Russell Davies, "A Prodigious One-Man Show," [London] *Times Literary Supplement* 28 Nov. 1986: 1331.

[6] Saul Bellow, *Herzog* (New York: Viking, 1967) 290.

[7] Diane Ackerman, *A Natural History of the Senses* (New York: Random, 1990) 67.

[8] Felix Rohatyn, "Becoming What They Think We Are," *New York Review of Books* 12 Apr. 1990: 6.

[9] Anatole Broyard, "Doctor Talk to Me," *New York Times Magazine* 26 Aug. 1990: 36.

[10] Annie Dillard, *The Writing Life* (New York: Harper, 1989) 3.

[11] Clifton Daniel, "Presidents I Have Known," *New York Times* 3 June 1984, sec. 6: 84.

[12] G[eorge] W. B[onham], "The Decline of Initiative," *Change* Apr. 1973: 16.

[13] Jenny Teichman, "Henry James among the Philosophers," *New York Times Book Review* 10 Feb. 1991: 24.

[14] Cynthia Ozick, "My Mother's Life Was a Life of Excellence: Insofar as Excellence Means Ripe Generosity," *Ms.* Jan. 1985: 45.

[15] Abigail Zuger, "Acrophobia in the Ivory Tower," *Harper's* Oct. 1975: 4.

[16] Robert Kerr, "EPA Smoke Report Should Fuel the Fire," *San Francisco Examiner* 2 Sept. 1990: A3.

VII
USAGE

USAGE

Whatever you have to say in your writing, you will want to say it within the rules of **standard written English**—*The "good English" that readers generally expect to find in papers, reports, articles, and books. Fortunately, you already follow most of those rules without having to think about them. In fact, if you did think about them while composing, you would have trouble concentrating on your ideas. The time to worry about correctness is after you have finished at least one draft. Then you can begin making certain that your points will come across without such distractions as incomplete sentences, spelling errors, and subjects and verbs that are incorrectly related.*

Problems with standard written English are usually divided into those of **usage** *and those of* **punctuation**—*that is, between rules for the choice and order of words (usage) and rules for the insertion of marks to bring out a sentence's meaning (punctuation). But usage and punctuation work together toward the same end of making sentences coherent, or fitting together in an easily understood way. Certain classic "usage" problems, such as the sentence fragment and the run-on sentence, are punctuation problems as well. Therefore, though we review the punctuation marks and their functions separately (Chapters 26–31), we also deal with punctuation in the present set of chapters. For example, if you are having trouble with modifiers or parallel constructions, you will find those topics treated as whole units, without artificial postponement of the relevant comma rules.*

18

Complete Sentences

COMPLETE SENTENCE	SENTENCE FRAGMENT
• One-lane country roads unnerve the best drivers.	x Which unnerve the best drivers.

Since a sentence is the basic unit of written discourse, you must be able to recognize complete and incomplete sentences in your drafts. A sentence begins with a capital letter and ends with a period, question mark, or exclamation point. Unfortunately, **sentence fragments** show those very features. You need to know, then, that a grammatically complete sentence normally requires a **verb** and its **subject** within an **independent clause**.

18a Recognize a verb.

A **verb** is a word that tells the state of its subject or an action that the subject performs. (If the verb consists of more than one word, as in *was starting* or *would have been accomplished*, it is called a *verb phrase*.) Every verb functions in one of three ways:

1. A **transitive verb** transmits the action of the subject to a **direct object**:

S V D OBJ
- The **doctor solved** the **problem**.

S V D OBJ
- The **technician took** an **x-ray**.

2. An **intransitive verb** in itself expresses the whole action:

S V
- The **patient recovered**.

S V
- **Dr. McGill lectures** often.

or

3. A **linking verb** connects the subject to a **complement**, an element that helps to identify or describe the subject:

S V COMPL
- Her **training has been scientific**.

S V COMPL
- **She is** a recognized **professional**.

The verb plus all the words belonging with it make up the **predicate**.

Verb Position

In normal word order for statements, the subject comes before its verb:

S V
- The **highway committee is meeting**.

S V
- The **law will remain** on the books.

But in some questions the verb comes before the subject:

V S
- **Are you** sure?

frag 18a

And in most questions the verb has two parts that surround the subject:

V
- **Is he driving** the Honda tonight?

S

V
- **Do you know** where she left the car?

S

Change of Verb Form

Verbs show **inflection**, or changes of form, to indicate **tense**, or time.

PRESENT TENSE	PAST TENSE	FUTURE TENSE
They **iron** their jeans.	They **ironed** their jeans.	They **will iron** their jeans.
He **fights** hard.	He **fought** hard.	He **will fight** hard.

Verb versus Verbal

VERB (In complete sentence)	VERBAL (In fragment)
V We **will break** our record.	VERBAL **To break** our record.
V Eve **was laughing** out loud.	VERBAL **Laughing** out loud.
V **Are** they **winning** the championship?	VERBAL **Winning** the championship.

Certain words resemble verbs and can even change their form to show different times. Yet these **verbals**—namely, **infinitives, participles,** and **gerunds**—function like nouns or modifiers instead of like verbs. Thus they do *not* supply a key element for sentence completeness.

Compare the complete sentences with the fragments in the box above. Note how you can tell that the three verbals in the right column are not functioning as verbs:

frag 18a

1. One kind of verbal, an infinitive, often follows *to (to break).* A true verb in a sentence stands without *to.*

2. A verbal ending in *-ing* is one word. When a true verb ends in *-ing*, it always follows a word or words that count as part of the verb *(was laughing, have been winning.)*

You can write complete sentences that include verbals, but only by supplying true subject-verb combinations:

S V
- **To break our record will be** difficult.

MOD S V
- **Laughing out loud**, **Eve ran** a victory lap.

S V
- **Winning the championship is** not easy.

18b Recognize a subject.

S
- My **uncle** prefers a big car.

A **subject** is the person, thing, or idea about which something is said or asked. Locating a subject therefore involves locating its accompanying verb.

Most subjects are **nouns**—words like *uncle, philosophy,* and *Eve*. Some subjects are pronouns, such as *she* or *they* or *someone*. Others are noun phrases like *a very fine day*. And still others, which we will call **nounlike elements**, are groups of words that function together as single nouns: *to run fast, winning the championship*, and so forth. Thus you cannot spot a subject simply by its form. Find the verb and then ask who or what performs the action of that verb or is in the state expressed by it:

V
- That law **affects** all drivers.

  What affects all drivers? *That law* is the subject.

V
- **Does** anyone **speak** Japanese?

  Does who speak Japanese? The subject is *anyone*.

V
- Whatever you see **is** for sale.

  What is for sale? *Whatever you see*. That whole clause is the subject.

frag 18b

Implied Subject

- [You] Watch out!

You cannot write a grammatically complete sentence without a verb, but in commands, the subject *you* typically disappears. Since that subject is implied, however, the sentence is not regarded as a fragment.

EXERCISES

1. Copy out the following sentences, and mark every subject (S), verb (V), direct object (DO), and complement (C) that you find.

   A. Biff grabs the opposing quarterback's face mask.
   B. A sore loser like Biff is not a credit to the game.
   C. The fans have become thoroughly disgusted.
   D. Why did Biff resent the quarterback's remark about his intelligence?
   E. The ape, after all, possesses many admirable traits.

2. Indicate which of the following items do not constitute complete sentences. In each faulty case, briefly explain the problem and offer an adequately revised version.

   A. Norbert has decided to become a guru.
   B. Giving advice even when it is not requested.
   C. Having completed years of strenuous self-discipline, and without encouragement from anyone.
   D. Take note of Norbert's progress.
   E. A noble achievement, to have earned the title "Norbert the Purified One of Daly City."

18c Distinguish an independent clause from a subordinate one.

INDEPENDENT CLAUSE	SUBORDINATE CLAUSE
S PRED	S PRED
Mike sells chickens.	Although **Mike sells chickens**, . . .

INDEPENDENT CLAUSE	SUBORDINATE CLAUSE
S / PRED: The **poster was badly printed**.	S / PRED: When the **poster was badly printed**, . . .
S / PRED: **Dogs were running wild.**	S / PRED: Because **dogs were running wild**, . . .

A **clause** is a cluster of words containing a subject-predicate combination (pp. 383–84, 18a). To avoid sentence fragments, you must be able to tell the difference between two fundamental kinds of clauses. An *independent clause* is a grammatically complete statement, question, or exclamation. It is capable of standing alone as a sentence. A *subordinate clause* (sometimes called a dependent clause) cannot stand alone, because it is typically introduced by a word that relates it to another part of the same sentence. Subordinate clauses serve important functions, but by themselves they are sentence fragments.

A subordinate clause is usually introduced by either

1. a *subordinating conjunction*, a word like *although, as, because,* or *when*, which subordinates (makes dependent) the following subject and predicate,

or

2. a *relative pronoun*, a word like *who, which,* or *that*, which begins a relative clause.

frag 18c

A **relative clause** is a subordinate clause that functions like an adjective by relating its statement to an earlier, or *antecedent*, part of the sentence.

ANT / REL CLAUSE

- George, **who was glad to have a working wife**, had never missed an episode of *General Hospital*.

Sometimes you will find that an independent clause, like many subordinate ones, follows a conjunction. But that word will always be one of the seven *coordinating conjunctions*. If you keep those seven words distinct in your mind from subordinating conjunctions and relative pronouns, you will have a head start toward distinguishing between independent and subordinate clauses.

COORDINATING CONJUNCTIONS (may precede independent clauses)			
and	for	or	yet
but	nor	so	

SUBORDINATING CONJUNCTIONS (begin some subordinate clauses)			
after	because	than	whenever
although	before	that	where
as	if	though	wherever
as if	in order that	till	while
as long as	provided (that)	unless	why
as soon as	since	until	
as though	so (that)	when	

RELATIVE PRONOUNS (begin relative subordinate clauses)			
who	whom	which	that

Remember, then, that each of your sentences will normally contain at least one independent clause—a construction which, like *Mike sells chickens*, contains a subject and predicate but is not introduced by a subordinating conjunction or relative pronoun:

frag 18c

- Acting on a hunch, **I removed the book from the shelf**. (IND CLAUSE)
- As I opened the book, **twenty-dollar bills fluttered to the carpet**. (IND CLAUSE)

- IND CLAUSE: **I stared intently**, and IND CLAUSE: **my palms began to sweat**.

- Although I am tempted to keep it, IND CLAUSE: **this money will have to be turned over to the police**.

EXERCISE

3. Submit five original sentences, each of which contains at least one subordinate clause. Use a different subordinating conjunction or relative pronoun to introduce each new subordinate clause. (Include at least two relative clauses.) In each sentence, underline the independent clause(s).

18d Eliminate an unacceptable sentence fragment.

A **sentence fragment** is a word or set of words beginning with a capital letter and punctuated as a sentence but lacking an independent clause (18c). Typically, a fragment is either a subordinate clause (18c) or a **phrase**—a cluster of words lacking a subject-predicate combination:

SUBORDINATE CLAUSE AS FRAGMENT:

x Because milk and eggs are still a bargain.

x Unless winning at chess is important to you.

x Which makes my uncle nervous.

PHRASE AS FRAGMENT:

x Such as milk and eggs.

frag 18d

x Winning at chess.

x My uncle being nervous.

Most unacceptable fragments are really detached parts of the preceding sentence that the writer has mistakenly set off with a period. The handiest way to correct most fragments is to rejoin them to that earlier sentence.

UNACCEPTABLE FRAGMENTS (Boldfaced)	COMPLETE SENTENCES
Local agencies will become overcrowded and ineffective. x **Unless the number of mental health services is increased.**	• Unless the number of mental health services is increased, local agencies will become overcrowded and ineffective.
Alex and Dolores played tennis in the park. x **Instead of at school**.	• Alex and Dolores played tennis in the park instead of at school.
They stood back and watched the crows. x **Wheeling and cawing over the splattered melon**.	• They stood back and watched the crows wheeling and cawing over the splattered melon.
When they had rested, they continued up a path. x **A winding path that led to the top**.	• When they had rested, they continued up a winding path that led to the top.

Again, the boldfaced parts of the following passage are unacceptable fragments.

CONTAINING FRAGMENTS:

On Thursday we reported the numbers of our missing traveler's checks. **Which were lost during our arrival in New Orleans that morning.** We sat down outside the American Express office and watched other tourists. **Who were sunning themselves on the levee.** We were feeling low because we thought we had missed our chance to hear some Dixieland jazz. We were overjoyed, though, when a group of musicians ambled by and set up their instruments. **Right there on the levee**. We spent the rest of the afternoon listening to their music. **The best open-air jazz concert in town**.

REVISED:

On Thursday we reported the numbers of our missing traveler's checks, which we had lost during our arrival in New Orleans that morning. We sat down outside the American Express office and watched other tourists sunning themselves on the levee. We were feeling low because we thought we had missed our chance to hear some Dixieland jazz. We were overjoyed, though, when a group of musicians ambled by and set up their instruments right there on the levee. We spent the rest of the afternoon listening to their music—the best open-air jazz concert in town.

How to Spot a Fragment

You can recognize many fragments by the words that introduce them—subordinating terms such as *although, because, especially, even, except, for example, including, instead of, so that, such as, that, which, who,* and *when*. Of course, many acceptable sentences also start with such words but are complete because they include a full independent clause (p. 387, 18c). When you see a draft "sentence" beginning with one of those words, just check to be sure that an independent clause is also present.

DRAFT (Fragments boldfaced):

I always helped my brother. **Especially with his car**. I assisted him in many chores. **Such as washing the car and vacuuming the interior**. He let me do whatever I wanted. **Except start the engine**. Now I drive my own car. **Which is a 1983 Chevy**. I am thinking of possible jobs to help pay the cost of upkeep. **Including driving a cab**. **Because maintaining a car these days can be expensive**.

REVISED:

I always helped my brother, especially with his car. I assisted him in many chores, such as washing the car and vacuuming the interior. He let me do whatever I wanted except start the engine. Now I drive my own car, a 1983 Chevy. I am thinking of possible jobs, including driving a cab, to help pay the cost of upkeep. Maintaining a car these days can be expensive.

Learn to recognize the following five types of fragments:

1. A subordinate clause posing as a whole sentence.

   DRAFT:

   frag 18d

   Living in the city is more dangerous than ever. **Especially if you are wearing a gold chain**. During the past several weeks gold snatchers have been on a crime spree. **Although the police have tried to track down the thieves**. Nobody with a chain is safe. **Because the victims range from drivers stalled in traffic jams to students in gym classes.**

   REVISED:

   Living in the city is more dangerous than ever, especially if you are wearing a gold chain. Although the police have tried to track down the thieves, during the past several weeks gold snatchers have been on a crime spree. Nobody with a gold chain is safe; the victims range from drivers stalled in traffic jams to students in gym classes.

2. A verbal (p. 385, 18a) or a phrase (p. 390, 18d) unaccompanied by an independent clause.

DRAFT:

Before the start of the race, the drivers sat in their cars. **Revving up their engines**. They all had the same dream. **To see that checkered flag waving when they crossed the finish line**.

REVISED:

Before the start of the race, the drivers sat in their cars, revving up their engines. They all had the same dream: to see that checkered flag waving when they crossed the finish line.

3. An appositive (p. 451, 21n) standing alone.

DRAFT:

I love to read about the Roaring Twenties. **A decade that had its own personality**. People did their best to blot out the horrors of the recent past. **The Great War, the worldwide flu epidemic, the ominous revolution in Russia.**

REVISED:

I love to read about the Roaring Twenties, a decade that had its own personality. People did their best to blot out the horrors of the recent past—the Great War, the worldwide flu epidemic, the ominous revolution in Russia.

4. A disconnected second verb governed by a subject in the sentence before.

DRAFT:

The speech for my film course took a long time to prepare. **And then turned out poorly**. I needed a live audience. **But didn't have one for the test**.

REVISED:

The speech for my film course took a long time to prepare and then turned out poorly. I needed a live audience but didn't have one for the test.

5. A "sentence" lacking a verb in an independent clause.

DRAFT:

If there are no more malpractice suits, the hospital to win its license renewal. But no one can be sure. **Because patients these days are very quick to go to court**.

REVISED:

If there are no more malpractice suits, the hospital will win its license renewal. But no one can be sure, because patients these days are very quick to go to court.

Sentence Beginning with a Coordinating Conjunction

Note that there is nothing wrong with beginning a sentence with a coordinating conjunction (p. 389, 18c) such as *and* or *but*, provided you want the effect to be informal or conversational.

ACCEPTABLE: COORD CONJ

- I said farewell to my friends in high school. **And in September I began a completely new life**.

EXERCISE

4. Using each of the five categories listed above, submit five unacceptable fragments followed by revisions that eliminate the problem. In each revision, underline the independent clause that makes for an adequately complete sentence.

18e Note the uses of the intentional sentence fragment.

Some composition instructors advise against any use of fragments in submitted work. They feel, understandably, that students ought to eliminate habitual mistakes before trying flourishes of style. But you should know that practiced writers do resort to an occasional *intentional fragment* when they want to reply to a question in the previous sentence or make a point concisely and emphatically. When you are sure you have the unacceptable fragment under control, you may want to try your hand at the intentional one.

ACCEPTABLE:

- He sets him up with jabs, he works to the body, he corners him on the ropes. INTENTIONAL FRAG **Then the finish, a left hook to the jaw that brings him down.**
- Many secretaries were outraged by the shift to a later working day. INTENTIONAL FRAG **But not quite all of them.**
- And now for the dessert. **Pecan pie and ice cream!**

You will see from your reading of published authors that intentional fragments usually possess a certain "shock value." Whereas an unacceptable fragment looks like a missing part of a neighboring sentence, an intentional fragment is a condensed means of lending punch to the previous sentence or, in some instances, the following one. For example:

> **Newspapers. Telephone books. Soiled diapers. Medicine vials encasing brightly colored pills. Brittle ossuaries of chicken bones and T-bones. Sticky green mountains of yard waste. Half-empty cans of paint and turpentine and motor oil and herbicide. Broken furniture and forsaken toys.** Americans produce a lot of garbage, some of it very toxic, and our garbage is not always disposed of in a sensible way.[1]

EXERCISE

frag 18e

5. All of the following items contain sentence fragments. Even though they lack the usual makings of a sentence, some of the fragments are of the intentional variety that readers generally accept. Others would be perceived as unacceptable or unintentional. Write a brief evaluation of each fragment, explaining what prompts you to regard each one as either intentional or unacceptable. Revise the unacceptable ones to form complete sentences.

A. This stock is selling at a price below its book value. What a bargain!
B. Its price-earnings ratio is 1:0. Which is hard to beat.
C. The market for laser death rays is expected to become firmer in the 1990s. Unless the peaceniks get control of the White House again.
D. Why do you suppose it is listed as an under-the-counter stock? To attract the small investor, perhaps?
E. Many people would kill for a chance to buy some shares. If they don't get killed first.
F. Although he happens to be in jail at the moment. The chairman of the board has high hopes for General Catastrophe.

NOTE

[1] William J. Rathje, "Rubbish!" *Atlantic* Dec. 1989: 99.

19

Joining Independent Clauses

19a Note the two common ways of joining independent clauses.

An *independent clause* is a grammatically complete statement, question, or exclamation—one that could stand alone as a full sentence, whether or not it actually does stand alone (p. 387, 18c).

INDEPENDENT CLAUSES:

- I need a rest. [statement].
- Have I ever been this tired before? [question]
- Leave me alone! [exclamation]

Comma and Coordinating Conjunction

There are two usual ways of joining independent clauses within a single sentence. The first way is to put a comma after the first independent clause and to follow the comma with a coordinating

conjunction—that is, one of the following seven connectives: *and, but, for, or, nor, so, yet.*

IND CLAUSE / COORD CONJ / IND CLAUSE

- George was lonely at first, **but** after a while he came to like having the whole apartment to himself.

IND CLAUSE / COORD CONJ / IND CLAUSE

- He ate constantly, **but** he still couldn't get enough food to satisfy his cravings.

Semicolon

Alternatively, you can join independent clauses with a semicolon alone if they are closely related in meaning and spirit or show a striking, pointed contrast:

IND CLAUSE / IND CLAUSE

- George's reliance on prepared foods was now total; Susan had gathered up her cookbooks before slamming the door for the last time.

IND CLAUSE / IND CLAUSE

- George's health soon improved; his diet had become rich in preservatives.

When using a semicolon, test to see whether what comes before it could make a complete sentence and whether what comes after it could also make a complete sentence. If either fails, your draft sentence is faulty.

DON'T:

X Susan, too, was lonely; especially since nobody had responded to her first "personals" ad for a man with no habits or distinguishing traits.

Especially since nobody responded . . . could not stand as a complete sentence.

DO:
- Susan, too, was lonely, especially since nobody had responded. . . .

or

- Susan, too, was lonely; nobody had responded. . . .

In some cases you will find it easier simply to eliminate the semicolon or replace it with a comma.

DON'T:
x He strode into the room; while flicking the light switch on.

DO:
- He strode into the room while flicking the light switch on.

DON'T:
x My grandparents said that they were too tired to see me; but that they would phone me later.

DO:
- My grandparents said that they were too tired to see me, but that they would phone me later.

EXERCISE

1. Submit five complete sentences, each of which contains two independent clauses. In the first three sentences, join the independent clauses with a comma and a coordinating conjunction. In the other two, use a semicolon. Make sure that the two parts of each sentence are properly related in meaning.

19b Avoid a run-on sentence.

RUN-ON SENTENCES	PROPERLY PUNCTUATED SENTENCES
x I need a rest, I must keep studying for the exam.	• I need a rest, but I must keep studying for the exam.
x I am not prepared I dread seeing the questions.	• I am not prepared; I dread seeing the questions.

If you remember how to join independent clauses, you will be able to spot and correct a **run-on sentence**—that is, a sentence in which two or more independent clauses are joined with only a comma between them or with no punctuation at all.

There are other ways to correct a run-on sentence besides inserting a semicolon or a comma and a coordinating conjunction—for example, by changing one of the independent clauses to a subordinate clause or a phrase (p. 390, 18d). But if you decide to keep your two independent clauses, remember the rules for joining them correctly (19a).

COMMA AND COORDINATING CONJUNCTION:

- I need a rest, **but** I must keep studying for the exam.

SEMICOLON:

- I am not prepared; I dread seeing the questions.

Comma Splice

A run-on sentence in which a comma alone joins two independent clauses is known as a **comma splice**. Such a construction does not seriously garble the statement being made, but it fails to indicate how its two clauses are related in meaning.

DON'T:

FIRST IND CLAUSE / SECOND IND CLAUSE

x Faulkner's novel is psychologically deep, they wanted to explore it further.

FIRST IND CLAUSE / SECOND IND CLAUSE

x They discussed Faulkner's novel, the class hour ended all too soon.

run-on 19b

How to Revise a Comma Splice

If you find a comma splice in one of your drafts, you can revise it in a number of ways, including the subordinating of one element to another.

COMMA AND COORDINATING CONJUNCTION (p. 397, 19a):

- Faulkner's novel is psychologically deep, **and** they wanted to explore it further.

SEMICOLON (p. 398, 19a):

- Faulkner's novel is psychologically deep; they wanted to explore it further.

SUBORDINATE CLAUSE (p. 387, 18c):

- **Although they did make some progress in discussing Faulkner's novel**, the class hour ended all too soon.

PHRASE (p. 390, 18d):

- The class hour came to an end, **leaving them unable to finish their discussion of Faulkner's novel**.

Exception: Note that a tag such as *she thought* or *he said* can be joined to a quotation by a comma alone, even if the quotation is another independent clause.

IND CLAUSE — IND CLAUSE

- "That is a matter of opinion," Emily replied.

For further ways of joining independent clauses, including another exception to the rule against committing comma splices, see page 406, 19d.

Fused Sentence

A run-on sentence in which independent clauses are merged with no sign of their separateness—neither a comma nor a coordinating conjunction—is called a **fused sentence**.

DON'T:

IND CLAUSE — IND CLAUSE

x Some people can hide their nervous habits I envy them.

IND CLAUSE

x Sometimes I have to stand up in front of other students

IND CLAUSE

it makes me sick.

How to Revise a Comma Splice

Revise by choosing from the same options given above for correcting a comma splice.

COMMA AND COORDINATING CONJUNCTION:

- Some people can hide their nervous habits, **and** I envy them.

SEMICOLON:

- Some people can hide their nervous habits; I envy them.

SUBORDINATE CLAUSE:

- I feel sick **whenever I have to stand up in front of other students**.

PHRASE:

- I feel sick **standing up in front of other students**.

If you habitually write run-on sentences, you may think you can solve your problem by keeping to safe, short sentences that scarcely combine clauses at all. But that can only be a stopgap measure; before long you will want to aim for more variety and logical development. Begin thinking, then, not of stripping down your sentences but of developing them by showing just how one element relates to another.

For further options in sentence variety, see Chapter 14, especially pages 318–27.

EXERCISE

2. Submit two original sentences illustrating the problems of a comma splice and a fused sentence, respectively. Under each faulty sentence, write four correct versions, illustrating in turn the use of (a) a comma and a coordinating conjunction; (b) a semicolon; (c) a subordinate clause; and (d) a phrase.

19c Watch especially for run-on sentences using connectors like *however, also,* and *then.*

RUN-ON SENTENCES	PROPERLY PUNCTUATED SENTENCES
x We planted a garden, **however** nothing grew.	• We planted a garden; however, nothing grew.
x We used a plastic mulch, **also** we watered vigorously.	• We used a plastic mulch, and we also watered vigorously.
x We scanned the gardening encyclopedia for help, **then** we phoned Ms. Green Thumb on WKGB.	• After scanning the gardening encyclopedia for help, we phoned Ms. Green Thumb on WKGB.

Look through the following terms, which often lead a writer to commit a comma splice (p. 400, 19b):

SENTENCE ADVERBS		
again	hence	nonetheless
also	however	otherwise
besides	indeed	similarly
consequently	likewise	then
further	moreover	therefore
furthermore	nevertheless	thus *(etc.)*

TRANSITIONAL PHRASES		
after all	for example	in reality
as a result	in addition	in truth
at the same time	in fact	on the contrary
even so	in other words	on the other hand *(etc.)*

A **sentence adverb** (also called a *conjunctive adverb*) is a word that modifies a whole previous statement. Note how such a term differs from an ordinary adverb.

ORDINARY ADVERB:

- She applied for the job **again** in March.
- **Then** she made arrangements to have her furniture stored.

SENTENCE ADVERB:

- **Again**, there is still another reason to delay a decision.
- We see, **then**, that precautions are in order.

An ordinary adverb modifies part of the statement in which it appears: she applied *again;* she stored her furniture *then*. But a sentence adverb modifies the whole statement by showing its logical relation to the preceding statement: after the already stated reasons to delay, here *(again)* is another one; because of the preceding statement, we therefore *(then)* see that precautions are in order. A **transitional phrase** is a multiword expression that functions like a sentence adverb.

What makes these modifiers tricky is that they "feel like" conjunctions such as *and, although, so,* and *yet*. If you treat a sentence adverb or transitional phrase as if it were a conjunction, the result will be a comma splice. You can revise such sentences in any of the ways previously discussed, either by properly joining the independent clauses (p. 397, 19a) or by changing the whole construction.

DON'T:

SENT ADV

x George turned the oven dial to the "Clean" position, **however** the dishes seemed dirtier than ever when he took them out.

DO:

SENT ADV

- George turned the oven dial to the "Clean" position; however, the dishes seemed dirtier than ever when he took them out.

run-on 19c

DON'T:

TRANS PHRASE

x Our garden was a disappointment, **in fact** it was a disaster.

DO:

TRANS PHRASE

- Our garden was a disappointment; **in fact**, it was a disaster.

If you are not sure whether a certain word is a sentence adverb, test to see whether it could be moved without loss of meaning. A conjunction must stay put, but a sentence adverb can always be moved to at least one other position:

- We planted a garden; **however**, nothing grew.
- We planted a garden; nothing, **however**, grew.
- We planted a garden; nothing grew, **however**.

When you are sure of the difference between conjunctions and sentence adverbs, you will be able to avoid putting an unneeded comma after a conjunction.

DON'T:

CONJ
x He swam for the island, **but**, the current exhausted him.

DO:

CONJ
- He swam for the island, **but** the current exhausted him.

DON'T:

CONJ
x The threat is serious, **yet**, I think we have grounds for hope.

DO:

CONJ
- The threat is serious, **yet** I think we have grounds for hope.

Setting Off Sentence Adverbs and Transitional Phrases

Since these expressions modity a whole previous statement, they are usually set apart by punctuation on both sides. Do not allow a sentence adverb or transitional phrase to "leak" at one end or the other.

DON'T:

SENT ADV
x John, **however** was nowhere to be seen.

DO:

SENT ADV
- John, **however**, was nowhere to be seen.

DON'T:

TRANS PHRASE
x Guatemala **in contrast**, has a troubled history.

DO:

TRANS PHRASE
- Guatemala, **in contrast**, has a troubled history.

In some cases you can omit commas or other punctuation around a sentence adverb *(And thus it is clear that . . .)*. But if you supply punctuation at one end, be sure to supply it at the other end as well.

EXERCISE (19a–c)

3. Correct any comma splices and fused sentences that you find here:

   A. Henry James was fond of Italy, in fact, he wrote a whole book about its civilized pleasures.
   B. This surprised Biff he had thought that Henry James had spent all his time playing the trumpet.
   C. This book is not illustrated, however its text is very clear.
   D. Dr. Dollar understands the rising concern for physical fitness, he also knows that many office workers cannot set aside time for an exercise period.
   E. Many potential readers are just now changing their habits, therefore many of them ought to buy *The Complete Book of Hopping to Your Place of Business*.

---

run-on 19d

19d Recognize exceptional ways of joining independent clauses.

Optional Comma after Brief Independent Clause

If your first independent clause is brief, consider the comma optional:

- **I was late** and it was already growing dark.

  But a comma after *late* would also be correct. When in doubt, retain the comma.

Optional Conjunctions in Series of Independent Clauses

When you are presenting several brief, tightly related independent clauses in a series (p. 500, 24k), you can gain a dramatic effect by doing without a coordinating conjunction:

- He saw the train, he fell to the tracks, he covered his head with his arms.

  By omitting *and* before the last clause, the writer brings out the rapidity and urgency of the three actions. This is a rare case of an acceptable comma splice.

Reversal of Negative Emphasis

If a second independent clause reverses the negative emphasis of the first, consider joining them only with a comma:

- That summer Thoreau did not read books, he hoed beans.

  The *not* clause leaves us anticipating a second clause that will say what Thoreau did do. The absence of a conjunction brings out the tight, necessary relation between the two statements.

Compare:

x Thoreau hoed beans all summer, he did not read books.

Lacking a "reversal of negative emphasis," this sentence shows a classic *unacceptable* comma splice.

run-on
19d

EXERCISE

4. Submit three original sentences illustrating, in turn, the three exceptional ways of joining independent clauses shown above.

20

Joining Subjects and Verbs

SUBJECT-VERB COHERENCE

20a Avoid a mixed construction.

DON'T:
x A hobby that gets out of hand, it becomes an obsession.

DO:
• A hobby that gets out of hand becomes an obsession.

If your subjects and verbs (pp. 383–84, 18a–b) are to work efficiently together, you cannot leave your reader wondering which part of a sentence is the subject. Do not start a sentence with one subject and then change your mind. In the DON'T example above, the reader begins by expecting that *hobby* will be the subject. After the comma, however, the writer serves up a new subject, *it*, leaving *hobby* grammatically stranded. The result is a **mixed construction**, whereby two elements in a sentence are competing to serve the same function.

DON'T:

x In doing the workbook problems was extremely useful.

> The sentence begins with a prepositional phrase (p. 725) that can only serve as a modifier (p. 430)—as it would, for example, in this sentence: *In doing the workbook problems I had trouble with quadratic equations*. But the writer has tried unsuccessfully to turn *In doing the workbook problems* into a subject.

When you suspect that a draft sentence suffers from mixed construction, first isolate the predicate (p. 384, 18a); then ask yourself what *one* thing makes that predicate meaningful. Thus, *what* was extremely useful? *Doing the workbook problems*. That phrase should become the subject.

DO:

• Doing the workbook problems was extremely useful.

The problem of mixed construction actually extends beyond subjects and verbs. Consider the following sentence:

DON'T:

D OBJ? D OBJ?

x They gave **it** to her for Christmas **what** she had been asking for.

> Here *it* and *what* are competing to be the direct object (p. 383, 18a) of the verb *gave*. The solution is to choose one or the other and make a consistent pattern.

DO:

• For Christmas they gave her what she had been asking for.

If your prose contains mixed constructions, review the essential sentence elements: subject, verb, direct object, complement (pp. 383–84, 18a). And be aware that in written prose you cannot make your meaning clear by changing your voice or by abandoning a sentence in the middle and starting over. The first element in a written sentence usually commits it to a certain structure that you must then follow. If you run into trouble, recast the sentence from the beginning.

EXERCISE

1. If your instructor has found no instances of mixed construction in your submitted work, skip this exercise. Otherwise, copy up to five noted examples of the problem. For each sentence containing a mixed construction, provide an adequate revision. Mark the subject (S) and verb (V) in each revised construction.

20b Watch for faulty predication.

Predication—saying something about a grammatical subject—is the essence of all statement. In first-draft prose, however, writers sometimes yoke subjects and predicates that fail to make sense together. A mixed construction (20a), which typically prevents the reader from knowing which word is the intended subject, shows faulty predication in an extreme form. But predication can also go awry if the writer asks a subject to perform something it could not possibly do.

DON'T:

S V

x The **capabilities** of freshmen in high school **function** on an adult level.

PRED

Can capabilities function? No; they are abstractions (p. 355, 16a), not agents. People or things function, and they do so because they possess certain capabilities. Thus the revised sentence must reflect that fact.

DO:

S V

- **Freshmen** in high school **are** capable of functioning like adults.

PRED

s–v coh 20b

or

S V

- **Freshmen** in high school **have** the capabilities of adults.

PRED

or

S V

- The **capabilities** of freshmen in high school **match** those of adults.

PRED

You can see that the problem in faulty predication often lies in treating an abstraction as if it were a performer of action. Once you have hit upon a subject like *capabilities* (or *inventiveness, symmetry, rationality, reluctance,* etc), your predicate must reflect the fact that you are not writing about an agent.

EXERCISE

2. Write five sentences that suffer from impossible predication. In each example, match an abstract subject with a verb that would require an agent as a proper subject. Add five adequately revised versions, and submit both sets of sentences.

SUBJECT-VERB AGREEMENT

20c Make a verb agree with its subject in person and number.

In grammar we refer to three **persons:**

	EXAMPLE	IDENTITY
First Person	I pull	the speaker or writer
	we pull	the speakers or writers
Second Person	you pull	the person or persons addressed
Third Person	he, she, it pulls the mother speaks the signal changes	the person or thing spoken or written about
	they pull the mothers speak the signals change	the persons or things spoken or written about

We also refer to the *time* of a verb as its **tense**—present, past, future, and so forth.

In standard written English, the ending of a verb often shows the **number** of the subject—that is, whether the subject is *singular* (one item) or *plural* (more than one item). A singular subject requires a singular verb; a plural subject requires a plural verb.

S V
- The **river flows** south.

 Here the *-s* ending on the verb *flows* indicates that the verb is in the third person, is singular, and is in the present tense.

The grammatical correspondence of subjects and verbs is called *agreement*. In *The river flows south* the verb *flows* is said to agree with its singular, third-person subject *river*. Note that the singular subject usually has no *-s* ending but that a singular, third-person verb in the present tense does have an *-s* ending: *flows*. Compare:

S V
- The **rivers flow** south.

 The lack of an *-s* ending on the verb *flow* indicates that the verb is plural, in agreement with its plural subject *rivers*. Notice that the *-s* on *rivers* marks it as a plural noun.

SINGULAR:

- The river flows.

PLURAL:

- The rivers flow.

Many native speakers of English use the same forms for both the singular and plural of certain verbs in the present tense: *she don't, they don't; he is, we is*. In standard written English, however, it is important to observe the difference: *She does not, she doesn't, they do not, they don't; he is, we are*.

s–v agr 20c

DON'T:

x They **is** having a party.

DO:

- They **are** having a party.

DON'T:

x He **don't** expect to rent a car.

DO:

• He **doesn't** expect to rent a car.

For further verb forms in various tenses, see pages 574–81, 32b–d.

EXERCISE

3. If your instructor has found no instances of subject-verb disagreement in your submitted work, skip this exercise. Otherwise, copy out as many as five noted examples of the problem, and indicate how you would now recast either the subject or the verb to bring them into agreement.

20d Be sure you have found the true subject.

Sometimes you will have a good stylistic reason for putting your subject after its verb. *(Chief among her virtues was her honesty)* or for separating the subject and verb with other language *(Her honesty, acquired from her strictly religious parents, was her chief virtue)*. Be careful, though, that you don't lose track of the subject and mistakenly allow the verb to be governed by another word. Here are the constructions—allowable but potentially tricky—that call for particular attention.

Intervening Clause or Phrase

DON'T:

S (subject); INTERVENING CLAUSE (over "that runs through these isolated mountain towns"); V (verb)

x The **highway** that runs through these isolated mountain towns **are** steep and narrow.

The subject, *highway*, is so far from its verb that the writer has absent-mindedly allowed that verb to be governed by the nearest preceding noun, **towns**.

s–v agr 20d

DO:

S V
- The **highway** . . . **is** steep and narrow.

Again:

DON'T:

S INTERVENING PHRASE V
x The **pleasures** of a motorcyclist **includes** repairing the bike.

DO:

S V
- The **pleasures** . . . **include** repairing the bike.

Learn to locate the true subject by asking who or what performs the action of the verb or is in the state indicated by the verb. Test for singular or plural by these steps:

1. Locate the verb and its subject.
2. Put the phrase between them into imaginary parentheses:
   The pleasures (of a motorcyclist) include / includes . . . .
3. Then say aloud:
   "The pleasures include"
   and
   "The pleasures includes."

The form of the verb that is correct without the element "in parentheses" is also correct with it. *The pleasures of a motorcyclist include. . . .*

A Phrase Like *along with* or *in addition to*

s–v agr 20d

DON'T:

S ADDITIVE PHRASE V
x **Jill**, along with her two karate instructors, **are** highly disciplined.

DO:
- Jill, along with her two karate instructors, **is** highly disciplined.

An expression that begins with a term like *accompanied by, along with, as well as, in addition to, including,* or *together with* is called an **additive phrase**. Though it is typically set off by commas (p. 445, 21l), it can "feel like" part of the subject. If you write *Jill, along with her two karate instructors*, you certainly have more than one person in mind. But grammatically, additive phrases do not add anything to the subject. Disregard the additive phrase, just as you would any other intervening element. If the subject apart from the additive phrase is singular, make the verb singular as well.

DON'T:

S — ADDITIVE PHRASE — V

x **Practical knowledge**, in addition to statistics and market theory, **enter** into the training of an economist.

DO:

- Practical knowledge, in addition to statistics and market theory, **enters** into the training of an economist.

Subject Following Verb

DON'T:

V S

x Beside the blue waters **lie Claire**, waiting for Henry to bring the towels.

To find the true subject, mentally rearrange the sentence into normal subject-verb word order: *Claire lies beside. . . .*

DO:

- Beside the blue waters **lies** Claire, waiting for Henry to bring the towels.

s–v agr 20d

Watch especially for agreement problems when the subject is delayed by an expression like *There is* or *Here comes*. By the time such a sentence is finished, its subject may be plural.

DON'T:

V S

x Here **comes a clown and three elephants**.

IMPROVED:
- Here **come** a clown and three elephants.

Or, since this example sounds strained:

PREFERABLE:
- Here **comes** a clown leading three elephants.

EXERCISE

4. For each sentence, identify the subject of the disputed verb, and choose the verb form that makes for subject-verb agreement.

   A. Above the wealthiest section of Rio *(stands, stand)* some of the world's most miserable slums.
   B. Baseball, along with all other sports, *(strikes, strike)* Priscilla as utterly meaningless.
   C. There *(is, are)* four candidates in this election.
   D. Any idea for improving the company's profits *(is, are)* welcome.
   E. Early darkness, together with cold weather and the usual miseries of flu, *(makes, make)* winter a difficult season to endure.

20e When the subject is a phrase or clause, make the verb singular.

PHRASE AS S — V
- **Having the numbers of several bail bondsmen is** useful in an emergency.

CLAUSE AS S — V
- **That none of his customers wanted to buy a matching fleet of De Sotos was** a disagreeable surprise for Harry.

A phrase or clause acting as a subject takes a singular verb, even if it contains plural items. Do not be misled by a plural word at the end of the phrase or clause. The two examples above are correct.

EXERCISE

5. Submit three original sentences correctly illustrating subject-verb agreement when the subject is a phrase or clause.

20f Usually treat a noun like *crowd* or *orchestra* as singular.

- The orchestra **is playing** better now that the conductor is sober.
- A strong, united faculty **is needed** to stand firm against the erosion of parking privileges.
- In Priscilla's opinion the middle class **is** altogether too middle-class.

A **collective noun** is one having a singular form but referring to a group of members: *administration, army, audience, class, crowd, orchestra, team*, and so forth. This conflict between form and meaning can lead to agreement problems. But in general you should think of a collective noun as singular and thus make the verb singular, too.

Once in a while, however, you may want to emphasize the individual members of the group. Then you should make the verb plural:

- The faculty **have** come to their assignments from all over the world.

Plural *of* Construction

A plural verb is especially common when a collective noun is followed by a plural *of* construction:

S V
- **A team of experts are** arriving by plane tomorrow.

In this sentence *is* would also be correct, but it would put emphasis on the collective *team* instead of on the individual *experts*.

s–v agr 20f

EXERCISE

6. Submit a pair of sentences in which you construe a collective noun as (a) singular and (b) plural, and add a sentence or two explaining the difference in emphasis between the two statements.

20g If a subject contains two parts, usually treat it as plural.

S V
- **A teller and a guard operate** the drive-in window at the bank.

S V
- **A bouquet and a box of candy are** no substitute for a fair wage.

A **compound** subject, such as *a clown and three elephants*, is made up of more than one unit. In most instances, such a subject calls for a plural verb.

Note, in the second example above, that *substitute* is singular even though the subject and verb are plural. Agreement does not extend to complements (p. 384, 18a)—words in the predicate that identify or modify the subject.

Exception: Both Parts Refer to the Same Thing or Person

Even when the parts of a compound subject are joined by *and*, common sense will sometimes tell you that only one thing or person is being discussed. Make the verb singular in such a case:

- My best friend and severest critic has moved to Atlanta.

One person is both friend and critic. By changing the verb to *have* the writer would be saying that two people, not one, have moved to Atlanta. Both sentences could be correct but their meanings would differ.

EXERCISE

7. Submit two original sentences in which you construe a compound subject as (a) singular and (b) plural, and add an explanatory sentence or two explaining the difference in emphasis between the two statements.

---

s–v agr 20g

20h Avoid a clash of singular and plural subjects linked by *or* or *nor*.

Compound subjects (20g) joined by *or, either . . . or*, or *neither . . . nor* are called **disjunctive.** They ask the reader to choose between two or more parts. Consequently, the verb should agree with only one of those parts—the one nearest the verb.

DON'T:

DISJUNCTIVE S — V

x **Either his children or his cat are** responsible for the dead goldfish.

BETTER:

NEAREST PART OF DISJUNCTIVE S

- Either his children or **his cat is** responsible for the dead goldfish.
V

But such conflicts of number are awkward. Rewrite to avoid the problem.

PREFERABLE:

S V

- Either **his children are** responsible for the dead goldfish or **his**
S V
cat is.

or

S V

- **No one** but his children or his cat **could have killed** the goldfish.

Some disjunctive subjects "feel plural" even though each item within them is singular, for the writer is thinking about two or more things. But so long as the individual disjunctive items are singular, the verb must be singular, too.

DON'T:

DISJUNCTIVE S — V

x **Neither WNCN nor WQXR carry** the country-western sing-off.

DO:

- Neither WNCN nor WQXR **carries** the country-western sing-off.

EXERCISE

8. Submit an original sentence in which an *either . . . or* construction results in subject-verb disagreement. In a second sentence, correct the problem by changing only the verb. Finally, add a sentence that avoids the problem by rephrasing the sentence in a more thoroughgoing way.

20i If you have placed *each* or *every* before a compound subject, treat the subject as singular.

S V

- **Every linebacker and tackle in the league was pleased** with the settlement.

S V

- Before being put away for the summer, **each coat and sweater is** to be mothproofed.

Each or *every*, if it comes before the subject, guarantees that the subject will be singular even if it contains multiple parts.

Note, however, that when *each* comes *after* a subject, it has no effect on the number of the verb:

S V

- **They** each **have** their own reasons for protesting.

EXERCISE

9. Submit two original sentences using the term *each*, with a singular verb in the first and a plural verb in the second. Add a sentence explaining why both sentences illustrate proper subject-verb agreement.

20j Observe the agreement rules for terms of quantity.

Numerical words (*majority, minority, number, plurality*, etc.) and plural terms of quantity (*three dollars, fifty years*, etc.) can take either a singular or a plural verb. If you have in mind the *totality* of items, make the verb singular:

s–v
agr
20i

S V

- The Democratic **majority favors** the bill.

But if you mean the separate items that make up that totality, make the verb plural:

S V

- **The majority of Democrats** on the North Shore **are** opposed to building a bridge.

The Word *Number*

When the word *number* is preceded by *the*, it is always singular:

S V
- The **number** of unhappy voters **is growing.**

But when *number* is preceded by *a*, you must look to see whether it refers to the total unit (singular) or to individual parts (plural).

TOTAL UNIT (SINGULAR):

S V
- A **number** like ten billion **is** hard to comprehend.

INDIVIDUAL PARTS (PLURAL):

S V
- **A number of voters have arrived** at their choice.

  Note that although *of voters* looks like a modifier of the subject *number*, we read *a number of* as if it said *many*.

When your subject contains an actual number, decide once again whether you mean the total unit or the individual parts.

TOTAL UNIT (SINGULAR):

S V
- **Twenty-six miles is** the length of the race.

INDIVIDUAL PARTS (PLURAL):

S V
- **Twenty-six difficult miles lie** ahead of her.

Mathematical Operations

s–v agr 20j

When adding or multiplying, you can choose either a singular or a plural verb:

- One and one **is** two.
- One and one **are** two.

When subtracting or dividing, keep to the singular:

- Sixty minus forty **leaves** twenty.
- Eight divided by two **is** four.

EXERCISE (20e–20j)

10. For each sentence, choose the verb form that makes for subject-verb agreement.

    A. Having to grow up with two brilliant and beautiful older sisters (*was, were*) hard on her ego.
    B. A number of people (*dislikes, dislike*) mushroom pizza.
    C. Each of them (*is, are*) equally certain of being right.
    D. A majority of votes (*is, are*) all you need to be elected.
    E. Neither age nor illness (*prevents, prevent*) her from laughing at the world's follies.
    F. Thirty less five (*leaves, leave*) twenty-five.
    G. The army in all its divisions (*is, are*) ready to fight.
    H. An honest politician and a caring woman (*has, have*) finally been elected as our governor.
    I. Every child throughout all the countries of Africa (*is, are*) facing an uncertain future.

20k As a rule, use a singular verb with a subject like *everyone* or *nobody*.

An *indefinite pronoun* leaves unspecified the person or thing it refers to.

INDEFINITE PRONOUNS

all	anything	everybody	most	no one	some
another	both	everyone	much	nothing	somebody
any	each	everything	neither	one	someone
anybody	each one	few	nobody	others	something
anyone	either	many	none	several	such

Some of these words serve other functions, too; they are indefinite pronouns only when they stand alone without modifying another term.

ADJECTIVE:

- **All** leopards are fast.

INDEFINITE PRONOUN:

- **All** have spots.

Some indefinite pronouns, such as *another*, are obviously singular, and some others, such as *several*, are obviously plural. But there is also a borderline class: *each, each one, either, everybody, everyone, everything, neither, nobody, none, no one*. These terms have a singular form, yet they call to mind plural things or persons. According to convention, you should generally treat them as singular:

S V
- **Everyone seems** to be late tonight.

S V
- **Neither has brought** the music for the duet.

Keep to a singular verb even when the indefinite pronoun is followed by a plural construction such as *of them:*

S V
- **Neither** of them **has** the music for the duet.

S V
- **Each** of those cordless phones **has** a touch-tone dial.

None

None is usually treated as singular:

S V
- **None** among us **is** likely to agree with Stanley's proposal to smash racism by blowing up Kentucky Fried Chicken.

But if you mean *all are not*, you can use a plural verb:

S V
- **None** of us **are** enthusiastic about Operation Fingerlicker.

  Since some writers would consider this sentence mistaken, keep to the singular whenever it does not sound forced.

EXERCISE

11. Choosing five indefinite pronouns from the "borderline" list—*each, each one, either, everybody, everyone, everything, neither, nobody, none,* and *no one*—submit five original sentences in which the indefinite pronoun serves as subject.

20l Note the special character of subjects like *politics* and *acoustics*.

Some nouns have an *-s* ending but take a singular verb: *economics, mathematics, mumps, news, physics,* and so forth:

S V
- **Physics has** made enormous strides in this century.

Some other nouns ending in *-s* can be singular in one meaning and plural in another. When they refer to a body of knowledge, they are singular.

AS BODY OF KNOWLEDGE:

S V
- **Politics is** an important study for many historians.

S V
- **Acoustics requires** an understanding of mathematics.

But when the same words are used in a more particular sense—not politics as a field but somebody's politics—they are considered plural.

IN PARTICULAR SENSE:

S V
- Gloria's **politics are** left of center.

V S
- How **are** the **acoustics** in the new auditorium?

s–v agr 20l

EXERCISE

12. Submit three pairs of original sentences in which the subject is a term like *politics, acoustics, aerodynamics,* or *optics*—a word that can be construed as either singular or plural. In each pair of sentences, make

the first verb singular and the second plural. Be prepared to explain the difference in meaning in each instance.

20m In a *that* or *which* clause, make the verb agree with the antecedent.

Consider the following correctly formed sentence:

REL CLAUSE
- The telephone bills **that are overdue** include a charge for a lengthy call to Paris.

Here *that are overdue* is a **relative clause**—a subordinate clause (18c, p. 387) that relates its statement to an earlier, or **antecedent**, part of the sentence. A relative clause usually begins with a word like *who, whom, whose, that*, or *which*. In this case the antecedent is *telephone bills*.

Relative clauses can make for tricky agreement problems. You will avoid trouble, however, if you remember that the verb in a relative clause agrees in number with its antecedent. Thus, in the example above, *are* agrees with the plural antecedent *telephone bills*. Again:

ANT V
- There have been complaints about **service** that **is** painfully slow.

Note, however, that you cannot automatically assume that the antecedent is the last term before the relative clause:

ANT V
- There have been **complaints** about service that **were** entirely justified.

ANT V
- The **oceans** of the world, which **have become** a dumping ground, may never be completely unpolluted again.

Ask yourself what the verb in the relative clause refers to:

What is painfully slow? Service.

What was entirely justified? Complaints.

What has become a dumping ground? Oceans.

Once you have an answer, a singular or plural term, you also have the right number for the verb in your relative clause.

Singular Complement in Relative Clause

Look at the following mistaken but typical sentence:

DON'T:

PLURAL ANT V SING COMPL
x **Math problems**, which **is** her **specialty**, cause her no concern.

A singular complement (p. 384, 18a) in a *who, which*, or *that* clause can trick you into making the verb in that clause singular when the antecedent is actually plural. Here the complement *specialty* has wrongly influenced the number of the verb *is*. That verb, like any other verb in a relative clause, must agree with its antecedent.

DO:

- Math problems, which are her specialty, cause her no concern.

One of Those Who

Consider the following sentences, both of which are correct:

ANT V
- Joe is one of those **chemists** who **believe** that science is an art.

ANT V
- Joe is the only **one** of those chemists who **believes** that science is an art.

The expression *one of those who* contains both a singular and a plural term—*one* and *those*. To avoid confusion, be careful to decide which of the two is the antecedent. In most cases it will be the plural *those* (or *those chemists*, etc.), but to be sure you must isolate the relative clause and ask yourself what it modifies.

s–v agr 20m

It Is and Plural Subject as Antecedent

Consider this imperfect sentence:

x It is the vegetables that makes Max feel queasy.

Here the writer has felt required to make the second verb agree with a singular antecedent, *It*. But *It* in this sentence is an **expletive**

(p. 715), not a pronoun. Its function is simply to anticipate the true subject, *vegetables*. And since *vegetables* is also the antecedent of the relative pronoun *that*, the plural *vegetables* should govern the number of the verb in the relative clause: *make*.

EXERCISE

13. For each sentence, choose the verb form that makes for subject-verb agreement.

    A. It is their own secret vices that (*allows, allow*) people to tolerate the vices of others.
    B. Death threats, which (*is, are*) a rarity in most people's lives, (*is, are*) all too familiar to famous athletes.
    C. Problems with a rebellious class that (*pays, pay*) no attention (*occurs, occur*) all too frequently these days.
    D. Max is one of those tourists who (*expects, expect*) all the natives to be wearing peasant costumes.
    E. There are difficulties with substandard care that (*requires, require*) immediate attention.

20n Prefer a singular verb with the title of a work.

Titles of works are generally treated as singular even when they have a plural form, because only one work is being discussed:

- Joyce's ***Dubliners*** (S) **has justified** (V) the author's faith in its importance.

- Camus's ***Lyrical and Critical Essays*** (S) **was** (V) required reading in Comparative Literature 102 last term.

  The plural verb *were* would misleadingly refer to the individual essays rather than the whole book.

s–v agr 20n

EXERCISE

14. Find or invent three book titles that take a plural form, and use those titles as the subjects of three sentences, as in the examples above.

PUNCTUATION BETWEEN A SUBJECT AND VERB

20o Omit an unnecessary comma between a subject and its verb.

DON'T:

S V
x **Ishi** alone, **remained** to tell the story of his tribe.

DO:

- Ishi alone remained to tell the story of his tribe.

An element that comes between a subject and its verb may need to be set off by commas, as in the sentence *Teenage suicide, which has become common in recent years, is a matter of urgent public concern* (p. 445, 21l). But beware of inserting commas simply to draw a breath, for the demands of grammar and of easy breathing do not always match up. You want to show your reader that a subject is connected to its verb.

DON'T:

S V
x **A pair of scissors, a pot of glue, and a stapler, are** still essential to a writer who does not use a word processor.

DO:

- A pair of scissors, a pot of glue, and a stapler are still essential to a writer who does not use a word processor.

S V
x **Those construction workers who had collected unemployment checks in the slump of December through March, were** delighted that spring had finally arrived.

DO:

- Those construction workers who had collected unemployment checks in the slump of December through March were delighted that spring had finally arrived.

EXERCISE

15. Indicate which of the following sentences are incorrectly punctuated, and why.

    A. Animals, vegetables, and minerals, all get involved in the exciting game of "Twenty Questions."
    B. One good reason for moving to San Antonio is that it is the cleanest city in the United States.
    C. Every person, no matter how incompetent at everything else is the world's foremost expert at deciphering his or her own handwriting.
    D. A woman who has so little tact as to keep her old boyfriend's picture in her wallet is surely courting trouble with her husband.
    E. Power as an end in itself, never brings true satisfaction.

20p Note where it is appropriate to insert punctuation between a subject and its verb.

Whenever you place an **interrupting element** (p. 445, 21l) between a subject and verb, you need to set that element apart by a pair of punctuation marks—usually commas:

S — INT EL — V

- The pilot, **having failed to secure clearance to land**, circled the field as she pleaded desperately with the chief traffic controller.

S — INT EL — V

- Tax simplification—**a major goal of this administration**—remains a distant promise.

EXERCISE

16. Submit three original sentences in which you place an interrupting element between the subject and verb. Be sure your sentences are correctly punctuated.

21

Modifiers

A **modifier** is an expression that limits or describes another element:

- **tall** messenger
- **the tall** messenger **with blond hair**
- **the tall** messenger **with blond hair who is locking his bicycle**
- **The tall** messenger **who is locking his bicycle** is **from Finland.**

A modifier can consist of a single word, a phrase, or a subordinate clause.

1. a single word:
   - The **tall** boy is from Finland.
   - A **new** star appeared in the **darkening** sky.
   - They did it **gladly.**
   - **That** proposal, **however**, was **soundly** defeated.
2. a **phrase,** or cluster of words lacking a subject-verb combination (p. 390, 18d):
   - The boy **with blond hair** is **from Finland.**

- **At ten o'clock** she gave up hope.
- **In view of the foul weather,** they remained **at home.**

3. a **subordinate clause,** or cluster of words that does contain a subject-verb combination but does not form an independent statement (p. 387, 18c):

   - The tall messenger **who is locking his bicycle** is from Finland.
   - The largest telephone company, **which once enjoyed a near monopoly on phone appliances,** is now being challenged in the open marketplace.

A single-word modifier is usually either an adjective or an adverb. An **adjective** modifies a noun, pronoun, or other element that functions as a noun. An **adverb** can modify not only a verb but also an adjective, another adverb, a preposition, an infinitive, a participle, a phrase, a clause, or a whole sentence.

All modifiers are subordinate, or grammatically dependent on another element. But there is nothing minor about the benefit that a careful and imaginative use of modifiers can bring to your style. Some modifiers lend vividness and precision to descriptions, stories, and ideas, while others establish logical relationships, allowing a sentence to convey more shadings of thought and complexity of structure.

DEGREES OF ADJECTIVES AND ADVERBS

21a Learn how adjectives and adverbs are compared.

Comparing Adjectives

Most adjectives can be *compared*, or changed to show three **degrees** of coverage.

POSITIVE DEGREE	COMPARATIVE DEGREE	SUPERLATIVE DEGREE
wide	wider	widest
dry	drier	driest
lazy	lazier	laziest
relaxed	more relaxed	most relaxed
agreeable	more agreeable	most agreeable

The base form of an adjective is in the *positive* degree: *thin*. The *comparative* degree puts the modified word beyond one or more items: *thinner* (than he is; than everybody). And the *superlative* degree unmistakably puts the modified word beyond all rivals within its group: *thinnest* (of all).

The comparative and superlative degrees of adjectives are formed in several ways.

1. For one-syllable adjectives: *wide, wider, widest* (but *less wide, least wide*).
2. For one- or two-syllable adjectives ending in *-y*, change the *-y* to *-i* and add *-er* and *-est: dry, drier, driest; lazy, lazier, laziest* (but *less lazy, least lazy*).
3. For all other adjectives of two or more syllables, put *more* or *most* (or *less* or *least*) before the positive form: *relaxed, more relaxed, most relaxed* (*less relaxed, least relaxed*).
4. For certain "irregular" adjectives, supply the forms shown in your dictionary. Here are some common examples.

POSITIVE DEGREE	COMPARATIVE DEGREE	SUPERLATIVE DEGREE
bad	worse	worst
good	better	best
far	farther, further	farthest, furthest
little	littler, less, lesser	littlest, least
many, some, much	more	most

Comparing Adverbs

Like adjectives, adverbs can be compared: *quickly, more quickly, most quickly; less quickly, least quickly*. Note that *-ly* adverbs—that is, nearly all adverbs—can be compared only by being preceded by words like *more* and *least*. But some one-syllable adverbs do change their form: *hard/harder/hardest, fast/faster/fastest*, and so forth.

21b Avoid constructions like *more funnier*.

DON'T	DO
x more funnier	• funnier
x least brightest	• least bright
x more quicklier	• more quickly

Be careful not to "double" the comparison of an adjective or adverb. A term like *funnier* already contains the meaning that is wrongly added by *more*.

CHOOSING AND PLACING MODIFIERS

21c Avoid a dangling modifier.

DON'T:

DANGL MOD

x **Pinning one mugger to the ground,** the other escaped.

DO:

MOD MODIFIED TERM

• **Pinning one mugger to the ground,** the **victim** helplessly watched the other escape.

When you use a modifier, it is not enough for you to know what thing or idea you are modifying; you must openly supply that modified term within your sentence. Otherwise, you have written a **dangling modifier**—one modifying nothing that the reader can point to. In the DON'T example above, the person doing the *pinning* is left out, and *the other* looks at first like the modified term. In the revised sentence, with its explicit mention of the *victim*, the uncertainty is resolved.

DON'T:

DANGL MOD

x **Once considered a culturally backward country,** Australian filmmakers have surprised the world's most demanding audiences.

> The writer, criticized for a dangling modifier, might protest, "Can't you see I was referring to Australia in the first phrase?" But where is *Australia* in the sentence? Since *Australian filmmakers* can hardly be called a *country*, the modifier does dangle.

DO:

MOD — MODIFIED TERM

• **Once considered a culturally backward country, Australia** has surprised the world's most demanding audiences with its excellent filmmakers.

DON'T:

DANGL MOD

x **To win in court,** an attorney's witnesses must convince the jury.

> Readers must do a double take to realize that it is the attorney, not the witnesses, who wants to win in court.

mod 21c

DO:

MOD — MODIFIED TERM

• **To win in court, an attorney** must choose witnesses who can convince a jury.

DON'T:

MOD

x **Embracing the astonished Priscilla,** a rash erupted behind Philo's left knee.

The possessive form *Philo's* cannot serve as the modified term; its function is adjectival, and one adjectival element cannot modify another.

DO:

MOD / MODIFIED TERM

• **Embracing the astonished Priscilla, Philo** felt a rash erupting behind his left knee.

DON'T:

MOD

x **Anticipating every taste,** it was decided to advertise the car as "an oversexed, pulse-quickening respecter of environmental quality."

Nobody is doing the anticipating here.

DO:

MOD / MODIFIED TERM

• **Anticipating every taste, the agency** decided. . . .

EXERCISE

1. Submit three pairs of original sentences. In the first sentence of each pair, illustrate the defect of a dangling modifier. In the second, correct the problem.

21d Avoid a misplaced modifier.

MISPLACED MODIFIER	REVISED
x **Driving to the basket unopposed,** it was an easy layup for Jordan.	• Driving to the basket unopposed, **Jordan** dropped in an easy layup.
x **Marinated in white wine and sprinkled with parsley,** Linda slid the halibut into the casserole.	• Linda slid the **halibut,** marinated in white wine and sprinkled with parsley, into the casserole.

Merely including a modifier and a modified term (pp. 433–34) is not enough; you need to get them close together so that the reader will immediately grasp their connection. Otherwise, a nearby noun or nounlike element may be mistaken for the modified term. Thus, in the left box column, a mysterious *it* appears to be driving to the basket, and poor Linda gets *marinated* before the party has even begun. In the right-hand examples, note how the true modified terms, *Jordan* and *halibut*, are properly placed.

DON'T:

MISPLACED MOD — MODIFIED TERM?

x **Stolen out of the garage the night before, my grandmother** spotted **my station wagon** on Jefferson Street. (MODIFIED TERM?)

The reader must reassess the sentence to get over the impression that it was the grandmother who was stolen from the garage.

DO:

MOD — MODIFIED TERM

• **Stolen out of the garage the night before, my station wagon** was on Jefferson Street when my grandmother spotted it.

DON'T:

MOD

x **Thinking that a Snoopy sweatshirt would win Priscilla over,** it only remained for **Philo** to choose an appropriate greeting card. (MODIFIED TERM)

Here the anticipatory pronoun *it* stands where the modified term ought to be.

mod 21d

DO:

MOD

• **Thinking that a Snoopy sweatshirt would win Priscilla over,** **Philo** turned his attention to the choice of an appropriate greeting card. (MODIFIED TERM)

Squinting Modifier

You may find that in a draft sentence you have surrounded a modifier with two elements, either of which might be the modified term. Such a modifier is called **squinting** because it does not "look directly at" the real modified term.

DON'T:

SQ MOD

x How Harry silenced the transmission **completely** amazed me.

Did Harry do a complete job of silencing, or was the writer completely amazed? Readers should never be left with such puzzles to solve.

DO:

MOD MODIFIED TERM

- How Harry **completely silenced** the transmission amazed me.

or

MOD MODIFIED TERM

- I was **completely amazed** by the way Harry silenced the transmission.

DON'T:

SQ MOD

x They were sure **by August** they would be freed.

Were they sure by August, or would they be freed by August?

DO:

MODIFIED TERM MOD

- They were **sure by August** that they would be free.

or

MOD MODIFIED TERM

- They were sure that **by August** they **would be freed.**

Notice how the insertion of *that* either before or after the modifier clarifies the writer's meaning.

EXERCISE

2. Submit three pairs of original sentences. In the first sentence of each pair, illustrate the defect of a misplaced modifier. In the second, correct the problem. At least one of your misplaced modifiers should be a "squinting" one.

21e Avoid a split infinitive if you can do so without awkwardness.

DON'T:

SPLIT INF
x It is important **to clearly see** the problem.

DO:

INF ADV
• It is important **to see** the problem **clearly.**

Some readers object to every **split infinitive,** a modifier placed between *to* and the base verb form: *to clearly see*. To avoid offending such readers, you would do well to eliminate split infinitives from your draft prose.

But when you correct a split infinitive, beware of creating an awkward construction that announces in effect, "Here is the result of my struggle not to split an infinitive."

DON'T:

x It is important **clearly to see** the problem.

> The writer has avoided a split infinitive but has created a pretzel. The "split" version, *It is important to clearly see the problem*, would be preferable. But *It is important to see the problem clearly* would satisfy everyone.

Even readers who do not mind an inconspicuous, natural-sounding split infinitive are bothered by *lengthy* modifiers in the split-infinitive position.

DON'T:

SPLIT INF
x We are going **to soberly and patiently analyze** the problem.

DO:

- We are going to analyze the problem soberly and patiently.

or

- We are going to make a sober and patient analysis of the problem.

EXERCISES

3. Submit three pairs of original sentences. In the first sentence of each pair, illustrate the defect of a multi-word split infinitive. In the second, correct the problem.

4. (21c–21e) Some or all of the following sentences contain dangling modifiers, misplaced modifiers, or split infinitives. Submit a corrected version of each sentence that you find faulty, and explain why you are leaving other sentences (if any) unrevised.

   A. She realized in a calmer moment everything would be all right.
   B. Before going to bed, the false teeth should be removed for maximum comfort.
   C. If you want to quickly, safely, and pleasantly make your way through the dense jungle at Disneyland, a native guide is necessary.
   D. His coach, though he was still very inexperienced, believed he detected some athletic promise in the eight-foot Elbows Lodgepole.
   E. He paid the penalty for his crimes in prison.

21f Place a modifier where it will bring out your meaning.

mod 21f

More often than not, adjectives and adverbs come just before the modified term (*a beautiful moon; We hastily adjusted the telescope*). In contrast, a *predicate adjective* always follows the verb: *The moon was beautiful.* There is nothing problematic about such placement.

In contrast, adverbs like *only, just,* and *merely* can be moved about rather freely without sounding nonsensical. The sense that they make, however, changes drastically from one position to another. Consider:

- **Only** I can understand your argument. [No one else can.]
- I can **only** understand your argument. [I cannot agree with it.]
- I can understand **only** your argument. [But not your motives; *or* The arguments of others mystify me.]
- She had **just** eaten the sandwich. [A moment ago.]
- She had eaten **just** the sandwich. [Not the rest of the food.]

You can see that it requires some thought to put "movable" adverbs exactly where they belong—namely, just before the terms they are meant to emphasize.

For the effective placement of whole modifying elements—that is, subordinate clauses and phrases—see p. 304, 13d.

EXERCISE

5. Submit three original sentences in which you use the adverb *just*, placing it in a different position each time. Add brief explanations of how the various positions affect the communicated meaning.

21g Do not hesitate to make use of an absolute phrase.

ABS PHRASE

- He rose from the negotiating table, **his stooped shoulders a sign of discouragement.**

Fear of dangling and misplaced modifiers (21c–d) leads some readers to shun the **absolute phrase,** a group of words that acts as a modifier to a whole statement. But a well-managed absolute phrase can be an effective resource. It allows you, for example, to craft a graceful **cumulative sentence** (p. 322, 14h)—one that sharpens or elaborates an initial main statement.

mod 21g

A classic absolute phrase differs from a dangling modifier by containing its own "subject," such as *his stooped shoulders* in the example above. Again:

"SUBJECT"

- **All struggle** over, the troops lay down their arms.

ABS PHRASE

"SUBJECT"
- The quarterback called three plays in one huddle, **the clock** having stopped after the incomplete pass.
ABS PHRASE

Some other absolute phrases do look exactly like dangling modifiers, but they are accepted as **idioms**—that is, as fixed expressions that everyone considers normal:

ABS PHRASE
- **Generally speaking,** Melody's memory is rather smoky.

ABS PHRASE
- **To summarize,** most of her energy has leaked into the cosmos at large.

EXERCISE

6. Submit three original sentences in which you make effective use of an absolute phrase.

21h Avoid a double negative.

DON'T:
x She **didn't** say **nothing.**

DO:
- She **didn't** say **anything.**

or

- She said **nothing.**

In written English the modifier *not* does all the work of denial that a negative statement needs. A **double negative,** though common in some people's speech, is considered a mistake rather than an especially strong negation.

Cumbersome Negative Formulas

Avoid certain negative constructions which are roundabout or confusing:

1. negatives following *shouldn't wonder, wouldn't be surprised*, etc.

   DON'T:
   x I shouldn't wonder if it **didn't** rain.

   DO:
   • I shouldn't wonder if it **rained.**

2. *cannot help but*

   DON'T:
   x They **cannot help but** think sadly about the soldiers who died in the Persian Gulf.

   DO:
   • They **cannot help thinking** sadly about the soldiers who died in the Persian Gulf.

3. *can't hardly, can't scarcely*, etc.

   DON'T:
   x We **can't hardly** wait to visit Mexico City.

   DO:
   • We **can hardly** wait to visit Mexico City.

4. *no doubt but what, no doubt but that*

   DON'T:
   x She does not **doubt but what** dreams foretell the future.

   DO:
   • She **does not doubt that** dreams foretell the future.

EXERCISE

7. If your instructor has found no double negatives in your submitted work, skip this exercise. Otherwise, submit up to five examples of the problem.

In each case, supply the single-negative expression that would have been preferable.

PUNCTUATING MODIFIERS

21i Place a comma after an initial modifying element that is more than a few words long.

SUBSTANTIAL SUB CLAUSE

- **After Susan had walked out on him**, George spent a few evenings reading Dr. Lincoln Dollar's helpful book of advice, *The Aerobic Kama Sutra*.

SUBSTANTIAL PHRASE

- **In the memorable words of Dr. Dollar**, "No modern home should be without a queen-sized trampoline."

If a modifying element preceding your main clause is itself a clause, as in the first example above, you should automatically follow it with a comma. A comma is also appropriate after an opening phrase (p. 390, 18d), as in the second example.

EXERCISE

8. Submit three original sentences, correctly punctuated, that begin with a substantial modifying clause or phrase.

21j If your sentence begins with a brief phrase, consider a following comma optional.

mod
21j

If a modifying phrase (p. 390, 18d) preceding your main clause is no more than a few words long, you can choose whether to close it off with a comma. A comma indicates a pause, and it marks a more formal separation between the modifier and the main clause. Follow your sense of what the occasion calls for.

WITH COMMA: MORE FORMAL	WITHOUT COMMA: LESS FORMAL
Until this week, I had kept up with my assignments.	**Until this week** I had kept up with my assignments.
For a beginner, she did remarkably well.	**For a beginner** she did remarkably well.

Note that an initial subordinate clause, however brief, automatically calls for a following comma; the optional comma applies only to a brief initial *phrase*.

BRIEF SUB CL
- **When Susan came back,** she found George sitting in the lotus posture and eating a Ho-Ho.

BRIEF PHRASE
- **Until that moment** she hadn't appreciated the spiritual side of his nature.

If you prefer not to worry about whether you are using an initial clause or a phrase, just include the comma; it is never wrong.

EXERCISE

9. Submit three original sentences, correctly punctuated, that begin with a brief phrase, and two more that begin with a brief clause. Among your five sentences, at least two should show the *absence* of a comma after the initial modifying element.

mod 21k

21k Use commas to set off a term like *however* or *on the contrary.*

SENT ADV
- Lori, **however**, finds the microwave oven too complicated to use.

TRANS PHRASE
- **On the contrary**, nothing could be simpler.

Look back to page 403, 19c, for lists of *sentence adverbs* and *transitional phrases*. Such modifiers, instead of narrowing the meaning of one element in a statement, show a relationship between the whole statement and the one before it. To bring out this function, be sure your sentence adverbs and transitional phrases are "stopped" at both ends, either by two commas, by a semicolon and a comma, or by a comma and the beginning or end of the sentence:

- A circus, **furthermore** [SENT ADV], lifts the spirits of young and old alike.
- Laughter is good for the soul; **moreover** [SENT ADV], it reduces bodily tension.
- **In reality** [TRANS PHRASE], she intends to stay where she is.
- The deficit has continued to grow, **as a matter of fact** [TRANS PHRASE]**.**

Exception: Sentence Adverbs without Pauses

If you find, in reading a sentence aloud, that a sentence adverb is not set off by pauses at either end, you can omit commas:

- We can **thus** discount the immediate threat of war.
- **Hence** there is no need to call up the reserves.
- Worry about the future has **therefore** subsided.

EXERCISE

10. Submit five original sentences, correctly punctuated, in which a sentence adverb or a transitional phrase appears somewhere other than the initial position. Instead of repeating the words and phrases illustrated above, draw on further items from the two lists on page 403. Include at least two transitional phrases among your five modifying terms.

21l Set off an interrupting element at both ends.

- A diet, **Betsy believed** [INT EL], called for strong discipline during the sleeping hours.

INT EL
- Reindeer droppings on the roof, **to be sure**, count as strong evidence for Santa's existence.

INT EL
- You, **George**, have been chosen by the computer to be Betsy's mate.

INT EL
- The computer, **an antique Univac**, is badly in need of repair.

In each instance above, the underlined words constitute an **interrupting element** (also known as a *parenthetical element*). An interrupting element can be a phrase, a clause, a sentence adverb like *however* or *furthermore*, a transitional phrase like *to be sure*, an appositive (21n), a name in direct address (*you, George*), or an inserted question or exclamation. Since an interrupting element comes between parts of the sentence that belong together in meaning, you must set it off by punctuation at both ends. Note the commas in all four examples above.

The main risk in punctuating an interrupting element is that you may forget to close it off before resuming the main sentence. The risk increases if the last words of the interrupting element happen to fit grammatically with the words that follow.

DON'T:

x The mayor's televised plea, which is rebroadcast every evening on the 6 o'clock news reaches everyone in town.

You can expect to come across such "unstopped" interrupting elements in your first drafts. When in doubt as to whether the element is truly an interruption, reread the sentence without it: *The mayor's televised plea reaches everyone in town.* Since that statement makes complete sense, you know that the omitted part *is* interruptive and must be set off at both ends.

Other Punctuation

Commas are the most usual but not the only means of setting off an interrupting element. Extreme breaks such as whole statements, questions, or exclamations are often better served by parentheses or dashes:

INT EL
- The sky in New Mexico (**have you ever been there?**) is the most dramatic I have seen.

INT EL
- Our recent weather—**what snow storms we have had!**—makes me long to be back in California.

When you need to interrupt quoted material to insert words of your own, enclose your insertion in brackets (p. 563, 30r).

Testing for an Interrupting Element

Note that an element is considered interrupting only if it comes between essential parts of a clause. If, instead, it merely follows a word like *and* or *but*, it is not truly interruptive. Consider:

- But **without hesitating for a moment,** Betsy sent away for Dr. Dollar's book about communicating with thin ancestors from the spirit world.

Despite the lack of a comma after *but*, this sentence is correctly punctuated, for nothing interrupts the main statement beginning with *Betsy*. (The comma after *moment* is well-advised, however; see page 443, 21i.)

EXERCISE

11. Submit five original sentences correctly illustrating the use of an interrupting element. In at least one of your five sentences, make use of parentheses or dashes instead of commas.

21m Learn how to punctuate restrictive and nonrestrictive modifying elements.

RESTRICTIVE	NONRESTRICTIVE
This is the lamp **we bought yesterday.**	This lamp, **which we bought yesterday**, is defective.

RESTRICTIVE	NONRESTRICTIVE
Suzanne is a woman **who started her own business.**	Suzanne, **who started her own business**, is an enterprising woman.
The coffee **that comes from Brazilian mountainsides** is the best.	The best coffee, **which comes from Brazilian mountainsides**, is also the most expensive.

To punctuate modifying elements in every position except the opening one (21j), you must recognize a sometimes tricky distinction between two kinds of modifiers—restrictive and nonrestrictive.

RESTRICTIVE: NO COMMAS	NONRESTRICTIVE: COMMAS REQUIRED
defining	nondefining
identifying	nonidentifying
essential to establishing meaning	meaning already established

Restrictive Element

A **restrictive element** is essential to the identification of the term it modifies. It restricts or narrows the scope of that term, identifying precisely *which* lamp, woman, or coffee the writer has in mind. Study the two columns in the box that begins on page 447 and you note that only the left-hand sentences contain modifiers of this kind. In the right-hand sentences the lamp, woman, and coffee under discussion do not need to be identified by restrictive modifiers; presumably the reader already knows which person or thing the writer intends.

mod 21m

Note also how the absence or use of commas marks the difference of function. A restrictive element can do its job of narrowing only if it is *not* isolated by commas.

DON'T:

x Women, **who are over thirty-five,** tend to show reduced fertility.

The commas absurdly suggest that all women are over thirty-five.

DO:

RESTR EL

- Women **who are over thirty-five** tend to show reduced fertility.

With the commas gone, the restrictive element narrows the subject to what the writer had in mind all along, women over thirty-five.

DON'T:

x I admire bus drivers, **who announce the streets as they come up.**

The comma suggests that all bus drivers announce the streets as they come up and that the writer therefore admires all of them. This is not what was meant.

DO:

RESTR EL

- I admire bus drivers **who announce the streets as they come up.**

Without a comma, the modifier restricts those bus drivers who are admired to just one kind, those who announce the streets.

DON'T:

x The discipline, **that George had recently adopted,** was called Transcendental Weight-watching.

Here a restrictive clause, serving to specify which discipline the writer has in mind, is wrongly punctuated as if it were nonrestrictive.

DO:

RESTR EL

- The discipline **that George had recently adopted** was called Transcendental Weight-watching.

Nonrestrictive Element

A **nonrestrictive element** is not essential to the identification of the term it modifies. Instead of narrowing that term, it adds some further information about it. To perform this task the nonrestrictive element must be set off by punctuation, usually commas.

DON'T:

x The reference librarian **who is a writer's best resource** is often acknowledged in the preface to a book.

> The absence of commas after *librarian* and *resource* implies that the italicized element is restrictive, telling us which reference librarian is meant. Notice that when the modifier is left out altogether, there is nothing misleading about the statement: *The reference librarian is often acknowledged in the preface to a book.* That is a sure sign that the modifier is nonrestrictive and that it therefore deserves to be set off.

DO:

NONR EL

• The reference librarian, **who is a writer's best resource**, is often acknowledged in the preface to a book.

DON'T:

x They snack on trail mix **which is a wholesome blend of nuts, seeds, raisins, and other dried fruit.**

> The absence of a comma after *mix* implies that one particular kind of trail mix is being identified. By adding a comma the writer can make it clear that trail mix in general is intended.

DO:

NONR EL

• They snack on trail mix, **which is a wholesome blend of nuts, seeds, raisins, and other dried fruit.**

mod 21m

The importance of setting off nonrestrictive modifiers at both ends may be brought home by this sentence from a newspaper:

x Noteworthy here are a painted settee and two armchairs, decorated with scrollwork and female figures that belonged to President Monroe.[1]

Female figures that belonged to President Monroe? A comma after *figures* is needed to head off wild ideas about the chief executive's leisure pursuits.

EXERCISE

12. Submit six original sentences illustrating the use of three restrictive and then three nonrestrictive modifying elements, with appropriate punctuation.

21n In punctuating an expression like *my sister Diane* or *Teresa, an old friend,* observe the restrictive/nonrestrictive rule.

- Teresa, **an old friend of mine** [APP], has scarcely changed through the years.
- What they saw, **a black bear approaching the baby's cradle** [APP], riveted them with fear.
- **A musical genius** [APP], he began playing Mozart at five.

An **appositive** is a word or group of words that identifies or restates a neighboring noun, pronoun, or nounlike element. Most appositives, like those above, are set off by commas. Nevertheless, you should not automatically make that choice. Instead, ask whether the appositive narrows down ("restricts") the term it follows or merely restates that term. To see why some appositives should appear without commas, compare these sentences.

- My sister, **Diane** [NONR APP], studied Portuguese in the Navy.
- My brother **Bert** [RESTR APP] played baseball in college, but my brother **Jack** [RESTR APP] was not athletic at all.

mod 21n

The commas in the first sentence tell us that the writer has only one sister—namely, Diane. The appositive does not restrict our understanding of *sister*; it merely supplies the sister's name. In contrast, the absence of commas in the second example reflects the fact that the writer has at least two brothers. *Bert* and *Jack* are restrictive appositives, since each name tells us *which* brother is meant.

The distinction here is a fine one, and few readers would object if the commas were dropped from the "Diane" example. But whenever you use an appositive to narrow the meaning of a term (which brother, which friend, etc.), you should omit the commas.

EXERCISE

13. Submit six original sentences illustrating the use of three restrictive and then three nonrestrictive appositives, with appropriate punctuation.

21o Use commas in constructions like *delicious, nutritious dinner* but not in constructions like *typical American meal.*

If a draft sentence contains two or more modifiers in a row, should you put commas between them? The answer depends on whether the modifiers all modify the same term. Usually they do; such modifiers are **coordinate,** or serving the same grammatical function. You should separate coordinate modifiers from each other by commas:

MOD MOD

- George fixed himself a **delicious**, **nutritious** dinner of Gatorade and Chun King Chop Suey.

  Here *delicious* and *nutritious* are coordinate, for they both modify the same noun, *dinner*.

mod
21o

But sometimes you will find that an apparent modifier is actually part of the term being modified. In that case, omit a comma after the modifier that comes before the whole modified term.

MOD MOD

- He wolfed down his **typical American** meal.

Here *American* modifies *meal*, but *typical* does not; it modifies *American meal.* A comma after *typical* would wrongly imply that *typical* and *American* modify the same word.

Again, note the contrast between the following sentences, both of which are correctly punctuated:

- She never forgave them for the way they insulted her on that
  MOD MODIFIED PHRASE
  infamous first day of school.

  The absence of commas reflects the fact that there are no coordinate modifiers here. *Infamous* modifies the entire phrase *first day of school.*

- She never forgave them for the way they insulted her on that
  MOD MOD MOD MODIFIED TERM
  infamous, **outrageous**, **unforgettable first day** of school.

  Now the sentence contains three coordinate modifiers, properly separated by commas. A comma after *unforgettable* would still be wrong, for *first day of school* continues to be the whole modified term.

To test whether you are dealing with coordinate modifiers, try shifting the order of the words. Truly coordinate terms can be reversed without a change of meaning: *a sunlit, windy day; a windy, sunlit day.* Noncoordinate terms change their meaning (*a blue racing car; a racing blue car*) or become nonsensical (*a popular rock group; a rock popular group*).

EXERCISE

14. Submit two pairs of original sentences illustrating the proper punctuation, within each pair, first of coordinate modifiers (*a haughty, commanding queen*) and then of a noncoordinate modifier (*a former beauty queen*). To make the contrast plain, try to repeat as much language as possible within each pair of sentences.

21p Omit a comma between the final modifier and the modified term.

When a modifier comes just before the modified term, no punctuation should separate them. Thus, however many coordinate modifiers you supply, be sure to omit a comma after the final one:

FINAL MOD

MODIFIED TERM

- O'Keeffe produced an intense, starkly simple, **radiantly glowing painting** of a flower.

  A comma after *glowing* would be mistaken. The whole set of coordinate modifiers—*intense, starkly simple, radiantly glowing*—already stands in proper relation to the modified term, *painting*.

For an exception to this rule, keep reading.

21q Consider enclosing a modifier in commas if it qualifies the modifier just before it.

PRECEDING MOD — MOD

- It was an **inaccurate**, **perhaps even deceitful**, account of the meeting.

If one modifier serves in part to qualify or comment on the modifier preceding it, you can bring out that function by enclosing it in commas. The sentence above would still be considered acceptable if the second comma were omitted, but here it shows that *perhaps even deceitful* is a "second thought" about the first modifier, *inaccurate*.

If you set off a "backward-looking" modifier at one end, be sure to supply a second comma at the other end.

DON'T:

x She told a fascinating, but not altogether believable story.

DO:

- She told a fascinating, but not altogether believable, story.

or

- She told a fascinating but not altogether believable story.

EXERCISES (21i–21q)

15. Some or all of the following sentences show a faulty use (or absence) of commas. Write a brief comment about each sentence, explaining *where* and *why* you would make changes, if any.

    A. Some judges have begun experimenting with a new concept, known as "house arrest."
    B. A convicted criminal, who is not considered dangerous, may be spared a prison sentence.
    C. The criminal, however, is not allowed to go completely free.
    D. Instead, he or she is required to stay within a restricted area venturing from home only to work and shop.
    E. This policy spares nonviolent offenders, the degrading and unnecessary experience of being locked away for years.

16. Most or all of the following sentences show a faulty use (or absence) of commas. When you find an adequately punctuated sentence, note that fact. For all the others, indicate what changes should be made.

    A. Airline passengers seem to prefer a safe trip with armed guards, to an unsafe trip without them.
    B. They won't lower the taxes, merely because people complain.
    C. Most tightrope walkers it seems, suffer from aching feet.
    D. Short-order cooks agree that soyburgers are the best, low-cost, high-protein, food to serve these days.
    E. A porcupine has approximately 30,000 quills for your information.
    F. As the press had expected the president announced on Friday that the price of steak, not gold, would henceforth define the value of the dollar.
    G. In a house work is more tedious than in an office.
    H. You Gertie are a woman of taste and sensitivity.
    I. The one mystery, that Biff couldn't explain, was why his smiling teammate was trying to inhale the twenty-yard line.

---

mod 21q

NOTE

[1] David Maxfield, "What Nancy Reagan Has Done to the White House," *San Francisco Chronicle* 23 Dec. 1981: 16.

22

Noun and Pronoun Case

22a Recognize the case forms and their functions.

CASES:	SUBJECTIVE	OBJECTIVE	POSSESSIVE
Personal Pronouns	I you he she it we they	me you him her it us them	my, mine your, yours his her, hers its our, ours their, theirs
Who	who	whom	whose
Nouns	car cars Janice Soviet Union	car cars Janice Soviet Union	car's cars' Janice's Soviet Union's

Nouns and pronouns change their form to show certain grammatical relations to other words within a sentence. These forms are called **cases.** They show whether a term is a subject of discussion or performer of action (*subjective case*), a receiver of action or an object of a preposition (*objective case*), or a "possessor" of another term (*possessive case*).

Most personal pronouns (*I*, *she*, etc.) show changes of form for all three cases, and so does the relative pronoun *who*. Nouns, however, do not change for the objective case.

A change in form helps to show which sentence function a word is performing. For example:

SUBJECTIVE CASE

1. Subject of verb (p. 386, 18b):
   - **He** went home.
   - **They** went home.
   - The one **who** went home was disappointed.
2. Complement (p. 384, 18a):
   - It was **she** who was guilty.
   - The victims are **we** ourselves.

OBJECTIVE CASE

1. Direct object of verb (p. 383, 18a):
   - They praised **him.**
   - We fed the child **whom** the agency had entrusted to us.
2. Indirect object of verb (p. 717):
   - They taught **him** a lesson.
   - The fine cost **them** a pretty penny.
3. Object of preposition (p. 725):
   - She explained the software to **us.**
   - For **whom** did you work last year?
4. Subject of infinitive (p. 731):
   - They wanted **her** to stay.
   - She expected **them** to give her a raise.

POSSESSIVE CASE

1. With nouns:
   - **Our** hats were all squashed.
   - **James's** case was the worst of all.
   - The **Beatles'** music still keeps its freshness.
   - **Whose** pen is this?
2. With gerunds (p. 385, 18a):
   - **His** departing left us sad.
   - **Their** training every day made them too tired for fun.
   - **Jane's** humming all day drove everyone wild.

In general, case forms must match sentence functions: subjective case for subjects of clauses, objective case for objects of several kinds, and possessive case for a possessing relation to the governed term.

We will see that in practice the choice of case can become tricky. Note at the outset that the "subject" of an infinitive takes the objective case and that the "subject" of a gerund usually takes the possessive case. The names are unfortunate, but most writers intuitively choose case by function, not by name.

22b Keep the subject of a clause in the subjective case.

DO:

S

- **He** and **I** were good friends.

DON'T:

S

x **Him** and **me** were good friends.

Standard usage requires that you avoid using objective-case pronouns for subjects of clauses.

See page 464, 22h, for a pronoun subject in a subordinate clause.

EXERCISE

1. If your instructor has not flagged sentences like *Him and me were friends* in your submitted work, skip this exercise. Otherwise, submit five original sentences correctly using a pair of pronouns as a subject.

22c Avoid awkwardly "correct" constructions like *I am she*.

WRONG	AWKWARD	PREFERABLE
I am **her.**	I am **she.**	I am the one you mean.
The person I miss is **her.**	The person I miss is **she.**	She is the person I miss.

The left-column examples above are wrong because pronoun complements (p. 384, 18a) should not appear in the objective case. Yet the "corrections" in the middle column sound pompous and prissy. Try, as in the right-column sentences, to find a natural-sounding way of conveying the same point.

EXERCISE

2. If your instructor has not flagged sentences like *I am her* in your submitted work, skip this exercise. Otherwise, submit two sets of original sentences showing a progression from "wrong" to "awkward" to "preferable" forms, as in the box above.

22d Watch out for constructions like *for you and I.*

The rule for pronoun objects of all kinds is simple: put them in the objective case.

DIRECT OBJECT OF VERB:

• Many differences separate **us.**

INDIRECT OBJECT OF VERB:

• She gave **me** cause for worry.

OBJECT OF PREPOSITION:

• Toward **whom** is your anger directed?

SUBJECT OF INFINITIVE:

• They asked **her** to serve a second term.

> Note that the "subject" of the infinitive appears in the objective case because it is at the same time the indirect object of the verb.

Choice of a correct objective form becomes harder when the object is **compound,** or made up of more than one term. Knowing that it is wrong to write *Him and me were good friends*, some writers "overcorrect" and put the subjective forms where they do not belong.

DON'T:

D OBJS

x They appointed **she** and **I** to a subcommittee.

DO:

• They appointed **her** and **me** to a subcommittee.

DON'T:

OBJS OF PREP
PREP

x That will be a dilemma for **you** and **I.**

DO:

• That will be a dilemma for you and **me.**

When in doubt, test for case by disregarding one of the two objects. Since you would never write x *That will be a dilemma for I*, you know that both of the objects must be objective in case.

The danger of choosing the wrong case seems to increase still further when a noun and a pronoun are paired as objects.

DON'T:

PREP / OBJS OF PREP \

x As for **Jack** and **I,** we will take the bus.

Would you write *As for I?* No; therefore, keep to the objective case.

DO:

• As for Jack and **me,** we will take the bus.

EXERCISE

3. If your instructor has not flagged expressions like *for you and I* in your submitted work, skip this exercise. Otherwise, submit five original sentences correctly using, in each instance, a pair of pronouns as an object of a preposition.

22e Observe the grammatical distinction between *who* and *whom*.

case 22e

In informal speech and writing, *whom* has become a rare form even where grammar strictly requires it. When the pronoun appears first in a clause, the subjective *who* automatically comes to mind.

COLLOQUIAL:

• **Who** did he marry?

• **Who** will you play against?

In standard written English, however, the question of *who* versus *whom* is still determined by grammatical function, not by speech habits. Note the reason for choosing *whom* in each of the following revisions:

D OBJ ⟋V⟍
- **Whom** did he marry?

Whom is the direct object of the verb *did marry*.

OBJ OF PREP PREP
- **Whom** will you play against?

or

PREP OBJ OF PREP
- Against **whom** will you play?

Whom is the object of the preposition *against*.

For more on *who* versus *whom*, see p. 464, 22h.

EXERCISE

4. If your instructor has not flagged expressions like *Who did he marry?* in your submitted work, skip this exercise. Otherwise, submit five original sentences correctly using *whom*. Try making *whom* serve, alternatively, as either a direct object or an object of a preposition.

22f Avoid an awkward choice of pronoun case after *than* or *as*.

case 22f

Many writers agonize over the case of a pronoun following *than* or *as*. Should one write *Alex is taller than I* or *Alex is taller than me?* Technically, the answer is that both versions are correct. In the first instance *than* serves as a subordinating conjunction: *Alex is taller than I [am]*. In the second, *than* has become a preposition with the object *me*.

In other sentences, however, one choice is clearly incorrect. Consider:

• The cows chased Margaret farther than $\left\{\begin{matrix} \text{I} \\ \text{me} \end{matrix}\right\}$.

Here *I* would indicate that Margaret was chased by both the cows and the writer: *The cows chased Margaret farther than I did*. Since that is surely not the intended meaning, the right choice is *me*.

When in doubt, consider your intended meaning and mentally supply any missing part of the clause:

• The cows chased Margaret farther than (they chased) me.

The added words will tell you which case to use for the pronoun.

Wherever both choices sound awkward, as in the "Alex" example above, look for an alternative construction:

SUB CLAUSE
• Alex is taller **than I am.**

By supplying the whole subordinate clause, you can avoid any hesitation between *I* and *me*.

22g Avoid constructions like *for we students*.

DON'T:

OBJ OF PREP APP
x Inflation is a problem for **we** students.

DO:
• Inflation is a problem for **us** students.

case
22g

When an appositive (p. 451, 21n) follows a pronoun, some writers automatically put the pronoun in the subjective case (*we*). As often as not, the result is a usage error. A wiser course is to test for the right pronoun case by leaving the appositive out of account. In the example above, *for we* is obviously wrong; so, then, is *for we students*. The rule is that a following appositive should have no influence on the case of a pronoun.

22h Choose a pronoun's case by its function within its own clause.

One of the hardest choices of case involves a pronoun that seems to have rival functions in two clauses.

DON'T:

x Wratto will read his poems to **whomever** will listen.

> The writer has made *whomever* objective because it looks like the object of the preposition *to: to whomever*. But the real object of *to* is the whole subordinate clause that follows it.

DO:

- Wratto will read his poems to **whoever will listen.** (S: whoever; V: will listen; SUB CLAUSE: whoever will listen)

> The subject of the subordinate clause *whoever will listen* belongs in the subjective case.

Whenever a subordinate clause is embedded within a larger structure, you can settle problems of case by mentally eliminating everything but the subordinate clause.

DON'T:

x Stanley had no doubt about **whom** would write the manifesto entitled "Smash Violence Now or Else."

> The test for case shows that *whom would write the manifesto* is ungrammatical. The object of *about* is the whole subordinate clause, which requires a subject in the subjective case.

DO:

- Stanley had no doubt about **who** would write. . . .

When a choice of pronoun case is difficult, the air of difficulty may remain even after you have chosen correctly. Your reader may be distracted by the same doubt that you have just resolved. It is therefore a good idea to dodge the whole problem.

DO:
- Wratto will read his poems to **anyone** who will listen.
- Stanley was sure that **he** would be the author. . . .

EXERCISE

5. Submit five original sentences in which a pronoun serves as both an object of a preposition and the subject of its own subordinate clause, as in *He will read his poems to whoever will listen.*

22i Use the possessive case in most constructions like *Marie's coming to Boston is a rare event.*

In the phrase *Marie's coming to Boston*, the word *coming* is a **gerund**—that is, a verbal (p. 385, 18a) that functions as a noun. Most gerunds, like this one, end in *-ing*, but there is also a two-word past form.

PRESENT GER
- There is less **swooning** in Hollywood movies than there used to be.

PAST GER
- **Having swum** across the lake made him generally less fearful.

A gerund can be preceded not only by a word like *a, the*, or *this*, but also by a governing noun or pronoun known as the subject of the gerund: *Wilson's achieving unity; his having achieved unity.* (A gerund can also take an object; see page 716.) The name *subject* is misleading, for most subjects of gerunds, just like words that "possess" nouns, belong in the possessive case.

case
22i

POSSESSION OF NOUN	POSSESSION OF GERUND
our departure	our departing
Marian's reliance	Marian's relying
Jules's loss	Jules's having lost

In general, then, put subjects of gerunds into the possessive case:

• **Esther's** commuting ended with her graduation.

Even if the subject of a gerund feels like an object, you should keep to the possessive form.

DON'T:

S OF GER GER

x Biff didn't know why everyone laughed at **him saying** he would like to be an astronaut and see all those steroids going by.

Here the writer has made *him* objective because it "feels like" the object of the preposition *at*. In fact, the object of that proposition is the whole gerund phrase that runs to the end of the sentence.

DO:

• Biff didn't know why everyone laughed at **his** saying. . . .

Note how the possessive *his* directs a reader's attention to the next word, *saying*. It is the activity, not the person, that inspired laughter.

Exceptions

When the subject of a gerund is an abstract or inanimate noun—one like *physics* or *chaos*—it can appear in a nonpossessive form.

ACCEPTABLE:

S OF GER GER

• We cannot ignore the danger of **catastrophe striking** again.

But *catastrophe's* would also be acceptable here. Rather than choose, however, why not recast the sentence?

PREFERABLE:

• We cannot ignore the danger that catastrophe will strike again.

When a gerund's subject is separated from the gerund by other words, the gerund tends to change into a modifier—specifically, a *participle* (p. 385, 18a). In such a sentence the possessive form is not used:

- People were surprised at him, a veteran speaker on many campuses, **having** (PART) no ready reply when Stanley seized the microphone and called him an irrelevant murderer.

  Without the intervening appositive (p. 451, 21n), *a veteran speaker on many campuses*, we would consider *him* to be the subject of a gerund and change the pronoun case accordingly: *People were surprised at his having. . . .* But in the sentence as it stands, *him* is a direct object modified by the whole participial phrase from *having no ready reply* through *irrelevant murderer*.

EXERCISE

6. Submit five original sentences in which you correctly use a gerund and a subject of the gerund. In your last two sentences, make the subject of the gerund nonpossessive.

22j Feel free to make use of constructions like *an idea of Henry's*.

The possessive relation for nouns is usually indicated either by an *-'s* or *-s'* (*Henry's; the three cats'*) or by an *of* construction (*of Henry; of the three cats*). But sometimes you can combine the two forms to avoid confusion. Compare:

- Priscilla remained unmoved by any thought of **Philo.**
- Priscilla remained unmoved by any thought of **Philo's.**

Both sentences are grammatical, but their meanings differ. The first sentence deals with any thought *about* Philo, the second with any thought *proposed by* Philo.

Some writers worry that the **double possessive,** like the double negative (p. 441, 21h), is a usage error. But everyone uses the double possessive with pronouns: a *peculiarity of hers; that nasty habit of his*, and so forth. Feel free to treat nouns in exactly the same way: *a bookkeeping trick of Harry's; that sawed-off shotgun of Bobo's*, and so on.

EXERCISE (22a–22j)

7. Some or all of the following sentences show a mistaken or awkward choice of case. Indicate which, if any, sentences are problem-free, and explain why you would make changes in the others.

   A. It is hard for we Americans to realize how rapidly the balance of power is shifting.
   B. Whom could you trust with the keys to a Lexus these days?
   C. For success in business, much depends on who you know.
   D. The customs officers gave her and we to understand that we would be thoroughly searched.
   E. Stanley is a man whom you could expect to lead a demonstration against Mother's Day.
   F. The person who we all want to serve as director is she.
   G. Bill hunting for an apartment for Sally and I proved exhausting.
   H. Biff can kick the ball twenty yards farther than me.
   I. A saying of Shakespeare's would appear to be applicable here.
   J. They admired her, a Canadian, enduring the heat of a Somali summer.

23

Pronoun Agreement and Reference

PRONOUN AGREEMENT	PRONOUN REFERENCE
Does the pronoun have the same gender, number, and person as its antecedent?	Can the reader see without difficulty which term is the pronoun's antecedent?
DON'T: x Although the union struck the **plant, they** remained open. The antecedent *plant* and the pronoun referring to it must be made to agree in number.	DON'T: x The strikers used violence against the management, **which** made a final reconciliation difficult. Does *which* refer to *violence* or to *management?*
DO: • Although the union struck the plant, **it** remained open.	DO: • It was the strikers' **violence that** made a final reconciliation with management so difficult.

Pronouns—words used in place of nouns—offer you relief from the monotony of needlessly repeating a term or name when your reader already knows what or whom you mean. But precisely because many pronouns are substitutes for other words, they raise a variety of usage problems, including subject-verb agreement (Chapter 20) and choice of the correct case (Chapter 22). Here we consider the two main kinds of relation between a pronoun and its **antecedent,** the term it refers to. First, a pronoun should show **agreement** with its antecedent in gender, number, and person. And second, the identification of the antecedent—that is, the pronoun's **reference** to it—should never be in doubt.

PRONOUN AGREEMENT

23a Make a pronoun agree with its antecedent in gender, number, and person.

GENDER	NUMBER	PERSON
masculine (*he*)	singular (*her, it,* etc.)	first (*I, we, our,* etc.)
feminine (*she*)	plural (*they, theirs,* etc.)	second (*you, your, yours*)
		third (*he, she, it, they, their,* etc.)

If the antecedent of a pronoun is explicitly female, make the pronoun feminine: *Ellen . . . she; her; hers*. If the antecedent is plural, make the pronoun plural: *cats . . . they; them; their; theirs*. And if the antecedent is first person, the pronoun should be first person as well: *I . . . me; my; mine*. The following examples show standard practice:

- **Philip** (ANT) still has not tried **his** (PRO) sailboard in rough weather.

  The antecedent and pronoun are both masculine, singular, and third person.

- Sooner or later, all **dancers** (ANT) suffer injuries to **their** (PRO) feet.

  The antecedent and pronoun are both plural and third person.

agr
23a

ANT PRO ANT PRO
- **We** should allow **our daughter** to decide on **her** own career.

The first antecedent-pronoun set is plural and first person; the second is singular, feminine, and third person.

All this looks straightforward enough, but points 23b–g below take up some potentially tricky applications of the rule.

For the problem of sexism in the use of pronouns, see page 346, 15f.

23b Usually refer to a noun like *mob* or *jury* with a singular pronoun.

ANT PRO
- The **mob** of angry demonstrators pushed **its** way into the mayor's office.

ANT PRO
- At last the **jury** came forward with **its** verdict.

A term like *mob* or *jury* is called a **collective noun** (p. 417, 20f) because, though singular in form, it designates a group of members. In most instances, like those above, a collective noun as antecedent calls for a singular pronoun.

When you wish to emphasize the separate members of the group, however, make the pronoun plural:

ANT PRO PRO
- The television camera followed the **jury** as **they** scattered through the courtyard to **their** waiting cars.

agr
23b

EXERCISE

1. Submit five original sentences in which you use a collective noun, such as *jury* or *mob*, as an antecedent. In your last two sentences, use a plural pronoun to refer to the antecedent, as in the example just above.

23c If the antecedent contains parts linked by *and*, usually refer to it with a plural pronoun.

ANT — PRO

- The **architect** and the **contractor** worked out **their** differences.

Two or more items in the antecedent generally call for a plural pronoun, as in the sentence above. But when both parts refer to the same thing or person, make the pronoun singular:

ANT — PRO

- My **son** and **chief antagonist** tries out **his** debating speeches on me.

  One person is both son and chief antagonist; hence the singular pronoun *his*.

EXERCISE

2. Submit four original sentences, correctly formed, in which you use an antecedent with parts linked by *and*. In the last two sentences, make the pronoun singular.

23d Avoid a clash of singular and plural antecedents linked by *or* or *nor*.

The schoolbook rule is that if two parts of an antecedent differ in number, the pronoun must agree with the *nearest* part.

"CORRECT":

NEAREST PART OF ANT — PRO

- Neither the coach nor the **players** will tell **their** story to the press.

NEAREST PART OF ANT — PRO

- Neither the players nor the **coach** will tell **his** story to the press.

agr 23c

But this "rule" often produces a strained effect, as in the second example above. You would do better to recast any sentence containing a conflict of number in the antecedent. Either eliminate that conflict (*Neither the coaches nor the players will tell their story . . .*) or do without the pronoun:

PREFERABLE:
- Neither the coach nor the players will tell the story to the press.

EXERCISE

3. Submit three sentences, all correctly formed, in which you show a clash of singular and plural antecedents, as in *Neither the coach nor the players will tell their story to the press*. Beneath each sentence, add a sentence recasting the statement in a way that avoids a clash of singular and plural antecedents.

23e If you have placed *each* or *every* before a noun, refer to it with a singular pronoun.

- **Each lion** [ANT] that was tranquilized has had a tag attached to **its** [PRO] ear.
- **Every pregnant woman** [ANT] in this exercise class is in **her** [PRO] third trimester.

Use a singular pronoun even if the term is compound (23c):

- **Every financial vice president and accountant** [ANT] gave **his** or **her** [PRO] budgetary projections for the coming year.

agr 23f

23f When in doubt, treat a pronoun like *everyone* or *nobody* as singular.

Review pages 422–23, 20k, which treat verb agreement with such indefinite pronouns as *each, everybody, neither*, and *none*. Those pronouns are singular in form but not necessarily in meaning. As antecedents, however, they generally require singular pronouns:

ANT PRO
- **Everyone** on the swimming team had remembered to bring **her** goggles and nose clip.

ANT PRO
- Tests on the two viruses show that **neither** has had **its** life span shortened by the new drug.

Keep to a singular pronoun even when the indefinite pronoun is followed by *of them:*

- **Each of them** has brought **her** accessories.
- **Neither of them** has had **its** life span shortened.

None, however, forms a partial exception to the rule. Although some writers insist that *none* is always singular (*None of them has surrendered his gun*), others construe *none* as plural when the intended meaning is *all* in a negative sense:

- **None** of them have memorized **their** automatic teller numbers.

EXERCISE

4. Submit five original sentences in which you correctly use indefinite pronouns such as *each, everybody, neither,* and *none* as antecedents, making sure in each case that the following pronoun agrees with its antecedent.

23g Watch for tricky antecedents like *politics* and *acoustics.*

agr
23g

ANT PRO PRO
- **Statistics** is a fine discipline, but **it** has **its** pitfalls.

ANT PRO
- His **statistics** were at **their** most impressive in the middle of the season.

Both of these sentences are correctly handled. In the first, *statistics* carries a plural *-s* ending but is rightly construed as a singular thing, the discipline of statistics. In the second example, the writer has in mind a collection of many numbers; hence the plural pronoun. Review page 424, 20l, for discussion of antecedents that take this form.

EXERCISE

5. Submit three pairs of original sentences in which a pronoun has as its antecedent a term like *politics, acoustics,* or *optics*—a word that can be construed as either singular or plural. In each pair of sentences, make the pronoun singular and then plural. Be prepared to explain the difference in meaning in each instance.

23h Avoid an abrupt pronoun shift.

Your choice of a noun or pronoun in one sentence or part of a sentence establishes a certain person and number; see page 470, 23a. When you refer again to the same individual(s) or thing(s), do not shift unexpectedly between persons and numbers—for example, from the singular *someone* to the plural *they*, from the third-person *students* or *they* to the second-person *you*, or from the third-person plural *people* to the second-person singular *you*. Keep to one person and number.

DON'T:

THIRD PERSON (someone) — SECOND PERSON (you)

x A good song stays with **someone,** making **you** feel less alone.

Having committed the sentence to a third-person pronoun, the writer jars us by switching to the second-person *you*.

DO:

PLURAL ANT (people) — PLURAL PRO (them)

• A good song stays with **people,** making **them** feel less alone.

Or, more informally:

SAME PRO (you — you)

• A good song stays with **you,** making **you** feel less alone.

EXERCISE (23a–23h)

6. Some or all of the following sentences show faulty pronoun agreement. Indicate which, if any, sentences are correct as they stand, and propose corrections for the others.

   A. The student body president hurled insults at the faculty as they sat in angry silence.
   B. When someone can type 120 words a minute, you never have to worry about being out of work.
   C. Whether it will be Leona's lawyers or Leona herself, they are sure to make an appearance in court today.
   D. Nobody could control their emotions on the day the war ended.
   E. The team is confident that its game plan will succeed.
   F. Although he tried to master aerodynamics, they are a subject best left to engineers.
   G. An officer and a gentleman would never lose his temper.
   H. A person would have to be crazy to want to risk their life in battle.
   I. Debate in the House of Commons shows politics at its best.
   J. Every dog in the world knows how to wag their tail.

PRONOUN REFERENCE

23i Make sure you have included a pronoun's antecedent.

In informal conversation, pronouns often go without antecedents, since both parties know who or what is being discussed: *He wants me to phone home at least once a week*. In writing, however, you want your antecedents to be explicitly (openly) stated.

ref 23i

DON'T:

x **They** say we are in for another cold winter.

Who is *They?*

DO:

ANT PRO

• **The weather forecasters** have more bad news for us. **They** say we are in for another cold winter.

DON'T:

x **It** explains here that the access road will be closed for repairs.

If the previous sentence has no antecedent for *It*, revision is called for.

DO:

ANT
- **This bulletin** tells us why the backpacking trip was postponed.
PRO
It explains that the access road will be closed for repairs.

EXERCISE

7. Submit three pairs of original sentences. In the first sentence of each pair, illustrate the defect of leaving a pronoun without a needed antecedent. Correct the problem in the second sentence of each pair.

23j Eliminate competition for the role of antecedent.

If you allow a pronoun and its antecedent to stand too far apart, another element in your sentence may look like the real antecedent. This confusion is usually temporary, but you should work to avoid confusing your reader even momentarily.

DON'T:

ANT? ANT? PRO
- Keats sat under a huge **tree** to write his **ode. It** was dense and kept him from the Hampstead mist.

The nearness of *ode* to *It* makes *ode* a likely candidate for antecedent, especially since an ode might be described as dense. With a little extra thought the reader can identify *tree* as the real antecedent—but a good revision can make that fact immediately clear.

DO:

ANT PRO
- Keats wrote his ode while sitting under a huge **tree, which** was dense and kept him from the Hampstead mist.

ref 23j

or

ANT PRO

- Keats wrote his ode while sitting under a huge **tree, whose** dense foliage kept him from the Hampstead mist.

DON'T:

ANT? ANT?

x Before I sold **cosmetics,** I used to walk by all the **clerks** in the
PRO
cosmetics department, amazed by **their** variety.

What was various, the cosmetics or the clerks?

DO:

- Before I sold cosmetics, I used to walk by all the clerks in the cosmetics department, amazed by the variety of makeup on display.

DON'T:

ANT? ANT? PRO

x Because Biff now loved **Suzie** better than **Alice,** he made **her** return his souvenir face mask.

After some reflection, a reader might see that *Alice* must be the intended antecedent. But why not make the meaning clear at once? Try *he made Alice return . . . ,* or rewrite the sentence:

DO:

- Because he had decided to split up with Alice, Biff made her return his souvenir face mask.

EXERCISE

8. Submit three pairs of original sentences. In the first sentence of each pair, illustrate the defect of confusion between two possible antecedents for the same pronoun. Correct the problem in the second sentence of each pair.

23k Watch especially for a *which* with more than one possible antecedent.

When you find a clause beginning with the relative pronoun *which*, check to see whether that word refers to a single preceding term or to a whole statement. If the antecedent is a whole statement, you risk unclarity.

DON'T:

x In the subfreezing weather we could not start the car, **which** interfered with our plans.

Although a reader can puzzle out that the antecedent of *which* is not *car* but the whole preceding statement, writers should not put readers to such pains.

DO:

- The subfreezing weather interfered with our plans, especially when the car would not start.

or

- Since the car would not start in the subfreezing weather, we had to change our plans.

DON'T:

x We skate on the frozen pond, **which** I enjoy.

What is enjoyed, the activity or the pond?

DO:

- I enjoy skating on the frozen pond.

DON'T:

x The improving weather allowed her to fly home, **which** is what she had been hoping for.

Had she been hoping that the weather would improve or

that she could fly home? Even though the two facts are connected, a reader needs to know which one is meant.

DO:

- The improving weather allowed her to fly home, as she had hoped to do.

or

- The improving weather, which she had been hoping for, allowed her to fly home.

EXERCISE

9. Submit three pairs of original sentences. In the first sentence of each pair, illustrate the defect of providing more than one possible antecedent for the relative pronoun *which*. Correct the problem in the second sentence of each pair.

23l Guard against vagueness in using *this, that,* or *it.*

Vague *This* or *That*

Study the following unclear passage:

DON'T:

x The town board voted to eliminate school crossing guards, even though a serious accident had recently occurred at the corner of Jefferson and Truman. **This** brought the parents out in protest.

Does *This* refer to the elimination of the crossing guards, to the accident, or to the whole preceding statement?

When the word *this, that, these*, or *those* is used alone, without modifying another word, it is known as a *demonstrative pronoun.* Inexperienced writers sometimes use the singular forms *this* and *that* imprecisely, hoping to refer to a whole previous idea rather than to a specific antecedent. The problem is that nearby terms may also look like antecedents. While all writers use an occasional demonstrative pronoun, you should check each *this* or *that* to make sure its antecedent is clear. The remedy for vagueness is to make *this* or *that* modify another term or to rephrase the statement.

DO:

- The town board voted to eliminate school crossing guards, even though a serious accident had recently occurred at the corner of Jefferson and Truman. **This dangerous economy** brought the parents out in protest.

  (MOD: **This**; MODIFIED TERM: **dangerous economy**)

The writer has gone from *This* to *This dangerous economy*, turning a vague demonstrative pronoun (*this*) into a precise modifier—a **demonstrative adjective.**

DON'T:

x The cat shed great quantities of fur on the chair. **That** made Mary Ann extremely anxious.

Though the antecedent of *that* (the whole previous sentence) is reasonably clear, the second sentence is not very informative. What was Mary Ann anxious about, the cat's health or the condition of the chair?

DO:

- The cat shed great quantities of fur on the chair. Mary Ann worried that when her mother saw the chair, the cat would be banished from the house.

or

- The cat shed great quantities of fur on the chair. The possibility that he was ill made Mary Ann extremely anxious.

ref 23l

Vague *It*

DON'T:

(INDEFINITE INDICATOR: **it**; PERSONAL PRO: **it**)

x Although **it** is a ten-minute walk to the bus, **it** comes frequently.

It can serve as both a personal pronoun *It is mine*) and an indefinite indicator (*It is raining*), but your reader will be momentarily baffled if you combine those two uses within a sentence.

DO:

- Although it is a ten-minute walk to the bus stop, **buses** come frequently.

EXERCISE

10. Submit three original sentences, illustrating in turn the vague use of *this, that,* and *it.* Add a corrected version below each faulty sentence.

23m Make sure the antecedent is a whole term, not part of one.

The antecedent of a pronoun should not be a modifier or part of a larger term.

DON'T:

x Alexander waited at the **train** (ANT) station until **it** (PRO) came.

> Here the word *train* is part of a larger noun, *train station.* The sentence contains no reference to a train, and thus *it* has no distinct antecedent. The pronoun "dangles" like a dangling modifier (p. 433, 21c).

DO:

- Alexander waited at the station for the **train** (ANT) until **it** (PRO) came.

DON'T:

x The peanut jar was empty, but Bobo was tired of nibbling **them** (PRO) anyway.

> There are no *peanuts* here to serve as the antecedent of *them.*

DO:

ANT

• The jar of **peanuts** was empty, but Bobo was tired of nibbling
PRO
them anyway.

DON'T:

x He was opposed to gun control because he felt that every
PRO
citizen should have **one** in case the cops staged a surprise raid.

The word *gun* appears in the sentence, but only as an attributive (adjectival) noun.

DO:

ANT

• He was opposed to the control of **guns** because he felt that
PRO
every citizen should have **one** in case the cops staged a surprise raid.

EXERCISE (23i–23m)

11. Some or all of the pronouns in the following sentences show faulty reference. Indicate which, if any, sentences are correct as they stand, and propose corrections for the others.

A. I want to drum some statistics into your heads which are concrete.
B. His father always told him what to do, but sometimes he wasn't familiar enough with the facts.
C. Although she was worried at first, it diminished after a while.
D. If your goldfish won't eat its food, feed it to the canary.
E. That storm is a dangerous one, which is why I intend to stay indoors.
F. She favored paper recycling because it could be used again for many purposes.
G. The tide is too high now, but it is certain that it will be low enough three hours from now.

---

24 Parallelism

When two or more parts of a sentence are governed by a single grammatical device, they are said to be structurally parallel, or in **parallelism.**

PATTERN	EXAMPLE
either *x* or *y*	either **boxing** or **wrestling**
neither *x* nor *y*	neither **tennis** nor **racquetball**
not only *x* but also *y*	He not only **sleeps soundly** but also **snores loudly.**
Let me *x* and *y*.	Let me **smile with the wise,** and **feed with the rich.** (Samuel Johnson)
It matters not *x* but *y*.	It matters not **how a man dies,** but **how he lives.** (Samuel Johnson)
The *x*'s are wiser than the *y*'s.	**The tigers of wrath** are wiser than **the horses of instruction.** (William Blake)
It is more blessed to *x* than *y*.	It is more blessed **to give** than **to receive.**
Do you promise to *x*, *y*, and *z*?	Do you promise to **love, honor,** and **cherish?**

PATTERN	EXAMPLE
I write entirely to find out *w, x, y,* and *z.*	I write entirely to find out **what I'm thinking, what I'm looking at, what I see,** and **what it means.** (Joan Didion)

Note from these examples that parallelism can include both *comparisons* (more *x* than *y*) and **series,** or the alignment of three or more elements (to *x, y,* and *z*). In general, parallelism entails matching the grammar, punctuation, and logic of two or more elements in a sentence.

As Chapter 14 makes clear (see especially pages 309–16, 14a–d), the matching of parallel elements can lend your prose clarity, conciseness, and emphasis. But under the pressure of composing a draft, it is sometimes hard to keep track of all the parts of a parallel construction. In this chapter we will focus on the typical problems of faulty parallelism you should look for when revising.

FAULTY PARALLELISM	ADEQUATE PARALLELISM
x The studio was large, square, and had a sunny aspect.	• The studio was **large, square, and sunny.**
x Not only did the painter splash her canvases, but also the floor.	• The painter splashed **not only her canvases but also the floor.**
x She wanted to express not so much the form of her subjects, but rather the nature of paint itself.	• She wanted to express **not so much the form of her subjects as the nature of paint itself.**
x She was not an easy person to understand, and neither was her work.	• **Neither she nor her work** was easy to understand.
x She loved obscurity as much as, if not more, than publicity.	• She loved **obscurity as much as publicity.**
x She was neither a fraud nor was she a major pioneer.	• She was **neither a fraud nor a major pioneer.**

JOINING PARALLEL ELEMENTS

24a Use like elements within a parallel construction.

However many terms you are making parallel, the first of them establishes what kind of element the others must be. If the first term is a verb, the others must be verbs as well. Align a noun with other nouns or nounlike elements, a participle (p. 385, 18a) with other participles, a whole clause (p. 387, 18c) with other clauses, and so forth.

DON'T:

- Melody was both habitually **late** (*x*) to work and a sound **sleeper** (*y*) on the job.

  The sentence awkwardly matches an adjective and a noun. Grammatically like elements—*late* and *sleepy*, or *latecomer* and *sleeper*—are needed for adequate alignment.

DO:

- Melody was both a habitual latecomer and a sound sleeper on the job.

DON'T:

x He enjoyed **rocking his torso** (*x*) and **to flail his arms.** (*y*)

The *x* element is a gerund phrase (p. 724), requiring the *y* element to be a gerund or gerund phrase as well. The infinitive phrase (p. 724) *to flail his arms* breaks the parallelism.

DO:

- He enjoyed **rocking his torso** (*x*) and **flailing his arms.** (*y*)

DON'T:

x She likes to **wear designer clothes,** **listen to classical music,** and **gourmet food is essential.**

(Brackets over the elements: x = wear designer clothes, y = listen to classical music, z = gourmet food is essential.)

The series begins with the completion of an infinitive: *to wear*. At this point the writer has two good options: either to keep repeating the *to* or to supply further verb forms governed by the original *to*.

DO:

- She likes **to wear designer clothes,** **to listen to classical music,** and **to eat gourmet food.**

(x = to wear designer clothes, y = to listen to classical music, x = to eat gourmet food)

or

- She likes to **wear designer clothes,** **listen to classical music,** and **eat gourmet food.**

(x = wear designer clothes, y = listen to classical music, x = eat gourmet food)

Either version adequately corrects the earlier one, in which a whole clause, *gourmet food is essential*, was forced into parallelism with two infinitive constructions. A further option, one that keeps the emphasis of the original statement, is to end the parallelism early.

DO:

- She likes to **wear designer clothes** and **listen to classical music,** and she finds gourmet food essential.

(x = wear designer clothes, y = listen to classical music)

Comparing Comparable Things

The problem of mismatched parallel elements arises most frequently in comparisons. The writer knows what is being compared with what, but the words on the page say something else.

DON'T:

x **The office in Boston** was better equipped than **New York.**

The sentence appears to compare an office to a city. The writer must add *the one in* to show that one office is being compared to another.

DO:

• **The office in Boston** was better equipped than **the one in New York.**

DON'T:

x The twins swore that **their lives** would be different from **their parents.**

The writer means to compare one set of lives to another, but the actual wording compares lives to people.

DO:

• The twins swore that **their lives** would be different from **those of their parents.**

or

• The twins swore that **their lives** would be different from **their parents'.**

// join
24a

DON'T:

x **Solar heating for a large office building** is technically different from **a single-family home.**

The writer is trying to compare one kind of solar heating to another, but the sentence actually compares one kind of solar heating to a single-family home.

DO:

x

• **Solar heating for a large office building** is technically different

y

from **that for a single-family home.**

EXERCISE

1. Submit five original sentences showing a failure to use like elements within a parallel construction. Follow each faulty sentence with a corrected version. Among your five defective sentences, include two illustrations of faulty comparison.

24b Make the second half of a parallel construction as grammatically complete as the first.

When you are aligning two elements *x* and *y*, be careful not to omit parts of your *y* element that are necessary to make it grammatically parallel with your *x* element. The problem tends to arise when the parallelism comes at the beginning of the sentence, especially if the formula being used is *not only x but also y*.

DON'T:

x

x Not only **did Mendel study the color of the peas,** but also **the**

y

shapes of the seeds.

Some good writers would find this sentence adequate; after all, its meaning is clear. But other writers would want to make a better match between *x* and *y*. Since the *x* element contains a subject (*Mendel*) and a verb (*did study*), the *y* element should follow suit.

// join 24b

IMPROVED:

V S

• Not only **did Mendel study** the color of the peas, but **he** also

V S

studied the shapes of the seeds.

But this revision is wordy. Such a construction can be made more concise by shifting the *not only* to a later position.

PREFER:

• Mendel studied not only **the color of the peas** (x) but also **the shapes of the seeds** (y).

For more about *not only . . . but also*, see pp. 496–97, 24h.

EXERCISE

2. Submit three original sentences showing a failure to make the second half of a parallel construction as grammatically complete as the first. Follow each faulty sentence with a corrected version.

24c Be sure to complete the expected parts of an anticipatory pattern.

Many parallel constructions are governed by **anticipatory patterns** (p. 311, 14b)—formulas that demand to be completed in a certain predictable way. If you begin the formula but then change or abandon it, your sentence falls out of parallelism.

Neither . . . nor

A *neither* demands a *nor*, not an *or*.

DON'T:

x Banging his fist on the table, he insisted that he had **neither** a drinking problem **or** a problem with his temper.

// join 24c

Change *or* to *nor*.

More like x *than* y

Do not sabotage this formula by adding the word *rather*.

DON'T:
x He seemed **more like** a Marine sergeant **rather than** a social worker.

Delete *rather*.

***No sooner* x *than* y**

Here the common error is to change *than* to *when*.

DON'T:
x **No sooner** had I left **when** my typewriter was stolen.

When must be changed to *than* if the anticipatory formula is to complete its work.

***Not so much* x *as* y**

Be sure that the necessary *as* is not replaced by an unwelcome *but rather*.

DON'T:
x She was **not so much** selfish, **but rather** impulsive.

DO:
• She was **not so much** selfish **as** impulsive.

or

• She was **not so much** selfish **as she was** impulsive.

Note the absence of a comma in the two satisfactory versions.

EXERCISE

3. Submit four original pairs of faulty and revised sentences illustrating, and then correcting, inadequate control over the four patterns *neither . . . nor, more like* x *than* y, *no sooner* x *than* y, *and not so much* x *as* y.

24d Watch for faulty parallelism with *not . . . neither.*

DON'T:

x The Marquis de Sade was **not an agreeable man,** and **neither are his novels.**

The complement *man* in the *x* element makes the sentence appear to say that the novels were not an agreeable man.

DO:

- The Marquis de Sade was **not agreeable,** and **neither are his novels.**

EXERCISE

4. Submit two pairs of original sentences illustrating, and then correcting, inadequate control over the *not . . . neither* pattern.

24e Beware of a suspended verb or a suspended comparison.

Suspended Verb

Be alert to likely difficulties with a **suspended verb**—the use of two forms of the same delayed verb, governed by the same subject: *The project can, and in all likelihood will, succeed.* That sentence, though cumbersome, is grammatically correct. But quite often the delayed verb turns out to fit with only one of the two expressions preceding it.

// join
24d

DON'T:

x Melody **can,** and indeed **has been, hitchhiking** in both directions at once.

The way to check such sentences is to read them without the interruption: *Melody can hitchhiking*, etc. To save the present form of the sentence, you could write *Melody can hitchhike, and indeed has been hitchhiking, in both directions at once*. But that sounds clumsy. A better solution would be to get rid of the double construction.

DO:
- Melody has been hitchhiking in both directions at once.

Suspended Comparison

Like those with a suspended verb, parallel constructions involving a **suspended** (delayed) **comparison** sometimes end in a tangle.

DON'T:
x Melody likes total strangers **as much,** if not **more than,** her closest friends.

The problem here, as in many suspended comparisons, is that the last part of the comparison fits with only one of the two elements that lead to it. *More than her closest friends* makes sense, but *as much her closest friends* does not. To be technically right, the suspended comparison would have to say *as much as, if not more than, her closest friends*. But why not do away with the clumsy suspended formula altogether?

DO:
- Melody likes total strangers at least as much as she does her closest friends.

EXERCISES

5. Submit two pairs of original sentences illustrating, and then correcting, inadequate control over (a) a suspended verb and (b) a suspended comparison.

6. (24a–24e) Some or all of the following sentences show a faulty handling of parallel structure. Indicate which, if any, sentences are correctly formed, and submit improved versions of the others.

A. He is not an outstanding swimmer, and neither is his running.
B. Her passion was to climb mountains and camping in the snow.
C. Not only is abortion a hotly contested issue these days, but also surrogate motherhood.
D. No sooner do I turn my back when you start going through my private papers.
E. They can, and furthermore they have been, making progress on the case.

24f Repeat *that* to show that two clauses are parallel.

When you are trying to make whole clauses parallel, watch out for allowing the parallel effect to lapse after the first clause. The danger is greatest when the *x* element is a *that* clause.

DON'T:

x Sue wrote **that she hated her job,** but **she was glad to be working.**

(*x* = that she hated her job; *y* = she was glad to be working)

As worded, this sentence allows the *y* element to become a direct statement about how Sue felt. But the writer's intention was to reveal two things that Sue *wrote*. A second *that* brings out that meaning.

DO:

- Sue wrote **that** she hated her job but **that** she was glad to be working.

// join 24f

EXERCISE

7. Submit two pairs of original sentences illustrating, and then correcting, the omission of a second *that* in two parallel clauses.

24g Do not use *and who* or *and which* unless you have already supplied a *who* or a *which*.

DON'T:

x She is a woman of action, **and who** cares about the public good.

DO:

- She is a woman **who** takes strong action **and who** cares about the public good.

  Alternatively, you can rewrite the sentence: *She is a woman of action, and one who cares about the public good.*

DON'T:

x That is a questionable idea, **and which** has been opposed for many years.

DO:

- That is a questionable idea, **and one which** has been opposed for many years.

or

- That is a questionable idea which has been opposed for many years.

EXERCISE

8. Submit two pairs of original sentences illustrating, and then correcting, the failure to include (a) *who* before *and who* and (b) *which* before *and which*.

24h Do not let an earlier term invade a parallel construction.

Remember that elements already in place before a parallelism begins should not be repeated *inside* it.

Either . . . Or, Neither . . . Nor

A parallelism involving one of these formulas may be grammatically dependent on an immediately preceding word or sentence element (*he wants either sausage or bacon*). Be sure to keep the preceding expression from reappearing inside the parallel construction itself.

DON'T:
x They serve **as** either guidance counselors or **as** soccer coaches.

The way to check such sentences is to take note of where the parallelism is introduced—in this case, at the word *either*. Next, isolate the whole parallelism—*either guidance counselors or as soccer coaches*—and see if it repeats the word that came just before it. Yes, the second *as* must go.

DO:
- They serve as either guidance counselors or soccer coaches.

or

- They serve either as guidance counselors or as soccer coaches.

Here *as* is repeated *within* the parallelism in order to make the *x* and *y* elements, *guidance counselors* and *soccer coaches*, fully parallel. Note how the two allowable versions differ from the faulty one:

as either *x* or as *y*	wrongly repeats an earlier element, *as*
either *x* or *y*	fully parallel
either as *x* or as *y*	fully parallel

// join
24h

Not Only x *but Also* y

This formula, useful when it works, can be easily misaligned. Once again, you must see where the parallelism begins and avoid repeating an earlier element.

DON'T:

x She remembered not only **her maps** but **she also remembered her tire repair kit.**

The first *remembered* comes just before the parallel construction and governs both of its parts. The second *remembered* thus breaks the parallel effect.

DO:

• She remembered not only **her maps** but also **her tire repair kit.**

Now *x* and *y* are parallel; they are the two things that were remembered. The sentence lines up like this:

She remembered { *not only* her maps / *but also* her tire repair kit.
(not only *x* but also *y*)

EXERCISES

9. Submit two pairs of original sentences illustrating, and then correcting, the faulty repetition of an element coming before the first of two parallel elements. In your first pair of sentences, use the *either . . . or* pattern; in the second, use *not only* x *but also* y.

10. (24f–24h) Some or all of the following sentences show a faulty handling of parallel structure. Indicate which, if any, sentences are correctly formed, and submit improved versions of the others.

    A. Harry told his angry customer that the car was indeed loaded with options, just as he had claimed, and one option was whether or not to start on cold mornings.
    B. She is an award-winning musician, but who never feels satisfied with her current level of achievement.
    C. You are either acting very hostile tonight or I am covered with bedbugs.

// join 24h

D. He disliked not only colonial rule, but he also distrusted the whole idea of parliamentary government.
E. She will neither commit herself to marriage, nor will she break off the relationship.

24i Carry through with any repeated modifier in a series.

If you begin repeating any modifier within a series, be sure to keep doing so for all the remaining items.

DON'T:

w *x* *y*

x He can never find **his textbooks, his tapes, calculator,** and

z

homework.

> The modifier *his* in the *w* element commits the writer to using the word again in *x*, *y*, and *z*. Note the options for revision.

DO:

w *x* *y*

- He can never find **his textbooks, his tapes, his calculator**, and

z

his homework.

or

w *x* *y*

- He can never find his **textbooks, tapes, calculator,** and

z

homework.

EXERCISE

11. Submit two pairs of original sentences illustrating, and then correcting, the failure to carry through with a repeated modifier in a series.

PUNCTUATING PARALLEL ELEMENTS

24j Join most pairs of elements without a comma.

To show that two elements are meant to be parallel, omit a comma after the first one.

DON'T:

x Last night's storm blew out **my electric blanket,** and **my clock radio.**

The comma implies that the only direct object of *blew out* has already been given and that the main statement is over. By removing the comma the writer can show that the *x* and *y* elements are parallel objects.

DON'T:

x Aspirin has been called **a blessing by some,** and **a dangerous drug by others.**

Aspirin has been called *x* and *y*; remove the comma to show that *x* and *y* are tightly related.

Pairing Independent Clauses

The no-comma rule above need not apply when the *x* element is an independent clause (p. 387, 18c), as in *Not only did they adjust the fan belt, but they also adjusted the brakes*. But in *either . . . or* constructions you should omit the comma to keep the *y* statement from escaping the controlling effect of the parallelism.

// punc
24j

DON'T:

x Either **you are wrong about the guitar strings,** or **I have forgotten everything I knew.**

Remove the comma and notice how the two statements then fit more tightly together.

EXERCISE

12. Submit two pairs of original sentences illustrating, and then correcting, the inclusion of an undesirable comma between two paired elements. Then add a final sentence in which a comma *is* correctly included after the first of two paired independent clauses.

24k As a rule, use commas and a word like *and* to separate items in a series.

- I used to sprinkle my writing with **commas,**^{x} **semicolons,**^{y} and **dashes**^{z} as though they were salt and pepper.

The normal way to present a **series** (three or more parallel items) is to separate the items with commas, adding a coordinating conjunction such as *and* or *or* before the last item.

Optional Final Comma

Many writers, especially journalists, omit the final comma in a series. So can you if you are consistent about it throughout a given piece of writing.

ACCEPTABLE:
- When George felt lonely in the kitchen, he drowned out the silence by turning on **the blender,**^{x} **the food processor**^{y} and **the garbage disposal.**^{z}

Note, however, that the *x*, *y* and *z* formula may not always allow your meaning to come through clearly.

AMBIGUOUS:

x The returning knight had countless tales to tell of ^{x}**adventure,** ^{y}**conquest of hideous monsters** and ^{z}**helpless damsels in distress.**

Did he conquer the damsels as well as the monsters? A comma after *monsters* would remove all doubt. If you keep to the traditional *x*, *y*, and *z* method, such problems will not arise.

Conjunctions without Commas

If all the members of a series are connected by conjunctions, no commas are needed:

- In his new frame of mind, George began to understand that every man must learn to live alone with ^{x}**his cable television** and ^{y}**his quadriphonic CD tape deck** and ^{z}**his video recorder.**

Emphatic Sequence of Clauses

You can sometimes omit a coordinating conjunction when presenting several brief, tightly related independent clauses in a sequence:

- George saw the frozen tamale pie, he yearned for it, he stuffed it eagerly into the shopping cart.

Here the lack of a conjunction before the third clause helps to bring out the rapidity and compulsiveness of the activities described.

EXERCISE

13. Submit three original, correctly formed sentences illustrating (a) the normal use of commas and a coordinating conjunction to separate items in a series, (b) the joining of all items in a series by conjunctions, without commas, and (c) the omission, for dramatic effect, of a coordinating conjunction in a series of independent clauses.

24l If an item within a series contains its own comma, use semicolons to show where each of the items ends.

Once you have begun a series, you may find yourself using commas for two quite different purposes: to separate the *x*, *y*, and *z* items and to punctuate *within* one or more of those items. If so, your reader may have trouble seeing where each item ends. To show the important breaks between the main parallel items, separate *x*, *y*, and *z* with semicolons:

- Wratto's poem said that lack of energy could keep people out of a lot of trouble; that moving around and doing things, burning calories unnecessarily, makes people forget about important things, such as supporting poetry; and that by sitting perfectly still, just letting the universe run down all by itself, you can actually get *with* entropy and make it beautiful.

  The semicolons help to show where each of the three items ends; otherwise the commas would be too confusing. Note that the items in a series punctuated by semicolons do not have to constitute independent clauses.

For other advice about the formation of effective series, see p. 313, 14c.

EXERCISES

14. Submit a long original sentence illustrating the correct use of semicolons to separate a series of items, some of which contain internal commas.

// punc
24l

15. (24i–24l) Some or all of the following sentences show inadvisable formation and/or punctuation of parallel constructions. Briefly comment on each, indicating where, why, and how you would make necessary changes.

    A. Whether the earthquake was caused by fault slippage, or by excessive drilling, could not be determined.
    B. Experimenters, who are slavishly admired by some people, and criticized as frivolous by others, have discovered that the taste for dill pickles declines after age sixty-five.

C. George couldn't remember whether Susan used to stock up on low-fat milk, condensed milk, defatted, reconstituted, or evaporated milk.
D. Stanley writes leaflets, makes underground broadcasts, tape recordings, and paints warnings on police station walls.
E. The Director of Food Services said that during the renovation the students would have priority in the dining halls; that faculty members should plan to cook at home, eat elsewhere, or bring bag lunches to their offices; and that the college's neighbors, including several retired professors living nearby, would be barred from the student halls until the work had been completed.

25 Relations between Tenses

Every time you write a sentence, you are expressing a **tense,** or time of action, through your verb. For a review of verb forms showing not only their tenses but also their **voices** and **moods,** see Chapter 32.

Some tenses are obviously appropriate to certain functions—the present for statements of opinion, the past for storytelling, the future for prediction. But choice of tense becomes trickier when you need to combine two or more time frames within a sentence (*He said he would have been ready if the plane had not been late; She will have finished by the day we get home;* etc.). When revising your work, check to see that your combinations of tenses follow the advice given below.

25a Choose one governing tense for a piece of writing.

Stating Facts and Ideas

The normal way to state facts or offer your ideas about any general or current topic is to use the present tense:

- Water boils at 100° Celsius.
- Does the new divorce law protect the rights of children?

Note how the following passage establishes a present time frame, departing from it only to narrate events that occurred previously:

- PRES
The great debate **continues** between heredity and environment.
PRES PRES
Both sides **have** strong arguments, but I **am convinced** that
PRES PAST
technology **adjusts** our fate. My grandfather, for example, **was**
PAST PERF
dead at forty from diabetes, a disease that my father **has lived** with for sixty years, thanks to this century's advances in medical research.

If you are stating ideas about the past, many of your verbs will be in the past tense. Even so, the present is appropriate for conveying your current reflections about past events:

- PRES PRES PAST
I **believe** we **can prove** that the Etruscans **had** much more
PRES
influence on Roman civilization than most people **realize.**

Narrating Events

The usual tense for narrating events is the past:

- PAST PAST
She **arrived** home in a fury, and she **was** still upset when the
PAST
phone **rang.**

- PAST
The solution **was allowed** to stand for three minutes, after
PAST
which 200 cc of nitrogen **were added.**

  In this second example the past verbs are in the passive voice (p. 580, 32d).

Sometimes, to get a special effect of immediacy, you may even want to use the present for narration:

tense
25a

PRES PRES
- When he **phones** her, she **tells** him to leave her alone.

But note that once you adopt this present-tense convention for storytelling, you have committed yourself to it throughout the piece of writing. Do not try to switch back to the more usual past.

DON'T:

PRES PRES
x When he **phones** her, she **tells** him to leave her alone. But he
PAST PAST PERF
acted as if he **hadn't understood** her point.

For consistency, the second sentence should read: *But he* *acts* *as if he* *hasn't* *understood. . . .*

25b Relate your other tenses to the governing tense.

Once you have established a controlling time frame, or **governing tense,** shift into other tenses as logic requires.

Present Time Frame

A present time frame, established by a present governing tense, allows you to use a variety of other tenses to indicate the times of actions or states. The following are ways of combining other tenses with the present:

- He **meditates** every day, and . . .

REST OF SENTENCE	TENSE
he **is meditating** right now.	present progressive (action ongoing in the present)
he **has meditated** five thousand times.	present perfect (past action completed thus far)
he **has been meditating** since dawn.	present perfect progressive (action begun in the past and continuing in the present)

tense 25b

REST OF SENTENCE	TENSE
he **meditated** for ten hours yesterday.	past (completed action)
he **was meditating** before I was born.	past progressive (action that was ongoing in a previous time)
he **had meditated** for years before hearing about the popularity of meditation.	past perfect (action completed before another past time)
he **had been meditating** for three hours before the interview.	past perfect progressive (ongoing action completed before another past time)
he **will meditate** tomorrow.	future (action to occur later)
he **will be meditating** for the rest of his life.	future progressive (ongoing action to occur later)
by next year he **will have meditated** for more hours than anyone ever has.	future perfect (action regarded as completed at a later time)
he **will have been meditating** for ten years by the time he is thirty.	future perfect progressive (ongoing action regarded as having begun before a later time)

Past Time Frame

When your time frame is in the past, choose other tenses according to the following patterns:

- There **were** rumors around school . . .

REST OF SENTENCE	TENSE
that the Dean **had been** a sergeant in Vietnam.	past perfect (action completed in an earlier past time)
that the Dean **had been lifting** weights all these years.	past perfect progressive (ongoing action that began earlier)
that the Dean **would take** disciplinary matters into his own hands.	conditional (later action)

Hypothetical Condition

Certain sentences containing *if* clauses set forth *hypothetical conditions*. That is, they tell what would be true or would have been true in certain imagined circumstances. Note that such sentences differ in both form and meaning from sentences proposing likely conditions.

LIKELY CONDITION	HYPOTHETICAL CONDITION
I **will dance** if you **clear** a space on the floor.	I **would dance** if you **cleared** a space on the floor.
If she **studies** now, she **will pass.**	If she **studied** now, she **would pass.**
If I **marry** your sister, we **will be** brothers.	If I **married** your sister, we **would be** brothers.

The "likely condition" sentences anticipate that the condition may be met, but the "hypothetical condition" sentences are sheer speculation: what would happen if . . . ? These require use of the **subjunctive mood** (p. 582, 32e) in the *if* clause. And in the "consequence" clause they require a *conditional* form, either present or past:

CONDITIONAL FORMS			
Present	*would* / *could*	+ base verb	would go could go
Past	*would* / *could*	+ *have* + past participle	would have gone could have gone

tense
25b

Thus:

IF CLAUSE	CONSEQUENCE CLAUSE
PRES SUBJN If you **worked** overtime,	PRES CONDL you **would have** more spending money.

IF CLAUSE	CONSEQUENCE CLAUSE
PRES SUBJN If they **won** a million dollars,	PRES CONDL what **would** they **do** with the money?
PAST SUBJN If she **had concentrated,**	PAST CONDL she **could have written** a perfect translation.
PRES SUBJN If you **had been** old enough,	PRES CONDL **would** you **have married** Barbara?

The most common mistake in combining tenses is to use *would* in both parts of a conditional statement. Remember that *would* goes only in the consequence clause, not in the *if* clause.

DON'T:
x If they **would** try harder, they would succeed.

DO:
• If they **tried** harder, they would succeed.

DON'T:
x If they **would have** tried harder, they would have succeeded.

DO:
• If they **had tried** harder, they would have succeeded.

25c Change the tense of a verbal only if it designates an earlier time than that of the verb.

When you use a **verbal** (p. 385, 18a)—an infinitive, a participle, or a gerund—ask yourself how it relates in time to the rest of your statement. Verbals change their form only if they characterize an *earlier* action or state than the main one.

tense 25c

Same or Later Time: Present Form

Use the present form of a verbal if it conveys an action or state no earlier than the time established in the rest of the sentence.

SAME TIME:

- We **try to snowboard** every day. (PRES: try; PRES INF: to snowboard)
- We **tried to snowboard** every day. (PAST: tried; PRES INF: to snowboard)
- We **tried snowboarding** every day. (PAST: tried; PRES GER: snowboarding)
- **Snowboarding** every day, we greatly **improved** our technique. (PRES PART: Snowboarding; PAST: improved)

LATER TIME:

- We **intend to snowboard** every day next winter. (PRES: intend; PRES INF: to snowboard)
- We **anticipate** months of **snowboarding.** (PRES: anticipate; PRES GER: snowboarding)
- We **hope** to become stronger, **snowboarding** every day. (PRES: hope; PRES PART: snowboarding)

Earlier Time: Past Form

In the rare case when your verbal is placed into relation with a later time, put it into a past form:

- We expect **to have improved** our snowboarding by next season. (PAST INF: to have improved)
- We wanted **to have made** a breakthrough before the new season began. (PAST INF: to have made)
- Our goal will be **to have made** a breakthrough by then. (PAST INF: to have made)
- **Having improved** so much the year before, we had good reason to feel hopeful. (PAST PART: Having improved)

tense 25c

EXERCISE (25a–25c)

1. Some or all of the following sentences show a faulty choice of tense. Indicate which, if any, sentences you find correct, and explain how and why you would change the others.

A. He knew she stopped smoking five years before.
B. She had wanted to have quit even earlier.
C. If I would have known Marilyn Monroe, I would have treated her respectfully.
D. She had always wanted to be named Mother of the Year, but she was not altogether pleased when the quintuplets had been born.
E. He was suffering quietly for years before his illness became public knowledge.

25d Learn how tenses differ between quotation and indirect discourse.

In the following chart, notice what happens to tenses when writers shift from what was actually said (quotation) to **indirect discourse,** or a report of what was said.

	QUOTATION	INDIRECT DISCOURSE
present verb in quotation	"I find it difficult to remember your name," she said.	She said that she **found** it difficult to remember his name.
past verb in quotation	"Your interest in bowling gave cause for alarm," she revealed.	She revealed that his interest in bowling **had given** cause for alarm.
present perfect verb in quotation	She protested, "I have never encouraged your crude advances."	She protested that she **had** never **encouraged** his crude advances.
past perfect verb in quotation	"Until then," she reflected, "I had never known how barbarous a male could be."	She reflected that until then she **had** never **known** how barbarous a male could be.
future verb in quotation	She added, "You will do better to bestow your 'date,' as you choose to call it, for the 'demolition derby' on some companion more keenly appreciative of such cultural gatherings than myself."	She added that he **would do** better to bestow his so-called "date". . . .

To summarize these changes of tense, indirect discourse:

	QUOTATION	INDIRECT DISCOURSE
makes a present verb past	want ⟶	wanted
makes a past or present perfect verb past perfect	wanted have wanted } ⟶	had wanted
leaves a past perfect verb past perfect	had wanted ⟶	had wanted
turns a future verb into *would* + a base (infinitive) form	will want ⟶	would want

You can deduce other tense changes in indirect discourse from these basic ones: *will have wanted* becomes *would have wanted, has been wanting* becomes *had been wanting*, and so on.

25e Do not shift between quotation and indirect discourse within a sentence.

Once you have begun to quote someone's speech or writing, do not suddenly move into indirect discourse (25d). Similarly, do not leap from indirect discourse to quotation.

DON'T:

x She said, **"I love science fiction movies,"** [QUOTATION] and **had I seen the one about the teenage Martians on a rampage?** [INDIRECT DISCOURSE]

DO:

• She said, **"I love science fiction movies,"** [QUOTATION] and asked me, **"Have you seen the one about the teenage Martians on a rampage?"** [QUOTATION]

tense 25e

DON'T:

INDIRECT DISCOURSE — QUOTATION

x My boss said **the key was gone** and **are you the one who took it?**

DO:

INDIRECT DISCOURSE — INDIRECT DISCOURSE

• My boss said **the key was gone** and asked **whether I was the one who had taken it.**

EXERCISE (25d–25e)

2. Some or all of the following sentences show a faulty use of tense in quotation and/or indirect discourse. Indicate which, if any, sentences you find correct, and explain how and why you would change the others.

   A. He protested that he never wanted to join the armed forces.
   B. He said that he will look into a career in photography instead.
   C. "It is still snowing," she remarked, and shouldn't we stay inside the cabin?
   D. She reminded him that until then, "you have a consistent record of getting lost in snowstorms."
   E. He replied, however, that this time will be different.

25f Use the present tense to write about action within a plot or about an author's ideas within a work.

Discussing Actions within a Plot

Unlike a real event, a scene within a work of art does not happen once and for all. It is always ready to be experienced afresh by a new reader, viewer, or listener. Consequently, the time frame for discussing such a scene is the present. Though you should use the past tense to write about the historical creating of the artwork, you should use the present tense to convey what the work "says to us." This function is called the **"literary" present tense.**

HISTORICAL PAST:

- Shakespeare **was** probably familiar with the plays of Kyd and Marlowe when he **wrote** his great tragedies. He **expressed** his deepest feelings in those plays.

"LITERARY" PRESENT:

- Shakespeare **reveals** Hamlet's mind through soliloquy.
- Hamlet's unrelenting psychological dilemma **drives** him toward catastrophe.
- The Misfit, in Flannery O'Connor's story "A Good Man Is Hard to Find," **murders** an entire family.
- In the 1949 film version of *Oliver Twist*, Alec Guinness **plays** Fagin.

    If the verb in this last example were *played*, the sentence would be making a statement not about the movie but about an event in Alec Guinness's acting career.

Discussing Ideas within a Work

No matter how long ago a book or other publication was written, use the "literary" present tense to convey the idea it expresses:

- In *The Republic* Plato **maintains** that artists **are** a menace to the ideal state.
- Thoreau **says** in *Walden* that we **can find** peace by staying exactly where we **are.**

    The present-tense verbs are appropriate because any book "speaks to" its readers in a continuing present time.

If, on the other hand, you want to refer to a noncontemporary author's ideas without reference to a particular work, use the past:

- Plato **believed** that artists **were** a menace to the ideal state.
- Thoreau **was convinced** that people **could find** peace by staying exactly where they **were.**

25g In discussing a plot, relate other tenses to the "literary" present.

Once you have established the "literary" present for action in a plot that is "happening right now" (25f), refer to earlier or later actions in that plot by using the past, future, and related tenses.

- When Hamlet's suspicions **were** (PAST) confirmed by the ghost, he **vowed** (PAST) revenge. But by Act Two he **fears** (PRES) that his self-doubts **have dulled** (PRES PERF) his purpose. He **engages** (PRES) a troupe of players to reenact the murder and **swears** (PRES) that the play **will "catch** (FUTURE) the conscience of the King. . . ."

  Notice how the writer has chosen a point of focus in Act Two of *Hamlet*. The use of the "literary" present for that time determines which tenses are appropriate for the other described actions.

25h Do not allow the past form of a quoted verb to influence your own choice of tense.

It is hard to keep to the "literary" present (25g) when you have just quoted a passage containing verbs in the past tense. The tendency is to allow your own verbs to slip into the past. Keep to the rule, however: use the present tense for actions or states under immediate discussion.

DON'T:

x D. H. Lawrence **describes** (PAST) Cecilia as "a big dark-complexioned, pug-faced young woman who very rarely **spoke** (PAST). . . ." When she **did speak,** (PAST) however, her words **were** (PAST) sharp enough to kill her aunt Pauline.

  Here *did speak* and *were*, influenced by the quoted verb *spoke*, wrongly depart from the "literary" present.

tense
25h

DO:

- D. H. Lawrence **describes** Cecilia as "a big dark-complexioned, pug-faced young woman who very rarely spoke. . . ." When she **does speak,** however, her words **are** sharp enough to kill her aunt Pauline.

EXERCISE (25f–25h)

3. Some or all of the following sentences show a faulty use of tense with regard to works of art. Indicate which, if any, sentences you find correct, and explain how and why you would change the others.

   A. Forster publishes *A Passage to India* in 1924.
   B. At the beginning of the novel, Aziz has no idea that he will be the defendant in a notorious trial.
   C. "I warned you before," said the hero of the novel, "and now you are going to be sorry."
   D. Two chapters earlier, Dimmesdale was sure he would be fleeing with Hester to England, but when he enters the pulpit to deliver his final sermon, he already knows that he will stay and confess his guilt.
   E. A specialist in UFO research worked as a consultant to *Close Encounters of the Third Kind,* a film in which alien creatures really did visit our planet.

VIII
PUNCTUATION

PUNCTUATION

Marks of punctuation are essential for clear meaning in written prose. Beyond showing where pauses or stops would occur in speech, they indicate logical relations that would otherwise be hard for a reader to make out. For example, parentheses, brackets, dashes, and commas all signal a pause, but they suggest different relations between main and subordinate material. The only way to be sure that your punctuation marks are working with your meaning, not against it, is to master the rules.

Part VII above, "Usage," covers a good many punctuation rules for handling such grammatical features as independent clauses, modifying elements, and parallel constructions. This part repeats those rules (giving cross-references to the fuller discussions), adds other rules, and shows how you can choose between punctuation marks that are closely related in function.

Note that the conventions of quoting are handled in Chapter 30. Apostrophes and hyphens are treated, respectively, in Chapters 33 and 34. To see how you should form and space the various punctuation marks, see Chapter 31.

26

Periods, Question Marks, Exclamation Points

PERIODS

26a Place a period at the end of a sentence making a statement, a polite command, or a mild exclamation.

STATEMENT:

- I think the Olympic Games have become too politicized.
- Art historians are showing new respect for nineteenth-century narrative painting.

POLITE COMMAND:

- Tell me why you think the Olympic Games have become too politicized.
- Consider the new respect that art historians are showing toward nineteenth-century narrative painting.

MILD EXCLAMATION:

- What a pity that the Olympic Games have become so politicized.
- How remarkable it is to see the art historians reversing their former scorn for nineteenth-century narrative painting.

Exclamation points at the end of these two sentences would have made them more emphatic; see p. 523, 26j.

26b End an indirect question with a period.

DON'T:
x Ted asked me whether I was good at boardsailing?

DO:
- Ted asked me whether I was good at boardsailing.

An **indirect question,** instead of taking a question form, reports that a question is or was asked. Thus an indirect question is a **declarative sentence**—one that makes a statement. As such, it should be completed by a period, not a question mark.

26c Consider a period optional after a courtesy question.

- Would you be kind enough to reply within thirty days.

or

- Would you be kind enough to reply within thirty days?

Some questions in business letters (Chapter 38) are really requests or mild commands. You can end such a sentence with either a period or a question mark. The period makes a more impersonal and routine effect. If you want to express actual courtesy toward a reader you know, keep to the question mark.

26d Eliminate an unacceptable sentence fragment [see discussion on p. 390, 18d].

DON'T:

x Most Americans should study recent changes in the tax laws. FRAG **Especially those affecting deductions for medical expenses, child care, and IRAs.**

DO:

- Most Americans should study recent changes in the tax laws, **especially** those affecting deductions for medical expenses, child care, and IRAs.

26e If a sentence ends with an abbreviation, use only one period.

DON'T:

x Send the money directly to Lincoln Dollar, M.D..

DO:

- Send the money directly to Lincoln Dollar, M.D.

QUESTION MARKS

26f Place a question mark after a direct question.

Most questions are complete sentences, but now and then you may want to add a question to a statement or insert a question within a statement. In every instance, put a question mark immediately after the question:

- Can a camel pass through the eye of a needle?
- I know that many strange things are possible, but can a camel really pass through the eye of a needle?

- It was just fifteen years ago today—remember?—that the camel got stuck in the eye of the needle.
- "Can a needle," asked the surrealist film director when he met the Arab veterinary surgeon, "pass through the eye of a camel?"

But if your sentence poses a question that is then modified by other language, place the question mark at the end:

- How could he treat me like that, after all the consideration I showed him?

26g To express doubt, use a question mark within parentheses.

- Saint Thomas Aquinas, 1225(?)–1274, considered faith more important than reason.

If the dates here were in parentheses, the question mark would go inside brackets: (*1225*[?]–*1274*).

Sarcastic Question Mark

No grammatical rule prevents you from getting a sarcastic effect from the "doubting" question mark. But if you are determined to be sarcastic, quotation marks will do a better job of conveying your attitude.

AVOID:

x The president expects to make four nonpolitical (?) speeches in the month before the election.

PREFER:

- The president expects to make four "nonpolitical" speeches in the month before the election.

?
26g

26h After a question mark, omit a comma or a period.

DON'T:
x Now I know the answer to the question, "Why study?".

DO:
• Now I know the answer to the question, "Why study?"

DON'T:
x "Where is my journal?", she asked.

DO:
• "Where is my journal?" she asked.

26i If a sentence asking a question contains another question at the end, use only one question mark.

• Why didn't Melody stop to ask herself, "Isn't it strange that I'm the only person in this whole zoo who is trying to feed peanuts to the elephant train?"

EXCLAMATION POINTS

26j Use exclamation points sparingly to express intense feeling or a strong command.

• "My geodesic dome! My organic greenhouse! My Tolkien collection! When will I ever see them again?"

• Standing in the bread line, he had a moment of revelation. So *this* was what his economics professor had meant by structural unemployment!

When you quote an outburst or want to express extremely strong feeling, end the sentence or intentional sentence fragment (p. 394, 18e) with an exclamation point. Frequent use of exclamation points, however, dulls their effect. And though an exclamation point, like a question mark, can be inserted parenthetically to convey sarcasm (26g), the effect is usually weak.

AVOID:

x Warren thought that a black-and-white photocopy (!) of the Rembrandt painting would give him everything he needed to write his art history paper.

In context, the folly of Warren's assumption would become apparent without the loud assistance of the exclamation point.

EXERCISE (26a–26j)

1. Submit corrections for any inadvisable handling of periods, question marks, or exclamation points in the following sentences.

   A. Aunt Sophia was disoriented by the family reunion. Never having played frisbee with thirty-five people before.
   B. He wondered if I would like to shoot the rapids with his novelist friend?
   C. I am not sure—will you correct me if I'm wrong—that porpoises are more intelligent than raccoons.
   D. She wanted her psychiatrist to tell her whether it was possible to get seasick in Iowa?
   E. His fellow workers at the car wash did not seem very impressed (!) by his Ph.D..

27
Commas

Primary discussions of most comma rules appear in other chapters; see the cross-references below. Here we bring all the rules together in an overview that shows (a) where you should use a comma or pair of commas, (b) where you should omit a comma, and (c) where you can include or omit a comma as you see fit. Wherever you need more examples or background, go to the cross-referenced discussions.

27a Learn where you should include a comma or pair of commas.

INCLUDE A COMMA OR PAIR OF COMMAS WHEN YOU . . .	
Join independent clauses (see p. 397, 19a):	• **Every blink is like fire,** and **tears well up constantly.**

The two clauses *Every blink is like fire* and *tears well up constantly* are independent because each of them could stand as a complete sentence. To avoid a comma splice or a fused sentence, you should join them either with a comma and a coordinating conjunction, as here, or with a semicolon: *Every blink is like fire; tears well up constantly.*

INCLUDE A COMMA OR PAIR OF COMMAS WHEN YOU . . .

Begin with a subordinate clause (see p. 443, 21i):

SUB CLAUSE
- **Since you asked,** I will admit that I am exhausted.

Since you asked is a clause because it contains both a subject (*you*) and a verb (*asked*). It is a subordinate clause because it cannot stand alone as a complete sentence. Whenever you begin a sentence with such a clause, add a comma.

Begin with a modifying phrase that is more than a few words long (see p. 443, 21i):

MOD PHRASE
- **In a spontaneous wave of enthusiasm,** the audience rose to its feet.

In a spontaneous wave of enthusiasm is a phrase because it forms a multi-word unit without a subject-verb combination. Unless an opening phrase is very brief, follow it with a comma.

Use an interrupting element (see p. 445, 21l):

INT EL
- The deficit, **as a matter of fact,** has continued to grow.

An interrupting element forces a break in the main flow of a sentence. Set it off on both sides.

Include a nonrestrictive (nondefining) modifying element (see p. 447, 21m):

NONRESTR EL
- Women, **who have rarely been treated equally in the job market,** still tend to be relatively underpaid.

The sentence refers to all women. Thus the subordinate clause *who have rarely been treated equally in the job market* does not serve to define or restrict the class of women who are meant. Such a nonrestrictive element should always be set off from the rest of the sentence.

Include items in a series (see p. 500, 24k):

- **Modems, plotters, baud rates,** and **programming languages** danced continually in Wilbur's busy mind.

A series, or set of three or more parallel items, requires commas after each item but the last.

, 27a

INCLUDE A COMMA OR PAIR OF COMMAS WHEN YOU . . .	
Present certain quotations (see pp. 558–59, 30l–m):	• **She said**, "I intend to be there early."
When you introduce a complete quoted sentence with a tag like *she said* or *he exclaimed,* follow it with a comma. If the tag appears later, surround it with commas: *"I intend," she said, "to be there early."*	
Present a place name with a more inclusive location:	• **Laramie**, **Wyoming**, celebrates its Jubilee Days every July.
When you add the name of a state, province, or country after a place name, set off the second name with commas on both sides.	
Present an address or a month-first date:	• 3945 Bushnell Road, University Heights, OH 44118 • March 17, 1964, was the date of his birth.
Note the commas both before and after *1964*.	
Include a title or degree:	• Monica Wu, **Ph.D.**, is holding office hours today.
Note the commas both before and after *Ph.D.*	
Include a number of more than four digits:	• 29,368,452
Set off every three digits, working from right to left.	

27b Learn where you should omit a comma.

OMIT A COMMA WHEN YOU . . .	
Join a subject and verb (see p. 428, 20o):	• A **bird** (S) in the hand **is** (V) worth two in the bush. [no comma after *hand*]
Note that *in the hand* does not interrupt the main statement; it is a restrictive element (see p. 528), showing which bird is meant. Thus a comma after *hand* would wrongly separate the subject and verb.	

, 27b

OMIT A COMMA WHEN YOU . . .

Join a verb and direct object (see p. 383, 18a):

- She **recognized** [V] in a flash the **meaning** [D OBJ] of her dream. [no comma after *flash*]

Since no comma sets off *in a flash* at the front end, a comma after *flash* would be inappropriate. The verb *recognized* must be allowed to hook up with its object *meaning* without a pause.

Join a verb and its complement (see p. 384, 18a):

- The laws against drug use **were** [V] not always so **strict** [COMPL] as they are today. [no comma after *always*]

A verb's complement, appearing in the predicate, identifies or modifies the subject—in this case, *laws*. Since there is no real interruption between *were* and *strict*, a comma after *always* would be wrong.

Join a subordinating conjunction and the rest of its subordinate clause (see p. 388, 18c):

- One further reason for using the shopping mall is **that parking is ample there.** [SUB CLAUSE; *that* = SUB CONJ; no comma after *that*]

That parking is ample there forms a subordinate clause—a subject-predicate combination that cannot stand alone. Since *that* is an essential part of the clause, a comma following it would be inappropriate.

Join a preposition and its object (see p. 722):

- My worries keep returning **to** [PREP] **inflation, unemployment, and natural disasters.** [OBJ OF PREP; no comma after *to*]

Even when the object of a preposition is lengthy, making you want to "catch a breath" just before it, you should resist the temptation to insert a comma. By omitting the comma, you honor the unity of the complete prepositional phrase. Note that a colon would also be unacceptable here (p. 536, 28g).

Include a restrictive (defining) modifying element (see p. 447, 21m):

- A child **who likes to play with electrical outlets** [RESTR EL; no commas] must be carefully watched.

, 27b

OMIT A COMMA WHEN YOU . . .

The subordinate clause *who likes to play with electrical outlets* serves to identify which child is meant. Thus it is defining, or restrictive. If you wrongly added commas after *child* and *outlets*, making that element nonrestrictive, you would be drastically changing the meaning of the sentence: every single child, everywhere, likes to play with electrical outlets and therefore must be carefully watched.

Join a final modifier and the modified term (see p. 454, 21p):

- It was an intensely vivid, compelling, **anxiety-producing** (FINAL MOD) **account** (MODIFIED TERM) (no comma) of the disaster.

No matter how many modifiers you string together, omit a comma between the final one and the modified term—in this case, *account*.

Join paired elements (see p. 499, 24j):

- The cause of the fire was either **a leak from the ancient gas heater** (x) (no comma) or **a short circuit.** (y)

The formula here is *either x* or *y*. To cement the connection between the *x* and *y* items, join them without a comma.

Include a day-first date:

- They were married on **23 January 1989.**

Note that a comma would be required if the month came first: *January 23, 1989.*

Include a numeral after a name:

- Oswald Humbert **IV** lost all his money in the crash. (no commas)

27c Learn where a comma is optional.

CONSIDER A COMMA OPTIONAL WHEN YOU . . .

Begin with a brief phrase (see p. 443, 21j):

- **After the storm,** the ground was strewn with leaves.

CONSIDER A COMMA OPTIONAL WHEN YOU . . .

- **After the storm** the ground was strewn with leaves.

When in doubt, you cannot go wrong by supplying the comma.

Use *thus* or *hence* (see p. 445, 21k):

- **Hence**, there is no need for alarm.
- **Hence** there is no need for alarm.

Invert the normal order of sentence elements:

- **What she calls happiness**, I call slavery.
- **What she calls happiness** I call slavery.

What she calls happiness is an objective complement—a complement of the direct object *slavery*. It normally follows the direct object, as in *They appointed him secretary*.

Use one modifier to qualify the preceding one (see p. 454, 21q):

- It was a difficult, **but by no means impossible**, assignment.
- It was a difficult **but by no means impossible** assignment.

Note how the second modifier, beginning with *but*, answers the modifier before it. Commas are optional in such a case.

Follow a month with a year:

- **May, 1968**, was the time of the famous uprising.
- **May 1968** was the time of the famous uprising.

If you add the date, commas are required on both sides: *May 14, 1968, was the time. . . .* Note also that a comma before the year obliges you to add another comma after the year.

Use a four-digit number:

- 8,354
- 8354

EXERCISE (27a–27c)

1. Some or all of the following sentences show a faulty handling (or absence) of commas. Indicate where and why you would recommend changes of punctuation.

, 27c

A. Did you know that, the first baseball game played under electric lights occurred in 1883?

B. The nutrition expert voiced some doubts about the health of American children raised on, "Crazy Cow, Baron Von Redberry, Sir Grapefellow, Count Chocula, and Franken-Berry."
C. What Shaw called the most licentious of institutions, other people call holy matrimony.
D. The old woodshed on the back lot, made a perfect clubhouse for the children.
E. As his weight-training program drew to a close, Biff found himself admiring, new curves in the most surprising places.
F. September 1939 was a bad time to be in Europe.
G. The issue of 16 October, 1975 contained some of the finest prose he had ever read.
H. New York, New York is a wonderful town.
I. Sammy Davis Jr. was a founding member of Hollywood's Rat Pack.
J. Last year the police reported 2571 more felonies than the year before.

28

Semicolons and Colons

SEMICOLON	COLON
Relates two statements	**Equates two items**
• We did not bully or threaten; we knew that justice was on our side. [The two parts of the sentence are logically connected; the second statement explains why no bullying or threatening was considered necessary.]	• We asked for just one thing: the return of our stolen land. [Everything following the colon serves to specify the *thing* preceding it. The colon means *namely*.]

SEMICOLONS

28a To keep two closely related statements within the same sentence, join them with a semicolon.

- My oldest sister is the boss in our family; what she says goes.

- The university conducts art history classes in Europe; the accessibility of great museums and monuments gives students a firsthand sense of the subject.
- Some of those painters influenced Cézanne; others were influenced by him.

The punctuation mark that comes nearest in function to the semicolon is the period. But whereas a period keeps two statements apart as separate sentences, a semicolon shows that two statements within one sentence are intimately related. When one statement is a consequence of another or contrasts sharply with it, you can bring out that tight connection by joining them with a semicolon instead of with a comma and a coordinating conjunction (p. 397, 19a).

Note that when a semicolon is used, the second statement often contains a sentence adverb or transitional phrase (p. 444, 21k) pointing out the logical relation between the two clauses:

- Misunderstanding is often the root of injustice; perfect understanding, **however,** [SENT ADV] is impossible to attain.
- Some parents weigh every word they speak; others, **in contrast,** [TRANS PHRASE] do not think twice about their harsh language.

28b Make sure that a semicolon is followed by a complete statement.

DON'T:

x I used to be afraid to talk to people; **even to ask the time of day.** [FRAG] I always let my brother speak for me; **because he was everyone's buddy.** [FRAG]

An unacceptable sentence fragment (p. 390, 18d) is just as faulty when it follows a semicolon as when it stands alone.

DO:

- I used to be afraid to talk to people; even asking the time of day was an ordeal. I always let my brother speak for me; he was everyone's buddy.

28c Feel free to use a word like *and* or *but* after a semicolon.

There is nothing wrong with following a semicolon with a conjunction, so long as the second statement is an independent clause (p. 397, 18c). Do so if you want to make explicit the logical connection between the statements coming before and after the semicolon:

CONJ
- All day long we loaded the van with our worldly goods; **but** when we were ready to leave the next morning, full of eagerness for the trip, we saw that the van had a flat tire.

  A comma after *goods* would also be appropriate, but the semicolon recommends itself because the second statement already contains two commas. Thus the semicolon helps to show the main separation in the sentence.

28d If an item within a series contains a comma, use semicolons to show where each of the items ends [see discussion on p. 502, 24l].

- Student dining halls include the Servery, which is located on the ground floor of the Student Union; the Cafeteria, temporarily relocated in Jim Thorpe Gymnasium; and the Rathskeller, now in the basement of Anne Bradstreet Hall.

COLONS

28e Use a colon to show an equivalence between items on either side.

A colon introduces a restatement, a formal list, or a quotation. Use a colon if you can plausibly insert *namely* after it:

- Dinner arrives: [*namely*] a tuna fish sandwich and a cup of tea.

- The bill is unbelievable: [*namely*] $8.50 for the sandwich and $1.95 for the tea.
- Samuel Johnson offered the following wise advice: [*namely*] "If you would have a faithful servant, and one that you like, serve yourself."

The *namely* test can help you avoid putting semicolons where colons belong and vice versa.

DON'T:

x The results of the poll were surprising; 7 percent in favor, 11 percent opposed, and 82 percent no opinion.

> *Namely* would be appropriate here; therefore the semicolon should be a colon.

x We slaved for years: we remained as poor as ever.

> *Namely* is inappropriate, since the second clause makes a new point. The colon should be a semicolon.

28f Make sure you have a complete statement before a colon.

Like a semicolon, a colon must be preceded by a complete statement.

DON'T:

FRAG

x **Occupations that interest me:** beekeeper, horse groomer, dog trainer, veterinarian.

DO:

COMPLETE STATEMENT

- **Occupations involving animals interest me:** beekeeper, horse groomer, dog trainer, veterinarian.

But remember that, unlike a semicolon (p. 533), a colon need not be *followed* by a whole statement.

28g Omit a colon if it would separate elements that belong together.

DON'T:

V D OBJ

x Before buying my Saturn, I **tested: a Toyota Corolla, a Ford Escort, and a Nissan Sentra.**

The colon separates a verb from its three-part direct object. Note that this practice would still be wrong if the direct object had any number of parts and extended for many lines.

V C

x Her favorite holidays **are: Christmas, Halloween, and the Fourth of July.**

The colon separates a verb from its three-part complement (p. 384, 18a).

PREP OBJ OF PREP

x The exhibit contained works by many famous photographers, **such as: Avedon, Adams, Weston, and Lange.**

The colon separates a preposition from its four-part object.

COMPLETION OF INF PHRASES

x The Renaissance naval adventurers set out **to: sack enemy cities, find precious metals, and claim colonial territory.**

The colon separates the infinitive marker *to* from the completion of three infinitive phrases (p. 724). Even if you had a long series of such phrases, the colon would be wrong.

In each of the four examples above, you need only drop the colon to make the sentence acceptable.

28h Use no more than one colon in a sentence.

DON'T:

x She needed three things: a new hat, warmer gloves, and boots that would be serviceable in all kinds of bad conditions: snow, slush, mud, and rain.

DO:

- She needed three things: a new hat, warmer gloves, and boots that would be serviceable in snow, slush, mud, and rain.

Once you have supplied a colon, your reader expects the sentence to end with the item or items announced by the colon. A second colon makes a confusing effect.

28i Use a colon to separate hours and minutes, to end the salutation of a business letter, and to introduce a subtitle.

HOURS AND MINUTES:

- The train should arrive at 10:15 P.M.

SALUTATION:

- Dear Mr. Green:

SUBTITLE:

- *Virginia Woolf: A Biography*

EXERCISE (28a–28c, 28e–28i; for 28d, see p. 502)

1. Correct any errors in the use of colons and semicolons:

   A. A penny saved is a penny earned: but rich people, I have noticed, tend to put their pennies into shrewd investments.

B. The planning commissioner said that in his judgment the new skyscraper had: "all the earmarks of an eyesore."

C. Rescuers found that the ferry had capsized too quickly for very many people to escape at once from the enclosed lower hall; that others, in desperation, had smashed windows and taken their chances in the 37-degree water; and that still others, whether through fear or calculation, had stayed put, counting on possible air pockets to save them from drowning.

D. The robber asked for only two things; her money and her life.

E. Biff told his teammates to watch out on the next play for one of the following: a quarterback sneak; a statue of liberty play; or a dropkick field goal.

29

Dashes and Parentheses

Both dashes and parentheses, as well as commas, can be used to set off interrupting elements (p. 445, 21l). The difference is that dashes call attention to the interrupting material, whereas parentheses suggest that it is truly subordinate in meaning.

Dashes	—	most emphatic	The monsoon season—with incessant driving rain and flooding—causes much hardship.
Commas	,	"neutral"	The monsoon season, with incessant driving rain and flooding, causes much hardship.
Parentheses	( )	least emphatic	The monsoon season (with incessant driving rain and flooding) causes much hardship.

Note that a dash is typed with two unspaced hyphens, without spaces before or after: `monsoon season--with. . . .` When typing, be sure not to use hyphens where dashes are called for.

DASHES

29a Use a dash or pair of dashes to set off and emphasize a striking insertion.

- Poets have been fascinated by Narcissus—**the most modern of mythological lovers.**
- Narcissus—**the most modern of mythological lovers**—fell in love with himself.

29b If your sentence resumes after an interruption, use a second dash.

When you begin an interruption with one dash, you must end it with another.

DON'T:

x Narcissus looked into a lake—**so the story goes,** and fell in love with his own reflection.

DO:

- Narcissus—**the most modern of mythological lovers**—fell in love with himself.

DON'T:

x Although Betsy took up massage—**somebody had told her it would increase her human potential**, she soon discovered that she was too ticklish.

DO:

- Although Betsy took up massage—**somebody had told her it would increase her human potential**—she soon discovered that she was too ticklish.

29c Make sure your sentence would be coherent if the part within dashes were omitted.

— 29a

The elements of your sentence before and after the dashes must fit together grammatically.

DON'T:

x Because he paid no attention to her—**he was riveted to his cable sports channel day and night**—so she finally lost her temper.

Ask yourself whether the sentence makes sense without the material between dashes: x *Because he paid no attention to her so she finally lost her temper*. Recognizing that this shortened sentence is grammatically askew, you can then correct the original.

DO:

- Because he paid no attention to her—**he was riveted to his cable sports channel day and night**—she finally lost her temper.

29d Note the other uses of the dash.

TO INTRODUCE AN EMPHATIC EXPLANATION:

- Narcissus was the most modern of mythological lovers—**he fell in love with himself.**

TO INTRODUCE A LIST ABRUPTLY:

- At least Betsy had accumulated some souvenirs—**a black eye from Encounter, bruised ribs from Rolfing, and a whiplash from Aikido.**

TO MARK AN INTERRUPTION OF DIALOGUE:

- "Run, Jane, run!" yelled Dick. "I see the principal and he's coming toward us with—"

  "It's too late, Dick, it's too late! The curriculum enrichment consultants have blocked the gate and—"

  "Oh, Jane, oh, Jane, whatever will become of us?"

If a character's speech "trails off" instead of being interrupted, an ellipsis (p. 560, 30o) is more suitable than a dash: "*We're not . . .*" Note that you should begin a new paragraph for each change of speaker.

TO ISOLATE AN INTRODUCTORY ELEMENT THAT IS NOT THE GRAMMATICAL SUBJECT:

APP
- **Depression, compulsion, phobia, hallucination**—these disorders often require quick and emphatic treatment.

In a sentence that makes a "false start" for rhetorical effect (p. 321, 14g), you want to give a signal that the opening element is an appositive (p. 451, 21n) rather than the subject of the verb. A dash serves the purpose.

29e Do not use more than one set of dashes in a sentence.

Dashes work best when used sparingly. Within a single sentence, one interruption marked by dashes should be the maximum.

DON'T:

x We cannot expect a tax reform bill—or indeed any major legislation—to be considered on its merits in an election year—a time when the voters' feelings—not the country's interests—are uppermost in the minds of lawmakers.

DO:

- We cannot expect a tax reform bill, or indeed any major legislation, to be considered on its merits in an election year—a time when the voters' feelings, not the country's interests, are uppermost in the minds of lawmakers.

29f Do not combine a dash with a comma or a period.

— 29f

DON'T:

x The people who knew Betsy most intimately,—her doctor, her pharmacist, and her lawyer—were eager to know what she would try next.

DO:
- The people who knew Betsy most intimately—her doctor, her pharmacist, and her lawyer—were eager to know what she would try next.

DON'T:
x She did find one organization that suited her temperament—the Cult of the Month Club—.

DO:
- She did find one organization that suited her temperament—the Cult of the Month Club.

EXERCISE (29a–29f)

1. Some or all of the following sentences show an inadvisable handling of dashes. Indicate where and why you would recommend changes of punctuation.

   A. He didn't want to accuse her of being forward with other suitors—after all, women were supposed to be more independent nowadays, but he couldn't help wondering why she had a toll-free telephone number.
   B. It is simply untrue,—and nothing you can say will convince me—that trees make wind by waggling their branches.
   C. Western clothes, rock and roll, student demonstrations for greater democracy—the Chinese government decided that things had gotten out of hand.
   D. Somehow my aunt sensed the danger—perhaps she realized that my uncle should have been home by then—and she phoned me to come over—the sooner the better—to wait with her.
   E. Since my calendar is so blank—hardly anyone has realized that I am back in town—so you can pick any date you like.

PARENTHESES

29g Use parentheses to enclose and subordinate an incidental insertion.

Parentheses are appropriate for showing the incidental, lesser status of an illustration, explanation, or passing comment.

ILLUSTRATION:

- Some tropical reptiles (**the Galápagos tortoise, for example**) sleep in puddles of water to cool themselves.

EXPLANATION:

- Julia Moore (**revered in her lifetime as "the Sweet Singer of Michigan"**) offered the memorable observation that "Literary is a work very difficult to do."

PASSING COMMENT:

- The Ouse (**a rather pretty, harmless-looking river**) is known to literary people as the body of water in which Virginia Woolf drowned herself.

29h Note the other uses of parentheses.

TO RESTATE A NUMBER:

- The furniture will be repossessed in thirty (30) days.

TO ENCLOSE A DATE:

- The article on race and gender in literary study appears in *Feminist Studies* 9, no. 3 (Fall 1983), pages 435–63.

TO ENCLOSE A CITATION:

- Guevara first began studying Marxism in Guatemala in 1954 (Liss 256–57).

29i Learn when to supply end punctuation for a parenthetic sentence within another sentence.

If your whole sentence-within-a-sentence is a statement, do not end it with a period:

- Shyness (**mine was extreme**) can be overcome with time.

But if you are asking a question or making an exclamation, do supply the end punctuation:

- Today I am outspoken (**who would have predicted it?**) and sometimes even eloquent.
- To be able to give a talk without panic (**what a relief at last!**) is a great advantage in the business world.

Notice that the parenthetic sentence-within-a-sentence does not begin with a capital letter.

29j When placing a parenthetic sentence between complete sentences, punctuate it as a complete sentence.

A whole sentence within parentheses, if it is not part of another sentence, must begin with a capital letter and contain end punctuation of its own, *within* the close-parenthesis mark:

- Shyness can be a crippling affliction. (**The clinical literature is full of tragic cases.**) Yet some victims suddenly reach a point where they decide they have been bullied long enough.

29k Do not allow parentheses to affect other punctuation.

Remember these two rules:

1. No mark of punctuation comes just before an open-parenthesis.
2. The rest of the sentence must keep to its own punctuation, as if the parenthetical portion were not there.

Thus, to decide whether a close-parenthesis mark should be followed by a comma, mentally disregard the interruption:

- After she had tried Primal Jogging and I'm-O.K.-You're-Not-O.K. (she still hadn't met any interesting men), Betsy resolved to become a Hatha Backpacker.

If you cross out the entire parenthesis, you can tell that the comma is needed (see p. 443, 21i).

• Betsy discovered (though not with true surprise) that swarms of mosquitoes were no remedy for loneliness.

Discounting the parenthesis, you can see that a comma would inappropriately separate a verb from its direct object: x *Betsy discovered, that swarms of mosquitoes were no remedy for loneliness.* (See p. 528, 27b.)

29l Use brackets, not parentheses, to interrupt a quotation.

Brackets (p. 563, 30r), not parentheses, are required when you want to insert information or commentary into quoted material.

DON'T:

x "Tatyana (Samolenko) has to be the favorite in this race," Nancy said.

DO:

• "Tatyana [Samolenko] has to be the favorite in this race," Nancy said.

EXERCISE (29g–29l)

2. Some or all of the following sentences show faulty handling of parentheses. Indicate where and why you would recommend changes of punctuation.

   A. "We'd better double-team Larry (Johnson)," the coach advised.
   B. Although some people suspect that the cocaine wave has been exaggerated by the media, most police chiefs (knowing the association between "crack" and violent crime), disagree.
   C. Student unrest reached a peak in the late 1960s. (Those were the years of strongest protest against the Vietnam War).
   D. Melody told the campers in her tent to be careful with matches, (she remembered her own early troubles) especially if they hadn't learned how to roll paper properly.
   E. A modem (a device for connecting a computer terminal to a central source of data), could easily be mistaken for an ordinary telephone.

() 29l

30 Quoting

THE LOGIC OF QUOTATION

30a Quote only when you need the quoted language to make your point.

Handling quoted material is more than a matter of being accurate, knowing where to put the punctuation marks, and giving proper acknowledgment of your sources (for the last of these, see page 181, 7a). Above all, it involves sensing when a quotation is called for and when it is not. For this purpose, review pages 97–98, 4d.

30b Recognize the punctuation marks used with quotations.

The marks used in handling quotations are double and single quotation marks, the slash, the ellipsis, and brackets.

MARK	FORM	FUNCTION
double quotation marks (30d)	" "	to mark the beginning and end of a quotation

MARK	FORM	FUNCTION
single quotation marks (30e)	‘ ’	to mark a quotation within a quotation
slash (30f)	/	to mark a line break in a brief quotation of poetry
ellipsis (30o)	. . .	to mark an omission from a quotation
brackets (30r)	[ ]	to mark an explanatory insertion within a quotation

Note that these marks have other functions as well.

MARK	OTHER FUNCTION	EXAMPLE
quotation marks	to show distance from a dubious or offensive expression	Hitler's "final solution" destroyed six million Jews.
slash	to indicate alternatives	Try writing an invoice and/or a purchase order.
	to mean "per" in measurements	ft./sec. (feet per second)
	to indicate overlapping times	the Winter/Spring issue of the journal
ellipsis	to show that a statement contains further implications	And thus he came to feel that he had triumphed over the government. How little he understood about bureaucracy. . . .
	to show that dialogue "trails off "	"What I am trying to tell youis . . . is. . . . "
brackets	to insert material into a passage that is already within parentheses	(See, however, D. L. Rosenhan in *Science* 179 [1973]:250–58.)

quot
30b

30c Avoid the unnecessary use of quotation marks.

Slang and Clichés

DON'T:

x He may be a little bit "goofy," but I think his "elevator" does, as they say, "go to the top floor."

DO:

• He may be eccentric, but I doubt that he is crazy.

When you have to apologize for your language by quarantining it within quotation marks, choose other language.

Widely Recognized Nicknames

DON'T:

x "Magic" Johnson may just be the most gifted basketball player ever.

DO:

• Magic Johnson may just be the most gifted basketball player ever.

or

• Earvin "Magic" Johnson may just be the most gifted basketball player ever.

Only when you are adding the nickname to the rest of the name, as in the last example, should you put the nickname in quotation marks.

The Title of Your Submitted Essay

DON'T:

x "Rebellion: Alternatives to Yuppiedom"

DO:
- Rebellion: Alternatives to Yuppiedom

DON'T:
x "'Nothing to Fear but Fear Itself': The Worst Days of the Depression"

DO:
- "Nothing to Fear but Fear Itself": The Worst Days of the Depression

When your title contains a quotation, indicate that fact with quotation marks. But your title itself, as it stands at the head of your essay, is *not* a quotation.

For the difference between quotation and **indirect discourse,** see p. 511, 25d.

INCORPORATING A QUOTATION

30d Use double quotation marks to set off quoted material that you have incorporated into your own prose.

If you are representing someone's speech or quoting a fairly brief passage of written work—no more than five typed lines of prose or no more than two or three lines of poetry—you should **incorporate** the quotation. That is, you should make it continuous with your own text instead of skipping lines and indenting it (p. 544, 30h). Be sure to enclose an incorporated quotation in quotation marks. In North American (as opposed to British) English, those marks should be double (" "):

- Betsy yelled, "You get away from those chocolate chips right now, you nasty old bear!"
- "Take a loftier view of your blisters," writes Dr. Dollar. "Regard them as so many lucky opportunities to expose the real inner you."

quot 30d

30e Use single quotation marks for a quotation within a quotation.

If the passage you are incorporating already contains quotation marks, change them to single marks (' '):

- E. F. Carpenter, writing in *Contemporary Dramatists*, says of Butterfield: "The playwright knows where his best work originated. 'Everything that touches an audience,' he told me, 'comes from memories of the period when I was down and out.'"

Similarly, if a title that belongs in quotation marks (p. 635, 36a) is contained within other quotation marks, make those "inside" marks single:

- "The concluding lines of Wratto's 'Ode to America,'" observes Pieper in *The Defenestrated Imagination*, "rest on an ingenious paradox."

Double Quotation within a Quotation

Try to avoid quoting a passage that already contains single quotation marks; the effect will be confusing. But if you find no alternative, change those single marks to double ones. Then check carefully to see that your *three* sets of marks are kept straight (" ' " " ' "):

- Orwell's friend Richard Rees informs us that "when Socialists told him that under Socialism there would be no such feeling of being at the mercy of unpredictable and irresponsible powers, he remarked: 'I notice people always say "*under* Socialism." They look forward to being on top—with all the others underneath, being told what is good for them.'"

  Here the main quotation is from Rees. Since Rees quotes Orwell, Orwell's words appear within single marks. But when those words themselves contain a quotation, that phrase ("*under* Socialism") is set off with double marks.

Note that British practice is just the opposite of North American: single marks for the first quotation, double marks for a quotation appearing within it, and single marks again for the very rare third quotation.

30f When incorporating more than one line of poetry, use a slash to show where a line ends.

You can incorporate as many as three lines of poetry instead of indenting them (30h). But if your passage runs beyond a line ending, you should indicate that ending with a slash preceded and followed by a space:

- Wratto tells us, "Ain't got my food stamps yet this month, & wonder if / Maybe this is fascism at last."

30g Learn how to combine quotation marks with other marks of punctuation.

1. Always place commas and periods inside the close-quotation marks. You do not have to consider whether the comma or period is part of the quotation or whether the quotation is short or long. Just routinely put the comma or period first:

   - Francis Bacon said, "To spend too much time in study is sloth."
   - "To spend too much time in study is sloth," said Francis Bacon.

2. Always place colons and semicolons outside the close-quotation marks:

   - "Sloth": that was Bacon's term for too much study.
   - Francis Bacon called excessive study "sloth"; I call it inefficiency.

3. Place question marks, exclamation points, and dashes either inside or outside the close-quotation marks, depending on

their function. If they are punctuating the quoted material itself, place them inside:

- "Do you think it will snow?" she asked.
- "Of course it will!" he replied.

But put the same marks *outside* the close-quotation marks if they are not part of the question or exclamation:

- Was Stephanie a sophomore when she said, "I am going to have a job lined up long before I graduate"?
- I have told you for the last time to stop calling me your "little sweetie"!

4. When the quotation must end with a question mark or exclamation point and your own sentence calls for a closing period, drop the period:

   - Grandpa listens to Dan Rather every evening and constantly screams, "Horsefeathers!"

5. Otherwise, the end punctuation of the quotation makes way for your own punctuation. For example, if the quoted passage ends with a period but your own sentence does not stop there, drop the period and substitute your own punctuation, if any:

   - "I wonder why they don't impeach newscasters," said Grandpa.

   The quoted passage would normally end with a period, but the main sentence calls for a comma at that point.

6. When a quotation is accompanied by a footnote number, that number comes after all other punctuation except a dash that resumes your own part of the sentence:

   - Bloomingdale's advertises women's skirts as "pencil-thin, get the point?"[6]
   - Bloomingdale's advertises women's skirts as "pencil-thin, get the point?"[6]—but in fact the skirts come in all sizes.

7. When a quotation is incorporated into your text (without indention) and is followed by a parenthetic citation (p. 188, 7c), the parenthesis comes after the final quotation marks but before a comma or period—even if the comma or period occurs in the quoted passage:

   - John Keegan begins his book about famous battles by confessing, "I have not been in a battle; nor near one, nor heard one from afar, nor seen the aftermath" (*The Face of Battle*, p. 15).

8. But if the incorporated quotation ends with a question mark or exclamation point, include it before the close-quotation marks and add your own punctuation after the parenthesis:

   - He raises the question, "How would *I* behave in a battle?" (Keegan, p. 18).

9. If you indent a quotation, setting it apart from your text, and if you then supply a parenthetic citation, skip two spaces and place the citation after all other punctuation:

   - I'm just sittin here washing television
washin telvsn
wshn t.v.
(yeah!)
wshn *tee veeee*. ("Ode to Amerika," lines 13–17)

INDENTING A QUOTATION ("BLOCK QUOTATION")

30h Indent a longer quotation.

PROSE	POETRY
Indent by ten spaces a passage of more than four lines.	Indent by ten spaces a passage of more than two or three lines; indent by fewer spaces if the lines are very long.

In the examples below, the red numbers are keyed to rules listed after the two pasages.

INDENTED PROSE:

Margot Slade points to the bond between siblings that is like no other connection between human beings: — 1

— 2

5

3,4

> Welcome to the sibling bond, that twilight zone of relationships between brothers and sisters, and any combination thereof, where parents must walk but often fear to tread. With good reason. As one well-seasoned father put it: "Under most circumstances, it can be suicide to interfere." — 6
> 7 — Siblings generally constitute an exclusive state--exclusive, that is, of parents. They are the keepers of each other's secrets and the supporters of each other's goals. They can be friends in the morning and enemies at night. (Slade 80)

5 — 2

Now let us see if this special relationship exists between the famous pair of siblings under consideration here.

The writer is quoting from Margot Slade's article, "Siblings: War and Peace." For proper citation form, see p. 188, 7c.

INDENTED POETRY:

In "Crossing Brooklyn Ferry" Whitman calls out to his fellow citizens of the future as well as the present: — 1

5 — 2

3,4,8

> I am with you, you men and women of a
>   generation, or ever so many generations hence.
> Just as you feel when you look on the river and
>   sky, so I felt.
> Just as any of you is one of a living crowd,
> I was one of a crowd, . . . — 5

— 2

By creating a bond with unborn Americans, Whitman prophesies the coming greatness of his country.

1. In most cases, introduce the passage with a colon.

quot 30h

2. Separate the passage from your main text by skipping an extra line above and below.

3. Indent the whole passage ten spaces from your left margin, or somewhat less if the quoted lines of poetry are very long.

4. If you are submitting a paper for a course, use single or double spacing according to your instructor's advice. But if you are writing for publication, double-space the passage, treating it just like your main text.

5. Omit the quotation marks you would have used to surround an incorporated quotation.

6. Copy exactly any quotation marks you find in the quoted passage itself.

7. In indenting prose, indent all lines equally if the passage consists of one paragraph or less. When you are quoting more than one paragraph of prose, indent the first line of each full paragraph by an additional three spaces.

8. In indenting poetry, follow the spacing (beginnings and endings of lines) found in the original passage (see p. 560, 30n).

30i When quoting dialogue, indent for a new paragraph with each change of speaker.

After you have completed a quotation of speech, you can comment on it without starting a new paragraph. You can also resume quoting the speaker's words after your own. But do indent for a new paragraph as soon as you get to someone else's speech.

> "I can't understand," I said, "how you can win world-class distance races without having been coached in high school or college."
>
> "Oh, but sir," he protested with a polite smile, "I have been running since I was a little child. In Kenya this is how we get from village to village."
>
> "Yes, yes, but where did you get your training?" This man seemed to defy everything I knew about the making of a great runner.
>
> "Oh, my *training*!" He threw his head back and laughed. "Mister reporter, *you* run every day, year after year, at 8,000 feet, carrying boxes and fuel and whatnot. Then please come back and tell me if you think you need some training!"

30j Learn how to punctuate a quoted speech that continues into a new paragraph.

In general, quotation marks come in pairs; for every mark that opens a quotation, there must be another to close it. But there is one exception. To show that someone's quoted speech continues in a new paragraph, put quotation marks at the beginning of that paragraph, and keep doing so until the quotation ends:

> "I have two things to bring up with you," she said. "In the first place, which of us is going to be keeping the stereo? I'd like to have it, but it's no big deal to me.
>
> "Second, what about the dog? I'm the one who brought her home as a puppy, and I intend to keep her."

Note that in such a passage, no close-quotation marks are used until the full quotation is completed.

EXERCISE (30a–30j)

1. Correct any errors in the use of quotation marks:

   A. "They don't call him "Doctor K" for nothing," said the commentator after Gooden's fifteenth strikeout.
   B. Is it true that the witness said, "I refuse to answer on the grounds that my answer might tend to incinerate me?"
   C. The poet tells us a good deal about his life when he writes,

      "Counted up Fri. and saw I still got
      Four lids and two caps,
      One lovin' spoonful,
      Three buttons from Southatheborder,
      Some coke but no Pepsi,
      And a bottle of reds.
      O Amerika we can still be friends fer a few more weeks."

   D. The secretary had never met anyone who *demanded* a MacArthur Fellowship before. "But Mr. Wratto," she protested, "That just isn't how we handle the selection process." "It is now, Toots," replied the poet. "Just write out the check for 350 grand and I promise you won't see me in here no more."
   E. That brazen young man with the tattoos and the buckskin shirt had the nerve to address me as "Toots!"

INTRODUCING A QUOTATION

30k If a quotation fits into your preceding phrase or clause, introduce it without punctuation.

The way to decide which punctuation, if any, to use in introducing a quotation is to read the quoted matter as part of your own sentence. Use introductory punctuation only if it would have been called for anyway, with or without the quotation marks:

- Macbeth expresses the depth of his despair when he characterizes life as "a tale told by an idiot."

  Since the quotation serves as an object of the writer's preposition *as*, a preceding comma would be wrong here (see p. 528, 27b). Note how smoothly the quoted passage completes the writer's sentence.

30l If a quotation does not fit into your preceding phrase or clause, introduce it with a comma or a colon.

- Reynolds comments, "A close look at Melville's fiction reveals that his literary development was even more closely tied to popular reform than was Hawthorne's."
- Baym's thesis rests on one central assumption: that "we never read American literature directly or freely, but always through the perspective allowed by theories."

In these examples, the quotations do not complete the writer's own statements—as would occur, for example, in *Baym's thesis rests on the assumption that "we never read. . . ."* You can choose between a comma and a colon to introduce a quotation that stands apart from your own prose. The comma is more appropriate for tags such as *She said* and *He remarked* (30m). When the quotation is long enough to be indented (30h), you should prefer the more formal colon (30n).

quot
30l

- Gandhi, when asked what he thought of Western civilization, smiled and replied, "I think it would be a very good idea."

  A colon would be equally correct here, but it would mark a more formal pause.

- Surrounded by surging reporters and photographers, the accused chairman tried to hold them all at bay with one repeated sentence: "I will have no statement to make before tomorrow."

  The colon is especially appropriate here because it matches *one repeated sentence* with the actual words of that sentence.

30m Follow an introductory tag like *He said* with a comma.

Even if you do not feel that a pause is called for, put a comma after an introductory clause such as *She said* or *He replied:*

- He said, "I'd like to comment on that."
- She replied, "Yes, you are always making comments, aren't you?"

If the tag follows or interrupts the quoted speech, it must still be set apart:

- "I'd like to comment on that," he said.
- "Yes," she replied, "you are always making comments, aren't you?"

30n As a rule, use a colon before an indented quotation.

Since an indented passage (p. 554, 30h) appears on the page as an interruption of your prose, you should usually introduce it with a colon, implying a formal stop.

- Here is Macbeth's gloomiest pronouncement about life:

```
                                 it is a tale
Told by an idiot, full of sound and fury,
Signifying nothing.
```

But if the passage begins with a fragment that completes your own sentence, omit the colon:

- Macbeth considers life to be

```
                                          a tale
Told by an idiot, full of sound and fury,
Signifying nothing.
```

A colon would be wrong here, since it would separate an infinitive (*to be*) from its complement (*a tale* . . .). Note that a comma would be unacceptable for the same reason.

OMITTING OR INSERTING MATERIAL

30o Use an ellipsis mark to show that something has been omitted from a quotation.

If you want to omit unneeded words or sentences from a quoted passage, accuracy requires that you show where you are doing so.

WHOLE PASSAGE:

- As I have repeatedly stated, those claims, which irresponsible promoters of tax shelter schemes continue to represent as valid, have been disallowed every time they have come before the IRS.

PARTIAL QUOTATION:

- Gomez reports that "those claims . . . have been disallowed every time they have come before the IRS."

30p Distinguish between three kinds of ellipses.

Three Dots

If an omission is followed by material from the same sentence being quoted, type the ellipsis mark as three spaced periods preceded and followed by a space:

- President Clearance declared that he had "nothing . . . to hide," and that "secrecy in University affairs is . . . contrary to all my principles."

If the sentence preceding your ellipsis ends with a question mark or exclamation point, keep that mark and add three spaced dots:

- "Is Shaw," she asked, "really the equal of Shakespeare? . . . That seems extremely dubious."
- The champion shouted, "I am the greatest! . . . Nobody can mess up my pretty face."

Four Dots

Use four dots—a normal period followed by three spaced dots—if you are omitting (1) the last part of the quoted sentence, (2) the beginning of the next sentence, (3) a complete sentence or more, or (4) one or two complete paragraphs.

- Clearance was lavish in his praise for the University: "Everything is fine. . . . We've tooled up to turn out a real classy product."
- "I resent the implication that nerve gas is being developed. . . . Besides, every safety precaution has been taken."

A four-dot ellipsis is appropriate whenever your quotation skips material and then goes on to a new sentence, whether or not you are omitting material *within* a sentence. But note that you should always have grammatically complete statements on both sides of a four-dot ellipsis.

DON'T:

x She wrote, "I am always bored. . . . nothing here to keep me occupied."

Here the four-dot ellipsis is wrongly followed by a fragment.

Row of Dots

Mark the omission of a whole line or more of poetry by a complete line of spaced periods.

Wratto continues:

What have U done fer yr poets O Amerika?
I'm sitting here waiting fer a call from the Nash
Ional Endowment fer the Arts and Humanities.
Is it arty to keep me waiting Amerika?
Is this yr crummy idea of a humanity?
. . . .
How much longer must I borrow & steal?
O Amerika I hold U responsible fer this hole in the seat of my Levis!

Notice that the line of spaced periods is about the same length as the preceding line of poetry. For nearly all omissions of prose, however, four dots should serve.

30q Avoid beginning a quotation with an ellipsis.

If you make a quoted clause or phrase fit in with your own sentence structure (p. 558, 30k), you should not use an ellipsis mark to show that you have left something out.

DON'T:

x The signers of the Declaration of Independence characterized George III as ". . . unfit to be the ruler of a free people."

DO:

• The signers of the Declaration of Independence characterized George III as "unfit to be the ruler of a free people."

quot 30q

30r Use brackets to insert your own words into a quotation.

To show that you are interrupting a quotation rather than quoting a parenthetical remark, be sure to enclose your interruption in brackets, not parentheses (p. 546, 29l):

- "None of us who saw Martina [Navratilova] play will ever forget her," he declared.

  Note that parentheses in place of brackets would imply a parenthetical remark by the speaker, not by the writer. Brackets are necessary to indicate that the quotation is being interrupted.

[*sic*]

The bracketed and usually italicized Latin word *sic* (meaning "thus") signifies that a peculiarity—for example, a misspelling—occurs in the quoted material:

- "Beachcombbing [*sic*] no longer appeals to me," Melody wired. "Send money."

Do not abuse the legitimate function of [*sic*] by applying it sarcastically to claims that you find dubious.

DON'T:

x Are we supposed to believe the "humane" [*sic*] pretensions of the National Rifle Association?

  The quotation marks are already sarcastic enough without [*sic*] to redouble the effect. But why not eliminate both devices and let the language of the sentence do its own work?

DO:

- Are we supposed to believe the humane pretensions of the National Rifle Association?

EXERCISE (30k–30r)

2. Correct any errors in the handling of quoted material:

   A. "Since I want to try a mountain gig anyway," wrote Melody on her application form, "I might as well pick up some bread being a counciler (sic)."

   B. Is Wratto referring to his high vocation when he writes that he is ". . . waiting fer a call"?

   C. In a snowstorm, says the noted Japanese poet Bashō

      "Even a horse
      Is a spectacle."

   D. Melody answered sharply "Just get off my cloud, will you"?

   E. Wordsworth writes: "O'er rough and smooth she trips along, / And never looks behind; / And sings a solitary song / That whistles in the wind."

NOTE

[1] Richard Rees, *George Orwell: Fugitive from the Camp of Victory* (London: Secker, 1961) 153.

31

Forming and Spacing Punctuation Marks

To see how punctuation marks are normally handled by typewriter or word processor, examine the typescript essays beginning on pages 147 and 217. In addition, note the following advice about forming marks and adding or omitting spaces around them.

31a Learn the three ways of forming a dash.

Dashes come in three lengths, depending on their function.

1. A dash separating numbers is typed as a hyphen:

- `pages 32-39`
- `October 8-14`
- `Social Security Number 203-64-7853`

2. As a sign of a break in thought—its most usual function—a dash is typed as two hyphens with no space between:

- `Try it--if you dare.`
- `They promise--but do not always come through with--overnight delivery.`

3. Use four unspaced hyphens for a dash that stands in the place of an omitted word:

- `He refused to disclose the name of Ms. ----.`

This is the only kind of dash that is preceded by a space; see 31g.

31b Learn how to form brackets.

If your typewriter lacks keys for brackets, you can improvise them by either

1. typing slashes (/) and completing the sides with underlinings: /_ _/
2. typing slashes and adding the horizontal lines later in ink: [ ]
3. leaving blank spaces and later writing the brackets entirely in ink: [ ]

31c Learn how to form the three kinds of ellipses.

1. An ellipsis (p. 560, 30o) is formed with three spaced dots if it signifies the omission of material within a quoted sentence. Note that a space is left before and after the whole ellipsis as well as after each dot:

- `"The government," she said, "appears to be abandoning its . . . efforts to prevent nuclear proliferation."`

2. A four-dot ellipsis, signifying the omission of quoted material that covers at least one mark of end punctuation, begins with that *unspaced* mark:

- "The government," she said, "appears to be abandoning its formerly urgent efforts to prevent nuclear prolifer-ation. . . . There may be a terrible price to pay for this negligence."

3. Leave spaces between all the dots of an ellipsis that covers a whole row, signifying the omission of one or more lines of poetry:

- The river glideth at its own sweet will:
  . . . .
  And all that mighty heart is lying still!

31d Learn the two ways of spacing a slash.

1. When a slash separates two quoted lines of poetry that you are incorporating into your text (p. 552, 30f), leave a space before and after the slash:

- Shakespeare writes, "Shall I compare thee to a summer's day? / Thou art more lovely and more temperate."

2. But if your slash indicates alternatives or a span of time, leave no space before or after the slanted line:

- We are not dealing with an either/or situation here.
- The article will appear in the Winter/Spring issue of the journal.

31e Leave two spaces after a period, a question mark, an exclamation point, or a four-dot ellipsis.

- The Chinese leaders appear to be ready for a new dialogue with the United States Should we let this opportunity

p/
form
31e

slip away? Certainly not! Remember the words of the Foreign Minister: "If we do not take steps to ensure peace, we may find ourselves drifting into war. . . . Our two nations can work together without agreeing about everything."

31f Leave one space after a comma, a colon, a semicolon, a closing quotation mark, a closing parenthesis, or a closing bracket.

- Here is the real story, we believe, of last week's disturbance: it was not a riot but a legitimate demonstration. The city police chief thinks otherwise; but his description of the "riot" is grossly inaccurate. The chief (a foe of all progressive causes) erred in more than his spelling when he wrote of a "Comunist [sic] uprising."

31g Leave no space before or after a dash, a hyphen, or an apostrophe within a word.

- Wilbur--a first-rate judge of toothpaste flavors--prefers Carter's Sparklefoam for its gum-tickling goodness.

31h When an apostrophe ends a word, leave no space before any following punctuation of the word.

- This ranch, the Johnsons', has been in the family for generations.

p/ form 31i

31i When a word is immediately followed by two punctuation marks, put them together without a space.

- Here is the true story of the "riot."

- When I heard the truth about the riot (as the police chief called it), I was outraged.
- The protest, which the police chief called the work of "Comunists" [sic], was actually organized by members of the business community.

31j Do not begin a line with any mark that belongs with the last word of the preceding line.

DON'T:

X Here is why Carol refuses to sign the petition
: she objects to the dangerously vague language
about waterfront development.

DO:

- Here is why Carol refuses to sign the petition:
she objects to the dangerously vague language
about waterfront development.

31k Do not divide an ellipsis between one line and the next.

DON'T:

X Carol objected to the petition because of "the . .
. language about waterfront development."

DO:

- Carol objected to the petition because of "the . . .
language about waterfront development."

For combining quotation marks with other punctuation marks, see p. 552, 30g. For the spacing of periods within an abbreviation, see p. 644, 36k.

EXERCISE (31a–31k)

1. If your instructor, in reading your submitted work, has found no incorrectly formed or spaced punctuation marks, skip this exercise. Otherwise, submit up to five sentences illustrating the accepted form that you now recognize.

IX

CONVENTIONS

CONVENTIONS

In this section we consider rules affecting the form a word can take. These are small matters—if you get them right. If you do not, you will be handicapped in communicating your ideas. It is essential, then, to spell and hyphenate correctly and to be accurate in showing different forms of verbs, nouns, and pronouns. And it is useful, if less urgent, to know where such conventions as italics, abbreviations, and written-out numbers are considered appropriate in a piece of writing. Once the conventions have become second nature, both you and your reader can put them out of mind and concentrate on larger issues.

32

Verb Forms

32a Note how verbs change their form to show person and number in the present tense.

Within most **tenses,** or times of action, English verbs show no differences of form for person and number. That is, the verb remains the same whether its subject is the speaker, someone spoken to, or someone (or something) spoken about, and whether that subject is one person or thing or more than one. The past-tense forms of *move*, for example, look like this:

	SINGULAR	**PLURAL**
First Person	I moved	we moved
Second Person	you moved	you moved
Third Person	he, she, it moved	they moved

But in the most common tense, the present, the third-person singular verb shows **inflection**—that is, it changes its form without becoming a different word.

	SINGULAR	PLURAL
First Person	I move	we move
Second Person	you move	you move
Third Person	he, she, it **moves**	they move

The third-person singular form of a present-tense verb ends in *-s*. If the base form of the verb ends in *-ch, -s, -sh, -x*, or *-z*, the addition is *-es*.

BASE FORM	THIRD-PERSON SINGULAR PRESENT
lurch	he lurches
pass	she passes
wash	Harry washes
fix	Betty fixes
buzz	it buzzes

In some spoken dialects of English, this third-person *-s* or *-es* does not occur. Standard written English, however, requires that you observe it. You may have to check your final drafts to be sure that your *-s* or *-es* endings are in place.

DON'T:
x When Meg **get** a new idea, she always **say** something worth hearing.

DO:
• When Meg **gets** a new idea, she always **says** something worth hearing.

32b Note how the verb tenses are formed in the active voice.

The various tenses are shown by changed forms of the base verb (*try—tried; go—went*) and through forms of *be* and *have* in combination with base (*try*) and participial (*trying*) forms (*will try, was trying, had tried, will have tried*). Here are all the active-voice forms—first, second, and third person, singular and plural—for a verb, *walk*, in eight commonly used tenses. (For passive forms, see 32d.)

ACTIVE VOICE		
Present:		
I	he, she, it	we, you (sing./pl.), they
walk	walks	walk
Present Progressive:		
I	he, she, it	we, you (sing./pl.), they
am walking	is walking	are walking
Present Perfect:		
I	he, she, it	we, you (sing./pl.), they
have walked	has walked	have walked
Past:		
I	he, she, it	we, you (sing./pl.), they
walked	walked	walked
Past Progressive:		
I	he, she, it	we, you (sing./pl.), they
was walking	was walking	were walking
Past Perfect:		
I	he, she, it	we, you (sing./pl.), they
had walked	had walked	had walked
Future:		
I	he, she, it	we, you (sing./pl.), they
will walk	will walk	will walk
Future Perfect:		
I	he, she, it	we, you (sing./pl.), they
will have walked	will have walked	will have walked

In the future tense, *I* and *we* can be accompanied by *shall* instead of *will*. *Shall* is normal in questions about plans:

- **Shall** we go to the movies?

In addition, some writers still keep to the once common use of *shall* for all first-person statements (*I shall go to the movies*) and for

verb
32b

taking a commanding tone (*you shall go to the movies!*) But *will* is now usual in these functions. Keep to *will* unless you want to make an unusually formal effect.

Principal Parts

	BASE	PAST TENSE	PAST PARTICIPLE
Regular	bake adopt compute	baked adopted computed	baked adopted computed
Irregular	choose eat write	chose ate wrote	chosen eaten written

All verbs have three **principal parts** used in tense formation: the infinitive or base form (*bake, choose*), the past tense (*baked, chose*), and the past participle (*baked, chosen*). The past participle is used with forms of *have* and with auxiliaries (*could have, would have*, etc.) to form various other past tenses (*had baked, would have chosen*, etc.). **Regular verbs**—those that simply add *-d* or *-ed* to form both the past tense and the past participle—cause few problems of tense formation. But you must take greater care to see how the following **irregular verbs** are formed.

PRINCIPAL PARTS OF IRREGULAR VERBS

BASE	PAST TENSE	PAST PARTICIPLE
awake	awaked, awoke	awaked, awoke, awoken
be	was, were	been
beat	beat	beaten, beat
become	became	become
begin	began	begun
bend	bent	bent
bite	bit	bit, bitten
bleed	bled	bled
blow	blew	blown
break	broke	broken

verb 32b

PRINCIPAL PARTS OF IRREGULAR VERBS		
BASE	**PAST TENSE**	**PAST PARTICIPLE**
bring	brought	brought
build	built	built
burst	burst	burst
buy	bought	bought
catch	caught	caught
choose	chose	chosen
come	came	come
cost	cost	cost
cut	cut	cut
deal	dealt	dealt
dig	dug	dug
dive	dived, dove	dived
do	did	done
draw	drew	drawn
dream	dreamed, dreamt	dreamed, dreamt
drink	drank	drunk
drive	drove	driven
eat	ate	eaten
fall	fell	fallen
feed	fed	fed
feel	felt	felt
fight	fought	fought
find	found	found
fit	fitted, fit	fitted, fit
fly	flew	flown
forget	forgot	forgotten, forgot
freeze	froze	frozen
get	got	gotten, got
give	gave	given
go	went	gone
grow	grew	grown
hang (an object)	hung	hung
hang (a person)	hanged	hanged
hear	heard	heard
hide	hid	hidden, hid
hit	hit	hit
hold	held	held
hurt	hurt	hurt
keep	kept	kept
kneel	knelt, kneeled	knelt, kneeled
knit	knit, knitted	knit, knitted

verb
32b

PRINCIPAL PARTS OF IRREGULAR VERBS

BASE	PAST TENSE	PAST PARTICIPLE
know	knew	known
lay (put)	laid	laid
lead	led	led
lean	leaned, leant	leaned, leant
leave	left	left
lend	lent	lent
let	let	let
lie (recline)	lay	lain
light	lighted, lit	lighted, lit
lose	lost	lost
make	made	made
mean	meant	meant
meet	met	met
pay	paid	paid
prove	proved	proved, proven
put	put	put
quit	quit, quitted	quit, quitted
read	read	read
rid	rid, ridded	rid, ridded
ride	rode	ridden
ring	rang	rung
run	ran	run
say	said	said
see	saw	seen
sell	sold	sold
send	sent	sent
set	set	set
shake	shook	shaken
shine	shone, shined	shone, shined (transitive)
shoot	shot	shot
show	showed	showed, shown
shrink	shrank	shrunk
shut	shut	shut
sing	sang, sung	sung
sink	sank	sunk
sit	sat	sat
sleep	slept	slept
slide	slid	slid
speak	spoke	spoken
speed	sped, speeded	sped, speeded

PRINCIPAL PARTS OF IRREGULAR VERBS

BASE	PAST TENSE	PAST PARTICIPLE
spend	spent	spent
spin	spun	spun
spring	sprang, sprung	sprung
stand	stood	stood
steal	stole	stolen
stick	stuck	stuck
sting	stung	stung
strike	struck	struck, stricken
swear	swore	sworn
swim	swam	swum
swing	swung	swung
take	took	taken
teach	taught	taught
tear	tore	torn
tell	told	told
think	thought	thought
throw	threw	thrown
wake	waked, woke	waked, woke, woken
wear	wore	worn
win	won	won
wring	wrung	wrung
write	wrote	written

32c Do not confuse the past tense with the past participle.

It is not enough to know the correct forms for the past participles of irregular verbs. You must also remember that past participles can form tenses only when they are combined with other words (*have gone, would have paid*). Do not use an irregular past participle where the past tense is called for.

DON'T:
x She **begun** her singing lessons last Tuesday.

DO:
• She **began** her singing lessons last Tuesday.

DON'T:
x They **seen** him put on the wrong jacket.

DO:
• They **saw** him put on the wrong jacket.

DON'T:
x We **swum** across the pool.

DO:
• We **swam** across the pool.

Similarly, do not use the past-tense form of an irregular verb with an auxiliary:

DON'T:
x We **have** already **swam** across the pool.

DO:
• We **have** already **swum** across the pool.

32d Learn the tense forms in the passive voice.

The **voice** of a verb shows whether its grammatical subject performs or receives the action it expresses. A verb is **active** when the subject performs the action (*Frankie shot Johnny*) but **passive** when the subject is acted upon by the verb (*Johnny was shot by Frankie*.)

ACTIVE VOICE:

• The paramedics **took** the old man to the hospital.

Note that the performers of the action (the paramedics) are also the grammatical subject.

PASSIVE VOICE:

• The old man **was taken** to the hospital by the paramedics.

Note that the performers of the action (the paramedics) are not the grammatical subject of the passive verb *was taken*.

One peculiarity of the passive voice is that you need not mention the performer of action at all: *Johnny was shot; The old man was taken to the hospital.* This feature can help you to remember the difference between the passive voice and the past tense. In *The ambulance went to the hospital*, the verb is past but not passive.

Here are the passive-voice forms of one verb, *show*, in the same tenses we reviewed in the active voice (p. 575):

PASSIVE VOICE		
Present:		
I	he, she, it	we, you (sing./pl.), they
am shown	is shown	are shown
Present Progressive:		
I	he, she, it	we, you (sing./pl.), they
am being shown	is being shown	are being shown
Present Perfect:		
I	he, she, it	we, you (sing./pl.), they
have been shown	has been shown	have been shown
Past:		
I	he, she, it	we, you (sing./pl.), they
was shown	was shown	were shown
Past Progressive:		
I	he, she, it	we, you (sing./pl.), they
was being shown	was being shown	were being shown
Past Perfect:		
I	he, she, it	we, you (sing./pl.), they
had been shown	had been shown	had been shown
Future:		
I	he, she, it	we, you (sing./pl.), they
will be shown	will be shown	will be shown
Future Perfect:		
I	he, she, it	we, you (sing./pl.), they
will have been shown	will have been shown	will have been shown

For the use of *shall* as an alternative to *will*, see page 575, 32b.

For the stylistic uses and limitations of the passive voice, see page 292, 12e.

32e Learn the forms and uses of the indicative, imperative, and subjunctive moods.

Verbs show certain other changes of form to convey the **mood** or manner of their action.

Indicative

Use the *indicative* mood if your clause is a statement or a question:

- The secretary of state **advises** the president.
- **Does** the secretary of state **advise** the president?

The forms of the indicative mood are those already given for normal tense formation (pp. 575, 581).

Imperative

Use the *imperative* mood for giving commands or directions, with or without an explicit subject:

- **Call** the police at once.
- You **stay** out of this!

The imperative mood uses the second-person form of the present tense.

Subjunctive

For a variety of less common purposes, use the *subjunctive* mood.

1. Hypothetical conditions:

   - He is, as it **were**, a termite gnawing at the foundations of our business.

     As it were is a fixed expression indicating that the writer is using a figure of speech (pp. 368–79, Chapter 17) instead of making a literal statement.

- If I **were** on the moon now, I would tidy up the junk that has been left there. [not **was**]
- I wish I **were** in Haiti now. [not **was**]

2. *That* clauses expressing requirements or recommendations:

- The IRS requires that everyone **submit** a return by April 15. [not **submits**]
- It is important that all new students **be** tested immediately. [not **are**]

3. Expressions of a wish in which *may* is understood:

- long **live** the Queen [not **lives**]
- **be** it known [not **is**]
- so **be** it [not **is**]
- **suffice** it to say [not **suffices**]

For nearly all verbs, the subjunctive differs from the indicative only in that the third-person singular verb loses its *-s* or *-es: come what may*, not *comes what may*. The verb *to be* uses *be* for "requirement" clauses (*I demand that she be here early*) and *were* for hypothetical conditions (*if he were an emperor*).

The following chart summarizes the contrast between the subjunctive and indicative moods. Subjunctive verbs are underscored. For further discussion of sentences proposing the imagined consequences of hypothetical conditions, see page 508, 25b.

	SUBJUNCTIVE	**INDICATIVE**
	Hypothetical conditions with imagined consequences:	**Possibilities or probabilities with real consequences:**
Verb *to be*	• If I <u>were</u> a parent, I **would carry** life insurance.	• When I **am** a parent, I **will carry** life insurance.
Other verbs	• If he <u>**married**</u> your sister, you **would be** brothers.	• If he **marries** your sister, you **will be** brothers.

verb
32e

	SUBJUNCTIVE	INDICATIVE
	***That* clauses expressing requirement or recommendation:**	**Actions that occur, have occurred, or will occur:**
Verb *to be*	• The government requires that tax returns **be** strictly accurate.	• My tax return **was** as accurate as I could make it.
Other verbs	• The art department insists that a lecturer **leave** all lights on during a slide show.	• Because my art lecturer **leaves** the lights on during every slide show, the class **stays** awake.

EXERCISES (32a–32e)

1. Consider the following one-word sentence: *Choose!*

   A. Name the person, tense, voice, and mood of that verb.
   B. Write a brief sentence using the same verb in a different person, tense, voice, and mood.
   C. Identify the person, tense, voice, and mood of the verb in your sentence.

2. Look through the list of principal parts for irregular verbs (pp. 576–79), and find three verbs whose past tense and/or past participle strike you as especially tricky. For each of the three verbs, submit four sample sentences, showing:

   (a) the past tense, active voice;
   (b) the past participle, active voice;
   (c) the past tense, passive voice; and
   (d) the past participle, passive voice.

3. Submit five original sentences illustrating different uses of the subjunctive voice.

33

Plurals and Possessives

33a Do not confuse the plural and possessive forms of nouns.

SINGULAR	PLURAL	SINGULAR POSSESSIVE	PLURAL POSSESSIVE
temple	temples	temple's	temples'
pass	passes	pass's	passes'
squash	squashes	squash's	squashes'
annex	annexes	annex's	annexes'
Ford	Fords	Ford's	Fords'

In making a noun plural (*two temples; three Fords*), *do not* use an apostrophe. (For the only exceptions, see 33h–j.) In making a noun possessive (*the temple's roof; the Fords' debt to their grandfather*), *always* use an apostrophe.

DON'T:
x The two **priest's** made many **contribution's** to the parish.

DO:
• The two **priests** made many **contributions** to the parish.

DON'T:
x The **Kennedy's** have been stalked by tragedy.

DO:
• The **Kennedys** have been stalked by tragedy.

DON'T:
x In many **place's** the **oceans** depth is unknown.

DO:
• In many **places** the **ocean's** depth is unknown.

DON'T:
x The **clocks** hands stopped all across the city.

DO:
• The **clocks'** hands stopped all across the city.

PLURALS

33b Form the plural of most nouns by adding *-s* or *-es* to the singular, as in *computers.*

bat	bats
class	classes
house	houses
song	songs
summons	summonses
waltz	waltzes

33c To form the plural of a noun ending in a consonant plus *-y*, change the *-y* to *-i* and add *-es*, as in *duties*.

army	armies
candy	candies
duty	duties
penny	pennies
warranty	warranties

33d Note the differences in plural form among nouns ending in *-o*.

Most nouns ending in a vowel plus *-o* become plural by adding *-s:*

patio	patios
studio	studios

Nouns ending in a consonant plus *-o* become plural by adding *-es:*

potato	potatoes
veto	vetoes

But some plurals disobey the rule:

piano	pianos
solo	solos
soprano	sopranos

And some words have alternative, equally correct forms:

zero	zeros/zeroes
cargo	cargos/cargoes

Where your dictionary lists two forms, always adopt the first, which is more commonly used.

33e To make a name plural, add *-s* or *-es* without an apostrophe, as in *the Smiths.*

Add *-s* to most names:

Smith	the Smiths
Perry	the Perrys
Helen	both Helens
Goodman	the Goodmans
Carolina	two Carolinas
Friedman-Bernal	Friedman-Bernals

When a name ends in *-ch, -s, -sh, -x,* or *-z,* add *-es*. The extra syllable that results should be pronounced:

Burch	the Burches
Jones	the Joneses
Weiss	the Weisses
Cash	the Cashes
Fox	the Foxes
Perez	the Perezes

33f Form the plural of a noun ending in *-ful* by adding *-s* to the end.

cupful	cupfuls
shovelful	shovelfuls
spoonful	spoonfuls

Beware of the "genteel" but incorrect *cupsful, shovelsful*, and so forth.

33g Follow common practice in forming the plural of a noun derived from another language.

A number of words taken from foreign languages, especially Greek and Latin, keep their foreign plural forms. But some foreign-based words have also acquired English plural forms. The rule for deciding which plural to use is this: look it up!

Even so, the dictionary cannot settle your doubts in every instance. It may not tell you, for example, that the plural of *appendix* is *appendixes* if you are referring to the organ but either *appendixes* or *appendices* if you mean supplementary sections at the ends of books. Similarly, your dictionary may not reveal that while an insect has *antennae*, television sets have *antennas*. The way to get such information is to note the practice of other speakers and writers.

When in doubt, prefer the English plural.

SINGULAR	**PREFER**	**NOT**
cherub	cherubs	cherubim
crocus	crocuses	croci
curriculum	curriculums	curricula
sanatorium	sanatoriums	sanatoria
stadium	stadiums	stadia

But note that certain foreign plurals are still preferred:

alumna	alumnae
alumnus	alumni
criterion	criteria
datum	data
phenomenon	phenomena
vertebra	vertebrae

Confusions between the singular and plural forms of these terms are common. Indeed, *data* as a singular is often seen in scientific publications. Many careful writers, however, while avoiding the rare *datum*, use *data* only when its sense is clearly plural: *these data*, not *this data*.

Note that Greek derivatives ending in *-is* regularly change to *-es* in the plural:

analysis	analyses
crisis	crises
parenthesis	parentheses
thesis	theses

33h To form the plural of a word presented *as* a word, add *-'s*.

Add an apostrophe and an *-s* to show the plural of a word you are discussing as a word, not as the thing it signifies:

- The editor changed all the ***he***'s in Chapter 4 to ***she***'s.

Note how the writer's meaning is made clearer by the italicizing of each isolated word but not of the -'*s* that follows it.

33i Add *-s*, without an apostrophe, to form the plural of most hyphenated nouns, capital letters, capitalized abbreviations without periods, written-out numbers, and figures.

- two stand-ins
- three *B*s
- four VCRs
- counting by fives and tens

- counting by 5s and 10s
- the 1980s

Use -*'s* wherever it is needed to avoid confusion.

DON'T:

x Charlene Armstrong Zeno uses her maiden name because she likes being called with the **As.**

> Here the plural of *A* looks confusingly like the preposition *as*.

DO:

- Charlene Armstrong Zeno uses her maiden name because she likes being called with the ***A*'s.**

When the first part of a compound term is the key identifying noun, as in *sister-in-law* and *president-elect*, add the *-s* to that noun: *sisters-in-law, presidents-elect.*

EXERCISE (33a–33i)

1. Write the plural forms of the following words:

A. ox	G. alloy	M. forkful
B. ax	H. ferry	N. phenomenon
C. phylum	I. Murphy	O. analysis
D. radio	J. tomato	P. 14
E. wish	K. wrong turn	Q. Ph.D.
F. woman	L. chairman-elect	

33j Add -*'s* to form the plural of an uncapitalized letter, an abbreviation ending in a period, or a lowercase abbreviation.

- ***a***'s, ***b***'s, and ***c***'s
- the two ***i***'s in ***iris***
- too many ***etc.***'s in your paper

poss
33k

- a shortage of **M.D.'s**
- thousands of **rpm's**

POSSESSIVES

A possessive form implies either actual ownership (*my neighbor's willow, Alice's computer*) or some other close relation (a *stone's throw, the governor's enemies*). Nouns and some pronouns form the possessive either by adding an apostrophe with or without an *-s* or by preceding the "possessed" element with *of: my husband's first wife, her parents' car, the wings of the canary.*

33k Do not add an apostrophe to a pronoun that is already possessive in meaning.

DON'T	DO
x his'	• his
x her's, hers'	• hers
x our's, ours'	• ours
x your's, yours'	• yours
x their's, theirs'	• theirs
x who'se	• whose

Note also that the possessive pronoun *its* (like *his*) has no apostrophe. *It's* is the correct form for the contraction of *it is* but a blunder for the possessive *its*. Similarly, *who's* is the correct contraction for *who is* but a blunder for the possessive *whose*.

DON'T:
x This album is **her's.**

DO:
• This album is **hers.**

DON'T:

x Why don't you drive **our's** and we drive **your's**?

DO:

• Why don't you drive **ours** and we drive **yours**?

DON'T:

x The dog seems to have lost **it's** collar.

DO:

• The dog seems to have lost **its** collar.

DON'T:

x This is the man **who's** stereo broke down.

DO:

• This is the man **whose** stereo broke down.

Again:

DON'T:

x The college canceled **it's** Saturday night film series.

x **Its** a baby girl!

x **Its'** a baby girl!

x **Whose** going to make the announcement?

DO:

• The college canceled **its** Saturday night film series.

• **It's** a baby girl!

• **Who's** going to make the announcement?

33l Add *-'s* to form the possessive of a singular noun, as in *the computer's power.*

• farm's

• Bill's

• Hayakawa's

Follow the rule even if the singular noun ends with an *-s* or *-z* sound:

- horse's
- bus's
- quiz's
- Les's
- Jones's
- Keats's

Exception for Certain Names

In names of more than one syllable, the *-s* after the apostrophe is optional when it might not be pronounced.

PRONOUNCED *-S*	UNPRONOUNCED *-S*
Dickens's	Dickens'
Berlioz's	Berlioz'
Demosthenes's	Demosthenes'

Whichever of these practices you follow, make sure you keep to it throughout a given piece of writing.

33m Watch for certain unusual singular possessives.

Where an added *-s* would make for three closely bunched *-s* or *-z* sounds, use the apostrophe alone:

- Moses'
- Ulysses'
- Jesus'

Note also that in certain fixed expressions (*for* —— *sake*), the possessive *-s* after a final *-s* sound is missing: *for goodness' sake,* *for conscience' sake, for righteousness' sake.* Some writers even drop the apostrophe from such phrases. But note the *-'s* in *for heaven's sake.*

33n Make most plural nouns possessive by adding an apostrophe alone, as in *the elephants' stampede.*

- several **days'** work
- the **Americans'** views
- the **dictionaries'** definitions
- the **Stuarts'** reigns
- the **Beatles'** influence

33o If a plural noun does not end in *-s,* add *-'s* to form the possessive.

- the **children**'s room
- those **deer**'s habitat
- the **mice**'s tracks
- the **alumni**'s representative

33p In "joint ownership" possessives like *Simon and Garfunkel's music,* give the possessive form only to the final name

When two or more words are "joint possessors," make only the last one possessive:

- Laurel and **Hardy**'s comedies
- John, Paul, George, and **Ringo**'s movie
- Sally and **Vic**'s restaurant

But give the possessive form to each party if different things are "owned":

- **John**'s, **Paul**'s, **George**'s, and **Ringo**'s personal attorneys once met to see whether the Beatles could be kept from splitting up.

33q In a phrase like *my father-in-law's car,* add *-'s* to the last of the hyphenated elements.

- the mayor-**elect**'s assistant
- a Johnny-come-**lately**'s arrogance

33r To avoid an awkward possessive, make use of the *of* construction.

DON'T:
x the **revised and expanded edition's** index

DO:
- the index **of the revised and expanded edition**

Wherever an *-'s* possessive sounds awkward, consider shifting to the *of* form. Suppose, for example, your "possessing" term or your "possessed" one is preceded by several modifiers. You can get rid of the bunched effect by resorting to *of.*

A possessive form following a word in quotation marks may sound all right but look awkward on the page. Again, prefer the *of* construction.

DON'T:
x **"La Bamba"**'s insistent rhythm

DO:
- the insistent rhythm **of "La Bamba"**

Watch, too, for an unnatural separation of the *-'s* from the word it belongs with.

DON'T:
x **the house on the corner's** roof

DO:
• the roof **of the house on the corner**

Finally, nouns for inanimate (nonliving) things often make awkward possessives.

DON'T:
x **the page's** bottom

x **social chaos's** outcome

DO:
• the bottom **of the page**

• the outcome **of social chaos**

33s Notice which indefinite pronouns form the possessive with *of*.

Some indefinite pronouns (p. 422, 20k) form the possessive in the same manner as nouns: *another's, nobody's, one's*. But others can be made possessive only with *of:*

of	all	few	several
	any	many	some
	both	most	such
	each	much	

DON'T:
x I have two friends in Seattle, and I can give you **each's** address.

DO:
• I have two friends in Seattle, and I can give you the address **of each**.

poss
33t

33t Learn the other uses of the apostrophe.

Contractions

Use an apostrophe to join two words in a contraction:

did not	didn't
have not	haven't
can not, cannot	can't
she will	she'll
we will	we'll
they are	they're
he is	he's
he has	he's
you have	you've

Beware of placing the apostrophe at the end of the first word instead of at the point where the omission occurs.

DON'T:

x He **did'nt** have a chance.

x They **have'nt** done a thing to deserve such punishment.

DO:

- He **didn't** have a chance.
- They **haven't** done a thing to deserve such punishment.

Omission of Digits

Use an apostrophe to mark the omission of one or more digits of a number, particularly of a year: *the summer of '92*. In dates expressing a span of time, however, drop the apostrophe: *1847–63*. And omit the apostrophe when you are shortening page numbers: *pp. 267–91*.

Certain Past-Tense and Passive Forms and Past Participles

Use an apostrophe to form the past tense or past participle of a verb derived from an abbreviation or a name:

- Martinez was **KO'd** in the twelfth round.
- They **Disney'd** the old amusement park beyond recognition.

"Possessives" Indicating Duration

- an **hour's** wait
- five **years'** worth of wasted effort

EXERCISES (33j–33t)

2. Write the alternative possessive form for each of the following:

    A. of the victor
    B. of the bystanders
    C. for the sake of goodness
    D. of a Pisces
    E. of the children
    F. of the louse
    G. a journey of four days
    H. the wives of the Yankee pitchers
    I. the partnership of Manny, Moe, and Jack
    J. the fault of somebody

3. In the following sentences, correct any inadvisable use (or absence) of apostrophes.

    A. The battered, barnacle'd, leaky ship's prow was a sorry sight.
    B. Melody was'nt altogether sure why she found herself on the ferry to Marthas Vineyard.
    C. In Advance'd Placement English we were Shakespeared to the point of crying, "Hold, enough!"
    D. In the spring of 87 she traded in her rusty Mazda '626.
    E. Its no simple matter to follow *One Hundred Years of Solitude's* plot.

34

Spelling and Hyphenation

SPELLING

If spelling causes you trouble, do not label yourself a poor speller and leave it at that; work to eliminate the wrong choices. You can attack the problem on two fronts, memorizing the right spellings of single words and learning rules that apply to whole classes of words. We will cover both of these strategies below.

If there is one key to better spelling, it is the habit of consulting your college dictionary whenever you are in doubt (p. 333, 15a). You need not pick up the dictionary until you have completed a draft, but you should check your final copy carefully for both habitual misspellings and typing errors.

With a Word Processor: If your word processing program contains a built-in spell checker, or if you have access to a stand-alone one, use it to search for errors and to locate the proper forms for correction. A spell checker can recognize only those words contained in its built-in dictionary, and it will miss erroneous word choices and typos that correctly form other words: *it's* for *its, envelope* for *envelop, jungle* for *jingle,* etc. You will have to evaluate each flagged instance and keep searching for unflagged problems. When your spell checker does turn up a habitual misspelling on your part, add the word to your spelling list (below).

34a Keep a spelling list.

Keep an ongoing spelling list, including not only the words you have already misspelled in your essays but also words whose spelling in published sources looks odd to you. To begin that list, review the "commonly misspelled words" on pages 603–9 below and the Index of Usage that begins on page 682. You will find that many problems of inappropriate meaning really stem from confusion over spelling.

The most serious misspellings are not those that would eliminate you from the finals of a spelling contest but slips with ordinary words. If you regularly make such slips, you may not be able to cure them simply by noting the correct versions. You will need to jog your memory with a special reminder. Try a three-column spelling list, using the middle column to show how the real word differs from the misspelling.

MISSPELLING	REMEMBER	CORRECT SPELLING
x (seperate)	not like *desperate*	sep**a**rate
x (alot)	one word is not *a lot*	a lot
x (hypocracy)	not like *democracy*	hypocr**is**y
x (heighth)	get the *h* out of here!	height
x (concieve)	*i* before *e* except after *c*	conc**ei**ve
x (wierd)	a *weird* exception to *i* before *e*	w**ei**rd
x (mispell)	don't *miss* this one!	mi**ss**pell
x (fiting)	doesn't sound like *fighting*	fi**tt**ing
x (beautyful)	*y* misspell it?	beaut**i**ful
x (goverment)	*govern* + *ment*	gover**n**ment
x (complection)	*x* marks the spots	comple**x**ion

34b Note how spelling differs among English-speaking countries.

Many words that are correctly spelled in British English are considered wrong in American English. Canadian English resembles

British in most but not all features. Study the following differences, which are typical.

AMERICAN	CANADIAN	BRITISH
cent**er**	cent**re**	cent**re**
col**or**	col**our**	col**our**
flav**or**	flav**our**	flav**our**
preten**se**	preten**ce**	preten**ce**
real**ize**	real**ize**	real**ise**
travel**er**	travel**ler**	travel**ler**

34c Check the spelling of words with unusual pronunciation.

Words Having Silent Letters

column

mortgage

sword

Wednesday

Words Having Letters Unpronounced by Some Speakers

environment

government

pumpkin

recognize

strength

withdrawal

Words Frequently Mispronounced

1. Added or erroneous sound:

athlete	(not (athalete)
escape	(not excape)
height	(not heighth)
memento	(not momento)

pejorative (not perjorative)
realtor (not realator)
wintry (not wintery)

2. Sound sometimes left unpronounced:

arctic
candidate
probably
quantity
sophomore
surprise
temperament
temperature
veteran

3. Sounds sometimes wrongly reversed:

jewelry (not jewlery)
modern (not modren)
nuclear (not nucular)
perform (not preform)
professor (not perfessor)
perspiration (not prespiration)

34d Review other commonly misspelled words.

A good way to begin your private spelling list (p. 601, 34a) is to look through the following commonly misspelled words, along with those already mentioned above, and pick out the ones that trouble you. (The letters *C/B* indicate Canadian and British forms wherever they differ from American.)

absence
accidentally
accommodate
acknowledgment
across
actually

address
adolescence, adolescent
aggravate, aggravated, aggravating
aggress, aggressive, aggression
allege
all right
a lot
altogether
always
analysis, analyses (*plural*)
analyze
anesthesia
annihilate
apparent
appearance
appreciate, appreciation
aquatic
argument
assassin, assassination
assistant, assistance
attendance
bachelor
balloon
beggar
benefit, benefited; *C/B:* benefitted
besiege
bigoted
bureau
bureaucracy, bureaucratic
burglar
bus
cafeteria
calendar
camouflage
category
ceiling
cemetery
changeable
commit, commitment
committee
competent
concomitant
conscience
conscious
consensus
consistent, consistency
consummate
control, controlled, controlling
controversy
convenience, convenient
coolly

corollary
correlate
correspondence
corroborate
counterfeit
criticism, criticize
decathlon
deceive
defendant
defense; *C/B:* defence
definite, definitely
deity
dependent
desirable
despair
desperate, desperation
destroy
develop, development
diarrhea
dilapidated
dilemma
disastrous
discipline
dispensable
divide
divine
drunkenness

duly
ecstasy
eighth
emanate
embarrass, embarrassed, embarrassing
equip, equipped, equipment
evenness
exaggerate
exceed
excellent, excellence
exercise
exhilarating
existence
exorbitant
expel
extraordinary
fallacy
familiar
fascinate
fascist
February
fiend
fiery
finally
forehead
foresee, foreseeable

forfeit
forty
fourth
friend
fulfill
fulsome
futilely
gases
gauge
glamour, glamorous
grammar, grammatically
greenness
grievance, grievous
gruesome
guarantee
guard
handkerchief
harangue
harass
heroes
hindrance
hoping
idiosyncrasy
imagery
immediate
impel
inadvertent
incidentally
incredible
independent, independence
indestructible
indispensable
infinitely
innuendo
inoculate
interrupt
irrelevant
irreparable, irreparably
irreplaceable, irreplaceably
irresistible, irresistibly
jeopardy
judgment; *C/B:* judgement
knowledge, knowledgeably
laboratory
legitimate
leisure
length
library
license; *C/B:* licence
loneliness
lying
maintenance
maneuver
manual

marriage

marshal (*verb and noun*), marshaled, marshaling

mathematics

medicine

millennium, millennial

mimic, mimicked

mischief, mischievous

missile

more so

naive (*or* naïve)

necessary

nickel

niece

noncommittal

noticeable, noticing

occasion

occur, occurred, occurring, occurrence

omit, omitted, omitting, omission

opportunity

optimist, optimistic

paid

pajamas

parallel, paralleled

paralysis, paralyze

parliament

pastime

perceive

perennial

perfectible, perfectibility

permanent

permissible

phony

physical

physician

picnic, picnicked, picnicking

playwright

pleasant

pleasurable

possess, possession

practically

practice; *C/B:* practice (*noun*), practise (*verb*)

predominant

privilege

probably

pronunciation

propaganda

propagate

psychiatry

psychology

pursue, pursuit

putrefy

sp 34d

quizzes
rarefied
realize
receipt
receive
recipe
recognizable
recommend
refer, referred, referring
regretted, regretting
relevant, relevance
relieve
remembrance
reminisce, reminiscence
repellent
repentance
repetition
resistance
restaurant
rhythm
ridiculous
roommate
sacrilegious
said
schedule
secretary

seize
sergeant
sheriff
shining
shriek
siege
significance
similar
smooth (*adjective and verb*)
software
solely
soliloquy
sovereign, sovereignty
specimen
sponsor
stupefy
subtlety, subtly
succeed, success
succumb
suffrage
superintendent
supersede
suppress
surprise
symmetry
sympathize

tariff	unnecessary
tendency	unshakable
terrific	unwieldy
than	vacillate
therefore	vacuum
thinness	vegetable
thorough	vengeance
threshold	venomous
through	vice
traffic, trafficked, trafficking	vilify, vilification
tranquil, tranquillity	villain
transcendent, transcendental	wield
transfer, transferred, transferring	withhold
	woeful
tries, tried	worldly
truly	writing
unconscious	yield
unmistakable, unmistakably	

34e Note how words change their spelling when certain suffixes are added to them.

A **suffix** is one or more letters that can be added at the end of a word to make a new word (*-ship, -ness*, etc.) or a new form of the same word (*-ed, -ing*, etc.). Since many spelling mistakes are caused by uncertainty over whether and how the root word changes when the suffix is tacked on, you should go over the following rules. (If a rule is hard to follow, you can get the point by studying the sample words that accompany it.)

sp 34e

1. **Beauty→Beautiful.** Change a final *-y* preceded by a consonant to *-i* when adding suffixes other than *-ing*.

easy	easily
happy	happier, happiest
hurry	hurries
imply	implies
ordinary	ordinarily
salty	saltier
tyranny	tyrannical
ugly	ugliness

2. **Hurry→Hurrying.** Do not drop the final *-y* of a word when adding *-ing*.

embody	embodying
gratify	gratifying
study	studying

3. **Desire→Desirable.** When adding a suffix that begins with a vowel, usually drop a final *-e*.

drive	driving
future	futuristic
hope	hoping
impulse	impulsive
mate	mating
sincere	sincerity
suicide	suicidal

Exceptions: In words ending in *-ce* or *-ge*, retain the "s" or "j" pronunciation by keeping the *-e* before a suffix that begins with *a* or *o*.

notice	noticeable
peace	peaceable
courage	courageous
manage	manageable

And note two further exceptions:

acre	acreage
mile	mileage

4. **Advance→Advancement.** Usually keep the final *-e* of a word when adding a suffix that begins with a consonant.

precise	precisely
safe	safely
tame	tameness

Exceptions: Look out for a few words that drop the *-e* before adding a suffix beginning with a consonant.

argue	argument
judge	judgment (in American English)
nine	ninth
true	truly

5. **Beg→Begging.** In a one-syllable word having a final consonant that is preceded by a single vowel, double the consonant before adding a suffix beginning with a vowel.

chop	chopper
clip	clipped
fun	funnier
thin	thinnest

6. In a word of more than one syllable having a final consonant that is preceded by a single vowel, follow these suffix rules.

   a. **Prefer→Preferring.** If the word is accented on its last syllable, double the consonant before adding a suffix that begins with a vowel.

begín	beginning
detér	deterrent
contról	controlled
occúr	occurrence
regrét	regrettable

   b. **Differ→Difference.** If the accent does not fall on the last syllable, do not double the final consonant.

ópen	opener
shórten	shortened
stámmer	stammering
trável	traveler (in American English)

   c. **Prefer→Preference.** If, when you add the suffix, the accent shifts to an earlier syllable, do not double the final consonant.

confér	cónference
infér	ínference
refér	réference

34f Remember the old jingle for *ie/ei.*

i before *e*	(achieve, believe, friend, grieve)
except after *c*	(deceive, ceiling, receive)
or when sounded like *a*	
as in *neighbor* and *weigh*	(freight, neighbor, vein, weigh)

Exceptions:

ancient	efficient	leisure	seize
conscience	foreign	science	weird

34g Overcome the confusion between *-cede, -ceed,* and *-sede.*

accede concede intercede precede recede secede	Several words end in *-cede.*
exceed proceed succeed	Only three words end in *-ceed.*
supersede	This is the only word that ends in *-sede.*

EXERCISE (34a–34g)

1. Go through all the previously graded papers (for this and other courses) that you have on hand, noting all the words that were marked as misspelled. Then carefully review the list on pages 603–9, checking the words you think you might misspell. From these two sources, begin a spelling list such as the one shown on page 601. Submit ten entries from your list, using the three-column format ("Misspelling," "Remember," "Correct Spelling").

HYPHENATION

34h Observe the conventions for dividing words at line endings.

In a manuscript or typescript, where right-hand margins are normally uneven, you can avoid breaking words at line endings. Just finish each line with the last word you can complete. A word processing program (Chapter 40) will do this for you automatically unless you specify otherwise.

When you do choose to hyphenate, follow these conventions:

1. Divide words at syllable breaks as marked in your dictionary. Spaces or heavy dots betwen parts of a word indicate such breaks: *en•cy•clo•pe•di•a*.
2. Never divide a one-syllable word, even if you might manage to pronounce it as two syllables (*rhythm, schism*).
3. Do not leave one letter stranded at the end of a line (*o-ver, i-dea*), and do not leave a solitary letter for the beginning of the next line (*Ontari-o, seed-y*).
4. If possible, avoid hyphenating the last word on a page.
5. If a word is already hyphenated, divide it only at the fixed hyphen. Avoid *self-con-scious, ex-pre-mier*.
6. You can anticipate what your dictionary will say about word division by remembering that:
   a. Double consonants are usually separated: *ar-rogant, sup-ply*.
   b. When a word has acquired a double consonant through the adding of a suffix, the second consonant belongs to the suffix: *bet-ting, fad-dish*.
   c. When the root of a word with a suffix has a double consonant, the break follows both consonants: *stall-ing, kiss-able*.

34i In terms like *ex-wife,* use a hyphen to separate certain prefixes from the root words to which they are attached.

A **prefix** is a letter or a group of letters that can be placed *before* a root word to make a new word. (Compare **suffix,** p. 609, 34e.) Dictionaries do not always agree with each other about hyphenation after a prefix, but the following guidelines will enable you to be consistent in your practice.

All-, Ex-, Self-

Words beginning with *all-*, *ex-*, and *self-*, when these are prefixes, are hyphenated after the prefix:

- all-powerful
- ex-minister
- self-motivated

Note that in words like *selfhood, selfish, selfless*, and *selfsame*, the accented syllable *self* is not a true prefix; no hyphen is called for.

Prefixes with Names

Prefixes before a name are always hyphenated:

- pre-Whitman
- un-American
- anti-Soviet

Words Like *Anti-Intellectual* and *Preempt*

Prefixes ending with a vowel usually take a hyphen if that same vowel comes next, or if a different following letter would make for an awkward or misleading combination:

- anti-intellectual
- semi-independent
- pro-organic
- co-worker

But prefixed terms that are very common are less likely to be misconstrued, and many double vowels remain unhyphenated:

- cooperate
- coordinate
- preempt
- reentry

Some dictionaries recommend a dieresis mark over the second vowel to show that it is separately pronounced: *reëntry*. In contemporary prose, however, you will not come across many instances of the dieresis.

Constructions Like *Post-Heart Surgery*

When a prefix applies to two or more words, attach it to the first one with a hyphen:

- a **pre-**aurora borealis phenomenon
- the **anti-**status quo faction

Constructions Like *Pre- and Postwar*

When a modifier contains compound prefixes, the first prefix usually stands alone with a hyphen, whether or not it would take a hyphen when joined directly to the root word:

- There was quite a difference between **pre-** and postwar prices.
- **Pro-** and antifascist students battled openly in the streets of Rome.

34j Follow your dictionary in deciding whether to hyphenate words like *bull's-eye* and *skydive*.

Many compound words (formed from more than one word) are hyphenated in most dictionaries: *bull's-eye, secretary-treasurer, spring-cleaning, water-ski* (verb only), and so forth. Many others, however, are usually written as separate words (*fire fighter, head start, ice cream, oil spill*, etc.) or as single unhyphenated words (*earring, scofflaw, scoutmaster, skydive*, etc.). To make matters more confusing, practice is always in flux; as compound terms become more familiar, they tend to lose their hyphens. All you can do, then, is be alert to the compound words you see in print and consult an up-to-date dictionary whenever you are in doubt.

34k Study the guidelines for hyphenating compound modifiers.

Compound modifiers (containing more than one word) such as *light sensitive* and *second-hand* pose especially tricky problems of hyphenation. The rules (below) are hard to remember and are not always observed by otherwise careful writers. You will often have to call on your assessment of the case at hand. If an expression would be ambiguous (uncertain in meaning) without a hyphen, include it; but omit the hyphen if you see that your reader can get along without it.

Before Modified Term: ***A Well-Trained Philosopher***

A compound modifier is usually hyphenated if it meets two conditions:

1. it comes before the term it modifies; and
2. its first element is itself a modifier.

These two conditions are met in the following examples:

- a **short-tempered** umpire (MOD)
- some **deep-ocean** drilling (MOD)
- **nineteenth-century** art (MOD)
- an **out-of-work** barber (MOD)

In such phrases the hyphens sometimes prevent confusion. Consider what would happen, for example, if you wrote:

X a short tempered umpire

X some deep ocean drilling

Is the umpire short in stature but tempered in judgment? Is it the drilling rather than the ocean that is deep? When hyphens are added, a reader can see at once that *short* is part of the compound modifier *short-tempered* and that *deep* is part of the compound modifier *deep-ocean*. In such a case the hyphen tells us not to take the next word to be the modified term.

If the first two words in a compound modifier are nouns, as in *school program administrator*, do not put a hyphen between them. A noun generally runs a low risk of being mistaken for a modifier of the next word. The following phrases are correct:

- the **ocean salinity** level (**ocean salinity** = MOD)
- a **barbecue sauce** cookbook (**barbecue sauce** = MOD)
- a **mercury vapor** lamp (**mercury vapor** = MOD)

But do use a hyphen if the initial noun is followed by a modifier:

- a **picture-perfect** landing (**picture-perfect** = MOD)
- that **time-honored** principle (**time-honored** = MOD)

> Here the hyphens are needed to show that the initial noun does not stand alone; it is part of a compound modifier.

Even when the first part of a compound modifier is itself a modifier, leave it unhyphenated if it forms a familiar pair with the following word and if there is no danger of confusion:

- the **Modern Language** Association (**Modern Language** = MOD)
- an **electric typewriter** store (**electric typewriter** = MOD)
- the **happy birthday** card (**happy birthday** = MOD)

After Modified Term: *A Philosopher Well Trained in Logic*

When a compound modifier *follows* the modified term, the hyphen usually disappears:

- A barber **out of work** resents people who cut their own hair.

Modifiers Like *Barely Suppressed*

When a compound modifier contains an adverb in the *-ly* form, it does not have to be hyphenated in any position. There is no danger of ambiguity, since the adverb, clearly identifiable *as* an adverb, can only modify the next word:

- a **barely suppressed** gasp
- an **openly polygamous** chieftain
- a **hypocritically worded** apology

Modifiers Like *Fast-Developing*

Adverbs lacking the *-ly* form do run the risk of ambiguity. Whether they come before or after the modified term, you should always hyphenate them:

- a **fast-developing** crisis
- a **close-cropped** head of hair
- The traffic was **slow-moving.**

Modifiers with Fixed Hyphens

If you find that a modifier is hyphenated in the dictionary, keep it hyphenated wherever it occurs:

- She was an **even-tempered** instructor.
- She was **even-tempered.**

Split Modifiers

In an expression like *a time- and money-consuming operation*, you want to be sure to put a hyphen after the first as well as the second part of the split modifier. Otherwise, that first part looks like a noun standing by itself. The result can be disastrous, as is shown by the following instructions on a bottle of car wax:

x You need only wipe your car with a damp cloth to reactivate its brilliant dirt and dust-repelling shine.

Reactivate its brilliant dirt? A hyphen after *dirt* is required to show that the writer means *dirt-repelling*.

34l Study the guidelines for hyphenating numbers.

Numbers *Twenty-one* to *Ninety-nine*

Always hyphenate these numbers, even when they form part of a larger number:

- Two hundred **seventy-five** years ago, religious toleration was almost unknown.

Number as Part of a Modifier

If the number and the term it modifies work together as a modifier, place a hyphen after the number:

- A **twelve-yard** pool is hardly long enough for swimming.

Noun Formed from a Number

Hyphenate all such nouns:

- Two **eighty-year-olds** were sitting on the bench.
- Three **sixty-five-year-olds** were standing nearby.

Fraction

Hyphenate all fractions, regardless of whether or not they serve as modifiers.

AS MODIFIER:

- The luggage compartment was **five-eighths** full.

NOT AS MODIFIER:

- **Five-eighths** of the space had already been taken.

34m Use a hyphen to connect numbers expressing a range, as in 1989-93.

- pages 37-49 [the pages 37 through and including 49]
- September 11-October 4 [from September 11 through October 4]
- 1987-1991 [from 1987 through 1991]

EXERCISES (34h–34m)

2. If it were necessary to hyphenate these words at the end of a line, where would breaks be appropriate? Indicate possible breaks by vertical lines.

   A. overripe
   B. ex-Republican
   C. passionate
   D. butted
   E. penning

3. Correct any errors of hyphenation in the following items:

   A. selfsufficient
   B. antiAmerican
   C. semi-incapacitated
   D. redesign
   E. pre and postinflationary
   F. suicide leap
   G. father-in-law
   H. an ill schooled student
   I. The doctor was poorly prepared.
   J. Teachers are under-paid.
   K. a bad looking thunderhead
   L. a finely-tuned violin
   M. sixty-five days
   N. a hundred-thirty-one times
   O. a three sixteenths opening
   P. four-elevenths of those people

Q. forty-three eighty-ninths
R. a delay of between 8-10 hours
S. between pages 45-50
T. a completely unsettling experience

35

Capitals

35a Capitalize the first letter of every sentence or intentional sentence fragment.

- **She** will need help when she moves.
- **Count** on me.
- **Will** you be able to come over on Sunday?
- **With** pleasure!

35b Learn when to capitalize within a quotation.

First Letter of the Quotation

Capitalize the first letter of a quotation if (1) it begins your own sentence, (2) it begins the sentence of a speaker or thinker whose words you are representing, (3) it is capitalized in the original and it doesn't help to complete a clause or phrase of your own, or (4) it is a customary capital beginning a line of poetry.

BEGINNING OF THE WRITER'S OWN SENTENCE:

- "**Cellular** telephones" was the phrase Max kept muttering to himself as he walked through Sofia, wondering how a society could have survived so long without the bare necessities of technology.

BEGINNING OF A SPEAKER'S OR THINKER'S SENTENCE:

- Bessie told Max, "**There's** nothing like a good American cup of freeze-dried coffee."

CAPITALIZED IN THE ORIGINAL:

- As Ben Jonson remarked, "**Talking** and eloquence are not the same: to speak, and to speak well, are two things."

Notice how the sentence from Ben Jonson stands apart from the language introducing it. But when a passage beginning with a capital letter does help to complete a clause or phrase of your own, change the capital to lowercase:

- Ben Jonson believed that "**talking** and eloquence are not the same: to speak, and to speak well, are two things."

Here, *talking* is part of the quoter's subordinate clause (p. 388, 18c) already under way, *that talking and eloquence are not the same*.

CAPITAL BEGINNING A LINE OF POETRY:

- One would have thought, writes Spenser, that nature had imitated "**Art**, and that Art at nature did repine."

Here, although the quotation helps to complete the quoter's own clause (*that nature had imitated art*), the capital *A* is retained because it begins a poetic line.

Significant Capital in the Quoted Passage

- Spenser fancies that "**Art** at nature did repine."

Even though this *Art* is not the first word in the line of poetry, its capitalization seems to be important in the original passage and thus is retained.

35c Learn when to capitalize after a colon.

As a rule, leave the next letter after a colon uncapitalized.

UNCAPITALIZED:

- Home was never like this: **twenty-four** roommates and a day starting at 5:00 A.M.
- I finally understood how the Air Force makes a pilot of you: **after** the crowded barracks, every cadet yearns for the solitude of flight.

Do use a capital letter, however, if (1) you are quoting a poetic passage that begins with such a letter, (2) you want to make an especially formal effect, or (3) the element following your colon consists of more than one sentence.

CAPITALIZED:

- At Antony's death, Cleopatra speaks her unforgettable lament: "**And** there is nothing left remarkable / Beneath the visiting moon."
- The sign at the gate left no room for misunderstanding: **Trespassers** would be shot.
- Jacqueline was left with two nagging questions: **To** whom could she turn for help? And would anyone believe her story?

35d Capitalize the first word of a sentence in parentheses only if the parenthetic sentence stands between complete sentences.

CAPITALIZED:

- Max and Bessie had a fine time in Moscow. (**They** especially liked shopping for used blue jeans and drinking Pepsi with Herb and Gladys.) But in Bulgaria Max missed the whole World Series because no one would lend him a shortwave radio.

UNCAPITALIZED:

- Dr. Dollar's best seller, *Be Fat and Forget It* (**the** publisher decided on the title after a brainstorming session with his advertising staff), has freed millions of Americans from needless anxiety.

cap
35f

35e Capitalize the first, the last, and all other important words in a title or subtitle.

If an article, a coordinating conjunction, or a preposition does not occur in the first or last position, leave it in lowercase:

- *The House* ***of the*** *Seven Gables*
- *The Mismeasure* ***of*** *Man*
- *Dr. Dollar Raps* ***with the*** *Newborn*

Do capitalize the first letter of a subtitle:

- *Peasants into Frenchmen:* ***The*** *Modernization of Rural France, 1870–1914*
- "Male Gymnasts: **The** Olympic Heights"
- "Working within the System: **A** Guide to Sewer Repair"

35f Capitalize both parts of most hyphenated terms in a title.

The Modern Language Association recommends that you capitalize both parts of a hyphenated term in a title:

- ***Fail-Safe***
- *Through the* ***Looking-Glass***
- ***Self-Consuming*** *Artifacts*

When an obviously minor element is included in a hyphenated term, however, leave it uncapitalized:

- "A Guide to Over-**the**-Counter Medications"

35g Capitalize the name of a person, place, business, or organization.

- Joyce Carol Oates
- Western Hemisphere
- New Canaan, Connecticut
- Lifeboat Associates
- Canadian Broadcasting Corporation
- Marvelous Max's Junktiques

35h Capitalize an adjective derived from a name.

- Shakespearean
- Malthusian
- the French language
- Roman numerals

But note the use of lowercase in *roman type* and *french fries*.

35i Capitalize a word like *father* only if you are using it as a name or part of a name.

NAME OR PART OF NAME (CAPITALIZED):

- Everyone has seen posters of **Uncle** Sam.
- Oh, **Mother**, you're so old-fashioned!

NOT PART OF NAME (UNCAPITALIZED):

- My **uncle** Sam wasn't the same man after the Dodgers moved to Los Angeles.
- You are the only **mother** on this block who objects to pierced noses.

35j Capitalize a rank or title only when it is joined to a name or when it stands for a specific person.

CAPITALIZED:

- **General** Norman Schwarzkopf
- The **Colonel** was promoted in 1983.

UNCAPITALIZED:

- Two **generals** and a **colonel** attended the parade.
- She was elected **mayor** in 1989.

35k Capitalize the name of a specific institution or its formal subdivision but not of an unspecified institution.

When you are designating a particular school or museum, or one of its departments, use capitals:

- **Museum** of Modern Art
- **University** of Chicago
- the **Department** of **Business Administration**
- Franklin **High School**

Subsequent, shortened references to the institution or department are sometimes left uncapitalized:

- She retired from the *university* last year.

But *University* would also be correct here.

Do not capitalize a name that identifies only the *type* of institution you have in mind:

- a strife-torn **museum**
- Every **university** must rely on contributions.

- She attends **high school** in the daytime and **ballet school** after dinner.

35l Capitalize a specific course of study but not a general branch of learning.

CAPITALIZED:

- **Physics** 1A
- **Computer Science** 142B

UNCAPITALIZED:

- He never learned the rudiments of **physics.**
- Her training in **computer science** won her a job as a programmer.

If a branch of learning is a language, however, capitalize it: *German, English, Japanese.*

35m Capitalize a sacred name but not a secular word derived from it.

Whether or not you are a believer, use capitals for the names of deities, revered figures, and holy books:

- the **Bible**
- **God**
- the **Lord**
- **Allah**
- the **Virgin Mary**
- **Buddha**
- the **Gospels**
- the **Koran**

But do not capitalize a secular word derived from a sacred name:

- **biblical** tones
- a **godlike** grandeur
- her **scriptural** authority
- the **gospel** of getting ahead

The pronouns *he* and *him*, when referring to the Judeo-Christian deity, have traditionally been capitalized, but this practice is less common today. You can consider it optional.

35n Capitalize the name of a historical event, movement, or period.

- the Civil War
- the Depression
- the Romantic poets
- the Bronze Age
- the Roaring Twenties

Note that *the* is uncapitalized in these examples.

35o Capitalize a day of the week, a month, or a holiday but not a season or the numerical part of a date.

CAPITALIZED:

- next **Tuesday**
- **May** 1988
- **Christmas**
- **Passover**
- **Columbus Day**

UNCAPITALIZED:

- next **fall**
- a **winter** storm
- July **twenty-first**
- the **third** of August

35p Capitalize the name of a group or nationality but not of a looser grouping.

CAPITALIZED:

- **Moslem**
- **Hungarian**
- **Friends** of the **Earth**

UNCAPITALIZED:

- the **upper class**
- the **underprivileged**
- **environmentalists**

35q Capitalize a word like *south* only if you are using it as a place name.

CAPITALIZED:

- **Northwest** Passage
- **Southeast** Asia
- The **South** and the **Midwest** will be crucial in the election.

UNCAPITALIZED:

- **northwest** of here
- Go **west** for two miles and then turn **south.**

cap 35r

35r Reproduce a foreign word or title as you find it in the original language.

- *Märchen* [Ger: fairy tale]
- *una cubana* [Sp.: a Cuban woman]
- *La terre* [title of a French novel: *The Earth*]

35s Notice that a word may have different meanings in its capitalized and uncapitalized forms.

- The Pope is **Catholic.** [He belongs to the Church.]
- George has **catholic** tastes. [His tastes are wide-ranging.]
- He became a **Democrat** after he married Rosa. [He joined the party.]
- Tocqueville saw every American farmer as a **democrat.** [He believed that they all supported the idea of equality.]

EXERCISE (35a–35s)

1. Correct any errors of capitalization:

   A. Our most musical president was Harry Truman, who, after reading a review of one of his Daughter Margaret's concerts, threatened to beat up the critic.
   B. Each year the Pelicans fly south to build their nests near the outfall pipe.
   C. Realizing that her marriage was in trouble, Susan went straight to the lingerie department and asked whether she could try on a Freudian slip.
   D. She wondered Whether it was really necessary for the management to frisk people who lingered near the meat counter.
   E. Stanley believed that the People, guided by himself and a few trusted friends, knew more about their true interests than any politician did.
   F. Max and Bessie spent the whole summer in Ireland, where they hoped to trace the ancestry of the Boston celtics.
   G. Dr. Dollar's Gospel was to worship the Almighty Goddess Success.

H. A University lacking an Art School is hardly worthy of the name.
I. Bob and Ray maintained that the prince of Wales ought to be a civil service position.
J. In a parisian cafe Bessie told Max, "you won't believe this, but some jerk in the kitchen must have accidentally dropped some stale bread into this Onion Soup."

36

Italics, Abbreviations, Numbers

ITALICS

Ordinary typeface is known as **roman,** and the thin, slightly slanted typeface that contrasts with it is **italic**—as in *these three words*. In manuscript or typescript, "italics" are indicated by underlining, although with a word processor and an appropriate printer, you can make direct use of italics.

MANUSCRIPT:

- The Great Gatsby

TYPESCRIPT:

- `The Great Gatsby`

PRINT OR WORD PROCESSOR:

- *The Great Gatsby*

36a Learn which kinds of titles belong in italics.

ITALICS:

One Hundred Years of Solitude	[a book]
Paradise Lost	[a long poem published as a whole volume]
Waiting for Godot	[a play]
Casablanca	[a film]
New York Times	[a newspaper]
Popular Mechanics	[a magazine]
Abused Children	[a pamphlet]
The Firebird	[a long musical work]
The Smithsonian Collection of Classic Jazz	[a record album]
Jazz Matinee	[a radio series]
The Bill Cosby Show	[a television series]
Van Gogh's *Starry Night*	[a painting]
Rodin's *Adam*	[a sculpture]
Quicken 1.5	[computer software]

QUOTATION MARKS:

"Araby"	[a short story]
"To Autumn"	[a poem]
"The Political Economy of Milk"	[a magazine article]
"Magic and Paraphysics"	[a chapter of a book]
"Smoke Gets in Your Eyes"	[a song]

Note the following special conditions:

1. In the name of a newspaper, include the place of publication in the italicized title:

   • She read it in the *Philadelphia Inquirer*.

   The article preceding the place name is usually not italicized (or capitalized).

2. The title of a poem, story, or chapter may also be the title of

the whole volume in which that smaller unit is found. Use italics only when you mean to designate the whole volume:

- "The Magic Barrel" [Bernard Malamud's short story]
- *The Magic Barrel* [the book in which Malamud's story was eventually republished]

3. Some publications, especially newspapers, use italics sparingly or not at all. If you are writing for a specific publication, follow its style. If not, observe the rules given here.

4. Do not italicize or use quotation marks around sacred works and their divisions.

   DO:

   - the Talmud
   - the Vedas
   - the Book of the Dead
   - the Bible
   - the New Testament
   - Leviticus

5. When one title contains another title that would normally be italicized, make the embedded title roman. That is, you should not underline it.

   - She was reading *The Senses of* Walden to get ideas for her paper.

36b Italicize a foreign term that has not yet been adopted as a common English expression.

STILL "FOREIGN" (ITALICIZE):

- *la dolce vita*
- *sine qua non*
- *La Belle Époque*
- *Schadenfreude*

FAMILIAR IN ENGLISH (DO NOT ITALICIZE):

- ad hoc
- blitzkrieg
- cliché
- de facto
- guru
- junta
- status quo
- sushi

Latin Abbreviations

Latin abbreviations are often italicized, but the tendency now is to leave them in roman. For example, according to the general practice these may be left in roman:

cf.	et al.	i.e.	viz.
e.g.	f., ff.	q.v.	vs.

See pages 639–40, 36g, for the meanings of these and other abbreviations used in documentation.

Translating a Foreign Term

When translating into English, put the foreign term in italics and the English one in quotation marks:

- The Italian term for "the book" is *il libro;* the French term is *le livre*.

The Modern Language Association also allows a translation to be placed within single quotation marks without intervening punctuation:

- *ein wenig* 'a little'
- They called the Fiat 500 *Topolino* 'little mouse.'

36c Italicize the name of a ship, aircraft, or spacecraft.

- *Queen Elizabeth II*
- *Cristoforo Colombo*
- *Air Force One*
- *Voyager 2*

But do not italicize abbreviations such as *SS* or *HMS* preceding a ship's name:

- SS *Enterprise*

36d Use italics or quotation marks to show that you are treating a word *as* a word.

- When Frank and Edith visited the rebuilt neighborhoods of their youth, they understood the meaning of the word *gentrified*.

 It would be equally correct to keep *gentrified* in roman type and enclose it in quotation marks: "gentrified."

36e To add emphasis to part of a quoted expression, italicize the key element.

If you want to emphasize one part of a quotation, put that part in italics. And to show that the italics are your own rather than the author's, follow the quotation with a parenthetical acknowledgment such as *emphasis added:*

- The author writes mysteriously of a "*rival* system of waste management" (emphasis added).

36f Use italics sparingly to emphasize a key element in your own prose.

To distinguish one term from another or to lend a point rhetorical emphasis, you can italicize (underline) some of your own language:

- No doubt she can explain where she was in the month of June. *But what about July?* This is the unresolved question.

Beware, however, of relying on emphatic italics to do the work that should be done by effective sentence structure and diction. Prose that is riddled with italics creates a frenzied effect.

DON'T:

x The hazard from *immediate radiation* is one issue—and a *very important* one. But the *long-term* effects from *improper waste storage* are *even more crucial,* and *practically nobody* within the industry seems to take it seriously.

This passage would inspire more confidence if it lacked italics altogether.

ABBREVIATIONS

36g Use abbreviations in parenthetical citations, notes, reference lists, and bibliographies.

For purposes of documentation (Chapter 7), you can use the following abbreviations.

ABBREVIATION	MEANING
anon.	anonymous
b.	born
bibliog.	bibliography
©	copyright
c. or ca.	about [with dates only]
cf.	compare [not *see*]
ch., chs.	chapter(s)
d.	died
diss.	dissertation
ed., eds.	editor(s), edition(s), edited by
e.g.	for example [not *that is*]
esp.	especially

ABBREVIATION	MEANING
et al.	and others [people only]
etc.	and so forth [not interchangeable with *et al.*]
f., ff.	and the following [page or pages]
ibid.	the same [title as the one mentioned in the previous note]
i.e.	that is [not *for example*]
introd.	introduction
l., ll.	line(s)
ms., mss.	manuscript(s)
n., nn.	note(s)
N.B.	mark well, take notice [*nota bene*]
n.d.	no date (in a book's imprint)
no., nos.	number(s)
p., pp.	page(s)
pl., pls.	plate(s)
pref.	preface
pt., pts.	part(s)
q.v.	see elsewhere in this text [literally *which see*]
rpt.	reprint
rev.	revised, revision; review, reviewed by [beware of ambiguity between meanings; if necessary, write out instead of abbreviating]
sc.	scene
sec., secs., sect., sects.	section(s)
ser.	series
st., sts.	stanza(s)
tr., trans.	translator, translation, translated by
v.	versus [legal citations]
viz.	namely
vol., vols.	volume(s)
vs.	versus [ordinary usage]

Note that *passim,* meaning "throughout," and *sic,* meaning "thus," are not to be followed by a period; they are complete Latin words. For the function of *sic,* see page 563, 30r.

36h Learn which abbreviations are appropriate in your main text.

Appropriate in Main Text

Some abbreviations are considered standard in any piece of writing, including the main body of an essay:

1. *Mr., Ms., Mrs., Dr., Messrs., Mme., Mlle., St.,* etc., when used before names. Some publications now refer to all women as *Ms.*, and this title has rapidly gained favor as a means of avoiding designation of marital status.
2. *Jr., Sr., Esq., M.D., D.D., D.D.S., M.A., Ph.D., LL.D.*, etc., when used after names: *Olivia Martinez, M.D.*
3. abbreviations of, and acronyms (words formed from the initial letters in a multiword name) for, organizations that are widely known by the shorter name: CIA, FBI, ROTC, NOW, NATO, UNESCO, and so on. Note that very familiar designations such as these are usually written without periods between the letters.
4. *B.C., A.D., A.M., P.M., mph*. These abbreviations should never be used apart from numbers (not x *I use the computer in the P.M.* but *I use the computer between 8 and 11 P.M.*). *B.C.* always follows the year, but *A.D.* usually precedes it: *252 B.C.*, but *A.D. 147*.
5. places commonly known by their abbreviations: *U.S., D.C., USSR*, etc. One writes *in the U.S.*, not *in U.S.* Do not use *D.C.* alone as a place name: x She commutes into *D.C.* Prefer *Washington*.

Inappropriate in Main Text

	DON'T	DO
1. titles	the Rev., the Hon., Sen., Pres., Gen.	the Reverend, the Honorable, Senator, President, General
2. given names	Geo., Eliz., Robt.	George, Elizabeth, Robert

	DON'T	DO
3. months, days of the week, and holidays	Oct., Mon., Vets. Day	October, Monday, Veterans Day
4. localities, cities, counties, states, provinces, and countries	Pt. Reyes Natl. Seashore, Phila., Sta. Clara, N.M., Ont., N.Z.	Point Reyes National Seashore, Philadelphia, Santa Clara, New Mexico, Ontario, New Zealand
5. roadways	St., La., Ave., Blvd.	Street, Lane, Avenue, Boulevard
6. courses of instruction	Bot., PE	Botany, Physical Education
7. units of measurement	ft., kg, lbs., qt., hr., mos., yrs.	feet, kilogram, pounds, quart, hour, months, years

Technical versus Nontechnical Prose

In general, you can do more abbreviating in technical than in nontechnical writing. See the following examples.

TECHNICAL WRITING	OTHER PROSE
km	kilometer(s)
mg	milligram(s)
sq.	square

Even in general-interest prose, however, abbreviation of a much-used term can be a convenience. Give one full reference before relying on the abbreviation:

- Among its many services, the Harvard Student Agency (HSA) sponsors the *Let's Go* series of travel books for students. HSA also functions as a custodial agency, rents photographic equipment and linens, acts as an employment clearinghouse, and caters parties.

36i Be consistent in capitalizing or not capitalizing abbreviations following times.

Authorities disagree over A.M. and P.M. versus *a.m.* and *p.m.* Either form will do, but do not mix them.

DON'T:

x She was scheduled to arrive at 11 **a.m.,** but we had to wait for her until 2 **P.M.**

DO:

- She was scheduled to arrive at 11 **a.m.,** but we had to wait for her until 2 **p.m.**

or

- She was scheduled to arrive at 11 **A.M.**, but we had to wait for her until 2 **P.M.**

36j Learn which kinds of abbreviations can be written without periods.

Good writers differ in their preference for periods or no periods within an abbreviation. Practice is shifting toward omission of periods. In general, you can feel safe in omitting periods from abbreviations written in capital letters, provided the abbreviation does not appear to spell out another word. Thus *USA* needs no periods but *U.S.* does, since otherwise it might be mistaken for a capitalization of the pronoun *us*. Other typical abbreviations without periods are:

- JFK
- USSR
- IOU
- NJ

Note that *N.J.*, with periods, is an option for abbreviating *New Jersey* but not for supplying a mail code before a ZIP number: *NJ 08540*.

But most abbreviations that end in a lowercase letter still require periods:

- Ont.
- Chi.
- Inc.
- i.e.

Note that there are commonly recognized exceptions such as *mph* and *rpm*. Also, abbreviations for metric measures are usually written without periods: *ml, kg,* etc.

36k Leave single spaces between the initials of a name, but close up all other abbreviations and acronyms, including postal abbreviations for states.

SPACED:

- T. S. Eliot
- E. F. Hutton
- A. J. P. Taylor

UNSPACED:

- e.g.
- A.M. (or a.m.)
- Ph.D
- CIA

POSTAL ABBREVIATIONS FOR STATES

Alabama	AL	Montana	MT
Alaska	AK	Nebraska	NE
Arizona	AZ	Nevada	NV
Arkansas	AR	New Hampshire	NH
California	CA	New Jersey	NJ
Colorado	CO	New Mexico	NM
Connecticut	CT	New York	NY
Delaware	DE	North Carolina	NC
District of Columbia	DC	North Dakota	ND
Florida	FL	Ohio	OH
Georgia	GA	Oklahoma	OK
Hawaii	HI	Oregon	OR
Idaho	ID	Pennsylvania	PA
Illinois	IL	Rhode Island	RI
Indiana	IN	South Carolina	SC
Iowa	IA	South Dakota	SD
Kansas	KS	Tennessee	TN
Kentucky	KY	Texas	TX
Louisiana	LA	Utah	UT
Maine	ME	Vermont	VT
Maryland	MD	Virginia	VA
Massachusetts	MA	Washington	WA
Michigan	MI	West Virginia	WV
Minnesota	MN	Wisconsin	WI
Mississippi	MS	Wyoming	WY
Missouri	MO		

num 36l

NUMBERS AND FIGURES

36l Know which circumstances call for written-out numbers.

Technical versus Nontechnical Prose

In scientific and technical prose, figures *(67)* are preferred to written-out numbers (*sixty-seven*), though very large multiples such as *million, billion,* and *trillion* are written out. Newspapers customarily spell out only numbers *one* through *nine* and such round numbers as *two hundred* and *five million*. In your nontechnical writing, prefer written-out numbers for the whole numbers *one* through *ninety-nine* and for any of those numbers followed by *hundred, billion,* and so on.

TECHNICAL PROSE	NONTECHNICAL PROSE
3/4	three-quarters
4	four
93	ninety-three
202	202
1500 (or 1,500)	fifteen hundred
10,000	ten thousand
38 million	thirty-eight million
101 million	101 million
54 billion	fifty-four billion
205 billion	205 billion

Special Uses for Written-Out Numbers

1. In nontechnical prose, write out a concise number between one thousand and ten thousand that you can express in hundreds: not *1600* but *sixteen hundred*. This rule does not apply to dates, however.

2. Write out round (approximate) numbers that are even hundred thousands:

- Over six hundred thousand refugees arrived here last year.

3. Always write out a number that begins a sentence.

   - **Eighty-four** students scored above grade level.

   But if the number would not ordinarily be written out, you would usually do better to recast the sentence.

   - The results were less encouraging for **213** other takers of the test.

     It would have been awkward to begin the sentence with *Two hundred thirteen.*

4. Write out a whole hour, unmodified by minutes, if it appears before *o'clock, noon,* or *midnight: one o'clock, twelve noon, twelve midnight.* Avoid x *twelve-thirty o'clock* or x *12:30 o'clock.*

Special Uses for Figures

1. Use figures with abbreviated units of measure:

   - 7 lbs.
   - 11 g
   - 88 mm

2. If you have several numbers bunched together, use figures regardless of the amounts:

   - Harvey skipped his birthday celebrations at ages **21, 35,** and **40.**

3. When two or more related amounts call for different styles of representation, use figures for all of them:

   - The injured people included **101** women and **9** children.

4. Use figures for all of the following:

   a. apartment numbers, street numbers, and ZIP codes:

      - Apt. 17C, 544 Lowell Ave., Palo Alto, CA 94301.

   b. tables of statistics.

c. numbers containing decimals: *7.456, $5.58, 52.1 percent.*

d. dates (except in extremely formal communications such as wedding announcements): *October 25, 1989; 25 October 1989.*

e. times, when they precede A.M. or P.M. (*a.m.* or *p.m.*): *8 A.M., 6 P.M., 2:47 P.M.*

f. page numbers: *p. 47, pp. 341–53.*

g. volumes (*vol. 2*), books of the Bible (*2 Corinthians*), and acts, scenes, and lines of plays (*Macbeth I.iii.89–104*).

36m Use Roman numerals only where convention requires them.

In general, **Roman numerals** (*XI, LVIII*) have been falling into disuse as **Arabic numerals** (*11, 58*) have taken over their function. But note the following exceptions.

1. In some citation styles, upper- and lowercase Roman numerals are still used in combination with Arabic numerals to show sets of numbers in combination. Thus *Hamlet III.ii.47* refers to line 47 in the second scene of the play's third act.
2. Use Roman numerals for the main divisions of an outline (p. 85, 3q).
3. Use lowercase Roman numerals to cite pages at the beginning of a book that are so numbered:
   - (Preface v)
   - (Introduction xvi-xvii)
4. Use Roman numerals as you find them in the names of monarchs, popes, same-named sons in the third generation, ships, and so forth:
   - George III
   - Leo IV
   - Orville F. Schell III
   - Queen Elizabeth II

The following list reminds you how to form Roman numerals.

1 I	10 X	50 L	200 CC
2 II	11 XI	60 LX	400 CD
3 III	15 XV	70 LXX	499 CDXCIX
4 IV	19 XIX	80 LXXX	500 D
5 V	20 XX	90 XC	900 CM
6 VI	21 XXI	99 XCIX	999 CMXCIX
7 VII	29 XXIX	100 C	1000 M
8 VIII	30 XXX	110 CX	1500 MD
9 IX	40 XL	199 CXCIX	3000 MMM

36n Distinguish between the uses of cardinal and ordinal numbers.

Numbers like *one, two,* and *three (1, 2, 3)* are called **cardinal numbers;** those like *first, second,* and *third (1st, 2d, 3d;* note the shortened spelling) are called **ordinal numbers.** The choice between cardinal and ordinal numbers is usually automatic, but there are several differences between spoken and written convention:

SPEECH	WRITING
Louis the Fourteenth	Louis XIV
July seventh, 1989	July 7, 1989 *or* 7 July 1989
But: July seventh [no year]	July 7th *or* July seventh

Note that the rules of choice between written-out numbers and figures are the same for cardinal as for ordinal numbers (36l).

Terms Like *Firstly*

The word *firstly* is now rarely seen; *first* can serve as an adverb as well as an adjective.

ADJECTIVE:

- The **first** item on the agenda is the budget.

num
36n

ADVERB:

- There are several items on the agenda. **First,** . . .

When you begin a list with *first,* you have the option of continuing either with *second, third,* or with *secondly, thirdly*. For consistency of effect, drop all the *-ly* forms:

- Let me say, **first,** that the crisis has passed. **Second,** I want to thank all of our employees for their extraordinary sacrifices. And **third,** . . .

But as soon as you write *secondly,* you have committed yourself to *thirdly, fourthly,* and so on.

Finally, beware of mixing cardinal and ordinal forms.

DON'T:

x **One,** a career as a writer presents financial hardship. **Second,** I am not sure I have enough emotional stamina to face rejection. **Third,** . . .

For consistency, change *One* to *First*.

EXERCISES (36a–36n)

1. Correct any errors in the use of italics, abbreviations, and numbers:

   A. Most drunk drivers would find it difficult to count backward from 135 to twenty-one by threes.
   B. He had only one reason for not wanting to ride—e.g., he was afraid of horses.
   C. 40 dollars will buy an adequate dinner for 1 at that restaurant.
   D. Four six'es are twenty-four.
   E. The attack was planned for precisely 7:42 o'clock.
   F. "Gone with the Wind" was the film that introduced profane language to the Hollywood screen.
   G. Alimony was never an issue for the ex-wives of King Henry the VIIIth.
   H. *The Falmouth Enterprise* is a typical small-town newspaper.
   I. You can still get a sporty sedan, fully equipped with roll bars, seat belts, impact-absorbing bumpers, and collision insurance, for nine thousand eight hundred forty-four dollars.
   J. Melody thought that *A Midsummer Night's Dream* was the most realistic play she had ever seen.

K. She made an appointment with Dr. Calvin Gold, D.D.S.
L. The Titanic at its launching was the world's largest, and soon thereafter the world's wettest, ocean liner.
M. Over the loudspeaker came an urgent and repeated request for a dr.
N. Criminals are treated leniently in Rome if they committed their offenses during lo scirocco, the hot, dry wind that supposedly makes people behave irrationally.
O. He won the primary election on June 8th, 1976.
P. Since he hoped to become a dog trainer when his football career was over, Biff was especially eager to read the article in "National Geographic" called *Sikkim*.

The following paragraph contains errors in the use or absence of italics, abbreviations, and numbers. Find the errors and make a list of your corrections.

> No piece of criticism has ever been harsher or funnier than Mark Twain's essay, *Fenimore Cooper's Literary Offenses,* which can be found in a vol. called "Selected Shorter Writings of Mark Twain." Twain asserts that Cooper, in novels such as *The Deerslayer, The Last of the Mohicans,* et al., has committed one hundred fourteen offenses against literary art out of a possible 115. "It breaks the record," says Twain. He proves that Cooper's Natty Bumppo, the indian Chingachgook, etc., perform physically impossible deeds and speak wildly different kinds of English from 1 page to the next. The attack is hilarious, but on a 2nd reading it can also be taken as seriously indicating Twain's allegiance to the literary realism of the later XIXth century.

X

APPLIED WRITING

APPLIED WRITING

Most of the skills you have developed for the writing of essays will serve you well in answering examination questions. At the same time, it is vital to understand the ways in which the in-class situation limits your options and calls for a more direct and emphatic style of writing (Chapter 37). And to operate successfully beyond the classroom, you must familiarize yourself with some new conventions. Chapter 38 indicates several standard ways of writing a business letter. Following one of those forms, you can make an impression of competence and confidence as you apply for a job, order merchandise, reply to correspondence, state a claim, or request information. The same chapter tells you how to prepare an increasingly common form of business correspondence, the facsimile transmission. And Chapter 39 gives you a model for your résumé—a summary of your background that will show your accomplishments to best advantage in the eyes of potential employers.

37

Examination Answers and In-Class Essays

37a Be prepared for the special conditions of an examination.

Most of the skills you are developing for the writing of essays will serve you well in answering essay questions on exams. At the same time, it is vital to understand the ways in which the exam situation limits your options and calls for a more direct and emphatic style of writing. Here are eleven points of advice, the first of which you can put into operation weeks before the exam.

1. *Try to anticipate questions.* Listen and take notes throughout the term. Attend especially to topics and theories that keep coming up week after week, so that you arrive at the exam with ideas that tie together the assigned material.

2. *Read through all instructions and questions before beginning any answer.* Determine whether you must answer all the questions. If you have a choice, decide which questions you can answer best. Responding to more than the required number may take time from your strong area to answer an unnecessary question in a weaker

area, and the grader will usually be under no obligation to count "extra credit" answers.

3. *Gauge your available time.* Translate the point value of a question into a time value. A 30-point question in a 50-minute, 100-point exam should not take much more of your time than 15 minutes (30 percent of 50). If you find yourself running over, stop and leave some blank space while you get something written on *all* other questions.

4. *Note the key instruction in each question.* Always pause and study the wording of each question. Be aware that most questions begin with a key word that tells you what to do: *compare, contrast, discuss, analyze, classify, list, define, explain, summarize, describe, justify, outline.* Let that word guide the writing of your answer. If you are asked to *describe* how lasers are used to unblock obstructed arteries, do not waste time *explaining* possible causes of the obstruction. And do not be tempted into writing prepared answers to questions that were not asked. If you are to contrast *X* with *Y*, be sure you are not setting out to give 90 percent of your emphasis to *X*. If you are to state the relationship between *A* and *B*, do not throw in *C* for good measure. And if the question tells you to analyze the content and style of a quoted passage, do not suppose that a double effort on content alone will gain you full credit. Break the question into its parts and attend to all of them.

5. *Plan your answer.* For longer answers, draw up a scratch outline (p. 86, 3q), and check the outline against the question to make sure it covers the required ground.

6. *Do not waste time restating the question.* A grader can only be annoyed by a hollow introductory paragraph that merely announces your willingness to address the question. Your grader will already be looking for ideas.

7. *Begin with a clear statement of your thesis in the opening paragraph.* Use your first paragraph to announce your main point and to establish the structure of everything that will follow. Do not fear that your strategy will be made too obvious. There is no such thing as being too obvious about your thesis in an examination answer. The danger, on the contrary, is that a harried grader will miss it.

8. *Highlight your main points.* Remember that your grader will be reading rapidly and will appreciate signals that make the structure of your answer clear. Consider enumerating key points, either with actual numbers (*1, 2, 3*) or with words (*First, Second, Third*); you can even underline the most essential statements to ensure that they will come to the grader's notice.

9. *Support your generalizations with specific references.* Most essay questions are broad enough to allow for a variety of "right" answers. Give your grader evidence that you have done the reading and have thought about it carefully. Your own ideas, backed by examples drawn from the assigned reading, will be much more impressive than unsupported statements taken directly from lectures and textbooks.

10. *Keep to the point.* In an examination answer you have no time for digressions—passages that stray from the case being made. You should not, for example, try to befriend your grader with humorous asides or pleas for sympathy.

11. *Read through your completed answer.* Try to leave time to go over your answer. Read it as if you were the grader, and try to catch inconsistencies, incoherent sentences, illegible scribbles, and unfulfilled predictions about what follows. Do not hesitate to cross out whole paragraphs if necessary or to send your grader, through an inserted arrow and a boldly printed note, to an extra page in the back of the blue book.

A Sample Answer

For a further idea of the way an examination answer typically goes straight to the point and reveals its structure, read this answer to a question on an American history final.

Question:
Summarize and explain the importance of Jefferson's reforms in the Virginia Legislature after 1776.

Answer:

Thesis first → Jefferson's purpose in revising the laws of Virginia was to get rid of all traces of aristocracy and to lay the foundations

Preview of supporting points → for democratic government. There were four key reforms—governing inheritance, education, and religion—that helped to change Virginia from a royal colony to a republican state.

First, the abolition of primogeniture. This ancient practice meant that the firstborn son inherited all the father's wealth. The importance of the reform was that wealth could now be distributed among several surviving offspring, thereby breaking down the holdings of large landowners and distributing ownership to a wider number of Virginians.

Each numbered point receives a paragraph of its own. Each paragraph both summarizes and explains the importance of its point.

Second, the repeal of the laws of entail. These laws provided that a landowner who had inherited an entailed estate had to leave it whole to a fixed line of heirs. Jefferson's reform allowed an owner to divide up his property and leave it to whomever he liked. The importance, again, was that the repeal broke the power of a landed aristocracy, a sure threat to a young democracy.

Third, the establishment of a system of general education. Jefferson felt it was the duty of the state to provide education and libraries for the poor. He felt that free education was the only guarantee against tyranny—that only educated people could become useful citizens by participating in the drafting of sound laws, thereby insuring the well-being and happiness of all citizens.

And fourth, the disestablishment of the state church and the guarantee of freedom of conscience. A deist himself, Jefferson supported the ethical teachings of religion but rejected a church/state alliance, which he felt unavoidably led to favoritism and tyranny. He proposed that Virginians be free of statutory taxation in support of a state church. Jefferson's legislation went beyond mere tolerance to guarantee freedom of religion for all by law.

A brief concluding paragraph emphasizes that the terms of the question have been met. → These four reforms broke down a landed aristocracy, educated a democratic citizenry to participate in government, and guaranteed for all a separation of church and state, thereby eradicating all traces of hereditary rank and privilege in Virginia.

37b Modify your composing method to suit the conditions of an in-class essay.

Nearly all the advice in this book applies to the writing of in-class as well as at-home essays. But an in-class essay resembles an examination (37a) in requiring you to make the "first draft" fully adequate. As in an exam, you must carefully gauge your available time, be absolutely sure you are meeting the terms of the questions, and foreshorten your planning and revision.

If you are given an hour to produce an essay, do not feel that you have been directed to write for exactly sixty minutes. Take out about ten minutes for planning, and try to finish in time to read through the whole essay and make emergency corrections. The key period is the beginning: you must not start writing until you have a clear idea of your thesis. If you search for ideas as you go along, your essay will probably show a meandering structure or even a self-contradictory one.

To guide your writing, make a scratch outline (p. 86, 3q) indicating the anticipated order of your points. Steer clear of elaborate or highly unusual structures that could turn out to be unworkable. Get your thesis into the first or second paragraph, and then concentrate on backing it with important points of evidence.

Your instructor will make allowances for the time constraint when judging your essay. Remember as you write, however, that it *is* an essay—one that should show such virtues as clear statement, coherent paragraph development, and variety of sentence structure. Do not, then, write like someone who has crammed for a test and who must now hastily spill out page after page of sheer information. The length of your in-class essay will be less crucial than the way it hangs together as a purposeful structure controlled by a thesis.

In your remaining time, check first to see that you have adequately developed your thesis, and insert any needed additions as neatly as you can. Then check for legibility and correctness of usage, punctuation, spelling, and diction, making needed changes as you go. Your instructor will not object to a marked-up manuscript if it remains reasonably easy to read.

38

Business Letters and Facsimile Transmissions

38a Master the standard features of the business letter.

Customary Elements

Examine the business letter on page 666. There you see:

1. *The heading*. It contains your address and the date of writing. Notice the absence of end punctuation.

2. *The inside address*. Place this address high (or low) enough so that the body of the letter will appear centered on the page. Include the name of the addressee, that person's title or office, the name of the company or institution, and the full address:

```
Joan Lacey, M.D.
Pioneer Medical Group
45 Arrow Avenue
Omaha, NE 68104
```

```
Mr. Kenneth Herbert
Director of Personnel
Cordial Fruit Cooperative
636 Plumeria Boulevard
Honolulu, HI 96815
```

3. *The salutation*. This formal greeting appears two lines lower than the inside address:

```
Dear Dr. Lacey:                    Dear Ms. Diaz:
Dear Mr. Herbert:                  Dear Reverend Melville:
```

Ms. is now the preferred form for addressing a woman who has no title such as *Dr.* or *Professor*. Use *Miss* or *Mrs.* only if your correspondent has put that title before her own typed name in a letter to you: (*Mrs.*) *Estelle Kohut*. And unless you see otherwise, you should assume that a woman wishes to be known by her own first name, not her husband's.

When writing to an institution or a business, you can avoid the possibly offensive *Dear Sir* or *Sirs* by choosing a neutral salutation:

```
Dear Personnel Manager:            Dear Editor:
Dear Sir or Madam:                 Dear Macy's:
Dear Bursar:                       To Whom It May Concern:
```

Note that business salutations end with a colon. Only if the addressee happens to be a friend should you use a comma to strike a more informal note: *Dear Estelle, Dear Andy,* . . . .

4. *The body*. Use the body of your letter to explain the situation and to make your request or response in a straightforward, concise way. You can write briefer paragraphs than you would use in an essay. Prefer middle-level diction, avoiding both slang and legalese: not x *You really put one over on me* or x *The undersigned was heretofore not apprised of the circumstances cited hereabove* but *I was not aware of the problem*.

Single-space the paragraphs of your letter, but leave a double space between one paragraph and the next.

5. *The complimentary close*. Type the complimentary close two lines below the last line of the body. The most common formulas are:

```
Sincerely,                         Yours sincerely,
Sincerely yours,                   Very truly yours,
Yours truly,                       Cordially,
```

Of these tags, *Cordially* is the only one that hints at actual feeling.

6. *Your typed name*. Leave four lines between the complimentary close and your typed name as you intend to sign it. If you have a professional title or role that is relevant to the purpose of the letter, add it directly below your name:

```
Elizabeth Pinsky                 Jackson Marley
Assistant Manager                Lecturer
```

In general, such titles are appropriate when you are using letterhead stationery.

7. *Your signature*. Always use blue or black ink. Match your signature and your typed name; a briefer signature is a sign of impatience.

8. *Special notations*. Lowest on the page, always flush left, come notations to indicate the following circumstances if they are applicable:

NOTATION	MEANING
cc: A. Pitts F. Adler	"Carbon copies" (probably photocopies) are being simultaneously sent to interested parties Pitts and Adler.
encl.	The mailing contains an enclosure (always mentioned in the body of the letter).
att.	A document has been attached to the letter.
BR: clc *or* BR/clc	The writer (initials *BR*) has used the services of a typist (initials *clc*).

Alternative Formats

There are three recognized ways of handling the arrangement of a business letter's elements on the page. You can choose any of the three, but they make somewhat different impressions. For extreme impersonality, the *block format* works best. A middle style, very commonly used, is the *modified block format*. And if you want your business letter to have some of the flavor of a personal letter, the *indented format* is available.

Here are the specifications for all three formats:

	BLOCK FORMAT	MODIFIED BLOCK FORMAT	INDENTED FORMAT
Heading	Flush left	Toward right margin	Toward right margin
Inside Address	Flush left	Flush left	Flush left
First Lines of Paragraphs	Flush left	Flush left	Indented 5–10 spaces
Complimentary Close, Name, and Signature	Flush left	Toward right margin	Toward right margin
Special Notations	Flush left	Flush left	Flush left

("Flush left" means that the lines begin at the left margin. "Toward right margin" means they should end at or near the right margin.)

These differences may sound complicated, but they are easy to see:

BLOCK FORMAT: page 665
MODIFIED BLOCK FORMAT: pages 666, 667
INDENTED FORMAT: page 668

Note that indented format is simply modified block format plus indentions for the first lines of paragraphs.

Form of Envelope

Make the address on your envelope identical to the inside address. In the upper left corner, type your address as it appears in the heading:

```
Kevin Oppenheimer
2264 N. Cruger Avenue
Milwaukee, WI 53211


                Mr. Robert F. Stone
                Customer Relations
                Kaiser Appliances, Inc.
                834 La Salle Street
                Chicago, IL 60632
```

38b Recognize the main purposes of the business letter.

Asking for Information

Make your inquiry brief, and limit your request to information that can be sent in an available brochure or a brief reply. Be specific, so that there can be no doubt about which facts you need.

Stating a Claim

Take a courteous but firm tone, setting forth the facts so fully and clearly that your reader will be able to act on your letter without having to ask for more information. If you are complaining about a purchase, supply the date of purchase, the model and serial number, and a brief description. If you have been mistakenly billed twice for the same service or product, state what that service or product is, the date of your payment, and the check number if you paid by check. If possible, enclose a photocopy of the canceled check (both sides). In a second paragraph, calmly and fairly state what adjustment you think you are entitled to. (See page 666 for a sample claim letter.)

Ordering Merchandise

Begin by stating which items you are ordering, using both product names and stock or page numbers. Tell how many units of each item you are ordering, the price per item, and the total price. If you want to receive the shipment at a different address, say so. Mention that you are enclosing payment, ask to be billed, or provide a credit card name and number and expiration date. (See the next page for an example of a letter ordering merchandise.)

Making an Application

Tailor your letter to the particular job, grant, or program of study you are applying for. Name the opening precisely. If you are asking to be considered for a job, explain how you heard about it. If a person in authority recommended that you apply, say who it was. Tell how you can be reached, and express your willingness to be interviewed.

When applying for a job, include your **résumé** (Chapter 39) and mention that you have included it. Emphasize those elements in the résumé that qualify you for *this* position. Avoid boasting and false modesty alike. The idea to get across is that the facts of your record make such a strong case for your application that no special pleading is necessary.

The letters on pages 667 and 668 illustrate how an applicant can state qualifications in different ways for different opportunities. Both letters pertain to the résumé appearing on page 672. Notice how each letter brings out "job-related" elements in the writer's background.

SAMPLE LETTERS

[BLOCK FORMAT]

36 Hawthorne Hall
University of the North
Bridgewater, CT 06413
February 15, 1992

MacWAREHOUSE, Inc.
P. O. Box 3031
Lakewood, NJ 08701

Dear MacWAREHOUSE:

Please send me, at the address above, the following software items as described in your insert in the January 1992 issue of Macworld magazine:

1 INIT Manager	UTI 0187	$35.00
1 T-Script Basic	FON0357	$55.00

I enclose a check for $93 to cover these items plus your standard $3 shipping charge. Thank you.

Sincerely yours,

Lily Marks

Lily Marks

[MODIFIED BLOCK FORMAT]

2264 N. Cruger Avenue — 1. heading
Milwaukee, WI 53211
February 22, 1992

Mr. Robert F. Stone
Customer Relations
Kaiser Appliances, Inc. — 2. inside address
834 La Salle Street
Chicago, IL 60632

Dear Mr. Stone: — 3. salutation

4. body

The Kitchen-Aid dishwasher I purchased in your store on February 14 was installed yesterday. Unfortunately, the installation was complete before the plumber and I noticed a large chip on the edge of the white front panel. Since the panel was still in its carton when the plumber arrived, it was probably defective upon delivery. The serial number of the dishwasher is T53278004; I enclose a copy of the bill, already paid.

In my phone conversation with you yesterday, I agreed to put this complaint in writing. I would like you to send a representative here to replace the damaged panel. To fix a time, please call me at home after 5:30 P.M. at (414) 565-9776.

Thank you for your prompt attention to this matter.

Sincerely, — 5. complimentary close

Kevin Oppenheimer — 7. signature

Kevin Oppenheimer — 6. typed name

KO: sms — 8. special notations
enc.

[MODIFIED BLOCK FORMAT]

137-20 Crescent Street
Flushing, NY 11367
August 17, 1992

F 1384
New York Times
New York, NY 10018

Dear Personnel Manager:

I am applying for the position of "Accounting Aide to CPA firm," which was advertised in yesterday's Times. I have completed my second year at Queens College as an Accounting major and plan to take a year off to supplement my education with relevant work.

From my enclosed résumé, you can see that I have been working in the business offices of Gristede's Food Stores, where I have assisted the bookkeeper in auditing procedures, including applications to computerized systems. My work requires strong mathematics skills and some familiarity with the Lotus 1-2-3 and Excel spreadsheets.

As a prospective accountant, I am especially interested in spending next year with a CPA firm. I can send you the names of references both at Queens College and at Gristede's and would be grateful for the chance to be interviewed. Please write to me at the above address or call me at (718) 317-1964 after 5:30 P.M.

Sincerely yours,

Janet Madden

Janet Madden

encl.

bus 38b

[INDENTED FORMAT]

137-20 Crescent Street
Flushing, NY 11367
August 17, 1992

Ms. Charlotte DeVico
Rock of Ages Health Related
  Facility
7481 Parsons Boulevard
Flushing, NY 11367

Dear Ms. DeVico:

Mr. Gene Connelly of the Flushing YMCA has suggested I write to you about working as a recreation assistant or bookkeeper in your facility beginning this fall. I am an Accounting major with a minor in Communications, and I plan to take a year off from school to supplement my education with relevant work.

From my enclosed résumé you can see that, in addition to a business background, I have experience in working with people. At the Flushing "Y" I have helped stage the annual talent show, held informal "chat" sessions, and presented films. I enjoy this work and find the elderly full of ideas and a willingness to make themselves happy.

Mr. Connelly has offered to write you about my work at the "Y," and I can also send you the name of my supervisor at Gristede's. I would be grateful for the chance to be interviewed. Please write to me at the above address or call me at (212) 975-1122 between 9:00 A.M. and 4:30 P.M.

Sincerely yours,

Janet Madden

Janet Madden

encl.

38c Master the standard features of a facsimile transmission.

A facsimile transmission, commonly known as a fax, is a document sent over phone lines from a sending "fax machine" to a receiving one. In the business world, faxes have become a standard way of communicating without the delay required by regular or even express mail. You can send and receive faxes in your workplace or, if no machine is handy, make use of a nearby machine—for example, in a photocopying center.

A letter sent by fax can be identical to one sent by mail, but you should begin the letter on the second page of your transmission. The first page should consist of a cover sheet. For example:

Goldman and Delmer Publishers, Inc.
16 Park Plaza
Boston, MA 02116
TEL: (617) 482-2397
FAX: (617) 482-9211

FAX TRANSMITTAL SHEET

ATTN: Elizabeth Nahem

COMPANY: Stock Responses, Inc.

FAX NUMBER: (415) 525-9742

FROM: Adela Herndon

DATE: 2/4/92 TIME: 1:30 E.T.

RE: Photographs for an upcoming publication

We are transmitting 3 page(s), including cover sheet. If there are any problems with this transmission, please call us immediately at (617) 482-2397. Thank you.

39

Résumés

39a Recognize the standard features of the résumé.

Your **résumé** is a brief (usually one-page) record of your career and qualifications. Along with your letter of application (p. 664, 38b), it can land you a job interview. To that end it should be clear, easy on the eye, and totally favorable in emphasis. Have your résumé typed by a professional if your typewriter or word processor cannot create a polished, near-printed look. Divide your résumé into the following sections:

1. *Personal information.* Provide only what is necessary: name, present address, permanent address, phone numbers. Add your age, marital status, and condition of health only if you know they are relevant to the job you want.

2. *Career objective.* Include a statement of your career goals. Avoid being so specific that you exclude reasonable opportunities or so broad as to be uninformative. Cite two goals if necessary, and mention any geographical limitations.

3. *Education.* Begin with the college you currently attend or have attended most recently, and work backward to high school. (If you have already graduated from college, omit high school.) Give dates of attendance, degrees attained, major and minor areas of study, and memberships in special societies. Briefly explain any outstanding

projects or courses. Include your grade-point average only if it happens to be high.

4. *Work experience.* Begin with your current or most recent employment, and list all relevant jobs since high school. Try not to leave suspicious-looking gaps of time. Give the name and address of each employer, the dates of employment, and a brief description of your duties. Include part-time or volunteer work that may be relevant. Remember that you can mention relevant skills learned on a job that seems unrelated. If you are seeking a teaching position, consider beginning this part of your résumé with a section called *Teaching Experience* and following it with another called *Other Work Experience.*

5. *Special skills, activities, and honors.* Include special competencies that make you a desirable candidate, such as proficiency in a foreign language, ability to operate equipment, or skill in unusual procedures or techniques. Mention any honors, travel, or community service.

6. *References.* Supply the address of your college placement office, which will send out your dossier (dáhss-ee-ay) upon request. The dossier is a complete file of your credentials, including all letters of recommendation and transcripts. You may wish to give the names, positions, and addresses of three people you can trust to write strong letters in your behalf. Be sure you have their permission, however.

Further advice:

1. *Keep the format clear and the text concise.* Single-space within each section, and double-space between sections. Try to keep your résumé to one page; do not exceed two pages.
2. *Do not mention the salary you want.* You will be considered for more openings if you stay flexible on this point.
3. *Update your résumé periodically.* Do not hesitate to ask for new letters of recommendation.
4. *Rewrite your résumé for a particular job opening.* Rewriting allows you to highlight those elements of your background and goals that will suit the job you are aiming for.

JANET MADDEN

Current Address:
137-20 Crescent Street
Flushing, NY 11367
(718) 317-1964

Permanent Address:
28 Pasteur Drive
Glen Cove, NY 11542
(516) 676-0620

CAREER OBJECTIVE:	Position as accountant or assistant accountant in an accounting firm. (Temporary position as a recreation assistant or bookkeeper in a recreational facility.)
EDUCATION:	Queens College (CUNY) B. A. expected June 1992 Majoring in Accounting Minoring in Communications
	Pratt High School, Glen Cove, New York Received Regents Diploma, June 1987
EXPERIENCE:	
Summers: 1991	Assistant bookkeeper, Gristede Brothers Food Stores, Bronx, New York
1990	Dramatics Counselor, Robin Hill Day Camp, Glen Cove, New York
1989	Volunteer, Flushing YMCA. Worked with elderly. Assistant director, annual "Y" talent show.
SKILLS:	Type 65 wpm. Use Lotus 1-2-3 and Excel spreadsheets.
REFERENCES:	Placement Office Queens College Flushing, NY 11367

XI

TOOLS

TOOLS

Have you made the leap from typing (or handwriting) to word processing? Sooner or later, you almost certainly will. Chapter 40 offers some orientation to this important aid to composing. In Chapter 41, we present an alphabetical listing of troublesome expressions that make for confusion of meaning and/or spelling. One way to discover where you have been misconstruing the language is simply to check each item in that Index of Usage. Finally, Chapter 42, the Glossary of Terms, explains all the concepts that appear in boldface type throughout this book. You can use the Glossary of Terms to "brush up on grammar" as well as for spot consultation.

40

Writing with a Word Processor

DEVICE	FEATURES
Typewriter:	
Manual or electric	type only
Electronic	some memory and display some formatting options may have spell checker and thesaurus
Computer with word processing program:	
Microcomputer	full memory and display revise whole document on screen many formatting options graphics, computations may have spell checker, thesaurus, and other aids to composition connection to printer modem access to databases
Mainframe and workstation terminals	same as microcomputer, plus larger memory, greater speed, and direct access to databases

Like it or not, you already live in a society that depends heavily on electronic information storage and retrieval. As a college-educated person, you will inevitably have to become familiar with computers in your work. As a college writer, meanwhile, you probably have access to word processing facilities on your campus. At many colleges and universities, a writing center or computer center houses a bank of *microcomputers* (such as Macintoshes or IBM PCs) or workstation terminals connected to a *mainframe computer* that serves many functions on a time-sharing basis. Even if your instructor doesn't require that you make use of a word processor, you should take advantage of scheduled demonstrations and get acquainted with this aid to composition.

As the chart on page 675 suggests, the revolution has extended downward to the (electronic) typewriter as well as upward to the vastly powerful mainframe. In this chapter, however, we assume that you will be working either with a freestanding microcomputer or a workstation terminal, both of which go far beyond what even a "smart" typewriter can do.

40a Learn the functions of a word processor.

ESSENTIAL TERMINOLOGY	
Central processing unit (CPU)	the "motherboard" of circuitry through which all instructions to the computer are routed
Monitor	the box housing the screen on which your text is displayed
Cursor	a blinking light on the screen that shows "where you are" in your document. By moving the cursor with keystrokes or a "mouse" (pointing device), you can make changes at different points in the text.
Software	a program, stored on a disk, that allows the computer to do a certain kind of work: word processing, graphics, spreadsheets, etc.

ESSENTIAL TERMINOLOGY	
Disk	a storage device containing a program and/or space for filing your documents. A *floppy disk* is a plastic record that you insert into the computer's *disk drive*. A *hard disk*, with vastly greater capacity, serves the function of many floppies.
Document	one essay, chapter, chart, letter, etc., that you create and display on the monitor screen
Edit	a mode that allows you to insert, delete, and move letters, words, or blocks of text in a document you are composing or revising on the screen.
File	a document that you have saved under a specific name, so that you can retrieve it for further editing or printing. You can save your drafts as separate files or, more usually, replace each discarded draft by keeping its file name for the new version.
Save	an instruction that the computer make a record of your document in its memory (or on a disk). You should periodically "save" while creating the document, so that an unexpected power failure cannot erase your work.
Backup	a second copy of your file. Always make backups of important documents; if you lose or botch one copy, you can easily switch to the other.
Formatting	your instructions about margins, tabs, typeface and size, italics, etc.
Hard copy	a printed version of what you have created on the screen

Think of a word processor as an electronic chalkboard on which you can scribble, erase, and move text from one spot to another until you are satisfied. Then with a keystroke or two, you can get unsmudged hard copy of your work from an adjacent printer. The following chart indicates what several kinds of printers can do.

KIND OF PRINTER	SPEED	QUALITY
Dot matrix:		
"draft" mode	fast	looks dotted
"near letter quality" mode	slower	closer to print
Daisy wheel	very slow	comparable to typewriter
Ink jet	fast	superior, approaching typeset clarity
Laser	very fast	superior, approaching typeset clarity

wp 40a

Since you will never have to retype a page, a paragraph, or even a line that is already in final form, word processing will save you much time and trouble. (With "word wrap"—the computer's knack of going automatically to the next line and readjusting all the prior spaces in an altered paragraph—every change will leave the whole text looking like new.) Thus, by making small and large changes so painless, the word processor will dissolve much of your reluctance to revise. Once you have effortlessly moved a whole block of paragraphs from one section of an essay to another in half a minute, you will wonder how you ever got along without one of these machines.

Many writers concede the advantages of a word processor but feel most comfortable when writing on a legal pad or marking up a crudely typewritten draft. You will quickly find, however, that you needn't make a final choice of medium. You can start in any way that feels right to you and take a break from composing by transcribing your text onto the computer screen for further editing. Then you can quickly get back to hard copy again by ordering a "draft mode" printout at any moment. A complete printout will help you revise by allowing large structural problems to become apparent. But you will always need to have your text back on the screen when you are tidying it for a final, flawless-looking version to be handed in.

With a word processing program you can also *format* your essay at the outset, determining what it will look like on the page, including margins, space between lines, tabs, paragraph indents, type size and face, and a "header" or "footer"—for example, the placement of your name and the page number in the upper right corner of each page. When you pare down a draft or add material to it, the program will continually repaginate for you. And a feature-rich program can do the same for footnotes or endnotes (p. 207, 7e), liberating you from any fuss over renumbering or trying to squeeze extra notes onto a crowded page. If you like, you can even command that the right margin of your document be *justified* (aligned, as on this page) instead of "ragged." But since right-justified margins make for oddly spaced words, you may want to inquire whether your instructor prefers ragged ones.

A word of caution. Especially when equipped with graphics, a computer program can be so absorbing that it may distract you from the essential task of composition. Choosing a clean, readable format for your essay is one thing; adorning it with multiple typefaces, customized borders, and cartoon figures is something else again—an annoyance for your reader. If you use the word processor simply to reproduce the look of a carefully prepared typewritten page, you can't go wrong.

40b Note the unique ways in which a word processor can aid your composing.

Combined with adequate software, a computer can help you as a writer in numerous ways, some of which we have already discussed in "With a Word Processor" boxes throughout the text:

1. *Freewriting* (p. 61, 3f). To keep yourself from pausing to edit when you are freewriting, turn down the brightness control knob on your monitor. Turn it back up again when the prescribed time for freewriting has elapsed. You may also want to use the computer's alarm function as a stopwatch.

2. *Aids to invention.* Some programs include tutorial aids such as reporters' questions (p. 64, 3g), designed to stimulate your initial thinking. By responding to the questions and then performing further operations on your answers, you can speed your search for an appropriate topic and thesis.

3. *Outlining* (p. 85, 3q). If your word processing program allows you to place "windows" on the screen beside your developing draft, fill one window with your outline. Consult the outline as you proceed from paragraph to paragraph. When you see that your essay must deviate from the outline, stop to revise the entire rest

of the outline, double-checking it for coherence. With some word processing programs or stand-alone applications, you can temporarily put your draft into "outline mode," turning key sentences into outline headings and handily rearranging the order of your points.

4. *Linking paragraphs* (p. 248, 9h). If your program can highlight the first and last sentences of every paragraph, make use of it. (If not, you can still "select" those sentences and make a document out of them.) Check to see that the connections between last and next (paragraph-opening) sentences are clear, and revise if necessary to make effective use of these naturally strong positions.

5. *Word mastery* (p. 338, 15b). Put your draft papers through a "search all" command for the words that you have previously tended to misuse. With each questionable instance highlighted, you can check to see whether you now have the problem under control. With an on-line dictionary or thesaurus, you can pause and search for just the word you have been groping for. Be aware, however, that an electronic thesaurus, like a printed one, works only for expressions that are already familiar to you (p. 338, 15b).

6. *Spell checker.* You can request that the checker search your whole document for possible misspellings. Unfortunately, being "suspicious" of every term not included in its resident dictionary, it will query some names and other correctly typed words that it doesn't recognize; you can simply bypass those queries. The spell checker will also overlook "invisible" mistakes such as *to* for *too, it's* for *its,* or *cod* for *cog.* But it will alert you to all other typos and some other errors that may be more chronic with you. Thus you can use the spell checker to add items to your ongoing list of expressions you habitually misspell (p. 601, 34a).

7. *Usage and style checker.* Various available programs can analyze your draft in search of common flaws of usage, punctuation, and style—sentence fragments, excessive use of *to be,* wordiness, slang, choppy sentences, and so forth. These tools can be useful if you clearly grasp their limitations. Their "judgment" is strictly mechanical; they have no way of telling, for example, that you may be aiming at a certain effect with an intentional sentence fragment, a passive form, or a colloquialism. A usage and style checker pays off when it highlights problems that you already recognize as common in your prose.

8. *Networking*. Some composition classes offer opportunities to share your draft with fellow students and the instructor through a "local area network." This is a set of terminals or whole computers linked by a "file server"—another computer that gives all members of the network access to one another's documents. By highlighting draft passages and exchanging messages about them, the participants can put editorial suggestions into immediate practice, displaying their revisions for further evaluation. Networking thus increases both the efficiency of peer editing and the number of people who can be involved in it.

9. *Access to databases*. If your terminal is connected to a mainframe or if your microcomputer is accompanied by a *modem*—a telephone that transmits electronic data—you may be able to search databases such as your library's catalog (p. 156, 6b) or an index of articles in a certain field (p. 162, 6c). Thus you can get a start on library research before you even enter the building. Note, however, that you may have to pay for some on-line searching.

41

An Index of Usage

The Index of Usage does not dwell on differences between dialect expressions, slang, and informal usage. It simply labels *colloquial* any terms that are inadvisable for use in college essays and papers.

above (noun, adjective) Stuffy in phrases like x *in view of the above* and x *for the above reasons*. Substitute *therefore* or *for these reasons*.

accept, except The first means *receive,* the second *exclude* or *excluding*.

A.D. Should precede the date: *A.D. 1185*. It is redundant to write x *In the year A.D. 1185,* since *A.D.* already says "in the year of our Lord" (Latin *anno domini*).

adapt, adopt To *adapt* is to *change for a purpose;* to *adopt* is to *take possession. She adapted her plan to the new circumstances. They adopted the baby.*

advice, advise The first is a noun, the second a verb: *He advised that he had no need of further advice.*

affect, effect As a verb, *affect* means to *influence: Rain affected the final score. Affect* may also be used as a noun meaning *feeling* or *emotion*. The verb *effect* means to *bring about* or *cause: She effected a stunning reversal.* When *effect* is a noun, it means *result: The effect of the treatment was slight.*

afraid See *frightened*.

again, back Redundant after words that begin with the prefix *re-*, which already contain the sense of *again* or *back: rebound,* *reconsider, refer, regain, resume, revert,* etc. Do not write x *She referred back to her notes* or x *He resumed his work again* or x *They reverted back to their life of crime.*

ain't Colloquial for *is not, are not.*

all, all of Use either *all* or *all of* with separable items: either *All the skillets were sold* or *All of the skillets were sold.* When there are no items to be counted, use *all* without *of: All her enthusiasm vanished; He was a hermit all his life.*

alright The preferred spelling is *all right.*

all that Colloquial in sentences like x *I didn't like her all that much.* How much is *that much?* Try *I didn't like her very much* or, more straightforwardly, *I disliked her.*

allusion, illusion, delusion An *allusion* is a *glancing reference: an allusion to Shakespeare.* An *illusion* is a *deceptive impression: Shakespeare created the illusion of enormous battlefields.* A *delusion* is a *mistaken belief,* usually with pathological implications: *He suffered from the delusion that he was Shakespeare.*

alot A mistake for *a lot.*

already, all ready The first means *by this or that time,* the second *all prepared. It was already apparent that they were all ready for the trip.*

also Do not use as a coordinating conjunction: x *She owned two cars, also a stereo.* Try *Along with her two cars, she also owned a stereo.* Here *also* serves its proper function as an adverb.

altar, alter The first is for worship: *The priest approached the altar.* The second is a verb meaning *change: He had altered the text of his sermon.*

alternate, alternative (adjectives) *Alternate* means *by turns: on alternate Fridays. Alternative* means *substitutive: Our alternative plan might work if this one fails.*

altogether, all together The first means *entirely,* the second *everyone assembled: I was altogether delighted that we were all together at last.*

A.M., P.M. These abbreviations, which most writers now capitalize, should not be used as nouns: x *at six in the A.M.* And do not accompany *A.M.* or *P.M.* with *o'clock,* which is already implied. Write *six A.M.* or *six o'clock* but not x *six A.M. o'clock.*

among, between *Among* is vaguer and more collective than *between,* which draws attention to each of the items:

- They hoped to find one good person *among* the fifty applicants.
- Agreement was reached *between* management and the union.

Many careful writers also reserve *between* for sentences in which only two items are involved. See also *between.*

amount, number For undivided quantities, use *amount of: a small amount of food.* For countable items, use *number of: a small number of meals.* The common error is to use *amount* for *number,* as in x *The amount of people in the hall was extraordinary.*

analyzation Always prefer *analysis.*

angry See *mad.*

ante-, anti- The first prefix means *before,* the second *against: In the antebellum period, there was much antiwar sentiment.*

anybody, any body; nobody, no body; somebody, some body The first member of each pair is an indefinite pronoun: *Anybody can see. . . .* The others are adjective-noun pairs: *Any body can be dissected.*

anyway, any way, anyways *Anyway* is an adverb: *I am busy on that day, anyway. Any way* is an adjective-noun pair: *I can't find any way to break the date. Anyways* is colloquial.

anywheres Colloquial for *anywhere.*

apt, liable, likely Close in meaning. But some writers reserve *liable* to mean *exposed* or *responsible* in an undesirable sense: *liable to be misunderstood; liable for damages. Likely* means *probably destined: She is likely to succeed. Apt* is best used to indicate habitual disposition: *When you tell those slouchers to work faster, they are apt to complain.*

argue, quarrel These can be synonyms, but *argue* also has a special meaning of *make a case,* without overtones of quarrelsomeness.

around If you mean *about,* it is better to write *about: about five months,* not x *around five months.*

as (conjunction, preposition) In the sense of *because,* the subordinating conjunction *as* is often ambiguous: x *As she said it, I obeyed.* Does *as* here mean *because* or *while?* Use one or the other of those terms. And do not use *as* to mean *whether* or *that:* x *I cannot say as I do.*

as, like Both *as* and *like* can be prepositions: *as a rule; like a rolling stone.* But when you want a conjunction that will introduce a subordinate clause, always prefer *as* to *like:* not x *Like the forecaster warned, it rained all day,* but *As the forecaster warned. . . .*

as, such as Not synonyms. Do not write x *The burglar's bag contained many items, as masks, screwdrivers, and skeleton keys. Such as* would be appropriate.

as far as . . . Be sure to complete this formula with *is/are concerned.* Do not write x *As far as money, I have no complaints.* Try *As far as money is concerned, I have no complaints,* or *As for money, I have no complaints,* or, better, *I have no complaints about money.*

as good as, as much as Colloquial when used for *practically:* x *He as good as promised me the job.*

author (verb) Widely used, but also widely condemned as substandard: x *He authors historical novels.* Prefer *writes,* and keep *author* as a noun.

back of Colloquial for *behind,* as in x *You can find it back of the stove.* Prefer *behind* to both *back of* and *in back of.*

bad Do not use as an adverb meaning *badly* or *severely,* as in x *It hurt him bad.*

bare, bear *Bare* is an adjective meaning *naked* and a verb meaning to *expose: She bared the secret about her bare cupboard.* To *bear* is to *carry* or *endure: Her guilt was hard to bear until she laid it bare.*

before, ago When referring to the past from a present perspective, use *ago: I told you to get ready two hours ago, and you still aren't even dressed.* When focusing on a past time and referring to an even more distant past, use *before: She had told him to get ready two hours before, but he still wasn't even dressed.*

being (participle) Often redundant: x *The city is divided into three districts, with the poorest being isolated from the others by the highway.* Either *with* or *being* should be dropped.

bemused Means *bewildered,* not *amused.*

beside, besides The first means *at the side of,* the second *in addition: Besides, she was beside the car when it happened.*

better than Colloquial as a synonym of *more than:* x *Better than half an hour remained.*

between Requires at least two items (see *among*). Do not write either x *Hamlet's conflict is between his own mind* or x *The poems were written between 1983–84.* In the second sentence *1983–84* is one item, a period of time. Try *The poems were written between 1983 and 1984.*

Between always requires a following *and,* not *or.* Avoid x *The choice is between anarchy or civilization.*

between each, between every Because *between* implies at least two items, it should not be joined to singular adjectives like *each* and *every:* x *He took a rest between each inning.* Try *He rested after every inning* or *He rested between innings.*

between you and I A "genteel" mistake for *between you and me.* As twin objects of the preposition *between,* both pronouns must be objective in case.

bias, biased The first is a noun meaning *prejudice,* the second an adjective meaning *prejudiced.* Do not write x *Some people are bias.*

bored Should be followed by *with* or *by,* not *of.* Avoid x *He was bored of skiing.*

born, borne The first means *brought into the world,* the second *carried: She had borne many sorrows before her baby was born.*

breadth, breath, breathe *Breadth* means *width;* the noun *breath* means *respiration;* the verb *breathe* means to *take breath.*

bring, take These words describe the same action but from different standpoints. You *bring* something *to* a location but *take* something *away* from it. Thus you can write *He took some flowers from the garden,* but you shouldn't write x *He took his mother some flowers.*

broke (adjective) Colloquial in the sense of *having no money* and as the past participle of *break:* x *The faucet was broke.* Prefer *broken* here.

bunch, crowd (noun) A *bunch* is a dense collection of *things; a crowd,* of *people* or *animals.* Avoid x *a bunch of my friends.*

business, busyness The first means *job,* the second *being busy.*

but that, but what These are awkward equivalents of *that* in clauses following an expression of doubt: x *I do not doubt but that you intend to remain loyal.*

buy, by If you write x *I want to by it,* you have confused the verb *buy* with the preposition *by.*

calculate See *figure.*

calculated See *designed.*

can, may Both are now acceptable to indicate permission. *May* has a more polite and formal air: *May I leave?*

can not, cannot Unless you want to underline *not,* always prefer *cannot,* which makes the negative meaning immediately clear.

capital, capitol *Capital* means either *governmental city* or *funds;* a *capitol* is a *statehouse.*

cause, reason Not synonyms. A *cause* is what produces an effect: *The earthquake was the cause of the tidal wave.* A *reason* is someone's *professed motive or justification: He cited a conflict* *of interest as his reason for not accepting the post.* Note that the actual *cause* of his refusal could have been something quite different.

cause is due to Redundant. Write *The cause was poverty,* not x *The cause was due to poverty.*

censor, censure (noun) A *censor* is an official who judges whether a publication or performance will be allowed. *Censure* is vehement criticism. *The censor heaped censure on the play.*

center around Since a center is a point, *center around* is imprecise. *Center on* or *center upon* would be better: *The investigation centered on tax evasion.*

character Often redundant. x *He was of a studious character* means, and should be written, *He was studious.*

chord, cord The first means *tones,* the second *rope.*

cite, sight, site To *cite* is to *mention.* A *sight* is a *view.* A *site* is a *locale.*

class (verb) *Classify* is preferable. Avoid x *She classed the documents under three headings.*

climactic, climatic The first means *of a climax,* the second *of a climate.*

coarse, course The first means *rough,* the second *direction* or *academic offering.*

commence Usually pompous for *begin, start.*

compare, contrast *Compare* means either *make a comparison* or *liken.* To compare something *with* something else is to make a comparison between them; the comparison may show either a resemblance or a difference. To compare something *to* something else is to assert a likeness between them.

To *contrast* is to emphasize *differences: She contrasted the gentle Athenians with the warlike Spartans.* As a verb, *contrast* should be followed by *with.*

complement, compliment As a noun, *complement* means *accompaniment: The salad was a perfect complement to the main course.* As a verb, *complement* means to *accompany: The salad complemented the main course. Compliment* means *praise: They all complimented her on the outstanding meal; She received a compliment.*

comprise, compose, constitute *Comprise* means *embrace, include: The curriculum comprises every field of knowledge. Compose* and *constitute* mean *make up: All those fields together compose* [or *constitute*] *the curriculum.* The most common mistake is to use *comprise* as if it meant *compose:* x *The parts comprise the whole. Is comprised of* is not an adequate solution: x *The whole is comprised of the parts.* Try *The whole comprises the parts* or *The parts compose the whole.*

concept, conception, idea The broadest of these terms is *idea,* and you should prefer it unless you are sure you mean one of the others. A *concept* is an abstract notion characterizing a class of particulars: *the concept of civil rights.* A *conception* is a stab at an idea, possibly erroneous: *She had an odd conception of my motives.* Note that *idea* would have been suitable even in these examples.

concur in, concur with You *concur in* an action or decision: *He concurred in her seeking a new career.* But you *concur with* a person or group: *He concurred with her in her decision.*

conscience, consciousness The first has to do with responsiveness to ideas of right and wrong, the second with mental awareness in general.

conscious, aware Almost synonyms, but you can observe a difference. People are *conscious* of their own perceptions but *aware* of events or circumstances.

consensus Avoid this noun unless you mean something very close to unanimity. And beware of the redundant x *consensus of opinion* and x *general consensus. Opinion* and *general* are already contained in the meaning of *consensus.*

considerable Colloquial in the sense of *many* (items): x *Considerable dignitaries were there.* Use the word to mean *weighty, important: The costs were considerable; The Secretary-General is a considerable figure.*

consist of, consist in Something *consists of* its components: *The decathlon consists of ten events. Consist in* means *exist in* or *inhere in: Discretion consists in knowing when to remain silent.*

contemptible, contemptuous Very different. *Contemptible* means *deserving contempt. Contemptuous* means *feeling or showing contempt. They felt contemptuous of such a contemptible performance.*

continual, continuous *Continual* means *recurring at intervals. Continuous* means *uninterrupted.* A river flows *continuously* but may overflow its bank *continually* through the years.

contrary to Since *contrary* is an adjective, avoid constructions in which *contrary to* serves as an adverbial modifier: x *Contrary to Baldwin, Orwell is not directly concerned with race.* This sentence makes it appear that Orwell is "contrary to Baldwin," whereas the writer means to compare the two authors' *concerns*. Try *Orwell, unlike Baldwin, is not directly concerned with race*. Save *contrary to* for sentences like *The order to surrender was contrary to everything they had been taught*.

convey Do not follow with a *that* clause: x *They conveyed that they were happy*. Choose a noun as object: *They conveyed the impression that they were happy*.

convince, persuade Often treated as synonyms, but you can preserve a valuable distinction by keeping *convince* for *win agreement* and *persuade* for *move to action*. If I *convince* you that I am right, I may *persuade* you to join my cause. Avoid x *He convinced his father to lend him the car*.

could of Always a mistake for *could have*.

council, counsel The first means *committee*, the second *advice* or *attorney*: *Her counsel sought counsel from the city council*.

couple, pair *Couple* refers to two items that are united. It is colloquial when the items are only casually linked: x *I have a couple of points I want to raise with you*. When you do use *couple of*, be sure not to drop the *of*: x *a couple reasons*.

Pair refers to two things that are inseparably joined in function or feeling: *The Joneses are a couple, but they are not much of a pair*.

Prefer *pairs* to *pair* for the plural: *four pairs of shoes*, not x *four pair of shoes*.

Verbs governed by *couple* or *pair* are generally plural, although a singular verb could be appropriate in a rare case: *A couple becomes a trio when the first child is born*.

criteria Always plural: *these criteria*. The singular is *criterion*.

cursor, curser The first is the blinking line on a computer screen; the second is someone who curses.

data Opinion is divided over the number of *data*, which is technically the plural form of *datum*. The safe course is to continue treating *data* as plural: *The data have recently become available*. Even so, the singular *data* is by now very commonly seen.

deduce, deduct Both form the same noun, *deduction*, but *deduce* means *derive* or *infer* and *deduct* means *take away* or *detract*. *He deduced that the IRS would not allow him to deduct the cost of his hair dryer*.

depend Do not omit *on* or *upon*, as in x *It depends whether the* *rain stops in time*. And avoid *it depends* without a following reason: x *It all depends* is incomplete.

descent, dissent The first means *lowering*, the second *disagreement*.

desert, dessert *Desert* means *barren area* or to *abandon; a dessert* is the last course in a meal.

designed, calculated Misused in passive constructions where no designing agent is envisioned: x *The long summer days are designed to expose your skin to too much ultraviolet light*. Try *The long summer days are likely to expose your skin to too much ultraviolet light*. Again, do not write x *This medicine is perfectly calculated to turn you into an addict*. Try *This medicine is likely to turn you into an addict*.

device, devise The first is a noun meaning *instrument;* the second is a verb meaning to *fashion*.

differ from, differ with To *differ from* people is to be *different from* them; to *differ with* them is to *express disagreement with* them: *The Sioux differed from their neighbors in their religious practices; they differed with their neighbors over hunting rights*.

different from, different than Because *from* is a preposition (p. 725) and *than* a subordinating conjunction (p. 389), you should avoid sentences like x *This book is different than that one*. Here the prepositional phrase *from that one* is required.

Is *different than* always wrong? Not if it introduces a subordinate clause, as in *The outcome was different than I expected*. When in doubt, however, you can spare yourself anxiety by falling back on *different from: The outcome was different from what I expected*.

discreet, discrete The first means *prudent*, the second *separate: It was discreet of him to put the documents into discrete piles*.

disinterested, uninterested Many writers use both to mean *not interested*, but in doing so they lose the unique meaning of *disinterested* as *impartial: What we need here is a disinterested observer*. Reserve *disinterested* for such uses. Avoid x *She was completely disinterested in dancing*.

doubtless(ly) Since *doubtless* is already an adverb, the *-ly* is excessive: *She will doubtless be ready at eight*.

drastic Once meant *violent*, and still retains a sense of harshness and grim urgency. Avoid x *a drastic improvement*.

dual, duel The first means *double*, the second a *fight*.

dubious, doubtful An outcome or a statement may be *dubious*, but the person who calls it into question is *doubtful* about it. Though some writers overlook the distinction, you would do well to keep *doubtful* for the mental state of harboring doubts.

due to Do not use adverbially, as in x *Due to her absence, the team lost the game.* In such a sentence use *because of* or *owing to,* and save *due to* for sentences like *The loss was due to her absence.*

dying, dyeing The first means *expiring,* the second *coloring.*

effect See *affect.*

e.g., i.e. Often confused. The abbreviation *e.g.* means *for example;* it can be used only when you are *not* citing all the relevant items. The abbreviation *i.e.* means *that is;* it can be used only when you are giving the *equivalent* of the preceding term. In the main text of an essay or paper, it is best to write out *for example* and *that is.*

Once you have written *e.g.,* do not add *etc.,* as in x *See, e.g., Chapters 4, 7, 11, etc.* The idea of unlisted further examples is already present in *e.g.*

elicit, illicit The first means *draw forth,* the second *unlawful.* Don't write x *His business dealings were elicit.*

eminent, imminent The first means *prominent,* the second *about to happen: The arrival of the eminent diplomat was imminent.*

enhance Does not mean *increase,* as in x *I want to enhance my bank account.* It means *increase the value or attractiveness of,* as in *He enhanced his good reputation by performing further generous acts.* In order to be enhanced, something must be already valued.

Note that the quality, not the person, gets enhanced. Avoid x *She was enhanced by receiving favorable reviews.*

enormity, enormousness Increasingly treated as synonyms, but many careful writers insist on keeping to the original meaning of *enormity* as *atrocious wickedness.* You would do well to avoid x *the enormity of his feet.*

envelop, envelope The first is a verb meaning to *surround;* the second is for mail.

escape (verb) When used with an object, it should mean *elude,* as in *They escaped punishment.* Avoid x *They escaped the jail.* Make *escaped* intransitive here: *They escaped from the jail.*

especially, specially, special *Especially* means *outstandingly: an especially interesting idea. Specially* means *for a particular purpose, specifically: This racket was specially chosen by the champion.*

Watch for meaningless uses of *special:* x *There are two special reasons why I came here.* This would make sense only if there had been many reasons, only two of which were special ones. Just delete *special.*

et al. Means *and other people,* not *and other things.* It belongs in citations, not in your main text.

etc. Means *and other things,* not *and other people. Et al.* serves that rival meaning. In formal prose, use a substitute expression such as *and so forth.*

Do not use *etc.* after *for example* or *such as:* x *America is composed of many ethnic groups, such as Germans, Poles, Italians, etc.*

eventhough A mistake for *even though.*

everyday, every day The first means *normal,* the second *each day.*

everyone, every one *Everyone* means *everybody; every one* means *each one* of specified items.

everywheres A mistake for *everywhere.*

exceeding(ly), excessive(ly) *Exceeding* means *very much; excessive* means *too much.* It is not shameful to be *exceedingly rich,* but to be *excessively rich* is a demerit.

except Do not use as a conjunction, as in x *She told him to leave, except he preferred to stay.* Keep *except* as a preposition meaning *excluding: He remembered everything except his toothbrush.*

expect Mildly colloquial in the sense of *suppose, believe:* x *I expect it will snow tomorrow.*

factor A *factor* is an *element helping to produce a given result,* as in *They overlooked several factors in seeking the causes of the riot.* Do not use *factor* simply as a synonym of *item* or *point.* Note that *contributing factor* is always redundant.

fair, fare *Fair* means *just* or *pretty;* a *fare* is what you pay on the bus.

faze, phase To *faze* is to *daunt;* a *phase* is a *period.*

feel, feeling Many careful writers prefer to keep *feel* a verb, saving *feeling* for the noun. Thus they object to x *She had a feel for trigonometry.*

few, little *Few* refers to things or persons that can be counted; *little* refers to things that can be measured or estimated but not itemized. *Few people were on hand, and there was little enthusiasm for the speaker.*

fewer, less, lesser, least *Fewer* refers to numbers, *less* to amounts; *fewer members; less revenue.* Beware of advertising jargon:

x *This drink contains less calories.* Since the calories are countable, only *fewer* would be correct here.

Lesser is an adjective meaning *minor* or *inferior: The lesser emissaries were excluded from the summit meeting. Least* is the superlative of *little.* As an adjective it should be used only when more than two items are involved: *That was the least of her many worries.*

Note that *fewer in number* is redundant.

figure, calculate Colloquial as synonyms of *think, suppose,* or *believe:* x *They figured she would be too frightened to complain.*

flaunt, flout Widely confused. To *flaunt* is to *display arrogantly: They flaunted their superior wisdom.* To *flout* is to *defy contemptuously: They flouted every rule of proper behavior.* The common error is to use *flout* for *flaunt:* x *The pitcher flouted his unbeaten record.*

flunk Colloquial for *fail,* as in x *He flunked Biology 23.*

for example See *e.g.*

forbear, forebear To *forbear* is to *refrain;* a *forebear* is an *ancestor. She forbore to criticize her forebears.*

forward, foreword The first means *ahead;* the second is a *preface.*

fortuitous Means *by chance,* whether or not an advantage is implied. Do not allow *fortuitous* to mean simply *favorable, auspicious,* or *lucky;* x *How fortuitous it was that fate drew us together!*

free, freely *Free* can serve as both an adjective and an adverb, meaning, among other things, *without cost.* But when you write *I give it to you freely,* you mean *I give it to you without mental reservation.*

frightened, scared, afraid You are *frightened* or, more informally, *scared* by an immediate cause of alarm; you are *afraid* of a more persistent danger or worry: *He was frightened [scared] by noises in the middle of the night; he was afraid he would have to buy a watchdog.*

fulsome Does not mean *abundant;* it means *offensively insincere.* Thus it would be wrong to write: x *I love the fulsome scents of early spring.*

fun Colloquial as an adjective, as in x *a fun party.*

gender Until recently, grammarians maintained that *gender* can refer only to grammar itself, as in *the feminine gender* of certain Latin nouns. By now, however, most writers extend the term to cover sexual differentiation among persons, as in *gender issues* or *He spoke for his gender but not for mine.*

good, well *You look good tonight* means that you are attractive. *You look well tonight* means that you do not look sick.

guess Colloquial as a synonym of *suppose:* x *I guess I should give up trying.*

had better Do not shorten to *better,* as in x *You better pay attention.*

half a Do not precede with a redundant *a,* as in x *He was there for a half a day.*

hangar, hanger A *hangar* is for airplanes, a *hanger* for coats.

hanged, hung The usual past participle of *hang* is *hung,* but many careful writers still use *hanged* when referring to capital punishment: *He was hanged for his heinous crimes; his lifeless body hung from the noose.*

hard, hardly Both can be adverbs. Fear of using *hard* as an adverb can lead to ambiguity: x *She was hardly pressed for time.* This could mean either *She was rushed* or, more probably, *She was scarcely rushed.* There is nothing wrong with writing *She was hard-pressed for time.* Note the hyphen, however.

high, highly *High* can be an adverb as well as an adjective. Prefer it to *highly* in expressions like *he jumped high; a high-flying pilot.* An antique vase may be *highly prized* and therefore *high-priced* at an auction.

hopefully Many readers accept this word in the sense of *it is hoped,* but others feel strongly that *hopefully* can mean only *in a hopeful manner.* Keep to this latter meaning if you want to give no offense. Write *He prayed hopefully* but not x *Hopefully, his pains will subside.*

how Avoid in the sense of *that,* as in x *I told her how I wouldn't stand for her sarcasm any more.*

how ever, however Distinct terms. *How ever are you going to untie that knot? You, however, know more about it than I do.*

However is correct in the sense of *in whatever manner; However you consider it, the situation looks desperate.*

i.e. Means *that is;* see *e.g.*

if not Potentially ambiguous, as in x *There were good reasons, if not excellent ones, for taking that step.* Does this mean that the reasons decidedly were not excellent or that they may indeed have been excellent? Try *but not excellent ones* or *indeed, excellent ones,* depending on the intended sense.

ignorant, stupid Often confused. To be *ignorant* of something is simply not to know it: *Newton was ignorant of relativity.* An *ignorant* person is one who has been taught very little. A *stupid* person is mentally unable to learn: *The main cause of his ignorance was his stupidity.*

imbue, instill You *imbue* somebody *with* a quality like courage; you *instill* that quality *into* the person. Don't write x *She imbued courage into him* or x *She instilled him with courage.*

implicit, explicit, tacit *Implicit* can be ambiguous, for it means both *implied* (left unstated) and *not giving cause for investigation.* Consider, e.g., x *My trust in her was implicit.* Was the trust left unstated, beyond question, or both? Try *My trust in her was left implicit* or *My trust in her was absolute.*

Explicit is the opposite of *implicit* in the sense of *implied: In his will he spelled out the explicit provisions that had previously been left implicit. Tacit* is close to this sense of *implicit,* but it means *silent, unspoken;* its reference is to speech, not to expression in general.

imply, infer Widely confused. To *imply* is to *leave an implication;* to *infer* is to *take an implication. She implied that she was ready to leave the company, but the boss inferred that she was bluffing.* The common error is to use *infer* for *imply.*

in back of See *back of.*

in case Can usually be improved to *if: If* [not *In case*] *you do not like this model, we will refund your money.* Save *in case* for *in the event: This sprinkler is provided in case of fire.*

in connection with See *in terms of.*

in terms of, along the lines of, in connection with Vague and wordy. Instead of writing x *In terms of prowess, Tarzan was unconquerable,* just write *Tarzan was unconquerable.* Similarly, x *He was pursuing his studies along the lines of sociology* should be simply *He was studying sociology.*

include Do not use loosely to mean *are,* as in x *The Marx Brothers included Groucho, Harpo, Chico, and Zeppo.* Use *were* in this instance. Only when at least one member is omitted should you use *include: The Marx Brothers included Harpo and Zeppo.*

individual (noun) Often pompous for *person:* x *He was a kind-hearted individual.* Use *individual* where you want to draw attention to the single person as contrasted with the collectivity, as in *Our laws respect the individual.*

inside of Widely regarded as colloquial; can always be shortened to *inside.* Write *inside the car,* not x *inside of the car.*

inspite of A mistake for *in spite of.*

irregardless There is no such word. But to correct a faulty sentence like x *Irregardless, we intend to complete our survey,* do not just insert *regardless* in place of *irregardless.* Be more specific: *Despite the objections that have been raised, we intend to complete our survey.* Note that if you used *regardless of the objections that have been raised* here, the sentence would be ambiguous, since *regardless of* could mean either *despite* or *refusing to heed.*

is because See *reason is because.*

is when, is where Often involved in faulty predication: x *A war is when opposing countries take up arms;* x *Massage is where you lie on a table and. . . .* Match *when* only with times, *where* only with places: *When she was ready, she went where she pleased.* Most predication problems can be solved by changing the verb: *A war occurs when. . . .*

it's, its The first means *it is,* the second *belonging to it.*

just because . . . doesn't mean Though common in speech, this construction is indefensible in writing: x *Just because you passed the written test doesn't mean you know how to drive.* A subordinate clause cannot serve as the subject of a verb. Try *The fact that you passed the written test doesn't mean you know how to drive.*

kind of, sort of, type of When used at all, these expressions should be followed by the singular: *this kind of woman.* But *such a woman* is preferable.

Sort of and *kind of* are awkward in the sense of *somewhat,* and they are sometimes followed by an unnecessary *a:* x *He was an odd sort of a king.* Do not use *sort of* or *kind of* unless your sentence needs them to make sense: *This kind of bike has been on the market for only three months.*

lead, led *Led* is the past tense of the verb *lead.* Avoid x *He lead her astray for years.*

leave, let Have different senses in clauses like *leave him alone* and *let him alone.* The first means *get out of his presence;* the second means *don't bother him* (even if you remain in his presence). Don't write x *leave him go in peace.*

lessen, lesson The first means to *reduce;* the second means *teaching.*

level (noun) Overworked in the vague, colorless sense illustrated by x *at the public level;* x *on the wholesale level.* Use only when the idea of degree or ranking is present: *He was a competent amateur, but when he turned professional he found himself beyond his level.*

lie, lay If you mean *repose,* use the intransitive *lie: lie down.* The transitive *lay* means, among other things, *set* or *put: lay it here.*

All forms of these verbs are troublesome. The following sentences use three common tenses correctly:

PRESENT	PAST	PRESENT PERFECT
I lie in bed.	I lay in bed.	I have lain in bed.
I lay down my cards.	I laid down my cards.	I have laid down my cards.

lightening, lightning The first means *getting lighter;* the second is a flash.

like See *as, like.*

likely Weak as an unmodified adverb: x *He likely had no idea what he was saying.* Some readers would also object to x *Very likely, he had no idea what he was saying.* Try *probably,* and reserve *likely* for adjectival uses: a *likely story.* See also *apt, liable, likely.*

likewise An adverb, not a conjunction. You can write *Likewise, Myrtle failed the quiz,* but not x *Jan failed the quiz, likewise Myrtle.*

literally Means *precisely as stated, without a figurative sense.* If you write x *I literally died laughing,* you must be writing from beyond the grave. Do not use *literally* to mean *definitely* or *almost.* It is properly used in a sentence like *The poet writes literally about flowers, but her real subject is forgiveness.*

loath, loathe The first means *reluctant,* the second to *despise.*

loose, lose *Loose* is usually an adjective meaning *slack* or *free: The door hinge was loose. Lose* means *mislay.* Avoid x *I loose my notes whenever I desperately need them.*

lot, lots Somewhat colloquial in the sense of *many:* x *I could give you lots of reasons. A lot* (note the spelling) and *lots* make colloquial modifiers, too: x *She pleases me lots.* Try *very much.*

mad, angry *Mad* means *insane.* It is colloquial in the sense of *angry:* x *They were mad at me.*

majority Do not use unless you mean to contrast it with *minority: The majority of the caucus voted to disband the club.* In x *the majority of the time,* the term is out of place because *time* does not contain members that could be counted as a majority and a minority.

many, much *Many* refers to countable items, *much* to a total amount that cannot be divided into items (see *amount, number*): *Many problems make for much difficulty*. Do not write x *There were too much people in the line*.

material, materiel *Material* means *matter* or *pertaining to matter*. *Materiel* means *military supplies*.

media Increasingly used as a singular term, but many good writers disapprove. Since *media* is the plural of *medium*, you would do well to keep it plural. Don't write x *The media is to blame*. Remember what someone once said: "TV is a medium because it isn't rare and it isn't well done."

militate, mitigate Often confused. To *militate* is to *have an adverse effect*. It is followed by *against*, as in *His poor eyesight militated against his becoming a pilot*. *Mitigate* means *reduce* (an unpleasant effect). It always takes an object, as in *The doctor's cheerful manner mitigated the pain*.

The common error is to use *mitigate* for *militate*, as in x *Their stubborn attitude mitigated against their chances of success*.

miner, minor A *miner* digs coal; a *minor* is not yet an adult.

mislead, misled *Misled* is the past participle of *mislead*. Avoid x *He mislead her several times*.

mix, mixture Some writers find it useful to keep *mix* a verb and *mixture* a noun. Thus they would avoid x *There was a fascinating mix of interests around the table*.

moreso A mistake for *more so*.

most Colloquial as an adverb meaning *almost*: x *We were most dead by the time we got there*; x *Most all the cows had found their way home*.

much less Avoid x *Skiing is difficult, much less surfing*. The *much less* construction requires an initial negation, as in *He has not even appeared, much less begun his work*.

muchly A mistake for *much*.

myself Do not use this intensive pronoun merely as a substitute for *I* or *me*: x *My friends and myself are all old-timers now*; x *She gave the book to Steve and myself*. Save *myself* for emphatic or reflexive uses: *I myself intend to do it; I have forgiven myself*.

naval, navel The first means *nautical*, the second *belly button*.

not too, not that Colloquial when used to mean *not very*: x *She was not too sure about that*; x *They are not that interested in sailing*.

nothing like, nowhere near Do not use in place of *not nearly,* as in x *I am nothing like* [or *nowhere near*] *as spry as I used to be.*

nowheres A mistake for *nowhere.*

numerous Properly an adjective. You can write *He still had numerous debts,* but avoid x *Numerous of his debts remained unpaid.*

occur, take place The narrower term is *take place,* which should be used only with scheduled events. Avoid x *The storm took place last Tuesday.*

of Do not try to make this preposition into part of a verb, as in x *She would of helped him if she could of.* Use *have.*

off of Should be either *off* or *from: She jumped off the bridge* or *She jumped from the bridge.* Avoid x *She jumped off of the bridge.*

oftentimes Colloquial for *often.*

old-fashion Colloquial for *old-fashioned.*

on, upon, up on *On* and *upon* mean the same thing, but you should save *upon* for formal effects: *She swore upon her word of honor.* Note that *up on* is not the same as *upon: He climbed up on the ladder.*

on account of Never preferable to *because of.*

only Do not use as a conjunction: x *He tries to be good, only his friends lead him astray.* Keep *only* as an adjective or adverb: *That is his only problem; He only needs some better advice.*

oral, verbal *Oral* means *by mouth; verbal* means *in words,* whether or not the words are spoken. Write *a verbal presentation* only if you have in mind a contrast with some form of communication that bypasses words.

other than that Considered awkward: x *Other than that, I can follow your reasoning.* Try a more definite expression: *except for one point, apart from this objection,* etc.

other times Do not use as an adverb, as in x *Other times she felt depressed.* Use the complete prepositional phrase *at other times.*

otherwise Allowable as an adverb meaning *in other respects* or *differently: Otherwise, I feel healthy; She decided otherwise.* But do not use *otherwise* to replace the adjective *other:* x *He loved old buildings, Victorian and otherwise.*

ourself Should be *ourselves.*

outside of Should be *outside.* And in figurative uses you should prefer *except for:* not x *outside of these reasons* but *except for these reasons.*

part, portion A *part* is a *fraction of a whole;* a *portion* is a *part allotted to some person or use*. Thus you should avoid x *A large portion of the ocean is polluted.*

passed, past Do not mistake the adjective, noun, or preposition *past* for the verb *passed,* as in x *They past the test*. The following sentences are correct: *We passed the tennis courts; The past has passed us by; Past the tunnel lies the railroad station.*

peace, piece The first means *tranquillity,* the second *part.*

persecute, prosecute To *persecute* is to *single out for mistreatment.* To *prosecute* is to *bring to trial. He was prosecuted for persecuting his neighbors.*

personal, personnel The first means *individual,* the second *employees.*

phenomena Not a singular word, but the plural of *phenomenon.*

place Some readers regard terms like *anyplace, no place,* and *someplace* as colloquial. It is safer to write *anywhere, nowhere, somewhere.* Note, in any event, the two-word spelling of *no place.*

plan The verb is best followed by *to,* not *on: He plans to run,* not x *He plans on running.* Note that since *plan* implies a future action, expressions like x *plan ahead* and x *future plans* are redundant.

plus Not a coordinating conjunction or a sentence adverb: x *He was sleepy, plus he hadn't studied.* Keep *plus* as a preposition with numbers: *Two plus two is four.* When no number is involved, avoid *plus:* not x *Her challenging work plus her long vacations made her happy* but *Along with her long vacations, her challenging work made her happy.*

poorly Colloquial in the sense of *ill* or *sick:* x *I feel poorly today.* Keep as an adverb: *I performed poorly in the exam.*

popular Implies favor with large numbers of people. Avoid when you have something smaller in mind: x *The hermit was popular with his three visitors;* x *That idea is not very popular with me.*

possible Do not use as an adverb: x *a possible missing airliner.* Try *possibly.*

pray, prey The first means *implore,* the second *victim.*

precede, proceed To *precede* is to *go ahead of;* to *proceed* is to *go forward. In the preceding announcement, we were instructed to proceed with caution.*

predominant, predominate The first is an adjective, the second a verb. *The Yankees were the predominant team; they predominated for years.*

prejudice, prejudiced The first is a noun meaning *bias;* the second is an adjective meaning *biased.* Do not write x *They were prejudice.*

pressure, press (verbs) Many good writers prefer to keep *pressure* as a noun; they would not be caught writing x *She pressured him to quit his job. Pressed* would raise no objection here.

principal, principle *Principal* is usually an adjective meaning *foremost; principle* is a noun meaning *rule. The principal reason for her success is that she keeps to her principles.* As a noun, *principal* usually refers to the head of a school. Do not write x *He had to go to the principle's office.*

prophecy, prophesy The first is a noun meaning *prediction,* the second a verb meaning to *make predictions.* Write *She prophesied his downfall,* not x *She prophecied his downfall.*

prostate, prostrate The first is the name of a gland; the second means *prone. His prostate pain left him prostrate.*

quote (noun) Often considered colloquial when used to mean *quotation,* as in x *this quote,* or when written in the plural to mean *quotation marks,* as in x *She put quotes around it.* In formal writing, take the trouble to use the full terms *quotation* and *quotation marks.*

rack, wrack The first is a *framework,* the second a *ruin.*

rain, rein, reign *Rain* is precipitation; to *rein* is to *restrain;* to *reign* is to *rule.*

raise, rise (verbs) *Raise* takes an object: *Raise your arm. Rise* does not: *Rise and shine.*

real Colloquial as an adverb, as in x *I am real committed.* Prefer *really.*

reason is because A classic predication error. You can write either *She stayed home because of her health* or *The reason was her health,* but it is redundant to write x *The reason she stayed home was because of her health.*

rebut, refute To *rebut* an argument is to *speak or write against* it; to *refute* an argument is to *disprove* it. The common error is to use *refute* for *rebut:* x *You may be right, but I will refute what you said.*

reckon Colloquial for *suppose, think:* x *I reckon I can handle that.*

Use in the sense of *count* or *consider: She is reckoned an indispensable member of the board.*

regardless See *irregardless.*

relation, relationship These overlap in meaning, and some writers use *relationship* in all contexts. But *relation* is preferable when you mean an abstract connection: *the relation of wages to prices.* Save *relationship* for mutuality: *the President's relationship with the press.*

relevant Requires a following prepositional phrase. Do not write x *The course was extremely relevant.* To what? Try *The course was extremely relevant to the issues of the hour.* Note, incidentally, that *revelant* is not a word.

ind usage 41

replace See *substitute.*

reticent Does not mean *reluctant,* as in x *They were reticent to comply.* It means *disposed to be silent,* as in *Reticent people sometimes become talkative late at night.*

scared See *frightened, scared, afraid.*

set, sit With few exceptions, *set* takes an object: *set the table. Sit* almost never takes an object: *sit down.* Avoid x *She set there sleeping* and x *I want to sit these weary bones to rest.*

similar Means *resembling,* not *same.* Avoid x *Ted died in 1979, and Alice suffered a similar fate two years later.* Try *the same fate.*

Do not use *similar* as an adverb meaning *like:* x *This steak smells similar to the one I ate yesterday.* Try *like the one.*

since An indispensable word, but watch for ambiguity: x *Since she left, he has been doing all the housework.* Here *since* could mean either *because* or *ever since.* Prefer one of these terms.

some Do not use as an adverb meaning *somewhat,* as in x *He worried some about his health.* Try *He was somewhat worried about his health.*

something Avoid as an adverb meaning *somewhat,* as in x *He is something over six feet tall.*

sometime, some time, sometimes *Sometime* is an adverb meaning *at an unspecified time; some time* is an adjective-noun pair meaning *a span of time. Sometime I must tell you how I spent some time in prison. Sometimes* means *at times.* Write *Sometimes I get lonely,* not x *Sometime I get lonely.*

somewheres A mistake for *somewhere.*

sort of See *kind of.*

special, specially See *especially.*

stationary, stationery The first means *still,* the second *paper.*

substitute, replace *Substitute* takes as its object the new item that is supplanting the old one: *He substituted margarine for butter. Replace* takes as its object the item being abandoned: *He replaced the butter with margarine.* Note that these sentences are recounting the same act.

such as See *etc.*

suppose to A mistake for *supposed to,* as in x *We are suppose to watch our manners.*

sure Colloquial as an adverb: x *She sure likes muffins.* Since *surely* would sound stuffy here, try *certainly.*

sympathy for, sympathy with, sympathize with To feel *sympathy for* someone is to experience compassion: *She has sympathy for the people of Ethiopia. Sympathy with* is a feeling of kinship or identity: *Her sympathy with Gloria Steinem made her a feminist.* To *sympathize with,* however, is once again to experience compassion: *She sympathized with the poor.*

tack, tact A *tack* is a nautical course; *tact* is *discretion.*

than, then *Than* is for comparison; *then* means *at that time.* Avoid x *It was later then she thought.*

that Beware of using *that* as an unexplained demonstrative adjective: x *He didn't have that much to say. All that much to say* would not improve matters. Just write *He didn't have much to say.*

that, which In restrictive clauses (p. 447, 21m), most careful writers prefer *that* to *which: Alberta is the province that fascinates me.* Use *that* wherever the clause serves to narrow or identify the term it refers to. Compare: *Alberta, which fascinates me, is my favorite province.*

their, there, they're Avoid confusing these terms, whose correct use is shown in *They're leaving their luggage there.*

theirself, theirselves Mistakes for *themselves.*

those kind, type, etc. Should be *that kind, type,* etc. But prefer *such,* which is more concise: *such people.*

thusly A mistake for *thus.*

till, until, til, 'til, 'till *Till* and *until* are interchangeable. The other three forms are inappropriate.

to, too, two *To* means *toward; too* means *also; two* is the number. *Too* is weak when used as a sentence adverb: x *It was dark and cold; too, the rain was heavy.* Try *moreover* or *furthermore.*

Avoid *too* as a synonym of *very:* x *It was too kind of them to come.* Just drop *too* here.

try and Should be *try to:* not x *Try and do better* but *Try to do better.*

type Colloquial in place of *type of:* x *You are a headstrong type person.* But *type of* is itself objectionably wordy; try *You are headstrong.*

usage, use Widely confused. Save *usage* for contexts implying convention or custom: *English usage; the usages of our sect.* Avoid x *They discouraged the usage of cocaine* or x *Excessive usage of the car results in high repair bills.* Substitute *use* in both sentences.

Even *use of* often proves wordy: x *By his use of symbolism Ibsen establishes himself as a modern playwright.* Why not just *By his symbolism Ibsen establishes himself as a modern playwright?*

use (verb), **utilize; use** (noun), **utilization** *Utilize* and *utilization* are almost always jargon for *use*. To *utilize* is properly to *put to use* or to *turn a profit on,* and it makes sense when coupled with an abstraction: *to utilize resources.* But the word has a dehumanizing air; prefer *use* in ordinary contexts. Note that *utilization* is almost four times as long as *use,* which can always stand in its place.

use to In an affirmative past construction, be sure to write *used to,* not *use to:* x *They use to think so;* x *They are not use to the cold.* In addition, certain past negative constructions with *use* always sound awkward: x *Didn't she use to take the bus?* Try *She used to take the bus, didn't she?*

verbal, oral See *oral.*

violently Not a synonym of *strongly,* as in x *I violently oppose your program.* Only thugs and terrorists oppose programs *violently,* causing actual physical damage.

waive, wave To *waive* is to *relinquish. Wave* is a verb meaning to *move to and fro* and a noun meaning a *spreading movement.* Avoid x *She waved her right to a jury trial.*

ways Avoid in the sense of *distance:* x *It was only a short ways.* The right form is *way.*

weather, whether *Weather* is the state of the atmosphere; *whether* means *if.*

what ever, whatever Distinct terms. *What ever will we do about the heating bills? Whatever we do, it will not solve the problem.*

where Do not use in place of *whereby,* as in x *T'ai-chi is an* *exercise regimen where one slowly activates every muscle group. Whereby,* the right word here, means *by means of which.* Save *where* for actual places: *That storefront studio is where we study T'ai-chi.*

where . . . at Redundant and colloquial, as in x *She had no idea where he was at.* Always delete the *at.*

who's, whose *Who's* means *who is; whose* means *of whom. Who's the person whose coat was left behind?*

-wise Acceptable when it means *in the manner of,* as in *clockwise* and *lengthwise,* and when it means *having wisdom: penny-wise and pound-foolish; a ring-wise boxer.* Note the hyphens in this second set of examples.

Avoid *-wise* in the sense of *with respect to:* x *taxwise; agriculturewise; conflict resolutionwise.* Such terms do save space, but many readers find them ugly. Look for concise alternatives: not x *the situation taxwise* but *the tax situation;* not x *America's superiority agriculturewise* but *America's superiority in agriculture.*

with See *being.*

would like for Colloquial in sentences like x *They would like for me to quit.* Try *They would like me to quit.*

would of Always a mistake for *would have.*

wreak, wreck To *wreak* is to *inflict: He wreaked havoc.* A *wreck* is a *ruin: a train wreck.*

your, you're The first is a possessive pronoun, the second a contraction of *you are.* Do not write x *Your certain to succeed* or x *Watch you're step!*

42

Glossary of Terms

The Glossary of Terms offers definitions of terms appearing in headings and **boldface** elsewhere in this book. Within the Glossary itself, words appearing in black boldface have separate entries which you can consult as necessary. The abbreviation *cf.* means "compare"—that is, note the difference between the term being defined and another. And *e.g.* means "for example."

abbreviation (p. 639) A shortened word, with the addition of a period to indicate the omission (*Dr.*).

absolute phrase (p. 440) A **phrase** that, instead of modifying a particular word, acts like an **adverb** to the rest of the sentence in which it appears:

ABS PHRASE
- **All struggle over,** the troops laid down their arms.

Absolute phrases are not considered mistakes of usage. Cf. **dangling modifier.**

abstract language (p. 10) Words that name ideas without involving any of the five senses: *agree, aspect, comprehensible, enthusiasm, virtuously,* etc. Cf. **concrete language.**

active voice See **voice.**

***ad hominem* reasoning** (p. 101) A **fallacy** whereby someone tries to discredit a position by attacking the person, party, or interest that supports that position.

additive phrase (p. 415) An expression beginning with a term like *accompanied by* or *as well as*. It is not strictly a part of a subject, and thus it should not affect the number of a verb.

adjectival clause See **clause.**

adjective (p. 431) A **modifier** of a **noun, pronoun,** or other **nounlike element**—e.g., *strong* in *a strong contender.* Most adjectives can be compared: *strong, stronger, strongest.* See **degree.** See also **interrogative adjective.**

adverb (p. 431) A word modifying either a **verb,** an **adjective,** another adverb, a **preposition,** an **infinitive,** a **participle,** a **phrase,** a **clause,** or a whole **sentence:** *now, clearly, moreover,* etc. Any one-word modifier that is not an adjective or an **article** is sure to be an adverb.

adverbial clause See **clause.**

agreement See **pronoun agreement, subject-verb agreement.**

allusion (p. 183) A passing reference to a work or idea, either by directly mentioning it or by borrowing its well-known language. Thus, someone who writes *She took arms against a sea of troubles* is alluding to, but not mentioning, Hamlet's most famous speech. The sentence *He did it with Shakespearean flair* alludes directly to Shakespeare. Quotation through allusion differs from **plagiarism** in that readers are expected to notice the reference.

"alternative MLA" style (p. 207) A documentation style, formerly preferred by the Modern Language Association, that makes use of **endnotes** or **footnotes** rather than **parenthetic citations.** Cf. **APA style, MLA style.**

analogy (p. 48) In general, a similarity of features or pattern between two things: *The nearest analogy to human speech may be the songs of whales.*

In **rhetoric,** an analogy is an extended likeness purporting to show that the rule or principle behind one thing also holds for the different thing being discussed. Thus, someone who disapproves of people leaving their home towns might devise this analogy: *People, like trees, must find their nourishment in the place where they grow up; to seek it elsewhere is as fatal as removing a tree from its roots.* Like most analogies, this one starts with an obvious resemblance and proceeds to a more debatable one.

analysis (p. 33) In a narrow sense, the breaking of something into its parts or functions and showing how those smaller units go to make up the whole. More broadly, analysis is the application of explanatory strategies to a given problem. In this book, analysis (or *exposition*) is treated as a rhetorical **mode,** along with **description, narration,** and **argument.**

antecedent (p. 425) The word for which a **pronoun** stands:

ANT PRO
- **Jane** was here yesterday, but today **she** is at school.

anticipatory pattern (p. 311) A structure, such as *both x and y* or *not x but y,* which gives an early signal of the way it will be completed.

APA style (p. 198) The **parenthetic citation** documentation style of the American Psychological Association. Cf. **MLA style, "alternative MLA" style.**

aphorism (p. 315) A memorably concise sentence conveying a very general assertion: *If wishes were horses, beggars would ride.* Many aphorisms show **balance** in their structure.

appositive (p. 451) A word or group of words whose only function is to identify or restate a neighboring **noun, pronoun,** or **nounlike element:**

APP
- Mike **the butcher** is quite a clown.

Arabic numeral (p. 648) A figure such as *3, 47,* or *106,* as opposed to a **Roman numeral** such as *III, XLVII,* or *CVI.*

argument (p. 33) The **mode** of writing in which a writer tries to convince the reader that a certain position on an issue is well-founded. Cf. **description, analysis, narration.**

article An indicator or determiner immediately preceding a **noun** or **modifier.** Articles themselves may be considered modifiers, along with **adjectives** and **adverbs.** The *definite article* is *the;* the *indefinite articles* are *a* and *an.*

attributive noun (p. 344) A **noun** serving as an **adjective:** *beach* in *beach shoes,* or *Massachusetts* in *the Massachusetts way of doing things.*

auxiliary A **verb** form, usually lacking **inflection,** that combines with other verbs to express possibility, likelihood, necessity, obligation, etc.: *She can succeed; He could become jealous.* The commonly recognized auxiliaries are *can, could, dare, do, may, might, must, need, ought, should,* and *would. Is, have,* and their related forms act like auxiliaries in the formation of **tenses:** *He is coming; They have gone.*

baited opener (p. 269) An introductory **paragraph** which, by presenting its early sentences "out of context," teases its reader into taking further interest.

balance (p. 315) The effect created when a whole sentence is controlled by the matching of grammatically like elements, as in *He taught us the intricate ways of the city; we taught him the simple ways of nature.* A balanced sentence typically repeats a grammatical pattern and certain words in order to highlight important differences.

base form of verb (p. 574) An **infinitive** without *to: see, think,* etc. Base forms appear with **auxiliaries** *(should see)* and in the formation of present and future **tenses** *(I see, I will see).*

begging the question (p. 71) The **fallacy** of treating a debatable idea as if it had already been proved. If, in a paper favoring national health insurance, you assert that only the greedy medical lobby could oppose such an obviously needed program, you are begging the question by assuming the rightness of your position instead of establishing it with **evidence.** Also called *circular reasoning.*

bibliographic note (p. 213) A supplementary note directing the reader to further sources of information. Cf. **substantive note.**

bibliography (p. 212) A list of consulted works presented at the end of a book, article, or **essay.** Also, a whole book devoted to listing works within a certain **subject area.**

See **indented quotation.**

bound element (p. 302) A modifying word, **phrase,** or subordinate **clause** which, because it is **restrictive,** is not set off by commas. Cf. **free element.**

brackets (p. 563) Punctuation marks used to insert an explanatory word or phrase into a sentence, as in *"I voted for [Dianne] Feinstein," she said.* Also called *square brackets.*

brainstorming (p. 63) The process of entertaining many suggestions for a topic without regard for links between them.

cardinal number (p. 649) A number like *four (4)* or *twenty-seven (27),* as opposed to an **ordinal number** like *fourth (4th)* or *twenty-seventh (27th).*

case (p. 457) The **inflection**al form of **nouns** and **pronouns** indicating whether they designate actors *(subjective case: I, we, they),* receivers of action *(objective case: me, us, them),* or "possessors" of the thing or quality modified *(possessive case: his Toyota, their indecision, Geraldine's influence). Personal pronouns* also have "second possessive" forms: *mine, theirs,* etc. Cf. **double possessive.**

choppiness (p. 318) The undesirable effect produced by a sequence of brief sentences lacking pauses marked by punctuation.

circular reasoning See **begging the question.**

circumlocution (p. 359) Roundabout expression, or one such expression—e.g., x *due to the fact that* for *because.*

clause (p. 388) A cluster of words containing a **subject** and a **predicate.** All clauses are either *subordinate* (dependent) or *independent.* (An independent clause is sometimes called a *main clause.*)

A subordinate clause cannot stand alone: x *When he was hiding in the closet.* An independent clause, which is considered grammatically complete, can stand alone: *He was hiding in the closet.*

There are three kinds of subordinate clauses:

1. A *relative* clause serves the function of an **adjective:**

   REL CLAUSE
   - Marty, **who was extremely frightened,** did not want to make a sound.

   The relative clause modifies the **noun** *Marty.*

2. An *adverbial* clause serves the function of an **adverb:**

   ADV CLAUSE
   - Marty held his breath for forty seconds **when he was hiding in the closet.**

   The adverbial clause modifies the **verb** *held.*

3. And a *noun* clause serves the function of a **noun:**

   NOUN CLAUSE
   - **That an intruder might slip through his bedroom window** had never occurred to him.

   The noun clause serves as the **subject** of the **verb** *had occurred.*

cliché (p. 364) A trite, stereotyped, overused expression: *an open and shut case; a miss is as good as a mile.* Most clichés contain

figurative language that has lost its vividness: *a heart of gold; bring the house down,* etc. When two clichés occur together, the effect is usually **mixed metaphor.**

collective noun (p. 417) A **noun** that, though singular in form, designates a group of members: *band, family,* etc.

comma splice (p. 400) A **run-on sentence** in which two independent clauses are joined by a comma alone, without the necessary coordinating conjunction: x *It is raining today, I left my umbrella home.* Cf. **fused sentence.**

common gender (p. 347) The intended sexual neutrality of **pronouns** used to indicate an indefinite party. Traditionally, indefinite *(one)* and masculine personal pronouns *(he)* were used, but the masculine ones are now widely regarded as **sexist language.**

comparative degree See **degree.**

comparison and contrast (p. 42) The analytic strategy of exploring the resemblances and differences between two or more things.

complement (p. 384) Usually, an element in a **predicate** that identifies or describes the **subject.** A single-word complement is either a *predicate noun* or a *predicate adjective:*

PRED NOUN
- He is a **musician.**

PRED ADJ
- His skill is **unbelievable.**

In addition, a **direct object** can have a complement, known as an *objective complement:*

D OBJ OBJ COMPL
- They consider the **location desirable.**

Infinitives, too, can have complements:

INF COMPL INF
- They beg him **to be** more **cooperative.**

compound, adj. (p. 418) Consisting of more than one word, as in a compound verb (*They whistled and sang*), a compound noun (*ice cream*), a compound preposition *(in spite of),* a compound subject (*He and she were there*), or a compound modifier (*far-gone*).

concession (p. 75) In **rhetoric,** the granting of an opposing point, usually to show that it does not overturn one's own **thesis.**

gloss
42

conciseness (p. 357) Economy of expression. Not to be confused with simplicity; conciseness enables a maximum of meaning to be communicated in a minimum of words.

concrete language (p. 10) Words that bring one or more of our five senses into play: *purple, car, buzz, dusty,* etc. Cf. **abstract language.**

conjunction (p. 389) An un**inflected** word that connects other words, **phrases,** or **clause:** *and, although,* etc.

A *coordinating* conjunction—*and, but, for, nor, or, so, yet*—joins grammatically similar elements without turning one into a **modifier** of the other: *You are sad, but I am cheerful.*

A *subordinating* conjunction joins grammatically dissimilar elements, turning one of them into a modifier and specifying its logical relation to the other—e.g., *Although you are sad, I am cheerful; I understand that you like jazz.*

Correlative conjunctions are matched pairs with a coordinating or a disjunctive purpose: *either/or, neither/nor,* etc.

Cf. **preposition.**

connotation (p. 344) An association that a word calls up, as opposed to its **denotation,** or dictionary meaning. Thus, the word *exile* denotes enforced separation from one's home or country, but it connotes loneliness, homesickness, and any number of other, more private, thoughts and images.

continuity (p. 240) The felt linkage between sentences or whole paragraphs, achieved in part by keeping related sentences together and in part by using **signals of relation** to indicate how sentences tie in with the ones they follow.

contraction (p. 598) The condensing of two words to one, with an apostrophe added to replace the omitted letter or letters: *isn't, don't,* etc. Contractions are used primarily in speech and informal writing.

coordinate modifiers (p. 452) Two or more **modifiers** that modify the same term, as in *a sunlit, windless day*. All coordinate modifiers but the last should generally be followed by commas.

coordinating conjunction See **conjunction.**

coordination (p. 397) The giving of equal grammatical value to two or more parts of a sentence. Those parts are usually joined by a *coordinating conjunction: He tried, but he failed; The lifeguard reached for her megaphone and her whistle*. Cf. **subordination.**

correlative conjunction See **conjunction.**

cumulative sentence (p. 322) A sentence that continues to develop

gloss 42

after its main idea has been stated, adding **clauses** or **phrases** that **modify** or explain that assertion: *She crumpled the letter in her fist, trembling with rage, wondering whether she should answer the accusations or simply say good riddance to the whole affair.* Cf. **suspended sentence.**

dangling modifier (p. 433) The **modifier** of a term that has been wrongly omitted from the sentence:

DANGL MOD
x **Not wishing to be bothered,** the telephone was left off the hook.

> The person who did not wish to be bothered goes unmentioned and is thus absurdly replaced by the telephone.

Cf. **misplaced modifier.**

dead metaphor (p. 364) A **metaphor** that has become so common that it usually does not call to mind an **image:** *a devil of a time, rock-bottom prices,* etc. When overworked, a dead metaphor becomes a **cliché.**

declarative sentence (p. 324) A sentence that presents a statement rather than a question or an **exclamation:** *Lambs are woolly.*

degree (p. 431) The form of an **adjective** or **adverb** showing its quality, quantity, or intensity. The ordinary, uncompared form of an adjective or adverb is its *positive* degree: *quick, quickly.* The *comparative* degree is intermediate, indicating that the modified term surpasses at least one other member of its group: *quicker, more quickly.* And an adjective or adverb in the *superlative* degree indicates that the modified term surpasses all other members of its group: *quickest, most quickly.*

demonstrative adjective (p. 481) A *demonstrative pronoun* form serving as a **modifier,** e.g., *those* in *those laws.*

demonstrative pronoun See **pronoun.**

denotation (p. 333) The primary, "dictionary," meanings of a word. Cf. **connotation.**

dependent clause See **clause.**

description (p. 9) The **mode** of writing in which a writer tries to acquaint the reader with a place, object, character, or group. Cf. **argument, analysis, narration.**

dialogue (p. 98) The direct representation of speech between two or more persons. Cf. **indirect discourse.**

diction (p. 332) The choice of words. Diction is commonly divided into three levels: formal *(deranged)*, middle *(crazy)*, and slang *(nuts)*.

digression (p. 238) A temporary change of topic within a sentence, paragraph, or whole discourse. In an **essay,** an *apparent digression*—one that later turns out to have been pertinent after all—may sometimes serve a good purpose. In general, however, digressions are to be avoided.

direct discourse (p. 23) The use of quotation, as opposed to summary, of a speaker's or writer's words. Cf. **indirect discourse.**

direct object (p. 383) A word naming the item directly acted upon by a **subject** through the activity of a **verb:**

S V D OBJ
- **She hit** the **jackpot.**

Cf. **indirect object.**

direct paragraph (p. 253) A **paragraph** in which the **main sentence** comes at or near the beginning and the remaining sentences support it, sometimes after a **limiting sentence** or two.

disjunctive subject (p. 418) A **subject** containing elements that are alternative to one another, as in *Either you or I must back down.*

distinct expression (p. 285) The forming of sentences in the clearest manner, without causing a reader to guess at the meaning or the relations between elements. Distinct expression is enhanced by effective punctuation, **subordination,** and **conciseness** of phrasing.

division (p. 36) The analytic strategy of spelling out the parts or stages that make up some whole.

double negative (p. 441) The nonstandard practice of conveying the same negative meaning twice: x *They don't want no potatoes.*

double possessive (p. 467) A possessive form using both *of* and *-'s: an idea of Linda's*. Double possessives do not constitute faulty usage.

either-or reasoning (p. 72) The depicting of one's own position as the better of an artificially limited and "loaded" pair of alternatives—e.g., x *If we do not raise taxes this year, a worldwide depression is inevitable.*

ellipsis (p. 560) The three or four spaced dots used to indicate material omitted from a quotation: "*about the . . . story.*" A whole row of dots indicates omission of much more material, usually verse.

emotionalism (p. 102) The condition of someone who is too upset to think clearly. Strong emotion can be a valuable aid to writing; emotionalism is always a handicap.

endnote (p. 207) A note placed in a consecutive series with others at the end of an **essay,** article, chapter, or book.

essay (p. 4) A fairly brief (usually between two and twenty-five typed pages) piece of nonfiction that tries to make a point in an interesting way. For the essay **modes,** see **analysis, argument, description, narration.**

euphemism (p. 362) A vague or "nice" expression inadvisedly used in place of a more direct one; e.g., *rehabilitation facility* for *prison,* or *disincentive* for *threat.*

evidence (p. 92) Facts, reasons, or testimony tending to support a **thesis.** One statement can be used as evidence for another only if there is a high likelihood that readers will accept it as true.

exclamation (p. 523) An extremely emphatic statement or outburst: *Get out of here! What a scandal!* Cf. **interjection.**

expletive (p. 426) The word *it* or *there* when used only to postpone a **subject** coming after the verb:

EXPL V S
- **There** are many reasons to doubt his story.

exposition

extended figure of speech (p. 376) A **figurative** image (metaphorical comparison) that is sustained for an extra sentence or more so that further implications can be drawn from it: *The last dinosaurs of Leninism are facing extinction. New political formations, like the mammals that sprang to prominence 65 million years ago, will surely prosper in the evolutionary niche that is now being vacated.*

fallacy (p. 94) A formal error or illegitimate shortcut in reasoning. See ***ad hominem*** **reasoning, begging the question, either-or reasoning, faulty generalization,** ***post hoc*** **explanation,** and **straw man.**

"false start" (p. 321) A device whereby a sentence appears to present its grammatical **subject** first but then breaks off and begins again, thus turning the opening element into an **appositive:** *Elephants, gorillas, pandas—the list of endangered species grows longer every year.* A false start can be a good means of seizing a reader's attention. Cf. **mixed construction.**

faulty generalization (p. 69) The **fallacy** of drawing a general conclusion from insufficient **evidence**—e.g., concluding from one year's drought that the world's climate has entered a long period of change.

figurative language (p. 368) Language that heightens expressiveness by suggesting an imaginative, not a **literal,** comparison to the thing described—e.g., *a man so emaciated that he looked more like an x-ray than a person.* See **metaphor, simile.** Cf. **literal language.**

footnote (p. 207) A note at the bottom of a page. Cf. **endnote.**

fragment See **sentence fragment.**

gloss 42

free element (p. 301) A **modifying** word, **phrase,** or subordinate **clause** that deserves to be set off by commas. Most but not all free elements are **nonrestrictive;** some **restrictive elements** at the beginnings of sentences can be treated as free—that is, they can be followed by a comma. Cf. **bound element.**

freewriting (p. 61) The practice of writing continuously for a fixed period without concern for logic or correctness. In *focused freewriting* the writer begins with a specific **topic.**

funnel opener (p. 267) An introductory **paragraph** beginning with a broad assertion and gradually narrowing to a specific **topic.**

fused sentence (p. 401) A **run-on sentence** in which two independent **clauses** are joined without either a comma or a coordinating **conjunction:** x *He is a dapper newscaster I love his slightly Canadian accent.*

gender (p. 347) The grammatical concept of sexual classification determining the forms of masculine *(he),* feminine *(she),* and neuter *(it)* personal pronouns and the feminine forms of certain nouns *(actress).* Also, sexual differentiation in general. Cf. **common gender, sexist language.**

gerund (p. 465) A form derived from a **verb** but functioning as a **noun**—e.g., *Skiing* in *Skiing is dangerous.* Gerunds take exactly the same form as **participles,** and they are capable of having **subjects** (usually possessive in **case**) as well as **objects:**

S OF GER — GER — OBJ GER

- **Elizabeth's winning** the **pentathlon** was unexpected.

Cf. **participle.**

governing pronoun (p. 78) The prevailing **pronoun** in a piece of writing, helping to establish the writer's **point of view.**

governing tense (p. 506) The prevailing verb **tense** in a piece of writing, establishing a time frame for reported events.

hyperbole (p. 379) **Figurative language** that works by overstatement, as in *I will love you until the sun grows cold.*

idiom (p. 339) A fixed expression whose meaning cannot be deduced from its elements—for example, *come around,* meaning *agree or acquiesce after initial resistance.*

image (p. 368) An expression that appeals to the senses. More narrowly, an example of **figurative language.** In both meanings, the use of images is called *imagery.*

imperative mood See **mood.**

implied subject (p. 387) A **subject** not actually present in a **clause** but nevertheless understood: *[You] Watch out!* The customary implied subject, as here, is *you.*

incorporated quotation (p. 550) A quotation placed within quotation marks and not set off from the writer's own prose. Cf. **indented quotation.**

indefinite pronoun See **pronoun.**

indented quotation (p. 554) A quoted passage set apart from the writer's own language. Prose quotations of more than four typed lines and verse quotations of more than two or three lines are customarily indented, without quotation marks. Also known as a *block quotation.* Cf. **incorporated quotation.**

indention (p. 554) The setting of the first word of a line to the right of the left margin, as in a new paragraph (5 spaces) or an **indented quotation** (usually 10 spaces).

independent clause See **clause.**

index (p. 162) A book, usually with a new volume each year, containing alphabetically ordered references to articles (and sometimes books) in a given field. Also, an alphabetical list of subjects and the page numbers where they are treated in a nonfiction book, as on pages 737–764 below.

indicative mood See **mood.**

indirect discourse (p. 511) Reporting what was said, as opposed to directly quoting it. Not *She said, "I am tired,"* but *She said she was tired.* Also called *indirect statement.* Cf. **direct discourse, indirect question.**

indirect object (p. 457) A word designating the person or thing for whom or which, or to whom or which, the action of a **verb** is performed. An indirect object never appears without a **direct object** occurring in the same clause:

- She sent **Fernando** (IND OBJ) a discouraging **letter.** (D OBJ)

indirect question (p. 520) The reporting of a question without use of the question form—not *She asked, "Where should I turn?"* but *She asked where she should turn*. Cf. **indirect discourse.**

infinitive (p. 385) The **base form of a verb,** usually but not always preceded by *to: to win; to prove; prove*.

inflection (p. 385) A change in the ending or whole form of a word to show a change in function without creating a new word. Thus *he* can be inflected to *his, George* to *George's, go* to *went,* etc.

intensifier (p. 360) A "fortifying" expression like *absolutely, definitely,* or *very*. Habitual use of intensifiers weakens the force of assertion.

intensive pronoun See **pronoun.**

intentional sentence fragment See **sentence fragment.**

interjection A word that stands apart from other constructions in order to command attention or show strong feeling: *aha, hey, wow,* etc. Cf. **exclamation.**

interpretation (p. 110) The making of judgments about the meaning or coherence of a piece of writing, a work of art, or an event or a movement.

interrogative adjective An interrogative **pronoun** form that combines with a **noun** to introduce a question—e.g., *Whose* in *Whose socks are these?*

interrogative pronoun See **pronoun.**

interrupting element (p. 445) A word or group of words that interrupts the main flow of a sentence:

INT EL
- You, **I regret to say,** are not the one.

Interrupting elements (also called *parenthetical elements*) should be set off at both ends by punctuation, usually by commas.

intransitive verb (p. 384) A **verb** expressing an action or state without connection to a **direct object** or a **complement**—e.g., *complained* in *They complained*. Cf. **linking verb, transitive verb.**

introductory tag (p. 559) A **clause,** such as *He said* or *Agnes asked,* introducing a quotation. A tag may also interrupt or follow a quotation.

inverted syntax (p. 325) The reversal of the expected order among sentence elements, usually for rhetorical effect: *After many bitter hours came the dawn*.

irony (p. 80) A sharply incongruous or "poetically just" effect—

created, for example, when the Secretary of the Treasury has to borrow a coin to make a phone call.

In **rhetoric,** irony is the saying of one thing in order to convey a different or even opposite meaning: *Brutus is an honorable man* [he really isn't]. Irony can be *broad* (obvious) or *subtle,* depending on the writer's purpose. Cf. **sarcasm.**

irregular verb (p. 576) A **verb** that forms its past **tense** and its past **participle** in some way other than simply adding *-d* or *-ed: go* (*went, gone*), *swim* (*swam, swum*), etc. Cf. **regular verb.**

italics (p. 634) Thin, slanting letters, *like these*. In handwritten or typewritten work, italics are indicated by underlining. Cf. **roman type.**

jargon (p. 349) Technical language used in inappropriate, nontechnical contexts—e.g., *upwardly mobile* for *ambitious, positive reinforcement* for *praise, paranoid* for *upset*.

leading idea (p. 235) The "point" of a **paragraph,** to which all other ideas in that paragraph should relate. Cf. **main sentence.**

limiting sentence (p. 252) A sentence that addresses a possible limitation, or contrary consideration, to the **leading idea** of a paragraph.

linking verb (p. 384) A **verb** connecting its **subject** to an identifying or modifying **complement.** Typical linking verbs are *be, seem, appear, become, feel, sense, grow, taste, look, sound:*

S LV C
- They **were** Mormons.

S LV C
- She **became** calmer.

Cf. **intransitive verb, transitive verb.**

literal language (p. 368) Words that factually represent what they describe, without poetic embellishment. Cf. **figurative language.**

"literary" present tense (p. 513) The present **tense** form of a verb when it is used to express the ongoing action or meaning of an art work or other text: *Willie Loman tries to hide from reality; The play addresses some of our deepest anxieties*.

main clause See **clause.**

main sentence (p. 235) The sentence in a paragraph that conveys its **leading idea.** Often called *topic sentence*.

metaphor (p. 371) An implied comparison whereby the thing at hand is figuratively asserted to be something else: *His fists were a hurricane of ceaseless assault*. Cf. **simile.**

misplaced modifier (p. 435) A **modifier** whose modified term is present in the sentence but not immediately identifiable as such:

MISPLACED MOD — MODIFIED TERM?
x **Laughing so hard,** Nancy was offended by **Ellen's** frivolity in a time of crisis.

Compare:

- Laughing so hard, Ellen offended Nancy by her frivolity in a time of crisis.

Cf. **dangling modifier.**

mixed construction (p. 408) The use of two clashing structures within a sentence, as in x *Even a friendly interviewer, it is hard to keep from being nervous.*

mixed metaphor (p. 374) A **metaphor** whose elements clash in their implications: x *Let's back off for a closer look;* x *He is a straight arrow who shoots from the hip.*

MLA style (p. 188) The **parenthetic citation** style of documentation now favored by the Modern Language Association. Cf. **APA style, "alternative MLA" style.**

mode A type of writing characterized by the purpose of its **rhetoric.** The modes recognized in this book are **analysis, argument, description,** and **narration.** One essay can make use of several modes.

modifier (p. 430) A word, **phrase,** or **clause** that limits or describes another element:

- MOD: the **gentle** soul
- MOD, MOD: **When leaving,** turn out the lights **on the porch.**
- MOD: **Before you explain,** I have something to tell you.

mood (p. 582) The manner or attitude that a speaker or writer intends a **verb** to convey, as shown in certain changes of form. Ordinary statements and questions are cast in the *indicative* mood: *Is he ill? He is.* The *imperative* mood is for commands: *Stop! Get out of the way!* And the *subjunctive* mood is used for certain formulas (*as it were*), unlikely or impossible conditions (*had she gone*), *that* clauses expressing requirements or recommendations (*They ask that she comply*), and *lest* clauses (*lest he forget*).

narration (p. 21) The **mode** of writing in which a writer recounts something that has happened. Cf. **analysis, argument, description.**

nonrestrictive element (p. 447) A **modifier,** often a **phrase** or a **clause,** that does not serve to identify ("restrict") the modified term and is therefore set off by punctuation, usually commas:

NONRESTR EL
- That woman, **whom I met only yesterday,** already understands my problems.

Cf. **restrictive element.**

gloss 42

noun (p. 386) A word like *Jack, Pennsylvania, house,* or *assessment,* usually denoting a person, place, thing, or idea. A noun can undergo **inflection** for both plural and possessive forms (*houses, house's, houses'*), and it can serve a variety of sentence functions (subject, direct object, etc.).

noun clause See **clause.**

noun phrase See **phrase.**

nounlike element (p. 386) A word or group of words having the same function as a **noun** or **pronoun,** but not the same features of **inflection**—e.g., *what you mean* in *He knows what you mean.* Also called *nominal* or *substantive.*

number (p. 412) In grammar, the distinction between *singular* and *plural* form. The distinction applies to **verbs** (she *drives,* they *drive*), **nouns** (*boat, boats*), and personal **pronouns** (*I, we*).

numeral (p. 648) A number expressed as a figure (*6, 19*) or a group of letters (*VI, XIX*) instead of being written out.

object (p. 383) A **noun, pronoun,** or **nounlike element** representing a receiver of an action or relation. See **direct object, indirect object,** and **object of preposition.** In addition, **infinitives, participles,** and **gerunds** can take objects:

OBJ OF INF
- to chair the **convention**

OBJ OF PART
- Chairing the **convention** impartially, she allowed no disorder.

OBJ OF GER
- Chairing a turbulent **convention** is a thankless task.

object of preposition (p. 460) A **noun, pronoun,** or **nounlike element** following a **preposition** and completing the prepositional **phrase**—e.g., *November* in *throughout November,* or *siesta* in *during a long siesta.*

objective case See **case.**

objective complement See **complement.**

ordinal number (p. 649) A number like *fourth* (*4th*) or *twenty-seventh* (*27th*), as opposed to a **cardinal number** like *four* (*4*) or *twenty-seven* (*27*).

outline (p. 85) A schematic plan showing the organization of a piece of writing. A *scratch outline* merely lists points to be made, whereas a *subordinated outline* shows, through indention and more than one set of numbers, which points are the most important ones. A further distinction is made between the *topic outline,* whose headings are concise **phrases,** and the *sentence outline,* which calls for complete sentences.

paragraph (p. 234) A unit of prose, usually consisting of several sentences, marked by **indention** of the first line (or sometimes by an extra blank line). A well-wrought paragraph of **analysis** or **argument** is expected to provide support for one **leading idea.**

paragraph block (p. 250) A group of paragraphs addressing the same part of a **topic,** with strong continuity from one paragraph to the next.

parallelism (p. 484) The structure or the effect that results from matching two or more parts of a sentence—e.g., the words *Utica, Albany,* and *Rye* in the sentence *He went to Utica, Albany, and Rye,* or the three equally weighted **clauses** that begin this sentence: *That he wanted to leave, that permission was denied, and that he then tried to escape—these facts only became known after months of official secrecy.* Cf. **balance, coordination.**

paraphrase (p. 178) Sentence-by-sentence restatement, in different words, of the meaning of a passage. Cf. **summary.**

parenthetic citation (p. 188) A reference to a work, given not in a **footnote** or **endnote** but in parentheses within a main text—e.g., (*Meyers 241–75*).

parenthetic element See **interrupting element.**

part of speech (p. 335) Any of the major classes into which words are customarily divided, depending on their dictionary meaning and their syntactic functions in sentences. Since many words belong to more than one part of speech, you must analyze the sentence at hand to see which part of speech a given word is occupying. The commonly recognized parts of speech are:

Verb	try, adopts, were allowing
Noun	Cynthia, paper, Manitoba
Pronoun	she, himself, each other, nothing, these, who
Preposition	to, among, according to
Conjunction	and, yet, because, although, if
Adjective	wide, lazier, more fortunate
Adverb	agreeably, seldom, ahead, together, however
Interjection	oh, ouch, gosh
Article	a, an, the
Expletive	it [is], there [were]

participle (p. 385) An **adjectival** form derived from a **verb**—e.g., *Showing* in *Showing fear, he began to sweat.* Participles can be present (*showing*) or past (*having shown*) and active or passive (*having been shown*). Like other **verbals,** they can have **objects** (*fear* in the sentence above), but unlike other verbals, they do not have **subjects.** Cf. **gerund.**

passive voice See **voice.**

past participle See **participle.**

peer editor (p. 115) In most instances, a fellow student who comments on another writer's drafts so that appropriate revisions can be made.

person (p. 411) In grammar, a characteristic of **pronouns** and **verbs** indicating whether someone is speaking (*first* person: *I go, we go*), being spoken to (*second* person: *you go*), or being spoken about (*third* person: *he, she, it goes; they go*).

personal pronoun See **pronoun.**

phrase (p. 390) A cluster of words functioning as a single **part of speech** and lacking a **subject-predicate** combination. Cf. **clause.**

A **noun** and its **modifiers** are sometimes called a *noun phrase* (*the faulty billiard balls*), and a **verb** form consisting of more than one word is sometimes called a *verb phrase* (*had been trying*). But the types of phrases most commonly recognized are *prepositional, infinitive, participial, gerund,* and **absolute.**

A *prepositional phrase* consists of a **preposition** and its **object,** along with any **modifiers** of those words:

OBJ
PREP MOD MOD MOD PREP
- **among her numerous painful regrets**

PREP PHRASE

An *infinitive phrase* consists of an **infinitive** and its **object** and/or **modifiers:**

OBJ
S INF INF MOD MOD MOD INF
- They asked **John to hit the almost invisible target.**

INF PHRASE

A *participial phrase* consists of a **participle** and its **object** and/or **modifiers:**

OBJ
MOD PART MOD MOD PART
- **Quickly reaching the correct decision,** he rang the bell.

PART PHRASE

A *gerund phrase* consists of a **gerund** and its **object** and/or **modifiers,** and it may also include a *subject of the gerund:*

S GER GER OBJ GER MOD
- **Their sending Matthew away** was a bad mistake.

GER PHRASE

An **absolute phrase** (see entry) may contain an **infinitive** or a **participle,** but it always modifies an entire statement.

pivoting paragraph (p. 255) A paragraph that begins with one or more **limiting sentences** but then makes a sharp turn to its **main sentence,** which may or may not be followed by **supporting sentences.**

plagiarism (p. 181) The taking of others' thoughts or words without due acknowledgment. Cf. **allusion.**

point of view (13) Literally, a place of observation—a vantage on a scene. More broadly, an attitude or mental perspective, a way of seeing things. An essay ought to imply a consistent point of view in this second sense.

positive degree See **degree.**

possessive case See **case.**

post hoc, ergo propter hoc (p. 70) A **fallacy** whereby the fact that one event followed another is wrongly taken to prove that the first event caused the later one. (In Latin, *post hoc, ergo propter hoc* means "after this, therefore because of it.")

predicate (p. 384) In a **clause,** the **verb** plus all the words belonging with it:

PRED

- He **had a serious heart attack.**

Cf. **subject.**

predicate adjective See **complement.**

predicate noun See **complement.**

predication (p. 410) The selection of a **predicate** for a given **subject.** The problem of *faulty predication* appears when subjects and predicates are mismatched in meaning: x *The purpose of the film wants to change your beliefs.* **Mixed construction** is a more radical form of faulty predication.

prefix (p. 614) One or more letters that can be attached before the root or base form of a word to make a new word: *pre-, with-,* etc., forming *prearranged, withstand,* etc. Cf. **suffix.**

preposition (p. 287) A function word that introduces a prepositional **phrase**, e.g., *to* in *to the lighthouse.* Other common prepositions include these:

about	below	from	since
above	beneath	in	through
across	beside	into	till
after	between	like	under
against	beyond	near	until
along	by	of	up
at	during	off	with
before	except	on	without
behind	for	out	

A preposition consisting of more than one word is **compound:** *along with, apart from,* etc. See also **object of preposition.** Cf. **conjunction.**

present participle See **participle.**

principal parts (p. 576) The **base** or simple **infinitive** form of a **verb,** its past **tense** form, and its past **participle:** *walk, walked, walked; grow, grew, grown.*

process analysis (p. 45) The **analysis** of a series of steps constituting a complete task (cooking a stew, making a candle, testing a product, etc.).

pronoun (p. 469) One of a small class of words mostly used in place of **nouns** for a variety of purposes:

1. A *demonstrative* pronoun (*this, that, these, those*) singles out what it refers to: *This is what we want.*
2. An *indefinite* pronoun (*anybody, each, whoever,* etc.) leaves unspecified the person or thing it refers to: *Anyone can see that you are right.*
3. An *intensive* pronoun (*myself, yourself, itself, ourselves,* etc.) emphasizes a preceding noun or pronoun: *She herself is a vegetarian.*
4. An *interrogative* pronoun (*who, whom, whose, which, what*) introduces a question: *Who will win the election?*
5. A *personal* pronoun (*I, you, he, she, it, we, they*) stands for one or more persons or things and is used in the tense formation of verbs: *They are willing to compromise.* Personal pronouns also have objective (*him, them*) and possessive (*his, their*) forms: *We asked her to recognize our rights.*
6. A *reciprocal* pronoun (*each other, each other's, one another, one another's*) expresses mutual relation: *We recognized each other's differences of outlook.*
7. A *reflexive* pronoun (*myself, yourself, itself, ourselves,* etc.) differs from an intensive pronoun in serving as a **direct** or **indirect object.** The reflexive pronoun shows that the **subject** of the **clause** is the same person or thing acted upon by the **verb:** *He hurt himself on the track.*
8. A *relative* pronoun (*who, whom, that, which*) introduces a relative or adjectival clause: *My uncle, who lives next door, slept through the earthquake.* Some grammarians also recognize an "indefinite relative pronoun" (one lacking an antecedent): *She knows what you mean.* See also **relative clause.**

pronoun agreement (p. 470) The correspondence of a **pronoun** to its **antecedent,** which ought to share its **gender, number,** and **person.**

gloss 42

Thus, in the sentence *When they saw Bill, they gave him a cool welcome,* the pronoun *him* properly agrees with the masculine, singular, third-person antecedent *Bill.* Cf. **pronoun reference, subject-verb agreement.**

pronoun reference (p. 476) The connection in a sentence between a **pronoun** and its **antecedent** whereby the antecedent is explicitly present and the pronoun's relation to it is clear. That is, no other word could be mistaken for the antecedent. Pronoun reference is faulty in a sentence like x *She smelled the cooking shrimp, which made her sick.* What made her sick, the shrimp or smelling them cooking? Cf. **pronoun agreement.**

punctuation marks (Chapters 26–31) Marks used to bring out the meaning of written **sentences.** They are:

.	period	( )	parentheses
?	question mark	[ ]	brackets
!	exclamation point	. . .	ellipsis
,	comma	'	apostrophe
;	semicolon	-	hyphen
:	colon	" "	quotation marks
—	dash	/	slash

racist language (p. 346) **Diction** that can give offense by using a derogatory name for an ethnic group or by perpetuating a demeaning stereotype: *greaser, dumb Pole,* etc.

reasoning (p. 93) The marshaling of premises from which a conclusion can be deduced: *If the raft has been at sea for two weeks, and if there was only enough water on board to last for a few days, any survivors are going to be desperately thirsty when they are found.* Reasoning is a classic means of marshaling support for the **thesis** of an essay.

reciprocal pronoun See **pronoun.**

redundancy (p. 358) The defect of unnecessarily conveying the same meaning more than once. Also, an expression that does so—e.g., *retreat back, ascend up.*

reference See **pronoun reference.**

reference (p. 186) A list of "Works Cited" or "References," supplied at the end of an **essay,** paper, article, or book, and showing where and when the cited or consulted materials appeared. The **parenthetic citations** within the text refer to items in the reference list.

reflexive pronoun See **pronoun.**

refutation (p. 75) The disproving of a point. By definition, all refutations are successful.

regular verb (p. 576) A **verb** that forms both its past **tense** and its past **participle** by adding *-d: hike (hiked, hiked),* etc. Cf. **irregular verb.**

relative clause (p. 388) A subordinate **clause** that functions like an adjective:

REL CLAUSE
- This is the tomb **that we visited.**

See also **clause.**

relative pronoun See **pronoun.**

restrictive element (p. 447) A **modifier,** often a phrase or clause, that "restricts" (establishes the identity of) the modified term. Unless it comes first in the sentence, a restrictive element is not set off by commas:

RESTR EL
- The woman **whom I met** has disappeared.

RESTR EL
- The man **in the black suit** is following you.

RESTR EL
- **On long ocean voyages,** seasickness is common.

(Because it is brief, the initial restrictive element in the last example could also appear without a comma; see page 443.) Cf. **nonrestrictive element.**

résumé (p. 670) A brief record of a person's career and qualifications, typically used in a job application.

rhetoric (p. 4) The strategic placement of ideas and choice of language, as in *His rhetoric was effective* or *His ideas were sound but his rhetoric was addressed to the wrong audience*. Note that *rhetoric* need not mean deception or manipulation.

rhetorical question (p. 324) A question posed for effect, without expectation of a reply: *Who can foretell the distant future?*

Roman numeral (p. 648) A figure such as *III, XLVII,* or *CVI,* as opposed to an **Arabic numeral** such as *3, 47,* or *106*.

roman type (p. 634) Plain letters, like these. Cf. **italics.**

run-on sentence (p. 399) A **sentence** in which two or more independent

clauses are improperly joined. One type of run-on sentence is the **comma splice:** x *She likes candy, she eats it every day*. The other type is the **fused sentence:** x *She likes candy she eats it every day*. Run-ons are typically corrected either with a semicolon (*She likes candy; she eats it every day*) or with a comma and a coordinating **conjunction** (*She likes candy, and she eats it every day*).

sarcasm (p. 522) Abusive ridicule of a person, group, or idea, as in *What pretty phrases these killers speak!* Cf. **irony.**

scratch outline See **outline.**

sentence (p. 284) A grammatically complete unit of expression, usually containing at least one independent **clause,** beginning with a capital letter and ending with a period, question mark, or exclamation point. See also **sentence fragment.**

gloss 42

sentence adverb (p. 403) An **adverb** that serves to indicate a logical connection between the modified **clause** or whole **sentence** and a previous statement—e.g., *therefore* in *She took the job; therefore, she had to find child care*. Also called *conjunctive adverb*.

sentence fragment (p. 390) A set of words punctuated as a **sentence** but either lacking a **subject-verb** combination (x *A day ago.*) or introduced by a subordinating **conjunction** (x *When they last saw her.*).

In general, sentence fragments are regarded as blunders. But an *intentional sentence fragment*—one whose context shows that it is a shortened sentence rather than a dislocated piece of a neighboring sentence—can sometimes be effective:

INT FRAG

- How much longer can we resist? **As long as necessary!**

sentence outline See **outline.**

series (p. 500) A set of more than two **parallel** items within a sentence:

SERIES

- They were upset about **pollution, unemployment, and poverty.**

sexist language (p. 346) Expressions that can give offense by implying that one sex (almost always male) is superior or of primary importance or that the other sex is restricted to certain traditional roles: *lady doctor; a man-sized job; Every American pursues his own happiness,* etc.

signal of relation (p. 241) A word or phrase, such as *therefore* or *subsequently* or *on the contrary*, that indicates how a sentence relates to the preceding one. Such signals contribute vitally to **continuity** between sentences and between whole paragraphs. A repeated word or a **pronoun** can also serve as a signal of relation.

simile (p. 371) An explicit or open comparison, whereby the object at hand is **figuratively** asserted to be like something else: *His eyes that morning were like an elephant's*. Cf. **metaphor.** Both similes and metaphors are called *metaphorical* or **figurative language.** See also **analogy, image.**

slash (p. 552) The punctuation mark /. A slash is used to separate alternatives (*either/or*) and to indicate line endings in **incorporated quotation** of verse. Sometimes called *virgule*.

split infinitive (p. 438) An **infinitive** interrupted by at least one **adverb:** *to firmly stand*. Some readers consider every split infinitive an error; others object only to conspicuously awkward ones such as x *Jane wanted to thoroughly and finally settle the matter*.

squinting modifier (p. 437) A **modifier** awkwardly trapped between sentence elements, either of which might be regarded as the modified term:

SQ MOD
x Why he collapsed **altogether** puzzles me.

Did he collapse altogether, or is the writer altogether puzzled?

stance (p. 79) The **rhetorical** posture a writer adopts toward an audience, establishing a consistent **point of view.** This book recognizes two stances, *forthright* and *ironic*. A forthright stance implies that the writer's statements are to be taken "straight"; an ironic stance implies that the reader is to "read between the lines" and uncover a different or even opposite meaning.

straw man (p. 100) The **fallacy** of misrepresenting an opponent's position so that it will appear weaker than it actually is. The writer "knocks over a straw man" by attacking and dismissing an irrelevant point.

subject (p. 386) The part of a **clause** about which something is **predicated:**

SUBJ
- **Ernest** shot the tiger.

The subject alone is called the *simple subject.* With its **modifiers** included it is called the *complete subject*—e.g., *The only thing to do* in *The only thing to do is compromise.*

Not only **verbs** but also **infinitives, gerunds,** and **absolute phrases** can have "subjects":

S OF INF INF
- They wanted **Alexander** to be king.

S OF GER GER
- **Alexander's** refusing upset them.

S OF ABS PHRASE
- **The conference having ended,** the diplomats went home.

ABS PHRASE

gloss 42

subject area (p. 53) A wide range of related concerns within which the **topic** of an essay or paper may be found. Cf. **thesis, topic.**
subject-verb agreement (p. 411) The correspondence of a **verb** with its **subject** in **number** and **person.** In *I stumble,* e.g., the verb *stumble* "agrees with" the subject *I;* both are singular and first-person in form. Cf. **pronoun agreement.**
subjective case See **case.**
subjunctive mood See **mood.**
subordinate clause See **clause.**
subordinated outline See **outline.**
subordinating conjunction See **conjunction.**
subordination (p. 297) In general, the giving of minor emphasis to minor elements or ideas. In syntax, subordination entails making one element grammatically dependent on another, so that the subordinate element becomes a **modifier** of the other element, limiting or explaining it. Thus, in *They were relieved when it was over,* the subordinate **clause** *when it was over* limits the time to which the **verb** *were relieved* applies.
substantive note (p. 214) A supplementary note which, instead of merely giving a reference for a cited passage or idea, makes further comments. Cf. **bibliographic note.**
suffix (p. 609) One or more letters that can be added at the end of a word's root or base to make a new word or form: *-ed, -ing,*

-ship, -ness, etc., as in *walked, singing, membership, weakness.* Cf. **prefix.**

summary (p. 176) A concise recapitulation of a passage. Cf. **paraphrase.**

supporting sentence (p. 252) A **sentence** that restates, elaborates, or provides **evidence** or context for some aspect of a paragraph's **leading idea.**

suspended comparison (p. 493) A comparison proposing two possible relations between the compared items, in which the second item is stated only at the end of the construction: *Taco Bell is as good as, if not better than, Pizza Hut.*

suspended paragraph (p. 258) A paragraph that builds, without a decisive shift of direction, toward a **main sentence** at or near the end. Cf. **direct paragraph, pivoting paragraph.**

suspended sentence (p. 326) A **sentence** that significantly delays completing the statement of its idea while **clauses** and/or **phrases** intervene: *The important thing is not to study all night before the exam, nor to try reading the instructor's mind, nor to butter up the TA, but to keep up with the assignments throughout the term.* Also called *periodic sentence.*

suspended verb (p. 492) A construction in which one subject governs two forms of the same delayed **verb:** *She can, and assuredly will, comply with the law.* Note how the verb *can comply* is "suspended" by the intervening element.

syllogism (p. 93) A chain of deduction from premises to a conclusion:

Premise:	All massive die-offs of fish in Lake Erie are caused by pollution.
Premise:	Last year there was a massive die-off of fish in Lake Erie.
Conclusion:	Last year's massive die-off of fish in Lake Erie was caused by pollution.

tense (p. 574) The time a **verb** expresses: present *(see),* future *(will see),* etc.

thesis (p. 54) The point, or one central idea, of an essay, paper, article, book, etc. Cf. **subject area, topic.**

thesis statement (p. 73) A one-sentence statement of the **thesis** or central idea of an essay or paper. In this book, a thesis statement is considered to be full only if it is complex enough to guide the essay's organization.

tone (p. 78) The quality of feeling that is conveyed in a piece of writing. Words like *factual, sober, fanciful, urgent, tongue-in-cheek, restrained, stern, pleading,* and *exuberant* may begin to suggest the range of tones found in **essays.** Cf. **stance, voice.**

topic (p. 53) The specific subject of an essay or paper; the ground to be covered or the question to be answered. Cf. **subject area, thesis.**

topic outline See **outline.**

topic sentence Replaced in this book by the term **main sentence,** since the key sentence in a paragraph is the one stating the **leading idea,** not the one announcing a "topic."

transitional phrase (p. 403) A **phrase** having the same function as a **sentence adverb,** modifying a whole **clause** or **sentence** while showing its logical connection to a previous statement:

TRANS PHRASE

- She says she simply can't bear to be late; **in other words,** she expects the rest of us to show up on time.

transitive verb (p. 383) A **verb** transmitting an action to a **direct object:**

TR V

- They **cast** the dice.

Cf. **intransitive verb, linking verb.**

trial thesis (p. 67) A possible **thesis,** or central idea, considered before a final thesis has been chosen.

trial topic (p. 64) A tentative **topic** that requires further evaluation before being judged suitable for an essay.

understatement (p. 378) A device of **rhetoric,** often used for **irony,** whereby the writer conveys the importance of something by appearing to take it lightly: *Living near the edge of a runway for jumbo jets is not altogether relaxing.*

verb (p. 383) A word or words like *goes, saw,* or *was leaving,* serving to convey the action performed by a **subject,** to express the state of that subject, or to connect the subject to a **complement.**

verb phrase See **phrase.**

verbal (p. 385) A form derived from, but different in function from, a **verb.** Verbals are either **infinitives, participles,** or **gerunds.** When mistakenly used as verbs, they cause **sentence fragments:**

VERBAL

x George **going** to the movies tonight.

voice (p. 574) The form of a **verb** indicating whether the **subject** performs the action (*active* voice: *we strike*) or receives the action (*passive* voice: *we are struck*.) Also, the "self" projected by a given piece of writing (p. 76). In the latter sense, this book recognizes two voices, the *personal* and *impersonal*.

weaseling thesis (p. 68) A **thesis** that fails to take any definite stand: x *People can be found who oppose gun control;* x *Abortion is quite a controversial topic*.

PERMISSIONS ACKNOWLEDGMENTS

NESTOR ALMENDROS Excerpt from "Lights, Camera, Communism," *The New Republic*, February 1988. Reprinted by permission of *The New Republic*, © 1988, The New Republic, Inc.

ROGER ANGELL Excerpt from *Five Seasons: A Baseball Companion*. Copyright © 1972, 1973, 1974, 1975, 1976, 1977 by Roger Angell. Reprinted by permission of Simon & Schuster, Inc.

RICHARD BLOW Excerpt from "Moronic Convergence," *The New Republic*, January 1988. Reprinted by permission of *The New Republic*, © 1988, The New Republic, Inc.

CHRISTINE R. B. BOAKE and ROBERT R. CAPRANICA Excerpt from "Aggressive Signal in 'Courtship' Chirps of a Gregarious Cricket," *Science*, November 5, 1982. Reprinted by permission of the American Association for the Advancement of Science.

WILLIAM BOLY Excerpt from "Downwind from the Cold War," *In Health*, July/August 1990. Excerpted from *In Health* magazine. Copyright © 1990.

GEORGE W. BONHAM Excerpt from "The Decline of Initiative," *Change*, April 1975. Reprinted with permission of The Helen Dwight Reid Educational Foundation. Published by Heldref Publications, 1319 18th Street, NW, Washington, D.C. 20036-1802. Copyright © 1975.

BRUCE BOWER Excerpt from "Murder in Good Company." Reprinted with permission from *Science News*, the weekly newsmagazine of science, copyright 1988 by Science Service, Inc.

CARL W. BUCHHEISTER and FRANK GRAHAM, JR. Excerpt adapted from "From the Swamps and Back: A Concise and Candid History of the Audubon Movement," *Audubon*, January 1973. Reprinted by permission from *Audubon*, magazine of the National Audubon Society.

JON CARROLL Excerpt from "The Picture of Good Health," *San Francisco Chronicle*, November 9, 1990. © *San Francisco Chronicle*. Reprinted by permission.

RACHEL CARSON Excerpt from *Silent Spring* by Rachel Carson. Copyright © 1962 by Rachel L. Carson. Reprinted by permission of Houghton Mifflin Company. All rights reserved.

PETER DE JONGE Excerpt from "When The Putting Goes Bad," *The New York Times*, March 13, 1988. Copyright © 1988 by The New York Times Company. Reprinted by permission.

J. A. DEUTSCH and H. S. KOOPMANS Excerpt from "Preference Enhancement for Alcohol by Passive Exposure," *Science*, March 23, 1973. Reprinted by permission of the American Association for the Advancement of Science.

JOAN DIDION Excerpts from *Slouching Towards Bethlehem* by Joan Didion. Copyright © 1968 by Joan Didion. Reprinted by permission of Farrar, Straus and Giroux, Inc.

DIANE DIVOKY Excerpt from "Waterproofing Your Baby: Too Good to Be True," *In Health*, May/June 1988. Excerpted from *In Health* magazine. Copyright © 1988.

DAVID EWING DUNCAN Excerpt from "The Long Good-bye," © David Ewing Duncan, originally appeared in *The Atlantic*, July 1990.

RICHARD J. EVANS Excerpt from "Towards Unification," *Times Literary Supplement*, May 4–10, 1990.

PETER GOLDMAN and LUCILLE BEACHY Excerpt from "One Against the Plague," from *Newsweek*, July 21, 1986. © 1986, Newsweek, Inc. All rights reserved. Reprinted by permission.

MEG GREENFIELD Excerpt from "The No-Fault Confession," from *Newsweek*, June 15, 1987. © 1987, Newsweek, Inc. All rights reserved. Reprinted by permission.

PAUL HENDRICKSON Excerpt from "Papa's Boys," *The Washington Post*, July 29, 1987. © 1987 The Washington Post. Reprinted with permission.

MIROSLAV HOLUB Excerpt from "Shedding Life," translated by Dana Habova and Patricia Debney, *Science 86*. Reprinted by permission of Family Media, Inc.

EDITH IGLAUER Excerpt from "The Strangers Next Door," *Atlantic*, July 1973. Reprinted by permission of Sterling Lord Literistic, Inc. Copyright © 1973 by Edith Iglauer.

MICHAEL IGNATIEFF Excerpt from "The Limits of Sainthood," *The New Republic*, June 1990. Reprinted by permission of *The New Republic*, © 1990, The New Republic, Inc.

PAUL JOHNSON Excerpt from *Modern Times: The World from the Twenties to the Eighties* by Paul Johnson. Copyright © 1983 by Paul Johnson. Reprinted by permission of HarperCollins Publishers.

ITZCHAK E. KORNFELD Excerpt from "Letters to the Editor," *The New York Times,* August 15, 1990. Reprinted by permission of Itzach E. Kornfeld.

BETTIJANE LEVINE Excerpt from "Living in the Shadows," *Los Angeles Times,* December 2, 1990. Copyright © 1990 *Los Angeles Times.* Reprinted by permission.

BOB MAIRS Excerpt from "How the Storm Developed," *Yachting,* November 1979. Reprinted by permission of *Yachting* Magazine, New York.

RIAN MALAN Excerpt from *My Traitor's Heart* by Rian Malan. Copyright © 1990 by Rian Malan. Used with permission from the Atlantic Monthly Press.

STEVEN J. MARCUS Excerpt from "How to Court a Cat," from *Newsweek,* March 22, 1982. © 1982, Newsweek, Inc. All rights reserved. Reprinted by permission.

LOUIS MENAND Excerpt from "Life in the Stone Age," *The New Republic,* January 1990. Reprinted by permission of *The New Republic,* © 1990, The New Republic, Inc.

PHILIP M. MERIKLE Excerpt from "Subliminal Auditory Messages: An Evaluation," *Psychology and Marketing,* 1988. Reprinted by permission of John Wiley & Sons, Inc.

MARK CRISPIN MILLER Excerpt from "Hollywood: The Ad," from *Seeing Through Movies* by Mark Crispin Miller. Copyright © 1990 by Mark Crispin Miller. Reprinted by permission of Pantheon Books, a division of Random House, Inc.

JOHN DAVID MORLEY Excerpt from *Pictures from the Water Trade* by John David Morley. Copyright © 1985 by Davis Morley. Used by permission from the Atlantic Monthly Press.

MOLLY O'NEILL Excerpt from "Getting Personal with a Lobster Doesn't Soften the Cook's Heart," *The New York Times,* August 8, 1990. Copyright © 1990 by The New York Times Company. Reprinted by permission.

GEORGE ORWELL Excerpt from "Politics and the English Language" by George Orwell, copyright 1946 by Sonia Brownell Orwell and renewed 1974 by Sonia Orwell, reprinted from his volume *Shooting an Elephant and Other Essays* by permission of Harcourt Brace Jovanovich, Inc., the estate of the late Sonia Brownell Orwell and Martin Secker & Warbury Ltd.

CYNTHIA OZICK Excerpt from "The Seam of the Snail," from *Metaphor & Memory* by Cynthia Ozick. Copyright © 1989 by Cynthia Ozick. Reprinted by permission of Alfred A. Knopf, Inc.

ROBERT M. PIRSIG Excerpt from *Zen and the Art of Motorcycle Maintenance* by Robert Pirsig. Copyright © 1974. Used by permission of William Morrow and Company, Inc./Publishers, New York.

THE RANDOM HOUSE COLLEGE DICTIONARY Entries for "fabulous," "strength," and "hardly." Reproduced by permission from *The Random House College Dictionary.* Copyright © 1984 by Random House, Inc.

READER'S GUIDE TO PERIODICAL LITERATURE Entries for "Heme," "Hemingson, Peter," "Hemingway, Ernest," and "Hemingway, Mary," reprinted by permission of the H. W. Wilson Co.

FELIX ROHATYN Excerpt from "Becoming What They Think We Are," *The New York Review of Books,* April 12, 1990. Reprinted with permission from *The New York Review of Books.* Copyright © 1990 Nyrev, Inc.

ROBERT STONE Excerpt from "Sunday Mornings with Fly Face," *Times Literary Supplement,* July 13–19, 1990. Reprinted by permission of Times Supplements Limited.

BEVERLY BELFER WIESNER Excerpt from "Stealing the Light," *Boston Review,* December 1987. Coyright © 1987 by Beverly Belfer Wiesner. Reprinted by permission of the author.

WILLIAM ZINSSER "Frankly, Miss Dodds," *Atlantic,* April 1973. Copyright © 1973 by William K. Zinsser. Reprinted by permission of the author.

ABIGAIL ZUGER Excerpt from "Acrophobia in the Ivory Tower." Copyright © 1975 by *Harper's Magazine.* All rights reserved. Reprinted from the October 1975 issue by special permission.

Index

Note: Main entries in **boldface** are defined in the Glossary of Terms (pp. 706–34). Page numbers in *italics* indicate the main discussion of a topic; go to those pages first.

Symbols for Comment and Revision

When commenting on your written work, your instructor may use some of the following marks. If a mark calls for revision, consult the chapter or section of the *Handbook* printed in boldface type.

✓	Excellent point; well said
✓ **arg**	Effective argument
✓ **concr**	Good use of concrete language
✓ **d**	Effective diction
✓ **det**	Effective supporting detail
✓ **dev**	Effective development of the point
✓ **fig**	Apt figure of speech
✓ //	Effective parallelism
✓ **p**	Effective choice of punctuation
✓ **trans**	Good transition

abbr	Faulty abbreviation, **36g–36k**
ad	Faulty comparison of adjective or adverb, **21a–21b**
agr	Faulty subject-verb agreement, **20c–20n**
awk	Awkward expression
cap	Capitalize this letter, **35**
case	Wrong pronoun case, **22**
chop	Choppy sequence of sentences, **14f**
cl	Cliché, **16f**
coh	Coherence lacking, **12**
colloq	Colloquial expression, **15h**
comp	Faulty comparison, **24a, 24e**
cs	Comma splice, **19b**
d	Inappropriate diction (word choice), **15c–15h, Index of Usage**
dm	Dangling modifier, **21c**
doc	Faulty documentation form, **7**
emp	Weak or inappropriate sentence emphasis, **14a–14e**
exag	Exaggeration; overstated claim, **3j**
fig	Inappropriate figure of speech, **17**
frag	Sentence fragment, **18d**
fs	Fused sentence, **19b**
G1	Look up this expression in the **Glossary of Terms**
hyph	Faulty hyphenation, **34h–34m**
ital	Use italics (underline), **36a–36f**
jarg	Jargon, **15g**
lc	Do not capitalize (leave in lowercase), **35**
livel	Stale language; rewrite for liveliness, **16**
log	Faulty logic, **3j–3k**
mis m	Misplaced modifier, **21d**
mixed	Mixed construction, **20a**
ms	Faulty manuscript form, **5i**
no ¶	Do not begin a new paragraph here, **10d**
num	Inappropriate form for a number, **36l–n**
p	Faulty punctuation, **26–30**
pass	Inappropriate use of passive voice, **12e**
p/form	Faulty form or spacing of punctuation mark, **31**